Penguin Special

Penguin Special
The Life and Times of Allen Lane

JEREMY LEWIS

VIKING
an imprint of
PENGUIN BOOKS

VIKING

Published by the Penguin Group
Penguin Books Ltd, 80 Strand, London WC2R ORL, England
Penguin Group (USA) Inc., 375 Hudson Street, New York, New York 10014, USA
Penguin Group (Canada), 10 Alcorn Avenue, Toronto, Ontario, Canada M4V 3B2
(a division of Pearson Penguin Canada Inc.)
Penguin Ireland, 25 St Stephen's Green, Dublin 2, Ireland (a division of Penguin Books Ltd)
Penguin Group (Australia), 250 Camberwell Road,
Camberwell, Victoria 3124, Australia (a division of Pearson Australia Group Pty Ltd)
Penguin Books India Pvt Ltd, 11 Community Centre,
Panchsheel Park, New Delhi – 110 017, India
Penguin Group (NZ), cnr Airborne and Rosedale Roads, Albany,
Auckland 1310, New Zealand (a division of Pearson New Zealand Ltd)
Penguin Books (South Africa) (Pty) Ltd, 24 Sturdee Avenue,
Rosebank 2196, South Africa

Penguin Books Ltd, Registered Offices: 80 Strand, London WC2R ORL, England

www.penguin.com

First published 2005
1

Set in 12/14.75 pt Monotype Bembo
Typeset by Palimpsest Book Production Limited, Polmont, Stirlingshire
Printed in Great Britain by Clays Ltd, St Ives plc

A CIP catalogue record for this book is available from the British Library

ISBN 0-670-91485-1

Note about the endpapers:
The endpaper penguins combine Edward Young's bulbous birds
with Jan Tschichold's more elegant fowl

To
Charles Sprawson,
intrepid swimmer and
best of friends

Contents

Acknowledgements   ix

Prologue   I

 1. Bristol Days   5
 2. Life with Uncle John   17
 3. *The Whispering Gallery*   36
 4. Goodbye to The Bodley Head   51
 5. Hatching a Penguin   71
 6. Pelicans Take Flight   101
 7. Red Alert   123
 8. Penguins Go to War   149
 9. Branching Out   171
10. The New Jerusalem   191
11. Transatlantic Blues   208
12. Scenes from Office Life   221
13. The Search for Perfection   236
14. Buildings and Classics   251
15. An Estate of the Realm   267
16. Flirting and Foreign Parts   283
17. Changing the Guard   301
18. Lady Chatterley Goes on Trial   315
19. Penguin Goes Public   334
20. The Rise and Fall of Tony Godwin   343
21. Closing Time   370

Epilogue   402

Reference Notes   404
Bibliography   442
Index   451

Acknowledgements

Allen Lane's papers, the Penguin files and Eunice Frost's papers are housed in the Library of Bristol University, and I'm extremely grateful to Hannah Lowery and her colleagues in Special Collections for looking after me and answering my questions with such courtesy and efficiency; Michael Estorick and Emma Russell lent me their house in Bath while I was working in the Library, which made life even more agreeable. It was a pleasure to work again with Michael Bott at Reading University, riffling through the papers of Chatto & Windus, The Bodley Head and Jonathan Cape, and to revisit the sumptuously renovated Harry Ransom Humanities Research Center at the University of Texas at Austin, where Tara Wenger and Pat Fox guided me through the labyrinth. I greatly enjoyed my sessions with Sue Bradley, who masterminds the 'Book Trade Lives' section of the British Library's National Sound Archive, and with Anne Bradley, the archivist at Bristol Grammar School; on a more melancholy note, John Seaton showed me round Harmondsworth in its dying days. Allen Lane's niece, Elizabeth Paton, very kindly showed me letters from her father, Richard Lane, and arranged for Tammie Gay at Penguin Australia to send me the correspondence between the two brothers. Charles Pick's unpublished memoirs are a gripping read for anyone interested in publishing, and his son Martin very generously allowed me to read them. I'm also very grateful to the staff of the Public Record Office, the St Bride's Printing Library, Book Trust and the London Library.

My indebtedness to those who have written about Allen Lane, Penguin and publishing is reflected in the bibliography. I'm particularly aware of my debt to Steve Hare's *Penguin Portrait: Allen Lane and the Penguin Editors 1935–1970* and the publications of the Penguin Collectors' Society, and to Nicholas Joicey's masterly essay 'A Paperback Guide to Progress' when writing about the pre-war Penguin Specials and Penguin's influence on post-war Britain.

I'd like to thank the following for their recollections of Allen Lane: Peter Buckman, Judith Burnley, Peter Calvocoressi, Ian Chapman, Jerry Cinamon, Charles Clark, Margaret Clark, Jim Cochrane, Joan and Evelyn Collihole, Elizabeth Creak, Arthur Crook, John Curtis, Alun Davies, Bob Davies, Ian Dickson, Lord Gibson, Ben Glazebrook, Fay Godwin, Martyn Goff, Gordon Graham, Graham C. Greene, John Gross, Betty Hartel, John Hitchin, Richard Hoggart, Lord Holme, Lord Hutchinson QC, Robert Hutchison, Malcolm Kelley, Joan Kite, John Letts, Ruari McLean, Tom Maschler, James Michie, Tony Mott, Jill Norman, Ian Norrie, Dieter Pevsner, June Pipe, James Price, Isabel Quigly, Tim Rix, Tom Rosenthal, Doug Rust, Edward and Stella Samuel, Paul Scherer, Doreen Scott, Sue Shaw, Raleigh Trevelyan, Shirley Tucker, Lord Weidenfeld and Patrick Wright.

Sara Wheeler and Geraldine Cooke urged me to get on with it during the course of a drunken party, and I'm very glad I followed their advice; Isabel Quigly fanned the flames, and introduced me to some of her old Penguin colleagues. Biographers rely on other people to a shaming degree, and I'm very grateful to the following for help, advice and information: Paul Addison, Iain Bain, Michael Barber, Sue Bradbury, Montagu Bream, James Chesterman, Ron Costley, Caroline Dawnay, Eric de Bellaigue, Maggie Fergusson, Christopher Foyle, Stephen Gardiner, Michael Geare, A. D. Harvey, J. C. Hall, Christopher Hawtree, Ernest Hecht, Valerie Holman, Michael Holroyd, Judy Taylor Hough, David Hughes, Lynn Hughes, Sam Humphreys, Richard Ingrams, Crispin Jackson, Andrew Kidd, Jim Knowlson, Lucy Lethbridge, Alistair McCleery, Belinda McGill, Peter Mayer, Huw Molseed, Jane Moore, John Moynihan, William Palmer, Clive Reynard, Steve Rubin, Hilary Rubinstein, Michael Sissons, Carol Smith, Jon Stallworthy, John M. Thomas, Nigel Viney, Ian Willison, Tanya Wolff and Martin Yates.

I'm extremely grateful to the following for reading the typescript in part or in whole, and for their comments and suggestions: Charles Clark, Jim Cochrane, John Curtis, Fay Godwin, Steve Hare, Alistair McCleery, Tom Maschler, Clare Morpurgo, Tony Mott, Dieter Pevsner, John Rolfe, Tanya Schmoller, Christine and David Teale, and Tony Weale, who – among many other good deeds – saved me from attributing Maupassant's 'Boule de Suif' to Balzac at the beginning of a chapter devoted to Allen Lane's insistence on the highest editorial standards. Further howlers were deflected by Nicolas Barker (typographical matters), Eric de Bellaigue (finance) and Lord Hutchinson (the trial of *Lady Chatterley's Lover*, in which he played an indispensable part). My editor at Penguin, Tony Lacey, reacted with his customary gusto when I suggested the idea of a biography of Lane at an *Oldie* literary lunch, since when he has been exemplary in his combination of enthusiasm and shrewdness, as well as being the most convivial of men; and sifting through the photographs with his assistant, Zelda Turner, proved an exceptionally enjoyable business. Annie Lee, my copy-editor, worked at Penguin in the Tony Godwin era and provided heartening evidence of the high standards set by the firm in those days. I am grateful to Elisabeth Merriman and Fiona Allen of Penguin for their help. My agent, Gillon Aitken, whose experience of publishing goes back to the Allen Lane era, has proved once again a sagacious and welcome source of advice; and I am very flattered that Douglas Matthews has once again undertaken the index. I am deeply indebted to Simon Brooke of Snake Eyes Computers, who was always at hand when I pressed the wrong button and the screen went blank.

The book would never have got off the ground without the support of Allen Lane's daughters, Clare Morpurgo and Christine Teale, and of Christine's husband, David Teale, an old colleague of mine from nearly forty years ago. I can't think of anything worse than to have an elephantine biographer blundering about in one's family history, and they fielded my questions with courtesy, kindness and admirable frankness. Tanya Schmoller, who knew Lane and the inner workings of Penguin better than anyone else, has been wonderfully helpful and encouraging. I have fond memories of bibulous afternoons with John Rolfe, who spent his working life at Penguin, knows more than most, and allowed me to read his own invaluable account of the firm's history. My greatest debt of all is to Steve Hare. A former editor of *The Penguin Collector* and the author of *Penguin Portrait*, published by Penguin in 1995, Steve lives surrounded by thousands of Penguin Books, and knows more about them than any man on earth: he has been unstintingly generous in allowing a newcomer to plunder a lifetime's knowledge, and has answered the most half-witted enquiries promptly and without a hint of impatience. And, of course, I owe everything to my wife Petra, who has had to put up with my pacing about the house in an absent-minded daze and getting up at five in the morning to type. She hosed me down when I despaired after reading the first draft, and suggested how I should rectify matters: whether she succeeded, only its readers can decide.

The author and publishers would like to thank A.M. Heath and the Estate of Sonia Brownell Orwell for permission to quote from *The Lion and the Unicorn* and other writings by George Orwell; and the Random House Group Ltd for permission to quote from *The Uses of Literacy* by Richard Hoggart, published by Chatto & Windus. The illustrations are reproduced by kind permission of the Library of Bristol University.

Prologue

Cyril Connolly once wrote that 'No two biographies are alike, for in every one enters an element of autobiography which must always be different', and this is no exception to his rule. Penguin Books were seven years old when I was born: I remember them all through my childhood, and since I have spent my entire working life in the publishing and literary world, Allen Lane and his colleagues have a certain familiarity. Writing about the years in which Penguin established itself as a national institution has been like revisiting a dimly remembered country, long gone but still familiar; and although I never met Lane, many of the figures who flit through these pages were known to me, by reputation or in person, from my early days in the publishing business.

As a second-generation Penguin reader, I looked out every month to see what new books were on offer, assumed that the only novels worth reading were those that had been paperbacked by Penguin in its famous livery of orange and white, and automatically turned to the blue-backed Pelicans if I wanted to know about the Ancient Greeks, the Hanoverians, the Roman Catholic Church, printing, Karl Marx or even the weather. For those of us who grew up in the Fifties and Sixties, Penguin seemed to be one of the benign monopolies that shaped our lives, along with the BBC and the National Health Service: a unique, unchanging institution, without rivals or compare. Quite who was responsible for it all, and how it had come into being, was a matter of complete indifference to me. The Penguin edition of *Lady Chatterley's Lover* was put on trial the year after I left school, but I remember nothing of it; and even when, seven years later, I went to work in the publicity department at Collins, the name of Allen Lane meant nothing to me.

In those days publishers were still newsworthy, and the colour supplements regularly carried admiring profiles of the two 'whizz

kids' of the book trade, Tom Maschler and Tony Godwin, both of
whom, as it happened, had worked for Allen Lane: but although
Lane had had more column inches devoted to his achievements than
any other publisher, most recently for sacking Tony Godwin, he was
tired and ill by the time I began to learn my way round the publishing
world, revered by his fellow-practitioners but less in evidence to the
world at large than such colourful figures as George Weidenfeld or
André Deutsch. Like a good many other people, I assumed, wrongly,
that he had invented the paperback, but since I knew next to nothing
about him, I had no reason to think otherwise.

I remember nothing of his death in 1970, but the previous year
I had gone to work as a junior editor at André Deutsch. Among
my colleagues was a young man named David Teale, who was
married to Lane's second daughter, Christine, and was gaining some
experience of hardback publishing before returning to Penguin: as
André Deutsch liked to remind us, his firm had been chosen for
the honour, and since his professionalism and dedication to
publishing equalled Allen Lane's, this made perfect sense. My wife
and I went to dinner with the Teales in their flat in the Old Mill
House, Allen Lane's elegant eighteenth-century house in West
Drayton, and since then I've often wondered whether Lane himself
might have been on the premises: soon afterwards we went our
separate ways, and I thought no more about David Teale until André
Deutsch's eightieth birthday party in 1997, when a genial figure
tapped me on the shoulder and reintroduced himself.

The publishing world which I joined in 1967 was that in which
Allen Lane had spent his working life. Although some mergers and
takeovers had occurred, most firms were still independent: many, like
Collins and John Murray, were still family firms; others, like André
Deutsch or Weidenfeld & Nicolson, were run by their founders.
Publishing offices were, as often as not, rickety Georgian houses in
Bloomsbury or Covent Garden: their entrance halls were invariably
clogged with brown paper parcels, while the offices upstairs combined
elegance and squalor, marble mantelpieces cluttered with dog-eared
showcards and half-empty bottles of wine, Victorian kneehole desks
awash with proofs, catalogues, readers' reports, old coffee cups, jacket

roughs, brimming ashtrays, unanswered letters and pristine finished copies. With one or two formidable exceptions, publishing was, in the upper echelons at least, masculine and middle-aged; its denizens sported fiery tweeds or chalk-striped suits, were keen members of the Garrick or the Savile, scribbled memos and did their sums on the backs of envelopes, and were firm believers in the long alcoholic lunch. Accountants and sales people were there to receive, not give, the orders; much was made of a publisher's 'nose' or 'hunch', and stories were told of how some book of the moment had been commissioned over the dinner table. Much of the hard work was done by a combination of old-fashioned clerking types, well-heeled ex public schoolboys with vague literary ambitions, and – most invaluable of all – a steady supply of middle-aged spinsters, all of whom were wretchedly underpaid, devoted their lives to the firm, and every evening lugged home baskets brimming with typescripts or proofs.

After I left André Deutsch I worked for A. P. Watt and Oxford University Press before spending ten long years at Chatto & Windus, and during my time in publishing the business changed in ways which Lane might not have enjoyed or approved. The firms he had known and done business with – Jonathan Cape, Hamish Hamilton, Secker & Warburg, Michael Joseph, Heinemann, Weidenfeld, Hutchinson, his beloved Bodley Head, even the seemingly impregnable William Collins – were taken over by conglomerates; Bloomsbury town houses were exchanged for a floor in a featureless office block; the middle-aged men in chalk-striped suits were elbowed aside by women who were no longer prepared to hover meekly in the background; the bibulous office lunch fell into disgrace, and steak and kidney pudding and claret gave way to a slice of salmon and Perrier water; bureaucracy triumphed as the computer and the photocopier spewed out mountains of bumph, and more and more meetings were held to discuss their contents; publishers ceased to be of interest to gossip-columnists and profile writers, giving way to PR men, celebrities, television cooks and the other heroes of a less literate age. And, as Tony Godwin had foreseen, Penguin lost its near monopoly at the literary end of the market as publishers set up their own rival paperback imprints, reserving for themselves books which would once have been published by Penguin, and reverting the rights in titles which had seemed part of Penguin's birthright. But some things never changed. Somehow Lane's principle of 'swings and roundabouts' survived: bestsellers and books on gardening or chess continued to subsidize first novels, unimportant memoirs and biographies of neglected eighteenth-century novelists.

Publishers with literary ambitions of their own seldom make it to the top, having one eye on the clock and another on the door, and lacking the monomaniacal intensity the trade demands. Like many of the best publishers, Lane was neither intellectual nor arty, but combined shrewd business sense with intuitive good taste and an ability to read the spirit of the age: he was, as has often been pointed out, a contradictory character, in that he was both affable and cold, ruthless and cowardly, loyal and fickle, but – like many of those who found and run business empires – he was an uncomplicated, single-minded man, more interesting for what he achieved than for his insights into the human condition and seldom afflicted by the ambivalence and indecisiveness endemic among writers and intellectuals. Though not the most bookish of men, he was a literary publisher in that he made the best writers of the past and the present available at prices everyone could afford, but his influence was cultural, social and even political as well as literary. Like David Astor at the *Observer* or Lord Beveridge or William Haley at the BBC or Kingsley Martin at the *New Statesman*, Allen Lane was one of the *éminences grises* who moulded the world in which I grew up, giving voice to the ideals that were made manifest by the post-war Labour government, prevailed through the 'Butskellite' consensus, and were only called into doubt with the rise of Mrs Thatcher. But unless they take to the soapbox, like Lane's great contemporary Victor Gollancz, publishers are curiously elusive and hard to pin down: politicians, sportsmen and soldiers busy themselves in public life, journalists and academics write it up, publishers commission the result, and the thread becomes ever more tenuous. Publishers loom large in their lifetimes, but are quickly forgotten: Allen Lane is – or should be – one of the rare exceptions to the rule. And his insistence on making the best available to the many, without dilution or simplification, makes him, in an age of dumbing down, an exemplary figure as well.

1. Bristol Days

Family trees are baffling at the best of times; Allen Lane's became more complicated than most when he learned that, as a condition of his joining The Bodley Head at the age of sixteen, he and his immediate family must exchange his father's surname, Williams, for his mother's maiden name of Lane. His parents and his three siblings dutifully traded names in order to advance the eldest son's career in publishing; and with that the Williamses – and, indeed, Allen Lane's Welsh connections – faded from the scene. Little enough was known about them in any event: it was said that undertaking ran in the family, and that Allen Lane's lifelong interest in funerals represented some atavistic urge, and he once suggested, implausibly, that the unconventional spelling of his Christian name, which he shared with his father, had something to do with a missionary who was killed, but not eaten, by cannibals. His Williams grandfather was a sea captain from Neath, in South Wales, and was given to running a flag up the flagpole in the garden to announce the birth of a child.

These included Allen Lane's father, Samuel Allen Gardiner Williams: according to family folklore, his two middle names were those of that same missionary, who had earlier been rescued in the Amazon by his nautical father. A round-headed, kindly-looking character with, in middle age, a balding pate, rimless specs and a walrus moustache, he was, according to his son's friend and colleague William Emrys Williams, 'a pleasant ruddy little man'. He was born in 1863; as a young man he prospected for gold in South Africa, without noticeable success, and when the Boer War broke out he joined a volunteer regiment attached to the Black Watch. Back from his African adventures, he settled in Bristol. In his eldest son's birth certificate, he is listed as an 'architect and surveyor'; elsewhere he is described, variously, as a clerk in the City Valuer's Office, a corporation surveyor and (according to Allen Lane) the Deputy or Assistant

City Valuer, working in the City Surveyor's Department at Bristol Corporation. Either way, he never earned more than £400 a year, and evidently felt that he had not done his family proud on the monetary front. In a 'goodbye letter' written shortly before his death in 1950, he apologized for his ineptitude at making money; Allen Lane, by then a rich and successful publisher, was touched and worried by his father's sense of inadequacy, assuring his mother that 'of the making of money itself there is not much to be proud especially if, as is so often the case, it has been done at the cost of suffering and hardship to others . . .' Out of office hours, the paterfamilias busied himself making vast quantities of homemade wines and cider, and when, in 1928, the Williams Lanes (as they had now become) moved to Falfield, in Gloucestershire, he maddened the cook by clogging up the kitchen with barrels and vats of fermenting parsnip and dandelion; unlike his three sons, all of whom were heavy and enthusiastic drinkers, he was abstemious by nature, but happily offered his potions to family and friends. He was also said to be a connoisseur of Cheddar cheese.

That the family should have switched surnames seems oddly apposite, since the Lane genes were gamier and more dominant than those of the Williamses, and Allen Lane was far more influenced by his mother than by his gentle and retiring father, and far keener on his Devonian ancestry than on anything originating from the Welsh side of the Bristol Channel. The Lanes – among them his remote relation John Lane, the founder of The Bodley Head – were farming folk; Allen Lane himself was to combine publishing with a passion for farming, and both his critics and his admirers – taking note of his stocky yeoman's build, ruddy cheeks and sharp blue eyes as well as his shrewdness as a publisher – were to make much, over the years, of his peasant cunning and rustic guile. Lane told the writer Ved Mehta that one of his maternal ancestors had invented the first self-binder for tying up bundles of straw, and had to protect his machine from being sabotaged by indignant farm-workers worried that it would do them out of a job. But not all his ancestors worked on the land; towards the end of the 1930s, when he took up sailing, he kept his boat, the *Penguin*, at Fowey in Cornwall, and claimed to know the area well, 'a number of my forebears having been pilots from the village of Polruan across the water'.

Lane's mother, Camilla, was the driving force in the family. In later years he rang her almost every day from work, and when, after her husband's death, she moved into a cottage a minute's walk from Silverbeck, the William IV mansion he owned a mile or two down the road from the Penguin headquarters in Harmondsworth, he made a point of calling in to see her after work on his way home from the office; a tradition he broke only when restlessly travelling round the world or trying to relax on holiday in France or Ireland, and continued till her death in 1958. Born in 1873 – the date must have been engraved on Allen's mind after he had, in a fit of absent-mindedness, set down her date of birth as 1893 when adding her name to the family plaque in Hartland church, an error that was remedied just in time by his brother Dick, who pointed out that, had that been the case, she would have been nine when her eldest son was born – she was a sturdy, large-featured woman: W. E. Williams, who thought her 'ruthless' on behalf of her family, remembered her as being 'manifestly the head of the house: a genial farmer's wife type of character, with a mop of curly hair twice as big as Jennie Lee's' – Jennie Lee being the fine-looking wife of Aneurin Bevan, a future Minister of the Arts and, at one stage, recommended to Lane by Williams as a possible heir-apparent at Penguin. Mrs Williams was also a good cook and an efficient and generous hostess – both qualities that Allen Lane came to expect of the women in his life, who would be called upon to entertain, often at short notice, printers, booksellers, authors and Penguin staff. Considered delicate as a child, she had been sent away from home to live with an uncle and aunt in Bristol; as a result, she was thought to be better educated than her Devonian sisters. For eight years she was engaged to be married to a Mr Harris, whose farm adjoined that of her parents, but, much to his indignation, her father's territorial and dynastic ambitions were thwarted when she chose instead to marry the mild and inoffensive Samuel Williams. Both Camilla and her future husband were Chapel folk, and she accompanied the services on the harmonium; despite his low–church leanings, he also sang in the choir of St Mary Redcliffe, the magnificent Perpendicular masterpiece in the middle of Bristol, and it was there that they were married.

Christened Allen Lane Williams, their eldest son was born on Sunday 21 September 1902, between nine and eleven in the evening: we know this because, for some reason best known to himself, Lane invariably inscribed the details of his birth in the front of his new pocket diary at the beginning of each year, along with the dates of birth and death of his parents and his brother John. His brother Richard (known as Dick to his friends and to the readers of this book, as 'Mr Richard' to his subordinates at Penguin) followed in 1905, John in 1908, and Nora in 1911. Samuel was earning £250 a year when they set up house together in Cotham Vale, a pleasant, hilly suburb to the north of the city centre, and in due course Camilla had to cater and provide for a family of six on an allowance of thirty shillings a week. Years later, Allen Lane attributed his 'awful compulsion to be doing something' to his having been 'brought up in the least affluent part of my father's and mother's families, and all my uncles and aunts were inclined to think that we were a curious brood and I wanted to show them'; but despite the shortage of funds, it was a happy household. 'That our upbringing was a good one there is no denying,' Lane told his mother in the letter he wrote her after his father's death: all the letters he had received since then had commented on 'the closeness of our family ties. Such solidarity could only spring from a happy and secure family life such as we enjoyed.' His own daughters, he went on, had been brought up more leniently than he and his brothers, and got away with crimes which would have earned a 'walloping' forty years earlier – but 'we none of us looked on Father as an avenging god, and what character-forming as he did was done more by example than precept'. Lane's closeness to his parents and his siblings, and to his mother and Nora in particular, was to become one of his most noticeable character-istics, presenting a daunting and seemingly impenetrable barrier to the outside world, and his father helped to set the pattern: 'During the whole of my life I don't remember ever having heard Father criticize you or any action of yours. He supported you in every act with I am sure at the back of his mind a full realization of the importance of a solid front being shown to the outside world and in particular to the family, which is the first to perceive any rift, however slight.'

Not long after Dick was born, the family moved down Cotham Vale from No. 40 to Broomcroft, a much larger house. Now marked with a plaque to commemorate its most distinguished resident, it was a handsome Italianate pile on four floors, with rounded windows and stone balls along the parapet, built from a pinkish local stone, and stood at the end of a terrace. A dark and gloomy basement housed the kitchen, the coal cellar, a scullery with a stone sink, a cold water tap and a copper to heat the water, and so many larders and store cupboards that over one school holiday the Lane boys were deputed to paint all seventeen doors in the basement; the dust-bins were put out in the area to await collection, and in his unpub-lished (and highly entertaining) 'Reminiscences' Dick remembered how vile they smelt in the hot summer months. There was no running hot water, and the top two floors had no water at all. Despite the modest salary on offer from the City Corporation, the Williamses, like the Pooters, could afford a maid; she worked from seven in the morning to eight at night, and was housed on the top floor. Of the five remaining bedrooms, one was used by Samuel as a photographic dark room; for some years Allen and Dick shared a bright and cheerful red-painted bedroom over the front door, and on winter evenings they were serenaded by a harpist who dragged her instrument behind her on a trolley, strummed in the street for twenty minutes or so, and was rewarded with a shower of pennies.

Although, in later years, Allen became increasingly impatient with Dick, they were, as children, extremely close. Both were exception-ally good-looking little boys. Allen was smaller, darker and sharper-featured, though never as lean and foxy-faced as brother John; Dick was large, blond, moon-faced, ruddy-featured and benign; both appeared in St Mary Redcliffe on Sundays in the guise of choir-boys, clad in ruffs and white cassocks. The Williamses were, according to Dick, a 'fairly religious family', and on Sunday evenings the head of the family sang hymns in the drawing-room in a deep bass voice: Allen – who never showed much interest in music in later life – sang in a madrigal society, attended a concert at the Colston Hall given by Clara Butt, and, when the First World War broke out, sang to the troops while his cousin Ducka Puxley collected the money. As an adult, Lane was a famously natty dresser, never appearing in public without a tie and a hip-hugging double-breasted suit, and bearing at times a curious resemblance to another dapper Bristolian, the actor Cary Grant; and in his childhood opportunities for dressing up were provided by membership of the Boy Scouts. A tinted photograph shows him in full regalia, peering anxiously out from under a gigantic tent-shaped fawn felt hat. Both boys were Scouts when war broke out, ready to shin up lampposts and turn off the gas in the event of an air-raid, spending odd nights on duty in a signal station somewhere beyond Clevedon, and – or so they told their friends – spotting a German submarine as it made its way up the Bristol Channel and arranging for its immediate arrest.

Mrs Williams liked to claim that her eldest son learned to read by studying estate agents' notices and advertisements when taken for walks by a governess, Mrs Hastings, who lived in the house next door. Printed matter of a more literary kind was in ample supply in the Williams household – their father kept old copies of the *Strand* magazine, exciting in his eldest a particular liking for the work of Conan Doyle, and Allen Lane once suggested that a regular diet of W. T. Stead's penny paperbacks, including Books for the Bairns, the Penny Poets and the Penny Shakespeare series, may have planted a Penguin seed – but neither boy was particularly bright or keen on learning. Dick was, according to the Puxleys, 'as dense as could be'; Allen, who thought he must have been 'probably rather dull' as a child, wanted, like any self-respecting Edwardian boy, to become an engine-driver, and six months before he died he referred, appreciatively, to the proximity of the main London to Exeter line to his farm at Chapmansford in Hampshire, 'which allows me to pander to my love of trains'.

The two older boys went to kindergarten together, and then on to a dubious establishment called Tellisford House, which they both loathed. The headmaster, Mr Crawford, was an old-fashioned sadist

who revelled in beatings and patrolled the corridors with his cane
at the ready; every now and then he would rap on the door of a
classroom with the handle of his cane, ask the master in charge
which boy was paying least attention, and administer a thwacking.
Despite his reign of terror – Dick claimed that they were beaten
several times a day – the Lane brothers were, more often than not,
on mischief bent: 'Allen and I were likened to the two facets of a
Seidlitz powder, harmless when separated but explosive when mixed.'

Over forty years later, after he had settled in Australia, Dick –
who, by then, felt bruised and aggrieved by the treatment he had
received at the hands of his older brother – wrote a long, nostalgic
letter to Allen describing, in almost Arcadian terms, their happy
childhood in Bristol, and wondering whether he too looked back
on those days with a comparable fondness. No doubt he received
back an awkward, businesslike letter, far more concerned with staff
problems or annual profits than with the tenderly remembered
minutiae of a distant past, but if Dick was wounded (though unsur-
prised) by the inadequacy of his brother's reaction, his own letter
provides some glimpses of their boyhood together. He recalled
summer holidays spent rowing on the river, clambering round Clifton
Gorge, fishing for sticklebacks at Coombe Dingle, and bringing
them home in jam-jars; and how they caught butterflies, raided
birds' nests, fished for eels in a claypit, took a sea journey in a tug
and made a trip by paddle-steamer from Hotwells to Clovelly. More
than once, they bicycled down to Devon to visit Lane relations: an
uncle owned a shop in Winkleigh, drew ice-cold water from a pump
in the garden, and allowed them to peer through a telescope mounted
in his sitting-room. They were there when an uncle got married;
the old father disgraced himself by taking the bell-ringers to the
pub before the service and filling them so full of beer that the celebratory peal of bells was discordant and out of tune. Did Allen
remember, Dick wondered, his friend Gale, who made gunpowder
and tested it on the tramlines in Whiteladies Road, so effectively
that the explosion could be heard for miles around? Or wandering
round Bristol docks, clambering over the boats and visiting 'old
Martin who had that delightful but rather dark old ships' repair

store-room down by the river, not far from Bristol Bridge', and how, one summer holiday, Allen supplemented his twopence a day pocket money by being apprenticed to a shipwright who worked on tugs and barges in the docks?

The family was on holiday in Highbridge when war broke out in August 1914: Dick remembered watching a train pass by full of Scottish soldiers, with flat freight trucks laden with field guns bringing up the rear. With the outbreak of war, Mr Williams, too old for the regular army, joined the Special Constabulary and the local Volunteers. Every now and then he did guard duty at the Filton Aircraft works, returning home at six in the morning for a wash before setting out for the office; as a sergeant in the Special Constabulary, he kept a record of ships' crews visiting Bristol, and augmented the family rations with tins of ships' biscuits, which he soaked in warm water before serving them up with sugar and hot milk. A concert party was given to raise money for the Blue Cross and the horses on the Western Front, and 'Father appeared dressed as the Kaiser, complete with German helmet and sword.' The Cotham Road tennis courts were converted to allotments: Allen and Dick applied for one, successfully, and set about the hard work of digging up their patch. At choir practice in St Mary Redcliffe, Allen offered his fellow choristers free sweets, cakes and lemonade in exchange for their manual labour; in his brief memoir of his old friend, W. E. Williams sees this as an early indication of Lane's entrepreneurial spirit, as well as his liking for Mark Twain's *The Adventures of Tom Sawyer*.

War brought changes, too, to John Lane at The Bodley Head: his large house in Lancaster Gate Terrace was hit by a bomb, and although the damage was fairly modest, some of his staff proved reluctant to return. Lane and his American wife, Annie Eichberg, decided to decamp for the duration to Bath; and, once installed, they got in touch with their relations in Bristol. Quite how Camilla Williams and London's most eminent publisher were related remains obscure: second cousins once removed might not be too far from the mark. Whatever the connection, the Williamses visited the Lanes in Bath, and were visited in turn in Cotham Vale, where the best china was brought out, Mrs Williams served up roast beef and Yorkshire pudding, and the boys were on their best behaviour. During the course of one of these uneasy gatherings, 'Uncle' John Lane – who had no children of his own, or any immediate family – first raised the possibility of Allen's joining The Bodley Head after he left school. Allen's initial reactions were understandably luke-warm: Dick's friend Gale had a cage full of rabbits, and when Uncle John raised the subject of a career in publishing, Allen muttered something about having to see to the rabbits, made his excuses and left. Sensing his kinsman's yeoman blood, perhaps, old Lane grumbled, prophetically, that if Allen was more interested in rabbits than books, he should probably become a farmer rather than a publisher; and his nephew would, in due course, combine a passion for farming with a single-minded devotion to the business of publishing.

Allen Lane once claimed that he left school and went to work in the rates office of Bristol Corporation, only to be 'yanked back to the Grammar School in Bristol' at the insistence of John Lane, who wanted him to transfer to the classical side of the school as a precondition of his being offered a job at The Bodley Head: but according to his woefully undistinguished school record, Lane clocked into Bristol Grammar School on 18 January 1916, when he was fourteen and a bit, and spent seven terms at the school before leaving on 11 April 1919 at the age of sixteen-and-a-half. It may be that he could take no more caning at Tellisford House, left as soon as he could, and put in a short stint at the rates office before enrolling at the Grammar School; or, more probably, that he took a holiday job in the rates office during his first summer at his new school with the vague idea that, since the school leaving age was then set at fourteen, he might abandon academic life if things worked out, but was persuaded to return to his studies.

Bristol Grammar School is a sixteenth-century foundation, duly equipped with an impressive and elegant set of Victorian Gothic buildings, including a dining-hall with a hammer-beam roof and portraits of heavily gowned and mortar-boarded headmasters glowering down from the walls. Despite a long and distinguished history, it had gone steadily downhill in late-Victorian times, but matters began to improve when Cyril Norwood, a former civil servant, was appointed Headmaster in 1906. The number of pupils shot up from 185 to 528, and new laboratories and sports facilities were laid on, as well as a gym and a library. 'We have a library of several hundred volumes and the school covered in pictures where there was not a book or a picture in 1906,' an exultant Head told the assembled parents and governors in his farewell peroration in 1916, when he left to become, successively, Headmaster of Marlborough, Headmaster of Harrow, and President of St John's College, Oxford; in 1944 he produced the hugely influential Norwood Report on the future of education, in which the teaching of science and technology was relegated to a paragraph, the classics were exalted above all else, and future Ministers of Education were urged to retain the existing divisions between grammar and secondary schools. Norwood was succeeded by J. E. Barton, in the same term in which Allen Lane joined the school. With a first in Greats and the Newdigate Prize already under his belt, Barton was said to have written the only book about Thomas Hardy which its subject could read with any pleasure; within the school, his great achievement was to enthuse his pupils about the pleasures of art and architecture. Although, in strictly academic terms, Lane seems to have learned almost nothing during his time at the school, it may well be that his visual taste and sense of style, which he put to such good effect as a publisher, were encouraged by a headmaster who 'opened [his] eyes to the significance of design and form'. Certainly Barton would have proved a more congenial figure than the austere Cyril Norwood: he was, according to a contemporary, 'a shorter, more substantial person, with ruddier cheeks and more than a suspicion of a nautical roll' and 'a robust sense of humour'. Revisiting his old school in 1952 to open a new building, Lane spoke of his 'real affection' for the school, and recalled how his 'education was taken in hand by Mr Barton, who commenced by introducing me to Palgrave and finished – I hasten to add that this was after I had left here – by introducing me to a very potent mixture of Russian stout and draught Bass in pint tankards'. Barton himself had nothing to say on the matter, but he did remember how 'the street lighting was dimmed by war regulations, and the school clock forbidden to strike, lest it might excite the interest of hovering zeppelins', and how, with most of the school lit by gas, the gas mantles in the classrooms below the Great Hall were damaged by 'the stamping exuberance of our Armistice Day assembly'.

Dick and John followed their brother to the Grammar School in due course, their father shelling out £5 per head per term for the privilege. Between them the three brothers appear not to have notched up a single public exam, nor made any impression whatsoever on the games field. All three records are a blank, revealing nothing beyond routine details of dates of entry and departure and father's occupation; none of them appears to have passed a single School Certificate, let alone the Higher School Certificate needed to go on to university. 'I wasn't very bright at school,' Lane once confessed; and although he occasionally turned out, reluctantly, for the Penguin cricket team when it took on neighbouring villages, he showed no interest whatsoever in games of any kind.

Early in 1961, Ernest Wilmott, a fellow-pupil who later became a builder in Bristol, heard Sir Allen Lane the publisher on the radio programme *Frankly Speaking*, and – discounting the change of name and the clipped, precise voice, oddly reminiscent of Noël Coward's in accent and intonation and lacking all traces of a Bristol burr – suddenly realized that the speaker had once been Allen Williams of Form IVA. In a letter sent only days before Lane's death, he recalled their feasting together on the gym roof and, wondering why his friend seemed to irritate the masters, attributed it to 'an incipient smile which was always on your face' – still present, he noted, in photographs of Lane in later life. Lane's humour, and his sense of mischief, would be evident in his career as a publisher, always more happy to tease and deride those who seemed to embody the established order; and so too was a loyalty to old friends that sometimes sat uneasily with volatility, fickleness and an alarming tendency to suddenly turn cold on those who had seemed, until recently, to be the favourites of the moment. His life would be threaded with characters who went back a long way, and among his more distinguished and diligent contemporaries at the Grammar School were Ivor Jennings, later the Master of Trinity Hall, Cambridge, and Oliver Franks, who went on to become an eminent civil servant, British Ambassador in Washington, Provost of Worcester College, Oxford, and (by now a peer) the author of the Franks Report into higher education. As a schoolboy, Franks was Lane's antithesis, serving as a school prefect, playing for the cricket and hockey elevens and the rugger fifteen, and winning a scholarship to the Queen's College, Oxford; and whereas Lane provides invaluable ammunition to those of us who long to be told that there is no correlation between success at school and success in life thereafter, Franks's school record, in the words of his biographer, 'offers no crumb of comfort to those who like their great men to be school dunces'. Unconcerned by his own failure to go on to university, and unabashed by the great gulfs of learning that lay between them, Lane would, in due course, publish Ivor Jennings's *The British Constitution* as a successful and long-lasting Pelican; he kept in touch with Franks via Old Bristolian dinners, and although nothing ever came of his approaches, he liked to touch him for advice and ponder his suitability as a possible Penguin director.

In the meantime, he accepted his Uncle John's offer of a place at The Bodley Head and, with his immediate family duly renamed, Allen Lane Williams Lane set off to London to seek his fortune.

2. Life with Uncle John

However tenuous the connections between Uncle John and his nephew-cum-protégé, the two men were extraordinarily alike. No doubt Allen Lane modelled himself in many ways on his eminent kinsman, even if he never sported an Elizabethan-looking beard, and made a better job of eliminating his West Country accent; and although mass-produced paperbacks seem a far remove from the exquisite limited editions with which John Lane first made his reputation, The Bodley Head and the experiences Allen Lane underwent there haunted and defined his career as a publisher. Both men had come to London when little more than schoolboys; both were stocky, dapper men, impeccably turned out, with china-blue eyes which, in Allen Lane's case, twinkled amiably enough for most of the time but, alarmingly, turned to chips of ice when unamused, whereas Uncle John's were prone to weeping – which 'mild affliction', the playwright Ben Travers recalled, 'lent kindliness to his expression', even if 'many of his authors must have accused him of shedding crocodile tears'. Both were impatient, bored by routine and the 'sombre tyranny of the desk', evasive, dilatory in replying to letters and liable to absent themselves at moments of crisis; both were unusually energetic, working all hours, seldom off duty, driving hard bargains and expecting a similar dedication from less driven colleagues and subordinates. Both men had a strong visual sense, manifesting itself in a care for the look of the books they published, and a passion for collecting paintings, antiques and *objets d'art*; most importantly, although neither was in any conventional sense a literary man, both were endowed with that inexplicable, almost psychic ability to sniff out a publishable book or series of books without reading more than a page or two of the works in question.

An ardent Devonian, John Lane was born in 1854, and was descended from a long line of farming folk. His father, Lewis, was a tenant farmer near Hartland in north Devon, a rolling landscape of bare, windswept hills and lushly wooded valleys, a mile or so down the road from the jagged black cliffs and foaming seas of Hartland Quay and Morwenstow. 'In this parish,' he wrote, 'I spent my happy, indeed I may say romantic, youth,' and although Allen Lane's own connections with the area were fairly remote, the grey little church at Hartland, with its high Perpendicular tower, was to become in due course a shrine to the Williams Lanes as well as to John Lane himself. Unlike his nephew, John Lane showed no interest in farming, but the headmaster of Chulmleigh Academy excited his interest in antiques: as a successful London publisher, he would collect furniture, glass, china, fans and eighteenth-century English portraits.

Eager to make his way in the wider world, John Lane left school at the age of fourteen and took a job in London as a clerk with the Railway Clearing House, which coordinated the activities and services of the innumerable railway companies responsible for shunting passengers and goods about the country. But the railways were not of all-consuming interest, and to supplement his wages Lane started dealing in second-hand books on the side, eventually going into business with the bookseller Elkin Mathews. Together they set up a bookshop on the north side of Vigo Street, naming it The Bodley Head in honour of another bookish Devonian, Sir Thomas Bodley, the founder of the Bodleian Library. But selling antiquarian books was small beer for the forceful, energetic and socially ambitious Lane. 'I have always been in doubt whether the writing of a great book or the capacity to appreciate it were the finest thing in the world; but I am convinced that the next in importance after the writing and the appreciating is the publishing of it. It was this that led me to regard the starting of a publishing business as a thing to be achieved sooner or later,' he declared, and in 1889, after Lane had raised £2,000 from a well-disposed lady friend, the two partners launched their new list with a collection of poems by Richard Le Gallienne. The books Lane went on to publish in the 1890s were, in effect, limited editions, with print-runs in the hundreds rather than the thousands; they were much admired for the elegance of their design and typography, with Aubrey Beardsley designing the title pages and bindings for eleven Bodley Head titles, including Oscar Wilde's *Salome*, and Charles Ricketts and C. H. Shannon providing a further whiff of the *fin de siècle*. Specializing in poetry and *belles-lettres*, the firm became synonymous, in the public mind at least, with the decadent, Romewards-inclined, absinthe-sipping writers of the Nineties – with Lionel Johnson, John Davidson, John Addington Symonds and, above all, with *The Yellow Book* and Oscar Wilde. Although Wilde never contributed to *The Yellow Book*, the two became inextricably entwined in the outraged and overcharged popular imagination: partly because both seemed redolent of sin and unmentionable goings-on, and partly because Wilde was rumoured, wrongly, to have been clutching a copy of the magazine when he was arrested in the Cadogan Hotel.

Like his nephew in due course, John Lane tried his hand more than once as a magazine publisher: most proved ephemeral and short-lived, and only *The Yellow Book* and *Blast* – promoted by Ezra Pound, edited by Wyndham Lewis, and published as war broke out in 1914 – are remembered today. Published in hardback at five shillings, with a sinuous Beardsley line drawing on the cover, the first issue of *The Yellow Book* appeared in 1894: 7,000 copies were printed, reduced to 5,000 for the second issue. Despite its lurid reputation, and a list of contributors that included Henry James, John Buchan, H. G. Wells, Baron Corvo, Edmund Gosse and Kenneth Grahame, its contents were, for the most part, highly respectable and even rather dull. Beardsley, its Art Editor, loathed Oscar Wilde, who was never asked to contribute; and although Wilde admired Max Beerbohm's article on cosmetics in the first issue, he told Ricketts how 'I bought it at the station, but before I had cut all the pages I threw it out of the window.'

John Lane had taken over the stock of Wilde's *Poems* from a publisher fallen on hard times, and had gone on to publish *Salome*, with Beardsley's illustrations, and *Lady Windermere's Fan*. But no love was lost between author and publisher. Wilde – who refused to be described as the 'author' in his contracts, insisting on 'poet' instead – treated Lane like a tradesman of the merest kind, and made sure that his publishers appreciated their lowly status by bestowing the names 'Lane' and 'Mathews' on the men-servants in *The Importance of Being Earnest*. Lane, for his part, was outraged to learn that Wilde had seduced the office boy and arranged assignations in the Vigo Street offices. He was on his first trip to New York when he learned of Wilde's arrest, and decided to stay there until the storm had blown over: the firm's offices were briefly under siege from a stone-throwing mob, *Punch* had declared that 'uncleanliness is next to Bodliness', and an anonymous wag had implored the publishers to

> Give us more of the godly heart
> And less of the Bodley Head.

While in New York he instructed Frederic Chapman, his loyal factotum, to withdraw all Wilde's books from the shops and cancel any outstanding contracts; and while he was at it, he decided to make a clean break with a decadent world by severing all connections with Beardsley as well. Beardsley's erotic drawings seemed to epitomize the effeteness and corruption of a literary avant-garde from which Lane wanted to distance himself: such forgotten grandees as the poet William Watson and Lord Leighton had threatened to withdraw their work and their support, and Lane sensed where his interests lay. Beardsley's title of Art Editor was removed from issue No.5, which was subsequently withdrawn; he transferred his allegiance to the short-lived *Savoy* magazine and the notorious Leonard Smithers, London's leading pornographic publisher, and although *The Yellow Book* limped on to a total of nine issues, it no longer gave off the same *frisson* as before.

As if to emphasize the need for a fresh start, Lane also dissolved his partnership with the mild and inoffensive Elkin Mathews. They divided their authors between them, and in 1894 Lane moved into a tiny, bow-fronted, black-bricked Regency house on the other side of Vigo Street, at the north end of the Albany: some seventy years later his nephew, in a spasm of nostalgia and family piety, reoccupied the same building as offices for his new hardback imprint, Allen Lane The Penguin Press. With the decadent Nineties firmly behind him, Lane set out to re-establish himself as a less *outré*, more conventional publisher. He continued to publish poetry, but no longer saw himself as a purveyor of limited editions; prepared to take on established firms like John Murray and Macmillan, as well as such new arrivals as William Heinemann, he branched out into fiction, history, biography, memoirs and the fine arts.

> How doth the little busy Lane
>   Improve the Bodley Head
> He gathers round him, day by day,
>   The authors who are read,

a versifier noted in the year in which Lane parted company with Elkin Mathews. Lane's change of tack was signalled by the publication of George Egerton's first novel, *Keynotes*, in 1895. 'George Egerton' was the pseudonym of the beautiful Mrs Egerton Clairmonte; anxious to do his best for his new author, he was keen to publish her novel in paperback but was overruled by cautious booksellers and librarians. He did, however, hijack her title for a new 'Keynotes' series of romantic novels; the most successful of his middlebrow novelists was the long-forgotten W. J. Locke, who joined The Bodley Head in the 1890s and went on to produce a stream of bestsellers over the next thirty years.

Occasional bestsellers combined with a dependable backlist were the lifeblood of publishing; but, then as now, publishing was a cash-hungry business, with money tied up in authors' advances, work-in-progress, slow-moving stock and booksellers reluctant to settle up a minute earlier than necessary; and, like any independent publisher without private means, Lane spent long hours juggling his finances and keeping a keen eye out for rich benefactors prepared to exchange a modest return on their investment for the *réclame* associated with the literary life. Sometimes referred to as 'Petticoat Lane', he enjoyed the company of women, and in 1896, the same year in which he opened a New York office, he met a rich American named Annie Eichberg. Her father, Julius Eichberg, was a musician of German origin. In due course he was appointed Director of the

Boston Conservatory, and at the age of fifteen Annie wrote the words for his patriotic hymn 'To Thee, O Country' – so earning a pat on the head from Longfellow, who told her that 'You have covered yourself in glory.' Annie and her middle-aged admirer were married in 1898, and moved into a large white house in Lancaster Gate Terrace. A generous hostess and an efficient housekeeper, she supervised literary salons, organized musical evenings, wrote books on Anglo-American cultural differences and advised her husband on what to publish at The Bodley Head. Lane's biographer and one-time employee Lewis May – another Devonian, whose vicar grandfather had married John Lane's parents – found her hard and somewhat daunting, noting how the shimmering grey metallic silk of her dresses and the whalebone corsets underneath gave her an alarmingly 'warlike' appearance.

Lane himself was, by now, a well-known figure on the literary and social scene. 'Alert, well-groomed, debonair', a keen clubman, he bustled between Lancaster Gate Terrace, the Bodley Head offices and his house in Brighton, made frequent trips to New York, and attended meetings of the quaintly-named Sette of Odd Volumes. Vigo Street became a kind of literary club where the likes of G. K. Chesterton, H. G. Wells and Arnold Bennett could meet for tea or the occasional slug of whisky. After an unhappy spell with a firm of wholesale grocers in the City, specializing in dried fruit, Ben Travers joined the firm as an apprentice in 1911, his father paying Lane £300 to enable his son to be taken on, in exchange for wages of a pound a week: he remembered how Lane worked in a 'dim, bottle-glassed little room tucked in beside the main office', with paintings propped on chairs and against the furniture, and teetering mounds of books and manuscripts all over the floor. The tiny outer office contained four assistants, a lady typist and an office boy, while another secretary and the cashier were housed in the upstairs rooms, reached via a circuitous winding staircase. Although, according to Lewis May, Lane's 'knowledge of literature was neither wide nor deep, he had an extraordinary "nose", as they say', and his enthusiasm was 'infectious, irresistible'; Ben Travers remembered how 'his soft voice and slow smile gave little evidence of his spirit

of wild enthusiasm and impulse in the discovery and exploitation
of talent', and was suitably awestruck when The Bodley Head's
reader told him how 'Lane had a sixth sense which enabled him to
discover merit in a derelict manuscript or in some original and revolutionary project without himself ever reading a page or investi-
gating a detail. He hated detail. The whole of his career was one
continuous flair.'

Not all Lane's colleagues or authors were equally admiring.
'You are such a *fraud*, you know,' Le Gallienne once told him,
while William Watson spoke of 'that villain Lane'; but the most
damning epithets of all were provided by the misanthropic
Frederick Rolfe, alias Baron Corvo, who, after contributing to
The Yellow Book, was briefly published by Lane before moving on
to Chatto & Windus. His publisher, he informed the reading
public, was 'a tubby little pot-bellied bantam, scrupulously attired
and looking as though he had been suckled on bad beer', 'a beery
insect', 'a snivelling little swindler' and 'a carroty dwarf with a
magenta face and puce pendulous lips'.

Despite the convivial atmosphere of Vigo Street and its high
standards of production, authors often followed Baron Corvo's
example and moved elsewhere after publishing their first books
with The Bodley Head. 'I think that authors of first novels received
a pretty good hiding from most of the other publishers, but John
Lane remunerated them with scorpions,' Ben Travers remembered:
as a tyro novelist, he was offered no advance, no royalties on the
first 1,000 copies sold, and a modest royalty on copies sold thereafter, with the same terms applying for the next four books under
contract with the firm. Like many publishers of his day, Lane hated
the new breed of literary agents, on the grounds that they disrupted
the agreeable partnership between publisher and author – or rather
the ability of the publisher to dictate terms to his authors, invariably to his own advantage.

But however strained and short-lived Lane's relations with his
authors may have been – after a particularly heated altercation with
a poet, who had smashed a table before stalking out of the office,
the publisher ruefully observed that this was 'one of the sacrifices

that mediocrity must needs make to genius' – he continued, in the years leading up to the First World War, to build up The Bodley Head into one of London's leading publishers; and this at a time when the number of new titles published every year continued to rise, from 6,456 in 1904 to 9,541 in 1913. He published Arnold Bennett's first novel, *A Man from the North,* Chesterton's *Orthodoxy* and Wells's *The New Machiavelli*; reissued classic authors in the cloth-bound New Pocket Library, selling at a shilling each, and paper-backed others in the Indian and Colonial Library; and made his mark as a humorist, albeit at one remove, by taking on Saki and Stephen Leacock. Aware of the importance to any publisher of dull but dependable steady-sellers, he started a line in gardening hand-books, published a book on the grapefruit written by Mrs Lane, and gave his support to *Airships in Peace and War* as well as Houston Stewart Chamberlain's *The Foundation of the Nineteenth Century*, a work that would be much admired by the Nazis and was translated from the German by Lord Redesdale, better remembered as the father of the Mitford sisters. When threatened with prosecution for publishing Hermann Sudermann's *The Song of Songs* – already toned down for the British market – he sent copies to Shaw, Hardy, Bennett and Wells in the hope that, if called upon, they would testify to its literary merit; so anticipating, albeit unnecessarily, his nephew's summoning of expert evidence in the *Lady Chatterley's Lover* trial fifty years later. He sustained The Bodley Head's louche reputation by publishing editions of *Moll Flanders*, Ovid's *Amores* and other works with suitably *risqué* illustrations; and, though no linguist himself, he happily sought his wife's advice about the work of Continental authors: of these, by far the most successful was Anatole France, the popular edition of whose collected works, priced at 2s. 6d. a volume, was reissued in a striking orange binding.

Ben Travers, best remembered as the author of *Rookery Nook* and other farces, left to enlist in 1914; other employees included Herbert Jenkins, who went on to found his own firm and publish the works of P. G. Wodehouse, and the long-suffering, ever-anxious Basil Willett, a small, bustling, bespectacled figure who joined the firm from Oxford in 1911 and soon found himself running errands for a boss who seemed to spend less and less time in the office. 'Will you procure me a box of cigars at about 8d. or 9d. each, as Mrs Lane wants them for Captain Norton-Taylor. Charge it to Mrs Lane, please,' Lane once instructed his harassed second-in-command. During the war Lane published *Ruggles of Red Gap* and Ford Madox Ford's *The Good Soldier*, interested himself in the plight of Belgian refugees (among them the poet Emile Cammaerts, whose daughter married J. E. Morpurgo, the biographer of Allen Lane and an editor at Penguin), and, after the bombing of 8 Lancaster Gate Terrace, moved to Bath, where he got in touch with his Williams relations in Bristol, and deluged Willett with an unceasing flow of instructions.

The sixteen-year-old Allen Lane started work at Uncle John's trade counter in Brewer Street on 23 April 1919, less than a fortnight after bidding farewell to Bristol Grammar School: in the years to come, Lane and his brothers would make a special point of celebrating St George's Day. On the other side of Regent Street from the editorial offices in Vigo Street, the trade counter dealt with the nuts and bolts of the trade – receiving and processing orders from booksellers and wholesalers, sending out review copies, arranging publicity, totting up authors' royalties – and, for all his family connections, young Lane was expected to learn the business from the bottom up. As office boy and general dogsbody, he worked as a packer and as a 'looker-out' – picking particular books off the shelves and matching them up with a bookseller's order – before graduating to royalties and the accounts department, and his understanding of the trade was improved still further when, in due course, he began to deal with printers, binders, blockmakers and paper merchants; but he really came into his own when he was allowed to go out on the road, first with Uncle John and then on his own account, visiting bookshops in London and the suburbs.

He enjoyed the camaraderie of the trade, the drinks and the gossip; like all the best publishers, he had a good memory for books published by rival firms as well as by The Bodley Head, and, without necessarily reading more than a page or two, had a shrewd sense of which books would, or would not, suit particular shops and buyers. His conviviality, his readiness to combine business with pleasure, and his dashing good looks made him a popular figure in the trade; he thought most bookshops dreary and offputting, but his understanding of and liking for booksellers themselves – not always shared by the grander or more literary type of publisher, uneasy in the company of tradesmen – was to serve him well in the years ahead. Llywelyn Maddock, later a Penguin employee, met Lane when both men were working as publishers' reps, and was struck by 'his bright, intelligent eyes, the neatness of his appearance, his charming smile of greeting and respectful friendly interest'; Eric Hiscock, then drumming up publishers' advertisements for the *Evening Standard*, and later to be courted by publishers as a tipster *par excellence* whose endorsement could create a bestseller, remembered him as a 'humorous, well-dressed figure', impeccably clad in 'a blue suit, white silk shirt, blue silk tie, with a fitting blue Melton overcoat over all', whose ability to extract orders from booksellers was lubricated by a wealth of 'smoking-room stories'. The reps gathered in Lyons in Ave Maria Lane for tea and gossip before going on to elicit orders from Simpkin Marshall, the once-mighty book wholesalers who were later to be bombed out in the Blitz and finally brought to their knees after being taken over by Robert Maxwell. Thirty years on, writing to thank an old colleague who had written to congratulate him on his knighthood, Lane looked back with a certain nostalgia. 'It is a far cry,' he wrote, 'from the days when you and I traipsed the city streets trying to sell a few books, but I am not sure that wasn't about the happiest period of my business life.'

Lane was always proud to have started at the bottom, believing that to have done so gave him an understanding of publishing as a whole denied to those who came into the business after university, usually at an editorial level. Jonathan Cape, a publisher he respected more than most, once told him that he didn't think 'flair amounts to anything more than having a real solid knowledge of what has gone on in the past, so that you can profit by people's mistakes and achievements, and you've got a smell for what can be done and what can't be done'. Lane evidently agreed, adding that a publisher 'can only have got where he is by sheer hard work, and working up from the bottom'. The 1920s saw the rise of the gentleman publisher, and the post-war Bodley Head was heavily staffed by rich young men, educated at public schools and Oxbridge and, as often as not, with money to invest in the firm; but the traditional publisher tended to be a self-taught tradesman from the lower middle classes, very often with a Nonconformist background, who went straight from school to a publisher's office. The great guru of the trade, Stanley Unwin, with whom Lane was to enjoy a prickly and embattled relationship, was a fine example of the breed. A high-minded, teetotal vegetarian, with a pointed Elizabethan beard not unlike that sported by Uncle John and a taste for open-necked shirts, he was omniscient about every aspect of publishing and bristled with self-importance; he had been invited into the trade by another childless uncle, T. Fisher Unwin, founded Allen & Unwin in 1914, and was said to have combined business with pleasure at his marriage by signing up the officiating clergy-man to write a book for the firm. But many of those with whom Allen Lane was to do business over the years – newcomers to the trade like Hamish Hamilton, Ian Parsons of Chatto & Windus, Fredric Warburg and Rupert Hart-Davis, as well as 'dynastic' publishers like 'Billy' Collins, Mark Longman and 'Jock' Murray – were gentleman publishers; and, unlike them, Lane would never feel entirely at home with the social and literary establishment, preferring to choose as his cronies and closest colleagues people who had been to a provincial university rather than Oxford or Cambridge, or had made their way in the publishing world without the benefits (and drawbacks) of a university education.

His starting wages were a guinea a week, ten shillings of which he put aside for board and lodgings, initially in the drearier suburbs of south-west London. He lodged in Raynes Park with Aunt Lily and Uncle Ted, and in Merton Park with his cousins Pat and Ducka Puxley, who had come up to London from Neath; unable to afford the 12s. 6d. fare back to Bristol at weekends, he gazed longingly at the steam trains as they puffed slowly out of Paddington in a westerly direction, and since he could use his season ticket on Sundays, he sampled a different church every week. Despite some modest rises, his earnings were barely enough to live on: writing to the firm three years after he joined, from a house in Worcester Park, he told his employers that although Mr Crockett, the trade director, had increased his wages by five shillings a week when he became the London rep, he was still out of pocket. His current income was 45s. a week, which boiled down to 43s. 10d. after deducting 'insurance and employment': as a result, he found it hard to 'be affable and keep smiling on my rounds . . . My two weeks experience in my new job has been full of interest to me, and I hope I can, with tact and intelligence, carry it through to your satisfaction.' He supplemented his earnings by writing the occasional reader's report. 'I like the writer very much; his plot is excellent, but I think he chose rather odd names for the people in the book,' he wrote of *That Girl March* by W. H. Rainsford. 'There is rather a large number of brackets and underlinings; also too many awkward adverbs. The characters are natural, but not like the characters in some books who never make mistakes – they have their little failings like ordinary people . . .'

In due course he left the suburbs and went to live with Uncle John and Aunt Annie at 8 Lancaster Gate Terrace. It was not, initially, an easy transition: Mrs Lane thought his cousin Pat Puxley a bad influence, and on one occasion he had to be locked in a broom cupboard when her tread was heard in the hall – while Allen found his uncle, who was ill-at-ease with young people, 'rather difficult to get on with'. But before long his natural sociability and ease of manner asserted themselves, and he was mixing happily with the literary and artistic grandees who flocked to Aunt Annie's soirées and dinner parties. Uncle John asked Ben Travers, who had rejoined the firm as an author, if he and his wife would keep an eye on his nephew and introduce him to the right sort of people: this proved, for Travers, 'as easy a job as I've ever been asked to do'. 'You will not suspect me of flattery when I say that I think your nephew is really a delightful fellow. I hope we may make good friends,' Travers wrote to his host after 'a most awfully jolly supper' at Lancaster Gate Terrace. The two young men were to remain friends for life: as for the induction into London life, 'within a week it was he who was looking after us', and the sociable young publisher found himself climbing into white tie and tails several evenings a week. One evening Travers invited him to a banquet at the Fishmongers' Hall, at the end of which the guests were each given a set of silver gilt cufflinks for themselves and a four-pound box of chocolates to take home to the ladies. Bored by the long-winded after-dinner speeches, they escaped the proceedings, only to find themselves in the room in which the guest speaker had been primed with brandy and cigars. After helping themselves to huge quantities of free drink, they set off back to Lancaster Gate Terrace for a night-cap: Lane skidded on the door-mat and grabbed hold of a grandfather clock which crashed down upon him, arousing an irate Uncle John from his slumbers.

Despite such débâcles, and his modest status in the firm, Lane began to be treated like an heir-apparent by Uncle John, who encouraged him to attend directors' meetings even though he was not yet in a position to do so, and sent him off to meet important authors. He visited W. J. Locke at his villa on the Riviera, where he was impressed by the seven bathrooms on offer, and no doubt took careful note of his host's much-quoted advice to 'Never lose an opportunity, nor a visiting card.' Uncle and nephew attended a dinner given by A. J. A. Symons's First Edition Club, along with such luminaries of the period as Sir Israel Gollancz, Ambrose Heal, Gordon Selfridge and Philip Sassoon, and the fresh-faced young man was sent down to Max Gate to meet the aged Thomas Hardy. The poet John Drinkwater and his wife made up the party, and it was suggested that Mrs Drinkwater might like to play a medley of Dorset folk-songs on the piano. Hardy bustled round looking for the scores, and 'when he found them he was as excited as a child, and listened with rapt attention while Mrs Drinkwater played his favourite tunes'. Hardy then offered his guests some chocolate biscuits wrapped in tinfoil; Drinkwater absent-mindedly twisted his foil into the shape of a chalice, and after tea was over Lane slipped it into his pocket as a souvenir. Hardy went on to complain about the pestilential ways of autograph-hunters, one of whom, an American, had bought up

the entire stock of his works from the bookshop in Dorchester and
trundled them out to Max Gate in a wheelbarrow for the great man's
signature. Little did he realize that his young guest would become
one of the foremost autograph hounds of modern times. One evening
Mrs Lane took the young publisher to a meeting addressed by Bernard
Shaw. Allen Lane asked GBS to autograph his programme, to which
the sage replied, 'Young man, why waste your time in chasing people
for their autographs when you might be using it so much more prof-
itably in making your own worthwhile?' Years later, undaunted by
Shaw's disapproval, Lane made a point of collecting a signed copy
of every Penguin he published. More often than not this was a
straightforward proceeding – the authors were flattered to be sent a
copy for signature, and happily obliged – but if a writer proved
unwilling or evasive, a signature would be scissored off the bottom
of a letter, or even a contract, and pasted into place. More than once
Lane or his secretary unwittingly asked for the signature of a long-
dead author; Ben Glazebrook at Constable returned a Penguin
awaiting signature with a note pointing out that Katherine Mansfield
had been dead for over forty years, while Roger Machell at Hamish
Hamilton regretted that he was unable to provide signatures from
Jean Paul Sartre, who never replied to letters, or from the reclusive
J. D. Salinger, who loathed all publishers, and paperback publishers
most of all.

Perhaps the most revered writer on The Bodley Head's list was
Anatole France, famed as an iconoclast and as the author of *Penguin
Island*. Since Allen was credited with schoolboy French, Uncle John
sent him to Paris to meet the magus. Lane and Lewis May were given
an audience at the Villa Said, at the same time as the excitable editor
of *Paris Soir*. Lane had prepared a long and gracious speech in honour
of his firm's eminent author, but was so over-awed and tongue-tied
by France's long white beard, ankle-length silk dressing-gown and
red skull-cap that he never got beyond 'Enchanté, monsieur'; after
which the editor of *Paris Soir*, who had seemed 'a little restive'
before they were admitted into the great man's presence, 'fell on
his hands and knees, pausing every now and again to bow' before
delivering a lengthy panegyric of 'fiery eloquence', at the end of

which he seized Anatole France's hand and pressed it to his lips. Uncle John sent his nephew back to Paris for France's funeral in 1924, and while there he paid the first of many visits to André Maurois. Lane claimed in later years that Maurois's *The Silence of Colonel Bramble* was the first book he worked on at The Bodley Head: *Ariel*, his biography of Shelley, was published by the firm in the year of Anatole France's death, and would be reissued in paperback as the very first Penguin book. Maurois was a well-known anglophile and had served as a liaison officer with the British Army during the First World War, so they almost certainly spoke to each other in English: Dick fondly believed that his older brother was 'bi-lingual' in French and English, but since he also tells us how Lane confused *fromage* with *homard* in a restaurant in Paris, so lumbering himself with two unwanted plates of lobster mayonnaise, he cannot be trusted on that score.

When not consorting with Bernard Shaw, John Galsworthy, Max Beerbohm and Sir Arthur Conan Doyle in Lancaster Gate Terrace, Lane hurried off to evening classes in design at the Regent Street Polytechnic, and struggled in vain to master shorthand and typing at Pitman's. Keen to ride in his spare time, he joined the Territorial Army, attending parades and even summer camps with the Sussex and Surrey Yeomanry and, later, the Essex Artillery. He was invited, in full uniform, to attend a levée at Buckingham Palace; his spurs locked together when he was summoned to meet the King, and he found himself gliding forward like an ice-skater in slow motion. He enjoyed another brush with royalty when Uncle John acquired a glass goblet which had once belonged to a Prince of Wales, and decided to present it to the current incumbent, the future Edward VIII. The Prince accepted Lane's offer, but told him that he wanted to sign its base with a diamond pen. Hurrying to obey the royal command, Lane sent his nephew off to a West End jeweller to borrow a pen and learn how to use it. Back in the office, Allen practised his signature on one of the mullioned windows before taking both goblet and pen round to St James's Palace. Eventually a rather nondescript young man sidled into the room, clad in flannels and a tweed jacket; Lane had no idea who he was, and paid him no attention until the Prince introduced himself and asked to be shown how to use the diamond pen. Unable to master it, he dashed the pen to the ground in a rage before finally inscribing his signature; Allen took the goblet back to the office, added his own signature alongside the Prince's, and posted it back to the palace. The mullioned window bearing his signature was still there when he re-acquired the Vigo Street offices in 1966.

At some point in the early Twenties, John Lane decided to turn The Bodley Head into a limited company. Rival publishers were providing stiff competition, entertaining in style was proving wretchedly expensive, costs were steadily rising, and the middle-class, middlebrow market on which hardback firms like The Bodley Head depended to make a living found its funds being steadily eroded by inflation and higher taxation. Despite Annie Lane's wealth, the firm was, as always, strapped for cash, and Lane needed to find some rich young men with money to spare. Neither Willett, who had been made managing director in 1920, nor Crockett had private means, and they could only afford a handful of shares, but two new directors who joined in 1919 were in a position to invest £10,000 apiece – an enormous sum in those days. Hubert Carr-Gomme, a former Liberal MP and private secretary to Sir Henry Campbell-Bannerman, was never much more than a sleeping partner, albeit of an irritable kind, but Ronald Boswell, who joined shortly after leaving Oxford, was a more influential and active participant. Of, presumably, German origin – as was the custom at the time, his original surname, Bussweiller, was printed in brackets under its anglicized version in the list of directors on the firm's notepaper – he was a man of liberal views, eager to publish books on current affairs and politics of a left-wing persuasion, and, according to Edward Young, later to be a key member of the original Penguin team, 'responsible for a tremendous library of psychology and sexology'. And in 1924 Allen Lane himself was made a director, as was an affable, well-connected character called Lindsay Drummond, who was a cousin of the Marquess of Northampton and invested another £10,000.

Unlike the old guard of Willett and Crockett, Allen Lane was soon on easy and familiar terms with the younger Bodley Head authors; and with none more so than Agatha Christie, who became a lifelong friend. She had written her first crime novel, *The Mysterious Affair at Styles*, when she was seventeen, and after it had been turned down by innumerable publishers she sent it to The Bodley Head. She heard nothing for two years, but was eventually summoned to meet John Lane, 'a small man with a white beard, behind a desk in a roomful of pictures, looking Elizabethan, as if he should have been a portrait himself, with a ruff round his neck'; with his 'shrewd twinkling blue eyes' he looked more like 'an old-fashioned sea captain' than a conventional publisher. The firm's reader thought her book 'worth publishing', though he doubted whether 'anybody would be allowed to give evidence in the way that the Belgian detective does it', and on the strength of this Lane decided that her novel '*might* have possibilities', and offered her an advance of £25 and a five-book contract: she always felt that he had taken advantage of her, and escaped to Collins as soon as she decently could. In Allen Lane, on the other hand, she found a kindred spirit, and whereas her letters to Mr Willett were stiff and plaintive, with much grumbling about the jacket artwork and his maddening inability to remember to include a dedication page, she was very quickly addressing her letters to 'Allen, my dear' and joshing him about his endless cocktail parties and over-convivial evenings. Lane liked to claim that he devoured her first novel while licking stamps in the office, and they first met after she had called in at Vigo Street to complain about a proposed jacket illustration for her second novel, which 'represented a man in pyjamas apparently having an epileptic fit on a golf links'. 'My first impression of Allen Lane has always stayed with me,' she wrote after his death. 'An impression of vigorous youth and a kind of attractive eagerness – someone very much alive, stretching out towards life and exhibiting a gaiety and friendliness that were immediately endearing.' But she had few illusions about her new friend where business was concerned. 'Allen, isn't it about a *year* since I had any royalties from you?' she would ask from time to time: 'I wondered whether you'd notice,' he'd reply, looking 'half-guilty, half-mischievous'. But for all that, she allowed him, in due course, to reissue *The Mysterious Affair at Styles* in The Bodley Head's unsuccessful series of ninepenny paperbacks and again in the first batch of ten titles to be published by Penguin; and although she remained faithful to Collins for the rest of her writing career, many years later she persuaded a reluctant Billy Collins, who was always uneasy about her friendship with Lane, to sub-lease a batch of her titles to Penguin.

Agatha Christie lived in Torquay, which appealed to the Devonian in Lane, and whenever he went to stay they trawled round the bookshops together and spent long hours 'popping in and out of antique shops'. They were joined by a third party when she wrote to say that she was marrying for the second time, to an archaeologist a good deal younger than herself who 'never speaks'. Silent or not, Max Mallowan was to become a good friend, and, in due course, the adviser to Pelican Books on archaeological subjects and authors. Years later, Mallowan and his wife invited Lane to visit them in Iraq, where they were excavating the ancient city of Nimrud; he remembered his guest as 'a man of boundless energy, an opportunist, a born pirate, ready to take on anything', who would 'ride roughshod over his best friend' and 'expected and never resented opportunism'.

The piratical Uncle John, in the meantime, showed few signs of slowing down. 'The burden of his seventy years lay, or seemed to lie, easily upon him,' Lewis May recalled. 'He was full of ideas, as full of energy as ever.' But the young J. B. Priestley, then employed by the firm as a reader, thought Lane 'ancient: small and bearded, puckered and peeping – his sight was so bad that he could no longer read'. In January 1925 Uncle John and Annie went down to their house in Brighton for the weekend. It was damp and foggy; Lane felt unwell and took to his bed, where he insisted on dictating letters and making phone calls. Pneumonia set in, and within a fortnight he was dead. DEATH OF FAMOUS PUBLISHER, ran a headline the following day; he was cremated at Golders Green, and after a memorial service in St James's Piccadilly his ashes were taken to St Nectan's church in Hartland. Allen Lane was ill with scarlet fever, but Dick – recently returned from four years in Australia, where he had worked on a fruit farm and as a jackaroo on a sheep station in the outback of New South Wales – accompanied Aunt Annie on the long journey down to Devon. Not long afterwards she received a letter from J. B. Priestley in which he spoke of her husband's 'friendly and very charming personality', and of how 'his confidence and unflagging zest made my work a pleasure'. But all was not well at The Bodley Head: according to Stanley Unwin, who was in a position to know, the firm was insolvent at the time of its founder's death, and remained so until a receiver was appointed eleven years later, in 1936. Faced with financial problems and, as it turned out, the hostility of his fellow-directors, Allen Lane set out to claim his inheritance.

3. *The Whispering Gallery*

Aunt Annie was now the majority shareholder in The Bodley Head, and although Uncle John's nephew only owned, as yet, a handful of shares, he had the benefit of her support, and was eager to make his mark as a publishing Lane. He continued to make useful contacts through the firm, among them the novelist Pearl Binder, who was to become a friend for life, and G. B. Harrison, who had been commissioned to edit a small-format series of Elizabethan and Jacobean dramatists for the firm, and would later edit the thirty-seven volumes of the Penguin Shakespeare; but it was not until some nine months after Uncle John's death that he took on a book that might, it was hoped, turn out to be a bestseller.

In the high summer of 1926, John Willis Dunbar, an editor at Odhams, got in touch with him about a book called *The Whispering Gallery*. The anonymous diaries of a retired diplomat, it was crammed with scandalous and revealing revelations about assorted politicians, tycoons and literary men, including Lenin, Mussolini, Kitchener, Churchill, the late Tsar, Henry James and Cecil Rhodes: it could hardly fail to be controversial, and, given the current appetite for memoirs, would almost certainly sell in vast quantities as well. The book had been put into shape by Hesketh Pearson, who was beginning to make his mark as a journalist and literary man; the American rights had been snapped up by the modish new imprint of Boni & Liveright, and *The People* had expressed keen interest in acquiring the serial rights. Dunbar would be happy to send a copy of the typescript to The Bodley Head: the only condition was that the diplomat's anonymity must be preserved, and divulged to no one, not even within the publishing house. 'The name on the manuscript is a fictitious one but the author will not have his identity disclosed. I happen to know that he is an ex-ambassador,' Dunbar told Lane, adding that 'in spots your people might consider it a bit *risqué*', and that it might be wise to have it read for libel.

All this sounded highly promising, and almost certainly appealed to the mischievous and subversive side of Lane's nature. Hesketh Pearson had a similar cast of mind, and although there is no evidence to support J. E. Morpurgo's claim that the two men were drinking pals before they met over *The Whispering Gallery*, they must have been kindred spirits. A tall, burly, jovial countryman with florid cheeks, an iron jaw and a pipe in one hand, Pearson was fifteen years older than his prospective publisher. After running a car show-room in Brighton with his brother, he had decided to become an actor and joined Beerbohm Tree's celebrated touring company in 1911; he had resumed his theatrical career after serving in Mesopotamia during the First World War, during the course of which a piece of shrapnel became lodged in his skull, but was now giving up his acting commitments in favour of the literary life. His first book had been published in 1921; he had written for various Odhams publications, and it was through them that he had met Mr Dunbar. To Dunbar, and none other, he had revealed that the diplomat Diarist's name was Sir Rennell Rodd. 'Who the dickens is Rodd?' Mr Dunbar had asked him; Pearson assured him that he had met the mysterious Rodd for lunch, and that the Diarist insisted that he had 'already published with other publishers perfectly respectable books of reminiscences, and he could not on any account allow his name to come out'.

At this stage in his career, Lane's fellow-directors were still anxious to 'give the boy every encouragement', and they suggested that he should pay a visit to Pearson, then on holiday in Bognor with his wife Gladys. Although his new Triumph motor-bike broke down *en route* to Sussex, Lane met the Diarist's amanuensis for a drink and a 'slight discussion' in the Dog & Duck in Bury on 3 September 1926, and again in the Norfolk Arms Hotel in Arundel the following day. Pearson told him that the Diarist had kept a diary since university; that he, Pearson, had known about the diaries for years, and had begged to be allowed to edit them into shape; that the Diarist had eventually agreed, and had given his blessing to Pearson's compilation and editorial labours. Lane offered an advance of £250, but insisted that, 'as an act of good faith, the firm will require the diarist's name to be divulged in confidence to one director'. 'If I can tell my co-directors that you have given me a name, that will be enough – provided I could satisfy myself the name was that of a man who was in my opinion in a position to have written the original diaries from which the book was written,' he told Pearson. Pearson promised to ask Boni & Liveright to delay their publication – the book was already in proof in the States – and said that although the Diarist was away on the Continent, he would obtain his consent to The Bodley Head's terms.

Back in the office, Lane was authorized to go ahead: he had read only about half the typescript, but although Carr-Gomme, as a former politician, expressed some reservations, his colleagues were all in favour of clinching the deal. Lane went back to the Dog & Duck on 10 September, bearing with him two copies of the contract. *The Whispering Gallery*, it declared, had been 'adapted by the author from the original Diary with the full consent and approval of the writer of the said original Diary'; and whereas the standard contract at the time allowed the author a niggardly six free copies, Pearson insisted on six for himself and six for the Diarist. He had already warned Lane that the Diarist – better described, he said, as an 'envoy extraordinary' than an 'ex-Ambassador' – would not and could not indemnify the publishers against any libel actions; for Pearson himself to assume responsibility 'rather puts me in the cart', since he was far from expert in the book's subject matter and could not, in any case, afford to fight a case. Lane told him that he could safely 'assure the Diarist that under no circumstances should we call upon him and you to go into the box in the event of an action being brought'; The Bodley Head's own lawyers seemed unworried, but Pearson readily toned down some of the Diarist's wilder flights at their suggestion, and *The Whispering Gallery* nudged its way towards publication.

Publishers like nothing better than a book that gives off positive vibrations, suggestive of both profits and prestige, and Lane's purchase was boding well. The *Sunday Chronicle* was now keen to serialize, but – to Pearson's intense irritation – The Bodley Head's directors rejected their offer on the grounds that it might damage sales of the book itself, but agreed to go ahead with post-publication serialization. Lane sent out letters to newspaper and literary editors, including Clement Shorter at the *Daily Telegraph* and the editors of the *Daily Mail* and the *Times Literary Supplement*, assuring them that this would be 'one of the most talked about books of the autumn season' and that 'we can vouch for the authenticity of the volume as we know the Diarist personally'; by the time the book was published on 19 November, 4,480 from an initial printing of 5,000 were out in the shops, and a reprint had been ordered. The sales, already promising, looked set to soar when, on the very day of publication, *The Whispering Gallery* was denounced in the *Daily Mail*. A SCANDALOUS FAKE EXPOSED, ran the headline, followed by MONSTROUS ATTACKS ON PUBLIC MEN and REPUDIATIONS BY FIVE CABINET MINISTERS. Lord Rothermere, it seemed, had been incensed by the Diarist's account of how his brother, the half-demented Lord Northcliffe, had, when crossed, stamped his feet on the floor and pounded the furniture; nor was so Conservative a paper likely to feel well-disposed to a book which seemed sympathetic to Lenin, who was depicted as a kindly character, while describing the Tsar as an 'ill-meaning skunk'. Although Pearson warned Lane that the Diarist was gravely upset by the *Mail's* assault – 'I was starting to read when the Diarist rang me up in the most agitated manner. In fact he could hardly speak he was in such a fury' – the publicity seemed all to the good.

But Rothermere was not alone. The *Observer* savaged the book as 'a reeking compost of garbage', its widely respected editor, J. L. Garvin, attacking the author as 'an impostor and a cad' who had come up with 'an unscrupulous farrago'; and he was followed by *The Times* and the Lord Chancellor, Lord Birkenhead. Tempers began to fray, and nerves to crack, at The Bodley Head: Carr-Gomme was so angry with the youngest director that he refused to speak to him again. Pearson warned Lane that he might well be 'sleuthed' by the Press, that he should make a point of leaving the office by a back door, and that they should not be spotted in public together.

As controversy steadily mounted, the editor-in-chief of Allied Newspapers wrote to Basil Willett, who had been all in favour of publication, to ask whether Lane would be prepared to submit a list of questions to the Diarist so that their papers could answer criticism levelled against the book, and possibly interview the author as well. Would the elusive diplomat take legal action against those papers which had described his book as a fraud? How would he answer those statesmen and public figures who had hastened to deny the claims made about them? Winston Churchill had claimed that he was on the Western Front at the very moment when, according to the Diarist, he was dining with Mr Asquith in Downing Street, and had described his alleged conversations with the Prime Minister as 'puerile in their ignorance'; Asquith, described by the Diarist as an 'old woman in trousers', had denied ever calling Lloyd George 'David'; Viscount Cecil was insistent that Lord Balfour had never called him 'Robert', nor had he ever smoked a cigar. Seemingly unabashed, the diplomat issued a statement, via his amanuensis, in which he refused to give his name and declared that 'I do not mind if I am believed or not'; Pearson issued another in which he said that it had always been understood that the Diarist's anonymity must be preserved. If the book was a fabrication, 'it is no fabrication of mine': his role was that of an 'intermediary and editor only', and as the book's editor he neither knew nor cared whether the Diarist was telling the truth; he had 'accepted the work in good faith from the source whence it emanated, just as the publishers accepted it in good faith from myself'.

By now, Lane's fellow-directors were in a state of panic, and they made it clear that it was up to him to sort things out. Pearson rang from 'a pal's flat' to say that he had got another statement from the Diarist; Lane met his managing director after dinner, and together they went back to Vigo Street to await Pearson's arrival. He eventually turned up at 11.30, looking rather flustered, and told them that he had had 'an awful time with the Diarist', and 'the greatest trouble' in extracting a handwritten statement, which he had then typed up at home. 'He is very excited and it is diffi-cult to keep him to the point. He says among other things that it is my fault that the book has got all this publicity, and that he did not want it,' he told the two publishers. He seemed curiously coy about showing the statement to Willett and Lane, but was prepared to read out the Diarist's replies to the questions posed by Allied Newspapers. Willett found him plausible enough: he felt 'for the moment satisfied as to his genuineness and that the *Daily Mail* attack was unjustified', though 'we formed the opinion that there was a little more "write-up" and a little less "diary" than we had at first imagined'.

Willett's optimism soon proved baseless; and his own position, and that of his colleagues, became a great deal more uncomfortable when the *Daily Mail* turned its attack on The Bodley Head. In a leader headed 'A Disreputable Publisher', the paper declared itself amazed that the publishers had not apologized to their readers. 'They have lent themselves to a fraud on the public and have debased the name of their firm. It remains to be seen whether reputable authors will be willing to have their works published by a firm which is capable of such disgraceful conduct,' the leader page declared. Stung into action, the directors held a board meeting on a Saturday at which Willett rang Pearson and told him to instruct the Diarist to withdraw his book, 'otherwise we shall have to sue the *Daily Mail* and call [him] as a witness'. Pearson told Lane that he had arranged to meet the Diarist at his home in Kensington – but when Lane at last got round to looking up Sir Rennell Rodd in *Who's Who*, he discovered that he lived in Cavendish Square. Whatever his home address, the Diarist was, Pearson reported, happy to have his book withdrawn; where possible, copies were taken back from the bookshops, and a planned reprint was cancelled.

Abandoning all hopes of a quiet weekend, the Bodley Head board met again on Sunday, two days after the *Mail* had unleashed its bombshell. Pearson, who had been chivvying Lane for £25 still owing on the advance, claiming that he had to pay over two-thirds of the proceeds to the Diarist, was summoned again to Vigo Street. He was told that he must provide firm evidence of the Diarist's existence; he should write at once to the Diarist, and Lane should deliver the letter in person. That, Pearson insisted, was quite impossible: not

only had he 'sworn not to communicate with the Diarist by letter',
but he could neither deliver letters through a third party nor phone
the Diarist in Lane's presence. Somehow overlooking the alleged
meeting in Kensington, he claimed that he had only ever met the
Diarist in a club or a flat belonging to a third party; but he would
be very happy to show Lane a cheque for the Diarist's two-thirds
share of the £225 already paid by The Bodley Head, drawn by
Pearson in the Diarist's favour and bearing his endorsement.

Ignoring Pearson's caveats about the use of intermediaries, Willett
told Pearson that 'if you will not do any of these things, our Secretary
will have to write to the man concerned, and deliver the letter in
person'. 'That, of course, would be much worse,' Pearson replied.
The ensuing silence was broken by Mr Crockett, the trade director,
a sturdy Scot and former Bodley Head rep who had knocked down
a picket who tried to stop him loading a van during the General
Strike earlier that year. Crockett was the only man in the firm to
have read the book in its entirety. 'Well now, not to mince matters,
is there a Diarist?' he asked the embattled ghost-writer. 'Of course
there is,' Pearson shot back, sounding suitably indignant. Unabashed,
Crockett then asked him whether he had written the book himself;
this was fiercely denied. Lane then left the room to make a phone
call; Pearson asked for a word in private with him, and joined him
in the Chairman's room. 'This is a very unfortunate business. It's
come at the worst possible time, as Rodd's daughter is being married
this week,' he told Lane. The two men rejoined the other directors, and Pearson told them that the Diarist might well have to start
proceedings against The Bodley Head, in which case he would have
to give evidence, and the name of the Diarist might be divulged:
but 'I should deny that I ever gave you the name.' 'Would you
throw us over?' Crockett asked him; to which Pearson replied, 'Yes,
I should be forced to do so.' Tempers were frayed when they
adjourned for lunch. Crockett, by now in the role of prosecuting
counsel, asked Pearson to go home to Abbey Road and return
bringing with him any correspondence with the Diarist, but when
they resumed after lunch, Pearson told him that he could not comply
with his request. 'Do you mean that you are not able to find *any*

document connecting you with the Diarist?' Crockett asked him. No, he was told: 'everything has been destroyed'. The board then turned on Lane and insisted that he should reveal the Diarist's name.

Lane initially refused, but the following day, after consulting his solicitor, he revealed that the elusive Diarist was, in fact, Sir Rennell Rodd; he had just been to see him in Cavendish Square, and had 'laid the facts before him'. Sir Rennell had denied any connection with *The Whispering Gallery*, Hesketh Pearson and The Bodley Head. By now in his late sixties, a product of Haileybury and Balliol and a former Ambassador to Rome, Sir Rennell was a highly respectable figure who had achieved a certain eminence as a literary man as well as a diplomat, and was planning to stand for Parliament at the next general election. He had won the Newdigate Prize at Oxford, and a collection of his poems, *Ballads of the Fleet*, had appeared in 1897: as a young man he had consorted with Burne-Jones, Whistler and Oscar Wilde, later to be the subject of Hesketh Pearson's most popular biography, paperbacked by Penguin: Wilde had written a foreword to a collection of Rodd's poems, but it was withdrawn by its recipient, who found it too effusive. A biography of the Prussian Crown Prince, written while Rodd was an attaché in Berlin, had given grave offence to its subject's family, and since then he had devoted himself to studies of Ancient Greece while serving with Lord Cromer in Egypt, in Abyssinia, as the Ambassador in Rome and, more recently, as a delegate to the League of Nations. Had Lane taken the trouble to consult the reference books, he would have discovered that he had recently written his memoirs in three volumes; the last of these had appeared only the previous year, which made it all the more unlikely that he would have written *The Whispering Gallery*.

Before long word got out, and The Bodley Head received a further battering in the press. 'Daily Mail Exposure Succeeds . . . Faked Book Withdrawn,' trumpeted the *Daily Mail*. 'The greatest literary scandal of recent times reached a dramatic climax last evening,' it informed its readers, before going on to refer to 'strong public indignation' and 'slanders upon public men'. The following day, it resumed the attack. The book was a 'shameless forgery' and

Pearson 'an impudent literary forger': 'the next step in the sordid affair lies with the Public Prosecutor'. Lord Birkenhead let fly another blast – 'The fate of *The Whispering Gallery* will I hope warn garbage manufacturers and their publishers that they cannot with impunity slander the dead and insult the living' – while Sir Rennell, who had already made clear his position through a letter to *The Times*, wrily observed that 'Perhaps the unkindest cut of all is that the author of the memoirs is said to have used such abominable English.'

Basil Willett, exerting himself at last, stopped the most recent cheque issued to Pearson, and strove to appease his assailants. Pearson claimed that The Bodley Head's directors hurried round to the *Mail* in search of absolution, and that 'under the influence of champagne, their tongues were loosened'. They told the paper that although Pearson had 'appeared to be a reputable literary man, whose books had been issued by other well-known firms', they now realized that they had been the victims of a hoax; and, far from accepting collective responsibility, they tried to pass all the blame on to the hapless Lane. Willett wrote abject letters to all the national papers, including the *Daily Mail*, in which he denounced 'our junior director' for having given newspaper editors and others his personal guarantee of its authenticity without consulting the other board members. He wrote on similar lines to Rodd's solicitors, who had asked how Lane could possibly have vouched for the authenticity of the diary on the grounds that 'we know the Diarist personally' when he had only recently met Sir Rennell for the first time: conveniently forgetting his own earlier backing for the book, Willett assured Sir Rennell's solicitor that it had indeed been taken on by 'the youngest partner in the firm in the course of business', and that it 'did not come to the knowledge of the other Directors until it was too late'. To Sir Rennell he expressed his 'deep regret that your name should have been dragged into this unfortunate business', and assured him that 'we are taking steps to bring to justice the miscreant who has made use of your name in this disgraceful way'.

The miscreant, as it happened, was out of London when this second storm broke, appearing in a play in Cardiff. The theatre was besieged by reporters; Pearson made his escape via the nearest pub, and from there he headed to the railway station and the London train, but was recognized by reporters and had to lock himself in the train's lavatory for the entire journey to Paddington. His house in Abbey Road was hemmed in by journalists, and a warrant for his arrest was lying on the hall table: his publishers had decided to sue him on the grounds of obtaining money from them under false pretences. He was eventually arrested in his solicitor's offices by Detective Inspector John Howell, and appeared before the Great Marlborough Street magistrates on 26 November, charged with having unlawfully obtained 'from one Allen Lane Williams Lane a certain valuable security to wit a banker's order for the payment of £225 by false pretences and with intent to defraud'. He was committed for trial at the London Sessions on 26 January 1927, and his brother-in-law, Colonel 'Dane' Hamlett, paid his bail of £1,000.

Although Sir Patrick Hastings, the most eminent barrister of the day and a keen theatre-goer, had agreed to act in Pearson's defence, he felt it to be a hopeless case, and urged Pearson to plead guilty. Bernard Shaw and Hugh Kingsmill were of similar mind. 'I am afraid poor old Hesketh Pearson will get it in the neck. He is fighting the case instead of caving in. I am very sorry for the poor old boy,' Kingsmill wrote to a friend, while Shaw suggested that Pearson should ask the court 'for no more consideration than to be treated as a fool rather than a scoundrel', and found it hard to believe that 'it was anything worse than the fictitious memoirs and travels that have often been published as genuine'. But Pearson, who had won the Military Cross in Mesopotamia, was determined to fight his corner. 'Pat [Hastings] gravely warned me to go home and talk matters over with my wife . . . I answered that if the prospect was from three to six years I would still refuse to confess that I had wronged a pack of cads, cowards and humbugs like the Lanes' – which seemed a little hard on the Lanes *en bloc*, given that Uncle John was dead and Allen was, as yet, the only other member of the family to be employed by the firm. Only the notorious lecher and arch-gossip Frank Harris – whose unexpected appearance in Vigo Street had once caused Uncle John to turn ashen with apprehension – insisted that Pearson should stick to his guns. 'Memoirs are a well-known form of fiction,' the moustachioed old rogue told Pearson from his bolt-hole in Nice. 'Say that a well-known literary man told you so. It will make the court laugh.'

Harris's words were all too prophetic: the court would have plenty to laugh at, both in the humiliation of The Bodley Head's directors, and the bizarre behaviour of the defendant. According to the *Daily Mail*, which took a keen interest in the proceedings, 'the well of the court and the gallery were filled, many of the public being women': no doubt they were both shocked and titillated, since Hastings decided that, in this apparently hopeless case, attack was the best form of defence, and that he would do his best to discredit the plaintiffs by portraying them as unabashed pornographers. He described, luridly and in unwholesome detail, the illustrated erotica published by the firm, laying special emphasis on Ovid's *Amores*, Balzac's *Contes Drolatiques* and Apuleius's *The Golden Ass*, Robert Graves's version of which would, years later, be among Lane's proudest achievements on the Penguin Classics list. Lane, struggling to keep his end up, would not admit that the Ovid was obscene, but refused to read an extract to the court; Hastings suggested that no 'decent woman' could bear to look at the illustrations by the Belgian Jean de Bosschère, and that one of those featured in *The Golden Ass* was almost certainly 'the foulest thing that any judge in any court has looked at'. The judge, helpfully enough, played his part to perfection: Pearson later told Kingsmill how he 'had to look at the drawings through the fingers of the hand that covered his face in horror', and how 'the jury (not the ladies) inspected these pictures with a care that led me to believe that their interest in them was not wholly legal. However, their faces showed a becoming sense of repugnance . . .' Hastings, who had evidently done his homework, then produced a modern novel published by The Bodley Head: 'Can you find a single page in that which is not utterly foul?' he wondered. After it was all over, Pearson ridiculed the firm's directors as so many 'dirty little rats' who had tried to send him to prison but 'daren't look their own publications in the face', and described how the wretched Willett, with his drooping moustache and pince-nez on the end of his nose, 'went greyer and greyer as he stood in that box; he aged ten years in as many minutes, and he spent the remainder of the day with his head buried in his hands'.

Lane's appearance in the witness-box was equally unimpressive. He was reproached for the careless way in which he appeared to have looked up Sir Rennell's entry in *Who's Who*, and for admitting that, until trouble loomed, he had only read about half of *The Whispering Gallery*. Far from quizzing Pearson about his part in the book, he admitted that 'I did not say "Now! How much of this work is yours?"': on the other hand, 'I didn't say "It doesn't matter a bit. He won't be asked to repudiate it because no one will ever know."' Nor, at his first meeting with Pearson, had he promised on his 'solemn word of honour' not to reveal the Diarist's name, though 'I probably said something to that effect at a later interview.' Recalled to give further evidence the following day, he denied having said that he'd try to forget the Diarist's name, or that Pearson had replied, 'Well in that case any name would do.' He denied having said, 'We want to publish the book. The name is a formality,' or that he had told Pearson that at least two of his fellow-directors thought the book a hoax fairly early in the proceedings; nor would he agree that Pearson had told him that 'of course you realize my book is going to cause trouble', to which he had replied that 'If a firm doesn't take risks it must put up its shutters,' and that he hoped the book would 'be attacked all over the place'. He admitted that the firm had initially welcomed the *Daily Mail*'s onslaught as valuable publicity, on the strength of which they had hoped to sell some 10,000 copies; and that, as far as Pearson was concerned, 'the whole of the time I was doing this business with the defendant I entirely and implicitly trusted him'.

After such directorial evasions, Pearson must have seemed a wonderfully frank and refreshing witness. When asked why he had used Sir Rennell's name, he admitted that he had done so 'because I could not think of anyone less likely to have written the book', and his words were greeted with 'laughter in court'. When Sir Henry Curtis Bennett, the prosecuting counsel, tried to discomfit him by asking him why he had continued to lie about the non-existent

Diarist, he thought this must have been 'because I was mad'. After
deliberating his case for twenty minutes, the jury returned a verdict
of 'not guilty'. Hastings told Pearson that 'you got yourself off by
your evidence in the witness-box', and in the pub afterwards a
member of the jury told him how his candour had won them round.

But the litigation was not yet over: Pearson decided that he, in
turn, would take out an action against The Bodley Head, claiming
damages for the 'pain and suffering' caused him by their prosecution. The publisher's solicitors recommended that they should settle
for the original advance of £250, and informed Pearson's lawyers
that the firm would not 'consent to pay a farthing to your client in
respect of his pain and suffering or expense, all of which he brought
entirely upon himself'. Once again, words proved stronger than deeds:
Pearson had asked for £250 plus £500 for the copyright in the book,
and The Bodley Head finally agreed to pay over to him £416 8s.
1d. – the entire profit from sales before the book was withdrawn –
much of which went on his defence costs. Nor had the firm's reputation been enhanced by the whole affair: Pearson told Kingsmill
that the publishers lacked 'the spunk of a boiled rabbit', and the
literary agent David Higham, then starting out on his career, remembered how they became known as 'John Lane The Badly Had'.
Certainly their behaviour seems to have been greedy, craven and
incompetent. Long before *The Whispering Gallery* came their way,
The Bodley Head's reader had found Pearson's *Parallel Lives* 'clever
and alert, but fundamentally unsatisfying' and had suggested that 'the
manuscript should be examined with exceeding care, both for libels
and faults of taste'. Pearson, who had polished his technique by
writing political profiles for *John Bull*, readily admitted to taking a
cavalier approach to the business of biography. 'No artist worth his
salt is concerned with accuracy in detail if it doesn't suit his purpose
. . . In order to achieve essential truth one often has to sacrifice the
essential facts,' he once declared. Michael Holroyd has suggested that
Pearson's *Modern Men and Manners*, replete with exaggerated and
often libellous tales of theatrical folk, may have been a dummy-run
for *The Whispering Gallery*, since when he had also published in John
Middleton Murry's *Adelphi* a collection of entirely imaginary

conversations between Bernard Shaw and G. K. Chesterton which were (and still are) widely regarded as authentic. He had read about Sir Rennell Rodd in *TP's Weekly*, and had written the book simply to make some money; it was, he happily admitted, 'an act of insanity', exacerbated by the lump of shrapnel in his head, and 'the work of an unbalanced person who, when he realized what he had done, acted like a lunatic'. To Pearson at least, 'it must have been obvious to the intelligent reader that conversations on that level of familiarity and comical repartee can never have taken place'; he was amazed at his publisher's readiness to be taken in, and 'had I been in possession of my wits I would have told them squarely that I had written the book, and that they could no more have believed it to be the work of a real diplomat than of a real dinosaur'. No publisher would look at Pearson's work for the next three years, after which he embarked on a successful career as an altogether more reliable biographer. Sir Rennell went on to become the first Baron Rennell, and died in 1941: his son, Peter Rodd, was married to Nancy Mitford, later to become a staple of the Penguin fiction list.

Given Lane's own mischievous cast of mind, his readiness to publish Pearson's biographies in Penguin and his refusal to bear a grudge despite the harsh things said about his family, it's hard to repress a suspicion that he may well have known that the whole thing was a hoax from the very beginning, and hoped to get away with it. Pearson himself had warned Lane that 'Lord Beaverbrook, you remember, thought it "too good to be true"'; and not long before his death, Lane told a retired army officer who had enquired about the case that 'there is no question that Hesketh Pearson did write the book himself, and I must say that despite the fact that the book got us into a great deal of hot water, I always had a high regard for him'. Lane's feelings towards his treacherous fellow-directors were a good deal less charitable, and from now on they regarded his every move with grave suspicion.

But the balance of power was about to change. Annie Lane had fallen ill during the trial, and died within weeks of its end: she left almost everything she had to the three Lane brothers and Nora, but whereas Dick and John inherited money, Allen was left her majority shareholding in The Bodley Head – a mixed blessing, since although it gave him control of Uncle John's publishing house, the firm never declared a dividend thereafter, and his shares were worthless when the business went into liquidation. Three months later, Basil Willett departed to work for a paper merchant, and Lane was left in charge.

4. Goodbye to The Bodley Head

For six months after Annie Lane's death, the two elder Lane brothers continued to live in style at Lancaster Gate Terrace; the house had come equipped with Mr Costin, the butler, a cook and two servants, and when not busying themselves with the sale of the leasehold and the contents of the house, they gave an endless succession of parties. The sale of Uncle John's paintings did little to improve Lane's relations with his colleagues at The Bodley Head: paintings and artwork commissioned and paid for by the firm had, as often as not, ended up on the walls of Lancaster Gate Terrace, and the other directors, already incensed by the *Whispering Gallery* fiasco, claimed that they belonged to the firm, not the family.

When not embattled in the office, Lane enjoyed a vigorous social life. The *Evening Standard* had dubbed him 'London's Youngest Publisher', and a cocktail had been invented in his honour; his genial manner and his liking for a party were converting the shy provincial into an urbane man-about-town. His new friends included another Bristolian, the precocious Beverley Nichols, and the formidable figure of Christina Foyle, who had thought up the notion of Foyles Literary Lunches at the age of nineteen, and was to mastermind them for the rest of her long career in the Charing Cross Road; but none was closer, for a time, than Ethel Mannin, then beginning to make her mark as a romantic novelist.

A letter-sorter's daughter from Clapham, Ethel Mannin went on to write over 100 books: well-read but entirely self-taught, she was happy to write for those who were 'philistines, and proud of it', admired Arnold Bennett, and hated writers she considered to be pretentious, obscure or deliberately difficult. An attractive, flamboyant and fine-looking girl, she had, at the age of nineteen, married a Mr Porteous, who had little to say for himself thereafter. She first met Lane at a PEN Club dinner. Noticing an 'incredibly good-looking young man' on the other side of the room, she asked a friend who he was. 'But that's Allen Lane!' her friend replied, amazed at her ignorance. She took to inviting him and Dick down to her country cottage for the weekend, along with Christina Foyle, Michael Joseph (then working as a literary agent, but soon to set up on his own account as a publisher), Ralph Straus, an influential middlebrow book reviewer, and the theatrical pair of Charles Laughton and Elsa Lanchester. Once installed, 'we drank a good deal of gin, and we led each other on, and there was a certain amount of nonsense, but no one rode a horse up the stairs, and no one threw anyone in the lily pond, and around 1 a.m. there would be a great deal of slamming of doors and starting up of engines'. Quite how involved with each other Lane and his hostess became – if at all – is a matter of conjecture. A devotee of 'modern' views and an advocate of trial marriages, she warned her friends not to call on her unannounced, since 'I am so liable to be caught in a "compromising situation", and that would be an embarrassment all round'; evidently Lane was not immune to embarrassment, for when he took her to the Authors' Club 'he told me to "dress quietly" and remember that his mother would be there'. But she did not remain true to her advanced beliefs. 'This is a very terrible book,' she told him apropos James Hanley's notorious novel, *Boy*, then on offer to The Bodley Head, and 'no amount of cutting or editing could possibly make it publishable . . . the whole book is nothing but buggery and brothels, and filth and horror piled upon each other in endless repetition'. Hanley had written Lane a series of harrowing letters – he was out of work, his father had lost his job at Cunard after forty-five years, and his mother was in hock to money-lenders – and begged for a loan of £50. Lane may or may not have lent him the money, but he decided not to take on *Boy*: it was eventually published by the short-lived firm of Boriswood, the manager of which, C. J. Greenwood, was later installed to run The Bodley Head by Stanley Unwin.

Although the three youngest Lanes had done best, in purely monetary terms, from Aunt Annie's will, all were entitled to £400 a year from what Dick referred to as an 'American Trust'; and some of this largesse seems to have found its way into the coffers of their parents, who moved from Coombe Dingle, near Bristol, to a large house in Gloucestershire with five bedrooms and seven acres of land. By now John was working in London for the London & Lancashire Insurance Company, and most weekends the three brothers would descend on the family home at Falfield. Badminton, the nearest station, was a request stop, but since only first-class passengers could avail themselves of the service, the brothers took to buying one first-class and two third-class tickets. Before long they were on the best of terms with the ticket-collector, who reserved a compartment for them, while the buffet staff set aside their favourite cuts of meat for dinner; and rather than shiver in the waiting-room with the hoi-polloi, they were given the freedom of the stationmaster's office, and its blazing fire in the winter.

Dick was finding it particularly hard to settle on a career. Allen found him work in a bookshop in the Finchley Road after his return from Australia in 1926, but no sooner had he come into his inheritance than he gave in his notice. The two brothers took part in a production of *Hamlet* in the Mill Hill School theatre. Lewis May played the Prince, and at a solemn moment in the proceedings the Lanes were deputed to carry Ophelia's body on stage; both were inflamed by drink, and she was ignominiously toppled from her bier. Although Allen was never a great theatre-goer, dutifully attending any new production of a play by Bernard Shaw but preferring lighter fare, Dick briefly contemplated a career on stage. Through Muriel Hines, a Bodley Head novelist, he met Robert Atkins, who persuaded him to join his Shakespearean touring company on a visit to Egypt, where they performed before King Farouk. With his brief theatrical career behind him, Dick was introduced by his brother to A. J. A. Symons, best remembered as the author of *The Quest for Corvo*. Symons ran the Wine and Food Society with André Simon as well as the First Editions Club, and needed some secretarial help: Dick was not the obvious man for the job, since he had no shorthand and could only type, very slowly, with two fingers, but he was set to work typing the menu for one of the Society's forthcoming lunches. This was followed by an unhappy spell with the National Bank of Egypt.

When Dick decided that banking was not for him, he began to work, initially as a freelance, for The Bodley Head. He vetted the reps' expenses, read manuscripts, and corrected proofs for five shillings per volume. A worrier over details, he found 2,000 mistakes in the translation of a book about a Swedish balloonist's attempt to fly over the North Pole; later, in the Penguin days, his detailed knowledge of cars and combustion engines was put to good effect, preventing thriller writers, in particular, from making too many motoring howlers. He was also an authority on guns. Once installed on a full-time basis, he went on the road as a rep, starting with the outer suburbs and East Anglia before graduating to the all-important bookshops of central London. As such, he masterminded a triumphant window-display in Selfridge's which featured a working model of the pancake-making machine from Norman Hunter's children's book *The Incredible Adventures of Professor Branestawm*: Allen had got in touch with Hunter after hearing him on the radio, given him toasted tea-cakes in Vigo Street, and commissioned W. Heath Robinson to provide the illustrations.

Throughout his career, Allen Lane both endured and encouraged the notion that he was not a great reader, but although he never claimed to be an intellectual or a literary man, he almost certainly read a good deal more, and more widely, than he let on, and to pose as an unbookish businessman was, in part, a useful subterfuge. Interviewed by the *Publishers' Circular and Booksellers' Record* in the spring of 1929, he remarked – apropos the familiar authorial complaint about publishers failing to read the books submitted to them – that 'it is sometimes unnecessary to drink the whole bottle of champagne in order to find out if it is flat'; he spent three-quarters of his time reading manuscripts, he informed its readers, and worked late in the office more often than not. Warming to his subject, he went on to say that word of mouth was the most effective way to make a bestseller, and that books should only be advertised if they were already being talked about: unlike his flamboyant contemporary Victor Gollancz, whose vast and strident advertisements in the Sunday papers were an unavoidable ingredient of literary life between the wars, Lane would always regard expensive publicity as a waste of good money, and at Penguin he preferred to advertise and promote the imprint and that month's new publications rather than particular titles. He concluded by hoping he might 'one day occupy the unique position of trust and affection which Mr John Lane held for so long in the London publishing world'.

As it turned out, he would be regarded, by his fellow publishers at least, with a wary if envious esteem, rather than with positive trust and affection. But although The Bodley Head's shaky finances were not conducive to trust, not least among its suppliers, in purely editorial terms the firm forged ahead over the next few years. Lane's busy social life netted him the memoirs of long-forgotten celebrities; *Good Housekeeping* applauded his 'surprisingly mature publishing judgement' in signing up Continental heavyweights like Pirandello and Roger Martin du Gard; he was rumoured to have taken on the memoirs of Gloria Vanderbilt while on a trip to New York; John Cowper Powys moved to the firm with *A Glastonbury Romance*, while Irving Stone's *Lust for Life*, a popular biography of Van Gogh, sold in its thousands. Agatha Christie may have moved on, but *Good Housekeeping* reported that he had 'found a storyteller of the first order in C. S. Forester', and although Michael Joseph would publish the Hornblower novels, Forester remained with The Bodley Head for thirteen books, including *The Gun* and *Brown on Resolution*. Lane's American authors included H. L. Mencken and Gertrude Stein, both eminent if unsaleable; a deal was worked out with Dodd, Mead in New York whereby the two firms gave each other the first offer of books in which they held the rights, and, on his increasingly frequent trips to the States, he got to know sympathetic publishers like Alfred and Blanche Knopf and Ben Huebsch of the Viking Press.

Two editorial developments were to have a particular bearing on Lane's future as a publisher: the buying in of rights from other publishers, and publishing books on current affairs. Like most publishers at the time, The Bodley Head reissued many backlist titles in 'cheap' hardback editions at 3s. 6d. each, so giving them a new lease of life at a lower price, but whereas his rivals usually contented themselves with cheap editions of their own books, Lane also bought the rights in other publishers' books for The Bodley Head's Modern Library. Taking in other people's washing sometimes proved problematic, especially when it involved the sale of stock as well as of rights: Jonathan Cape tried to buy back The Bodley Head's remaining stock of their cheap edition of André Maurois's *Byron* and reissue it himself at 7s. 6d., but Lane turned him down on the grounds that the book was still selling very nicely; Basil Blackwell wrote to complain about the confusion caused by the firm's habit of buying up competitors' overstocks, overblocking the spine, pasting in a cancel title page, and reissuing these books under their own imprint.

By the end of the decade, following the Great Crash and the onset of mass unemployment, Lane thought of himself as a socialist, albeit of the intuitive rather than the analytical variety: in later years he attributed this to his coming across homeless or unemployed men and women sleeping on benches, wrapped in newspaper against the cold, as he strolled home across Hyde Park, clad in white tie and tails. Such sights proved no bar to further social activity – he was, he readily admitted, 'quite a social bird' and 'a bit of a partygoer', more at home in the Café Royal or the 400 Club than in Toynbee Hall with Major Attlee – but, as a publisher, he could do his bit to remedy matters. Ronald Boswell, with his Continental connections, was already making the firm's reputation for publishing topical books on current affairs, and however keen Lane may have been to see the back of the old guard at The Bodley Head, Boswell included, he was all in favour of publishing Edgar Mowrer's *Germany Puts the Clock Back* (later reissued, in an updated version, as the very first Penguin Special), Hubert Griffith's *Seeing Soviet Russia* and H. R. Knickerbocker's *Germany: Fascist or Soviet?* A year after Hitler's rise to power Boswell published *Heil!*, which juxtaposed unflattering photographs of the Nazi leaders with an equally disobliging commentary, and may have led to a rumour that some members of staff at The Bodley Head had been put on a black list by the *Völkischer Beobachter* for publishing anti-Nazi books. Not only did Boswell anticipate the Penguin Specials, but he employed Krishna Menon, a wild-eyed Indian barrister equally devoted to Socialism and Indian independence, as the editorial adviser on the Twentieth Century Library: contributors included Eric Gill on Art, Norman Bentwich on the Jews, Naomi Mitchison on the Home, Winifred Holtby on Women and Ralph Fox on Communism.

With his liking for the nuts and bolts of the trade, Lane spent the greater part of his Bodley Head career in the firm's Brewer Street trade counter, finding life there more congenial than it might have been among the gentleman publishers in the more elegant if equally cramped editorial offices in Vigo Street. Grubby, dusty and down-at-heel, Brewer Street was a Dickensian maze of cubbyholes, high stools and old-fashioned clerks carefully noting, by hand and in large leather-bound stock books, the exact number of copies sold and despatched that day. Those books that were not still with the printer or the binder, attracting unwelcome storage charges, were stored in the cellar in brown paper parcels; on the ground floor, just inside the front door, was the trade counter itself, where orders from booksellers and wholesalers were processed and despatched by men in brown cotton coats of the kind once worn by old-fashioned ironmongers. A tiny, twisting staircase led up to cubbyholes containing an accountant, poring gloomily over the figures, and a royalty clerk, totting up the sums due to authors and paying them out at the last possible moment. Lane's office was on this floor; it had two doors, so enabling him to make a quick get-away when Doris Leslie, a successful romantic novelist, turned up in search of royalties, clad in riding-breeches and clutching a whip. And despite their differences over *The Whispering Gallery*, he may well have had a soft spot for Mr Crockett, the Trade Director, now in charge in Brewer Street: every now and then Crockett would disappear in a purposeful way, clutching a set of golf clubs while claiming that he had to spend the afternoon in Vigo Street. This pleasant way of life came to an end when Basil Willett handed in his notice and the somnolent but resentful Carr-Gomme retired. Lane took over as Chairman and Managing Director, joining his editorial colleagues in Vigo Street, and the golf-loving Mr Crockett died in 1930.

One of the perks of Vigo Street was the use of two attic rooms in Albany. Lane had these redecorated – a starry constellation was

painted on the blue bedroom ceiling – and installed a bathroom
and lavatory, and when he and Dick were too late or too tired or
too drunk to make their way home to Lancaster Gate Terrace, they
could spend the night next door to the office. But once the leasehold in Uncle John's old house had been sold, they had to find
somewhere else to live. They took a cramped and squalid set of
rooms above a doctor's surgery in Southwick Street, off the Edgware
Road, and when John came to London he joined them there,
sharing a bedroom with Allen. There were no lights in the bathroom – 'the dirtiest, darkest place of ablution I have ever met', in
Dick's opinion – or in Allen's bedroom; the geyser was operated
by feeding pennies into a padlocked meter, but Dick, ever the
handyman, kept a large collection of keys about his person, so
enabling him to undo the padlock and recycle their pennies. When
the brothers decided that the time had come to move on, they
took with them as many fittings as they could unscrew, unbolt or
otherwise remove: alerted by the clattering on the stairs of John's
partially dismantled bed, the landlord hurried out in his dressing-
gown to find a policeman, and they quickly made their escape.
From there they moved, in 1929, to 16 Talbot Square in Paddington,
wedged between Praed Street and Sussex Gardens. The white
stuccoed terraces north of Hyde Park were then regarded as slums;
but the Lanes were to spend 'ten very happy years' there, and Dick
and Allen would look back on them with the sadness and nostalgia
reserved for a vanished youth.

Eager to learn what the future held, Lane took the advice of at
least two astrologers and fortune-tellers. Evangeline Adams was hopelessly wide of the mark – 'There is little to indicate that you should
go into business for yourself,' she observed – but Kate Murray from
Golders Green was surprisingly perceptive. 'You appear to be much
more fixed and determined than you really are,' she told him. 'You
are rather inclined to waver and be indecisive, but you have a fine
intuitive mind,' even if 'you seem to need the stimulation of another
person's mind and character to do your work'. Though 'warm-
hearted and affectionate', he was not a passionate man, but was
liable to be over-anxious about his love affairs. 'I do not think you

will ever get very stout,' she concluded, but he needed to watch his diet and 'be very careful to limit the alcohol'.

Prepared for all emergencies, Lane continued his battle to keep The Bodley Head afloat; and Dick was always beside him, like a kindly, anxious and infuriating bank manager, clucking over his brother's extravagance, his passion for running risks, his faith in his hunches, and his worryingly left-wing views. Among the purchases which must have given Dick sleepless nights were the 'Silly Symphonies', a series of Walt Disney pop-up books which Lane bought on one of his American trips, and which included such old favourites as *The Three Little Pigs* and *The Big Bad Wolf*. The books sold well at 2s. 6d. a piece, and Woolworth's expressed interest in taking an edition; since items sold in Woolworth's were never sold for more than sixpence, this would have involved selling copies to them at well below the costs of production, and at an infinitely higher discount than the third off the published price offered to conventional retailers; but whereas Dick may well have been tearing his hair, Allen saw the Woolworth's offer as a challenge worth accepting, whatever Dick's costings might suggest.★

Lane's fellow directors were horrified by Lane's seemingly cavalier ways, and to circumvent their caution and hostility he suggested

★ Then, as now, publishers costed their books via a combination of the formulaic and the intuitive. The formulaic method involved marking up, or multiplying, the production costs per title (setting, printing, paper, blockmaking, binding, etc.) by a multiple of x to allow for overheads, author's royalties and a modest profit for the publisher: if, for example, the current mark-up was five times the production cost, and a particular book cost a pound to produce, the published price would be £5. Publishers who stuck too rigidly to the mark-up could well find themselves losing readers, or profits, or both: the mark-up provided an approximate price, but this could be reduced or inflated, depending on the publisher's judgement of what the market would bear, or what he could get away with. Although royalty rates are lower today than they were in the Thirties, overheads – rent, rates and salaries – are, proportionately, far higher than they were, and whereas a mark-up today might be seven or eight times the production cost, in the Thirties it was often as low as three times the cost. Dick can hardly be blamed for turning pale at the thought of selling 'Silly Symphonies' to Woolworth's at 4d. each.

that the Lane brothers should publish certain titles at their own risk and expense while making use of The Bodley Head's imprint and publishing services; and it was on this basis that Penguin Books would be launched from within The Bodley Head. He tested the waters with two very different items. Peter Arno was a well-known *New Yorker* cartoonist, and Lane bought *Peter Arno's Parade*, a book of his cartoons, on one of his trips to New York. Back in England, he showed his new purchase to Ben Travers, who shared his enthusiasm to the full. 'I cherish always the memory of Allen that morning, full of that exhilarated eagerness of his and with the quick words tumbling out of his mouth,' he remembered many years later. Lane's dealings with authors were to become fewer and more intermittent as the years went by, but in the meantime 'one of the greatest pleasures in publishing is derived from coming in touch with writers of every degree, and in the making of literary friendships'.

Lane's other item of personal risk-taking not only involved him with what is regarded by many as one of the masterpieces of English literature, but proved that, despite his tribulations over *The Whispering Gallery*, he was still prepared to risk prosecution in the courts. James Joyce had begun to write *Ulysses* in 1914, when he was living in Zurich. Three years later, he approached Harriet Weaver at the Egoist Press about the possibility of her serializing the completed early chapters in the *Egoist*, but it proved impossible to find a printer prepared to run the risk of prosecution. T. S. Eliot, in the meantime, had spoken to Leonard and Virginia Woolf about Joyce's troublesome manuscript, and the following year Miss Weaver paid them a visit in the hope that the Hogarth Press might be prepared to take it on. She handed over the manuscript wrapped in a brown paper parcel, and, Leonard Woolf later recalled, 'we put this remarkable piece of dynamite into the top drawer of a cabinet in the sitting-room, telling her that we would read it and, if we thought well of it, see if we could find a printer to print it for us'. Virginia Woolf, waspish as ever, was amazed that so torrid a novel should boast so spinsterish a midwife. 'Her table manners were those of a well-bred hen,' she wrote. 'How did she ever come into contact with Joyce and the rest? Why does this filth seek exit from her mouth?' After sounding out various printers, none of whom were prepared to commit themselves, the Woolfs withdrew from the fray.

In 1920 Joyce moved to Paris, where he met the American Sylvia Beach, who had just opened her avant-garde Left Bank literary bookshop, Shakespeare & Co. She agreed to publish the complete and uncut version of his novel, and 1,000 copies were published in a de luxe edition in 1922. It enjoyed an immediate if scandalous *réclame* among literati and book collectors – Winston Churchill was among its subscribers – and when Sylvia Beach's edition went temporarily out of print, Harriet Weaver printed 2,000 copies, using the same French printer but a less opulent presentation. Getting them across the English Channel was more of a problem. The Post Office was at liberty to intercept suspicious-looking mail, and the Customs and Exercise were empowered, under the 1876 Customs Consolidation Act, to confiscate and destroy imported copies of offending works: 499 copies of the Egoist Press edition were seized by the Customs at Folkestone in 1923, and burned in the picturesquely named King's Chimney. Some years later a retired Customs official told C. H. Rolph that those caught trying to smuggle in a copy of *Ulysses* almost invariably surrendered without a struggle: some had found its language too ripe, some found the whole thing unintelligible, and none wanted to see their names in the papers next morning. Sir Archibald Bodkin, the Director of Public Prosecutions, took a particularly dim view of the book: sent a copy by an official in the Home Office, he complained that it had no discernible story, contained 'a great deal of unmitigated filth and obscenity' and read, in parts, 'as if composed by a more or less illiterate vulgar woman'. When Sir Archibald discovered that F. R. Leavis, a 'dangerous crank or worse', was lecturing on *Ulysses* at Cambridge, he threatened to prosecute the misguided academic.

Nor were matters any better on the other side of the Atlantic. Desperate to have his book published, uncut and unbowdlerized, in London and New York, Joyce had asked Ezra Pound to intervene on his behalf with Margaret Anderson, the editor of the *Little Review*. She was ready to go ahead with serial publication in her magazine; it was hard to find a printer, but she eventually entrusted the work to a Serbian who could not understand a word of it. Mainstream publishers like Viking and Boni & Liveright were contemplating publication when 500 copies imported from France were seized and burned by the US Post Office: the New York Society for the Prevention of Vice swung into action, Margaret Anderson and her fellow-editor were fined $50 each and forbidden to publish any more extracts from the offending work, and a dealer was imprisoned for importing copies of Sylvia Beach's edition, which was reprinted seven times between 1922 and 1930.

Eventually, however, Bennett Cerf, the forceful and flamboyant co-founder of Random House, decided to take the plunge after overhearing a New York lawyer say that he would like to act on behalf of *Ulysses*. A furniture salesman turned lawyer, Morris Ernst was an ardent defender of free speech, a champion of the American Civil Liberties Union who had defended Radclyffe Hall's notorious lesbian novel *The Well of Loneliness* as well as works by Marie Stopes and Havelock Ellis. During the Thirties he became a friend of President Roosevelt and a supporter of the New Deal; as a man who made a point of being in the know, not least where publishing was concerned, he would also become one of Allen Lane's closest confidants in America, a source of tips and not entirely disinterested advice. In March 1932, a month after he'd acquired the American rights, Cerf asked Ernst if he'd fight the case in the courts. He was not able to pay him a large fee, but it was agreed that if they won Random House would pay Ernst a royalty on every copy sold for the rest of his life. Ernst then set about collecting statements of support from academics, librarians, clergymen and writers, among them Arnold Bennett, Edmund Wilson and Rebecca West. Rather than risk losing an entire edition in the event of a successful prosecution – and, given its bulk, *Ulysses* was an expensive book to produce – Ernst suggested that Cerf should invite prosecution under the 1930 Tariff Act by having a copy of a French edition mailed to him from Paris, with the contents clearly marked: any action against the book would be a civil rather than a criminal case, so there was no risk of either of them going to prison, and all they could lose was that single copy. The copy arrived at the docks in

New York in May, and a Random House employee was standing by to receive it (or not). To his frustration, the Customs waved it through without a second glance, so he made a point of drawing it to their attention. Once again, nothing happened: *Ulysses* had been allowed into the States at last, and Random House felt free to move ahead. But the obscenity lobby was not yet through with it, and the book was put on trial in the US District Court in October. In a famous decision, Justice John M. Woolsey declared in its favour. 'I am quite aware that owing to some of its scenes *Ulysses* is rather a strong draught to ask some sensitive, though normal, persons to take,' he declared. 'But my considered opinion, after long reflection, is that whilst in many places the effect of *Ulysses* on the reader undoubtedly is somewhat emetic, nowhere does it tend to be aphrodisiac.' An appeal against his judgement to the Circuit Court of Appeals was rejected on the same day that Prohibition came to an end, and Random House sold 33,000 copies between the two court cases; a jubilant James Joyce declared that 'Thus one half of the English-speaking world surrenders. The other half will follow.'

Such optimism seemed unfounded, at least as far as his regular publishers were concerned. Jonathan Cape had taken over the stock and rights in *Dubliners*, *Portrait of the Artist*, *Exiles* and *Chamber Music* from Harriet Weaver, but he didn't care for *Ulysses* unless it was read out loud, and he was not prepared to run the risk: three years earlier, his edition of *The Well of Loneliness* had fallen foul of one of the periodic purges initiated by Sir William Joynson-Hicks, a famously puritanical and censorious Home Secretary, after James Douglas in the *Sunday Express* had declared that he would 'rather put a phial of prussic acid into the hands of a healthy girl or boy than the book in question', and Cape had lost his taste for litigation. T. S. Eliot at Faber, Joyce's ideal choice, had agreed to publish *Finnegans Wake*, and already had *Work in Progress* and *Pomes Penyeach* in hand; but he was worried about a possible prosecution of *Ulysses*, and was not reassured when civil servants at the Home Office and in the Solicitor-General's office warned him that whatever the Government's attitude, there was nothing to prevent a private individual launching a prosecution. Eliot was given five days in which to make up his mind, but while he dithered, Allen Lane took action. He had met Joyce in Paris in 1929 through Sylvia Beach; he was in New York when Random House decided to publish, and Bennett Cerf thought him the ideal publisher for the book in Britain. Following Morris Ernst's example, and displaying a very Lane-like mixture of caution and bravado, he had a copy of the book sent from France bearing a label which read 'This parcel contains a copy of James Joyce's *Ulysses*', and after this had been ignored by both the Post Office and Customs and Excise he took out a nine-month option on the novel, paying £50 for the option itself, a further £50 when and if he decided to publish, and £100 on the day of publication. The old guard at The Bodley Head disapproved of the whole business, and although the Lanes were using their own money to publish and publicize the book, Lane's fellow-directors insisted on their putting down a further sum as a guarantee against any legal costs incurred by a prosecution, and to hold off publication for another year or two. Publishing contracts were finally exchanged in May 1936: Lane committed his firm to publishing a 'limited [i.e. expensive] edition', but Joyce, resentful of anything that suggested his book was unavailable to the world at large, deleted the words 'for private circulation only'. Lane's belief that the sensible thing would be to issue the book initially in a limited, expensive edition, inaccessible to the susceptible and the impoverished, ran counter to his customary urge to make books cheap and easy to obtain, but shrewdly reflected the thinking of the nation's moral guardians: on learning from the Metropolitan Police and Foyle's bookshop that publication was imminent, a Home Office official minuted a colleague in the Director of Public Prosecution's office that 'a book costing £6. 6. 0. or £3. 3. 0. was not likely to get into the hands of anyone likely to be corrupted by it and that probably the best course was to do nothing'.

Ulysses was eventually published in October 1936, at five guineas, in an edition of 1,000 copies, 100 of which were signed by the author. Francis Meynell, the typographer and publisher of the Nonesuch Press, had designed some specimen pages, but neither Lane nor his young colleague Edward Young were very taken with them; nor did they warm to the suggestion that Matisse might provide some line drawings to enliven the text. 'Allen and I had fairly similar tastes in many ways, and we decided, no, we wouldn't have any of this nonsense,' Young later recalled. In the event, the only decoration was Eric Gill's cover drawing of Ulysses' bow. A cheaper, trade edition was published the following year, making a valuable contribution to the reviving fortunes of The Bodley Head; but by then the Lanes had severed all connections with the family firm, and although they had financed its publication, a hardback edition of *Ulysses* had no place on the Penguin list, and they had to leave it behind.

While *Ulysses* was inching its way into print, John Lane decided that he would make a two-year world tour, meeting publishers' agents, wholesalers, booksellers and local publishers, and, since he would be paying his own way, representing the interests of various London publishers as well as The Bodley Head. As bright, energetic and forceful as his eldest brother, John had decided to throw up his job with the London & Lancashire and join his brothers in the firm; and just as Allen and Dick had familiarized themselves with the domestic market, John wanted to do the same for the export trade, which had been in the doldrums throughout the 1920s. Talbot Square was deluged with price lists, proofs and publishers' catalogues; there were endless farewell parties, all of them drunken, with seventeen people staying the night before his departure, and an oyster lunch on his last day. His brothers had arranged to sail with him in the *Carthage* from Tilbury to Southampton, and a fleet of taxis, laden with luggage and revellers, drew up on the dockside. More carousing took place when the ship drew alongside a Canadian Pacific liner in Southampton: John knew several of its officers, and they were invited on board for drinks. Awash with brandy and soda, Dick and Allen eventually staggered down the gangway of the *Carthage*; Dick, clutching two brimming glasses, was accused of stealing ship's property, and John lowered two more glasses, also brimming, down the side of the ship in a gesture of farewell. As they wove their way to the station, it turned out that Dick had enough money to get them home but was incapable of speech, while Allen could speak but had not a penny to his name. On his travels John was frequently mistaken for Uncle John, and fêted accordingly; he acquired a knowledge of publishers' overseas markets that would prove invaluable to Penguin Books, and on his return he was appointed The Bodley Head's export director. 'The trip had aged him,' Dick noted after his return, and left him 'getting a little thin on top'.

Not to be outdone on the foreign front, Allen took motoring holidays in the South of France with the printer Raymond Hazell, visited Paris several times a year, skied in Switzerland with John, and, as an *aficionado* of the bullring, brought home posters from Spain to decorate the walls of Talbot Square. And, if Dick is to be believed, he had a brief fling with someone else's wife. 'Allen's last affair was a very bad one indeed,' Dick told John in Australia. 'It lasted nearly four months, and was very bad for business. He asked everyone's advice and took nobody's. It created several records as far as long distance phone calls were concerned, including one 45-minute call from Manchester to Paris and one of 72 minutes from Manchester to London. Some of the local calls exceeded two hours.' At one stage the husband was seen lurking outside Talbot Square, but Lane had been alerted and did not return that night.

No sooner had John returned home in the summer of 1934 than Allen announced that Talbot Square was to be redecorated from top to bottom: he could stand the squalor no longer, and if his brothers did not agree with his plans he would move out and leave them to pig it together. (He was, Agatha Christie noted, very much the head of the family, and 'regarded his two brothers and his young sister as his responsibility in life'. It was, she thought, 'a touching and lovable attitude'.) At the cost of £1,000, the white-fronted early Victorian house was converted into the epitome of 1930s elegance, a cross between Peter Jones and a transatlantic liner. The sitting-room carpets were replaced with a pale brown parquet floor; there was a bar in one corner, with glass shelves and hidden lighting; tubular furniture abounded, and the kitchen was fitted out with a gas-powered fridge (none of the brothers could master its controls, and Agatha Christie, hoping for supper, was confronted with a rock-hard frozen rabbit). The bathroom and lavatory were moved up a floor, and provided with the most up-to-date shower and bath-tub. John's bedroom remained a plain undecorated box, while Dick's was fitted out with a work-bench, including a vice and a lathe; Allen, in fine period style, insisted that his must be green throughout, from the walls and the carpet to the bedding and the telephone.

Despite their passion for parties, far and away the most impor-tant ritual of the day, lasting sometimes up to an hour and involving endless discussion and debate about the recent past, the immediate future and what should be done with The Bodley Head, took place in the early morning in the bathroom, when the Lanes took turns in the bathwater, with one brother perched on the lavatory seat reading the day's papers, another shaving at the basin, and a third lolling in the bath: Lane liked to bath before shaving, Dick to shave before bathing, John had no strong feelings, and they all shared the same bathwater. They were less united in the evenings: Allen was out in his white tie and tails three or four times a week, while Dick and John toyed with a chop in the Edgware Road or visited a music hall. Living in Lancaster Gate Terrace had accustomed them to the services of a butler, and in Talbot Square their every need was met by a 'gentleman's gentleman' called Knight. An ex-marine, Knight lived nearby in Praed Street: he made tea in the morning, ran the all-important bath, cooked breakfast and an evening meal special-izing in steak and kidney pies, did the housework and claimed, misleadingly, to be teetotal.

But while the Lanes were leading the lives of well-heeled young men about town, The Bodley Head was teetering on the edge of bankruptcy. 'Candidly the situation is desperate and demands that you take the most desperate steps,' the firm's accountants told Lane in October 1932 (he had asked them to address all such letters to Talbot Square, away from the prying eyes of the other directors), and 'on the present volume of sales it is only a matter of time before the business will have to cease trading'. They suggested that the Brewer Street office should be closed, that Boswell and Drummond should be made to share an office, and that a huge remaindering exercise should be set in motion; unless they came up with a bestseller the firm was unlikely to survive another year, and given recent losses the directors could face some awkward questions if an official receiver moved in. He should bear in mind the fact that, under the 1929 Companies Act, the directors would be personally responsible if, in the event of the firm's being wound up, it should be discovered that anything had been done 'with apparent intent' to defraud creditors. These could include authors and suppliers. Ben Travers called in at the office to complain about the non-payment of royalties owed to him; Lane had earlier agreed to pay the money in instalments, but nothing had materialized. Eventually he was paid the money due, after a meeting with Lane that 'was of a very friendly nature as usual'. Eric Hiscock was, in retrospect at least, 'conscious that there might have been rather a lot of unpaid printers' bills lying around', many of which had not been settled by the time The Bodley Head went into liquidation, and stock was consistently over-valued. By June 1934 the firm had a cumulative debt of £42,367, and a year later – two months before Lane launched Penguin Books from within The Bodley Head – this had increased by a further £4,968.

Since the death of Uncle John and the *Whispering Gallery* fiasco, Lane had been determined to get rid of the old guard, or what remained of it. His solicitors informed him that since he did not control three-quarters of the voting shares, he could not carry an extraordinary resolution to remove a fellow-director, so attrition had to take its course. After the amiable Lindsay Drummond left to found his own (unsuccessful) publishing house, only Ronald Boswell remained *in situ*. 'We shall have to watch Mr Boswell very carefully,' Lane's solicitor noted, but Boswell eventually bowed to the inevitable and found a job at the BBC.

With or without the old guard, The Bodley Head's days were numbered, at least in its current incarnation. Desperate as he was to keep it afloat, all Lane's energies were, by 1935, tied up in the successful launching of the first Penguin titles. Awash with Penguin cash, he transferred £2,360 to The Bodley Head's bank account, and six junior members of staff lost their jobs in a 'slaughter of the innocents'; but all to no avail. 'It is expecting too much for authors and trade creditors to wait indefinitely for their money, and one of them may become troublesome, exercise pressure and force the bank to appoint a receiver,' his solicitors warned him in May 1936, nine months after Penguin had been launched. After fending off an offer of £40,000 for both Penguin and The Bodley Head from Wilfred Harvey of Purnell's the printers, Lane's old firm was put into voluntary liquidation, with its creditors receiving only a small proportion of the moneys owing to them. Among the royalties not paid were those on Nehru's *Autobiography*. Philip Unwin, whose offer of £50 for the rights in the book had been rejected in favour of £150 from The Bodley Head, felt a frisson of *Schadenfreude*; his Uncle Stanley, in the meantime, hurried to the rescue of his ailing rival. 'It is astonishing for how many years a book publishing house can continue its insolvent way before the showdown comes,' he later wrote. 'It suddenly occurred to me that it would be amusing to run the John Lane business cooperatively with two of my competitors.' Wren Howard of Jonathan Cape and W. G. Taylor of J. M. Dent also 'thought it an amusing idea', and The Bodley Head's future was secured. Still unreconciled to his loss, Lane brooded on a scheme to buy the firm from the receiver – according to Morpurgo, he may have hoped to borrow the money from Jonathan Cape – but by then it was too late. '*Ultimately* it may be possible for you to realize your wish,' Wren Howard told him, 'but that "ultimately" may be far off.'

'If I had been a little wiser and less precipitate I would have kept the firm going,' Lane wrote to a colleague many years later, and his longing to recover The Bodley Head never left him. When, in 1952, Basil Willett wrote to congratulate him on his knighthood, Lane, in his letter of thanks, referred to rumours 'that it might be possible for The Bodley Head to return to the Lane name': some years later he sent W. E. Williams to investigate after Fred Warburg had told him that Sir Stanley Unwin was thinking of selling the firm, but Williams was given short shrift, and 'a most unpleasant proceeding it proved'. In the early Sixties Penguin took over the distribution of Bodley Head titles, and in 1963 Tony Godwin, the most brilliant and tumultuous of all Lane's protégés, referred to the possibility of

the firm joining the Penguin group in light of 'the long and sentimental association between The Bodley Head and Sir Allen Lane'.
Nothing ever came of it, but six years later, in what was, in effect,
his last great achievement on behalf of Penguin, Lane bought the
paperback rights in *Ulysses* from Max Reinhardt of The Bodley
Head. It was published on 23 April 1969, fifty years to the day after
the sixteen-year-old Allen Lane had gone to work for Uncle John.

5. Hatching a Penguin

Quite when, where and even whether Allen Lane first had the notion of Penguin books is a matter of debate. According to the standard version of events, he was coming back to London from a weekend with Agatha Christie and Max Mallowan in Devon, realized he had nothing to read on the train, and was so appalled by the rubbish on offer at the railway bookstall on Exeter station that he decided, there and then, that he would remedy matters by producing a line of paperbacks that cost no more each than a packet of cigarettes, looked bright and elegant rather than garish, and included worthwhile works of literature instead of lightweight ephemera. Others came up with very different versions of the story, or were keen to deny him the originality claimed on his behalf. Lane, for his part, combined personal modesty with single-minded determination, an entrepreneur's instinct for the spirit of the age, and a readiness to exploit and realize the talents and achievements of others: he made Penguin into one of the most famous and distinctive brand names in British business life, as instantly recognizable as Guinness or Rolls-Royce, and if, in later years, he was irritated by the way in which – like 'hoover', 'mackintosh' or 'biro' in their respective fields – 'Penguin' was used as a synonym for 'paperback', he had only his own success to blame; nor was it surprising that the world at large should assume that he, and he alone, had invented the paperback. Like many others at the time, he was convinced that there was a vast new readership waiting to be tapped: intuitive as ever, he set about putting his hunches into effect at a time when Britain was coming out of recession, yet the conventional book trade retained the siege mentality of men who felt that their livelihood was under threat, not least from his activities. Quick, impatient and possessed of a contagious enthusiasm, Lane was, by 1934, poised to put his plans into action.

One of the constants of English history is an ever-rising middle class, and never more so than in the fifty years that led up to the outbreak of the Second World War. An expanding middle class with a degree of disposable income was good news for publishers of books, magazines and newspapers, and Lane – like Northcliffe, Newnes and, later, Lord Beaverbrook – was to make his fortune from its desire to be entertained and instructed by means of the written word. Forster's Education Act of 1870 was bearing fruit by the turn of the century; the proliferation of office jobs – in the financial sector, in estate agencies, in businesses of every kind – presupposed a degree of literacy, and although the intelligentsia despised and feared the perky, lower-middle-class clerks of the kind immortalized in *Three Men in a Boat*, *The Diary of a Nobody* and the early novels of H. G. Wells, publishers saw them as welcome new recruits. George Newnes's *Tit-Bits* combined hints on social etiquette, bicycling columns and snippets of self-improvement with extracts from the classics, leading John Carey to suggest, subversively, that 'as a means of awakening interest in books, arousing curiosity and introducing its readers to new ideas, *Tit-Bits* must compare very favourably with more acclaimed organs such as T. S. Eliot's *Criterion* and F. R. Leavis's *Scrutiny*, and its effects were infinitely more widespread'; Newnes's *Strand Magazine* was, as we have seen, a popular item with the Williams family in Bristol. And the most famous press baron of all, Lord Northcliffe, had founded the *Daily Mail* in 1896 to cater for the new world of office-workers, and followed it up, five years later, with the *Daily Mirror*, designed at first for lady readers.

Book publishers were equally anxious to tap this new market. Years earlier, in 1848, W. H. Smith had inaugurated its chain of railway bookstalls. Their immediate effect was to trigger off a proliferation of cheap reprints – shilling in hardback, sixpence in paper – aimed at the bookless traveller avid for something to read on the journey. Printed, for the most part, in double columns in a typeface so small as to be almost illegible, they included such long-forgotten series as Bohn's Shilling Library, Routledge's Railway Library and the Fireside Library; most were ephemeral trash, with lurid covers and advertisements printed on the back and the inside covers, though John Dicks's Illustrated Novels, published in the 1880s at sixpence each, included works by Dickens, Harrison Ainsworth and other eminent Victorians. New paper-making techniques – esparto grass was used from the 1860s, wood pulp from the 1880s – made such cheap editions still cheaper to produce, to the horror of the literate classes: in the vanguard of those who hurried to defend the heights of literature was Matthew Arnold, who attacked 'a cheap literature, hideous and ignoble of aspect, like the tawdry novels which flare in the bookshelves of our railway stations, and which seem designed, as so much else that is produced for our middle class seems designed, for people with a low standard of life'.

Although the demise of the mid-Victorian three-decker novel in favour of shorter works meant that the price of a new novel fell from 31s. 6d. for a set of three to 7s. 6d. for a single volume – a price for new fiction that remained constant from the turn of the century until the outbreak of the Second World War – new novels remained far too expensive for all but the well-heeled. The classics, on the other hand, had always lent themselves to cheap editions: royalties were not payable on out-of-copyright titles, and competition among publishers was intense from the 1830s onwards. W. T. Stead's Penny Poets and Penny Novels, both familiar from Lane's childhood, began to appear in the mid-Nineties, and went on to sell some 9 million copies *in toto*; but the best-remembered series of all – appealing, in part, to those earnest, high-minded, self-taught working-class and lower-middle-class readers who, more often than not, professed themselves Fabian socialists, rode bicycles, read H. G. Wells and Bernard Shaw, wore 'rational' clothing, and attended university extension courses and, in later years, the Workers' Educational Association – were the product of the Edwardian age. Grant Richards founded the World's Classics in 1901 – when he went bankrupt four years later, the list was acquired by Oxford University Press – and he was quickly followed by Collins Pocket Classics and Nelson's Classics: but the best known of all was Everyman's Library, founded by J. M. Dent in 1906.

The son of a Darlington house-painter, self-taught and Nonconformist, Dent was typical of the old-fashioned tradesman publisher. 'My aim was to publish a volume of 500 pages for one shilling,' he wrote – a shilling being 'the democratic price'. Anticipating Allen Lane's practice at Penguin, he published new titles in batches, reckoning he had to sell 10,000 of each to cover its costs, and insisted that his books should be good to look at as well as to read: the early Everymans are redolent of William Morris and the Kelmscott Press, all twining shrubbery and sinuous forms, but in the 1930s they were given a cleaner, more modern look, including end-papers, jackets and title-page motifs designed by Eric Ravilious. By then they were also buying in the hardback reprint rights from other publishers. Back in 1907 H. G. Wells had asked Macmillan to sub-lease his *Kipps* to the Nelson's Sevenpenny Library, where it sold 43,000 copies in the first year alone, and Everyman's Library went on to include works by Virginia Woolf, Conrad, Synge, Aldous Huxley and E. M. Forster among the 1,000-odd titles it had on offer. Not all Everyman readers were upwardly mobile spirits, bent on self-improvement: but a generation after the first Everyman appeared, the same kind of readers would be snapping up Penguins, Pelicans and, in due course, Penguin Classics.

By the 1920s most publishers were reissuing titles in the hardback 'cheap editions' familiar to Lane at The Bodley Head. At 3s. 6d., or occasionally 2s. 6d., apiece, these were more expensive than the Classics lists: their titles were almost invariably in copyright and were burdened with royalties, and the print-runs were generally shorter. A book would be published first as a conventional hardback – 7s. 6d. for a novel, 12s. 6d. for a travel book, biography or history – and then, when the publisher reckoned that sales of the full-priced edition had ground to a halt, it would be reissued, for a 'further bite of the cherry', as publishers liked to put it, in a cheap edition. Many of these, like Cape's Travellers' Library or Chatto's Phoenix Library, were elegant, pocket-sized volumes; others included Heinemann's Windmill Library, Secker's Adelphi Library and, at two shillings each, the Hodder Yellow Jackets, which reissued such fine storytellers as Sapper, Buchan, Baroness Orczy and A. E. W. Mason, and would, in due course, be dealt a 'murderous blow' by the sixpenny Penguins.

Paperbacks were generally regarded as a lower form of life; and, if the old order had its way, would remain forever incarcerated in the literary bargain basement. Book trade historians trace them back to the days of Aldus Manutius in the early sixteenth century, but by the time Lane was pondering Penguins, the paperback had fallen on hard times. As the publisher Robert Lusty recalled in his memoirs, sixpenny paperbacks were a commonplace long before Penguins appeared. A good many of them were published by the half-mad, power-crazed Walter Hutchinson, who collected publishing houses in much the same way as others collect stamps or racehorses; George Hutchinson, the founder of the firm, had initiated a series of paper-back Sixpenny Blacks, but by the time Lusty joined the ramshackle empire paperbacks were reserved for the most rubbishy thrillers and romances, printed in double columns and with lurid covers to match.

There were, however, sporadic exceptions to the assumption that paperbacks were synonymous with tosh. In the 1920s, Victor Gollancz, who had abandoned schoolmastering for life as a publisher and was learning the trade at Ernest Benn, started, with Douglas Jerrold, Benn's Sixpenny Library, a line of small format, very short paperbacks designed to provide the lay reader with useful background information and introductions to seemingly daunting subjects: Bertrand Russell produced a primer to philosophy, C. E. M. Joad pondered *The Mind and its Workings*, and the history of England was summarized in the minimum number of pages. By enlisting well-known academics to explain their subjects to the lay reader, they had something in common with Lane's Pelicans, but their brevity and dingy brown paper covers told against them. A few years later Gollancz, by now the master of his own firm, decided to have another crack at paperbacks. In 1930 he published several new novels as paperback originals, selling at 3s. each and bearing the generic name of Mundanus paperbacks. 'VG' declared his new series to be 'both socially desirable and commercially profitable', but although the first three titles sold between 10,000 and 20,000 each, newsagents withheld their support and the scheme collapsed. 'How dare you! I am incapable of error!' the volcanic Gollancz once roared at a literary agent who had dared to disagree, but the failure of Mundanus suggests that he was as fallible as any of his rivals.

A longer-lasting and more valuable contribution to the notion that paperbacks and quality were compatible was provided by the Tauchnitz and Albatross Continental Editions. Baron Tauchnitz had begun to reissue his Continental editions of works by British and American writers in 1847, and by the 1930s the firm had published over 5,000 books. Tauchnitz editions could only be sold on the continent of Europe, and this gave them a certain glamour, indicative of foreign travel and exotic goings-on: Allen Lane remembered his father reading to him from a Tauchnitz edition of Kipling's *Just So Stories*, smuggled over the Channel by some intrepid traveller. From the earliest days, Tauchnitz had insisted on paying royalties to the authors on his list, at a time when piracy was rife, particularly in the United States; Tauchnitz editions had come to be well regarded by writers and their agents, who were happy to assign them the Continental rights in their books, however much their publishers in London or New York may have resented losing sales in Europe to cheaper German paperbacks.

By the early 1930s, Tauchnitz editions, with their squat format, drab covers and impossibly long lines of type, were beginning to look dowdy and old-fashioned. In 1931 Kurt Enoch, a young German publisher, was approached by the British Holding Company about the possibility of their setting up a rival firm which would break the Tauchnitz monopoly on Continental editions, and a year later Albatross Verlag was in business. Its ultimate owner, Sir Edmund Davis, was a South African copper magnate; its chairman was Arnoldo Mondadori, the Italian publisher, and there were two members of the Collins family on the board. Kurt Enoch, based in Hamburg, looked after promotion and distribution; Max Christian Wegner, who had been sacked from Tauchnitz after suggesting that they should modernize the appearance of their books, supervised editorial and production matters from Paris; the great typographer and book designer Hans (or Giovanni) Mardersteig, a German based in Verona, designed a narrow, elegant and legible page and a spare, modern-looking cover design, both far removed from Tauchnitz's lumpish equivalents; and John Holroyd-Reece, fluent in German, French, Italian and English, liaised with the British Holding Company and negotiated with publishers, agents and authors in London or at his villa on the Côte d'Azur.

Of all those involved, Kurt Enoch would have the longest asso-ciation with Allen Lane, and make the strongest mark on the publishing world; but John Holroyd-Reece – 'that urbane and pictur-esque international', in the words of the literary agent Curtis Brown, who claimed to have introduced him to Wegner – was by far the most fascinating. Born Hermann Riess in 1897 to a German Jewish father and an English mother, he had been educated at Repton, where he was allegedly cited as a precocious co-respondent, and had turned down a place at King's College, Cambridge, in order to join the Dorset Yeomanry; he became a member of the Egyptian Expeditionary Force, and in 1918 was said to have been appointed Governor of Zable and Malloake in Sudan. A director of various Paris banks and insurance companies, and of the Musée Ethno-graphique du Trocadéro, he was, at some stage, made a Knight Commander of the Crown of Italy. He had worked for Ernest Benn in the 1920s and got to know Victor Gollancz, who sporadically employed him as a European 'scout'. An enthusiastic collector of antiques, he founded the Paris-based Pegasus Press in 1927, special-izing in expensive and handsomely produced books on fine art: his Odyssey Press, based in Hamburg, took over publication of Sylvia Beach's edition of *Ulysses* in 1932, and with Jonathan Cape he co-published Radclyffe Hall's *The Well of Loneliness*, so making it avail-able in Europe at least after its condemnation in the British courts. Kurt Enoch, an austere soul, thought Holroyd-Reece extravagant and prone to delusions of grandeur, with a 'personality bordering on that of an adventurer', and disapproved of his appetite for hunting and the aristocracy; although Paul Léon, James Joyce's secretary, remembered him as being rather red in the face, David Higham, the literary agent, recalled him as a pallid, monocled figure, invariably clad in black, who 'somehow gave off a sinister vapour' and turned up in London from time to time 'with a handsome wife – never ask him whose' (in addition to other people's wives, he had five of his own); Nicolas Barker has described him as a 'creature of grandiose schemes' who 'flashed across the typographical world like a comet', dragging in his wake such eminences as Stanley Morison, Mardersteig, Oliver Simon and Beatrice Warde, each of whom he dropped in due course, leaving them 'breathless, exhilarated and sometimes very much the poorer'.

Albatross published in batches of four new titles a month, and their books were more up-to-date than those on offer from Tauchnitz: James Joyce's *Dubliners* was the opening title, published in 1932, and before long he had been joined by Aldous Huxley, Virginia Woolf and Sinclair Lewis. At a less elevated level, A. A. Milne and Edgar Wallace were admitted to the list, and the various categories of book – travel, crime, *belles-lettres* or whatever – were designated an identifying colour, in much the same way that Penguins would be coded orange for fiction, blue for biography, green for crime and magenta for travel: emulation is endemic to publishing, and the Albatross colour-coding was itself a variant on the coloured bands used by Tauchnitz to identify different types of book. Unable to compete with its stylish new rival, Tauchnitz began to discuss a possible merger between the two firms. The Nazis, by now in power in Germany, objected to British ownership of Tauchnitz, and still more so since Sir Edmund Davis was Jewish, so a deal was worked out whereby Oscar Brandstetter, the firm's printer in Leipzig, bought the company but handed over editorial, sales and distribution to Albatross.

Despite its elegance, and the distinction of its list, Albatross's moment was all too brief. Kurt Enoch, who was Jewish, left Hamburg and settled in Paris, where he continued to work on behalf of Albatross; Stanley Unwin later claimed that authors resented having to sign a form declaring that they were of suitably Aryan descent. Tauchnitz and Albatross coexisted for a time, with the older firm looking after the more old-fashioned or middlebrow authors; Tauchnitz editions were remodelled along slimmer, more elegant lines, with a large letter 'A' on the front, designed by Reynolds Stone. But eventually Penguin would deprive both lists of their *raison d'être*: with all the world its marketplace, it could, with far longer print-runs, undercut and outsell its German competitors. With the outbreak of war, Tauchnitz began to specialize in German-language books; after the war, efforts were made to revive both imprints, but to no avail. The influence of Albatross in particular on the development of Penguin, in terms of both design and content, was both beneficial and undeniable. While still at The Bodley Head, Lane had been in touch with Holroyd-Reece about the possibility of their two firms sharing printing costs on certain titles; years later, Holroyd-Reece told Ved Mehta that Lane adopted the Penguin format 'as a result of detailed discussions with me before he formed his company', but that it would be wrong to suggest that he simply copied Albatross. Mardersteig, he claimed, had been working on some unpublished notebooks of Leonardo da Vinci, in which Leonardo had 'determined an ideal page size'; Mardersteig had then followed this ruling, and Lane, in turn, 'copied it no more than I did'.

By the late 1920s the British book trade felt increasingly embattled, and although it weathered the Depression better than some trades, a vague feeling that something should be done to tap new markets and make books more accessible was combined with innate conservatism and hostility to change. And new media were competing for the public's attention and pocket money. By 1935 there were 4,500 cinemas up and down the country, and the British were being acclaimed (or reviled) as the world's most ardent film-goers. The BBC came into being, albeit under a slightly different name, in 1922, and although under the austere and high-minded control of Lord Reith, its Director-General from 1927 to 1938, it only offered one station to its listeners, 71 per cent of the population had a radio licence by 1939; and whereas in 1918 the national daily newspapers sold some 3.1 million copies per day *in toto*, that figure had soared to 10.6 million twenty years later, with two papers boasting circulations of over 2 million, and a further three with over a million each. Shrewd publishers exploited radio and the Press via reviews, free publicity and the sale of serial and broadcasting rights; their less adventurous colleagues trembled and hoped for the best.

Equally worrying to the old order of publishers was their increasing dependence on the library market, and, in particular, on the 'twopenny libraries' which lent books to subscribers at twopence a time. Boots, with 460 branches up and down the country, combined the sale of aspirins and toothbrushes with the loan of books, as did their rivals Timothy Whites; although W. H. Smith had fallen between its pharmacist rivals, Foyles soon entered the market, boasting that at any one time some three-quarters of a million books were out on loan. Some cheap editions were bestsellers in their own right – Cassell sold 20,000 of Warwick Deeping's *Sorrell and Son* at the full price of 7s. 6d., over a million at 3s. 6d. – but most publishers relied on the library market for their well-being; and anything which threatened that benign dependence was to be deplored.

Heretical spirits, however, came up with ideas that threatened the status quo. W. H. Smith, which took a dim view of any new initiatives, whether book tokens, book clubs or sixpenny paperbacks, were committed to keeping prices high in the interests of both publishers and booksellers, but in 1929 a Mr Chapell of their advertising department suggested that they should start a line of 'cheap shops' selling 'cheap books' as a means of boosting trade in the year of the Great Crash, and attracting new business. 'This is an age of cheapness,' he declared, 'and all classes – even the Queen herself – have patronized Woolworth's. There is a limit to the amount of business to be obtained from the cultured classes to whom our handsome shops mainly appeal.' His suggestion that Smith's should follow the example of Woolworth's, famed for selling nothing over sixpence, was rejected by his superiors: but it was a straw in the wind, and Woolworth's was to loom large in the whole vexed issue of cheap reading matter, and Penguins in particular.

The more conventional publishers and booksellers were united in their initial hostility to new ideas. Harold Raymond of Chatto & Windus came up with the idea of book tokens in 1928, but it took four years before his scheme was put into effect by booksellers worried that parents would use the tokens to buy their children's school textbooks; Tommy Joy, who ended his career running Hatchard's bookshop in Piccadilly, suggested that publishers should reduce their 'over-stocks' (books that had ceased to sell and were clogging up the warehouse) by means of an annual National Book Sale, but had to wait till the 1950s before his plan was accepted; when Collins, the most commercially minded of publishers, tried, in 1934, to launch a line of clothbound 'Sevenpennies' they were forced to withdraw on the ground that such books would destroy the market for hardbacks, and for cheap editions in particular. Despite a resolution made two years earlier by a joint committee of publishers and booksellers to the effect that 'in the present times of economic depression the book-buying public could not afford large and expensive books and therefore attention should be directed to books of lower price', rhetoric and action remained far removed from one another.

Further irritants took the form of book clubs, and the sale of books by newspapers in exchange for coupons. German by origin, book clubs sprang up in America in the 1920s in the form of the Book of the Month Club and the Literary Guild, both of which offered their members new books at prices lower than those in the shops. In 1929 Alan Bott founded the Book Society: although its members were not offered a discount on their choices, the publishers whose books were chosen could, in principle, take advantage of the longer print-runs resulting from the Society's order to reduce the published price to members and bookshop buyers alike. Bott's selection committee included Hugh Walpole and J. B. Priestley, and the Society was felt to embody the solid, unadventurous tastes of a public devoted to thrillers, P. G. Wodehouse, A. J. Cronin, golf and crossword puzzles: the Cambridge-based critic Queenie Leavis, who would soon be savaging the debased values of commercial publishing, the mass market and the metropolitan literary scene in *Fiction and the Reading Public*, despised it for promoting a 'middle-brow standard of values', and the writers it exalted were exactly those whom Cyril Connolly so lethally derided in his *New Statesman* fiction reviews and in his parodies of literary life. Later in the decade the wrath of the booksellers would be excited by those clubs which provided books to their members at a fraction of the published price – John Baker's Readers' Union, founded in 1937, offered 15s. and 10s. books to its 17,000 members for as little as 2s. 6d. – on the grounds that they not only deprived long-suffering booksellers of legitimate full-price sales, but implied that all hard-back titles were grossly overpriced.

A more immediate menace resulted from the newspaper circulation wars of the early 1930s. Increasingly dependent on advertising, and desperate to bolster their circulations, the middlebrow papers sought to win new readers by offering them the complete works of

Dickens and Shakespeare, cookery books and encyclopedias far more cheaply than they were available in the shops. The *Daily Mail* offered a complete set of Shakespeare in exchange for 5s. 9d. and six coupons cut from the paper; in 1934 the *Daily Herald* offered a special edition of all Bernard Shaw's plays – including three not included in the Constable edition, priced at 12s. 6d. – in exchange for six coupons and 3s. 9d. Shaw's ready acceptance of the *Herald*'s offer, despite the opposition of his publisher, was widely resented in the trade. Utterly unrepentant, GBS wrote a defiant letter on the subject to the *Bookseller*. 'This particular transaction will increase the business of every bookseller in the country by adding to the book-reading public many thousands of customers to whom 12s. 6d. books are as inaccessible as Rolls-Royce cars,' he declared. 'If the Woolworth firm sends me an order of sufficient magnitude to enable it to sell copies through its stores for 6d. and yet give me a better return from my labour than I can obtain through prices that are prohibitive for nine-tenths of the population, I shall execute that order joyfully. And let the bookseller who would do otherwise cast the first stone at me.' To Basil Blackwell, who claimed that the newspaper's edition had 'placed those booksellers in the unfortunate position of having deceived the public', he was equally unbending. 'I can do nothing for the booksellers but tell them not to be childish,' he wrote. He had recently received from America 'two orders of 50,000 copies each from book clubs, to be given away to their members *for nothing*, as a bonus', and 'of course, I accepted both'. He was, he went on, 'looking forward to an order from Woolworth's for a sixpenny edition'. 'Have you no bowels of compassion for the millions of your fellow-countrymen who can no more afford a twelve-and-sixpenny book than a trip round the world? I am really surprised at you. When we met at Bumpus's you seemed quite an intelligent youth.' Authors were, on the whole, far better disposed towards the notion of cheap books than publishers or booksellers, and Shaw was more passionate than most. He would, in due course, become a keen supporter of Penguin Books, and be a godfather to the Pelican list; no doubt Allen Lane read his defiant letter in the *Bookseller*, and was heartened by his words.

That same year another highly successful champion of the 'little man', J. B. Priestley, published *English Journey*, based on his travels round the country. In it he famously declared that there were now three Englands: the old, rustic England of castles and yokels and country inns; the England of the Industrial Revolution, blighted by unemployment and now in apparently irremediable decline; and 'the new post-war England, belonging far more to the age itself than to this particular island'. It was, he suggested, American in inspiration, a land of 'arterial and by-pass roads, of filling-stations and factories that look like exhibition buildings, of giant cinemas and dance-halls and cafés, bungalows with tiny garages, cocktail bars, Woolworth's, motor coaches, wireless, hiking, factory girls looking like actresses, greyhound racing and dirt tracks, swimming-pools and everything given away for cigarette coupons'. Based, for the most part, in the London suburbs and the Home Counties, this new England was 'essentially democratic . . . You need money in this England, but you do not need much money. It is a large-scale, mass-production job, with cut prices. You could almost accept Woolworth's as its symbol.' Seven years later another astute observer of the English social scene came to similar conclusions. 'The place to look for the germs of the future England is in light-industry areas and along the arterial roads,' George Orwell wrote in *The Lion and the Unicorn*. 'It is a rather restless, cultureless life, centring round tinned food, *Picture Post*, the radio and the combustion engine. It is a civilization in which children grow up with an intimate knowledge of magnetos and in complete ignorance of the Bible. To that civilization belong the people who are most at home in and most definitely *of* the modern world, the technicians and the higher-paid skilled workers, the airmen and their mechanics, the radio experts, film producers, popular journalists and industrial chemists.'

It was also a world with money to spare. The British economy had begun to haul its way out of the Depression, thanks in part to a consumer-led spending boom. Average real wages were 30 per cent higher in 1938 than in 1931, and between the wars the average working week went down from 55 to 45 hours: there was more money around, and more leisure time in which to spend it. Although poverty and unemployment still blighted rural areas and the old manufacturing regions of the Midlands and the north, in the affluent south people had time and money to spend on holidays, charabanc outings, electrical goods, cars and entertainment; the service industries flourished, and the relative costs of food, clothing, housing, furniture and the humdrum necessities of life steadily declined. Book-buyers, then as now, were a minority sect, drawn mainly from the middle classes: neither Orwell's tinned-food-eaters nor Priestley's good-looking factory girls may have seemed natural book-buyers, but if Allen Lane was right in his belief that there was an army of potential readers waiting to be recruited, all of whom shared his own feeling that old-fashioned bookshops were off-putting and intimidating, and their contents far too expensive, then some at least might be found along the arterial roads and in the new industrial estates.

Disposable income and time to spare were not the only factors working in his favour. Orwell noted the spread of middle-class ideas and habits among the working classes, and how 'the habit of reading has become enormously more widespread. To an increasing extent the rich and the poor read the same books, and they also see the same films and listen to the same radio programmes.' As the old working class, the labourers and the navvies, were elbowed aside by shop- and office-workers, a 'general softening of manners' had taken place, with the result that 'in tastes, habits, manners and outlook the working class and the middle class are drawing together'. Cyril Connolly and Virginia Woolf would have been appalled to be bracketed with suburban clerks – the Book Society and A. J. Cronin were bad enough – but Orwell was not alone in his sense of a cultural coming together. 'Notice how the very modern things, like the films and wireless and the sixpenny stores, are absolutely democratic, making no distinction whatsoever between their patrons,' Priestley wrote in *English Journey*. The Twenties, the great age of Modernism, had seen a widening of the gulf between the 'brows': the arts, like the sciences, were, by their very nature, accessible only to the sensitive, the well educated and the unusually perceptive, and whereas *Ulysses*, Picasso and Schoenberg could be understood by the highbrows, by Bloomsberries and the enlightened men and women who haunted senior common rooms, the middlebrows had to make do with Hugh Walpole and Louis Golding, and the lowbrows with the cartoon characters Pip, Squeak and Wilfred. The Thirties were more socially conscious, and although social and intellectual snobbery were as sharp and as callous as ever, they were masked or mitigated by a tendency, among the thinking and literary classes, to espouse left-wing causes and proclaim their faith in the Common Man. Seventy years on, Orwell's and Priestley's faith in a common culture seems idealistic and almost naïve, but their views would not have seemed absurd between 1939 and 1945, or in the socially optimistic years of the post-war Labour government: Penguin would benefit from, and cater to, this new constituency, and if Lane's own tastes were instinctively middlebrow, the proliferation, over the years ahead, of Pelicans, Penguin Poets, *Penguin New Writing*, Penguin Modern Painters and the rest would appeal as much to the highbrow literati as to the Wellsian clerks who so excited their disdain.

In the meantime, of course, the great mass of the population had no strong views on the matter, whatever their class or education. It was, Harold Raymond ruefully remarked, 'a marked and regrettable characteristic of so many Englishmen of the public school type that they find no pleasure or relaxation in the use of their intellect. "I'm no reader" are words which one often hears uttered without shame or regret.' 'Before the war the English on the whole were not a book-buying people,' Christina Foyle recalled. 'We in the book trade remember with horror an advertisement that depicted a woman worrying over her small boy. There he is, poring over a book, a pitiable spectacle. "You don't want your boy to be a bookworm," ran the caption. "You want him to be a normal healthy boy." A few doses of Dr So-and-so's pills averted the tragedy, and you see him in the next picture chasing a football with a happy grin on his little idiot face.' Leaving aside the caution or hostility of his professional colleagues, Lane had quite a mountain to climb.

When, after Basil Willett's departure from The Bodley Head, Allen Lane moved his office from Brewer Street to Vigo Street, he took with him Stan Olney, the trade manager, and an office junior named

H. A. W. Arnold. Olney was a loyal, likeable, under-nourished-looking character, with heavily Brylcreemed hair swept back from his forehead and thick round horn-rimmed specs that made him look like a leaner version of Arthur Askey. He was essentially a clerk, at home in the world of ledgers and double-entry book-keeping, but – as was the way at The Bodley Head, and in the early years of Penguin – he was expected to turn his hand to anything: he was, for a time, in charge of press advertising, supervising the work of Edward Young, a shy and good-looking young man who had recently graduated from pasting reviews into a scrapbook to designing ads and display material. Arnold was a bookish youth from south London who had joined The Bodley Head at the age of fifteen on wages of 15s. a week, and was now earning twice as much. One day in the summer of 1933 Arnold told Edward Young that he felt convinced there was a market for a series of sixpenny paperbacks, ideally of out-of-copyright classics, undercutting the hardback Everyman's Library and tailor-made for people like himself, keen readers who could never afford to spend a sizeable slice of their wages on hardback books. Young urged him to talk to the boss about his plans, but since Lane was seldom in the office, and was hard to pin down, some time went by before Arnold could, with due diffidence, raise the matter with him. To his disappointment, Lane showed little interest, though he promised to think about it: Arnold must realize that the firm had done extremely badly with its own series of 9d. paperbacks, that they still owed the printers £9,000 for printing the thirty-odd titles, so adding to the firm's overdraft, and that his fellow-directors would never lend their support to such a scheme. Lane never subsequently referred to this conversation, but some weeks later Olney handed Arnold two paperbacks, a Tauchnitz and an Albatross: they were to get estimates from printers and papermakers, do their own sums, and work out how many copies they would need to print (and sell) in order to publish at 6d. a volume. Over the next six months, to the disapproval of the old guard, or what remained of it, the two men pored over the figures. Eventually they came up with a calculation which not only turned in a modest profit but, by allowing a farthing a copy royalty, enabled them to publish books that were still in copyright.

After a spell at The Bodley Head's new trade counter in Galen Place, near the British Museum, Arnold left publishing for the Museum itself: Max Mallowan, knowing of his interest in archaeology, found him a job there, and in due course he became a world authority on some of the lesser-known Oriental languages. We may never know to what extent Lane had been influenced by his suggestion – or, indeed, exactly when he inspected the stock at the Exeter railway bookstall, on his way home from a weekend with the Mallowans – but by the spring of 1934 he must have been pondering the possibility of chancing his arm with sixpenny paperbacks. Later, when Penguins had proved the publishing phenomenon of the decade, if not the century, he explained in articles and interviews what his thoughts had been. 'From the moment when somebody invented a way of duplicating books from movable types, the mass-produced sixpenny became inevitable,' he told the *Penrose Annual*, the bible of the printing trade. The man in the street, accustomed to the penny newspaper, could not understand why books were so expensive: 'he compared the price of a new novel with, for instance, the number of pints of beer he could get for the same money, and naturally chose beer every time'. Although something of an anti-smoker – Edward Young remembered how, in the early days of Penguin, staff were only allowed to smoke when entertaining visitors – his most famous analogy was with tobacco rather than drink: 'quite obviously', he declared, 'the thing to aim at was the sixpenny book, something that could be bought as easily and as casually as a packet of cigarettes'. His motives were 'both missionary and mercenary': it was 'very important that books *should* be mass-produced if there is to be any meaning in liberty of opinion, and if knowledge is to be accessible to everyone', and he resented the notion that 'the only people who could possibly want a cheap edition must belong to a lower order of intelligence'. Years later he told Woodrow Wyatt that he wanted to make the point that 'a man who may be poor in money is not necessarily poor in intellectual qualities', and that far from publishing lurid-looking nonsense, 'I wanted to make the kind of book which, when the vicar comes to tea, you don't push under the cushion. You are rather more inclined to put it on the table to show what sort of person you are.'

Like the cigarette packet, the visiting vicar was to become a recurrent if oddly old-fashioned presence in Lane's interviews with the Press; and so too was his dislike of the frowstier type of book-shop, with its snooty-seeming staff and reverential hush: Penguins, he told the *Bookseller*, were 'designed primarily to reach these people, where they congregate on railway stations and in chain stores, with the hope that when they see these books are available in the regular bookshops, they will overcome their temerity and come in'. As for his fellow-publishers, the day of the 'quiet, "gentle-manly" publisher' had passed, as had that of 'the publisher who imagines that the majority of people are stupid, interested only in entertainment that enables them to escape from their environment'. In short, 'the only conclusion we can come to is that for several years the book trade has been sitting on a gold mine and not known it. It is quite clear that the time has come to wake up to the fact that people want books, that they want good books, and that they are willing, even anxious, to *buy* them if they are presented to them in a straightforward, intelligent manner at a cheap price.' At a more practical level, such books would, for the time being at least, be published under The Bodley Head imprint, with the Lanes putting up the money, taking all risks and profits, and paying their old firm a commission for sales, distribution, publicity and other services: to such good effect, as it turned out, that when The Bodley Head went into liquidation, Penguin Books were its largest debtors.

Armed with these thoughts, Lane set out, in September 1934, to attend a conference of publishers and booksellers at Ripon Hall, near Oxford. As Presidents of the Publishers' and the Booksellers' Associations, Stanley Unwin and Basil Blackwell had invited forty-eight eminent colleagues, twenty-four from each side, to bemoan rising costs, sluggish sales and reduced profit margins and, or so Blackwell claimed years later, 'to discuss the new reading public which we felt was just round the corner'. As it turned out, the only person prepared to take up the challenge was Allen Lane. The Canadian publisher and author Rache Lovat Dickson remembered that 'he combined with a handsome appearance an air of incisiveness, as though he was about to make a great decision' – and that the assumption that they had all gathered for a genial session of grousing was shattered once he rose to his feet. Lane dared to suggest that there was a new market which, at present, was met by Woolworth's, the twopenny libraries and the chain stores, and that he intended to tap this market via a line in sixpenny paperbacks. His audience was neither pleased nor impressed. A well-known Glaswegian bookseller said he would have 'naething' to do with Lane's paperbacks, since 'if we can't make money at seven and six, how are we going to make it at sixpence?' but the most vociferous opponent was David Roy, the head of W. H. Smith's book department. Roy had earlier led book trade opposition to the Book Society, and more recently worked himself into a frenzy of rage over a scheme, supported by authors but eventually withdrawn in the face of booksellers' hostility, whereby Kensitas cigarettes offered books in exchange for coupons. According to Frank Morley from Faber, Roy, 'a large, rugger-playing sort of figure, burly, very red-faced, *very* angry, proceeded to blast off': he interrupted Lane's speech incessantly, reminding Morley of a Spanish galleon trying to see off Sir Francis Drake. Stanley Unwin claimed to remember nothing of Lane's speech, though he thought the vexed issue of paperbacks might have been discussed informally; Blackwell, on the other hand, recalled how '47 of [the delegates] went away on the Monday morning with no further thought on the subject. The 48th was Allen Lane, who told me that the idea of Penguins came to him under an aged apple tree in my garden.'

Despite support from a few of his fellow-delegates, Wren Howard of Cape among them, Lane returned from the Ripon Hall conference 'flaming mad' with his fellow-publishers (or so H. A. W. Arnold recalled), and set about putting his Newtonian moment of revelation into practice. This involved deciding what the books should look like, finding a name for the list, and, since it would be a reprint list, approaching other publishers to see if they (and their authors) would be willing to sub-lease him the rights. 'I have never been able to understand why cheap books should not also be well-designed, for good design is no more expensive than bad,' he once wrote, and although Penguins only realized their full elegance after the war, when the great Swiss typographer Jan Tschichold was persuaded to join the staff, they were always striking and pleasing on the eye: 'We aimed at making something pretty smart, a product clean and as bright as two pins, modern enough not to offend the fastidious high-brow, and yet straightforward and unpretentious.' Like Victor Gollancz, he instinctively disliked picture jackets. 'I have always thought it one of the worst days in the world for the British book trade when "picture jackets" began to come in,' stormed the hyper-bolical VG: Lane may well have been influenced by the striking yellow, black and magenta lettering jackets that Stanley Morison was designing for Gollancz, who had decided, after exhaustive tests at a London railway bookstall, that yellow jackets were the most notice-able of all. Penguins were, by comparison, a model of sobriety. Edward Young, though never trained as a typographer, designed the famous horizontal bands, using a fashionable Gill Sans Bold for the title's lettering: Lane, he recalled, wanted 'a consistent and easily recognizable cover design' as well as a 'good trade mark that would be easy to treat pictorially, easy to say, and easy to remember'. The texts themselves were set, initially, in a variety of typefaces, but in 1937 the compact but legible Times New Roman, the typeface which Morison had designed for the remodelling of *The Times* in 1932, was chosen for the new Penguin Shakespeare series, and it remained the standard Penguin typeface until the arrival of Jan Tschichold. And whereas many publishers bulked out their books to make them look value for money, Lane insisted that his books should fit easily into a pocket or a handbag.

He was anxious to promote Penguin as a brand, to sell the imprint as well as individual books: paperbacks might be, in theory, as dispos-able as newspapers or cigarettes, but he wanted people to collect Penguins, so that each book helped to sell its companions. Penguins were, he wrote in 1938, 'the first serious attempt at introducing "branded goods" to the book trade'. Notions of 'corporate image', 'house style', 'logos' and the like were being promoted by up-to-the-minute advertising agencies like Crawford's, by Frank Pick at London Underground, who imposed a 'house style' on the Tube with Edward Johnston's sans serif lettering, and by that inimitable patron of poets and painters, Jack Beddington at Shell; and Lane was in tune with the times. The Thirties had a passion for design, and if Lane did not consciously subscribe to the Bauhaus notion that well-designed objects – fridges, vacuum cleaners, typewriters, ocean liners, the lettering on the side of a department store – should be works of art, he was moving in that direction.

Equally important was a memorable and, ideally, endearing name-cum-trade mark for the new publishing house. Edward Young recalled how a long morning was devoted to the subject, the participants sitting round a table in a 'dark little office' in Vigo Street while Allen Lane's secretary, Joan Coles, typed busily away on the other side of a partition and, every now and then, 'elderly and benign Bodley Head gentlemen sauntered in and out with gentle smiles and mutters of "hare-brained schemes" under their breath'. 'Phoenix' was considered, suggestive of the new firm rising from the ashes of The Bodley Head, but Chatto already had its Phoenix Library. A dolphin was suggested, redolent of a Renaissance printer's device and the Bristol coat-of-arms, but failed to find favour. According to Young, they had Albatross's example in mind – 'As to the name of the series, who knows whether the Penguin was not subconsciously hatched from an Albatross egg?' the Penguin typographer Hans Schmoller once wondered – when Joan Coles suddenly piped up from the far side of her partition with 'What about Penguins?' Lane liked it at once – it had, he felt, 'a certain dignified flippancy' that seemed entirely appropriate – and Young, supplied with funds from petty cash, was sent off to the Zoo in Regent's Park to sketch a penguin for the covers.

Years later Ethel Mannin recalled how, 'in the old days, when *you* had much *less* money, and *I* had much more', and she was 'young and beautiful, as we all were then', she met the Lane brothers in a pub in Piccadilly. 'They had a cardboard model of a penguin, with which they fooled about, waddling it about the table at which we sat; they were laughing, yet deadly serious,' she wrote in her memoirs. '"Our idea was paperbacks at sixpence, and calling them Penguins," Allen said. I enquired, through a ginny haze, "Why Penguins?" They laughed and remarked "Why not?" To which there was no logical answer . . .' Robert Lusty called in at Vigo Street and found Lane 'quick, alert, emphatic', and far removed from conventional notions of a 'revolutionary prophet'. 'How well I remember our holiday in Spain when you were far gone in Penguin pregnancy, and as dreamy and uncomfortable as any woman in her ninth month,' the printer Raymond Hazell recalled. His firm produced a dummy and specimen pages for the first ten titles, but the actual printing order would go to a rival firm, the Athenaeum Printing Works in Redhill, whose quote was cheaper 'by some percentage of a farthing per copy' – so demonstrating that, when it came to business, 'shrewdness always counted more than sentiment with Allen Lane'. Sensibly spreading his debts, Lane printed the subsequent batches with Clay's, Wyman and Purnell, and Hazell's had to wait until some of the early titles were reprinted before their services were called upon.

'In choosing these first ten titles,' Lane told the *Bookseller* shortly before they appeared, 'the test I applied to each book was to ask myself: is this a book which, if I had not read it, and had seen it on sale at 6d., would make me say, "This is a book I have always meant to read; I will get it now."' That was all very well, but persuading publishers to fall in with his plans was a very different matter. Penguin No. 1 – André Maurois's *Ariel* – was no problem, since The Bodley Head was its hardback publisher; but thereafter he came across fierce resistance. Although Lane always denied that Penguins would cheapen books or reduce hardback sales, on the grounds that the books had long been available anyway and 'any sales we effect will be extra sales and not at the expense of existing editions', publishers worried that Penguins would destroy the sale of their cheap editions and ruin their business with the all-important library market. The most eloquent spokesman for the old order was Harold Raymond, a former schoolmaster who had joined Chatto & Windus after the First World War and remained there for the rest of his working life. 'Your suggestion of the sixpenny series has led to long discussions among us here, but I am sorry to tell you that we have decided not to cooperate,' he told Lane. Were he to agree to sub-lease titles to Penguin, 'the sale of the other editions of the other titles in the series [i.e. the 3s. 6d. cheap editions] would suffer very severely'. As he had told Lane on his visit to Chatto, 'The steady cheapening of books is in my opinion a great danger in the trade at present, and I sometimes think that the booksellers have to be saved from themselves in this respect. It is they who have so constantly clamoured for us publishers to "meet depression with depression prices". Yet it is this lowering of prices which is one of the chief reasons why our trade is finding it so hard to recover from the slump.' Raymond returned to the subject in a lecture at Stationers' Hall three years later, by which time his firm was doing brisk business with Penguin Books. He conceded that Penguins looked good, published worthwhile books and appealed to authors once their hardback sales of the sub-leased books had begun to drop away, but worried whether 'the book trade can afford to cut its profits to the fine point which a sixpenny novel now involves'. Were Penguins tapping a new market, or would people spend even less on books now that cheap books were so readily available? Booksellers were reporting a falling-off in the sales of hardback cheap editions – so much so that they soon ceased to exist – and he worried that the 7s. 6d. novel, and the still more expensive works of non-fiction, would be seen by the public as a 'ramp', and the publishers themselves as gentlemanly wide-boys. High prices, he concluded, were in the interests of publishers, booksellers and authors: whereas a successful author could expect a royalty of 20 per cent or even 25 per cent on a 7s. 6d. hardback, the most he could expect from Penguin was the equivalent of 2 per cent of sixpence, or half a farthing per book.

Nor was Raymond alone in his opposition. Sir Newman Flower at Cassell refused to have any dealings with Penguin, though his son Desmond changed all that when he took over the family firm in 1938; Charles Evans of Heinemann was adamant in his hostility, convinced that Penguin would destroy authors' livelihoods and do terrible damage to his firm's profitable cheap editions. When Enid Bagnold begged him to offer her bestselling novel *National Velvet* to Penguin, he refused even to consider the idea. Heinemann had sold 19,655 copies of the 7s. 6d. edition alone, and for him to sub-lease the rights to Penguin would ruin sales of the cheap edition. 'It is best for everybody's sake to get the last drop of milk out of the coconut,' the avuncular publisher told her. Eighteen months later she returned to the attack, but was once again beaten off. 'It is my considered view, based on facts, figures and experience, that the sales of Penguins have done more harm to publishing and authors than any movement for a great many years. There are many booksellers who would tell you that since the demand for Penguins they can sell practically nothing else,' he warned her. 'Nobody can live off sixpenny books. Nobody makes any money out of them except the Penguin publishers and possibly their printers.' Penguin, he went on, were making their profits 'at the expense of writers and other publishers', and 'in the long run, all authors who have given encouragement to the Penguin series are helping to cut their own throats'. Defeated but unconvinced, Enid Bagnold made one last plea for mercy. '*National Velvet* is now dead,' she told her unbending publisher. 'Dead as mutton. But it could have this huge second life, and I feel desperate when I think that I can't have it, and *National Velvet* can't have it. That it is shut away in a 7s. 6d. coffin, decent, rich, with brass handles, and it might have sixpenny wings. *National Velvet* is like a child who is eating his heart out to go on the music halls.'

But not all authors shared her passion for paperbacks. Writing in the *New English Weekly*, George Orwell pronounced Penguins

splendid value for sixpence, so splendid that if the other publishers had any sense they would combine against them and suppress them. It is, of course, a great mistake to imagine that cheap books are good for the book trade. Actually it is just the other way about. If you have, for instance, five shillings to spend and the normal price of a book is half-a-crown, you are quite likely to spend your whole five shillings on two books. But if books are sixpence each you are not going to buy ten of them, because you don't want as many as ten; your saturation point will have been reached long before that. Probably you will buy three sixpenny books and spend the rest of your five shillings on seats at the 'movies'. Hence the cheaper books become, the less money is spent on books. This is an advantage from the reader's point of view and doesn't hurt trade as a whole, but for the publisher, the compositor, the author and the bookseller it is a disaster.

Harold Raymond and Charles Evans could hardly have hoped for a more eloquent advocate.

Both Stanley Unwin and Victor Gollancz were determinedly unhelpful. Unwin was generally thought to know more about publishing than any man alive, and was determined to prove that cheap paperbacks were doomed to failure: Lane liked to imagine him scurrying round the bookshops, peering at the Penguins through his pince-nez and scribbling costs and calculations in his notebook. Unwin was convinced that only a limited number of books could justify, in sales terms, the long print-runs needed to publish at 6d., and that Penguins would die of inanition in due course. He also predicted that rising costs of printing and paper would erode Lane's wafer-thin profit margins, making it impossible for him to continue in business, or stick to the terms of his agreement to publish at sixpence: but although Lane would always remain wedded to the notion of cheap books, he would, in due course, reluctantly put up the prices of his books to allow for rising costs, knowing perfectly well that Penguins were, by then, too well established to lose their market.

Whereas Unwin's reaction was cool and analytical, Gollancz's was that of a sulky child who resents a newcomer hogging the limelight and succeeding where he had earlier failed. He refused to reply to Lane's standard letter about the possibility of his acquiring the rights in particular Gollancz titles: in the end – or so it was said – Lane sent him a pre-paid postcard reading, 'I shall be happy to negotiate/I am sorry but I cannot consider leasing to Penguins the following titles . . . Please delete whichever phrase is inappropriate', only to have it returned 'with everything struck out up to and including the words "I am sorry"'. Lane was able to take some kind of revenge by including in his first batch a novel by Dorothy Sayers, an author about whom Gollancz was particularly possessive: he persuaded Benn to release *The Unpleasantness at the Bellona Club*, in which they still controlled the rights, and honour was satisfied. Gollancz refused to have any dealings with Penguin until the 1950s, when he wrote to 'my dear Allen' to ask whether Penguin could be persuaded to paper-back one of his own books, *A Year of Grace* ('It is said to be the most successful anthology of its kind since Robert Bridges's *Testament of Man*,' he assured his old enemy, who was duly persuaded). The two men had much in common, as it happened: neither had any time for trade organizations like the Publishers' Association ('I refuse to be manacled by fools!' VG once shouted); both paid below-average wages to their employees but would indulge in sudden acts of generosity; like Jonathan Cape in Bedford Square, both combined courage and ruthlessness in their business dealings with moral cowardice, sacking people on an impulse but leaving it to others to execute their orders. But their temperaments could hardly have been more different. The novelist Norman Collins, a director of Gollancz in the Thirties, remembered how 'Victor exuded a greater dynamism than any man I've ever known. Even to see him coming through the front door was like a tempest coming in. He sat down in a chair; the chair creaked. I remember going in to see him one day. He was sharpening a pencil; it was like any lesser man hewing down an oak tree.' VG was emotional, impulsive, shambolic in appearance and given to roaring and pounding the table in a rage; AL − as Lane's Penguin employees soon came to call him − was cool, reserved and dapper, and when he was angry he never raised his voice but his lips thinned and his bright blue eyes turned to slivers of ice.

One publisher was prepared to give Lane the benefit of the doubt; and where he led, others would follow. A well-dressed, hard-headed countryman who had begun as an errand boy at Hatchard's before working for Gerald Duckworth, Jonathan Cape was, according to his former employee Rupert Hart-Davis, 'one of the tightest-fisted old bastards I've ever encountered'. 'A publisher of outstanding genius with the heart of a horse-coper' in Eric Linklater's opinion, he had started his own firm in 1921, and before long it was widely agreed to be the most stylish and fashionable publisher in London, admired for the elegance of its production, masterminded by Cape's partner, Wren Howard, and for a literary list that was second to none. Lane was determined to win them round, and paid a visit to No. 30 Bedford Square. 'I went to see Jonathan and said: "I want 10 to start and 10 to follow, and I want 10 of them from yours."' He told Cape which titles he was after, and offered him an advance on each of

£25, payable on publication, against a royalty of a farthing a copy. Cape replied that he would accept advances of £40, payable on signature of the contract, against royalties of three-eighths of a penny, and the deal was done. Years later, Lane recalled,

I was talking to Jonathan and he said, 'You're the b . . . that has ruined this trade with your ruddy Penguins.' I replied, 'Well, I wouldn't have got off to such a good start if you hadn't helped me.' He said, 'I know damn well you wouldn't, but like everybody else in the trade I thought you were bound to go bust, and I thought I'd take 400 quid off you before you did.'

Cape provided six of the first ten titles, Hemingway's *A Farewell to Arms*, Eric Linklater's *Poet's Pub*, Susan Ertz's unmemorable *Madame Claire*, Beverley Nichols's *Twenty-five*, E. H. Young's *William* and *Gone to Earth* by Mary Webb, an author much admired and publicly acclaimed by the Prime Minister, Stanley Baldwin; The Bodley Head provided *Ariel* and Agatha Christie's *The Mysterious Affair at Styles*; Compton Mackenzie's *Carnival* came from Chatto, now reluctantly eating their words, and the Dorothy Sayers concluded the opening salvo. (According to Steve Hare, the Penguin historian, the famous first batch of ten was, in fact, eleven: Agatha Christie's *The Mysterious Affair at Styles* was, thanks to a contractual misunderstanding, included in the opening ten, but was immediately withdrawn and replaced with her *Murder on the Links*. Both books remained on the Penguin list.)

Persuading booksellers to stock them was to prove quite as daunting a task as winning round the publishers. While John Lane put his new-found knowledge of overseas markets to miraculous effect – he simply wrote to the booksellers and wholesalers he had met on his world tour to tell them how many copies he would be sending, and later wished he'd been even bolder in the quantities recommended – Dick and Allen devoted the early summer of 1935 to the dispiriting task of trying to win round booksellers in the home market. Dick concentrated on London and the suburbs; Allen visited bookshops in England and Scotland, and since he liked to involve his family whenever possible, he took his mother along for the ride. Neither of them can have been cheered by the trade's reactions. Many booksellers refused to allow Penguins into their shops or, if they condescended to place an order, confined the offending items to a bin on the pavement outside. They complained that the profit margin on sixpence was too small to be worth bothering with, that such small books would fall prey to shoplifters, that they would soon look grubby and tatty, that the dust-jackets worn by the early Penguins would be torn by the public, that they would 'simply add to the bad stock with which every bookshop was already unpleasantly full'. 'Who's ever heard of *Pooet's Poob*?' grumbled a Manchester bookseller on being shown a dummy of Eric Linklater's novel. Selfridge's had reserved a window, and the famous J. G. Wilson of Bumpus in Oxford Street had promised his support, but Lane was so dispirited that he almost abandoned hope. 'It's a flop. Nobody will want them. I've got to pack it up. Do you know anyone who would take the whole thing off my hands?' he asked Llywelyn Maddock after learning that neither W. H. Smith nor Simpkin Marshall had shown any interest. 'Poor Allen was knocked for six – the only time in my life when I have seen him really down,' Maddock recalled. Lane had printed 20,000 each of the ten titles, 10,000 of which had been bound: each copy had cost twopence-halfpenny to manufacture, the gross margin was a penny a copy, and they would break even when sales reached between 17,000 and 18,000 per title. So far they had subscribed a miserable 7,000 each, and the future looked grim indeed.

Then, quite suddenly, everything changed. According to publishing folklore, three weeks before publication, on a Saturday, a despondent Lane called at Woolworth's head office. Although Clifford Prescott was the buyer for the haberdashery department, books formed part of his empire, and Lane had got to know him when he sold him *The Three Little Pigs*. Most of the books sold in Woolworth's were at the lower end of the market – Collins did brisk business with them, and they produced their own Readers' Library – and Prescott took a dim view of the Penguins. 'I don't know about these, with no pictures on the front. Readers' Library is better value,' he told Lane, and his assistant was equally unenthusiastic. Just then Mrs Prescott arrived, fresh from shopping and eager for lunch. She recognized, and approved of, several titles on the Penguin list, and (or so it was said) had a soft spot for their handsome young publisher. 'I think they're very good too, we'll give them a trial,' said Mr Prescott, suddenly converted. He told Lane that he would take a consignment order; back in the office, Lane rang Sydney Goldsack, the sales manager of Collins, to find out what was meant by a consignment order, and was told that every branch of Woolworth's would have Penguins on sale, but that if he failed to meet the order in full by the agreed date he could lose it *in toto*. A day or two later an order for 63,500 copies came through; other shops followed suit, and Penguin's future was assured. Not all of this quite rings true:

cynics have suggested that Lane set up the meeting with Prescott far earlier than he later claimed, and engineered the entire episode so as to extract maximum publicity and create a surge of last-minute orders; nor does it seem credible that so experienced a salesman as Lane would have been ignorant about consignment orders.

The first ten Penguins were published on the Tuesday before the August Bank Holiday of 1935. On the Friday Lane jumped off a bus outside Selfridge's on his way to work, and was told by the book-buyer there that the initial 100 copies of each title had almost sold out, and he needed another 1,000 at once. Back in the office, the phone was ringing with booksellers demanding copies. Penguins had arrived in strength, and were already confounding their critics.

6. Pelicans Take Flight

The *Times Literary Supplement* may have ignored the first batch of Penguins, but, for the most part, reactions in the Press and from private individuals echoed the enthusiasm of the book-buying public. 'These Penguin Books are amazingly good value for money. If you can make the series pay for itself – with such books at such a price – you will have performed a great publishing feat,' J. B. Priestley told Lane. 'Let me congratulate you greatly on your Penguin Books, perfect marvels of beauty and cheapness. You have nipped in at just the proper time for getting them floated, for they are the ideal books for holiday-makers,' wrote Mr Bulloch of Allied Newspapers.

Nowadays it is hard to imagine a publishing house hitting the headlines, let alone a brave new venture, but things were very different in an age when television was in its infancy, the printed word prevailed, and Victor Gollancz was a figure of national importance. 'A PUBLISHING TRIUMPH,' blared the *Sunday Referee*, hardly the most highbrow of papers. 'Not since the halcyon days of the pre-war period has so courageous a venture been launched,' the paper's correspondent declared. 'I don't know how it is done. For apart from the fact that every title is in copyright – and authors have to live – the production is magnificent: strong, limp binding, good paper, clear type, and even a dust-jacket. The venture is bound to succeed. The courage behind it is as admirable as the volumes. The publishers have placed the reading public under a debt of gratitude.' Howard Spring, an influential middlebrow novelist and literary panjandrum, voiced his approval; at a higher-brow level, Herbert Read decreed that the disposable Penguin 'makes literature as fluid a commodity as cigarettes or chocolate, a thought which would have horrified a Ruskin or a Morris' – so partly missing the point, since one of the more obvious manifestations of Penguin fever was that people kept (and sometimes collected) them in exactly the same way as conventional hardback books. The *Observer* thought the new list made 'perfect reading for sixpence a time, in the jolliest coloured paper bindings. Perfect for seashore, wood, moorland and even the train or aeroplane', and forecast that 'every suitcase in the family' would soon be 'bursting with treasure'. The *Saturday Review* declared them ideal for being 'carried in a man's pocket or a lady's handbag'; the *Bookseller* reported a week after the launch that 150,000 copies had been sold in four days, and that 'one of the great Continental air transport companies' was thinking of giving free copies to their passengers. James Agate in the *Daily Express* confirmed the fears of those publishers who worried that Penguins would disrupt the delicate ecology of their business. Under the heading '7/6 is too much for a novel: the new sixpenny ones prove it', he suggested that the book trade was 'in my considered view the biggest ramp in the country . . . Publishers are the door-keepers and valets of men of letters, and were I in charge of the next revolution I should give every publisher of my acquaintance a choice between the sixpenny novel and the lamppost!'

Influential as he was, Agate was in no position to match rhetoric with action; but publishers are an imitative breed, and in no time Lane's rivals were following his example. The *Evening Standard* reported that Hutchinson, the veteran paperback publishers, had started a sixpenny list of Toucan Books, while Collins introduced its White Circle list of thrillers, with Peter Cheyney its star author. If Penguin's success was anything to go by, they were well advised to follow Lane's example. The second batch of Penguins had included Norman Douglas's *South Wind*, Samuel Butler's *Erewhon*, Liam O'Flaherty's *The Informer*, Dashiell Hammett's *The Thin Man* and W. H. Hudson's *The Purple Land*, and others followed in a steady stream: in January 1936 the *Evening Standard* informed its readers that a million Penguins had been sold in the first four months after publication. The business made a net profit of £4,500 in its first nine months' trading, and by July 1936 over 3 million books had been sold: a Penguin was being bought every ten seconds, the firm boasted in a *Bookseller* advertisement, and 'placed end-to-end they would reach from London to Cologne'.

Some of the profits were siphoned off for the ailing Bodley Head: Lane still nourished vain hopes of buying the firm for £10,000 after a receiver had been appointed, and using it as a 'feeder' for Penguin titles, but the umbilical cord linking Penguin with its parent firm was finally severed shortly after the entire staff of Penguin had celebrated their first Christmas together with dinner at Talbot Square, followed by a visit to the Metropolitan music-hall in the Edgware Road. Fearful that his new enterprise could be dragged under by an insolvent parent, Lane arranged for Penguin Books Ltd to be incorporated on 1 January 1936. The three brothers were its directors: Dick had recently claimed from his insurers after losing various items during a burglary at their parents' house in Falfield, so he put up the initial capital of £100; and the deeds of the parental home were lodged with the bank as collateral. A £7,000 overdraft at the Cocks Biddulph branch of Martins Bank enabled them to keep afloat, and would become a permanent feature of Penguin life for the next quarter of a century; and despite the bad debts at The Bodley Head, printers and other suppliers were prepared to give Lane extended credit. Dick took to visiting the bank once a fortnight with a copy of that day's *Times* tucked under his arm; he knew that the two managers liked to do the crossword every morning after opening the post, and, eager to keep in their good books, and to give 'an air of friendliness' to the proceedings, Dick made a point of opening each discussion with 'Have you got one across yet?'

Before long, other publishers were following where Cape had led. Harold Macmillan of the family firm may have refused to consider an offer for the paperback rights in Hardy's novels, but Harold Raymond at Chatto was proving more emollient than expected. Two months after the launching of Penguins, he wrote to Lane to say that he had discussed the matter with his partners, and 'though our general feeling still is that the Book Trade as a whole may come to rue the day of the advent of this particular line of publication, we are quite willing to approach some of our authors and invite them to join in our venture. Although I shall not beg them to accept, I shall certainly not do the reverse.' A few days later Raymond was in touch with T. F. Powys about the possibility

of Penguin publishing *Mr Weston's Good Wine*. 'Chattos have been
rather coy about their blandishments from a general feeling that
there is a danger of books becoming too cheap,' he told his author.
'However, the series has been very successfully launched and the
Lanes are in a position to offer terms that are distinctively attractive' – and, he could have added, better than those being offered
to other publishers, consisting as they did of an advance of £100
per title against 30s. per 1,000 copies sold for a five-year exclusive
licence. All the same, 'I cannot help feeling that the day may come
when the book trade as a whole may regret these very cheap books,
and that authors and publishers may find it increasingly hard to
scratch a living. I think it would pay you to take advantage of the
proposal, for it would take a long while for *Mr Weston* to earn £50
from our Phoenix Library.' Chatto, as the hardback publisher, would
be keeping 50 per cent of the Penguin advance and royalties: hence
the reference to £50.*

Writing to the Hogarth Press about his new series, Lane assured
Leonard Woolf that 'one of the interesting features has been the
way in which it has not affected adversely the sales of more expensive books'. Cape had already licensed five titles from their Florin
Library – priced, inconsequentially, at 2s. 6d. apiece – and had
received no complaints about cheap editions becoming unsaleable
in the face of sixpenny Penguins: 'in fact we have definitely been
able to trace sales of more expensive editions of books by the same
author directly to sales of Penguin Books.' (Such optimism was
premature: by the time war broke out, sales of hardback cheap
editions had been virtually annihilated.) Lane offered an advance of

---

* A 50–50 split between author and hardback publisher on sub-leased paperback
earnings became standard practice in the trade: such a division of spoils suggests
that the hardback publishers' claim that the paperback damaged or diminished
hardback sales had prevailed over Lane's belief that Penguin sales were additional
to hardback sales and opened up a new market for the author's work. The 50–50
split lasted well into the 1970s, when hardback publishers started their own mass
market paperback lists, paying authors a 'full' (i.e. undivided) royalty on such sales;
at the same time literary agents insisted that a larger proportion of the income
from sub-leased paperbacks should find its way into their authors' pockets.

£40 for Vita Sackville-West's *The Edwardians*; despite all the publicity, the author had never heard of Penguin Books, but since 'it sounds rather a paying proposition' she was all for going ahead. By September 1936 her novel had sold 64,349 copies in paperback, earning her £56 10s. 5d in royalties over and above her original advance; another 23,885 had been sold by the following spring, and the same rate of sale was sustained in the next two half-yearly statements. In October 1939 Lane asked if he could reduce the royalty from 30s. per 1,000 to £1 per 1,000, and Woolf urged his author not to accept. 'I cannot see why you should be expected to subsidize the Lanes,' he told her. 'I think it wrong in principle to agree,' she wrote back. 'It is spoiling the market for other people who may be absolutely dependent upon their earnings.' On the other hand, being published in Penguin 'does provide a good advertisement for an author from which you as my publisher naturally benefit', so perhaps they should agree to 25s. per 1,000? But Woolf would have none of it. He had refused to accept a reduced royalty, and had made no mention of a compromise 'as it seems to me to give away the principle and I really think the whole thing is a try-on on the part of Penguins'.

Try-on or not, the shrewd and parsimonious Woolf was prepared to deal further with the Lanes, discussing terms for the 'sixpenny rights' in C. H. B. Kitchen's *Death of My Aunt* and doing battle with Dick over the farthing royalty proposed for Vita Sackville-West's *All Passion Spent*; but Stanley Unwin remained unconvinced. Three years after the launching of Penguins, and a year after the appearance of the non-fiction Pelican list, he was still on the warpath. Writing in the *Times Literary Supplement* under the heading 'Concerning Sixpennies', he affected the world-weary note of the sage who has seen it all before and knows it is doomed to failure. There was nothing new about sixpennies, he claimed: in August 1914, publishers' warehouses had been crammed with the wretched things after the initial flurry of sales had been followed by the inevitable slump when the novelty wore off. 'As a member of the public I appreciate them,' he assured his readers, gritting his teeth the while; but in publishing terms they couldn't and didn't make sense. Mass production techniques could be applied to a limited number of

items, and only a modest quantity of bestselling books would sell
well enough to justify the 50,000 print-runs needed to price them
at 6d. each; a farthing per copy on sales of 50,000 would earn an
author a mere £50, a sum made in no time via a 15 per cent royalty
on a 7s. 6d. hardback. He quoted Ruskin's insistence that 'a book
is not worth anything unless it is worth *much*', and a recent essay
in which J. M. Keynes blamed a benighted public for 'their wrong
psychology towards book-buying, their mean and tricky ways where
a book, the noblest of man's works, is concerned'.

Years later Sir Stanley's nephew, Philip Unwin, pointed out that
his uncle had been disingenuous in comparing Penguins with the
paperbacks of 1914, which had consisted of works by the likes of
Ethel M. Dell, printed on newsprint in tiny type in double columns;
but a more immediate champion was to hand in the form of Margaret
Cole, a keen Fabian whose husband, G. D. H. Cole, would be
commissioned to write *Practical Economics* for the opening batch of
Pelican Books. Said by some to have a soft spot for their debonair
young publisher, Mrs Cole had already enthused at length about
Penguins and other paperbacks in the *Listener*, noting how they had
changed the perception of the book 'from something that was only
suitable to members of an upper or educated class to something
which anybody may enjoy or possess without being thought odd,
highbrow or "apeing one's betters"', and citing the sales by Collins
of 3 million White Circle thrillers within three months as further
evidence that 'we are now only at the beginning of a stage in the
democratization of books'. Spurred into print by Stanley Unwin's
article, she hurried to put the other side of the story to *TLS* readers.
Penguins, like the Readers' Union book club and Gollancz's Left
Book Club, had created new readers. Book-buying, she declared,
was blighted by poverty and snobbery, and 'if books are to be
purchased by the poor, or the middling poor, they must be as cheap
as cigarettes'. Until recently, publishing for the lower orders had
been regarded as 'either a piece of philanthropy or a patent medicine racket', in which trash was served up in a suitably hideous
guise. 'It is high time that book-owning should cease to be the
preserve of a small class,' she concluded: by 'giving them the best

you can, not either by playing down to them or lecturing them on their "duty" to uphold literature', Lane had discovered a new market of the hitherto disenfranchised. Unconvinced, as yet, by her passionate defence, the *TLS* sided with the old order: a leader writer worried that sixpennies were 'debauching' buyers of contemporary literature, who would be tempted to wait for the paperback rather than invest in the hardback, that they encouraged the notion that mainstream publishing was, as James Agate had suggested, a 'ramp', and that they owed their success to 'the action of a few very rich authors or very determined propagandists', but consoled himself with the knowledge that they were 'already sowing the seeds of their own destruction'. *The Economist*, on the other hand, declared that 'to bring serious, well-printed books and genuine literature to homes where ephemeral trash has been the staple diet has been a notable step'.

In the meantime, Lane shocked his more conservative colleagues by installing a 'Penguincubator', a slot-machine book-dispenser, in the Charing Cross Road, and by inserting business reply cards in some of his books, asking readers for suggestions and putting them on a mailing list: given the initially lukewarm response from conventional booksellers, he was, for many years, an enthusiastic advocate of selling directly to his readers – a practice abominated by the Booksellers' Association – and only closed down his direct mail service when it proved too expensive to sustain. The warehouse in which he stored and despatched his books was equally unconventional. The earliest Penguins, those published under the umbrella of The Bodley Head, had been warehoused all over London, but now they were brought under one roof. Designed by Sir John Soane, the architect of the Bank of England, and completed in 1828, Holy Trinity, Marylebone, is a Greek Revival church on the Euston Road. Its crypt was lying empty, so Lane rented it as a warehouse, paying the Church Commissioners a rent of £150 per annum. A dank and gloomy spot, it was reached by a metal spiral staircase. The walls were plastered with plaques commemorating long-dead parishioners, and it suffered sporadic infestations of mice, the whiff of which was known to linger in the pages of the books. Two empty tombs were fitted with metal doors; one was used for petty cash, while the other held the invoice books. The light filtered in through shallow windows high up on the walls; the grille was removed from one of these and replaced with a set of folding doors opening on to a chute, down which new deliveries were hurled from the church-yard above. Wrapped in brown paper parcels, the books were stacked all round the walls, waiting to be despatched to booksellers all over the world, making their escape by means of an ancient lift, formerly used to convey the coffins of the recently deceased, many of them retired civil servants from the West Indian island of St Lucia. Paraffin stoves provided a modicum of warmth in winter. A tin bucket served as a communal lavatory, and at the end of the day it was emptied on to the flagstones of the churchyard; each employee was provided with a penny a day in case they needed to use the public lavator-ies on the other side of the Euston Road, adjacent to Great Portland Street tube station.

Allen Lane always liked to embellish the past with a patina of myth, and the crypt loomed largest of all in Penguin mythology. H. A. W. Arnold, by now happily ensconced at the British Museum, visited Stan Olney 'all among the skeletons': the crypt was, he decided, 'a grim place. There were moaning sounds from running water, that kind of thing.' It was rumoured that Bill Rapley, a devout Catholic given to profanities, had fallen through a coffin and found himself embracing a skeleton, and that a member of staff – Rapley, perhaps – hammered his thumb while nailing up a crate of books and let out a terrible oath, interrupting a wedding service in the church above at a critical moment in the proceedings. Edward Young noted the nude pin-ups taped to the walls, and how 'they had to have a curtain which they could drop at a moment's notice because the vicar used to come and see how the dear boys were getting on downstairs'. Survivors of the crypt acquired an almost heroic status, and many went on to devote their working lives to the firm: in addition to Olney and Rapley, they included Bob Maynard, recently arrived from Chatto, the muscular Peter Kite, Jack Summers, the sixteen-year-old Bob Davies and, briefly, the piratical travel writer Eric Muspratt, two of whose books appeared in Penguin. For

Muspratt, Penguin 'represented an ideal in the business of publishing, of giving good books to the world at only sixpence each. There was a Soviet touch in this, and Allen Lane had a true touch of the Napoleonic.' The work was long and exhausting: Lane himself often helped pack and invoice books, and on one occasion Dick and John worked for forty-eight hours without sleep. When involved in such marathon sessions, the two younger brothers, having worked all night, would breakfast in a nearby Lyons Corner House, return to Talbot Square for a bath and a shave, row on the lake in Regent's Park, and then head back to work. Lane took to visiting Champney's health farm near Tring for restorative sessions: famed for its regime of orange juice, steam and colonic irrigation, its literary clientele included Hugh Walpole and Cyril Connolly, whose recurrent visits excited the unkind derision of Evelyn Waugh. In later years, when the trousering of his impeccable dove-grey double-breasted suits began to strain at the leash, Lane would book himself in for a session of citrus fruit and salads, returning home slimmer but more fractious than usual.

When not helping out in the crypt, he was busy in a new office on the other side of the Euston Road. Joan Coles had noticed how, towards the end of his time at The Bodley Head, he spent little time in the office and was even harder to pin down than usual: was he, she wondered, trying to dodge persistent creditors brandishing unpaid invoices? Now, with Vigo Street no longer at his disposal, and the creditors off his back, he had taken a couple of rooms above a car showroom in Great Portland Street, over the road from the unofficial office lavatories. A journalist from a trade paper was struck by his lack of self-importance and his nervous energy – he paced up and down his tiny office, seemingly incapable of sitting still – and how very different his was from a conventional publisher's office: there were no pictures on the wall, the furniture consisted of a small desk and two upright chairs, the phone rang incessantly, and in the room next door, in charge of production, sat the 'square-jawed, tallish, modest Edward Young, who seems much too young to tackle such big problems'. Jean Osborne, who went there as a secretary, soon found that she 'was in love with all the Lanes, and

Edward Young too'; but Allen made her feel gauche and 'seemed to take a delight in scrutinizing me at close range', so much so that 'I began to think I must smell or look quaint or dowdy'. She came to rather distrust him: he was often kind, but then 'spoiled his actions by being quite heartless'. John, on the other hand, she liked unreservedly. 'I felt he was less complex and could cope better with his humour and "ways"': he was 'usually so twinkly', and she liked the way he strutted about the office in his light grey 'peacock suit'. Bob Davies, who went on to make his career in the sales side, specializing in the European market, found John a kindly and helpful mentor, and was duly grateful when he covered up for him after he had given a retailer a wholesaler's discount, a cardinal sin in the founder's book. Others found John an angular, difficult character; all seem to agree that he was the 'brainy' brother. Morpurgo suggests, without citing his sources, that John and his eldest brother became increasingly scratchy and competitive with one another; whereas the cautious, benign and stolid Dick, however irritating he may have been, in no way posed a threat. Dick, in Jean Osborne's opinion, 'was a dear, and even then I could sense that he was something of an outsider in the trio'.

'Of one thing I'm sure; there's no money in it for anybody,' Lane had told his close friend Edmund Segrave, the editor of the *Bookseller*, shortly before he launched his list, and elsewhere he wrote that 'there is no fortune in this series for anyone concerned'. Penguins would, in due course, make him a millionaire, and by the end of the Thirties he was already a very rich man; but in the early days money was in short supply, and although he paid himself £1,000 a year – a handsome wage in those days – both Dick and John worked for nothing for the first two years, and Jean Osborne remembered how the brothers used to cadge 9d. off each other for a haircut. But Lane would always combine modest pay with extraordinary acts of generosity and kindness, usually performed on the sly and a matter of some embarrassment to him: years later, when he learned that Bob Maynard's wife had been ill during her pregnancy, he found out who was the best gynaecologist in London and booked her into University College Hospital to give birth, and others benefited from his covert good deeds. Before long the success of Penguins enabled him to lash out, for himself and for his staff. His own salary increased by leaps and bounds – in October 1937 the *Star*, one of London's three evening papers, ran a large feature on Penguin's '£10,000 a year employer, five feet six or so, sturdy in build, intelligent and commanding in face, quick in thought and decision' – but he partly compensated for miserly wages by passing his staff 10 per cent of the profits every six months. 'I wouldn't dream of running a business any other way,' he told *Rover World*, 'because it makes for the maximum efficiency in every department. The staff themselves see that every individual pulls his weight, and that makes expensive supervision unnecessary.' Very much in advance of its time, his profit-sharing scheme was soon abandoned: during the war all members of staff were paid a regular bonus based on profits, but this was discontinued in the austere post-war era. Of more immediate interest were staff outings to France. In Boulogne, the *Bookseller* reported, 'even the King Penguin behaved in a manner incompatible with his usual austere dignity' as the alcohol flowed; for the day trip to Dieppe staff members were each provided with a cardboard disc carrying the Penguin colophon and worn round the neck on a string, and one over-charged member of staff, eagerly examining the girls lined up in a brothel for his inspection, noted that one of them was clad in nothing save high-heeled shoes and a Penguin disc round her neck.

Life was not all work, but it seemed impossible to keep the Penguins at bay. Lane took his parents on a cruise to Portugal in September 1937, and on his birthday they asked the Dutch steward if he could produce a penguin-shaped pudding, but were presented instead with a stork; and when, a year earlier, he decided to buy himself a boat, it was named, inevitably, the *Penguin*. Some years earlier Lane had got to know Norman Clackson, then employed on *Yachting Monthly*, and he turned to him for advice. They tracked down a nine-ton yacht on the Crouch, had her refitted, and arranged for Eric Muspratt to sail her round to Fowey in Cornwall. Dick far preferred fishing to sailing, but Allen and John spent long weekends sailing near Fowey or on the Beaulieu River in Hampshire.

He kept the *Penguin* till the early 1950s, and his interest in the
subject took profitable shape in Peter Heaton's Pelican on *Sailing*,
which was taken on after the war and, despite Clackson's predic-
tion that it would sell, at most, 15,000 copies, went on to notch
up sales of over 350,000.

The *Times Literary Supplement* may have had its reservations about
paperbacks, but its parent paper had noted 'the emergence of a new
social habit on a large scale'; and Lane widened the scope of
that social habit when, in August 1936, Bernard Shaw urged him
to reissue in paperback Apsley Cherry-Garrard's classic of Antarctic
exploration, *The Worst Journey in the World*. Lane dutifully took up
the suggestion, but in his letter of thanks he told Shaw that what
he really wanted was to reissue *The Intelligent Woman's Guide to
Socialism, Capitalism and Sovietism*, published by Constable in 1928.
To his amazement, Shaw leapt at the idea. 'Right, how much do
you want to pay for it?' he asked – a reaction which, Lane told the
News Chronicle, 'rather knocked us'. Nor was that all: Shaw was keen
to add two new chapters to his book, and asked that the word
Fascism should be added to the title. 'Prepare for a shock,' he told
the printer William Maxwell. 'The Penguin Press wants the *Intelligent
Woman's Guide*. A sixpenny edition would be the salvation of
mankind.' Shaw liked Lane's businesslike approach and lack of
pretension, and Penguins provided the perfect answer to his yearning
to see his work in cheap editions. 'If a book is any good, the cheaper
the better,' he told *Penguins Progress*, the magazine which kept
Penguin readers informed about forthcoming books and their
authors. 'I should have all my books priced at sixpence or less if
there had been bookshops enough in these islands to make such a
price remunerative.' He welcomed 'the great enterprise with open
arms. Thanks to them I am becoming almost a known author now
that I am between eighty and ninety.'

The Penguin list had always included non-fiction, but Shaw's
book was to form the opening title of a new list. Shortly after he
had acquired the rights, Lane was standing by the bookstall at King's
Cross station when he overheard a woman asking for 'one of those
Pelican books'. Presumably she meant a Penguin, but with Toucan

Books and Bluebird Books already caged in the paperback aviary, Lane worried that a rival might snap up pelicans as well. Back in the office, he rang his solicitors, Rubinstein, Nash, and was told that he could only claim exclusivity in the name by using it. 'You can't protect the word, it's an existing object,' Harold Rubinstein told his client. 'Publish quick, if you're going to, and we can get them ['them' being any rival firm anxious to use the name] for passing off.' Pelican Books were inaugurated forthwith, appearing in the familiar Penguin horizontal livery but with pale blue replacing the fictional orange, and a line drawing of a pelican standing in for Edward Young's penguin. H. G. Wells's *A Short History of the World*, already available in Penguin, was immediately transferred to the new list. Both Wells and Shaw were to prove keen supporters of Pelican Books, and their combination of accessibility, clear and forceful prose, and leftwards-leaning politics, far closer in spirit to the pragmatists of the Fabian Society than to the ideologues of the far Left, was to infuse and inform the Pelican list. Bearing in mind their age and eminence, Lane was in awe of both men. He took tea but no liberties with Shaw, who deluged him with his comical postcards; he approached Wells with 'some misgivings', knowing of his reputation as an author who switched publishers as carelessly as he changed his shirts, but found him entirely benign – 'perhaps because we both had the same birthday' – and Wells, for his part, recommended books and authors, and later described Lane as 'one of the greatest educationalists alive'.

In a letter to Cecil Franklin of Routledge, dictated in August 1936 and typed on old Bodley Head notepaper, Lane said that he was starting a new series called Pelicans, 'which are to be similar to Penguins only a little more serious in tone'. He was on the hunt for new titles, and was determined that his new list should 'become the true everyman's library of the twentieth century, covering a whole range of the Arts and Sciences, and bringing the finest products of modern thought and art to the people': but who, apart from Lane himself, thought up the idea of Pelican Books was the subject of rival claims. 'Bookish Krishna Menon's dark eyes were wide open for new developments in the publishing world, and he took due notice of the Penguins' progress. Also he had an idea, which he hastened to bring to the attention of the enterprising Lanes. The idea was even more enterprising: to move heavily into the non-fiction field, and to publish not only reprints, but also original works by big names,' wrote a supporter of one of the two contenders; W. E. Williams, in the opposite corner, claimed that 'When I first met Allen I suggested that Penguins might join the current crusade by starting a parallel series of cheap books on a wide range of intellectual interests – philosophy, psychology, history, literature, science. He responded immediately and enthusiastically, and I went off to put the idea on paper . . .' Writing to Williams during the war, Lane referred to how 'when you and I first discussed the Pelican idea my eyes were immediately opened to an exciting new possibility', and how 'it all began in that quiet little back-room of yours in 29, Tavistock Square', but it seems most probable that Lane himself had the idea, and used both men to put it into effect. Like all good publishers, he was nimble at exploiting the gifts of others, and in particular of those better educated and more literate than himself; and they were happy to claim credit for themselves, and to patronize him as a shrewd but ignorant businessman, ill-at-ease in the world of writers and thinkers. Since Krishna Menon was described as the 'General Editor' of the series on the title page of the first thirty Pelicans, it makes sense to start with him.

In later life, Krishna Menon became the Defence Minister and Foreign Minister in the governments of his close friend Pandit Nehru, but when Lane got to know him he was a penniless agitator and pamphleteer living off tea, potatoes and twopenny buns in a garret near St Pancras. A lean, ascetic figure with blazing black eyes, a hawk nose and a mane of long grey hair, he had been born in Kerala in 1896. His father, descended from a long line of rajahs, was a well-heeled lawyer and landlord, and the youthful Krishna grew up in luxury. After taking two degrees at Madras University, and dabbling in Madame Blavatsky's theosophism, he moved to London in 1924. He taught for a time at a school in Hertfordshire, and set about adding to his collection of degrees: these included a BSc at the London School of Economics, taken at night classes, an MA in psychology at University College London, and an MSc on eighteenth-century English political thought. He was also called to the Bar at the Middle Temple; a natural inclination to side with the underdog had been inflamed by Harold Laski at the LSE, and as a lawyer he specialized in defending indigent Indians. A passionate politician, he devoted every minute of the day to the causes of Socialism and Indian independence. Though spurned as a parliamentary candidate for Dundee, he was, from 1924, a member of the Labour Party; he was also, at various times, a member of the Independent Labour Party and the Socialist League. A keen committee man, he was Vice-Chairman of the St Pancras Borough Labour Party (Barbara Castle was a fellow-committee member), Chairman of the St Pancras Tenants' Defence League, a member of the Haldane Club of socialist lawyers and the National Council for Civil Liberties, and served on the Central Committee of the China Campaign and the Spain-India Committee. He was a familiar figure among the soap-box orators of Hyde Park Corner, as well as producing a constant flow of articles and pamphlets; he was the European representative of the Indian Socialist Party, the international representative of the Indian National Congress, and the Secretary of the India League. He found little time for sleep, allegedly averaging two hours a night, was said to consume between 100 and 150 cups of tea a day, and would often work at the League's offices till four in the morning, typing and draining his endless cups of tea. He was a vegetarian, unmarried, teetotal and a non-smoker; his only known vanity consisted of a large collection of well-made suits, a passion he shared with Allen Lane; his eyes would glaze over in mid-conversation as his mind wandered away from what the other person was saying, but his brusque and arrogant manner was combined with sudden acts of kindness and generosity, and on the few occasions when money came his way he would spend it on his friends. He was a famously fast reader, and it was said that he could polish off a detective novel in forty minutes. The journalist Shiela Grant Duff, who helped him organize Nehru's visit to Britain in 1935, found him 'an impressive and rather frightening figure' who 'looked as if he had stepped out of the tomb of Tutankhamun, saturnine, emaciated and limping heavily on a tall walking stick'.

Menon's political enthusiasms and his rapidity as a reader had already been exploited by publishers eager to tap the market for books on current affairs. He had edited a series of Topical Books for Selwyn & Blunt, one of the many imprints under the wing of the demented Walter Hutchinson, where Robert Lusty remembered him as a 'wild-eyed, emaciated, limping Indian'. On being told that his half-starved editor was on the verge of death, Lusty hurried round to a garret off Gray's Inn Road and found Menon lying on what looked like a bed of nails. 'I am dying, Lusty, and I want to see you and say goodbye,' Menon told him, holding out an emaciated hand, and Lusty, in return, 'muttered some embarrassed good wishes for the journey'. Such narrow escapes had not prevented Menon from editing the Twentieth Century Library for Ronald Boswell at The Bodley Head, where he and Lane first met.

It was through Menon that Lane was introduced to the other claimant to the Pelican throne, W. E. Williams; and whereas the austere and abstemious Menon was never a kindred spirit, and soon fell out of favour with Lane, the convivial and bibulous Williams was a very different matter. Born in 1896, and very much a Welshman in looks and accent – both his parents were Welsh-speakers – he grew up in Manchester, and won a classics scholarship to Manchester University. While a student there he met his wife, Gertrude Rosenblum, who later taught at Bedford College in the University of London and wrote, for Pelican, *The Economics of Everyday Life*. Williams then trained as a Congregationalist minister, but abandoned his studies after losing his faith and moved into education instead: he brought to adult education in particular the same 'evangelistic fervour' that might have marked him out as a clergyman, claiming that he 'defected to education because in that field I could find scope for my deep social concerns and idealistic beliefs'. They moved to London, where he taught at Leytonstone High School for Boys before being appointed a staff tutor in English Literature at London University's Extra-Mural Board. His commitment to adult education led on to a long and close association with the Workers' Educational Association.

Leftwards-leaning in a pragmatic, non-Marxist, very English way, the WEA was a fine embodiment of the earnest, nonconformist, self-improving tradition that had inspired J. M. Dent to found Everyman's Library. During the Twenties and Thirties some 60,000 men and women, many of them future trades union or Labour Party leaders, took its courses: a survey in 1938 revealed that fifteen of the current batch of Labour MPs had studied with the WEA. In due course Williams was appointed to its National Executive, joining such luminaries as R. H. Tawney, Richard Crossman, Archbishop Temple and A. D. Lindsay, the high-minded Master of Balliol; this gave him an entrée into an intellectual and academic milieu, closely associated with the Fabians and the LSE, that would prove highly compatible with the aims of Pelican Books: as he once put it, 'the emergence of Penguin seemed a heaven-sent opportunity for making it an ally and collaborator in the mission in which I was deeply involved'. He edited and greatly improved the WEA's hitherto rather dour publications, including *The Highway*, *The Travel Log* and *Adult Education*, persuading well-known writers and academics to contribute to them. In 1934 he became the Secretary to the British Institute of Adult Education, with an office in Tavistock Square, and when he became involved with Penguin, he and Lane would hold editorial meetings there. Despite a stammer, he became a frequent broadcaster, and wrote a regular column in the *Listener*. In 1935 he broadened his passion for bringing culture to the masses with his 'Art for the People' scheme, whereby modern paintings were borrowed from rich collectors and sent on tour, with lecturers like John Rothenstein and Eric Newton (author of the Pelican *European Painting and Sculpture*) on hand to explain what they were all about. Two years later he fell in love with a beautiful young Danish journalist named Estrid Bannister; although he remained married to Gertrude until his death in 1977, he and Estrid shared a basement flat in Swiss Cottage, and she advised Penguin and other publishers about Scandinavian writers as well as promoting Danish glassware and furniture. She was promiscuous as well as beautiful, and an affair with a journalist caused Bill Williams particular anguish. 'But Estrid, darling, not the *News Chronicle*,' he begged her, while

at the same time giving vent to his loathing for popular culture. 'Be
raped by *The Times* if you must, but not by a vulgar democratic
organ. Tell the bastard that if he makes a pass at you, I'll choke him
with his own infamous paper and stuff it by the yard down his lewd
and licentious throat.'

Bill Williams was a large, crumpled, amiable-looking character,
with wavy black hair brushed back from his forehead, humorous
hangdog eyes, a dapper line in overcoats and what Richard Hoggart
described as a 'heavy cherub's face'. He was bustling, benign, shrewd,
well-connected, a consummate operator and fixer who flourished
in the Byzantine, claustrophobic world of cultural bureaucracy; he
was also endearingly idle, a man for the broad brushstrokes who left
others to fill in the details. He wanted to write, but his contributions to the printed page amounted to little more than brief introductions to collections of essays or anthologies of poetry, and since
(or so he once told Lane) he sometimes sat up all night trying to
perfect a 300-word blurb for a new Penguin, he was hardly a fast
mover. Although he had plans to write Lane's biography, his memoir
of his old friend, perceptive and evocative as it is, amounts to no
more than ninety-three small-format pages; he suggested authors
and ideas, and was happy to open up his address book, but little
evidence remains of his editorial labours. H. L. Beales of the London
School of Economics, a man of comparable conviviality and
authorial indolence, described him as being broad-minded, tolerant,
undogmatic and humorous: he was 'not the man to wear hair shirts',
and 'if the barricades ever go up in this country, don't blame Williams
for it. His is the quality that dissolves the barricade spirit.'

Despite his long involvement with Penguin, Williams liked to
keep his distance: he was never on the staff, working, as he put it,
'in a strictly extra-mural capacity and virtually for out-of-pocket
expenses' in the belief that his independence gave him 'special terms
of confidence' with Lane. Though the buttoned-up Lane never fully
reciprocated Williams's eloquent expressions of affection and admiration, he enjoyed him as a drinking companion and appreciated his
connections in the wider world; and whereas Oxbridge dons
inflamed his sense of social and intellectual inferiority, Williams,

like Richard Hoggart in later years, was the kind of academic – lower middle-class, of provincial origin, educated at a 'red-brick' university – with whom he felt at home. Williams, for his part, was to find Lane 'an infuriating, mercurial colleague who was dearer to me than any other man in my life'. 'We are a funny pair, seldom communicating our feelings but, I think, always aware of them,' Williams told Lane in one of the many letters in which he poured forth his feelings without exciting a comparable response. 'We think for ourselves, and never try to please each other by acquiescence; but with uncanny frequency we reach the same conclusions.'

The other members of the Pelican advisory panel were to prove more transient figures. Lance Beales of the LSE reinforced the leftish flavour of the list, specializing in historians, economists and sociologists. Quick-witted and well-informed, his 'favourite posture', according to Williams, 'was a semi-horizontal one . . . He looks like the advertisement for Buoyant Easy Chairs, the embodiment of easy affability.' 'Wistfully cynical and always very relaxed, Beales struck me as a rather lazy man', was the verdict of George Weidenfeld, who employed him in an advisory capacity some ten years later; a 'Falstaffian Fabian socialist', in Weidenfeld's words, Beales drank like a fish, so much so that Williams 'sometimes imagined his inside must resemble the delta of the Nile or the Mississippi'.

Sir Peter Chalmers-Mitchell, who advised Pelican on scientific matters, was another heavy drinker: according to Dick, who knew about such things, he mixed 'the largest and most powerful dry Martinis I have ever been privileged to consume', and he was once reported as 'getting in a mess with a car and a lamppost'. Chalmers-Mitchell was in his seventies when he joined Pelican as an advisory editor in exchange for £50 a year (or, Lane promised, £100 if the series proved a success). A biologist by training, he was best known as the founder of Whipsnade Zoo, and had recently retired from a thirty-year stint as the Secretary of the London Zoo, which, according to Solly Zuckerman, he had ruled 'with a rod of iron'. He commissioned Berthold Lubetkin to design the famous Penguin Pool, which was opened in 1933 and visited two years later by Edward Young with sketchbook in hand; two of his fellow-directors, Solly

Zuckerman and Julian Huxley, would both have connections with Penguin Books, and Lane himself would, in due course, become a director of the Zoo and entertain guests to lunch in its restaurant. Despite being a keen member of the Savile Club, Chalmers-Mitchell's political sympathies were 'with the extreme Left', according to the *DNB*, albeit of the anarchist variety. After his retirement from the Zoo in 1935, he went to live in Málaga. The following February he was unexpectedly joined there by Arthur Koestler, who was covering the Civil War for the *News Chronicle* and in flight from Franco's forces, and they sat in deckchairs on his veranda swigging gin and french as the fascists tightened their grip on the town; Sir Peter was whisked away at the last minute in a British destroyer but Koestler, well-known for his left-wing views, was led away to prison and possible execution. Back in Britain, Sir Peter was invited to replace an equally eminent scientist, Lancelot Hogben, on the advisory panel of Pelican Books. He offered his views on all kinds of books, including *The Oregon Trail*: he severed his connection with the firm in 1939, but not before he had effected fruitful introductions to fellow-scientists like J. B. S. Haldane, whom Lane first encountered at a 'leftish party' in Park Lane.

The first Pelican list included, in addition to the works by Shaw and Wells, Julian Huxley's *Essays in Popular Science*, Leonard Woolley's *Digging up the Past*, Olaf Stapledon's *Last and First Men* and G. D. H. Cole's *Practical Economics*; although the others were all reissues of books bought from hardback publishers, the G. D. H. Cole marked a new departure as a venture into original publishing, and was the first book to be commissioned by Penguin. In December Lane sent Krishna Menon a list of new titles approved by the Editorial Committee, including R. H. Tawney's *Religion and the Rise of Capitalism*, Halévy's *History of the English People*, James Jeans's *The Mysterious Universe*, Freud's *Psychopathology of Everyday Life*, Clive Bell's *Civilization* and Woolley's *Ur of the Chaldees*; but relations between the two men were rapidly deteriorating. Both complained of poor communications, with Lane grumbling that he had heard nothing for months from Menon about which titles he proposed to take on, and Menon complaining that Lane had not been in touch about the contractual negotiations for these books: but the truth of the matter was that Lane, mercurial and easily bored, found the austere and unconvivial Menon a far from kindred spirit, and was happy to freeze him out. Menon lectured him for an hour in a Soho restaurant in a low monotone, and Lane, who could neither hear nor understand what he was trying to say, finally lost patience and called him a 'bottleneck', at which Menon stormed out in a rage; Menon, ill, under-nourished and overworked, felt bruised and isolated. He complained that Lane never returned his calls or kept him informed, and seemed to inhabit 'a world which paralyses all action and makes decent people feel they don't fit in with things'. 'I shall be most grateful if you will make an appointment for me to see you,' he told Lane in November 1938. 'I have made several efforts to get in touch with you and I have also written, but I have never been able to get any reply.' Menon's solicitors and Rubinstein, Nash began an exchange of letters, and eventually, after Lane had left on a tour of India and the Middle East, Dick wrote to terminate Menon's agreement with the firm. 'Last time when we met you promised to put in order before you left for the East arrangements with regard to the Pelican Books,' Menon wrote to his departed boss. 'Your letter takes me by surprise. Each time we meet you make a promise which you fail to keep . . .' Menon was paid off with a cheque for £125; his solicitor made off with the money, and Menon refused to press charges on the grounds that he had a wife and child, and needed the money far more than he did. Freud's *Totem and Taboo* was the last Pelican to bear his name. It was a sad end to the story; but although it was sometimes claimed that Krishna Menon's political hostility to the West was directly attributable to his treatment by Lane, his entries in *Who's Who* always mentioned the fact that he had been the first editor of Pelican Books. Lane, it seems, was less forgiving: years later, Tony Godwin noticed how, at the mere mention of Menon's name, Lane's 'voice seethed with venom. It gave me goose pimples merely to hear such animosity.' 'The reason for our split with Menon was that we found him so dilatory and so incapable of making up his mind,' Lane himself recalled. 'It was a unanimous decision that we could not continue with him.'

Writing in *Left Review* in May 1938, Lane declared that more and more people were demanding 'access to contemporary thought and to a reasonable body of scientific knowledge', that 'we are now in a position to control our future in the light of our knowledge of the past', and that 'we have within our grasp the elements of true civilization, the ending of a pre-historic age'. His sixpennies provided 'access to some of that knowledge on which a reasonable life must be based . . . There are many who despair at what they regard as the low level of the people's intelligence. We, however, believed in the existence in this country of a vast reading public for *intelligent* books at a low price, and staked everything on it' – and in doing so Penguin had 'provided a complete answer to those who despair of the state of England'. These were noble words, and no doubt Bill Williams would have claimed their authorship, but Lane was not alone in his views. The *Spectator* described Pelicans as 'a fact of enormous importance in the struggle to overcome economic restrictions to knowledge'. The series was proving 'a decisive influence on the growth of popular understanding of the world', and 'if there is any sense in saying that the culture of the world should be accessible to all without distinctions of wealth, such publications are helping to make it true'. Lane could not have asked for a finer tribute.

7. Red Alert

Bill Williams was not the only key figure to join Penguin at this time, but whereas he remained deliberately detached, devoting less than half his time and energy to the firm, Eunice Frost could hardly have been more different. Like her slightly older contemporary, the even more formidable Norah Smallwood of Chatto & Windus, Eunice Frost was one of the first women to rise to the top (or near the top) of what had always been an exclusively male preserve: this in itself was enough to make her both pushy and prickly, and the fact that both women had started at the bottom of their respective firms, as secretaries, and neither had been to university or received that much in the way of 'higher education', made them still more sensitive to slights, and more aware than necessary of their own intellectual and literary shortcomings. Both were feared and sometimes detested by those who worked for them in junior capacities – one embattled secretary summed up Eunice as 'plain horrible' – and both were addicted to large and eye-catching hats; but whereas Mrs Smallwood managed, through force of personality, to cling on to power at Chatto until well into her seventies, Eunice Frost was only in her early forties when – neurotic, bronchitic and increasingly out of touch with changes in the publishing and literary worlds – she was edged out of Penguin to spend the rest of her life in exile in Lewes, grumbling about the sad falling-off of the firm, bombarding former colleagues with letters and interminable phone calls, and nursing that sense of grievance that is all too liable to afflict those who have entrusted their all to a firm or institution. Though she never lost her sense of humour or her contagious laughter, she was, by the end of her life, a melancholy and pathetic figure: but for twenty years she did more for Penguin, in terms of sheer effort and hard work, than anyone except its founder; and although, to her intense irritation, it was always assumed that she

concerned herself exclusively with the fiction list – an honourable
enough activity, but essentially second-hand in that it involved buying
the rights in books already published by other firms – she busied
herself, as a tireless editor, with every kind of book published by
the firm, from Pelican philosophers and Penguin Modern Painters
to King Penguins and John Lehmann's *Penguin New Writing*.

After her death in 1998, the papers of this very private woman –
including tax returns for 1939, unopened copies of the *Bookseller*,
still in their brown paper tubes, the proceedings of the Lewes
Horticultural Society for 1961, and every letter and Christmas card
she had received over forty years – were acquired by Bristol University
Library; and from comments scribbled on the backs of envelopes
and scraps of paper it is possible to discover something of who she
was and where she came from. She was born in the Midlands in
1915, 'the fourth, last and unwanted child of parents who should
never have had children at all'. She loathed her father, and longed
to learn that he had been killed when he went away to fight in the
First World War: he was, she wrote, 'a proud, weak and intolerant
man', given to terrible rages, and 'there was never anything but hate
between us, and on my side a great fear and, later, a contempt'. She
grew up in Burton-on-Trent, was educated at a convent school, and
sent out to make her way in the world. 'Never really had any self-
confidence,' she noted. 'Have simply made my way. My pride has
been a method of keeping going.' As 'a fighter, but not for myself',
she would always be worried about money: with reason, since her
salary at Penguin would always be pitifully low. At the age of eighteen
she went to work as a secretary-cum-receptionist in a 'well-known
country hotel', and she came to London to work as a secretary at
the Milk Marketing Board. From an early age she had literary and
artistic ambitions: in later life she took up painting, storing her work
in fridges dotted about the house, but in her twenties she wrote
stories, articles ('Nature Decorations for Your Home') and poems.
Several of her poems – 'Song for Lost Love', 'The Toad', 'Some
Have Yet Writ with Sorrow' – were published in a literary magazine called *The Decachord*, other contributors to which included Ernest
Raymond, T. Sturge Moore and Eden Phillpotts. 'They strike me as

being fresh and full of the spirit of the countryside,' a publisher told her in a kindly rejection letter. 'What a pity that poetry is not a commercial proposition.'

She was working as a secretary at the Chelsea Arts Club – helping, among other things, to organize the Coronation Costume Ball in 1937 – when she learned, through a small ad, that Allen Lane was looking for a new secretary. Always stylishly turned out despite the shortage of funds, and the owner of a vast collection of shoes, she turned up for her interview in Great Portland Street in an enormous black cartwheel hat. Lane was in his shirt-sleeves, half-hidden behind the publisher's familiar detritus of typescripts, proofs, letters, estimates, review cuttings and seasonal catalogues. He had a soft spot for good-looking women: Eunice could hardly be described as a beauty – she had a long horse face framed by shoulder-length hair, and her expression was usually on the morose or lugubrious side – but he must have taken to her at once. 'In my first week, instead of being told what to do, I was expected to do the extraordinary,' she recalled in a brief memoir entitled 'How I Became a Literary Midwife'. 'Allen said, "How do you like reading?" and pushed a whole pile of books across his desk. And that's how I learned that you had to take the baby home with you every night.' Elsewhere she noted how 'at the quixotic instigation of Allen Lane I was almost immediately catapulted from secretarial to editorial functions', becoming as a result 'the first in-house Penguin editor'. She found her new employer like 'an extraordinary spinning-wheel, though even that may give too simple an idea of his complexities'. He was, as she soon discovered, 'powerfully possessive, and found difficulty in sharing his kingdom. He lived his work, and you ignored this at your peril.' She quickly became devoted to Lane and, offices being the way they are, it was assumed, probably incorrectly, that they must have had an affair. 'Deep as her devotion to you is, she is inclined to get jumpy and hysterical when she is too close to you,' Williams once told Lane, but whatever her feelings about Lane she seems to have been a neurotic and highly-strung woman who sought refuge in her work, was given to peals of nervous laughter and announced her presence with a warning cough. Although he exploited her ruthlessly in terms of both her workload and her pay, Lane valued her very highly; and whereas he was, to varying degrees, critical of all his colleagues, however close, he never ran her down behind her back but worried constantly about her neuroses and her poor health. 'You don't need me to have to tell you again that if one had to pick on the two people most responsible for the creation of the firm it would be us,' he told her not long before she vanished into her forty-year exile in Lewes. Lane's secretary, Jean Osborne, thought her 'the ultimate in sophistication and savoir-faire', but for most of the staff 'Frostie' was a daunting and alarming presence: according to the typographer and book designer Ruari McLean, who worked for the firm before and after the war, 'while Allen was always charming and pliant, and did not always mean what he said, Eunice was the tough one you had to listen to'. (Tough or not, she took a shine to McLean, and even suggested that they should get married; but by then the war had broken out, he had enlisted as a submariner, and he held her at bay with a cry of 'Not now – perhaps later!')

No sooner had Frostie installed herself in Great Portland Street than the firm was on the move. A council official inspected the crypt after the firm had applied for permission to install a lavatory, and was shocked by what he saw. 'We were breaking every known by-law,' Lane remembered, and 'as he left he said, "If anyone says this place exists I will have to deny it. I just haven't seen it. If anyone says I have, I will say they're a liar." That's when we decided we'd better find real premises.' Rather than remain in central London, the brothers decided to investigate the outer suburbs, where property and rates were cheaper; and since the Lanes still spent most week-ends with their parents in Gloucestershire, it made sense to head in a westerly direction. Dick was deputed to visit estate agents and possible sites in his Morris Cowley, and eventually he plumped for a field of cabbages near the village of Harmondsworth in Middlesex, immediately opposite the future Heathrow airport. The Great West Road, famed for its roadhouses, ran past the cabbage field, epitomizing the new England of arterial roads and industrial estates celebrated by Priestley in his *English Journey*; Croydon airport had yet to be supplanted by Heathrow, and the surrounding country-side was flat, undistinguished and faintly scruffy, a not unpleasant world of pollarded willows, fields full of ponies, market gardens and red-brick walls. Morpurgo suggests that the decision to house Penguin in what was still – just – open country reflected Lane's rural nostalgia, and that he had been influenced by visits to Port Sunlight, Bournville and the *Reader's Digest* headquarters at Pleasantville in upstate New York; be that as it may, he bought the three-and-a-half-acre site for £2,112, though negotiations nearly broke down when the farmer insisted on being paid an additional £200 for his crop of cabbages. Dick (or so it was said) was told to sell off the cabbages, or give them to members of staff; an architect was commissioned to design a building that would combine publishing offices and warehouse; old Mr Williams Lane laid the foundation stone in August 1937, and three months later Harmondsworth was in business. Some members of staff moved out from London and settled in Harmondsworth or West Drayton, and Lane helped them with a loan of £25 each to cover the move; others stayed put, and commuted against the flow. Edward Young, by now sharing a flat with Ruari McLean in Hammersmith, took the Greenline bus, and reported a 'tremendous hoo-ha' when he asked that his salary should be raised to £10 a week to cover the extra costs of travel.

Some years later, in one of the firm's celebratory publications, a smug and anonymous Penguin – Bill Williams, no doubt – wrote of Harmondsworth that 'plain men, in cars, passing it, say to each other, "That's where the Penguin Books come from," and know that they have thereby established their status in the cultural life of our time'. Although Lane sporadically opened London offices, in Portman Street and later in Holborn, he was proud to publish in a place far removed from Bloomsbury or Covent Garden, but editorial decisions were made, more often than not, in Bill Williams's office in Tavistock Square or, more congenially, in the Barcelona, a Spanish restaurant in Beak Street in Soho. Run, according to Williams, by a 'genial gastronome called Carbonnel', it was well regarded by A. J. A. Symons in his capacity as restaurant critic of

Night and Day, London's short-lived equivalent of the *New Yorker*:★ though a modest establishment – its other patrons included George Orwell and assorted refugees from the Spanish Civil War – it had an 'excellent chef', a monopoly on Alicante and Jijona *turrones*, laid in by Señor Carbonnel before the outbreak of the Civil War, and a good line in 'inexpensive Habana panatellas'. Better still, for Williams and the Lanes at least, was a fathomless supply of wine from the owner's family vineyards. Allen, Dick, Williams and Frostie formed the nucleus of the Barcelona lunchers, meeting there once a week to sift through and debate the books or proposals on offer to the firm; the typescripts were piled on the floor beside the table, and brought out one by one for dissection and discussion. Their deliberations were lubricated with innumerable glasses of wine, and favoured candidates were placed at the bottom of the pile on the understanding that the greater the number of bottles drunk, the better the chances of a positive decision. In later years, when Penguin had become larger, more institutionalized and part of the publishing establishment, Lane and Bill Williams and Frostie would look back at those happy days in the Barcelona with the fondness reserved for a paradise lost; nor was it simply a matter of their invariably drinking, as Lance Beales put it, 'far more sherries than was good for us'. It was, Frostie recalled over fifty years later, 'a time of very high idealism', and together they seemed to 'inhabit a time of innocent awareness, dedication towards ideals, and a constant determination in pursuit of the best that each could give or do'.

Their idealism was political as well as literary and educational. The Thirties was a period in which dictatorships and rival ideologies

★Published by Chatto & Windus between July and December 1937, and very obviously based on the *New Yorker*, *Night and Day* was as stylish and evocative of its period as Penguin Books or Brian Cook's brilliant, poster-like jackets for Batsford's topographical books. Graham Greene was its literary editor, its contributors included Evelyn Waugh, John Betjeman, Nicolas Bentley, Cyril Connolly, Elizabeth Bowen and Robert Byron, and among its directors was Lane's friend Raymond Hazell. It was famously closed down after Shirley Temple, incensed by unkind remarks from Graham Greene, threatened a libel suit; it had been steadily losing money, and she provided the *coup de grâce*.

provoked a corresponding idealism, particularly on the Left, and the radicalization of a youthful middle class racked with guilt, and anxiety about unemployment, the rise of fascism and the persistent threat of war, were reflected in their reading habits. The Labour Party had been divided and demoralized by Ramsay MacDonald's decision to head the National government in 1931, with the result that many of its supporters defected to other left-wing parties, including the Communists, while the mass unemployment and the hunger marches of the early Thirties had moved Lane and others like him to declare themselves socialists. But as the economy began to recover, the fears and aspirations of the intelligentsia were increasingly focused on foreign affairs: the Nazis came to power in Germany, Mussolini invaded Abyssinia, Hitler reoccupied the Rhineland, the Japanese annexed Manchuria and the Spanish Civil War broke out. Pacifism, disarmament, collective security and the League of Nations were proclaimed as universal panaceas by the idealistic Left; the USSR, with its five-year plans and beaming peasant girls gathering in the harvest, was hailed as a new civilization by Shaw and the Webbs despite the show trials and strong reservations on the part of Malcolm Muggeridge and George Orwell, who had witnessed first-hand the ruthlessness employed by the Communists against Trotskyites and Anarchists in Republican Spain. Memoirs of the First World War and the horrors of the trenches – Remarque's *All Quiet on the Western Front*, Sassoon's *Memoirs of an Infantry Officer*, Graves's *Goodbye to All That*, Blunden's *Undertones of War* – were read in their thousands, confirming a determination that such wars should never be fought again; there was much talk about the iniquities of armaments manufacturers and the devastation that could be unleashed on our cities from the air. Despite some dissenters, T. S. Eliot, Wyndham Lewis, Evelyn Waugh and Roy Campbell among them, writers, academics and the intellectual classes, and not least the scientists, tended to be on the Left; some, like Stephen Spender and C. Day Lewis, were – briefly, and uncomfortably – members of the Communist Party. The outbreak of the Spanish Civil War provided a unique opportunity to match idealism with activity: some, like Orwell and John Cornford, went to fight for the Republicans; some, like Koestler and Claud

Cockburn, went out as war correspondents; some, like Auden and T. C. Worsley, served as ambulance men. In the early Thirties Hitler had benefited from the widespread notion, articulated above all in Keynes's *The Economic Consequences of the Peace*, that Germany had been hard done by at the Treaty of Versailles, in terms of both territory lost and economic reparations, but once his territorial ambitions in Europe became more evident, along with his treatment of the Jews, the Left's earlier devotion to pacifism and disarmament dropped away, and appeasers and the 'men of Munich' replaced cosmopolitan arms dealers as the villains of the hour.

Although the *Daily Mail* and its readers – characterized by the literati as golf-loving, pipe-smoking suburbanites devoted to dogs, crossword puzzles, organized games and detective stories – remained impervious to the intellectual currents of the age, the media in general registered a perceptible shift to the Left that was to become still more explicit during the war, and make itself manifest in the election of a Labour government in 1945 and the establishment of the Welfare State. Nowhere was the swing to the Left more apparent than in the transformation of the *Daily Mirror*. Then as now, newspaper proprietors were regarded with deep suspicion, exerting undue power behind the scenes and dictating policy to their editors. Lord Rothermere, with his soft spot for Hitler, was a particular bogeyman, but in 1933 he made amends of a kind by selling the *Daily Mirror*. Under Cecil King, Hugh Cudlipp and its legendary editor Harry Guy Bartholomew, it was transmogrified into a campaigning paper of the Left, with its most famous columnist, Bill Connor, alias 'Cassandra', relishing his role as the scourge of the established order. Nor was the *Mirror* a solitary voice. Gerald Barry became editor of the liberal-minded *News Chronicle* in 1936; the *Manchester Guardian* already had impeccable liberal credentials; Geoffrey Dawson of *The Times* supported Chamberlain at Munich and was close to the Cliveden Set, but the appointment as a leader-writer of E. H. Carr, the left-wing Cambridge don and expert on Soviet Russia, and the presence behind the scenes of the Jesuitical, black-clad figure of Stanley Morison, who combined left-wing views with a devotion to the Catholic Church, suggested that changes were on the way. David Low, the scourge of Hitler and Colonel Blimp, had moved to the *Evening Standard* in 1934; Ritchie Calder was writing for the *Daily Herald* and Vernon Bartlett for the *News Chronicle*; Kingsley Martin's *New Statesman* was more highly regarded and more influential than its right-wing rival, the *Spectator*, while *The Week* – edited by the mischievous Claud Cockburn, who also wrote for the *Daily Worker* under the pseudonym of Frank Pitcairn – could be relied on to expose skulduggery in high places.

In 1938 the Hungarian émigré Stefan Lorant and Tom Hopkinson founded the legendary magazine *Picture Post*, a kindred spirit to Penguin Books until its demise in the early 1950s. Despite the huge success of Lorant's pocket-sized *Lilliput*, launched the previous year and priced at sixpence, W. H. Smith, cautious as ever, placed an initial order of only 70,000 copies of *Picture Post*: Lorant printed 750,000, and within four months the magazine was selling 1,350,000 a week. With its modern layout, bold use of photography and hard-hitting approach to domestic and foreign politics, *Picture Post* not only reflected the influence of documentary film-makers like John Grierson, whose GPO Film Unit was set up in 1933, but literary fashion as well. Throughout the Thirties writers sought to record the lives of the hitherto inarticulate, both at home and abroad: though embarrassed by Orwell's claim that the working classes smelt – so embarrassed that he insisted on writing a foreword in which he apologized for, and distanced himself from, his author's tactless observations – Victor Gollancz published *The Road to Wigan Pier*, and working-class memoirs and exotic reportage were snapped up by publishers. *Fact*, a magazine devoted to documenting working-class life, included in its editorial team Storm Jameson, Stephen Spender and Arthur Calder-Marshall, providing prose equivalents of Humphrey Spender's bleakly evocative photographs of slums in the North of England; and the anthropologist Tom Harrisson and the poet Charles Madge founded Mass Observation, a body devoted to interviewing, through teams of volunteers, the man and the woman in the street, collating their findings, and using the results to influence politicians and opinion-makers in a leftwards direction.

Nor were publishers immune to the prevailing political climate.

Victor Gollancz was firmly established as the leading left-wing publisher. He had decided to set up a book club devoted to left-wing writing, both polemical and documentary, after a lunch with Stafford Cripps. The Left Book Club, he told the *New Statesman*, had been formed to 'help in the terribly urgent struggle for world peace and *against* fascism, by giving all those who are willing to take part in that struggle such knowledge as will immensely increase their efficiency', and he cited the 'almost incredible circulation of books in the Soviet Union' as a 'glorious example' to be followed. The books were chosen by Gollancz, John Strachey and Harold Laski; club members were expected to buy the monthly choice for a minimum of six months, but whereas members of the public could buy the books from bookshops at 7s. 6d. or 5s., members paid a mere 2s. 6d. for their choices, each of which came in the celebrated orange limp binding. Advertisements for the Club made their first appearance in the spring of 1936; Gollancz had estimated that, for it to be commercially viable, he needed 2,500 members, but by May some 9,000 had enrolled, reaching 40,000 by the end of that year and 57,000 by 1939. Gollancz liked to boast that his chauffeur had been particularly effective as an enroller of new members, but elsewhere 5,000 or so volunteers helped to spread the word. Lectures, discussion groups and social evenings were held up and down the country, as were weekend and summer schools; trips to Russia were organized by the Club, along with Russian lessons; the first national rally of the LBC was held in the Albert Hall in February 1937, followed a year later by anti-appeasement rallies; working-class readers who found some of the choices fairly heavy going were offered 'B' membership, and were free to take alternative choices. Though never a Communist himself, unlike John Strachey, VG keenly supported their policy, dictated from Moscow, of a Popular Front in which all left-wing parties would be united against fascism; he fought hard not to alienate or offend the Party, and did battle with those, like Leonard Woolf in *Barbarians at the Gates*, who were critical of Stalin. 'I should explain that I am a rather peculiar kind of publisher in that, on topics which I believe to be of vital importance, I am anxious to publish nothing with which I am myself not in agreement,' he once declared. He declined to publish *Homage to Catalonia*, with its bitter denunciations of Communist practices in Spain, but although Orwell soon placed his book with Fredric Warburg, then making his name as the publisher of non-Communist left-wing writers, he sold a mere 1,500 copies through Secker & Warburg, whereas the LBC edition alone of *The Road to Wigan Pier* had chalked up sales of 42,000. Orwell went on to dismiss most of the Club's output as 'slick books of reportage, dishonest pamphlets in which propaganda is swallowed whole and then spewed up again, half-digested', and in this he was not alone: the Labour Party, according to A. J. P. Taylor, disliked the LBC on the grounds that it 'was diverting high-minded schoolteachers into reading Communist tracts when they ought to have been joining the Labour Party or working for it', and stalwarts like Herbert Morrison, Ernest Bevin and Hugh Dalton denounced it as a Communist front, a 'dangerous type of vermin' and an apologist for the Soviet Union. An attempt to set up a rival Social Democratic book club, with titles chosen by Tawney, Dalton and G. D. H. Cole, collapsed: a Low cartoon devoted to the Battle of the Book Clubs – Douglas Jerrold's Right Book Club had now joined the fray – carried the caption 'A fierce battle is now taking place on the reading front, the Blimp Book Club advancing strongly against the Left. Heavy casualties are reported including twenty-nine unconscious and General Gollancz's spectacles blown off.'

Taylor may have dismissed the LBC as a harmless safety valve whereby members 'worked off their rebelliousness by plodding through yet another orange-coloured volume', but although Lane shared none of Gollancz's fervid political convictions or aspirations, or his yearning to make his mark as a public figure, he must, however grudgingly, have been impressed by the LBC as a display of stylish and opportunistic publishing which made a good deal of money as well; and he, too, was eager to alert the public to what was going on in the world about them, while at the same time profiting from the chance to do so. But whereas Gollancz wanted the Left Book Club to 'provide the indispensable basis of *knowledge* without which a really effective United Front of all men and women of good faith cannot be built', Lane was less dogmatic about the uses to which that knowledge might be put. 'People want a solid background to give some coherence to the newspapers' scintillating confusion of day-to-day events,' he told the *Penrose Annual*; later he recalled how 'It was pretty obvious to many of us that we were drifting rapidly into a dangerous situation internationally, and some of us felt that the general public was perhaps not as well informed as to the shape of things to come as they might be.'

Inherent in the philosophy of Penguin Specials was the notion, spelled out in Wickham Steed's Special on *The Press*, that the news as presented in newspapers was shaped and coloured by the interests of proprietors, advertisers and big business: the Specials could not only go into far greater detail and background, but – as G. T. Garratt, author of *Mussolini's Roman Empire*, told the *Bookseller* – could reveal the 'news behind the news'. The Penguin Specials were, on the whole, shorter and more accessible than the LBC choices, and whereas Gollancz's books were sold in large numbers to the converted, Lane's reached a far wider and less ideologically committed market. Both series were aimed, above all, at the young, radicalized middle classes, and Specials were often on sale at Book Club meetings. Edward Young, responsible for designing the red and black typographical jackets of the Specials, each different from the other, not only found the job a pleasant change from the standard Penguin and Pelican jackets, but happily admitted his debt to Stanley Morison's forceful lettering on Gollancz's titles.

The first Penguin Special, published in November 1937, was an expanded reissue of *Germany Puts the Clock Back* by the American journalist Edgar Mowrer, first published by Ronald Boswell at The Bodley Head in 1932; over-optimistically, Mowrer dedicated Lane's signed copy 'To Allen Lane, who helped to prevent what should have been prevented'. Shortly after it was published, Lane had lunch with Gerald Barry of the *News Chronicle*, who urged him to get in touch with the French journalist Geneviève Tabouis about her book *Blackmail or War*, in which she warned of the drift to war and berated the British and the French for their failure to stand up to Hitler. Although, to Dick's distress, Madame Tabouis turned out to be a teetotal vegetarian, Lane flew to Paris for lunch with his new author; her book was translated and published within two weeks of its delivery to Penguin, and over 200,000 copies were sold, so setting a pattern whereby Specials were printed and published at speed, and often went on to sell a quarter of a million copies or more. 'Cassandra' wrote about her at length in the *Mirror*; other reviewers included 'Frank Pitcairn' in the *Daily Worker*, and a curious character called A. S. B. Glover, later to loom large in the Penguin story.

Later that year, at the time of the Munich crisis, Shiela Grant Duff's *Europe and the Czechs* was published at still greater speed, appearing in the shops within a week of the typescript being delivered by the author. Edward Young worked on the typescript with her in trains, buses, and a dentist's waiting-room, and remembered her as 'a tremendous fire-eater'; she told him he ought to be doing his bit in Czechoslovakia, and he 'felt awfully wet just being here publishing books'. As publication neared, the residents of Harmondsworth saw lights in the Penguin warehouse on a Sunday evening: suspecting burglars, they summoned the police, who rushed to the scene of the crime, only to find staff packing 50,000 copies for delivery first thing on Monday morning. Its author returned from Prague to be greeted with posters in Victoria Station announcing the Munich Agreement: her book had been overtaken by events, but 'with bitter irony it became a bestseller now that the cause it championed was lost'.

'Are these Penguin Specials any good?' Bernard Shaw asked Lane: he had written 'a lot of stuff knocking adult suffrage into a cocked hat', and was torn between publishing 'a Constable book which no one will buy at Constable prices, and a Penguin book'. His book never materialized, though Dick was soon involved in a long and whimsical correspondence about the apparent impossibility of keeping both volumes of *The Intelligent Woman's Guide* in print at once, given the maddening tendency of Volume I to sell more briskly than Volume II. Shaw or no Shaw, the list of Specials steadily expanded. Norman Angell advocated an armed League of Nations in *The Great Illusion*; Stefan Lorant drew on his own experiences of Nazi Germany in *I Was Hitler's Prisoner*, and published an extract in

Picture Post; Louis Golding discussed *The Jewish Problem*; Tom
Harrisson and Charles Madge reported on *Britain by Mass Observation*;
Edgar Mowrer moved on to *Mowrer in China*; Shiela Grant Duff
resurfaced as a contributor to E. O. Lorimer's *What Hitler Wants*,
G. T. George reinforced her original warnings in *They Betrayed
Czechoslovakia*, and *The Air Defence of Britain* provoked a flurry of
leading articles and a thunderous denunciation of governmental
apathy by 'Cassandra', who insisted that 'Someone Has Got To Clean
Up The Mess We Are In . . . Or Fifty Million People Will Want
To Know The Reason Why'. But whereas Left Book Club contributors were expected to toe the line, Penguin Special authors were
free to express divergent and even heretical views. C. E. M. Joad,
the popular philosopher whose career came to ruin after he had
been discovered travelling on the Oxford to London train minus a
ticket, promoted the pacifist cause in *Why War?* The Marquess of
Londonderry, a former Air Minister who thought Hitler a 'kindly
man with a receding chin and an impressive face' and a peace-loving
character who 'dreads war', set out his views in *Ourselves and
Germany*, the cover copy of which announced that his book
'represents a point of view which is in many respects opposed to
that expressed in most of the previous Specials . . . We publish it
because it is the clearest exposition so far of the policy of rapproche-
ment with Nazi Germany and a plea for a more sympathetic understanding of Herr Hitler's point of view.' It was serialized in the
Evening Standard, and the author made sure that complimentary copies
were sent to Hitler, Goering, Ribbentrop, von Papen, and his cousin
Winston Churchill, who thoroughly disapproved of his views.

At the opposite end of the political spectrum, D. N. Pritt, a genial
Pickwickian barrister, unrepentant fellow-traveller and far-Left
Labour MP who later became a neighbour of Lane's in the Berkshire
countryside, got in touch after dictating 3,000 words on what he
regarded as the unfair anti-Soviet hysteria prompted by the signing
of the Nazi–Soviet Pact in August 1939. Lane suggested he should
convert his essay into something more substantial. Pritt (or so he
later claimed) produced the extra words within a day: anticipating
large sales of *Light on Moscow*, Lane urged him to alter the proofs

in response to the changing political situation, telling him not to worry about the costs and to 'tear it up if you like!' Lane, Pritt recalled, 'always seemed to be bubbling when I saw him': understandably, perhaps, since *Light on Moscow* sold 12,000 a week after its appearance in November 1939, and with its successor achieved sales of over 250,000. Published during the Russo-Finnish War, *Must the War Spread?* exposed an alleged conspiracy on the part of the capitalist West to make common front with the Nazis against the Soviet Union; it gave the Labour Party a longed-for opportunity to expel the pestilential Pritt, though he clung on as the MP for Hammersmith North. After being told that it was 'seditious', Lane reneged on the contract to publish Pritt's *Choose Your Future*, which went on to sell 15,000 for Lawrence & Wishart, the Communist publishers: but although Pritt referred the matter to arbitration (and won), he still referred to Lane as a 'superb publisher'. Lane was, he recalled in later years, 'an old-fashioned liberal' at heart: 'I never thought of him as a socialist: I just thought he had the generous mind which would lead a man halfway to socialism. If you are a Welshman, you are either a fool or in favour of the underdog . . .'

Thirty-five Specials were published between November 1937 and the outbreak of war, including two 'topical' novels, Jaroslav Hašek's *The Good Soldier Schweik* and Phyllis Bottome's *The Mortal Storm*. Lane actively commissioned titles, and suggested to Basil Liddell Hart, without success, that he should write a book on Blitzkrieg. Chalmers-Mitchell, abandoning his scientific brief, put him in touch with the 'Red' Duchess of Atholl for a book on the Spanish Civil War. A passionate partisan of the Republican cause, the Duchess aroused the wrath of the Catholic Press. 'Have you noticed the titles of the first three Penguin Specials?' asked the *Catholic Herald*'s reviewer of *Mussolini's Roman Empire*. 'I don't say the Penguin owners are responsible but someone must have been pushing hard to achieve this propagandist coup. I am told that the real reason why these books are left is that the publishers consider only leftish books can sell in sufficient quantity to justify the venture.' The *Tablet* thought little of the Duchess's book – 'To believe all evil of the Nationalists and to make every excuse for the Republicans may be forgivable in an ardent partisan, especially in times of war, but persons who write and feel like that should not degrade the high name of historian' – and George Orwell, drawing on his own experiences of Communist methods in Republican Spain, was equally unimpressed. The Duchess's book, he declared, was a straightforward apologia for the Communists, and had nothing new to say, but was an interesting phenomenon in itself. 'Anti-fascists in high life' – people like the Duchess, in other words – were 'simply part of the national war preparation':

The people who read the *New Statesman* dream of war with Germany, but they also think it necessary to laugh at Colonel Blimp. However, when the war begins they will be forming fours on the barrack square under Colonel Blimp's boiled blue eye. That, I think, is the real function of books like this of the Duchess of Atholl's and Mr G. T. Garratt's *Mussolini's Roman Empire*, and the prophetic utterances of Madame Tabouis and various others of the same kind. These people are forming – not consciously, of course – the link between Left and Right which is absolutely necessary for the purpose of war.

Towards the end of his life, Lane looked back on the Specials as 'perhaps the most interesting things we did', but not all his friends shared his enthusiasm. Referring to rumours that Lane was thinking of starting a journal devoted to current affairs, Ethel Mannin told him that 'there is some feeling current about the fact that your proposed magazine is going to be edited by a Communist, John Lehmann, and be generally in the hands of Communists. If this is indeed a fact, I do think it is a pity.' Lehmann was indeed sympathetic to the Left, but Mannin and her informants seem to have got hold of the wrong end of the stick. Undaunted, she resumed the attack a few days later. 'Your name is associated with the Communist Party for very obvious reasons,' she wrote in August 1938. 'It was John Lehmann who edited *New Writing*, and Krishna Menon who edited (or was anyhow associated with) the series of non-fiction books done by The Bodley Head – the Twentieth Century Library. Both are Communists.' To make matters worse, Penguin had published Ralph Bates's book about the Spanish Civil War, *Lean*

Men, as well as polemics by the notorious Professor Laski. 'If a Communist edits your proposed paper, whether you like it or not you'll be lined up with Gollancz as far as publishing is concerned,' she warned her old friend. 'If you did something by George Orwell it would balance the Communist stuff. I wish you could do his *Homage to Catalonia*, but I fear it's too newly out; but there are his novels, only I don't suppose Gollancz would release them.' In due course Penguin would publish all Orwell's major works, but in the meantime Lane was irritated by Ethel Mannin's charges. 'I'll be damned if I'll supply any evidence except the Penguin list against such fool accusations,' he told her, in a rare display of temper. She promptly climbed down − 'I shall firmly contradict *any* party labels attaching to Penguin, and intend to track down this particular one to its source' − but the damage had been done: Lane had published three of her novels in Penguin, but only one more was to follow, and they were never as close thereafter.

Rather less contentious was a short-lived series of Pelican Specials, launched in June 1938 to 'deal with matters of non-political significance, particularly the arts and sciences'; as Lane himself put it in an article entitled 'Books for the Million' in the *Left Review*, 'In the books on Science and Art you will find no abstruse technical treatises or highbrow art criticism. We believe in treating art *as a human activity*, in historical and social perspective.' Lane took Arnold Haskell, formerly of Heinemann, out to dinner, and suggested he should write *Ballet* for the series: 'I never discovered if Allen read the many books he sponsored or whether his success came from an immense flair and an idealistic outlook, which he certainly possessed,' Haskell wrote in his memoirs. *Modern German Art*, written by the German art critic O. Bihalji-Merin under the pseudonym of Peter Thoene, was published to coincide with an exhibition at the New Burlington Galleries, organized by Herbert Read in response to the Nazis' exhibition of 'degenerate' art in Munich. Lane asked John Betjeman to write a book on English churches: it was never delivered, but may well have resurfaced some years later in the two-volume *Collins Pocket Guide to English Churches*. J. G. Crowther, the scientific correspondent of the *Manchester Guardian*, was asked to advise on scientific books; adept as ever at knowing whom to approach for expert advice, Lane consulted James Fisher, author of the Pelican on *Watching Birds*, about the possibility of his advising on natural history books, and J. M. Richards, who had succeeded John Betjeman as assistant editor of the *Architectural Review*, for suggestions about architecture. Fisher went on to edit Collins's famous New Naturalist series with Julian Huxley, but although Richards's part-time career as an editorial adviser was cut short by the war, he wrote, at Lane's suggestion, *The Modern Movement in Architecture* for Pelican. When Lane asked him who would be the best person to write a history of European architecture, he promptly suggested a colleague on the 'Archie Rev', so effecting an introduction to Nikolaus Pevsner, later to become the best-known of all Lane's 'outside' or advisory editors. Richards later recalled that Lane's 'flair and judgement were remarkable considering that when one met him his conversation did not even seem to be intelligent. His manner was detached and brisk. He listened more than he talked and seemed to arrive at decisions by a process different from other people's.'

Until he left Penguin to join Alan Bott's Reprint Society, Edward Young combined editorial labours with designing jackets and press advertisements: he enjoyed a jocular relationship with Anthony Bertram, the author of a Pelican Special on *Design*, reporting that his secretary was 'violently hiccupping after the most fearful binge last night' before adding that 'It's a good thing the bosses manage to keep sober these days.' Both young men had their serious sides: Bertram confessed, apropos his book, that 'behind all this business of taps and teapots and where to put the electric light there lies a very big idea – the idea of civilized man planning and making a civilized life', an attitude which reflected the ethos of Penguin Books and of contemporary designers and architects like Maxwell Fry, Ralph Tubbs and Ernö Goldfinger, all of whom shared a belief that good design enhanced spiritual as well as material life; Ruari McLean was well aware that, charming as both Young and Lane invariably were, 'iron determination was hidden under a thick layer of velvet'.

One side effect of the Penguin Specials was to bring Lane into contact with the austere figure of Kurt Enoch, the co-founder of

Albatross Books. Now based in Paris, Enoch oversaw the distribution of Albatross Books throughout Europe outside Germany, as well as distributing works published by Jack Kahane's Obelisk Press – the precursor of the post-war Olympia Press, run by Kahane's son Maurice Girodias, which was effectively put out of business in the 1960s after Penguin's publication of *Lady Chatterley's Lover* led to a falling off of prosecutions under the Obscene Publications Act. Enoch and John Holroyd-Reece had gone their separate ways in 1938; Holroyd-Reece, who took a tearful farewell of his old partner, had been dividing his time between his house in Lincoln's Inn and a luxurious flat-cum-office on the Île de la Cité, and the punctilious Enoch had found his approach to publishing finances lax and wildly optimistic. Early that year, Holroyd-Reece and Lane defended paperbacks at a dinner held by the Double Crown Club, the members of which were publishers, printers, typographers and artists. Ian Parsons of Chatto and the bibliophile John Carter read papers on 'Cheap Reprints' to a gathering that included Geoffrey Keynes, Noel Carrington, Bill Williams, Jock Murray, Reynolds Stone and Barnett Freedman. Most of the diners were too busy inspecting the samples that were passed round the tables to pay much attention to the proceedings, but after the main speeches Harold Raymond ventilated his familiar views on the matter: according to the minutes of Holbrook Jackson, an authority on printing, typography and the *fin de siècle*, Lane made a 'spirited rejoinder' – 'Cocky little sparrow, that chap,' Noël Carrington's neighbour commented afterwards – while Holroyd-Reece's 'acute sense of values contributed a note to the discussion which was cynically overwhelming'. 'With the greatest skill and charm you blunted the attack against yourself by claiming that it was all my fault since your brilliantly successful efforts were derived from the instigation and impetus of the Albatross,' Holroyd-Reece told Lane many years later; in the meantime he faded from the scene, briefly resurfacing shortly after the war, when he was rumoured to have landed in Kent in a light aircraft without the requisite authorization.

Enoch replaced Holroyd-Reece as his London representative with the young Charles Pick, who had started out as Gollancz's London

rep, was now working for the fledgling firm of Michael Joseph, and
– with Joseph's permission – was happy to boost his earnings by
acting for Continenta, Enoch's distribution firm. Pick had come to
Lane's attention after he had imported a line of French paperback
classics, selling them on at 6d. each, and together they made several
trips to Paris to see Kurt Enoch in his offices in the Place Vendôme
and discuss the possibility of reissuing French and even German
translations of Penguin Specials under the imprint of Penguin Paris:
Lane agreed to put up £5,000, and André Maurois was prepared to
lend his name to the enterprise. The outbreak of war prevented
such schemes from coming to fruition, but Pick was impressed by
Lane's insistence on staying in cheap, bug-ridden fleapits in Paris –
on one occasion he was so badly bitten that he finally agreed to
move into Pick's more salubrious quarters – and the way in which,
when the train from Dieppe to Paris broke down, Lane wandered
off into the surrounding fields while Pick and John Lane stayed
dutifully on board, worrying that the train would drive off without
him: it was, Pick concluded, 'exactly the sort of mild Russian
roulette that Allen played'. Enoch, for his part, paid a couple of
visits to Harmondsworth, greatly relishing the huge English break-
fasts served aboard the Hercules biplanes on the Paris to London
morning flight.

Penguin Specials were not the only innovation of those frantic
pre-war years. *Penguin Parade*, an occasional magazine carrying original stories, poems and essays, made its appearance in December
1937 under the editorship of Denys Kilham Roberts; although fourteen numbers were published between then and 1948, it never
acquired either personality or purpose, and would soon be eclipsed
by John Lehmann's *Penguin New Writing*. (A convivial barrister who
divided his time between the office and the racecourse, Kilham
Roberts was a hard taskmaster, according to Julian Maclaren-Ross,
the great chronicler of Soho literary life. Penniless as ever, and
working at the time as an ineffectual vacuum-cleaner salesman,
Maclaren-Ross submitted a story to *Penguin Parade* not long before
the outbreak of war. It was accepted, and he was offered a fee of
£4. When he asked when he could expect to be paid, he was told

that nothing would be paid on acceptance, nor was it clear when exactly the money would be forthcoming. Maclaren-Ross then tried to discover when the story would be published, in the hope that this might clarify matters, as a result of which his story was returned with a note regretting that he was not prepared to abide by the magazine's rules of payment. Ruefully wondering how Kilham Roberts reconciled his behaviour with his other role as Secretary of the Society of Authors, Maclaren-Ross wrote that 'I was back where I started with no story published, and Denys Kilham Roberts has since been awarded the OBE.' Maclaren-Ross is not the most reliable of witnesses, but, as ever, his story provides a colourful insight into the travails of the literary life, the bedrock on which all publishing ultimately rests.) Still more unsuccessful was a short-lived list of paper-back Illustrated Classics, designed to undercut such long-established lists as Everyman's and the World's Classics. Its editor, Robert Gibbings, was a jovial, red-bearded, Chestertonian Irishman of prodigious size and girth who like to set type in the nude; a celebrated wood-engraver, he had run the Golden Cockerel Press from 1924 to 1934, publishing exquisite limited editions illustrated by Eric Gill, David Jones and Paul Nash. The Penguin series was launched with a party in Talbot Square in May 1938; Gwen Raverat had provided the woodcuts for an edition of Sterne's *A Sentimental Journey*, while Gibbings himself had provided those for Melville's *Typee*. 'I must say, though I says it myself, these first ten volumes seem to me ruddy fine, and I hope they create a revolution. Young's arrangement of the covers is masterly,' Gibbings told his publisher; but the war put paid to the series, which never got beyond the initial ten.

The Illustrated Classics may have been a doomed venture, but Lane's last pre-war innovation, King Penguins, are remembered with huge affection, and hoarded by those lucky enough to own them; yet they were entirely different from anything that had hitherto appeared in Penguin in that they were mostly hardback originals, aimed at the collector or the casual buyer in search of an elegant and entertaining gift, and devoid of any educational pretence. They were modelled, unashamedly, on the work of German publishers. In 1912 the firm of Insel Verlag had started a line of small-format hardbacks, and in due course the list ran to nearly 1,200 titles. Full colour illustrations were introduced in 1933; the books were published at the equivalent of 9d. each, in print-runs of between 50,000 and 100,000, and were given over to a wide variety of subjects, from birds and wild flowers to minerals and folklore. The series soon found admirers and potential imitators on this side of the English Channel. In 1935 Ian Parsons approached Lane about the possibility of his collaborating with Chatto on an English equivalent, but although Edward Bawden produced some sample illustrations, nothing came of it; two years later Chatto started the small-format Zodiac Books, but without the illustrations or colour work that distinguished the Insel Verlag exemplars.

That year two German refugees, Wolfgang Foges and Walter Neurath, founded Adprint, a prototype 'book packager' designing, editing and producing illustrated books for publishers who lacked the time or the expertise to undertake the work themselves. Adprint is best remembered for producing the wartime 'Britain in Pictures' series for Collins, and Neurath would, in due course, found Thames & Hudson with his wife Eva. In the meantime Foges suggested to Lane that Penguin might be interested in an Insel-style edition of Redouté's famous roses. Lane was taken with the idea of a series; his ideal price would be a shilling, necessitating a print-run of 25,000 copies. Elizabeth Senior, from the staff of the British Museum, was appointed series editor, and there was keen debate about where the proposed series should be printed. Adprint favoured a firm in the Sudetenland, hardly the most suitable venue in 1938; Edward Young and Lane arranged to take the boat train to Holland to visit 'old man van Leer' from a firm of Dutch printers, but 'we went to some party and got rather tight and missed the train', so they had to take the plane instead, and the hungover Young was impressed by the efficient way in which Lane, equally reduced, got on to Croydon airport and rearranged their trip. With war imminent, British printers were finally given the work, and the first two King Penguins, *A Book of Roses* and *British Birds on Lake, River and Stream*, were published in November 1939. After producing four titles in the series, Adprint were given their marching orders; their standards of production were not thought high enough, and

Nikolaus Pevsner, who had been contracted to produce a book on illuminated manuscripts, told Elizabeth Senior that, given the poor quality of the colour work, he wanted to pull out. After Elizabeth Senior's death in an air-raid, Lane asked Pevsner if he would edit the series: Pevsner told him he would only do so on the condition that he had a printer as co-editor, so R. B. Fishenden, the editor of the *Penrose Annual* and an authority on colour printing, was put in charge of their production; and the art historian E. H. Gombrich wrote *Caricature*, the first 'in-house' King Penguin. Seventy-six King Penguins were published between 1939 and 1959, when the series was discontinued; print-runs hovered around the 20,000 mark, though Gwen White's *Book of Toys* eventually sold 55,000 copies. Including reprints like Ackermann's views of Oxford and Cambridge and cartoons by Max Beerbohm as well as original work by modern artists like Ronald Searle, Edward Bawden and Lynton Lamb, the King Penguins are, perhaps, the most loved of all the birds in Lane's aviary; and, like the Christmas books which he occasionally produced for his friends, they enabled him to indulge his passion for the finely printed hardback.

They were a luxury the firm could well afford: Penguin was becoming a national institution, so much so that Merle Oberon appeared in Alexander Korda's *The Divorce of Lady X* reading a Penguin. Jonathan Cape may have complained about the non-payment of royalties, while Lane was alerted to the 'complete disintegration of the old Bedford van' used to ferry books around London, but in the autumn of 1938 he told the *Evening Standard* that he had sold over 17 million books in the previous three years, was shifting six tons of books a day, and never printed fewer than 50,000 copies of any new title. Penguin's press advertising had always been livelier than most, and the firm's high profile was reinforced by a front cover advertisement in the *Bookseller* featuring penguins gambolling at the Zoo: the photograph was taken by Howard Coster, commissioned by Lane to take the authors' back cover portraits, and one of the most sought-after photographers of the day.

A celebratory dinner of 'Penguin Elders' was held at the Hind's Head in Bray, conveniently coinciding with 'Father Beales's' departure to the States 'to preach the Gospel of the True Penguin Faith to the eternal confusion of Adolf Hitler, Benito Beelzebub, Krishna Moloch and other servants of the Devil'. Lane, Dick, Bill Williams, Frostie and Edward Young were served Krug 1928 and oysters on arrival; the giblet soup was washed down with sherry, and the lobster soufflé with Bâtard Montrachet; Château Lafite, Haut Brion and two other wines accompanied the subsequent courses. Such self-indulgence was well deserved. Lane's conviviality was accompanied by an engaging lack of pomposity, made pleasingly apparent when a seventeen-year-old schoolboy, Kenneth A. Mason, submitted *An Anthology of Animal Poetry*. 'Let's see the boy. This is a fine selection,' Bill Williams reported. 'I note that you are at school,' Lane wrote to his newest and youngest author, 'but I assume that you will have at least one free afternoon during the week, and if you could arrange to come down here to see me I would much appreciate it.' An author of an older generation reported on the popularity of Penguins in the Baltic states. 'It is obvious that the greatest difference in the knowledge of English during the last few years has been made by your sixpennies,' Lane was informed by Holbrook Jackson, whose *The Eighteen Nineties* would shortly be reissued as a Pelican, and the students in Latvia and Estonia 'carry a Penguin in their pockets as Americans used to carry a flask'.

'I guarantee you twelve months from today we shall be at war with Germany,' Lane warned Dick after Neville Chamberlain had returned from Munich waving his scrap of paper and promising 'peace in our time', and despite the apparent inevitability of war, and the fact that his empire was expanding in so many different directions, Lane decided to take six months off, leaving the firm in the hands of Dick and John. The Governor of Aden had invited him to stay, and, never happy if alone for too long, Lane asked if he could bring his sister Nora with him; she had done some repping in the West Country and manned the Penguin stand at the Ideal Home Exhibition at Earl's Court, and, quite apart from the pleasure of her company, she too deserved a break. They left in December 1938, after giving sixty friends a premature Christmas party which involved a showing of *Night Mail* at the GPO theatre in Soho Square, a tour of the Oxford Street lights and dinner in Talbot Square. From

Aden he decided to travel on by P&O liner to Bombay; he cabled home for a further £500, and for the next three months he and Nora travelled all over India by train, visiting rajahs and politicians, enjoying a long talk with Nehru, and professing themselves shocked by the 'pitiful conditions' endured by the great mass of Indians. He had noticed that Pelicans sold far better than Penguins in India, and 'the reason was not far to see': the Indian student had to scrimp and save to secure an education, and 'he was not inclined to waste his time on poor escapist literature, but wished to use his new knowledge to the full by reading such books as might make him fitted for a better job, a higher rank in the Civil Service'.

According to Morpurgo, Lane wrote long and eloquent letters home about what they had seen, and, for the only time in his life, contemplated writing a book of his own based on their travels; but the letters were lost, and, once back in England, the pressures of publishing life carried all before them. He had told Bernard Shaw that he was making the trip 'in connection with a proposal that we should publish a number of titles in basic English for native populations', but although nothing more was heard of this, he told A. C. Bouquet that his travels in India had made him realize that 'one of the greatest needs was for a book on Comparative Religion', and promptly commissioned him to write a Pelican on the subject. In Ceylon he contracted dengue fever; the *Times of Ceylon* devoted a full page to the distinguished visitor, noting how 'this rather serious young man takes everything else but himself seriously', how he was 'about medium height, well built, with a slight suspicion of a stoop', and how 'his face might well have made him a fortune on the screen. It is finely chiselled, with a broad forehead, straight nose, firm mouth and very resolute chin. His eyes look at you directly all the time he is talking.'

Back in London, the lease on Talbot Square was about to expire, so Dick and John scoured the property pages for a house they could all share, ideally not too far from Harmondsworth. Eventually they decided on Silverbeck, a handsome William IV mansion, a couple of miles from the office and now at the end of one of the main runways at Heathrow airport. For £2,250 they acquired seven bedrooms, three bathrooms, a dining-room, a library-cum-billiards room, a cellar, a large greenhouse, a potting-shed, a garage, a mushroom house, nine acres of surrounding field, a half-mile frontage on the River Colne, and a large garden complete with walnut trees; in later years Lane added a rose garden with an ornamental pond complete with fountain and goldfish, hemmed in with a yew hedge interspersed with alcoves and seats: the perfect place to give a party. The river was deep enough to swim in, but before long a swimming-pool was installed, and an aviary replete with budgerigars. Desperate to get the place ready before the master returned, Dick and John supervised decorations and alterations, scraped and polished the floors, installed an Aga, fitted kitchen cupboards, hung the curtains, trimmed the hedges, dug the garden and mowed the lawn. Mr Knight, the butler from Talbot Square, found country life too quiet and quickly returned to London, but two maids, a gardener and an all-purpose boy were enlisted. All was finally in order when Lane and Nora returned from their travels with forty pieces of luggage, including rugs, ebony elephants and tea-chests crammed with tea. No sooner had they unpacked than the parties began. Since none of the brothers was married, their cousin Joan Collihole was summoned from Devon and, to her initial alarm, told to act as hostess to a stream of authors, printers, journalists and publishers; she was also put in charge of the chickens, preserving their eggs in isinglass, while her sister Evelyn, a more sporadic visitor, cleaned the Aga, already in a 'shocking state'. The brothers, in the meantime, were photographed prancing about the grounds in their tight-hipped double-breasted suits, like Cary Grant in triplicate. All in all, it seemed a good place in which to await the outbreak of war.

Camilla and Samuel Williams (later Lane) with Allen (left) and Dick

Allen and sister Nora in holiday mood

'Uncle' John Lane, complete with Elizabethan beard: from a portrait by Ernst L. Ipsen

AL as a dapper young publisher-about-town

The Vigo Street offices of The Bodley Head; later, Allen Lane The Penguin Press

Hard at work in the Crypt: note the pin-ups on the wall

AL at the wheel

The Penguincubator, AL's own slot machine

A streamlined Penguin delivery van

The brothers Lane at Silverbeck. Dick (left) was a keen angler; John is in the middle

The brothers prancing for Nora Lane's camera

The brothers in front of the original Penguin building at Harmondsworth. Dick (left) and John (right) had yet to be called up; note the anti-bomb blast tape in the windows

AL and his sister Nora on their pre-war trip to Aden and India

AL in India, 1939

The *Penguin*: AL can be dimly discerned through the rigging

AL and Lettice's big day, 26 June 1941, with a cardboard-Penguin guard of honour

Recently married

Dick in pensive mood

Packing books in the blackout

Harmondsworth at war: note the David Low cartoon of Colonel Blimp

Despatching books by hand

The fiery Krishna Menon in one
of his many tailor-made suits

Eunice Frost ponders a typescript

AL and Frostie inspecting some
of Low's wartime cartoons

W. E. Williams,
AL and Nikolaus
Pevsner. Drinks
loomed large in
Penguin life

John Lehmann

Jan Tschichold

Frostie and Bill Williams

Editorial meeting at 117 Piccadilly. Left to right: TK (Tanya Schmoller),
J. E. Morpurgo, Dick Lane, AL, Bill Williams, Eunice Frost, Alan Glover

8. Penguins Go to War

Allen Lane was digging an air-raid shelter at Harmondsworth when, at 11.15 on the morning of 3 September, Neville Chamberlain informed the nation over the wireless that Britain was now at war with Germany. By all accounts, Lane and his fellow-diggers downed tools and headed off for a ruminative drink: in Dick's version of events, they made for the Peggy Bedford, a local roadhouse in which a good deal of Penguin business and pleasure would be conducted over the years; another veteran of the event feels sure they retired to Silverbeck, where Lane briskly set about mixing cocktails of a suitably incendiary strength ('They were like dynamite – they used to go off halfway down and nearly blow your head off,' the veteran recalls). Little work was done for the rest of that day, but, like the phoney war that followed the announcement of hostilities, the lull

was misleading: over the next six years, with all the pre-war staff except Stan Olney and Eunice Frost away in the Forces at various times, and a wartime staff that never exceeded forty people, Penguin would publish over 600 titles, almost half of which originated within the firm, start up nineteen new series, and, thanks in part to the popularity of Penguin Books among some (but by no means all) of the armed forces, see the firm established as a national institution. The titles published would range from archaeology to crossword puzzles, from green-covered detective stories to 'Planning, Design and Art Books' devoted to the reconstruction of post-war Britain, from the six volumes of Penguin Hansard to such invaluable aids to the war effort as G. H. Goodchild's *Keeping Poultry and*

Rabbits on Scraps and R. A. Saville-Sneath's *Aircraft Recognition*, the bestselling title on the Penguin list until the arrival of *Lady Chatterley's Lover*; the new series would include Puffin Books, Penguin Handbooks, Penguin Poets, John Lehmann's *Penguin New Writing* and Penguin Modern Painters, as well as more modest and shorter-lived enterprises like Editions Penguin, published initially for the Free French forces, the larger-format, buff-coloured Editions Pingouin, the single volume issued by Edizioni di Pinguino, and a set of four prints produced by Feliks Topolski. The Topolski prints included a drawing of Churchill in bulldog mood, and a less flattering one of Hitler – the accompanying verses to which, by D. B. Wyndham Lewis, alias Timothy Shy, strike a fine note of comic defiance:

> Dolf Hitler gif a barty,
> Der RAF komm by,
> Day in der pants his troops gekick
> Und sock dem in der eye.
>
> Der Fuehrer cry: 'So! Hermann!
> Du winnst anodder maddle!
> Wohl auf, my bully Kavaliers,
> Boots offgepull und paddle!'

To begin with life went on much as before. Three weeks after the declaration of war, Lane bustled into Harold Nicolson's chambers in the Temple, commissioned him to write a 50,000-word Penguin Special on *Why Britain is at War*, took delivery of the typescript a fortnight later, published on 5 November, and sold 100,000 copies, quite a few of them in the United States; he went skiing in Chamonix, calling *en route* at the Allied Headquarters in Arras and inspecting the supposedly impregnable Maginot Line; he and Dick went to a wine-tasting in the City, thought it a pity to waste so much good wine by spitting it out, swigged four or five bottles between them and somehow staggered back to Silverbeck, where Dick made incomprehensible phone calls while Lane slept in the car outside. With petrol rationing imminent, the brothers bought themselves bikes, and pedalled to work each day. 'There is really an astonishing lack of interest in the whole affair, and except for the fact that there are more people about in uniform, and that there are occasional slight hitches in getting through supplies, there is very little to denote that there is really a war on,' he told Elsa Lanchester, who was now living in the States.

Lane was in his late thirties when the war broke out, at the upper limit of those eligible for the Forces, and as the head of Penguin Books he belonged to a 'reserved' profession, more valuable for his non-military contribution to the war effort than for his martial prowess; and it was agreed that while his two younger brothers would do their bit in the Navy, he would be better employed in keeping the family firm afloat. According to Dick, he started the war as a captain in the Territorial Army, and remained as such for the duration, albeit in an honorific capacity. He also served as a corporal in the Local Defence Volunteers, later renamed the Home Guard, doing guard duty in the Harmondsworth area and taking part in Sunday manoeuvres: he was soon bored by the proceedings, and happily allowed his platoon to be captured after learning that the 'enemy' was based in a nearby pub. His biographer, Jack Morpurgo, who was proud of his own war record, liked to think that Lane felt guilty and embarrassed at not having fought in the war, and relished his discomfiture. 'Only much later,' he wrote of Lane, 'when the war was already won, did he so much as hint that he felt in any way deprived of being just too young for active service in the First War and too important to join in the more obviously military activities of the Second; and even then such unease as there was in his conscience he revealed only by sulky silences when in the company of old soldiers and forced to listen to their reminiscences.' Morpurgo had his own agenda, but others have suggested that Lane's refusal, in the early 1950s, to compete with publishers like Billy Collins for bestselling wartime memoirs like *The Wooden Horse*, *The White Rabbit* and *The Colditz Story* reflected a sense of inadequacy or guilt. None of this quite rings true. Good publishers, like Lane, know where their strengths and weaknesses lie: he had a very strong sense of what a Penguin book should be, and since he would rather step aside than publish books which might in any way dilute or corrupt the image of his firm, it seems far more likely that he felt, instinctively, that however well war books might do for Collins, Hodder or Pan, they were not right for the Penguin list. But he was also a sentimental man, and when the time came to choose the thousandth Penguin, in 1954, he bought the rights from Rupert Hart-Davis to one of the finest of all war memoirs, his former colleague Edward Young's *One of Our Submarines*. (The first RNVR officer to command an operational submarine during the war, Young was awarded the DSO and the DSC, and was once described as 'one of our greatest submarine captains'.) Nor was Lane averse to action at the time of Dunkirk. Bob Maynard, who had replaced Young as production manager without knowing the first thing about printing, paper or design, remembered how Lane stuck his head round his office door, told him that he had heard on the radio that boats were assembling on the South Coast to take part in the evacuation of British troops, and asked if he would be willing to help out: Maynard was happy to go along, but the *Penguin*, now tied up at Bucklers Hard on the Solent, was in no fit condition, and nothing ever came of the idea.

Dick and John had both been RNVR reserve officers before the war, and shortly after Dunkirk they received their call-up papers and joined the training ship *King Alfred*. In due course Bob Maynard also joined the Navy. Lane took him out for a farewell drink, plied him with a vast Tom Collins, followed by several more, and promised to keep his job open and his salary paid while he was away. Maynard was not the only old hand to benefit from Lane's generosity. Members of staff away on active service received Christmas cards and 'comfort parcels' including the latest Penguins; one serving in North Africa was disappointed to receive *Keeping Poultry and Rabbits on Scraps* and *Social Life in the Insect World*, and a covering note in which Stan Olney apologized for problems with the printers.

Problems with printers became endemic during the war, not least because they lost many skilled men to the Forces, found it hard to replace machinery damaged or destroyed in air-raids, and could find their services being requisitioned by the Government at short notice; but paper shortages were the real nightmare, made worse when the German invasion of Denmark and Norway in 1940 cut Britain off from Sweden and Finland, its traditional suppliers of newsprint, while the fall of France made it hard to acquire esparto grass. Paper rationing was introduced in March 1940, and the annual quota allowed each publisher was set as a percentage of the paper used by that firm between August 1938 and August 1939: it started at 60 per cent, was reduced to 37.5 per cent in 1942, went up to 42.5 per cent in 1944, and remained in force until 1951. Most publishers complained, bitterly, that 1938–9 had been an exceptionally lean year, and that 1937 should have been chosen instead; Lane, on the other hand, had enjoyed a phenomenal success with Penguin Specials during that time, selling 9 million books in 1939, and, much to the irritation of his rivals, he not only qualified for a far heftier paper ration than most, but by supplying special editions to the armed forces and prisoners of war he was able to corner additional supplies as well. But paper shortages were a problem for even the best endowed publishers. Publishers' requirements were not regarded as a top priority: in 1944, a representative year, HMSO was allocated 100,000 tons, newspapers (many of them reduced to a mere four pages) 250,000 tons, magazines and periodicals 50,000 tons, and the entire publishing industry a miserly 22,000 tons. Despite some vigorous lobbying led by Stanley Unwin, the House of Lords, debating the matter in October 1941, was unmoved by revelations that, with the Allied fortunes at their lowest ebb, 30 per cent of publishers' turnover still consisted of exports, 20 million volumes had been lost in air-raids and needed to be replaced, and demand for books, and not least for technical and scientific books, had never been greater. That same year, however, the Ministry of Supply released another 250 tons, to be shared out among members of the Publishers' Association on the understanding that it should be used in a responsible manner. Despite initial opposition from Victor Gollancz and Douglas Jerrold from Eyre & Spottiswoode – both of whom, despite their very different political affiliations, resented being told how they should use any extra paper – the Moberley Pool, as this annual allocation came to be known, remained in being until 1949.

Quality as well as quantity was also under siege. From January 1942 book publishers were expected to comply with the Book Production War Economy Agreement: a committee consisting of Billy Collins, Stanley Morison and Wren Howard laid down rules about type size, width of margins and quality of paper to be used, and those who refused to cooperate were threatened with a reduced paper quota. Books became shorter and slimmer as a result; although the price of a Penguin went up from 6d. to 9d. in 1942, Bob Maynard did away with dust-jackets, dutifully trimmed the margins and type sizes and eventually replaced sewn binding with hideous metal staples which rusted in damp weather, turning the grey, straw-based paper orange in the afflicted areas. 'Since my return from America I have been very much perturbed by the very shabby condition of our publications on a number of bookstalls,' Lane had noted in 1941, even before the Agreement came into force; for a publisher who placed so much emphasis on the production and design of his books, it must have been a dismal state of affairs. Reprinting *Sir Isumbras at the Ford* was proving a tricky business, he informed its author, D. K. Broster: paper rationing made it impossible to publish books of more than 256 pages, and he was reluctant to reduce the type size below 10-point. Most writers were resigned to the worst, but G. H. Goodchild was anxious to be of help: 'If the question of paper presents any difficulty, I might be able to get some concession, as the Government attach great importance to Rabbit Breeding,' he informed his publisher. Books were pulped and re-pulped, and in 1943 the Ministry of Supply mounted a salvage drive to collect and pulp unwanted books. Black market paper merchants did brisk business; Lane was tempted to buy from a paper spiv, but when Stan Olney and Bob Maynard pointed out that to do so would make him liable to prosecution, he asked Maynard to disengage, and hurried off on holiday.

Shortages of paper, blockages at binderies and shortages of machinery and manpower in the printing industry coincided with an unprecedented demand for books. Publishers could sell whatever they had in stock: as Stanley Unwin pointed out, conditions were both ideal and deeply frustrating, in that editorial fallibility, 'the most expensive item' in any publisher's business, was no longer a problem, yet shortages of materials and printing capacity often made it impossible to print as many copies as they could sell, or to reprint strong-selling titles and keep backlists in print. Like other publishers, Penguin had to ration their customers, providing them with only a proportion of their orders. There were two reasons for this seemingly insatiable demand for books: the destruction of existing stock, and the conditions endured by soldiers and civilians alike. On 29 December 1940, Paternoster Row, the heart of the book trade since the sixteenth century, was flattened in a German bombing raid: a clear night helped the Luftwaffe to pinpoint the City, and a low water level in the Thames made it harder for firemen to fight the blaze. Simpkin Marshall lost 6 million books; Longmans, resident in Paternoster Row since 1724, went up in flames; Blackwood's, Hodder, Collins, Nelson, Eyre & Spottiswoode and Hutchinson suffered heavy losses. 'I went to look at Paternoster Row and that area,' Raymond Postgate told his American publisher, Alfred Knopf. 'It was much as you suppose, but the ruins were all orange . . . There was a bright blue sky, and the whole effect was exotic, as if a view of Algiers had been concealed behind the brick of Ludgate Circus.' 'The Germans have done what Constable's have never succeeded in doing,' observed a sardonic Bernard Shaw. 'They have disposed of 86,701 sheets of my work in less than twenty-four hours.'

Nor was this the only disastrous day for the trade: Allen & Unwin later lost 1.4 million books from a single bomb, and much of Secker's stock was destroyed when their printers in Plymouth were bombed during the Blitz. Libraries, both public and private, were destroyed, and desperately needed to replace their stock. Publishers were compelled to pay war insurance premiums, so adding to their overheads; to pay the new Excess Profits Tax – designed to thwart shady operators, as well as raising money for the Treasury – publishers sold off their backlists, which they then found it impossible to replace. By 1942, 580 out of 970 titles in Everyman's Library were out of print, at a time when demand for the classics, and the supposedly 'escapist' Trollope in particular, had never been higher.

Although Christina Foyle noted, in May 1940, 'a general falling-off of sales of political books', the war witnessed an extraordinary resurgence of reading. Civilians had to endure the blackout, or fill in the long hours of fire-watching; soldiers, sailors and airmen carried a book to while away the boredom of interminable journeys by train or in troopships, and reading made life in camp or in barracks more bearable. Some read to escape the tedium and unpleasantness of war, some to improve their minds, some to learn skills or obtain qualifications for when they eventually returned to civilian life. Although the great majority preferred comic books or the comic-strip adventures of the semi-naked Jane in the *Daily Mirror* to *What Happened in History* or the latest Evelyn Waugh, there was an extraordinary appetite for culture in general, and books in particular. 'The average intellectual level of the books published has markedly risen,' George Orwell noted early in 1942, and

the average book which the ordinary man reads is a better book than it would have been three years ago. One phenomenon of the war has been the enormous sale of Penguin books, Pelican books and other cheap titles, most of which would have been regarded as impossibly highbrow a few years back. And this in turn reacts on the newspapers, making them more serious and less sensational than they were before. It probably reacts also on the radio, and will react in time on the cinema.

Shortly before the outbreak of war, Stanley Unwin had bemoaned 'the literary indifference and morbid tastes of our public', which he saw as 'of danger not merely to our intellectual but to our national life in general', while Sir Geoffrey Faber claimed that all publishers had noted a 'progressive decline in the quantity and quality of worthwhile manuscripts' submitted to them; five years later, Unwin observed how

Young people were buying books, and not merely books but good books. They wanted the best. The war created a new reading public. Many acquired the reading habit who had never turned to books before, and there is much comfort in the realization that they did so for the acquisition of knowledge and the enjoyment of good literature, and not merely as an escape from the war.

Unlike Orwell, Unwin remained reluctant to give Lane or Penguin any credit. Towards the end of the war, his nephew Philip asked him whether he had changed his mind about Penguin. 'No, not a bit of it,' the sage replied. The phenomenal sale of Penguins was 'entirely due to war conditions – you'll see, as soon as the war is over, the demand for paperbacks will decline'.

Lane would have agreed with Unwin that 'the chief feature of wartime publishing has been the prolonged struggle in defence of books with one government department after another'; where they differed was in their readiness to act on behalf of the trade as a whole. Unwin was the quintessential committee man, a passionate team player who busied himself in the Publishers' Association and other trade bodies, campaigning against paper rationing and other iniquities; Lane was, and remained, a loner and a maverick, happy to enjoy the benefits accrued from the labours of others, but hating bureaucracy and bumph. Lane's more public-spirited colleagues resented his disdain for bodies like the PA, and his refusal to lend his weight to their activities. When, in 1940, the Chancellor of the Exchequer, Kingsley Wood, decided that publishers were liable for Purchase Tax, and a campaign was mounted by A. P. Herbert, J. B. Priestley, Hugh Walpole, A. D. Peters, R. H. Tawney and others to keep the tax at bay, it was left to such stalwarts of the trade as Geoffrey Faber, David Roy, Wren Howard and Harold Macmillan to lead a successful delegation to 11 Downing Street. Lane enjoyed good relations with Mr Reed, the all-important Paper Controller, but he made his own rules and went his own way, and his fellow publishers looked on with envy and indignation.

He had close ties, too, with the Ministry of Information, not least through Kenneth Clark, the Controller of Home Publicity. Based in Senate House, and employing what Clark described as 'an uneasy mixture of so-called intellectuals, ex-journalists and advertising men, ex-politicians and *éminences grises*' which included Graham Greene, Peter Quennell and the literary agent A. D. Peters with a leavening of civil servants, the Ministry was simultaneously concerned with propaganda, both at home and abroad, and censorship of the written word: according to Orwell, who later blamed his problems in finding a publisher for *1984* on the Ministry's devious machinations, it was up to publishers to show the Ministry worrisome or problematic typescripts or proofs, and 'the Ministry of Information "suggests" that this or that is undesirable, or premature, or "would serve no good purpose". And though there is no definite prohibition, no clear statement that this or that must not be printed, official policy is never flouted.' Given the informal nature of the Ministry's interventions, it is hard to know to what extent Penguin was affected, but even contributions to *Penguin New Writing* were submitted to Senate House if they were thought to contain 'sensitive' material. And the Ministry, for its part, liked, if possible, to get its message across through conventional publishing channels – including Oxford University Press, Penguin, Foyles and *Picture Post* – and was in a position to make extra paper available if need be.

Although Lane too preferred to work behind the scenes, and loathed making speeches or performing on a podium – 'I have a distinct phobia about speaking,' he had earlier confessed – he had a brief incarnation as a public figure in the early years of the war. He turned up in canteens and dockyards and barracks, debating the issues of the day with other well-known names; with C. Day Lewis and Cyril Connolly, he took part in a broadcast debate about publishing and literary life, chaired by Alistair Cooke (he could not sell enough books, he declared, and his 'superior publishing friends' said the same); the *Daily Mail* organized a lunch at the Savoy, early in 1940, at which Lane, the film director Alexander Korda, William Crawford the advertising agent, Sidney Bernstein and the managing director of Harrods discussed wartime propaganda (Lane suggested that the work could be done by a 'small nucleus' of people, and should involve 'taking the people more into our confidence, showing them what we are aiming at, and the steps we must take to reach our goal'). Such excitements soon palled – Morpurgo, typically, suggests that Lane was neither cultured nor quick-witted enough to hold his own – but Penguin's propaganda value was recognized by both sides: at some stage in the war the Germans produced an imitation Penguin Special, and Paul Fussell has claimed that, in 1942, rumours were spread about paper being set aside for a million Penguin French–English phrase books in the hope that this would mislead the Germans into thinking that the Allies were planning to land in mainland France rather than francophone North Africa.

'I can appreciate more than ever how our books must be needed by the services, and I think we ought to concentrate more than ever on them,' Lane wrote to Eunice Frost on his way to Montreal in August 1941. In terms of size and weight – if not always of brow level or subject matter – Penguins were perfect for troops on the move or at rest. Richard Hoggart remembered how 'only a mean-minded sergeant would spot them and demand that they be removed. They became a signal: if the back trouser pocket bulged in that way that usually indicated a reader, a rare spirit in Initial Training Camp.' Paul Fussell, on the other hand, located the 'Penguin pocket' above the left knee of the battledress, and claimed that it was also used to carry copies of Cyril Connolly's *Horizon*; according to Morpurgo, Penguins also fitted perfectly into the pocket of the haversack in which gas masks were carried. From very early on in the war, friends and relatives sent Penguins to soldiers, sailors and airmen drumming their heels in barracks or transit camps. 'If you were to advertise or let it be known that you would send off direct parcels of, say, not less than six Penguins, it would be a good thing, and I think popular,' G. B. Harrison advised Lane in October 1939. 'If one does want to send books to people at the Front it is a bore to order them from Smith's and then subsequently pack them oneself.' Lane replied that he was working on a scheme whereby books could be sent to individuals in cartons of five or ten; individual benefactors could place orders directly with Penguin, and the books would be delivered via the Services Central Book Depot.

In the summer of 1940 Lane received a letter from Ifor Evans, whose recently published *A Short History of English Literature* was selling briskly on the Pelican list. Evans had shown a copy of his book to Lord Macmillan, the Chairman of the philanthropic and culture-loving Pilgrim Trust, who had written to say that he had had discussions with Tom Jones, Lloyd George's former Cabinet Secretary, about the possibility of providing copies of the book to the Forces, since 'the men in our Services nowadays are drawn from all classes and there must be many among them who would find in your history just the sort of reading they want in their scant leisure'. 'Here surely is an idea bigger than anything that affects my book,' Evans told Lane. 'I think you should consult William Emrys Williams who knows Tom Jones . . .' An inveterate fixer and puller of strings, Tom Jones was, with Kenneth Clark and Bill Williams, a founder-member of the Pilgrim Trust.

Quite apart from his part-time work at Penguin, Williams was heavily involved in two other high-minded, acronymic projects, both of which reflected and helped to create a world in which Penguins and Pelicans could flourish: the Council for the Encouragement of Music and the Arts (CEMA), which became the Arts Council in 1945, under the Chairmanship of Lord Keynes; and the Army Bureau of Current Affairs (ABCA), set up to teach members of the Forces why they were fighting the war, and what kind of Britain they were fighting for. Funded, in part, by the Pilgrim Trust, CEMA was set up in January 1940 to bring culture to the people. Many theatres and concert halls had closed at the outbreak of war, and the contents of the major art galleries had been taken to safe locations, far removed from the bombs; and yet, as publishers quickly realized, the demand for culture was greater than ever: 'My feeling is that after the first shock of war there will be a great need for books along cultural lines,' Lane told Ifor Evans. The best-remembered manifestation of this thirst for culture was Myra Hess's piano recitals in the National Gallery, the Director of which, Kenneth Clark, had shipped all the Old Masters to safety caves in North Wales, and replaced them with contemporary works. 'The public seemed to be quite suddenly transformed. The change was as pervasive as it was mysterious,' John Rothenstein recalled, adding that 'whatever the cause, the results were manifest everywhere, whether in an increased demand for the cheap editions of the classical authors, an increased desire to listen to the classical composers and to see fine painting'. 'At no time in the pre-war years was there so large and varied a public for good literature, pictures, plays and music as there is at present. In fact the demand hugely exceeds the supply,' the critic Eddie Sackville-West noted in 1943, while Mollie Panter-Downes, writing for the *New Yorker*, observed how 'more and more Londoners have taken to reading poetry, listening to music, and going to art exhibitions, although there is less of all three in this shabby, weary capital', and Philip Hope-Wallace noted the enthusiastic 'Penguin-educated audience' for such plays and concerts as were available: up to 8,000 people squeezed into the Albert Hall for the Proms after Malcolm Sargent took over in 1944. CEMA encouraged and catered to these needs, arranging concerts in factories and canteens, and encouraging amateur dramatics and local choral societies. Before long a split became apparent between the populists, including Bill Williams, who valued the efforts of amateurs as well as professionals, and those like Kenneth Clark and Maynard Keynes who had no time for Morris dancers or Northumbrian bagpipers, and insisted on the highest professional standards within conventional 'artistic' terms of reference. The perfectionists prevailed after Keynes replaced Lord Macmillan in 1942, and Williams nimbly changed sides; but in the meantime, as head of the Arts Panel, he was able to continue the good work he had begun in 1935 with his 'Art for the People' scheme, exhibiting the work of war artists in the depleted National Gallery and arranging for paintings by Graham Sutherland, John Piper, Barnett Freedman, Duncan Grant and others to be shown in workplaces and canteens.

Such activities bore fruit for Penguin, most obviously in Kenneth Clark's editorship of the Penguin Modern Painters series, but Williams's involvement with the Army Bureau of Current Affairs proved of equal value. No sooner had war broken out than various bodies were set up to deal with army education, which was thought to be good for morale, a useful antidote to boredom and inactivity, a safety valve, and a means of teaching skills that would be of use when the war was over. The Central Council for Army Education involved teachers and university lecturers in extra-mural classes administered by the Army Education Corps, and the Haining Report recommended that officers should give informal talks and lectures to the soldiers under their command. Gertrude Williams claimed to have had the idea for ABCA while she and her husband were on holiday in Wales; it came into being in 1941, with the full support of Sir Ronald Adam, the newly appointed and liberal-minded Adjutant-General, and Bill Williams as its Director. An unmartial figure, Williams refused to wear uniform or accept a rank – since his deputy was a brigadier, he should have been a major-general – and eschewed a staff car in favour of his battered old Hillman.

Within six months over half the units in the Army boasted ABCA discussion groups: compulsory sessions were held for one hour every week, with officers leading the discussions of prearranged topics. The ABCA handbook promoted the Cromwellian notion of the citizen-soldier who 'must know what he fights for and love what he knows'; A. D. Lindsay, the Master of Balliol, suggested that 'There had not been any army in England which discussed like this one since that famous Puritan army which produced the Putney Debates and laid the foundations of modern democracy.' The Bureau published two regular bulletins, *War* and *Current Affairs*; exhibitions were mounted, plays put on, films shown, and a course in 'citizenship' provided. Although ABCA was viewed with grave suspicion by many Conservatives, who saw it as part of a left-wing conspiracy, even the diehard Tory Lord Croft acknowledged its Director to be 'a very vital personality', and 'a man of ideas as well as of push and drive'.

Both ABCA and CEMA encouraged a receptive readership for Penguin Books; and Lane made use of Williams's innumerable connections and intuitive understanding of the bureaucratic mind when following up Ifor Evans's suggestion. He was already on good terms with Lt-Col. Jackson of the Services Central Book Depot, which had shipped 200,000 selected Penguins to the ill-fated British Expeditionary Force in February 1940; three months later the Postmaster-General authorized the free transmission of books and periodicals to the Forces, and – on the assumption that a Penguin reader might, in due course, become a Penguin buyer as well –

many new Penguins carried a message urging its purchaser to drop the book off, once it had been read, at the local Post Office for posting on to the troops. In the first year of the war, half a million second-hand books, many of them Penguins, were donated to the Forces by the public through voluntary organizations like the Red Cross, but before long the Blitz and paper rationing had taken their toll: on the home front, and among the Forces, demand was far exceeding supply. Late in 1941, just before the paper ration was reduced yet again, Lane had a bright idea which, he hoped, would increase his paper ration. Penguin, and Penguin alone, would supply titles for what would be known, misleadingly, as the Forces Book Club, which would in turn supply units rather than individual servicemen. With Williams playing a key role in the negotiations between Penguin and the War Office, of which ABCA formed a part, Lane suggested to Colonel Jackson that he should produce ten titles a month for the Services Central Book Depot, supplying 75,000 copies of each title at 5d. each. The Paper Controller, Jackson reported, would be happy to cooperate provided all the extra paper provided was used solely for books for the Forces, and the scheme did not include any reprints.

News of the scheme soon leaked out, and was greeted with cries of outrage from Lane's rival publishers, who felt that his already bloated paper allowance was being unfairly augmented, and that he had been given a monopoly in this particular market. Cape, Cassell, Chatto, Dent, Murray, Faber, Heinemann and Harrap set out to beat Lane at his own game by publishing Guild Books, a jointly owned paperback imprint publishing reprints from their backlists at 6d., 9d. or 1s. Walter Harrap was its driving force, but although a trade paper reported that he 'paces his office throwing off witty cracks like an electric train spitting sparks', his dealings with the Army authorities were lethargic and condescending. 'Sooner or later the Services will have to do something to make the publication of such books possible if they really feel the troops must have light reading,' he told the Services Committee for the Welfare of the Forces in April 1942, three months before Colonel Jackson gave the go-ahead for the Forces Book Club. What Harrap failed to realize was that Bill Williams, wearing his Penguin trilby and his ABCA peaked cap, was reading all his correspondence and passing copies on, duly and derisorily annotated, to Allen Lane. 'If I know anything of the PA [the Publishers' Association], I think we may well be in for a protracted correspondence and at the end of it get nowhere,' Lane noted, displaying his habitual contempt for trade bodies and the spirit of cooperation. He was right to ignore the competition: although Guild Books limped on into the post-war years, it was fatally weakened by having no paper quota, its members drawing on their own reserves for those titles they decided to reprint themselves in paperback rather than sub-leasing to Penguin.

Bill Williams, in the meantime, assured his military masters that 'Allen Lane in this matter is mainly a philanthropist, he wants to give the Services priority in book supplies and he wants to mitigate for them the consequences of the impending book famine'; and although Lane initially wanted to keep Penguin's name off books supplied to the Club for fear of annoying other publishers, it was thought best to come clean and print in the prelims 'Published for HM Forces by Penguin Books Ltd'. The first batch of ten titles was published in October 1942. Although Lane took advantage of the Club edition to run-on copies for the trade, so reducing the overall unit cost, the scheme was a failure, with print-runs nearer to 10,000 a title than the anticipated 75,000. It proved popular with the chosen authors, who made a windfall of £75 each in what seemed a good cause, but its readers were less happy. Few soldiers, it seemed, were that keen to read *Howards End* or Margaret Mead's *Growing Up in New Guinea*. 'Could you please arrange to increase a more liberal supply of fiction and adventure books, as we find that the majority of the books are of a heavy type, and seldom find any demand by the men of this unit,' a unit commander informed the Central Book Depot. Lane was frustrated by the failure of his scheme, which was discontinued in September 1943, after 120 titles had been published in their own distinctive bindings. 'It seemed to me to be obvious that we are not supplying the types of book which you feel are best suited for the Services,' he told the Depot. 'You mentioned three categories stressed by you – "warm" fiction, Westerns and crime –

and as we have never published any books in the first two categories and not more than two titles a month out of a total of ten for the last category, I can readily understand how unsuitable as a whole our list must be.'

Lane's other efforts to publish special editions for the Forces were more modest and, probably, more successful: an Egyptian printer was licensed to produce editions for troops serving in the Middle East, and the Prisoner of War Book Service capitalized on the 'permit' scheme whereby publishers were allowed to 'export' books to prisoners of war via the Red Cross. The contents of such books were vetted by the authorities to make sure that no references were made to such sensitive subjects as docks, airfields, navigation tables or tidal charts. In March 1943, *The Prisoner of War*, a magazine for the relatives of the incarcerated, announced a scheme whereby they could place orders with booksellers for Penguins to be despatched to individual prisoners. The books were specially produced and included works by Margery Allingham, L. A. G. Strong, Ngaio Marsh, Stella Gibbons and T. H. White, as well as *The German Lebensraum* and two books about escape attempts by the British in the First World War. According to the printer Elliott Viney, who served as the librarian in a German camp, all went well until that 'fatal day in 1942' when the German censor spotted an advertisement, drawn by Bob Maynard, for a short-lived Penguin Pen, in which a British Tommy, wielding an outsize fountain pen, was shown hoisting a runtish and terrified Hitler aloft by his trousers on the point of the nib. After that (or so it was said), all Penguins coming into the camp were confiscated. The ban was lifted shortly after the Normandy invasions, and some 25,000 pent-up Penguins flooded into the camp; a few were read, but the great majority were put to good use as fuel or lavatory paper.

Lane's time was not solely given over to publishing. He had decided to become a farmer as well as a publisher, and after lunch one day at the Hind's Head in Bray, he and John, then home on leave, went along to an auction in Reading. He liked to make out that he acquired Priory Farm after the auctioneer had mistaken John's picking his nose for a bid; either way, the farm was acquired by the three brothers, on the understanding that, until the war was over, Allen would be responsible for its running. It was less than an hour's drive from Silverbeck, and Lane set out to learn about farming with the same thoroughness and professionalism he had brought to his life as a publisher.

Farming was to become a source of great pleasure, but acquiring Priory Farm was not the only change to his domestic circumstances. One evening in the spring of 1941, Lane went to a party in Cambridge, given by Lance Beales. The LSE had moved to Cambridge for the duration, and every now and then a Pelican editorial meeting was held in the town; hence Lane's presence at the party. Among the guests was a short, pretty, strong-featured girl named Lettice Orr. Clever, quick-witted and possessed of a caustic tongue, she was the eldest daughter of Sir Charles Orr, a Woolwich-trained soldier who, after serving in India, had entered the colonial service, working under Lugard in Nigeria and in Cyprus and Gibraltar before ending his career as Governor of the Bahamas. Lettice's mother was a good deal younger than her husband, and when he was sent to the Bahamas she refused to go with him, partly because she disapproved of her children consorting with black people, and partly because she was having an affair with his aide-de-camp, so she stayed behind in England and taught her children at home. Lettice took a diploma in the social sciences at Bedford College, where she was taught by Gertrude Williams; she had trained as a psychiatric social worker, and was now working at Addenbrooke's Hospital in Cambridge. She went to the party in the hope of meeting her old tutor's husband, Bill Williams, but noticed instead a 'short, powerful-looking man in country gentleman's tweeds', standing by himself and talking to no one. She went up to him and said, 'You're looking sad'; he told her that both his brothers were in the Navy, she persuaded him on to the dance floor, and, a week later, he invited her to stay at Silverbeck. After her return to Cambridge, Jean Osborne and Joan Collihole used to stand at the top of the stairs at Silverbeck, just outside Lane's 'huge bedroom', and listen in to his two-hour telephone marathons with his new girlfriend.

The net result was that Lettice and Lane got engaged, and were photographed for *Tatler* and the *Sketch*, a terrier posing at their feet. They were married on 28 June 1941, a contingent of cardboard Penguins forming a guard of honour outside the church; Joan Collihole returned to Devon, and Jean Osborne was 'unceremoniously' told to leave Silverbeck once Lettice was installed.

Their marriage was to prove an embattled affair, and although they were still together, just, when Lane died, they had spent much of the intervening time apart. Writing to Eunice Frost four years before his death, Lane admitted that his brothers' joining the Navy, leaving him alone for the first time, 'was the reason for my getting married. If the three of us had stayed together I very much doubt if I would ever have married.' His sense of isolation was heightened when Nora got married and went to live in Newcastle. Her fiancé, Frank Bird, had been put out when Lane whisked his wife-to-be off to India for three months, and then insisted on sending her to America with John just as war broke out, checking up on the newly opened New York office; and as soon as they returned he made her Mrs Bird and carried her off to Northumberland, far removed from the clannish, possessive and overpowering Lanes. All three brothers were bachelors by nature, hating change, stuck in their ways and wanting things done their own way. Dick and John resented their elder brother getting married, and John in particular: he regarded Lettice as an interloper, and would burst into the newly-weds' bedroom, talking Penguin business non-stop and paying her no attention whatsoever, and she disliked him heartily in return.

For all his good looks and urbane demeanour, Lane's reputation as a ladies' man was misleading, and the sexual side of their marriage may well have been blighted by an imbalance between the demands and expectations of the two partners. As a young man, Lane once confessed to Frostie, 'somehow I got the idea that sex was wrong'. He had indulged in odd affairs before meeting Lettice, but 'I remained a rather self-contained and aloof being, and although at the beginning Lettice and I had relations of a sort, they were never of the intensity which I now know they should be in a happy union.' She was still involved with a Cambridge don when they met, and the affair continued even after her marriage; it had made Lane very unhappy, and he had thought of postponing the wedding for six months. Sad and familiar as their predicament was, it made for an inauspicious start.

Nor was life that easy on the domestic front. Though neurotically neat and tidy in his appearance, and a devil for detail in the office, Lane was disorderly and impulsive in his manner of living: he would roll up late (or not at all) for meetings, change his mind on a whim, fill Silverbeck with an ever-changing cast of people, and liked nothing better than to throw an impromptu party in the grounds. Throughout the war staff continued to work and even live at Silverbeck, particularly after Harmondsworth had been requisitioned by Lord - Beaverbrook's Ministry of Aircraft Production for the repair of fighter aircraft in 1941. 'Every time a stack of books was moved you'd find the fuselage of a Hurricane or a Spitfire, all bullet holes,' a veteran recalled: the warehouse and staff were moved to a building in West Drayton formerly occupied by the Rotary Photographic Company, a firm specializing in postcards of royalty, actresses and seaside resorts, but although editorial and production stayed put for a time, the noise was so unbearable that Bob Maynard, Frostie and Jean Osborne decamped to Silverbeck. June Pipe, who joined the firm in 1944 at the age of seventeen, used old Mrs Lane's dressing-table as a desk, arranged for her employer's shirts to be recollared and recuffed when required, and soon learnt to gauge his mood from the look in his eyes; Elizabeth Creak, another teenager who joined that year, remembered paying six shillings a week for communal lunches cooked by Lettice, who had never boiled an egg until she got married. Lane expected her to run his household efficiently and well, provide meals on time for as many people as might be around, bring up their children – Clare was born in April 1942, to be followed by Christine in 1944 and Anna in 1947 – and entertain the guests at their parties: but, clever and well-read as she was, he never asked her opinion on books, and she never attended meetings held at Silverbeck or set foot in Harmondsworth. Nor were his attempts at jocularity always benign. 'I want you to meet Lettice

Orr,' he told Bob Maynard, when the two men were on fire-watching duty together. 'The "W" is silent.'

Despite being called up, Dick and John kept in touch with Penguin affairs: Dick was given leave by the RNVR, who had no immediate call on his services, to visit Penguin's New York office in May 1940, while John, writing from HMS *Mollusc* later that year, worried about the American office and suggested giving W. H. Smith a 'solus' discount. But the Navy brought the two brothers together in a world from which Allen himself was, for once, entirely excluded. On their last voyage together, their ship was torpedoed, and after the order to abandon ship had been given John, immaculate as ever, insisted on returning to their cabin and changing into his best suit. Back on dry land, they went down to visit their parents, where, after lunch washed down with 'quite a few glasses of home-made wine', they got out the deckchairs and sat under a chestnut tree. 'After gazing idly at some magazines we both decided that a little shut-eye would be a very good thing,' Dick remembered.

I woke first and looked at John, who was still peacefully sleeping. And I thought of all that we had just been through together. Then I remembered early childhood days, happy times at Coombe Dingle, his world tour when he wrote us such amusing letters, the day when he and I moved from Talbot Square to Silverbeck, the occasion when we were at *King Alfred* and father came to dinner with us and John took him off on a tour of nightclubs, the day we joined the ship together, 'Lane Bros reporting for duty, Sir,' the monumental week in Ireland when Nora joined us, and then back to our last voyage . . .

Later that year, in November 1942, Dick was on leave at Silverbeck when a telegram arrived to say that John was missing, and presumed dead: his ship, the *Avenger*, had been sunk off the coast of North Africa while taking part in the landing of Allied troops; only four out of some 800 men had survived. Quite how Lane received the news remains uncertain. According to one version of events, Lane's father was the first to hear the news and rang Lettice, who then passed it on to her husband; according to another, Lane received the telegram, read it, folded it up, put it in his jacket pocket and then, without saying a word, went on talking to Bill Rapley, the London rep, about an order from Bumpus. John's death had a devastating effect on his eldest brother. Agatha Christie thought Lane 'loved John better than anyone in the world and when John was killed in the war Allen was inconsolable. For a time it seemed to change his character completely. He became in many ways unapproachable.' According to Morpurgo, Lane forgot his recent animosity towards his youngest brother, and thereafter 'encased himself in a spiritual armour which he hoped would keep him free from similarly generous relationships and from the consequent danger of suffering hurt'; for a time he took to 'solitary drinking', ate very little, and avoided looking at the baby Clare because she reminded him of John.

Lane's reserve, his combination of affability with unapproachability, a sense that even those he loved most could get so close but no closer, was remarked upon by all who knew him – including, much as they loved him, his daughters – and John's death accentuated this aspect of his character: as Lane himself once put it, 'I have got a little barrier around myself that I find very difficult to let anybody inside. People confide in me and I enjoy it and try to help them if I can, but I find it very hard to discuss anything which brings people into a very close relationship with me.' But he was not the only one to suffer from John's death. Dick, dependable as ever, was granted a temporary shore posting to enable him to sort out his dead brother's affairs, but his own survival was a permanent reminder of what had been lost. It was said that, in an unguarded moment, Lane blurted out that the wrong brother had been killed; and, however close they may have been in the past, he became increasingly irritated by Dick's torpid and cautious approach to life. Eager as ever to keep things in the family, Lane made Nora a 'temporary director' of Penguin while on his way to the States in 1944: but John's death marked the transition from youth to maturity, from the carefree, optimistic, uninhibited life of the pre-war years to the wary, more calculating wastes of early middle age. Nothing would ever be quite the same again.

9. Branching Out

One evening in June 1940, shortly after Dunkirk, Solly Zuckerman invited Allen Lane to a meeting of the Tots and Quots, a left-of-centre dining club devoted to discussing the interaction of science and society. The club had been founded in 1930, and its members included radical young scientists, often of a fashionably Marxist hue, such as J. D. 'Sage' Bernal, Lancelot Hogben, J. B. S. Haldane, C. H. Waddington, P. M. S. Blackett and J. Z. Young, economists like Roy Harrod and aspiring Labour politicians like Richard Crossman and Hugh Gaitskell. In the year of Munich, Bernal and Zuckerman had written a paper on the importance of mobilizing the full resources of the scientific world in the event of war, and at the June dinner – also attended by the ubiquitous Kenneth Clark – the diners returned to the attack, giving vent to their shared frustration at the Government's failure on this front. As they were preparing to leave, Lane expressed his regrets that no record had been made of the proceedings, since he sensed in the subject a useful and saleable Penguin Special. Zuckerman, rising to the bait, said that he could deliver a typescript within a fortnight if Lane could guarantee to publish within a fortnight of delivery. The deal was done, and although books with multiple contributors – twenty-five in the case of *Science in War* – usually move at the speed of the slowest, both men stuck to their promises. Tots and Quots and Penguin Books had, between them, made a valuable contribution to the war effort, and – putting theory into practice – both Zuckerman and Bernal went on to become scientific advisers to Lord Mountbatten.

One of the original members of Tots and Quots was V. Gordon Childe, a Professor in the Department of Prehistoric Archaeology at Edinburgh University who, egged on by Lane, wrote a bestselling Pelican on his academic speciality. 'I should love to appear flapping as a Penguin,' the Professor had confessed to H. L. Beales in October 1938. A year later Lane took him out to lunch at the Athenaeum and urged him to write a book. Progress was slow, but Lane persisted. The Clarendon Press, Childe told him two years later, had approached him about reprinting a series of lectures, 'but what I really want to do this time is to reach the much wider, more democratic circles that I imagine buy 6d. books and show such that archaeology is not after all so useless and dull'. The lure of the paperback prevailed, and Lane's hunch paid off: European prehistory may not have seemed the most seductive of subjects, but *What Happened in History* went on to sell over 500,000 copies.

Unlike the professor, H. G. Wells had no need to be coaxed from his lair. 'I think the Roman Catholic organization the most evil and dangerous thing in the world,' he told Lane in February 1943, when the extermination of the Jews was in full frenzy on the far side of the English Channel. 'If – after that warning – you ask me to put together a Penguin on that subject, I'll be quite ready to oblige.' Lane was happy to go ahead, and in *Crux Ansata*, his fourth Penguin Special, Wells gave vent to his 'intensely anti-Roman Catholic' prejudices. 'It is delightful to find one publisher exists who does not suffer from contagious cold feet,' the gratified author told Lane, but it was unlikely that Penguin would have spurned suggestions from Wells or Bernard Shaw, however eccentric. Wells's *The Rights of Man* was promoted as 'a handbook of World Revolution'; Shaw was an enthusiastic devotee of schemes for a simplified and rationalized spelling and alphabet, and left money in his will for the publishing of a bi-alphabetical edition of *Androcles and the Lion* which is unlikely to have sold a single copy as a Penguin paperback, though a hardback edition was distributed free to every public library.

In the meantime, Lancelot Hogben, another member of the Tots and Quots brigade, wrote to Lane in 1942 to announce that, as a contribution to a much-needed understanding among the nations, he had invented a new language: a mixture of Latin and Romanian, it had no grammar, was intelligible within a matter of hours, and could be mastered in a week. Hogben's bestselling *Mathematics for the Millions* and *Science for the Citizen* had been published by Allen

& Unwin, but (or so he assured Lane) they had not enough paper to take on his new project, entitled *Interglossa*. Hogben's proposal, Lane replied, 'has interested me more than any other that I can remember since I have been in publishing', and he hurried to sign it up before his old adversary came across a hidden cache of paper. Hogben proved a demanding and eccentric author, insisting on proofs in triplicate and heaping derision on the printers as they struggled to set material in a language hitherto unknown to man. 'These printing johnnies are confoundedly dilatory,' he told Lane, and to make matters worse 'they have some phoney idea about italics not being quite genteel'. Despite being temporarily over-whelmed by a tidal wave of author's corrections, amounting to 'six foolscap sheets', Hazell, Watson & Viney eventually printed 100,000 copies, plus a steady stream of erratum slips as baffled readers wrote in with queries and corrections. 'I am afraid *Interglossa* has not come up to our joint expectations, and we are finding it extremely diffi-cult to maintain any enthusiasm for it in the trade,' Lane told the disappointed linguist when declining a planned Interglossa–English dictionary. Stanley Unwin, who had made a show of indignation when his author briefly defected to Penguin, was no doubt mightily relieved to have dodged the issue, and delighted at his rival's discom-fiture; Lane, ever the professional publisher, muttered his customary mantra about 'swings and roundabouts', whereby profitable and strong-selling titles subsidize less successful books, before quickly moving on to other things.

Literary magazines are famously unprofitable, depending for their survival on the support of philanthropic millionaires and a tiny, dedicated staff prepared to work for next to nothing, and Lane's readiness to subsidize worthwhile ventures from profits made else-where was never more evident than in his backing for John Lehmann's *Penguin New Writing*: it became more grudging and intermittent as idealism fought a losing battle with the demands of commerce, but it lasted ten years, an eternity in the short-lived world of literary magazines, and enabled Lehmann to edit one of the finest maga-zines of the century, and one which, in the early years at least, made a valuable contribution to turnover and profits. Lane's dealings with

John Lehmann dated back to his days at The Bodley Head, but it was never an easy association. Some five years younger than Lane, a product of Eton and Trinity, Cambridge, at home in Bloomsbury and Garsington Manor, a friend (uneasily, at times) of Auden, Spender and Isherwood, waspish, touchy, ambitious and uncompromisingly homosexual, Lehmann was calculated to arouse Lane's dormant feelings of social, educational and literary inadequacy, and was far from a kindred spirit; but he was also a brilliant and dedicated editor of the kind that Lane valued and admired.

Tall and fair-haired, with the aquiline features of an ill-tempered eagle, Lehmann spent much of the Thirties in Weimar Germany and then in Vienna, combining a theoretical adherence to left-wing politics with the keen pursuit of boys in lederhosen; and it was while he was in Berlin, shortly before the Nazis came to power, that he first discussed with Isherwood the possibility of his starting a magazine, modelled partly on *The Yellow Book*, which would publish long short stories, poems and non-fiction pieces that were either too long or too uncategorizable for more conventional outlets. Isherwood urged him to press ahead, and promised his support; as did Denys Kilham Roberts, his co-editor of *The Year's Poetry*, who suggested he should approach their publisher at The Bodley Head. Lane and Lindsay Drummond eventually agreed to publish *New Writing* on a twice-yearly basis, paying an advance of £60 per issue to cover editorial and contributors' costs: it would be published in hardback, and contain around 150,000 words. '*New Writing* is first and foremost interested in literature, and though it does not intend to open its pages to writers of reactionary or fascist sentiments, it is independent of any political party,' Lehmann famously declared in his opening editorial. Such sentiments chimed with the spirit of the age; and, like the Penguins which were launched that same year, the magazine was intended to 'bridge the gap between the middle-class, well-educated world and the less fortunate working-class world'. It was, Lehmann recalled in later years, 'a spirit, a near-revolutionary mood of the time I was after; something anti-mandarin, anti-establishment in both style and outlook'. Lehmann was as good as his word: among the items included in the three issues of *New Writing* published by The Bodley Head were Auden's 'Lay Your Sleeping Head' and Orwell's 'Shooting an Elephant', as well as contributions from Louis MacNeice, E. M. Forster, V. S. Pritchett, Edward Upward, Berthold Brecht and Ignazio Silone. 'George Orwell's story of the shooting of the elephant is, I think, particularly fine,' Lane informed the editor; but by then his own energies were concentrated on setting up Penguin, and The Bodley Head was slipping from his grasp.

Lehmann was gratified by the excellent reviews of the second number – 'thus giving the lie to the gloomier forebodings of Drummond and others in your office' – but modest sales and new ownership of The Bodley Head put paid to the connection. The next three numbers were published by Lawrence & Wishart, the Communist publishers; a further three, confusingly entitled the New Series, were then brought out under the auspices of Leonard and Virginia Woolf's Hogarth Press, where Lehmann had recently become a partner and half-owner. Unconvinced by Lehmann's claim that publishing *New Writing* attracted new and young authors to the Hogarth Press, Leonard Woolf disliked having to publish the magazine, on the grounds that it lost him money, and No. 3 of the New Series, published on the outbreak of war, seemed to mark the end of a brave if erratic literary adventure.

One immediate result of the outbreak of war, akin to the closing of theatres and the removal of Old Masters to Welsh caves, was the sudden death of various well-known literary magazines, including T. S. Eliot's *Criterion*, Geoffrey Grigson's *New Verse*, Julian Symons's *Twentieth-Century Verse* and the *London Mercury*. No sooner had they announced their demise than others – sensing, like Lane, that war brought with it a hunger for culture – hurried to plug the gap: the most famous of these was Cyril Connolly's monthly *Horizon*, briefly co-edited by Stephen Spender and funded by Peter Watson, an art-loving margarine millionaire, but others included George Woodcock's *Now* and Tambimuttu's *Poetry (London)*; before long they would be joined by the most successful of them all, edited by John Lehmann under the Penguin umbrella. Once again, a shortage of paper was combined with a seemingly insatiable demand: George

Woodcock bought his paper on the black market, and reckoned that whereas before the war he would have done well to sell 700 copies per issue, wartime sales of *Now* hovered between 3,000 and 4,000; *Horizon*, launched in the nick of time, escaped the ban on new magazines, while *Penguin New Writing* passed itself off as an integral part of Penguin's book publishing programme, and had access to Penguin's relatively generous paper quota.

In the early years of the war, Lane read John Lehmann's pamphlet 'New Writing in England' – itself published to coincide with his *Folios of New Writing*, a 'lean war substitute' for the discontinued New Series – and suggested that it should be expanded into *New Writing in Europe*; and in May 1940 he floated the idea of a new monthly magazine. The original idea was to reproduce, in paperback form, the best of the material already published in *New Writing*'s various incarnations, but after the two men had met for 'an extremely harmonious and sanguine discussion', it was agreed that the new magazine should eventually consist of new material, specially written or commissioned, and amounting to some 60,000 words per issue. The details were, Lehmann later recalled, settled at 'incredible speed': this was, as other 'outside' editors would soon discover, very typical of Lane; they might, in due course, feel abandoned or betrayed if Lane lost interest or decided to cut his losses, but in the early stages at least he was an exemplary publisher, quick and decisive in giving a new project his full support, and, while keeping a keen eye on the financial and business implications, happy to let his chosen editor get on with the job with the minimum of interference. Lehmann submitted a curious CV to Eunice Frost, in which he described himself as, among other qualifications for the job, 'an authority on the international control of the Danube'; striking a more relevant note, he told Lane that he had 'the advantage of backing something you know is good and not too highbrow'. Stephen Spender, who had recently resigned from *Horizon*, was happy to be involved, as was Lehmann's sister Rosamond: all in all, 'I think I can say without boasting that the three of us could produce a magazine to beat anything of the sort in England.' Spender, anxious to keep a foot in both camps and reluctant to give offence to either Connolly or Lehmann, tied himself in knots and agonized aloud, but Lane was more decisive. 'I have no hesitation in saying "go ahead" with the scheme as fast as you like,' he told Lehmann in October 1940. He was prepared to pay an advance of £75 per issue, to cover Lehmann's own labours and secretarial help, as well as contributors' fees: 'if the sales exceed our expectations and we can afford to pay a higher advance', he would be happy to do so, and it was increased to £150 after Volume 3. Bearing the contributors in mind, he was prepared to allow thirty free copies rather than the customary six, and to commit himself to publish 'one issue each month, and in no case allow the interval to be more than six weeks' – though (and here the cautious publisher intervened) 'it might be dangerous to commit myself to a definite contract for this in these uncertain times'.

Averting his gaze from Lane's caveat, Lehmann hurried to put his plans into practice. Spender agreed to write a regular column on 'The Way We Live Now' and look after book reviews, G. W. Stonier discussed the pleasures of 'Shaving through the Blitz', and approaches were made to, among others, V. S. Pritchett and George Orwell. The original plan for a paperback selection of reprinted *New Writing* pieces was published in December 1940, and the first issue of *Penguin New Writing* appeared a month later. It sold 80,000 copies; Volumes 2 and 3 sold 55,000 each, and sales peaked at 100,000 just after the end of the war. Without the sales support of a major publishing house, Cyril Connolly's *Horizon* never sold more than a tenth as many copies, starting out with sales of 3,500, doubling them the following month, and peaking at 10,000 in 1947. The two magazines shared readers and contributors, engaged in friendly if wary competition, helped sustain literary life, and provided solace and pleasure to soldiers and civilians alike: though less remembered and less liked than Connolly, Lehmann was, perhaps, the finer and bolder editor, and among those he published in *PNW* were newcomers like Julian Maclaren-Ross, Denton Welch, William Sansom, Alan Ross, Lawrence Durrell, Saul Bellow and James Michie, alongside such established writers as Graham Greene, Elizabeth Bowen and Henry Green.

Lehmann's hopes of monthly publication were soon in doubt as paper shortages and the bombing and disruption of printers and binders began to take effect. 'It is only fair to tell you that what I have in mind at the moment is making *Penguin New Writing* a quarterly publication in place of the present monthly basis,' Lane told him only two months after the magazine had been launched. Lehmann was understandably upset. 'I was rather surprised to find you sounding a note of discouragement about *PNW*, considering how short a while ago you spoke of it with enthusiasm and confidence,' he replied. Making it a quarterly would be 'a real disaster for both of us. To abandon a monthly after only six months must appear to the public as a real admission of failure.' A brief respite was offered by Bill Williams, who spoke to Lane and then wrote to say that 'it would be absurd to alter things at this stage. Lane's decision, which I think will be final, was to continue on the monthly basis for at least twelve months and then perhaps reconsider . . . He is perfectly satisfied with *PNW*, both from the prestige and financial points of view: his only uncertainty was whether he could reasonably spare so much paper for one enterprise.'

Despite a letter from Lane in June 1941 in which he told Lehmann that a friend who spent time 'among dockside workers tells me she hears *New Writing* being spoken of constantly in terms of the highest praise' – a pleasing notion, though more reminiscent of Soviet propaganda than of everyday life in Liverpool or Rotherhithe – Lane was forced to renege on his promises; and, as was so often the case, he did his best to avert his gaze, or leave it to others to break the bad news. 'I hope you won't think me disagreeable if I say that I find it increasingly hard to carry out my job as editor of *Penguin New Writing* while I am kept so completely in the dark about the publication date each month,' Lehmann protested, while at the same time urging Lane to buy the rights in F. M. Mayor's melancholy masterpiece *The Rector's Daughter*, recently published by the Hogarth Press. In December that year, by which time the paper quota had been reduced from 42 per cent to 37.5 per cent, Lane decreed that from now on the magazine would be a quarterly. Lehmann was shocked by Lane's letter, which 'seemed entirely in contradiction to everything you have said to me'. 'Why don't we have lunch together some time and talk about it a little less hurriedly?' he suggested, almost certainly in vain. But the news was not all bad. Lane had promised that he would contemplate increasing the number of pages, and this he now honoured; he also agreed to include a section of black-and-white photogravure illustrations, devoted for the most part to ballet and theatre productions and the work of neo-romantic artists like Graham Sutherland, John Piper, John Craxton, Keith Vaughan, Michael Ayrton and Leonard Rosoman, and Bob Maynard's rather amateurish lettering jackets were replaced by stylish John Minton woodcuts, with typography to match. Colour illustrations followed in 1945, and better paper was made available; a long-postponed meeting between the two men left Lehmann 'impressed by your keenness to make *Penguin New Writing the* literary and artistic magazine for this country, and *the* cultural ambassador for abroad'. Lane was equally reassuring when, in 1945, Tom Hopkinson suggested that American magazines, with their large format and colour illustrations, represented the way forward. Lehmann was half-persuaded by his arguments, but Lane seemed unconvinced:

American magazines concentrated far too much on 'flashy presentation', and, as far as *PNW* was concerned, 'I think we should make up our own minds on what meets with our approval and stick to it, as I think our standards are sufficiently high to make this a good criterion.'

Brave words indeed; but as the magazine's circulation dropped away from its peak of 100,000 copies in 1945 to 80,000 by 1947, 40,000 by 1949 and 25,000 each for the last two issues, it became harder to match deeds with rhetoric. 'I liked a great deal of what was in *New Writing*, and I have to a certain extent basked in reflected glory,' Lane wrote. 'Hard facts, however, must have their place in this unholy business of publishing, and with the many difficulties which I see ahead, I think it is fairer to all concerned to clear our minds of delusions and face these facts now.' In November 1946 Lehmann reluctantly agreed to quarterly publication, but in January 1947 he was told that *PNW* would now be appearing three times a year; in between, convinced that the end was imminent, he wrote to Lane lamenting the demise of 'a venture that looked as if it was going to change the whole nature of literary periodical publications, and was recognized as a big cultural bulwark in an age when the breakers are dashing so violently against the walls'. 'I do hope you will be able to let me have a word about this new turn in Dr Lane's view of the patient, my little child,' an unexpectedly saccharine Lehmann told Frostie. 'His strength is very low, and he keeps on asking his Daddy in a faint voice whether it wouldn't be better to send for another doctor. Naturally his Daddy is unwilling to do so, as long as the old family practitioner has a prescription or two up his sleeve.' Such glutinous whimsicality was unavailing. The length of the magazine was reduced to 128 pages in 1949, and Lehmann was told that the most he could hope for was twice-yearly publication. He was, he told Lane, already losing money by editing the magazine, in that it left little time for his own writing and he had to pay his assistant, Barbara Cooper; and now he would be even worse off. 'I am devoted to the little magazine, with its romantic wartime fortunes, but I am not so well off that I can face with equanimity supporting my (and your) child out of my own pocket,' he told Lane. Cyril Connolly's *Horizon* was about to go under – he had recently offered it to Lehmann 'at a reduced price' over a bottle of champagne at the Athenaeum – and 'it seems particularly wrong when *Horizon* is collapsing that a literary magazine, one of the very few left, still badly needed, with a circulation four or five times *Horizon*'s, should follow it'. But nothing could postpone the evil moment, and *Penguin New Writing* followed *Horizon* to the grave in the autumn of 1950, after the publication of the fortieth issue. When Frostie wrote to ask for his comments on the end of *PNW* for a forthcoming issue of *Penguins Progress*, Lane scribbled on the bottom of her letter that he had nothing to say 'except tears, idle tears'. 'It is the worst loss so far, and for the greatest number of people,' Stephen Spender declared. However unappealing in person, Lehmann had been an incomparable editor, and *PNW* remains one of the great literary magazines, along with *Horizon*, *Encounter* and Alan Ross's *London Magazine*, founded by Lehmann in 1955; and although, in the end, he had to play the killjoy role of the money-minded proprietor, Lane deserves huge credit for supporting it for as long as he did.

Both men had much to be proud of in *Penguin New Writing*, but although book publishers have often been tempted into magazine publishing, gratified by the speed of production and a more immediate impact on the literary, cultural and political scene, books and magazines have such different gestation periods and are sold in such different ways that the experiment seldom works. Penguin Specials, written to supplement and expand upon the news, and published within weeks rather than months, may have given Lane a taste for magazine publishing which it took time to expel from his system. *Penguin New Writing* was the most durable and distinguished runner in his stable, but other wartime and post-war contestants were published, albeit – to the frustration of their editors – in a sporadic and seemingly *ad hoc* manner.

The brainchild of the ubiquitous Moura Budberg, the former mistress of H. G. Wells and Maxim Gorky, *Russian Review* mirrored changing attitudes towards the Soviet Union as the Cold War replaced wartime enthusiasm for kindly 'Uncle Joe' Stalin. In October 1944, as the Russian army was advancing into Germany, Lane, Frostie, Bill Williams, Count Benckendorff and Baroness Budberg met and agreed to publish at least three issues of the magazine. The second issue contained a long piece about Polish prison camps; though recently returned from the Nuremberg Trials, Lane felt that 'everybody has had enough of this "death camp" business, and the sooner we all block it out of our minds, the better for everybody'. By early 1946, Lane was losing heart. He had, he confessed to the Count, embarked on the magazine on a 'somewhat idealistic basis', but sales were 'fairly catastrophic', with 4,000 of the 25,000 copies of the most recent issue winging their way back from the shops. Tempers flared – Bill Williams reporting that 'the Baroness stormed in on me yesterday' – and the Count was replaced by the journalist Edward Crankshaw. But to no avail: at the end of 1947 Lane told Crankshaw that they had come to the end of the road, for 'with the present feeling regarding Russia there really was no alternative'.

Post-war Penguin magazines included the *Penguin Film Review*, edited by Roger Manvell, which boasted Michael Balcon, Basil Wright, Anthony Asquith and Michael Powell among its contributors but lacked both advertising and bookshop support, and was closed down after nine issues despite regular sales of 25,000 per issue; the *Penguin Music Magazine*, published sporadically between 1946 and 1949, and featuring work by Neville Cardus and John Barbirolli; and the quarterly *Penguin Science News*, suggested by C. H. Waddington of the Tots and Quots at a time when few national newspapers had science correspondents, which was published between 1946 and 1960 but was eventually rendered redundant by the rise of the *New Scientist* and *Scientific American*. But whereas they all adhered to the conventional Penguin book format, *Transatlantic* represented a very different foray into magazine publishing: it looked far more like a slightly smaller version of *New Yorker* or the short-lived *Night and Day*, and had the inestimable advantage of appearing on a regular monthly basis between 1943 and 1946. Designed to explain our new American allies to the British public, it carried advertisements, was enlivened by a four-colour *New Yorker*-style jacket, changed for every issue, and was initially edited by the economist Geoffrey Crowther, who had a lifelong interest in Anglo-American relations and had, since 1938, been the editor of *The Economist*. The first issue carried pieces by D. W. Brogan, William Saroyan and Paul Gallico, and later contributors included Alistair Cooke, John dos Passos and the New Zealand writer Janet Flanner.

Full-colour jackets of the kind flaunted by *Transatlantic* would prove a bone of contention on both sides of the Atlantic in the years to come, but in one area of the Penguin empire at least they were never seen as a problem. The youngest brother of the painter Dora Carrington, Noël Carrington was, like Lehmann, a veteran of the Bloomsbury world; but whereas Lehmann, with his ice-blue eyes and petulant manner, was a daunting figure – so much so that he was sometimes likened, unkindly, to an SS officer – Carrington was a good deal more amiable and easy-going. His sister thought him 'almost as beautiful as Rupert Brooke', though she worried that he was 'so governed by conventions and accepts the "public school" opinions'. He had rowed for Christ Church, and worked for OUP in India; Kathleen Hale, best remembered for Orlando the Marmalade Cat, recalled him as 'a fine figure of a man, tall and distinguished. He had lost the use of his right arm in the 1914 war. He had always lived in the country and dressed accordingly, in a rather "arty" style, in faded and scrupulously clean blue shirts, corduroys washed until they were pastel shades, brightly coloured socks, and very shabby brown walking shoes or even shabbier check bedroom slippers. I was never to see him in a collar and tie or city suit, whatever the occasion.'

Noël Carrington would have worn a tie, and probably a suit as well, when he and Lane first met, at that meeting of the Double Crown Club at which John Holroyd-Reece had galloped to Penguin's defence. He was then, among other duties, the Chairman of the Design and Industries Association – he had a keen interest in practical design, and years later pressed for the use of lower-case lettering on motorway signs – and when the meeting broke up Lane asked him if he'd like to write a Pelican Special on the subject. He declined, recommending Anthony Bertram instead, but the connection had been made. When not pondering the shape of things to come, Carrington worked on the book publishing side of *Country Life*; he was present when Orlando the Marmalade Cat was born, and published the celebrated *High Street*, with a text by J. M. Richards and illustrations by Eric Ravilious.

With three children of his own to educate – one of whom had had polio and had to be taught at home – Carrington found himself brooding on children's books of the informational variety. Eager to stimulate their interest in natural history and the man-made world around them, and to use illustrators rather than photographers, he was already much taken with the French Père Castor series of illustrated children's books when Pearl Binder drew his attention to an inexpensive and brightly coloured series of Russian children's books produced by auto-lithography. Whereas conventional colour printing involved photographing a painter's artwork three or four times through different filters, auto-lithography was cheaper and, ideally, produced a finished object far closer to the artist's original, in that the artist drew his own colour separations directly on to the stone or lithographic plate, so cutting out the expense of camera work and the possible distortions of mechanical separation. Days before Lane set out on his pre-war tour of Aden, India and Ceylon, he had lunch with Carrington, who suggested a series of cheap children's books, rather along the lines of *How Aeroplanes Fly*, which he had just published at *Country Life*. Lane told him in less than a minute that he liked the idea, suggested that Carrington should do some costings to find out how many they would need to print in order to publish at 6d., and set off on his travels. Carrington continued his investigations into auto-lithography with the printer Geoffrey Smith of W. S. Cowell in Ipswich, but heard no more from Penguin until, early in 1940, Lane rang to say that the war had made such books more necessary than ever, and that he was keen to press ahead. Newnes, the new owners of *Country Life*, told Carrington that 'There's no money in sixpennies' and, greatly relieved, he felt free to accept Lane's offer: like Lehmann and the other outside editors employed by Penguin, Carrington was never a member of staff, and for much of the war he worked part-time for John Murray in Albemarle Street.

Landscape in format, and sporting a puffin drawn by Bob Maynard, the first Puffin Picture Books were published later that same year. The first three titles – *The War on Land*, *The War at Sea* and *The War in the Air* – had a topical edge, and in due course David Garnett described *The Battle of Britain*, but thereafter the series concentrated, for the most part, on natural history and arts and crafts. Subjects surveyed included insects, wild flowers, stamps and fireworks; among the artists commissioned for the series were Edward Bawden, Enid Marx and C. F. Tunnicliffe. Bernard Venables explained the mysteries of *Fish and Fishing*, E. G. Boulenger, the Curator of the Aquarium at the London Zoo, revealed *The Wonders of Sea Life*, Harold Curwen of the Curwen Press pronounced on *Printing*, and Gordon Russell, the pioneer of modernist furniture design and one of those responsible for wartime Utility furniture, told *The Story of Furniture*.

Once a fortnight Carrington visited Lane at Harmondsworth, Silverbeck or, since his own farm in Hampshire was no distance away, Priory Farm. Far from being a blasé tycoon, Lane displayed all the childlike interest and enthusiasm which, it was hoped, the series would arouse in its readers. According to Carrington, he loved to escape from the office, playing truant 'like a schoolboy ready to take the day off'; he liked to discuss artists' work with them, making them feel that, however modest the rewards, it was a privilege and a pleasure to work for Penguin. He insisted on the books being as accurate as possible, drawing on his own expertise when it came to the cattle and farm buildings displayed in *On the Farm*: when, in 1946, James Gardner revised his illustrations, both Allen and Dick, by now more experienced farmers, had forceful views on the matter, Allen finding his drawing of a milking machine 'rather confused', while Dick noted that 'the plough is an old-fashioned type without tripping gear'. Dick was asked for his views on *About a Motor Car*, and produced a detailed critique of sodium valves, gudgeon pins and cylinder heads, while Baroness Budberg pointed out, apropos *Waterways of the World*, that the Rhine ran through four countries rather than three. When Carrington showed Lane Paxton Chadwick's watercolours for *Wild Flowers*, he displayed all the enthusiasm of an old-fashioned schoolboy. 'But this is absolutely tops!' he cried. 'Who is this chap? Of course we must do it.' Carrington pointed out that Chadwick insisted on having colour on every page rather than alternate openings, that he wanted an extra colour, grey, to be used for the shadows, and that his book should not be more expensive than others in the series. The production manager had declared this to be impossible. 'Nonsense,' Lane said. 'Nothing is too good for Penguins. We will double the print to bring the cost down. Bring this chap along to our next meeting. I want to see him!' Lane must have prevailed over the doubters, since Chadwick went on to produce *Wild Animals in Britain* and *Pond Life*. Nor would Lane be dictated to by the sales department: he valued their views, and relished their support, but saw them, like accountants, as servants of the firm who should never be allowed to dictate policy or decide what should or should not be published. When booksellers were consulted about what eventually became one of the most successful of all Puffin Picture Books, the anatomically explicit *The Human Body*, they were both shocked and gravely pessimistic: mild enough by modern standards, it took ten years to find its way into print, and sold in huge quantities.

Published under Carrington's aegis, Kathleen Hale's *Orlando's Evening Out* was the first 'fictional' Puffin Picture Book, and it was not long before Penguin started to publish full-length children's books under the Puffin imprint. Eleanor Graham, its originator, was a veteran of the children's book world. Her first children's book had been published in 1925; two years later she started work in the children's book department of Bumpus, the legendary Oxford Street bookshop, and she began to review children's books for the *Sunday Times* in 1934. In the early days of Penguins, Lane talked to her about starting a children's list, and they saw eye to eye about the kind of list they wanted. Neither was interested in merely reprinting out of copyright classics; both believed that a Penguin children's list should, like its adult equivalent, publish the very best work that was then being written, the classics of the future; both were swayed by childhood memories of W. T. Stead's *Books for the Bairns*. Eleanor Graham was working at the Board of Trade when the war broke out, and in the autumn of 1940, at the height of the Blitz, Lane rang her to say that he was now ready to start a Puffin list, and invited her down to Harmondsworth. She arrived at Hounslow West station in the middle of an air-raid, was told by the ticket collector that someone from Penguin was waiting for her in the pub opposite, and was driven to Silverbeck under a hail of flak. German bombers were as nothing to the opposition of the children's book world. Librarians, teachers and the hardback publishers were united in their hostility to the very notion of paperbacks for children; even Jonathan Cape was adamant in his refusal to sub-lease the rights in *Swallows and Amazons* and the other Arthur Ransome titles, or the Dr Dolittle books. Unfazed by the opposition, Lane and Eleanor Graham pressed ahead. The first batch of Puffin Story Books was published in 1941, and included Barbara Euphan Todd's *Worzel Gummidge*; another steady seller, Eve Garnett's *The Family from One End Street*, was among those published in the following year. The early Puffins were, Eleanor Graham remembered, 'thin little books, not at all impressive, with red and white covers and an ad for Kiltie shoes on the back'; but however modest their earliest manifestations, they pioneered a reading revolution, and although they came to be associated, above all, with the glamorous and flamboyant figure of Kaye Webb, it was Eleanor Graham who set the wheels in motion.

Like the *Radio Times, Lilliput*, Shell, London Transport and innumerable advertisements for cigarettes, stout and petrol, Puffins and Puffin Picture Books provided invaluable outlets for British artists and illustrators; and the British genius for painting, so long decried and undervalued, was celebrated in a new Penguin series, published at a time when art-lovers were cut off from the Continent and better disposed than usual to home-grown products. 'For some time I have been interested in trying to do the same sort of work for the modern British artist as we have been doing for their opposite numbers, the authors,' Lane wrote to Kenneth Clark in June 1942. As Chairman of the War Artists Advisory Committee, responsible for commissioning painters to cover every aspect of the war, and Controller of Home Publicity at the Ministry of Information, Clark was already thinking along similar lines: proclaiming the virtues of British artists helped boost morale on the home front and the image of Britain overseas, and coincided with a yearning, part patriotic and part escapist, for the music of Elgar and Vaughan Williams, for poets and writers who celebrated the English countryside and a lost Arcadia of country houses and Trollopian cathedral closes.

Pre-war art books had been long, cumbrous affairs, horribly expensive and designed for the art historian and not the lay reader: what Lane had in mind was a paperback series, in landscape format, priced at half-a-crown each and carrying an introduction by a well-known writer; and whereas OUP had earlier published a series of booklets at a shilling each, carrying a mere eight pages of mono-chrome illustrations, his would be illustrated half in colour and half in black-and-white. Clark had earlier suggested, through Bill Williams, that the 'Art for the People' scheme should be converted into book form, and he happily rose to Lane's bait. 'I was very much excited by your proposal of doing Penguin monographs on painters, and I could not help thinking how I would enjoy editing the series myself,' he told Lane – though 'you may feel I could not give enough time to it, and you would rather have an editor whom you could hustle'. In the event, most of the hard work was done by Eunice Frost, heavily laden as she was with editing Pelican ori-ginals, ploughing through new novels and soothing John Lehmann's brow: her health was already being undermined by overwork, so much so that Bill Williams told her to take some rest 'instead of carrying Penguin on your resolute and overburdened shoulders – take it easy, Frostie my love, or I'll beat hell out of you . . .' It was up to her to chivvy the authors, negotiate with the painters, deal with the owners of the paintings, keep tabs on the pictures them-selves – Clark allowed her to use the National Gallery to store paint-ings in transit between owners and blockmakers – and nudge the books into print. Each artist was paid £100, and was expected to provide Lane himself with a painting, so enabling him to build up a superb collection of contemporary British art: introducers were paid £50, and Clark himself received £50 for each new title commis-sioned. This was far too much, he protested. 'The greater part of the work has been done by Miss Frost,' he told Lane, and he had done little more than suggest artists and writers, choose the pictures and check the proofs. More than once he asked to have his name removed from the series. A year or two later Lane told Bernhard Baer, the editor of the short-lived series of Penguin Prints, that 'the firm is now so well known for the quality of its productions that anonymity of the editors, as is done with the correspondents of *The Times*, not only gives strength to the enterprise, but if anything enhances the value of the particular editor or correspondent': but rules are made to be broken, Clark's name carried more weight than most, and Lane had no intention of losing it.

The new series was called Penguin Modern Painters: 'If there are people who are put off by this title because they think Penguin is publishing a series of books on house painters, they would probably be too simple-minded for our books anyway,' Clark told Frostie, who was briefly worried by the title. The opening number, Geoffrey Grigson introducing a selection of Henry Moore's work, was published in April 1944. Nineteen titles would be published in the series over the next fifteen years, including John Betjeman on John Piper, Raymond Mortimer on Duncan Grant, Herbert Read on Paul Nash, Philip Hendy on Matthew Smith, Edward Sackville-West on Graham Sutherland, J. M. Richards on Edward Bawden, Clive Bell on Victor Pasmore, John Rothenstein on Edward Burra, and Eric Newton on Stanley Spencer. Not everything ran smoothly: Clark was not keen to include abstract artists, doing battle with Herbert Read about the inclusion of Ben Nicholson, and reluctantly giving way, while R. B. Fishenden, the great authority on colour printing, was baffled by modern art of any kind. Clark opposed the decision to include Klee and Braque, and used this as an excuse to withdraw from the series. 'The old scheme seemed to me valuable because it helped people to understand painters whose work they could buy, and it thereby helped the painters. I remember that this was in Allen Lane's mind when he first proposed it,' he told Frostie. (Lane's attitude may well have reflected the influence of Lettice, who liked to support young and indigent writers and painters, and made a point of only buying works by artists who were alive and needed the money.) Clark felt that painters like Braque were already well known and widely admired, and 'whether there is really any point in introducing the people of South Shields, at this late hour, to Matisse and Picasso, I am far from certain'. Competition to Penguin Modern Painters soon manifested itself in the form of Kurt Maschler's Faber Gallery and, in due course, the co-editions pioneered by Walter Neurath at Thames & Hudson and Bela Horovitz at Phaidon; but the series had served to introduce the work of its subjects to an entire generation, and survived, intermittently, into the 1960s. 'They are an extraordinary example of what can be done with a little courage, enterprise and good will,' Kenneth Clark told Lane after four titles had appeared, and after he resigned from the editorship in 1946 he wrote to say that it had done 'a great service to modern painting'. Like *Penguin New Writing*, Penguin Modern Painters was a memorable manifestation of the idealism and ingenuity of Penguin at war.

10. The New Jerusalem

'London certainly seems to have caught a hell of a packet,' John Lane wrote to his eldest brother in November 1940, at the height of the Blitz, 'but I am hoping that there will be a silver lining to that cloud and that it will lead to a remodelled city – what a marvellous Pelican to publish on Armistice Day.' He never lived to see VE Day, let alone the New Towns or the Green Belt or the Festival Hall, or any of those other innovations, all too often redolent of rusting concrete and windswept, litter-strewn public spaces, whereby the post-war Labour government sought to realize wartime dreams of a sunlit, brand-new, egalitarian England in which planners prevailed, poverty was abolished, and a happy, culture-loving citizenry marched confidently into the future: but he voiced sentiments which Penguin Books would both reflect and reinforce. Or, as Lane himself put it in his letter to Elsa Lanchester, written earlier that year, he would, where Penguin Specials were concerned, be switching the emphasis from international affairs to 'discussing the possibility of a new world order when this mess is over'.

Although it would be absurd to claim that the entire nation, and not least its thinking classes, lurched to the left during the war – Evelyn Waugh and Anthony Powell were two obvious exceptions to the rule – people from very different political backgrounds were united in a belief that there should be a larger role for the state in the ordering of post-war Britain, and that society should be seen in 'organic' or 'holistic' terms; and such ideas, and their partial implementation once the war was over, would form the basis of the 'consensus' or 'Butskellite' politics that were shared by both the major political parties and prevail until their demolition at the hands of Sir Keith Joseph and Mrs Thatcher. Those who subscribed to such collectivist notions came from across the political spectrum. Some, like T. S. Eliot, were Christians, placing their trust in an ordered, hierarchical society of duties and obligations; some, like R. A. Butler and Harold Macmillan, were what became known as 'one-nation' Tories, heirs to Disraeli, fiercely opposed to the harsh, uncaring views of Manchester Liberalism, eager to embrace those of Lords Keynes and Beveridge, and to distance the Conservative Party from images of the dole queue and the hunger march; some were statists, anxious for the state to intervene in every aspect of life, some libertarians, some Communists, some cranks, some – the great majority, perhaps – of no fixed views beyond a desire not to return to the 'bad old days', and a vague, benign belief that the war should be fought in a good cause on the home as well as the international front.

As always, war was a great leveller. German bombers made no distinction between rich and poor, and neither did conscription, evacuation or the ration book; servants vanished from the social scene; the air-raid and the air-raid shelter were, in A. J. P. Taylor's words, 'a powerful solvent of social antagonisms'. This was, it was said at the time, a 'people's war', and although class distinctions remained firmly in place, there was a sense in which the country was united by sacrifice, and more open than ever before to egalitarian notions, irrespective of political party. As George Orwell declared in *The Lion and the Unicorn*, 'Progress and reaction are ceasing to have anything to do with party labels. If one wishes to name a particular moment, one can say that the old distinction between Left and Right broke down when *Picture Post* was first published. What are the politics of *Picture Post*? Or of *Cavalcade*, or Priestley's broadcasts, or the leading articles in the *Evening Standard*? None of the old classifications will fit them.'

Dunkirk, the fall of France, the replacing of the discredited Neville Chamberlain as Prime Minister by Winston Churchill, and the participation of the Labour Party, led by Clement Attlee, in a Coalition government, all contributed to a new readiness among politicians to consider ideas that had hitherto been the preserve of radical journalists, idealistic writers and impractical academics. Conveniently forgetting their pre-war enthusiasm for pacifism and disarmament, left-wing politicians and theorists blamed military defeats on the 'old gang' associated with the 'men of Munich' and the Cliveden Set and, by implication, with all that was most benighted, selfish and socially undesirable in the old Conservative Party (and, indeed, the old social order). Harold Laski suggested that the price of Labour participation in a Coalition government should be a commitment to what came to be known as 'reconstruction', or the building of a 'New Jerusalem'. In the days after Dunkirk, the Ministry of Information's Home Morale Committee recommended a 'statement on peace principles', while the Ministry's Director-General declared that 'the opportunity should be taken of an all-party government to make some promises as to social reforms after the war', and that 'our aim should be to redress grievances and inequalities and create new opportunities'. Ever alert to the mood of the moment, Harold Nicolson, a National Labour MP, announced that 'we should proclaim that we intend to make a better world at home in which the abuses of the past shall not be allowed to re-appear. Unemployment, education, housing and the abolition of privilege should form the main planks of such a platform.'

Churchill himself was indifferent to, and occasionally irritated by, such subversive notions, but his eagerness not to be distracted from saving the country from invasion by Hitler, and then winning the war, left ample opportunities for those more concerned with life on the domestic front. In July 1940, shortly before the Battle of Britain, the War Cabinet instructed Duff Cooper, the then Minister of Information, to set up the War Aims Committee to 'consider means of perpetuating the national unity achieved during the war through a social and economic structure designed to secure equality of opportunity and service among all classes of the community'. Touring the country that same year, J. B. Priestley found that although the war itself was inevitably the prime topic of conversation, the second 'was always the New World after the war. What could we do to bring our economic and social system nearer to justice and security and decency? That was the great question.' Before long 'reconstruction' was itself a 'war aim'. According to Laski, 'the way to victory lies in producing the conviction now among the masses that there are to be no more distressed areas, no

more vast armies of unemployed, no more slums, no vast denials
of genuine equality of educational opportunity'. And whereas many
of his fellow-writers from the Thirties had abandoned the political
struggle – Auden and Isherwood had famously decamped to America
shortly before the outbreak of war, while Cyril Connolly, never the
most political of men, was urging his colleagues in the pages of
Horizon to ignore the war as far as they could, to cultivate their art
and not allow their talents to be wasted or diluted by propaganda
work for the BBC or the Ministry of Information – John Lehmann
reflected the mood of the moment in his editorial for the March
1941 issue of *Penguin New Writing*. 'A new consciousness is stirring,
both among those who have joined the armed forces and those who
are still left in so-called civilian life,' he declared: 'a consciousness
that, not merely as a matter of self-preservation for the moment,
but in order to equip ourselves for a far more strenuous future when
the results will be far worse if we do not avoid the dismal, sleep-
walking mistakes of the past, the old ways of life and the old slogans
will have to be scrapped'.

Poets and novelists may have retired from the fray, exalting the
private and the pastoral at the expense of politics, but journalists,
academics, politicians and well-intentioned middle-class reformers
busied themselves envisioning the New Jerusalem. The Press was
increasingly sympathetic to notions of reconstruction, and to the
Left in particular: so much so that a Tory MP, writing in 1944,
lamented that conservatism had 'allowed itself to be deprived of the
intellectual leadership of the nation' and noted how 'if you spend
the weekend with an educated man, the odds are that you will find
that the *New Statesman* is the only weekly taken. Your host may
affect to laugh at its politics; he may say he only takes it for its
literary articles or its film criticism; but the point remains that he
does take it, and that he and his like have been reading it and its
predecessor since the last war.' Writing the 'London Letter' for the
Partisan Review three years earlier, George Orwell remarked on how
newspapers 'print articles which would have been considered hopelessly above their readers' heads a couple of years ago', and how 'to
get any straightforward expression of reactionary opinion . . . you

now have to go to obscure weekly and monthly papers, mostly Catholic papers'. As evidence of the pervasive swing to the left, David Astor followed J. L. Garvin at the *Observer*, employing Orwell and Arthur Koestler as columnists, and displaying an unmillionaire-like sympathy for left-wing views; Michael Foot took over as editor of the *Evening Standard*; Robert Barrington Ward replaced Geoffrey Dawson at *The Times*, where the influence of the left-wing Cambridge historian E. H. Carr and Stanley Morison led one Tory MP to describe the paper as 'the threepenny edition of the *Daily Worker*'; most influential of all was the *Daily Mirror*, which increased its circulation from 1,750,000 in 1939 to 3,000,000 in 1946, championed the Beveridge Report, and – like J. B. Priestley's 'Postscripts', his hugely successful and influential series of BBC broadcasts – claimed to articulate a sense of community and to speak up for the hitherto neglected 'little man'.

Nor were book publishers inactive on the Left. The Left Book Club had been given a knock by the Nazi-Soviet Pact, and had some explaining to do, but Gollancz soon bounced back with his yellow-jacketed Victory Books, referred to by some as 'Yellow Perils', which called for a Labour victory once the wartime coalition had been dissolved. Far and away the most successful of these was *Guilty Men* by 'Cato', alias Michael Foot, which savaged the 'men of Munich' and, despite W. H. Smith's refusal to handle it, went on to sell 220,000 copies. Not to be outdone by his more left-wing rival, Fred Warburg started a list of Searchlight Books, edited by Orwell and Tosco Fyvel, designed to 'criticize and kill what is rotten in Western civilization' and discuss the ways in which Britain could be transmogrified into 'an up-to-date socialist community that could inspire the world'. Published in 1941 and 1942 at two shillings each, the list included Orwell's *The Lion and the Unicorn* and Cassandra's *The English at War*.

The promoters of the 'New Jerusalem' were, almost invariably, middle-class intellectuals who had little experience of business or industry, and were, irrespective of cost or the ability to pay, far more concerned with spending money on housing and social services than with industrial renewal, reviving exports and rebuilding the infrastructure once the fighting was over: the country was hope-lessly in debt, deprived of currency reserves and dependent on American Lend-Lease, yet according to a 1944 Treasury report 'the time and energy and thought which we are all giving to the Brave New World is wildly disproportionate to what is being given to the Cruel Real World', and, Correlli Barnett sardonically suggests, the country's most influential and articulate spokesmen were concerned only with 'a vision of a garden-city society filled with happy, healthy children, smiling mothers, bustling workers, serene elderly souls in a golden twilight of state pensions; all living in houses furnished in Gordon Russell's simple good taste; and, having been equally well educated in a reformed educational system, all busy in cultural pursuits other than dog-racing or going to the pictures'. What is certainly true is that the same names recur again and again. Members of the pressure group or think-tank known as Political and Economic Planning (PEP) included Julian Huxley, Maxwell Fry and Tom Harrisson, as well as Maynard Keynes, the great advocate of the managed economy and the notion that capitalism should be improved rather than abolished, and Lord Beveridge, 'the people's William', whose celebrated report, unveiled in 1942, heralded the Welfare State, advocating the funding, through a national insurance scheme, of a national health service and protection for all against the ravages of illness, unemployment and old age. The report sold 645,000 copies, was accepted grudgingly by Churchill and with huge enthu-siasm by the Labour Party and the Tory left wing, and – like Butler's 1944 Education Act, the establishment of a Ministry of Town and Country Planning, and the 1944 White Papers on the National Health Service, employment policy and national insurance – set the scene for the reforms of the post-war Labour government.

Early on in the war, such ideas were being ventilated, by a similar cast of characters, through the pages of *Picture Post* and the delib-erations of the 1941 Committee. Kenneth Clark at the Ministry of Information persuaded Edward Hulton, the immensely rich and temporarily left-wing owner of *Picture Post*, to devote a special issue of the magazine to the reconstruction of post-war Britain. Julian Huxley was co-opted as joint editor with Tom Hopkinson, and the forty-page special issue, entitled 'A Plan for Britain' and published on 4 January 1941, carried pieces by Maxwell Fry on planning, Thomas Balogh on the state management of the economy, A. D. Lindsay, the Master of Balliol, on education, J. B. Priestley on culture and recreation and Huxley himself on 'Health for All'. In his editorial, Hopkinson argued for a minimum wage, a planned economy and full employment, and insisted that their plan was 'not something outside the war, or something *after* the war. It is an essential part of our war aims. It is, indeed, our most positive war aim. The new Britain is the country we are fighting for.'

Such views would have received a warm welcome at meetings of the 1941 Committee, held at Hulton's house in Hill Street, off Berkeley Square. Chaired by Priestley, the Committee's members included Victor Gollancz, David Astor, Kingsley Martin of the *New Statesman*, H. G. Wells, Gerald Barry of the *News Chronicle*, Ritchie Calder, A. D. Peters the literary agent, Tom Wintringham, Thomas Balogh, Douglas Jay, Tom Hopkinson, Lady Violet Bonham-Carter, David Low the cartoonist, the left-wing MP Konni Zilliacus, Richard Titmuss and Sir Richard Acland. In May 1942 the Committee published a Nine-Point Declaration calling for free education for all, full employment and a degree of nationalization, after which it merged with Sir Richard Acland's Forward March to form the Common Wealth Party. An earnest, bespectacled Devon landowner and former Liberal MP who believed in the common ownership of industry, urged the middle classes to abandon their privileges to create a classless society, and looked forward to the creation of a 'new society' and the 'emergence of a new kind of man, with a new kind of mind, new values, a new outlook on life, and, perhaps most important of all, new motives', Acland had founded Forward March in order to give the people what was good for them, on the understanding that it was 'the right and duty of the progressive not merely to give people what they desire, but to teach them what they should desire'. Both Forward March and the Common Wealth Party were supported by teachers, solicitors, doctors and other members of the high-minded and well-meaning middle classes, Penguin-readers incarnate. Membership of the Common Wealth

Party never exceeded 15,000, but for as long as the Labour Party was locked into the wartime coalition, it provided some kind of opposition, winning three by-elections in the process; it lost its *raison d'être* once the coalition was dissolved, and the Labour Party felt free to campaign on its own account, but in the meantime it helped to spread faith in the New Jerusalem among those whom Michael Frayn would later describe as life's 'herbivores'.

Allen Lane has, all this time, been notable for his absence, so much so that a reader might assume he had dropped out of the story, or that an inattentive typesetter had wandered into another book: yet Penguin Books and its creator were central to the development of the post-war consensus, not just through the books they published but because Penguin itself was coming to be seen as a benign monopoly in a country which had a more 'concentrated' or mixed economy than most by the end of the 1930s, with four railway companies replacing 130, and nationally owned corporations running the BBC and the airlines. Lane was never a political animal in the sense of belonging to a particular party, subscribing to an ideology or adhering to a consistent point of view, but he instinctively sided with the underdog and liked to annoy those in authority, and he was on good terms with people like Hulton, Kingsley Martin, Tom Hopkinson, Tom Wintringham, Gerald Barry and Tom Harrisson; as he told the historian Paul Addison, 'We were anti-They. We were against the privileged classes.' His diary for 1942, for example, records attendance at several meetings of the Fabian Society, and one of the Socialist Propaganda Committee, but whereas radicals like Victor Gollancz were keen committee men, forever passing resolutions and writing letters and joining together to protest against this or that, Lane, with his hatred of committees and paperwork, left far fewer traces behind: in later life he was occasionally dragooned into signing a round robin – Gollancz persuaded him to lend his name to his campaign against capital punishment, and he signed a letter of support to *The Times* in support of George Weidenfeld's decision to publish Nabokov's *Lolita* – but this was not the kind of thing he relished. In public life as in publishing, he was a loner, and happy to keep it that way.

Invisibility and influence are perfectly compatible: Lane exercised influence through the books he published, so much so that the *Daily Herald* once suggested that he had done more than Shaw, Wells or Beveridge to 'influence the tastes, the thoughts, the knowledge and perhaps even the character of the English'. The outbreak of war was followed by a flurry of Penguin Specials explaining why Britain was at war, but although foreign affairs occasionally intruded – K. S. Shelvankar's *The Problem of India*, published in 1940, was described as a subversive work in the House of Commons by Duff Cooper, then the Minister of Information – most of those published thereafter dealt with life on the home front and the kind of society they hoped to see in post-war Britain. Sir Richard Acland's Forward March appealed to Lane's liking for outsiders and eccentrics, and his manifesto, *Unser Kampf*, was published as a Penguin Special in 1940; it sold 150,000 copies, and gave Penguin as well as the House of Commons as a forwarding address for those eager to ventilate their views or learn more about the party. Another Special, *People's War*, provided an additional pulpit for Forward March and its belief that the war should be fought for 'fair play and food, freedom and homes': its author, Tom Wintringham, was a Communist Party member who had commanded the British battalion of the International Brigade in Spain, and was now in charge of training the Home Guard in guerrilla warfare at Osterley Park, a project partly funded by *Picture Post*. In *Where Do We Go from Here?* a more conventional left-winger, Harold Laski, called for a 'revolution in the spirit of man if we are to enter the Kingdom of Peace as our rightful inheritance'. Though not a religious man, Lane was happy to publish books by churchmen which invoked the New Jerusalem, and nine Penguin Specials of a religious nature were published between 1940 and 1944, all of them calling for the creation of a better society. Archbishop Temple's Penguin Special on *Christianity and the Social Order* sold 140,000 copies, while James Parkes, the author of *God in a World at War* and *God and Human Progress*, argued that God was 'a thoroughly intelligent and capable personality', a supreme planner who bustled about 'in his shirt sleeves' and believed in 'getting on with his job'; 'For the first time in the progress of the human race, religious, scientific and creative artists are united in aim and moving forward co-operatively and simultaneously in the same direction,' Phyllis Bottome declared in *Our New Order or Hitler's*, published in 1944, before invoking a new order 'founded and built upon a state educated to Courage, Truth, Freedom and Love'.

Nor were the practicalities of the New Jerusalem ignored. C. H. Waddington's *The Scientific Attitude*, another by-product of the Tots and Quots, argued for the importance of the scientific mind in developing a new culture, and its relevance to modern architecture in particular. Published in 1942 in a landscape format, Ralph Tubbs's *Living in Cities* looked eagerly forward to the glass and concrete Le Corbusier-inspired cities that (or so it was fondly believed) would rise on the ruins of those destroyed in the Blitz and later by doodle-bugs, the tower blocks punctuated with un-English piazzas populated with brightly clad citizens teetering about on pointed triangular legs. Invoking the spirit of 'swings and roundabouts', Lane was happy to publish, initially, at a loss. 'Our cost of production will amount to exactly twice the amount we will receive from the trade,' he told Tubbs, 'but so convinced am I of the "worthwhileness" of the venture, that this causes me no qualms.' He was as good as his word: in due course Tubbs's book spawned the 'Planning, Design and Art' series which included *The County of London Plan*, edited by Ernö Goldfinger and E. J. Carter, and Hugh Casson's *Homes by the Million*. Lionel Brett's *Houses*, Gordon Fraser's *Furniture* and books on gardens, public transport, ships and pottery formed part of another new series, 'The Things We Can See', inspired by an exhibition boldly entitled 'Britain Can Make It'.

Bill Williams, in the meantime, was propagating similar attitudes through ABCA, and making himself unpopular with right-wing Tories in the process. 'I am more and more suspicious of the way this lecturing to and education of the Forces racket is run,' the Conservative MP Maurice Petherick memoed Churchill's PPS. 'I maintain most strongly that any of these subjects which tend towards politics, even if the lecturers are Tories, are *wrong* . . . for the love of Mike do something about it, unless you want the creatures coming back all pansy-pink.' Churchill himself regarded the whole business with grave suspicion. 'Will not such discussions only provide opportunities for the professional grouser and the agitator with the glib tongue?' he asked the Conservative Chief Whip, David Margesson, in 1941; and a year later he returned to the attack, hoping that 'you will wind up this business as quickly and decently as possible, and set the persons concerned to useful work'. 'We are fighting not only for the Britain we know, but for the better Britain it could become,' Williams informed readers of his *Current Affairs* in October 1942; his wife, Gertrude, explained Keynesian demand management in a piece entitled 'Work for All', and an article on 'Building the Post-War Home' discussed the need to build between 3 and 4 million new homes in the ten years that followed the end of the war. As early as 1942 *The Times* conceded that 'the ABCA habit may develop in the demobilized soldiers such a social consciousness as may make them a shrewder electorate than their fathers were'; Richard Hoggart recalled how ABCA pamphlets 'did not talk down, and underestimated neither the subject nor the capacity of the readers – getting across without selling out . . . They were rare English examples of that *haute vulgarisation* which the French respect and the English fear' – he could well have been describing what Williams and Lane were striving to achieve with the Pelican list – and how they 'did a great deal to make many soldiers vote for Attlee – not because ABCA's activities were barely disguised socialist propaganda (they were not), but because they helped reduce the power of the mandarin voices, accelerated the decline in deference, made soldiers realize that they did have the right to think for themselves'.

All this bore fruit in the election of 1945. All parties, including the Conservatives, gave greater priority in their manifestos to full employment, housing and social security than to industrial reconstruction or reviving exports. A total of 1.7 million servicemen voted, returning 393 Labour MPs and 213 Tories; and there were many among the liberal-minded middle classes who, like the film-maker Michael Balcon, 'voted Labour for the first time after the war: this was our mild revolution'. 'Your bloody *Picture Post* is responsible for this,' Tom Hopkinson was told at an election party (or wake), and Penguin too came in for blame or credit. 'After the WEA, it was Lane and his Penguins which did most to get us into office at the end of the war,' Attlee was reported as saying, albeit in old age and to a Penguin editor at the end of a party; and when, in 1947, the Conservative Party mounted an exhibition entitled 'Trust the People', devoted to showing 'how the people were told a story' and the ways in which 'Socialist propaganda was "put across" in spite of the Party Truce', the rogues' gallery of those responsible included Allen Lane, along with Michael Foot and Hannen Swaffer of the *Daily Herald*.

Victor Gollancz may well have wondered at his exclusion, since his own firm had made its own flamboyant contribution to a Labour victory; and despite his earlier hostility, he was happy to cooperate with Penguin over a book on which he had an option. John Hersey's *Hiroshima* had been published, *in toto*, in the *New Yorker* in the autumn of 1946. Victor Weybright, then in charge of editorial matters at Penguin's New York office, tipped off his colleagues in Harmondsworth, should they want to nip in ahead of Gollancz; the book would come at a price, since Knopf, the American publishers, were looking for an advance of $2,000 and a guaranteed first printing of 250,000 copies. Lane was in Switzerland at the time, and neither Dick nor Frostie was enthusiastic. It was, Dick told Weybright, an 'able piece of work', but there was a bottleneck in production, and to have to print so many copies would only make matters worse. Back from holiday, Lane was appalled to discover what had been going on in his absence. 'INTENSELY ANXIOUS TO SECURE NEW YORKER HIROSHIMA ARTICLE,' he cabled Weybright, adding, in a letter, 'I am frantically excited about the Hiroshima book . . . What thrills me even more is this instance of cooperation from your side. It will I hope prove to be the forerunner of many such plans, and it demonstrates how usefully we can run in double harness.' Lane acquired the paperback rights – Gollancz seemed happy to follow on with a hardback edition for the libraries – and Dick was left to make amends. 'I can quite see Allen's point of view,' he told Weybright. 'It is something new and exciting; it involved cables and transatlantic phone calls, which he loves; and also there is the question that if we got the book, a certain other publisher would not . . .'

VG and Lane may have come to an accommodation over *Hiroshima*, but they were still rivals when it came to publishing left-wing politicians. 'Now that Gollancz's Left Book Club is out of action for all practical purposes, the Penguins are far and away the most effective means of diffusion left,' wrote the maverick Labour MP Konni Zilliacus in 1948, and Lane seemed happy to publish William Gallagher's *The Case for Communism*. The only Communist MP, Gallagher had noted Penguin's publication of Quintin Hogg's *The Case for Conservatism* and John Parker's *Labour Marches On*, and approached Lane with his proposal on the grounds that 'you say in your Publisher's Note that "As Publishers we have no Politics"'. Lane told Gallagher that he planned to publish his book at the same time as two new books on Roman Catholicism, by Douglas Woodruff and Barbara Ward, and 'they will undoubtedly be read in conjunction with your book as expositions of the two great rival philosophies with which the world is now confronted'. But before long his nerve began to crack. Bill Williams had initially supported publication on the grounds that 'much as some of us may dislike the policy advocated, I don't feel we as publishers can afford to ignore it', but now reported a 'lingering sense of unease' about the effect publishing such a book might have on Penguin's reputation; and the book's prospective editor was already spending long hours at the Communist Party's headquarters in King Street. Lane tried to wriggle out on the grounds that the typescript was shorter than agreed – Hogg's, on the other hand, had come in at twice the contracted length, and had to be published as a Penguin Double – but by now it was too late. The book went on to sell over 100,000 copies, but it marked the end of a line. Although they were revived towards the end of the 1950s, Penguin Specials came to a halt in 1945; Gollancz had printed a mere 6,250 copies of the last Left Book Club title, G. D. H. Cole's *The Meaning of Marxism*, in 1948, and when, three years later, Lane turned down another proposal from Zilliacus, he blamed continuing paper shortages, the rising cost of living, a tendency among book-buyers to go for 'permanent' rather than 'topical' titles, and the fact that it now took at least eighteen months to get a book published: for all of which reasons 'I am fighting shy at present of all books on Current Affairs'. And he told the *Daily Telegraph* that 'the demand is now for cultural books', and not for more overtly political works.

Bernard Shaw would have regretted Lane's decision – he thought 'Zilly' should be the Foreign Secretary rather than Ernest Bevin, and deplored the Government's assumption that Stalin was 'a twentieth-century Attila instead of the mainstay of peace in Europe' – but the old Fabian retained his admiration for Penguin, and remained as anxious as ever to have his work made available in paperback. Dick took pains to remind Lane that the 'old boy' was extremely fond of him, and that he should pay him the occasional visit; and Lane dutifully obliged, calling on Shaw at Ayot St Lawrence or in Whitehall Court, the pinnacled, lavatory-tiled pile on the Embankment where, before long, he took a flat himself. From time to time Shaw disagreed with what Penguin had in mind, and a jocular correspondence ensued: he strongly objected when Lane insisted on retaining the word 'unpleasant' in *Plays Pleasant and Unpleasant*, warning him that he would 'lose sales on any book you label Unpleasant', but caved in when Lane refused to budge ('Well, have it your own way . . .').

Equally contentious was the vexed issue of Topolski's illustrations. One of the most fashionable artists of the day, Feliks Topolski had been published by Lane at The Bodley Head. Shaw had been happy enough with his pre-war illustrations for the Penguin *Pygmalion*, seeing them as a 'genuine independent attraction' and far preferable to photographs, but his proposed cover illustration was going too far. 'Topolski's cover for *Pygmalion* is a ghastly mistake,' he told Lane, ready for once to abandon his objections to illustrated covers. 'Ask yourself whether the pictures of a repulsive old man and an unpleasant middle-aged one, both of them badly dressed and unwashed, would induce you to buy . . . Tell Topolski his business is to design an attractive cover and not cry stinking fish.' Penguin's New York office were keen to have Topolski illustrate *St Joan* and *Major Barbara*, but Shaw would have none of it. Topolski's style was 'so individual and masterly that he can illustrate nobody but himself. His St Joan is not my St Joan, nor anybody's but his own,' he told Lane; and Lane, for his part, saw the need to tread warily. 'The pleasant relations which have existed between Shaw and myself have been a little disrupted of late by the appearance of others on the scene at Ayot St Lawrence, and I don't want to make a false step, particularly as the old man has always been so frightfully generous in all the transactions I have had with him,' he told the rejected artist.

Writing to Shaw in November 1945, Lane revealed that he planned to celebrate the old boy's ninetieth birthday the following July by reissuing ten of his works in print-runs of 100,000 each. Inspired by gratitude and commercial acumen, the 'Shaw Million' was the first of several 'Millions', or 'Tens' as they were also known, awarded to bestselling authors on the Penguin list: later recipients included Evelyn Waugh, H. G. Wells, D. H. Lawrence, Georges Simenon and Agatha Christie. GBS was understandably chuffed, and said he would happily agree 'provided Willie can do it' – 'Willie' being William Maxwell of R. & R. Clark in Edinburgh, the firm responsible for printing all Shaw's works on an exclusive basis. In fact Clark's could undertake only a proportion of the work; the rest, unknown to Shaw, was farmed out to other printers but carried R. & R. Clark's imprint on the copyright page. 'No venture which I have undertaken in thirty years of publishing has given me so much pleasure,' Lane told Shaw. His pleasure was still greater when, on the day of publication, the manager of W. H. Smith in Baker Street tube station rang to say that a seemingly interminable queue building up outside his shop did not consist of stranded commuters but eager buyers of Bernard Shaw. The Million sold out in six weeks, and the birthday itself was celebrated with a party at Silverbeck. Shaw was unable to attend, but the guests included Sybil Thorndike, Wendy Hiller, Topolski, William Maxwell, Stanley Morison and his close friend Beatrice Warde, the historian of printing and typography. 'We had sherry on a smooth lawn that sloped down to a little weir, and a Siamese cat came and conversed with us,' Beatrice Warde remembered. 'The dinner was superb – Scotch salmon and chicken and a compote of raspberries which Richard Lane had canned himself, and home-grown peaches: iced hock and no end of champagne.' The guests were presented with a cased set of the Million, and Morison toasted 'the most significant event in publishing in our time'. The austere old typographer may have been carried away by the excitement of the moment and a surfeit of champagne, but the Shaw Million, and those that followed after, reflected Lane's combination of generosity and shrewdness, and his belief that a publisher should concentrate on an author's work *in toto*, on the backlist as well as the book of the moment.

Shaw's Fabian beliefs had been a huge influence on Pelicans and Penguin Specials, and on most of those who had set out to create the New Jerusalem in post-war Britain, and his death in 1950 marked the end of an era. The following year saw both the end of a Labour government which had introduced the Welfare State and national-ized large swathes of the economy, and the public celebration of that high-minded, idealistic, leftwards-leaning spirit which had brought it into being. The Festival of Britain originated with Lane's old acquaintance Gerald Barry. 'A glamorous figure in the worlds of journalism, the arts and left-to-middle-of-the-road politics', according to George Weidenfeld, Barry had suggested the idea to Sir Stafford Cripps, the President of the Board of Trade, in 1945, and three years later he was made its Director-General. 'The tone of the Festival', according to Michael Frayn, 'was not unlike the tone of the *News Chronicle*, which he had edited for eleven years – philanthropic, kindly, whimsical, cosy, optimistic, middlebrow, deeply instinct with the herbivorous philosophy so shortly doomed to eclipse.'

If the cartoonist Roland Emmett, with his model railway trundling round Battersea Park, epitomized the whimsicality of the Festival, Ralph Tubbs was its idealistic manifestation. Tall, rosy-cheeked and elegantly suited, convinced that architecture 'lives by the very passion to stir the human heart', Tubbs was, with Mischa Black and Hugh Casson, in charge of the Festival's overall design; he also designed its famous Dome of Discovery, then the largest dome in the world.

Back in the Thirties, when Lane got to know him, he had worked with Gropius, Maxwell Fry and Ernö Goldfinger; a passionate, idealistic believer in planned cities and the public ownership of land, thereby cutting out property speculators, he had most recently spelt out his ideas in *The Englishman Builds*, published by Penguin in 1945. The new architecture, he declared – the uncluttered tower blocks, the pedestrianized shopping malls, the swathes of gleaming white concrete – would 'achieve a place among the great architectures only if we have a set of values which are not entirely materialistic, if we have faith in the Spirit of Mankind'. It was a fine and noble sentiment – and one which Lane, hard-headed as he was, both valued and sought to realize.

11. Transatlantic Blues

Another new world was waiting to be developed on the other side of the Atlantic, and it was one that would never prove congenial. America and Allen Lane were curiously incompatible, at least in publishing terms: to his tweedier, old-fashioned colleagues in the London book world, Lane may have seemed an alarmingly modern and mid-Atlantic figure, bustling about in his Van Heusen shirts and Cary Grant suits and demolishing the sacred tenets of the trade, but once in New York he seemed almost reactionary, radiating disapproval of American business methods and refusing to recognize that what worked in a country like Britain might not be applicable in Chicago or Arizona. America brought out the worst in him, and in his dealings with American publishers, and with those he employed to run the Penguin operation in the States, he revealed himself at his most elusive and duplicitous.

Contrary to expectations, mass-market paperbacks were a later arrival in the States than in England. In the summer of 1938 Robert de Graff, a former salesman with Doubleday, set up Pocket Books, 'complete and unabridged' paperback editions of recently published titles and classics, selling at 25 cents apiece. Unlike Penguins, they boasted picture jackets, some designed by McKnight Kauffer; they were squatter in shape, the pages had red coloured edges to disguise the poor-quality paper, and the colophon consisted of a bespectacled kangaroo named Gertrude, who lost her glasses when redesigned by Walt Disney. Unlike Lane, de Graff decided to do some market research before he took the plunge. A questionnaire was sent to 40,000 prospective readers in New York City, and he test-marketed 1,000 copies of Pearl Buck's *The Good Earth*. Reactions were favourable, but even so de Graff moved ahead with caution. Anxious to cut his prices to the bone, he immediately opted for 'perfect' binding, whereby the folded 'sections' of the book were not sewn, as in hardbacks or the early Penguins, but were guillotined on all four sides and then glued along the spine; he offered authors or their hardback publishers a modest 4 per cent royalty; and, to begin with, he made his books available only within New York City. The first ten titles included Agatha Christie's evergreen *The Murder of Roger Ackroyd*, Thornton Wilder's *The Bridge of San Luis Rey* and James Hilton's *Lost Horizon*, as well as the out-of-copyright *Wuthering Heights*, *The Way of All Flesh* and five of Shakespeare's tragedies. Hardback publishers were hostile at first, with Cass Canfield refusing to sub-lease Harper & Row titles on the familiar ground that a paperback edition would undermine hardback sales: but then Simon & Schuster, de Graff's partners in the business and its eventual owners, decided to let him have the rights in Dale Carnegie's *How to Win Friends and Influence People*, and the floodgates were opened. A total of 1.3 million copies had been sold by 1941, by which time the total sales of Pocket Books had reached 8.5 million. The paperback revolution had arrived in America, and others hurried to join in: Avon Books was set up in 1941, the Popular Library in 1942, and Dell in 1943.

America was far too large and rich a market to be ignored, and, where the rights were free, Penguins were available in the States from the very beginning: but, as Lane was soon to discover, the book trade was run on very different lines, at least where paperbacks were concerned. Bookshops were in short supply outside the major cities and university campuses, which specialized in academic monographs and set texts: like its rivals and successors, Pocket Books did 80 per cent of their business through independent magazine distributors, who then sold the books on to news-stands, drugstores, cigar stores and variety stores. Magazine distribution was a viciously competitive world, violent and gangster-ridden: in Chicago, where the Annenberg family made their fortunes as magazine distributors, twenty-seven news-dealers had been killed in the turf wars of the early years of the century. American paperbackers believed in saturating the market, and then treating as 'returns' those copies that could not be sold. In England returns, if agreed to at all, involved exchanging a few unsaleable books for credit or other titles of comparable value, but in America the front covers were torn off and returned as evidence, while the books themselves were destroyed; and, even in those early days, up to 50 per cent of copies sold could end up as returns. Like magazines, paperbacks had a short shelf-life, and were treated accordingly.

Quite forgetting his initial dependence on Woolworth's, his contempt for the hidebound British book trade and his readiness to experiment with book-dispensing machines and the like, Lane regarded American sales and distribution methods as a barbarous business to which he was loath to lend his name; he disliked, too, the American insistence on illustrated covers, and would find his American managers' eagerness to publish books in the States for the American market increasingly hard to accept. But these horrors were undreamed of when, shortly before the outbreak of war, he set up Penguin Books Inc. to handle the sales and distribution of his books in the States. He chose as his American manager a twenty-two-year-old American named Ian Ballantine, who had, until recently, been doing postgraduate work at the LSE under the supervision of H. L. Beales. Ballantine had written a thesis on the book trade: Lane may or may not have read it, but either way he was sufficiently impressed by the young man to offer him the job. Ballantine's fiancée, Betty, was only eighteen, and working in a bank in the Channel Islands, when she received a cable asking her to marry him at once and come to New York. She handed in her notice and took the first boat to London, where Lane gave the couple lunch and offered them a 49 per cent share in Penguin Inc.; and within a week they were on board ship, married and bearing with them $500, a gift from her father, with which to start out on their new life together.

Once in New York, they took a first-floor room on East 17th Street, bought some second-hand furniture, agreed to pay themselves $15 a week each, and got down to work. 'I think I have come back from England with a combination that will finally make the quarter book a permanent feature of American publishing,' Ballantine observed: already he was anticipating something more than the mere importing of Harmondsworth Penguins, for 'if one can build up sales in America on the basis of importations and so organize a distribution system which can handle 25,000 of a single title, the point will have been reached at which Penguin Books Inc. starts publishing in America.' In the meantime a friend from *Ice Cream World* magazine helped with the advertising, while the Ballantines set about importing books from England for sale at 25 cents apiece. These arrived, by sea, in crates of 1,000; the books had, somehow, to be manhandled up to the first floor before, with luck, being sent on their various ways. Some titles had no obvious appeal in America, so they ordered a mere 200 of these; others, like Harold Nicolson's *Why Britain is at War*, went on to sell 20,000 copies, with some copies being airmailed out via Lisbon while others made their way through Italy. On the day war broke out John and Nora Lane were sent to New York to sign the deeds of incorporation: John signed them as 'John Lane' rather than 'John Lane on behalf of Penguin Books', which caused problems after he died without leaving a will, since the American company now passed by default to his old parents in Oxfordshire.

One of the problems with importing books from England was that under the notorious 'manufacturing clause', a feature of US copyright law designed to keep American printers in business, it was only permissible to import 1,500 copies of books printed outside the United States: reprinting the book in America would entitle its author to the protection of American copyright, but any imported copies over the minimum permitted would instantly forfeit copyright. While working on his thesis for the LSE, Ballantine had discovered, or thought he had discovered, that it would be possible to import books with 'resigned' copyrights, though whether the authors 'resigned' their American copyrights to Penguin Inc., or whether Penguin Inc. 'resigned' any copyright claims in imported titles, remains unclear: either way, as the war began to take effect, and the U-boats took their toll on transatlantic convoys, the whole business of importing Penguins into America became increasingly vexed. Ballantine was frustrated by Lane's refusal to answer letters about shipping out printing plates, so enabling him to print in America and publish titles excluded by the manufacturing clause; he was disappointed by Lane's refusal to accept that there might be a market for Tom Wintringham's Penguin Special, *New Ways of War*, still more so since John Wheeler-Bennett, the Head of the British Press Service in Washington, had told him he 'thought it the best possible propaganda as it dramatizes for every American, no matter what his class, how completely the entire population of Britain is involved in the war'; he even begged Lane to bring some much-needed books with him as hand luggage on his next trip to the States. Equally problematic was the wartime deterioration of production standards: straw-coloured paper, rusting staples and cramped typography might be tolerable – obligatory – in Britain, but not in the States, where the competition was not, as yet, shackled by paper quotas. 'The paper got to be the same colour as the ink,' Ballantine later complained to Lane. 'That was acceptable in England, because you read what you could, but it was not accept-able here.' American department stores were not prepared to stock shoddy-looking English paperbacks, however fine their contents: he needed laminated and, ideally, illustrated covers if he was to keep Penguins on the news-stands, and if he could print them in the States, so much the better.

While Ballantine nursed his frustrations, and entertained Dick on a flying visit in May 1940 – according to reports in the Press, he had come over to mastermind the sale of 50,000 copies of the cartoonist David Low's *Europe since Versailles* to a mysterious Englishman based in the States – a figure from Lane's past was about to impinge on the American scene. When war broke out, Kurt Enoch, still based in Paris, had been interned as an enemy alien, and separated from his wife and daughters. They had made their various ways to Marseilles, where they had been provided with US visas, crossed the Pyrenees, travelled on to Lisbon, and taken a Greek ship to New York. Once installed, Enoch began to size up the American publishing scene with the eyes of a veteran, noting the shortage of bookshops, the importance of literary agents, the huge sums spent on advertising and promotion, and the neglect of back-lists and the classics, not least by Pocket Books. When, in 1941, Lane made his way to New York by way of Montreal, he invited Enoch round to his hotel and told him that he was thinking of closing down Penguin Inc. if matters didn't improve. Enoch, echoing Ballantine, told him that he should print and publish in the States, and at the same time give him a job. Lane pointed out that, under wartime exchange regulations, it was impossible for him to transfer the necessary funds to the States; when Enoch suggested that he should try to raise start-up funds in New York, Lane gave him 'a quick and decisive "yes"', and promised him a 5 per cent share in the reconstituted Penguin Inc. Kurt Wolff, another German-Jewish publisher recently arrived in the States, lent Enoch some money, later used to set up Pantheon Books; and after meeting Ballantine, whom he found a 'polite, serious young gentleman with whom I should be able to establish a good working and sympathetic personal relationship', Enoch set about putting the business on a firmer footing. It was agreed that Ballantine would look after sales and distribution, while Enoch was responsible for production and design, and until some more furniture arrived, the new Vice-President of Penguin Inc. perched on an empty crate.

The bombing of Pearl Harbor proved the salvation of Penguin Inc., and the huge demand for cheap, stapled Armed Services Editions as well as for conventional paperbacks made fortunes for those involved; as the New York *World Telegram* put it, 'Pocket-sized Books, turned out like cars, are turning over Pocketfuls of Money.' Ballantine got in touch with Colonel Greene of the *Infantry Journal*, who was keen to publish a line of paperbacks for new recruits; realizing that Harmondsworth's hugely successful two-volume *Aircraft Recognition* failed to cover Japanese fighters and bombers, the Ballantines and their young editor, Walter Pitkin, working at the kitchen table, produced *What's That Plane?* for the colonel, nipping in ahead of a planned Pocket Book on the same subject and eventually selling over 400,000 copies. Other Fighting Forces publications produced by Penguin Inc. included *The New Soldier Handbook* and *How the Jap Army Fights*. When paper quotas, based on past use, were introduced in 1943, Enoch was able to tap into the *Infantry Journal's* allowance.

With sales to the services providing a large and reliable turnover of books originated and published in the States, Ballantine felt free

to flex his muscles as a fully-fledged paperback publisher. He cultivated hardback publishers with a view to buying paperback rights;
the powerful Curtis Circulating Company, the distribution arm of
the group that published the *Saturday Evening Post* and the *Ladies'
Home Journal*, agreed to act as the firm's national distributor, providing
access to thousands of new outlets; longer print-runs made it possible
for Enoch to print on faster and cheaper rotary presses and make
full use of 'perfect' binding. But all was not well. Back in England,
Lane resented Ballantine's increasing independence, his addiction to
picture jackets, and his readiness to accept the norms of American
paperback life; Ballantine, for his part, was preparing to set up on
his own under the imprint of Bantam Books. In 1944 Marshall Field
III, the department store tycoon, bought Simon & Schuster and
Pocket Books; worried by a pending imbalance of power, a cartel
of hardback publishers, including Random House, Harper's,
Scribner's, Little, Brown and the Book of the Month Club, bought
Grosset & Dunlap, a hardback reprint firm specializing in bestsellers.
Convinced that the future lay with popular mass-market paperbacks
of the kind published by Pocket, Dell and Avon, Ballantine
approached Bennett Cerf of Random House, the head of the cartel,
about the possibility of their backing Bantam as a rival to Pocket
Books, with Grosset & Dunlap and Curtis between them covering
bookshop and magazine outlets.

Kurt Enoch knew nothing of this, but was anxious that Penguin
Inc. should follow in the Penguin tradition. In 1944, at the start of
a six-month tour of North and South America, Lane arrived in
New York, and instantly sided with Enoch. The following year
Bantam was incorporated, with Curtis and the Grosset consortium
each owning 42.5 per cent of the shares. Ballantine and Betty sold
back their 49 per cent share in Penguin Inc. for a dollar, and took
with them most of the staff and the *Infantry Journal* contract. 'Kurt,
in six months you'll be broke,' Ballantine told his former colleague,
whom he left sitting in an empty office.

Since Enoch needed help and had, as yet, an imperfect command
of English, Lane sent Frostie to New York in the summer of 1945
to lend him a hand. She made her mark at once, commissioning,

as the first American Pelicans, books by the anthropologist Ruth Benedict and the political pundit Walter Lippmann, appointing two full-time editors, and employing as a reader Saul Bellow, who remembered her as being 'angelic' and 'dovelike and forbearing'. With Enoch beside her, she slogged round American publishers' offices, trying to persuade them to license books to Penguin Inc. and to ignore Ballantine's oft-repeated claim that 'Penguins will be out of business in six months'. She found Enoch 'the most lugubrious and depressing person to work with', and spending time with him was 'like living with the Gestapo'. 'There is something about his "Pardon me" and his pale little stare which brings out the worst in one,' she told Lane. Nor did they see eye-to-eye on the vexed issue of covers, since 'his major stand is that the covers must have art work in the case of fiction, and that each one, within the frame-work of a consistent design, must be treated as an individual book'. Enoch's view would, in due course, prevail on both sides of the Atlantic, but it would not be an easy victory.

Lane was a master of divide and rule, and, unknown to Enoch, he had another candidate in mind to help run Penguin Inc. Victor Weybright was a convivial, rubicund anglophile, keen on bow ties, rolled umbrellas and hunting in the country round his farm in Maryland. During the war he had run the London branch of the Office of War Information, attached to the American Embassy, and had busied himself entertaining and getting to know writers, publishers and newspaper editors. He and Lane got on well together, so much so that he was appointed Christine's godfather (Agatha Christie was her godmother). Although his pre-war experience of publishing had been fairly modest – he had been an editorial adviser to *Reader's Digest*, and had worked for some obscure technical publishers – Lane asked him if he would be his personal representative and report back to him about Penguin Inc. in particular, and American paperback publishing in general.

Back home in the States, Weybright was unimpressed by the fare on offer from American paperback firms, finding it 'devoid of the taste and vision which had characterized ten years of Penguins and Pelicans in England'. His researches concluded, he turned up unannounced at the offices of Penguin Inc., now housed in a scruffy building occupied by rug and toy manufacturers. Enoch, who knew nothing of Weybright's mission, kept him waiting for two hours: he assumed his visitor was 'a stooge for Lane and an intruder', but although the two men had little in common beyond the smoking of pipes, he found Weybright 'amiable and congenial', and suggested that, since they were to be colleagues, he should buy half the notional 40 per cent of Penguin Inc. recently promised him by Lane.

Enoch was not best pleased when the shareholding failed to materialize, and after Lane had threatened to wind up Penguin Inc. unless Weybright could convince him that its operations were editorially compatible with those of Harmondsworth, Dick was despatched to sort matters out. Despite the apparent urgency of his mission, he travelled out on a slow-moving freighter; according to Weybright, 'the tall, apple-cheeked countryman' seemed completely baffled by his mission, though down in Maryland Dick 'moved among the workers and talked with the farmers in the manner of a beardless Tolstoy, never so happy as when his boots were muddy and his sleeves rolled up'. Dick dutifully disapproved of the American desire for picture jackets, while at the same time retailing a strong line in louche naval stories; he was, Weybright concluded, 'a lovable man, so accustomed to reflecting the buoyancy and energy of Allen Lane that he was generally accepted as a mysterious partner full of deep and unutterable wisdom'. Although Enoch and Weybright got what they wanted, Lane retained his grip on the voting shares: the whole affair, Enoch later wrote, 'put me on my guard and raised doubts with regard to Allen's personal reliability and credibility', and he noted how, in the years to come, other American publishers would find themselves at the receiving end of Lane's 'unfortunate arbitrariness and inconsistencies'.

With the shareholding sorted out, however unsatisfactorily, Frostie was able to return home while Enoch and Weybright set about building up a list. 'We will continue to aim for the consistent rather than the casual reader. Our books will be of permanent value rather than one-shot,' Weybright reported back to Lane. Works by Virginia Woolf, E. M. Forster, D. H. Lawrence, Joyce, dos Passos, Moravia,

Silone and Carson McCullers were published; and although the firm was chronically under-capitalized – not least because currency restrictions made it almost impossible for Lane to provide funds from Britain – matters were momentarily improved when Erskine Caldwell's *God's Little Acre*, published by Penguin Inc. in March 1946, sold over a million copies. Pocket Books, the market-leaders, were being successfully attacked on their own ground, but Lane was unimpressed. Once again, picture covers were the problem. 'I am convinced more than ever that if we want to attract the American masses to good literature, we have got to display on our covers more than a beautiful bit of typography, no matter how distinguished it may be. Frostie thinks otherwise,' Weybright told Lane, who had voiced objections to the covers as well as the contents of novels by Faulkner, Caldwell, James M. Cain, James T. Farrell and other authors from what he referred to as the 'Porno Books' section of the list. Pocket Books copied the magazines, Bantam copied Pocket Books, and Penguin could not afford to lag too far behind: Americans, Weybright suggested, were 'more elementary than the Britishers' and had been 'schooled from infancy to disdain even the best product unless it is smoothly packaged and merchandised'.

Penguin Inc.'s jackets were unusually elegant, cleverly designed and made use of such fine artists as Robert Jonas, but Lane's hostility was more than aesthetic. The post-war lifting of paper restrictions had triggered an orgy of over-production: the market was glutted with unwanted paperbacks, vast numbers of which had to be pulped. Having to write off a sizeable chunk of each print-run added further strains to the under-funded Penguin Inc., which had become increasingly dependent on credit from printers, and from the giant Chicago firm of W. F. Hall in particular. Lane worried that Hall might end up taking over Penguin Inc., and would then be able to use the Penguin name in the States. He wanted Penguin Inc. to take more books from Harmondsworth, and he remained as hostile as ever to American sales and distribution methods. According to Weybright, he agreed to provide Penguin Inc. with the funds they needed to reduce their dependence on Hall, but reneged on his promise while in the States; Lane later claimed that he could not have committed himself without the formal permission of the Bank of England. Whatever the truth of the matter, an *ad hominem* argument broke out between the two men, and words were exchanged which Lane, for his part, found hard to forgive.

Matters went from bad to worse, with suspicion and resentment mounting on both sides. According to Weybright, Lane worried that, with America now the major English-speaking nation, Penguin Inc. could become larger and more powerful than its English parent, and that he would lose control; on a visit to London, Weybright noticed that Allen Lane underneath was 'a "little Englishman" as only a Welshman can be'. In the spring of 1947 Weybright visited London again on what turned out to be a fruitless mission, lugging with him, via Shannon, some fifteen-foot-tall dogwood trees which Lane wanted to plant at Priory Farm in memory of John, who had once written a lyrical letter home about the dogwood trees in blossom in the Hudson Valley. Later that year Lane and Lettice went to the States. After staying with Weybright in Maryland, they moved back to New York to a suite in the Elysée Hotel, much favoured by visiting publishers and often referred to as the 'easy lay'. When Weybright arrived there for what he had expected to be a serious business meeting, he found the suite crammed with heavy-drinking party-goers, and Lane in no mood for a deep discussion. It was, for Weybright, a moment of revelation: Lane had refused to provide credit in the dealings with the Chicago printers; Weybright could no longer stand his suspicious attitude, and was fed up with having to spy on Enoch. After the Lanes had returned to England, taking with them thirty-two items of luggage, both sides prepared for a divorce. In London that autumn a separation was agreed. Lane came to see Weybright and Enoch at their hotel; he had covered a black eye with a patch, and seemed unamused when Weybright, attempting levity, made a crack about the Nelson touch. 'Allen was as grim as any member of the Royal Family seeing the Union Jack come down on a liberated colony,' Weybright remembered, adding that 'Billy Williams and Eunice Frost sat sadly in the sidelines': in Williams's opinion, Weybright had 'discharged his responsibilities admirably', not least by resisting the temptation to lower editorial standards in pursuit of sales. It was agreed that Enoch and Weybright should be able to use the Penguin and Pelican imprints for a further year, until their own new firm, grandly entitled the New American Library and brought into being on 1 January 1948, was in a position to publish its first books under the Signet and Mentor imprints.

NAL went on to become one of the most distinguished and successful American paperback imprints; early Signet bestsellers included novels by Truman Capote, Gore Vidal and William Faulkner, while the Mentor list, closely modelled on Pelicans, published a philosophy series edited by Isaiah Berlin. No love was lost between the former partners in London and New York. 'The cover of *The Tyranny of Sex* makes me sick, and I shall be very glad indeed when our name stops being used for books of this nature,' Lane told Morris Ernst, who was to act as his intermediary and informant in his dealings with American publishers over the next decade or so. Harry Paroissien, who had joined Penguin in 1947, was sent out to look after the sale of Penguin titles in America, initially under the Allen Lane imprint. 'Whatever comes, we keep absolutely clear of this pair, and of any organization with which they may be concerned,' Lane told his lieutenant apropos Messrs Weybright and Enoch, and Paroissien reported home about 'that unpleasant couple, the bouncing Victor and the cold, fish-like Enoch', whom he professed to 'dislike more than anyone I have met on either side of the Atlantic'. Nor, as it turned out, would the alliance between Weybright and Enoch prove harmonious: Weybright found his partner 'dictatorial' and prone to a 'secret authoritarianism', while the austere Enoch disapproved of Weybright's love of hunting, in much the same way as he had earlier frowned upon Holroyd-Reece. Ian Ballantine, in the meantime, turned up in London to enquire about the possibility of his buying Penguin Inc. Paroissien had found him 'not quite such a squirt as I had expected', and Lane thought him 'not a bad egg', but despite his years at the LSE, Ballantine mistook English self-deprecation for the genuine article: Lane told Paroissien how, 'after having ladled out my usual line on my being too old for the turmoil of publishing, and that what I craved for was a pleasant and quiet old age in the country, he took me more seriously than I intended'. Similar mis-apprehensions had bedevilled Lane's American adventures, and worse were to come in the years ahead.

12. Scenes from Office Life

'I'm afraid the pre-war spirit is absent from me for good,' Lane told Dick in the summer of 1947; and although Dick, for his part, felt that 'there hasn't been a definite enough breakaway from the old don't-care-a-damn years', and that his brother was far too tolerant of the 'slipshod methods' of the early days, it is hard to avoid a sense that although Penguin in the second half of the 1940s remained as innovative as ever, Lane had lost some of his old sparkle, matching restlessness on the home front with the intrigues and anxieties endemic to tycoonery. He remained as mischievous and subversive as ever, mercifully free of pomposity and self-importance, and intolerant of bureaucracy and paperwork; but as Penguin grew larger and more subject to the disciplines and priorities of a conventional business, he found himself devoting more and more of his time to the manipulation of his colleagues and employees, and to his dealings with the outside world, and less to the everyday workings of the firm. The number of titles sold increased modestly in the ten years after the end of the war, and it was only in 1957 that Lane made a conscious decision to double the turnover; but Penguin had become a national institution, and Lane a public figure, and there was a price to be paid for fame and success as his firm changed from being, in effect, an extended family to a more conventional kind of business.

Large as the firm was, Lane and Dick were still the sole directors. Dick lived with his brother and Lettice at Silverbeck, where he busied himself as a handyman, made vats of tomato juice and jars of horseradish sauce, and helped with the running of Priory Farm. In the office, he saw himself as a steadying influence, a solid, dependable, commonsensical figure, full of sound advice; and, as such, he proved a major irritant to his more volatile and impetuous sibling. He worried about the seemingly insouciant way in which

Lane, reliant on his publisher's instincts, took on a book after meeting a man at dinner the night before, launched a new series after scribbling some sums on the back of an envelope, dictated letters in the back of a car, was invariably late for meetings, and every summer took a month or more on holiday with his family in the Scilly Isles, Cornwall or the South of France. Lane, who never enjoyed being told what to do, and was far more amenable to the circuitous than to the direct approach, came to see Dick as a bore and a drag on the proceedings. But he was happy to use him as a front man, sorting out (or seeming to sort out) awkward predicaments in which Lane, eager as ever to avoid a direct confrontation with the enemy, could pull the strings from a distance while benefiting from the general fondness felt for his brother. Interviewing Lane two years after the end of the war, a journalist who had known both brothers in their Bodley Head days claimed that Lane never worried over problems because Dick was on hand to do the worrying for him: he remembered Lane asking Dick whether he was worried about a particular problem, and when Dick admitted he was, Lane replied, 'Then there's no need for me to worry too.'

A kind and unalarming figure, 'Mr Richard' was popular with the staff, and even if his secretaries claimed that he dictated so slowly that they could take his letters down in longhand, and that most of them had to do with the cows at Priory Farm, his readiness to consider picture jackets, and his worries about poor standards of production and inadequate blurbs, suggest that he was far from being the fuddy-duddy of Penguin folklore; but his homilies, however sensible and well-meant, grated on his brother's nerves. He told Lane he should try to get into the office earlier, for 'although I dislike people who call themselves directors, as this is our job we should aim to carry it out'; he understood why Lane, after a busy day in the office, wandered off to weigh up parcels and fuss about the postage, but 'this is not our main function in the firm'. Lane might not like it, but he should, from time to time, invite the heads of departments and their wives to dinner; he had to organize his time better, keep a diary, note 'what he has discussed with whom', and spend at least ten minutes a day dictating letters. The firm's editorial policy, Dick declared, was far too slapdash. 'You write a couple of letters, see a couple of interesting persons, and go off for six months,' he complained. The firm was too much a 'one-man concern': problems were caused by Lane's 'having led people on', since 'possibly you don't realize how infectious your enthusiasm can be, and people not knowing you are apt to consider that you mean everything you say'. He wasted too much time following up 'unnecessary people and ideas', and 'it would do you more good wandering about the garden contemplating than burning up effort talking to tiresome nitwits'. It would be good to know which nitwits Dick had in mind: whoever they were, far too much of the firm's money was tied up in advances for books that had yet to be written, and his brother seemed 'rarely if ever worried by the amount of capital required for any particular venture'. Matters were very different when Dick was left in charge: on one occasion he refused to sign any cheques until Stan Olney reminded him that the staff might well leave if not paid. 'Sometimes I am rather under the impression that you think nothing happens while you are away,' Dick once told his absent brother. 'Possibly we are not as efficient, but to balance this we are much more cheerful, and several types who had signs of gastric ulcers are now recovering slowly.'

Any ulcers in the making were more likely to occur among the upper echelons of Penguin. Although Frostie insisted that Lane knew everyone by name, and made a point of going from office to office when he arrived, junior staff found 'AL' benign but remote – among them a young woman called Margaret Clark, who started work as a secretary at Penguin in the year of the Festival of Britain. She began by typing letters for Mr Gale, the newly appointed office manager, who was ignored by everyone from Lane downwards; in due course he departed, unremarked, and she was shunted down the corridor to work for Lane himself. The main offices, she noted, ran along the front of the building; a corridor linked them together, and since the partition walls were glass from above the dado line, the overall effect was of lightness and brightness. Lane's office was in a corner of the building; his desk was twice as large as anyone else's, and was covered with green leather embossed with golden scrolls. His last secretary had hated every minute – her father was said to have stormed into the office with a horsewhip, promising to exact revenge – but Margaret Clark was unalarmed. Her new boss 'worked impulsively and restlessly, walking up and down, looking out of the window, biting his nails (the only outward sign that his volatile temperament, often so injurious to others, affected him equally), dictating in fits and starts, much of his negotiation done on the telephone'. She noted how he seemed to crave affection and attention, and how, when he began to dictate, his 'magnetic' blue eyes 'dropped the twinkle and were cold as cold'. His dedication to his work was combined with an apparent levity and a refusal to seem too serious. He was prone to vanish suddenly and without explanation, was given to quick, darting movements, and used to run his stubby fingers along his beloved leather-bound stock books – which, according to office rumour, he took home to read in bed, poring over the details of that month's sales.

Every now and then some luckless member of staff was sacked. A fellow publisher once remarked of Lane that 'he was bad at hatchet work unless he could put the hatchet into someone else's hands', and he invariably deputed the wretched business to one of his lieutenants, who would be instructed to take the victim to lunch at the Berkeley Arms; at the critical moment Lane let himself out of a back door, and Margaret Clark would catch a glimpse of his stocky, grey-clad, neatly suited rear view bustling through a gap in the hedge *en route* for the car park. In his memoir, Bill Williams wrote that Lane was 'gay, volatile, insecure, capricious and unreliable', combining ruthlessness with a 'lack of moral fibre' and even 'a decided streak of sadism': 'you could be top dog one day – and in the dog house the next', and if Lane decided that a face no longer fitted, lunch at the Berkeley Arms would soon be on the agenda. Far and away the most painful sacking – or forcible retirement – was that of the loyal, clerk-like Stan Olney, who had devoted his life to Penguin but was increasingly out of his depth in a firm that, by the end of the decade, would have some 200 employees and a turnover far exceeding those of its rivals. Lane combined, as he had to, sentimentality about the past with the ruthlessness inherent in running a business, and old retainers like Olney were particularly prone to the delusion that long association would prevail over commercial imperatives. It was said that he never recovered from losing his job, and that the rep Bill Rapley, another veteran of the Crypt, was so shattered by Lane's failure to attend his sixty-fifth birthday that he died shortly afterwards: tragic testimony to the folly of those who invest too much hope, faith and devotion in anything as fickle and heartless as a place of work. Others were more fortunate: Ashton Allen, who met Lane first in 1922 at The Bodley Head, and spent much of his life as Penguin's North of England rep, lasted through until his retirement in 1968.

Williams never saw Lane lose his temper, but he tended to sulk if thwarted or displeased, with his lips clamped shut and his head sunk into his neck. He was never pompous or boring, loved gossip, preferably malicious, and 'was good company at a party but never set a table at a roar nor broached a lively conversation. He was simply a cordial presence and a willing and contented participant.' He used to stick his head round Williams's office door in London like a jack-in-the-box, 'eyebrows raised enquiringly and a smile at the ready in his bright blue eyes . . . He would come briskly in and start talking in his rapid staccato manner, jacket buttoned up, as always, and a quick pull at the knot of his tie.' His moods were reflected, above all, in his eyes. 'One might be gossiping with him of this and that, and he would be attentive and involved,' Robert Lusty remembered. 'Some word, some name, some project might strike a certain chord and on the instant Allen would be neither attentive nor involved. Cold little shutters would close upon the light in his eyes. Someone, something, somewhere had had it. The unpredictable was predictably about to happen: and nearly always rightly so.'

Although, in Bill Williams's opinion, Lane had done 'nothing to cultivate his mind or enlarge his knowledge' since leaving school, he was 'an inveterate and diligent quizzer' who listened to other people with 'modesty and eagerness', and was adept at picking their brains. He had, Williams felt, 'picked up a lot about books and their authors without actually reading them, and in this respect he was unique among all the publishers I have known' – which suggests that, for all his important connections, Williams had little understanding of Lane's fellow publishers, the best of whom worked in exactly the same way. According to Williams, Lane was never a nimble mathematician, and his letters, 'whether dictated or written in his own hand, were devoid of any distinction: they were pedestrian, often awkward, and never felicitous'. Ruari McLean observed that Lane 'did not appear ever to have read a whole book, but had a superb instinct for books', and that his 'façade was that of a clubman, most at home when telling stories in front of the smoking-room fire': meetings with printers were constantly interrupted by phone calls to Lane's farm manager, and were invariably brought to an end with a cry of 'Now let's all go across to the Peggy Bedford and have a drink!' Lane's eagerness to escape to the pub was never more apparent than at meetings: he would writhe in his seat, say little, and do his best to subvert the proceedings, playing 'ducks and drakes' with the agenda, as Bill Williams put it. Sometimes meetings were held in the Peggy Bedford, which made the proceedings more bearable: Bernhard Baer, the serious-minded German editor of Penguin Prints, was shocked to find an editorial meeting taking place in a rowing-boat at Silverbeck, lubricated with lashings of gin.

But Lane's bonhomie was matched by his reserve. 'He had an easy, likeable way,' Bernard Venables recalled, 'but I always felt there was some guard behind that. That you'd be talking with apparent intimacy, but there was another Allen Lane standing by, making notes . . . But he had the ideal mix of mercenary and missionary for what he did.' Lane's reserve was sadly apparent in the long letters written him over the years by two of his closest associates, Bill Williams and Harry Paroissien. Paroissien had joined Penguin in 1947, the year of the famously frozen winter, when coal and fuel stocks ran critically low, the grimness of post-war austerity seemed set to last for ever, and many printers and binders had to close down (one ingenious binder defied the shortages by attaching bicycles to his machines). A mole-like character who smoked a pipe, Paroissien was dour, loyal, diligent and devoted to the interests of Lane and Penguin Books, a natural lieutenant who did what had to be done efficiently and well, resented change, and took pains to see off any threats to his own position in the firm. A cultivated character, if his handwriting is anything to go by – when young he had dealings with John Betjeman, who thanks him warmly in the foreword to *A University Chest* – he had worked for Simpkin Marshall, edited *Books of the Month*, and spent the war working for the British Council in North Africa and the Middle East; most recently he had been the managing director of the Book Export Scheme, designed to revive exports at a time when American publishers, bolstered by Marshall Aid, were making inroads into British markets while their London equivalents, still battered by paper quotas and currency restrictions, struggled to regain their old ascendancy. 'I found that Harry and I had so much in common in our knowledge of this odd publishing business, and that our reactions were so similar, that I now have no doubts on at least one member of the team,' Lane assured Paroissien's wife Eileen; a year or two later, in case Paroissien had any doubts, he insisted that 'I am slow to give my allegiance or friendship, and I am not more honest than the next man, but once given I am pretty constant.'

Paroissien was a good deal more reserved than the garrulous and bonhomous Williams, but they were as one in their eagerness to write Lane the office equivalents of love letters. Both are touchingly eager to prove their admiration and affection, and to break down his impenetrable reserve. They tell him, again and again, how highly they esteem him, and how working for Penguin has been the single most important ingredient in their lives: yet, like frustrated lovers, they get little in return, at least in letter form, and their outpourings of emotion elicit nothing more than conventional business letters, dictated on the hoof, in which the humdrum details of discounts and quantities ordered are interlaced with snippets of office gossip, welcome in themselves but hardly the response they craved. Reserved as he was, Lane's failure to reciprocate may have been a deliberate technique: he relished power, and one of the means whereby the powerful keep their subordinates on their toes is by promising intimacy, and whipping it away when those to whom it is offered hurry forward to claim their reward; the half-open gate clangs to, and they are left to begin all over again. Because Lane seemed so amiable, it was easy to misread the signs; and, of course, he was far busier than most, and, as head of the company, needed to retain a degree of detachment and reserve.

He continued, as ever, to combine parsimony with sudden acts of hidden generosity. He insisted that pencil stubs should be handed in before new ones were issued, and when Bob Davies, the European rep, asked for a new briefcase when his eventually collapsed, he was handed an old one of Lane's, in even worse condition; but when he learned that the daughter of Jimmy Holmes, the production manager, had leukaemia, he gave her a pony and invited her to ride it at Priory Farm. He made any excuse for a party, including the redecoration of the ladies' lavatories; and the firm's twenty-first birthday was celebrated with a party at Silverbeck – 'nothing fancy, but rather jovial and alcoholic' – and every member of staff was given a history of the firm with a freshly minted one pound note for every year of service tucked inside. Cricket matches were organized with neighbouring villages and firms, and the annual office outing was resumed. Before setting out for Le Touquet in 1950, Lane addressed the fifty-odd members of staff about the vexed matter of 'lavatory accommodation' in France, and warned them about the dangers of drinking too much Pernod, while Dick reminded them that 'On the other side of the Channel you have to speak up.' The outing had been a great success, he told Paroissien: 'The plane trip, a new experience to the majority of the staff, caused some mild apprehension, but fears were soon allayed, and no paper bags were put into use.' Several members of staff viewed French food with grave suspicion, but, with rationing still in force, happily returned home laden with bananas, brandy, nylons, chocolate and sugar.

Most members of staff admired Lane for what he had achieved, and their idealism about Penguin and pride in their work made up for modest pay packets and austere working conditions. According to Isabel Quigly, who joined as an editorial assistant in 1948, fresh from Cambridge, the offices were sometimes so cold that she and her colleagues worked in their overcoats. She was particularly taken by Lane's unpretentiousness and lack of pomp: towards the end of his life, years after she had left the firm, he spotted her in the Tube – in itself a commendation – and he let out a cry of 'Quigles!' and bounded across the compartment to greet her. Employees were expected to turn their hands to anything, irrespective of qualifications or expertise. David Herbert wangled a job by writing in with such persistence that Lane felt obliged to employ him. He knew nothing about selling books, but one day Lane told him, 'I want you to go on the road tomorrow. Borrow my wife's car – she won't like it – and go to the mining valleys': but despite reversing Lettice Lane's Morris Minor up vertiginous Welsh slopes, Herbert failed to sell a single copy. As Nikolaus Pevsner soon discovered, cars – or the shortage of cars – loomed large in Penguin deliberations. David Hedges, the London rep, was given the use of Dick's Rover, the proprietorial owner of which regularly inspected it for telltale scratches and abrasions; and when Dick was sent out to Melbourne to run the Australian office, and Harry Paroissien was posted to Baltimore, much time and correspondence was given to shunting second-hand cars around the world.

With a few honourable exceptions – Trollope, Sinclair Lewis, Dickens, Roy Fuller and P. G. Wodehouse among them – writers have tended to neglect office life, but in 1947 an insight into Harmondsworth life was provided by Tom Harrisson's Mass Observation: eight years earlier, the organization had been responsible for the Penguin Special *Britain by Mass Observation*, but this report was for internal consumption only. The report began, soberly enough, by trying to define the average Penguin reader. Basing their findings on questionnaires fielded in Hammersmith, Bethnal Green, Middlesbrough and Worcester, the MO teams discovered that 41 per cent of middle-class respondents were Penguin readers, as opposed to 17 per cent of the artisan class and a mere 8 per cent of the working classes, and that 44 per cent of Penguin readers had benefited from some form of secondary education whereas 8 per cent had never got beyond the primary stage; and that although those who never read books at all tended to be working-class women over forty, more women than men read Pelicans. After quoting *Tribune* to the effect that 'Penguin Specials broke into a new book-reading market. Millions of people who had never before been touched by socialist propaganda or by the Labour Party found themselves guided daily to the left by their reading,' MO revealed that – according to their polls – Penguin readers were five times more likely to vote Labour than non-Penguin readers. 'There is no doubt,' it declared, 'that Penguin's public is pre-eminently a "Keep Left" public.'

With the statistics behind them, the observers moved into Harmondsworth itself. Although some Penguin employees, and in particular those editorial types who insisted on living in central London, faced long bus or train journeys to work, others bicycled or walked across the fields. The hours were eight to five or nine to six, with half an hour off for lunch in a 'drab and cheerless canteen', inherited from the Air Ministry along with a Nissen hut which housed accounts, and an aircraft hangar which served as a bulk store. The directors and senior staff ate in the canteen along with everyone else, and fetched their own meals, but tended to stick together; the door invariably jammed open, causing icy blasts to rush through and exciting loud cries of 'Shut that door', and the leftovers were fed to the pigs on Priory Farm. The buildings were unheated; the ladies' lavatory was arctic, and staff were expected to bring their own soap and towels. Those with time to spare after lunch could entertain themselves with a game of table-tennis, and all members of staff benefited from a free medical once a month. There was a strong sense of camaraderie among survivors from the Crypt – Dick remembered how the rustling of mice sometimes gave them a fright when writing invoices in the middle of the night – and a good many references, emanating usually from Lane and Bill Williams, to the need for a 'snifter', particularly after a meeting. The meetings themselves were genial, informal affairs: Frostie kept her colleagues informed about 'the younger contemporary intellectual circles', and contemporary writing usually aroused stronger feelings than academic works. At the annual Christmas party, the canteen was decorated with satirical drawings, dinner was served on long trestle tables and paper hats were worn; directors and senior staff donned white waiters' jackets and served at table, and Lane mixed cocktails in a silver shaker shaped like a penguin.

Despite the visiting doctor and the celebratory snifters, those interviewed were not entirely complimentary about their presiding genius. 'He's got no sympathy with people he thinks are no good,' said one. 'You can never get hold of him, and when you do get him, the phone rings, people keep coming in, and this that and the other, and you never really get through,' complained another, seemingly unaware of a trait shared with many other monomaniacal publishers, and tycoonery at large. Lane's wealth excited a degree of resentment. 'He'll be buying himself his own aeroplane before long,' suggested one respondent, while another, who had damaged an office door by using it to prise the crown top off a beer bottle, was duly unapologetic: 'Oh, Mr Lane's door. Good job he's got a lot of money . . .' A satirical drawing pinned up in the canteen over Christmas showed Lane at his desk with a memo pad which read:

1. Lunch at Ritz
2. Recover from above
3. Must sign my letters

Dick's equivalent listed all the things he needed for a journey:

1. Sloe gin
2. Fishing rods
3. Sloe gin
4. Cigars
5. Hooks
6. Clothes
7. Sloe gin
8. Sloe gin
9. Penguins to read on train . . .

The onset of middle age may have dimmed some of Lane's youthful zest, but neither he nor Dick had lost their taste for booze.

'I suppose it is a result of too much party-making in my youth, but in recent years I have tended to shun them more and more,' he told Carrington, who had suggested a party at which Lane could meet Puffin authors and illustrators involving 'say a dozen gins and half a dozen sherry, which should be enough to raise spirits without indulging in an orgy', but he continued to host innumerable parties at Silverbeck, and drink loomed large in letters and repartee. In 1947, the year in which he inaugurated a pattern of taking at least a month off every summer, he wrote to Dick from France to say that he liked to consume two large glasses of *vin blanc* at 12.30, snooze all afternoon, and return to the *vin blanc* in the early evening. Despite the snoozing and the *vin blanc*, work was never far from his mind: over the years, colleagues back in the office would become inured to a steady bombardment of letters and phone calls in which he ventilated his worries about the firm, plans for the future, and grouses about the inadequacies of other members of staff, and insisted on being told every detail of that day's sales figures.

Back in England, Lane told Dick that he had decided to abandon spirits for wine, far less accessible then than now, so that 'we can have our own bottle mid-day or on the way home': be that as it may, when he and Lettice attended a farewell dinner at the Junior Carlton Club for Clifford Prescott of Woolworth's, and they were offered a post-prandial choice of rum or kummel, Lane instantly ordered 'Both!' and Ruari McLean would have us believe that when the Lanes came to dinner and were offered a choice of gin or sherry, Lane opted for 'Oh, half and half, thank you.' According to Nikolaus Pevsner, Lane 'couldn't take the drink, he was so easily just slightly sozzled, nicely sozzled but emphatically sozzled'. No doubt he was emphatically sozzled whenever he got together with Peter Heaton, the author of *Sailing*. Time, Lane told him, was always in short supply, but 'this never kept me long from the bottle, and I would welcome a foregathering in the near future'. One thing led to another, and before long Lane was writing to ask whether Heaton would be interested in 'some (serious this time) heavy drinking in the near future???' Despite his fondness for Bernard Shaw, he was far removed from Orwell's lethal stereotype of the teetotal and vegetarian high-minded left-winger, and sometimes seemed immune to the privations of post-war England. His birthday dinner in 1946 was attended by Tatyana (Tanya) Kent, a new member of staff recently arrived from Uruguay, Bill Williams and Estrid Bannister, Frostie, Dick and his girlfriend, Ifor Evans and the typographer Oliver Simon and his wife Ruth, about to embark on her long affair with Rupert Hart-Davis: Evans and Williams sang and made speeches in Welsh, and the meal consisted of caviare followed by roast goose, washed down with liberal quantities of champagne, claret and port.

Tatyana Kent was to become one of Lane's closest and most dependable colleagues. He had met her first in 1944, when he set out to investigate the competition posed by American publishers in the South American market. Whereas British publishing had always been aware of, and reliant on, export markets, their American equivalents, with their vast home market, had never paid much attention to foreign parts. During the war, however, they began to encroach on markets which the British had always regarded as theirs – and not only countries in the open market, where both Americans and British were contractually free to compete, but in those English-speaking countries of the British Empire which the British retained as part of their exclusive market. Although the British book trade had, miraculously, continued to export a sizeable chunk of its turnover throughout the war – in Penguin's case this had sometimes involved the local manufacture of books under licence, not least in Australia – the problems involved in shipping stock out through submarine-infested seas had taken their toll, and the relative unavailability of British editions had made far-flung markets vulnerable to American competition. To make matters worse, American paperbacks looked better, were printed on better paper, and – most alluring of all – came wrapped in full-colour picture jackets: something that appealed in particular to Canadians and Australians, with their New World tastes. Although South America had never formed part of the British publishers' exclusive market, American publishers had hitherto paid little attention to it until Alfred Knopf, the most stylish of New York literary publishers, alerted his colleagues to its potential in terms of sales and publishable authors. Bearing letters of introduction from the British Council and the Ministry of Information, Lane visited Colombia, Peru, Brazil, Chile, Uruguay and Argentina, and while in Montevideo and Buenos Aires he was taken in hand by Tatyana Kent, who was employed by the British Council in Montevideo and acted as an interpreter in his dealings with local publishers. Bilingual and a keen Penguin reader, she had grown up in Uruguay and was anxious to continue her studies at the LSE. Lane encouraged her to come to England: he was toying with the idea of starting a series of Spanish-language Penguins, but although the scheme soon petered out, Tatyana (or 'TK', as she was always known) arrived in England in November 1945, by way of New York, where she stayed with Eunice Frost. Once in England, she was immediately plunged into Penguin life, translating from the Spanish where necessary, trying to make sure that Lane arrived at meetings on time and stayed to the end, and taking dictation in the back of his chauffeur-driven car as they drove to and from London for editorial meetings in Bill Williams's office at the Bureau of Current Affairs in Piccadilly (now that the war was over, the prefatory 'Army' had been dropped). Lettice invited her to stay at Silverbeck, where she lived for a year: she remembered bowls of clotted cream on top of the Aga, Dick cooking the occasional evening meal (on one occasion badger was served), and Lane dictating letters while having his hair cut: 'as likely as not', she told her mother back in Uruguay, 'you would find him scrubbing out the larder or cleaning out the tool cupboard'. Lane's friend Elwyn Jones, who was married to the novelist Pearl Binder and went on to become Attorney General under Harold Wilson, was a member of the British prosecuting team at the Nuremberg Trials, and invited him to attend in 1946: Lane was made a brigadier for the occasion, and TK was deputed to iron his uniform in readiness.

Elsewhere in Silverbeck life seemed, on the surface, harmonious enough. Lane was devoted to his three daughters, who, in the summer months, splashed naked in the pool at Silverbeck while a steady stream of guests clutching gin and tonics sauntered round the well-kept gardens; old habits persisted, with Bernard Shaw writing to say that he thought it 'perfectly wicked to start an innocent child wasting her time with the useless practice of autograph-hunting (except at the foot of cheques). Why not buy her a teddy bear? But I suppose I must oblige you.' But for all the jollities and the long family holidays in France, marital life was increasingly fraught. In the spring of 1949 Lane told Frostie that he and Lettice were seeing a psychiatrist: though 'genuinely sorry' for Letttice, he felt that her upbringing was to blame, and worried about the children, 'to whom I am devoted'. He would love to talk to Frostie about it, since 'I would value your opinions more than anyone else's'. 'What a life!' he added, ruefully enough, though 'I do feel I mustn't so change my own character and way of life as to make my own contribution to the world less vital.' There seemed little chance of that.

13. The Search for Perfection

While on holiday with the family in France in the summer of 1947, Lane found himself worrying about the use of slang in a Penguin Classics translation of Maupassant's 'Boule de Suif' and other stories. He wrote to Dick on the subject, with special reference to page 240. 'Each book which goes to press should be as perfect as possible and carry with it the feeling that it is not just another paperback but a book on which considerable thought has been expended,' he told his brother, adding that he had just finished *Moll Flanders* and was about to embark on *Barchester Towers*, and that while on holiday he had taken to drinking an iced vermouth before lunch and two-thirds of a bottle of wine with the meal, 'and now I'm off for my mid-morning snort'. The fact that he had got as far as page 240, was evidently reading the book with some care, and asked Dick at the same time to investigate the running heads for the new Penguin Shakespeare *Coriolanus*, gives the lie to those who like to believe that he never read anything except P. G. Wodehouse's *Performing Flea* and Rachel Carson's *Silent Spring*: and the whole episode is indicative of what John Betjeman once described as 'the innate sense of quality that runs through all you do'. Lane's perfectionism was not infallible – referring to some editorial 'blemishes' in *The Romans*, the accompanying volume to H. D. F. Kitto's evergreen Pelican on *The Greeks*, Bill Williams pointed out that there was 'only yourself to blame' since although it had been agreed that between them they should vet every new book before it went into production, this particular title 'was on your desk from the time you were on holiday' – but to make sure that his publications came as close as possible to his ideal, he employed two of the most demanding and insistent perfectionists ever to have worked for a publishing house. Lane might come up with the bright ideas – on another French holiday he made a point of visiting the recently opened caves at Lascaux, sensing a book in their Stone Age paintings – but it would be up to A. S. B. Glover to make sure that every statement in the resulting book was correct, while Jan Tschichold brought the same scrupulous attention to detail to every aspect of its layout and typography.

Over the years, Alan Glover had subjected Penguin to such a steady stream of letters pointing out factual and typographical errors that Lane decided the only way to stem the flow was to offer him a job. Glover was, by all accounts, one of the most extraordinary men ever to grace a publisher's office: his range of knowledge and almost photographic memory were of immeasurable value not just to those titles, mostly Pelicans, which were first published by the firm but, since in those days titles bought in from outside were always reset in the Penguin house style, to reprints as well, and did more than anything else to establish the notion of Penguin's reliability and near infallibility. An owlish figure, hidden behind a pair of heavy horn-rimmed specs and parading an arsenal of fountain pens in his breast pocket, he was invariably clad, according to Isabel Quigly, in a 'dark shirt, heavy tweed jacket, woolly tie and a single grey cotton glove, or rather mitten, with the fingers chopped off'. His entire body other than his left hand was rumoured to be covered with tattoos, from his heels (these were sometimes glimpsed through a hole in his socks) to his balding pate; those on his cheeks – an Indian on one side, a cowboy on the other – had been partially removed, and his name was visible behind one ear.

Baptized Allan McDougall in 1895, Glover had spent four months at Christ's Hospital before moving to the City of London School, where he had mastered Sanskrit; although he had come top in every possible exam, he had not gone on to university, and his awareness of this inflamed his urge to omniscience. He had, at some stage, enrolled as a Franciscan tertiary – medieval Latin remained a particular enthusiasm, and he had translated hymns, liturgical fragments and stretches of St Thomas Aquinas – but since then he had become a Quaker and, more recently, a Buddhist, his knowledge of which faith he put to good effect when editing Christmas Humphreys's Pelican on the subject. As an extreme conscientious objector, he had spent much of the First World War being shunted from prison to prison: he spoke with authority on the amenities on offer in Pentonville and Durham, and, having a waggish sense of humour, liked to disconcert strangers by referring to his time at Winchester, later revealing that he had in mind the prison, not the school. With Stanley Morison, he had edited a prison newspaper, written on sheets of lavatory paper; it was claimed that, in addition to going on hunger strike, he had worked his way through the entire *Encyclopaedia Britannica*, committing much of its contents to memory; he also knew Bradshaw's Railway Guide by heart, and was unusually well informed about cricket scores and the varieties of religion. He made an appearance in Morchard Bishop's novel *The Green Tree and the Dry*, published by Cape in 1939, five years before he joined the Penguin staff:

Though only twenty-eight, he looked a good deal older. For this his four years in prison were no doubt responsible. His hair, which was thick and curling and originally quite black, was already beginning to turn grey at the sides. It was too long, which gave him an untidy and shaggy appearance. He had a big nose, and large, round-lensed horn-rimmed spectacles, and he carried himself very upright, perhaps because he was rather short. He wore a light tweed suit and a dark green shirt with a pink tie, and his voice was on the loud side, high-pitched, its original Cockney basis over-laid by an acquired refinement.

In the novel, 'Norton' and his wife dabble in theosophy and read Aquinas to one another of an evening, and she leaves him for another man; in real life, Glover's first wife died in childbirth, while his second went on to make a bigamous marriage. When Glover joined the firm he was living in West Hampstead with a schoolteacher called Janet Morrell, immured by books and gramophone records: marriage would have been frowned upon at the school where she worked, so was never contemplated.

Before being invited to Penguin, Glover had worked for Burns & Oates, the Catholic publishers, for Routledge & Kegan Paul, for Odhams and, improbably, for the *Reader's Digest*. A workaholic by any standards, he continued to work for Routledge long after he left Penguin in 1960, as well as for the Bollingen Foundation, which was sponsoring publication of the Complete Works of Jung: in his addendum to Glover's *Times* obituary, Lane – his mind on other things no doubt – referred to it as the 'Bollinger Foundation'.

J. E. Morpurgo claimed that Glover was 'the only man I have ever known who could correct galley-proofs whilst strap-hanging in a busy rush-hour tube', and his editorial feats were equally impressive. 'You say on page 78, near the bottom, "A Salesian father did so and so",' he told Evelyn Waugh, apropos the Penguin edition of his *Edmund Campion*. 'This refers to 1580, but at this date St Francis of Sales was only thirteen years old and the order known by his name, the Salesian, founded by Don Bosco, did not come into existence until the nineteenth century.' 'It was, of course, "Silesian",' replied the over-awed author: it was 'extraordinary that the book can have been read aloud in refectories, commended to students and so on for years, and no one should have spotted it. I am most grateful.' Glover drew on another area of expertise when corresponding with Freeman Wills Croft, the detective story writer:

You say of your hero at the beginning of the second para: 'He reached Wembley to find a steam train about to start for town,' but this is surely impossible. Under the act passed at the end of the last century which provided for the extension of the Manchester, Sheffield and Lincolnshire railway to London along the lines of the Metropolitan, it was expressly provided that no Great Central trains should stop between Harrow and London, and therefore they never stopped at Wembley Park.

A similar knowledge was brought to bear when reading the proofs of a new edition of *Major Barbara*. The play, he told Shaw, was riddled with anachronisms of a kind that would 'strike those who are familiar with the waste between West Ham and Bermondsey': the characters should travel by trolleybus – the last tram had been withdrawn in 1939 – and a particular eating-house should be an ABC, since the chain referred to had disappeared in the 1920s.

Ruari McLean, who returned briefly to Penguin after wartime service in the Navy, thought Glover 'by far the most pleasant and admirable man on the staff'; Isabel Quigly relished his 'quizzical, mysterious air' and recognized him as 'the main influence on (such as it is) my intellectual life'. For younger editorial members of staff, many of whom had joined the firm straight from university, Glover was a mentor and a spokesman. Though overworked and under-paid himself, he wrote long memos to Lane on behalf of his younger colleagues, urging him not to take their good will for granted, and to provide longer holidays and better pay. It was important, he told Lane, that they should be kept informed about what was going on in the firm, that they should, in the firm's interests as well as their own, have enough time to follow up their own interests, and keep up with changes in the political, cultural and literary worlds; they should, he suggested, 'be recompensed for their work with some-thing more concrete than kind words and smiles', and to do so would dispel the notion, widespread in the world at large, that Penguins were 'produced by sweated labour'. Lane almost certainly resented Glover's well-meant if long-winded interventions, in much the same way as he resented Dick's bank-managerly advice. Nor can he have been best pleased by a long letter from Glover, received on holiday, in which the older man, blundering benignly but misguid-edly into unfamiliar and hostile terrain, presumed to criticize, as an equal, Lane's colleagues from the early days. 'I do feel more and more that Bill's judgement, though by no means without its value, is often questionable if only because too hasty,' Glover suggested, adding that Lane shouldn't 'let Bill get away with things too easily'; as for Frostie, 'Do, please, when you get back try and keep EEF on the rails' – she was 'looking ghastly again' and was 'as preoccupied and nervey and worried as before'. He was almost certainly right on all counts: but his opinion had not been sought, nor was he, in Lane's opinion, in a position to tender his views. Glover's editorial labours were invaluable, but he would never become one of the cronies or courtiers upon whom Lane increasingly depended, or a member of the inner circle. Lane referred to him as 'that old Buddhist'; and whereas Williams was, by Glover's standards, both indolent and lightweight – too lazy to walk the short distance from his office in Piccadilly, he asked Eunice Frost if she, or some editorial underling also working in Harmondsworth, could pop round to the London Library in St James's Square to pick up some books he needed for an anthology of English essays he was compiling for Penguin – he was, unlike Glover, a convivial boozing companion from the carefree days before the war, and someone with whom to spend the time of day.

If Glover was the means whereby Lane could realize his insistence on the highest possible editorial standards, Jan Tschichold was responsible for giving the Penguin list its incomparable elegance and quality of design and production. Once again, it was Lane who knew what he wanted, and insisted, against the advice of his colleagues, on appointing him to do the job; and he did so at a time when, in Oliver Simon's words, 'the typographical care and experience that had been lavished on the *edition de luxe* was ready to be used for the mass-produced book'.

Although some publishers of the late nineteenth and early twentieth centuries – Grant Richards, William Heinemann, J. M. Dent and John Lane himself – were interested in typography and the design of their books, a great gulf was set between the rarefied, art for art's sake perfectionism of the private presses, of which William Morris's Kelmscott Press was the most celebrated example, and the routine work churned out for commercial publishers by jobbing printers. The productions of the private presses were too few in number, and far too expensive, to be bought by the general reader, and catered only to the very rich and to full-time collectors; the new techniques of mass production made it possible to produce books faster and more cheaply than before, but seemed to have little relevance to those who regarded the book as, ideally, a thing of beauty in itself as well as a means of conveying information and entertainment. Gradually, however, the two strains began to converge. Dent's Everyman's Library combined echoes of William Morris in their elaborate title pages and endpapers, yet were produced in such quantities that the firm had to build its own printing works and bindery at Letchworth to cope with the flow; and in 1922 Stanley Morison was appointed typographical adviser to the Monotype Corporation, set up in 1897 to exploit an

American invention unable to find backers in the States. Just as the invention of the punch-cutting machine in the late nineteenth century had made it possible to cast typefaces mechanically rather than by hand, so firms like Monotype were able to combine the design standards of the private presses with mechanical composition: a scholar of lettering and typography, and of the Italian Renaissance practitioners in particular, Morison favoured elegant, legible, classical faces, and he revived several classical typefaces as well as producing his own Times New Roman. With Francis Meynell, the founder of the Nonesuch Press, he edited the journal *Fleuron*, published between 1923 and 1930, in which they campaigned for their ideals of legibility, elegance and practicality, and criticized both the Arts and Crafts movement and some modernists for producing work that was striking but illegible; and, as the typographical adviser to Cambridge University Press, Morison was able to put his principles into practice.

Lane's own instinctive elegance and sense of style had, with the help of Edward Young and others, manifested itself in the simple but appealing lines of the early Penguins; but although the spirit had been willing, he had not, as yet, been able to draw on the kind of professional expertise embodied in Morison, Meynell and Simon; nor had the war made life any easier. Both production and design had been run in a spirit of inspired amateurism: Bob Maynard, with no previous experience, had been left in charge after Edward Young's departure, and when he left to join the Navy design matters became the responsibility of John Overton, né Hans Oberndorfer, whose father was said to have been a Viennese friend of Lane's, and whose office experience had hitherto been of a clerical kind: according to McLean, Overton became at some stage the typographical adviser to the Emperor of Abyssinia before moving on to Australia, Uganda and Pakistan, but further evidence of this is not forthcoming. Dealing with printers and papermakers had fallen to the equally inexperienced Jimmy Holmes. At the end of the war Charles Prentice, a former chairman of Chatto & Windus, helped out on the design side, but he was too tired and ill to make much impact. Ruari McLean briefly resurfaced, but saw no future for himself in the firm so long as Overton was *in situ*, since 'I wanted to design books, not go on fighting Germans': he went on to design *Eagle*, the bestselling comic for middle-class schoolboys in the 1950s, redesign the *Observer* for David Astor, and become an authority on matters typographical.

By 1947 Lane was determined to sort out the future appearance of Penguin Books. He asked Oliver Simon who was the best typographer and book designer in Europe, or perhaps the world, and when Simon recommended Jan Tschichold he picked up the phone to Switzerland, told Tschichold what he had in mind and, within a matter of days, was on a plane to Basel, with Simon at his right hand: according to Dick, who disapproved of the whole business, the pilot wore civilian clothes and a cloth cap, and added a few more gallons of fuel at the last minute 'just to be on the safe side'. A neat, beaming, cherubic-looking character, given to rimless specs and bow ties, Tschichold had been born in Leipzig in 1902, the son of a sign-painter. As a young man in the 1920s he had been associated with the Bauhaus; a passionate devotee of asymmetrical lettering and the use of uncapitalized sans serifs – a look much favoured by modish advertising agents like Crawford's when they wanted to emphasize modernity and speed – he became well known during the Weimar period for his elegant if indecipherable film posters, in which the image was set askew and explained by means of a thin ribbon of type, also set at an angle. The Nazis, with their enthusiasm for gothic blacklettering or *fraktur*, denounced his work as 'Kultur-Bolshevismus', and he was arrested in his Munich flat and stripped of his job. Released from prison after six weeks, he and his wife moved to Switzerland, where they lived in a flat that was entirely white except for the shiny black floor; and whereas the Nazis abandoned blackletter in 1941, partly because it was considered illegible in the conquered countries of Europe, Tschichold abruptly abandoned his Bauhaus principles in favour of classic typography of the most severe and elegant kind, with headings and text centred on the page and, in the main body of the text at least, not a sans serif to be seen. He had visited England in 1935 when, at the suggestion of McKnight Kauffer, Lund Humphries staged an exhibition of his work; while in the country he redesigned the *Penrose Annual* for his hosts, and addressed a meeting of the Double Crown Club.

A ruthless perfectionist, Tschichold once declared that it was 'more difficult to design a book than to draw a landscape'. Before he left for England he insisted on being sent an example of every printed item produced on Penguin's behalf, from books and posters to labels, headed notepaper and invoice forms; these were then marked up, and his conclusions (invariably scathing) distributed to, in particular, the Penguin editors. Once installed in Harmondsworth, he found English printers maddeningly slow, old-fashioned and aesthetically unaware. Standards of composition were far lower than in Switzerland: 'Fine typefaces, bad composition and appalling hand composition are the characteristics of the English printing house,' he declared. There were, it seemed, no composition rules to be followed: typesetters worked to nineteenth-century conventions, seemed to have no real interest in their work, sent everything by post in the most leisurely manner, and, if forced to send revises, took an age to produce them. Paid by the key-stroke, and therefore more interested in quantity than quality, they maddened Tschichold by inserting far too much white space between words and after full stops, while at the same time refusing to allow any horizontal light into the page by means of leading. The hand compositors, responsible for the all-important title page and prelims, proved even more benighted and uncooperative than their colleagues on the Monotype machines; to Tschichold's intense frustration, they seemed to have no idea of spacing letters by eye rather than by rote, so he had a rubber stamp made which read 'Equalize letter-spacing according to their visual value.' Baffled by his insistence that 'Capitals must be letter-spaced', some of the bolder spirits tried to revolt, at which – according to McLean – Tschichold 'produced a bland smile and could not understand English'. He sometimes insisted on as many as ten revises for a title page, and told an elderly Hazell, Watson & Viney compositor that he would never achieve perfection unless he used tissue paper to separate the settings of type rather than wafer-thin strips of metal. Printers' costings allowed for one revise rather than seven or ten, and it may well be that when, in the late 1960s, it was discovered that Penguin was paying far more than its rivals for composition and printing, this almost certainly reflected the high standards insisted on by Tschichold and his equally punctilious successor, Hans Schmoller, as a result of which printers were building the cost into their estimates. Lane was delighted with his new appointment. 'I think he could produce perfection,' he told Dick, who was outraged to learn that Tschichold was being paid more than anyone else on the staff, and he relished the 'quick and decisive moves he makes when he appreciates the problem'.

Tschichold worked at Penguin for twenty-nine months, and during that time he designed and prepared for press over 500 books, on a page-by-page basis. In doing so he combined discipline with flexibility: he designed a standardized grid or layout for the various Penguin series, but whereas Stanley Morison at Victor Gollancz had insisted on uniform title pages, Tschichold designed the title pages – some austere, others ornate – that seemed to suit a particular book or subject. Nor did he insist on uniformity of typeface: he thought Times New Roman better suited to newspapers than books, but made good use of those classic faces – Baskerville, Garamond, Bembo and Caslon – which Morison had resurrected for the Monotype Corporation. Nor did he confine himself to lettering: he redrew Edward Young's portly penguin ('deformed' was his epithet) eight times before settling on the elegant bird we know today; when drawing the lettering for the new cover of the Penguin Shakespeare series – his own typography perfectly complemented by Reynolds Stone's woodcut of the bard – he worked, painstakingly, with a pin held in a pen-holder. Like Glover, he was not afraid to beard the mighty. His most celebrated battle was with Dorothy Sayers, who had taken exception to his use of decorative asterisks in her Penguin Classics translation of Dante's *Inferno*. 'In your letter you express the opinion that no self-respecting title page should ever carry an asterisk,' he told her, his mastery of English magically rising to the occasion. 'I wonder where you learned this, but in any case it is the master who establishes the rules and not the pupil, and the master is permitted to break the rules, even his own.'

After the devaluation of the pound in 1949 Tschichold returned to Switzerland, where he worked for the pharmaceutical firm of Hoffman-La Roche and, according to his successor at Penguin, 'squandered' his gifts on 'brochures and leaflets for tranquillizers and other ephemera for a doctor's wastepaper basket'; but during his time with the firm, Ruari McLean has suggested, he 'had probably done more for British book production as a whole than any other single book designer', while in Alan Bartram's opinion, 'No British typographer had the finesse, the ruthlessness or the obsession to carry out the job.' His influence spread far beyond Penguin, affecting publishers, printers and typographers alike. His insistence, shared by Schmoller, that book designers should produce detailed layouts and instructions for printers was something hitherto unheard of in the British book trade, but soon became the norm; his detailed Penguin Composition Rules were used or adapted by innumerable firms, and their iron grip within Penguin itself was only diluted when, in the early 1980s, the firm abandoned the tradition of resetting all books bought in from outside, and offset (i.e. photographed) the existing pages instead. He also won a long battle to improve the quality of the paper used by Penguin, replacing a dirty grey with a smooth cream stock. Tschichold's reforms were inevitably expensive, but, in Lane's opinion, well worth it. Compromising standards of design or production gave Lane positive displeasure: he was reluctant to replace stitched with 'perfect' binding, and sent Raymond Hazell a copy of *Anatomy of Peace* – 'You will see by the position of the bus ticket that I have got to page 48' – and asked him how much more expensive it would have been if bound in the old way.

Far removed from the austere perfectionism of Glover or Tschichold, Bill Williams continued to provide an endless stream of advice, and not just on editorial matters: he recommended, for example, that A. J. Ayer should be appointed editor of a new Pelican philosophy list, a suggestion that was swiftly taken up, and he spoke sound sense on Penguin's role in the world at large. 'My overall hunch is that Penguins will be the last to feel the cold wind of austerity now blowing up again,' he told Lane as another sterling

crisis loomed following the restoration of the pound to full convert-
ibility. 'The general reaction will be to buy cheaper commodities,
and my bet is that book-buyers will be more disposed than ever to
buy the cheaper Penguins rather than the hardback book. I have
always felt that Penguin Books was particularly well-rigged in the
nautical sense to stand up to the slump . . .' Brooding on the vexed
issue of exports, Bill Williams urged Lane not to spread his wings
too wide, to concentrate on the home market and the under-
developed markets of India and Africa at the expense of the rest of
the world: the Marshall and Truman Plans both came with strings
attached in favour of dollar purchases, and there seemed little point
in trying to compete.

As he moved into middle age, and Penguin expanded along with
his waistline, Lane became more akin to the Roi Soleil, with an
inner circle of dark-suited cronies who fought for his favours and
whom he played off one against the other: Penguin became increasingly political, a place of machinations and conspiracies, with Lane
the spider at the centre of the web. 'Tishy' – Tschichold – was too
transient, and Glover too high-minded, to become members of the
inner circle, but Bill Williams, with his instinctive understanding
of the corridors of power, was in his element, conspiring and
conspired against. He continued to keep his distance in terms of
both the time he gave to the firm and his conditions of employment, but for a brief moment he and Lane discussed the possibility of his upgrading his involvement from that of a part-time
adviser to taking charge of the editorial department at
Harmondsworth. 'I feel far more constructive zeal in the outfit
than I have felt for a long time,' he told Lane in the summer of
1947 – acting as Lane's hatchet-man, he had just given J. E.
Morpurgo the sack, of which more later, and the adrenalin was
running high – 'and I like to think that I will have more to do in
the future with our developments than I have had in the past.' 'Bill,
I think, feels rather lost when there is no meeting on and he has
nothing to do but hang around in my room,' Lane informed Dick:
he should be given an office of his own, and 'with Bill as Chief
Editor, Tishy as Typographer and Paroissien as sort of General

Manager, we ourselves should be able to spare more time for farming and other like pursuits'.

Lane's devotion to his farm was as great and as genuine as his devotion to Penguin, and from now on the dream – or the threat – of early retirement, or at least of taking a back seat in the running of the firm, was to become a recurrent motif in his letters and conversation, misleading friends and colleagues alike and causing havoc among those unwise enough to take him at his word. Williams, for his part, suggested an 'inner cabinet' consisting of himself, Lane, Paroissien, Dick and Tschichold, since the rapid growth of the firm 'involves, so far as you personally are concerned, the exercise of the habit of delegation . . .'

By 1948, Lane had changed his mind about Williams's role in the firm. The consummate cultural bureaucrat, Williams was now spending part of his time with Unesco in Paris, and before long he would become Secretary-General of the Arts Council. As such, Lane told him, he was 'in the unparalleled position of having contacts in so many fields: Unesco, the Bureau, the Arts and British Councils etc., all of which are of inestimable value to us, and enable you to keep your finger on the pulse'. Working full-time for Penguin would 'bore you stiff'. Writing from Paris, Williams hurried to agree. Although Penguin was 'my permanent love' and 'the most constructive and exciting job I know, or am ever likely to know', he and Lane were far too alike: Lane must be the leader, and for them to duplicate their roles would be pointless.

Williams used his contacts to bring editors and authors to the firm, but Frostie and Glover were left to knock their offerings into shape and deal with the innumerable small but time-consuming chores involved in transforming an author's typescript into a published work: Frostie, not Williams, was expected to edit the contributors to A. J. Ayer's philosophy list, a formidable team of academics that included Stuart Hampshire, G. J. Warnock, T. D. Weldon, Richard Wollheim, Father Copplestone and Ayer himself. However waspish, temperamental and crushing she may have seemed to junior members of the firm, Lane trusted her entirely, and confided to her his anxieties about his private as well as his professional life.

Writing to Frostie from the *Queen Elizabeth* in the summer of 1949, he asked her to buy him a cuckoo clock in Switzerland in exchange for some much sought-after nylons from New York, before moving on to the perennial topics of her health and the running of the firm. 'We must jointly see that there is no recurrence of the condition,' he insisted, though whether her 'condition' was neurotic or her 'TB thing', or a mixture of the two, remains unclear. 'There is a lot to be done which only you and I can do and we must conserve our energies and delegate as much as we can to leave ourselves enough time for policy planning,' he told her, for 'you and I bear the bulk of the responsibility for the running of the firm, and we mustn't do anything which would jeopardize our fitness to carry on the work.' Recent attempts to hand over responsibility to a committee had not been a success, not least because the two most important members – Frostie herself, and Paroissien – had been absent: Stan Olney 'is, we know, of no importance', Overton 'lies like a trooper', and Glover 'has no integrity [a curious charge] or at least not sufficient strength of character'. As for Bill Williams, Lane confided, he was 'a problem in a class by itself'. He was becoming increasingly irritable and unreliable, and never more so than over the matter of some rather low-grade thrillers by Peter Cheyney which Lane had agreed to buy from Sydney Goldsack at Collins: for Williams to 'oppose Cheyney and recommend Sax Rohmer (I've just read one of each) shows a complete lack of responsibility'. He had no illusions left about Williams: 'I am moving with considerable caution, and my spies tell me that he on his side takes a somewhat dreary view of me. We must have less temperament in the operation, more working on a solid basis as opposed to hunches.' With that off his chest, Lane confessed that he had jumped off the wagon after being invited to drinks in Ernest Bevin's suite: Williams had alerted him to the fact that the Foreign Secretary kept 'a pretty selection in alcohol', and he was intent on sampling what was on offer.

Frostie shared his views on their colleagues, describing Williams and Glover as 'sources of infection' within the firm, and warning him of how Glover was unable to keep a confidence, appeared to need adulation from its younger members in particular, and would 'say anything, especially to the younger members of the staff, in order to ingratiate and give the impression that he is very close to you and that you rely on him a lot'. Frostie's reference to her colleagues as 'sources of infection' strikes a chilling, almost Stalinist note; and in due course she too would be carried off, a victim of a rapidly changing world that she neither liked nor understood.

14. Buildings and Classics

If office life was becoming ever more Byzantine, Lane's readiness to back new ideas remained as fresh and ardent as ever; and his readiness to run risks, and his faith in backlist publishing, were fully vindicated when, in 1946, he defied the doubts of his colleagues by publishing E. V. Rieu's translation of Homer's *Odyssey*, which went on to become one of the best-selling titles in the history of the firm, selling over 3 million copies, and to form the foundation stone of the Penguin Classics.

A benign, granitic-looking character, keen on garden gnomes, prep-school jokes, cats and light verse, of which he was a nimble practitioner, Rieu was fifteen years older than Lane. His father had been Keeper of Oriental Manuscripts at the British Museum; after St Paul's and Balliol he had gone out to run OUP's first Indian branch before serving in the Mahratta Light Infantry during the First World War. He had then gone to work at Methuen, where, at the recommendation of Graham Greene, he added Christopher Isherwood to the list, and sold Lane the reprint rights in Eileen Powers's *Medieval People* and Olaf Stapledon's *Last and First Men*. He began to translate the *Odyssey* in 1931, reading it aloud to his wife, Nellie; as the translator of the Babar the Elephant books, she knew a good story when she heard one, and urged him to continue – and to do so in prose, rather than attempt a verse rendition. He mentioned his translation to Lane, who liked what he read and, ignoring those of his colleagues who warned him that there was already a glut of translations on the market, decided to go ahead and publish. The book was an immediate success, and Lane told Victor Weybright that Rieu was 'bucked as a dog with two tails over the magnificent reception the book has had here'.

But that was not the end of the story. Two years before the *Odyssey* was published, Rieu wrote to say that he had Methuen's

consent to his editing for Penguin a new series devoted to translations from the Greek and Latin classics; he had made a long list
of potential titles, and was looking into the possibility of including
translations from other languages as well. Colour-coded by language,
and sporting engraved roundels on the cover, Penguin Classics
proved a huge success, elbowing Everyman's and World's Classics
aside in their chosen area, and including translations from Russian,
Portuguese, French, Arabic, Norwegian, Icelandic, German and
Italian: Rieu himself went on to translate the *Iliad*, Virgil's *Pastoral
Poems*, Apollonius's *The Voyage of Argo* and *The Four Gospels*. The
translations commissioned by Rieu were to be free of notes and
academic paraphernalia, and although he began by approaching
academics he found that few could write decent English and many
were 'enslaved by the idiom of the original language'. As often as
not, he commissioned translations from professional writers: among
those who contributed to the series were Dorothy Sayers, earlier
seen doing battle with Tschichold over the asterisks in her translation of Dante; the novelist Rex Warner, responsible for
Xenophon's *The Persian Expedition*; that tireless polyglot J. M.
Cohen, who not only translated *Don Quixote*, *Gargantua and
Pantagruel* and Rousseau's *Confessions* but edited the *Penguin
Dictionary of Quotations* and innumerable Penguin anthologies,
including *Comic and Curious Verse*, wrote *A History of Western
Literature* for Pelican and was the General Editor of the marvellous
poetry list; the poet David Wright, who made *Beowulf* intelligible
to the world at large; and Robert Graves, who not only provided
a popular rendition of Suetonius's *The Twelve Caesars*, but worried
that his version of Apuleius's *The Golden Ass* might be prosecuted
for obscenity. 'I personally am not at all apprehensive on this score,
and would be prepared to consider the deletion of the usual libel
and obscenity clause from the contract in this instance,' Lane told
his anxious author. 'My view is that we are publishing for a sophis-
ticated audience, and I would be perfectly willing to justify this
policy were it brought into the courts.' Graves continued to dither,
so Bill Williams was quoted as saying 'without hesitation that it
would be a crime if we were to cut a word from the edition as it

stands'. 'My dear Allen, All right. Have it your own way. WEW ought to know,' Graves scribbled on the bottom of Lane's letter, and the book was put into production forthwith. By the time Rieu retired in 1964 there were over 200 titles on the list, and at his farewell party, which was adorned with a bust of Homer borrowed from the British Museum, Lane declared that 'If I were asked which I considered to be the series which had given me personally the greatest pleasure, I would without question say it was this.'

Paper shortages and a sluggish economy made it hard to keep existing titles in print – Lane told Blanche Knopf that 'by husbanding our reserves we can only manage to keep some 200 titles on our active list' – but Penguin Classics was not the only ambitious new series to be launched in the aftermath of war. One day, towards the end of the war, Nikolaus Pevsner and his wife Lola were sitting in the garden at Silverbeck when Lane suddenly said, 'You have done the King Penguins now, and we are going on with them, but if you had your way what else would you do?' Without hesitating for a moment, Pevsner outlined his ideas for a multi-volume guide to the buildings of England. Lane took out his gold propelling-pencil, scribbled some figures on a scrap of paper and said, 'Yes, we can do them both.' No salesman was consulted, no costings produced, no battle was done with a literary agent: Lane had given both series his support, and it was up to Pevsner to justify his faith.

An austere but kindly figure, lean, balding and sporting a pair of wire-rimmed spectacles, Nikolaus Pevsner was the same age as Lane. After taking his doctorate at Leipzig University, he had been Assistant Keeper at the Dresden Art Gallery before becoming a lecturer in the History of Art and Architecture at Göttingen University. Despite his blond looks and conversion to Lutheranism, he was, as a Jew, removed from his post when the Nazis came to power. He made his way to England, where he worked for a time as a fabrics buyer for Gordon Russell, the furniture-maker, and published his *Pioneers of the Modern Movement* in 1936. While on a research fellowship at Birmingham University he wrote to J. M. Richards at the influential *Architectural Review*; his future bugbear, John Betjeman, was also associated with the magazine, but this did not prevent Pevsner from becoming a regular contributor, writing pieces on carpets, light fittings and kitchenware. Interned when the war broke out, he was released in 1941, thanks to the efforts of Kenneth Clark and Frank Pick; after a brief spell helping to clear bomb debris, he took over as editor of King Penguins and began to teach on a regular basis at Birkbeck College. By now Pelican had commissioned him to write *An Outline of European Architecture*: reviewing the typescript in 1942, Richards told Frostie that Pevsner had done the job of condensing a vast amount into very little space 'extraordinarily well', but that it was 'a little bit dull to read and may not seem very inspiring to the general reader'. When Richards went off to war, Pevsner became an increasingly influential figure on the *Architectural Review*: though an admirer of the austere lines of the Bauhaus and a champion of the functional, undecorated, anonymous 'international' style of architecture, seeming to embody the idealistic, egalitarian notions of planning, standardization and modernity that appealed to advocates of the New Jerusalem, most of the articles he wrote for the magazine had to do with the history of architecture rather than its most modern manifestations.

Despite rationing, austerity and a shortage of cars and petrol, it was a good moment to launch a series which would, inevitably, take years to complete: signposts, removed during the war, had been restored to the roads and lanes of England, and by the time the first three titles were published life was beginning to improve for the footloose middle classes, whose forays to the Continent were severely curtailed by currency restrictions. There was little competition. Back in 1933, John Betjeman and John Piper had persuaded Jack Beddington at Shell to sponsor a series of architecturally-based county guides, each to be written by a suitable enthusiast; by the time war broke out thirteen titles had been published by Faber, but lively and entertaining as they usually were, they were never intended to be scholarly or exhaustive. Shortly before the war broke out, Penguin itself had published a series of guides, edited by L. Russell Bone, but they were thought feeble compared with the Blue or Shell Guides, and although they were revived after the war and survived until 1960, they soon expired. Pevsner had, in vain, tried to interest publishers in a series based on a German model; and now Lane had offered him all he desired.

Pevsner decided that he would try to polish off two counties a year, travelling round with notebook in hand during the vacations from Birkbeck and writing up his findings as he went. To help him on his way he employed two émigré German art historians, and although he was unable to drive, he set about wangling the use of a car. Lane lent him a 1933 Wolseley Hornet, plus thirty gallons of petrol, and – since it was the nearest county, and conveniently flat – the Pevsners set out to explore the wilds of Middlesex, with Lola at the wheel. Pevsner was a superhumanly hard worker, but even he found the regime exhausting. 'The journeys are just not human,' he reported back to base. 'To bed 11, even 11.30, too tired even to read the paper. Up this morning at 6 to scribble, scribble, scribble . . .' Much of his correspondence was devoted to cars and their faults. In October 1947 he sent Lane a list of all that had gone wrong with the Hornet, including a faulty indicator, a punctured spare wheel and a broken solenoid ('Is there such a thing?' Pevsner wondered). Nine months later he wrote in to say that travelling round by bus was far too slow: he was hoping to pass his driving test in time for the next county, but in the meantime wondered whether he could use the car once again; that autumn he reported difficulties in starting the Hornet, and confessed that he had 'succeeded in making several dents and scratches'.

No doubt Dick was intensely irritated by the dents and scratches, and he was understandably concerned when an inspector from Scotland Yard called to say that several country-house owners had reported a suspicious-looking character with a German accent who, after writing to ask if he could inspect their houses, turned up with a tape measure in his hand. The first three titles – Middlesex, Cornwall and Nottinghamshire – appeared in 1951, initially in paperback. Simultaneous hardbacks were introduced the following year: the jackets and the intricate but elegant text layout were designed by Tschichold's successor, Hans Schmoller, and the woodblock roundels on the front covers were often the work of Berthold Wolpe, best remembered for his Albertus typeface, employed to stunning effect on the book jackets he designed for Faber. Sales were disappointing, and print-runs had to be reduced to 20,000 copies per title. Penguin lost £30,000 on the first twelve volumes, and Lane took to introducing Pevsner as 'my best-losing author': but although the two men were never close ('I don't think he opened up very easily,' Pevsner told Schmoller after Lane's death. 'He was very pally, but I think this went up to a point, and not beyond'), Pevsner remembered, with gratitude, that he had never seen Lane 'put finance first and the quality of a book or a man second'. Financial disaster was averted when Pevsner managed to drum up subsidies from, among others, the Leverhulme Trust; and he himself went on to write thirty-four of the titles in the series, and co-author a further ten.

Lane's support was unstinting when it came to Pevsner's other brainchild, the Pelican History of Art, a large-format hardback series that might have looked more at home with a university press. Authoritative and impeccably produced, with a Pelican colophon specially drawn for the series by Berthold Wolpe, they were old-fashioned in spirit and approach, looking back to the ponderous, monochrome art books of the Thirties and far removed from the full-colour, co-production art books which were being pioneered at Phaidon and Thames & Hudson. Pevsner warned Lane of the large sums of money that would inevitably be tied up in books that were expensive to produce and slow to move out of the shops (or, indeed, the publisher's warehouse): once again, Lane unscrewed his gold propelling-pencil, scribbled on the margin of his newspaper, and declared, 'No, that's all right – there's no need to worry.' The Pelican History of Art was very different from anything Lane had published hitherto, at least at Penguin, and Kenneth Clark, for one, thought it a great mistake: Bill Williams reported a meeting in New York at which Clark said, 'We are departing from our chosen function of cheap accessibility.'

Whatever Clark's views, a party was held in the garden behind Pevsner's office in Gower Street in July 1949 to celebrate the fiftieth King Penguin: some penguins were brought from the Zoo, one of which lost control and savaged a guest. Some better-behaved birds were in evidence when Ralph Tubbs and his wife drove Pevsner down to Priory Farm to one of Lane's parties; they squeezed him into the dickey of their open Alvis, and he chortled with pleasure as his sparse grey locks fluttered in the wind. When they got there they spotted some penguins staggering about the lawn and, still more conspicuous among the dinner-jacketed guests, Aneurin Bevan in a heavy tweed suit, queuing outside the marquee for his dinner.

Not all Lane's editorial initiatives had the critical or commercial success of Penguin Classics or the Buildings of England. During these post-war years he wanted to excel in areas already dominated by long-established firms like Oxford University Press or Collins, and sometimes lost his bearings as a result. A Penguin atlas was not a great success, and an attempt to break into the costly and competitive world of natural history publishing proved an expensive write-off, and one that exemplified the old axiom that sensible publishers work within their strengths and limitations, and stray outside them at their cost. The story of *British Wild Flowers* is not, of itself, of great importance, but both its author and its illustrator wrote sprightly prose, and provided entertaining and perceptive accounts of Lane's business methods.

Best remembered, perhaps, for his jacket illustrations for the Cape editions of the James Bond novels, Richard Chopping was a meticulous artist who had been introduced to Noël Carrington by Kathleen Hale, and had already provided the artwork for *Heads, Bodies and Legs*, a Baby Puffin, and *Butterflies in Britain*, a Puffin Picture Book. Towards the end of the war, he went to see Lane at Whitehall Court to discuss a book on spiders. Walking across Green Park afterwards, Lane said he wanted to 'publish a book of English wild flowers so that I can throw it on the desk of other publishers and say, "Well, there you've got a flora of the British Isles with the Scarlet Pimpernel, the Blue Pimpernel, every bloody pimpernel."' Lane's competitive urge may have been inflamed by their passing close by the offices of Collins in St James's Place, just off Green Park. Not long afterwards, Billy Collins started the New Naturalist series, edited by James Fisher and Julian Huxley: it went on to become one of the great achievements of post-war publishing, but whereas Collins would eventually insist on illustrating his series with

colour photographs, Lane was contemplating a fantastically expensive nine-colour printing, with the artwork to be provided by
Chopping, who told Lane that he would need to be paid a full-
time salary for as long as was needed. The text was to be written
by his friend Frances Partridge, a junior member of the Bloomsbury
world and a close friend of Noël Carrington; she remembered
Chopping as a 'very sweet character, affectionate, gentle, kind and
inquisitive', and was impressed by the fact that he washed his socks
every day and hung them on the line. It was agreed that each flower
should be given a full page illustration, with explanatory text on
the opposite page, and that *British Wild Flowers* could well run to
twenty-two hardback volumes. Seemingly undaunted, Lane agreed
terms, and author and artist set to work.

Every now and then Chopping would show some work-in-
progress to an 'ever-appreciative' Lane; and, when not concentrating
on the minutiae of British flora, he subjected his publisher to the
same exacting scrutiny. 'A pocket Napoleon', Lane tended to be

inscrutable, lips shut in a tight line only opening for essentials, no small
talk. Grey, well-cut suits, as if he had been too well tailored and poured
into the mould of his clothes when there was just a little too much of
him for them. Very well manicured, shaved, hair never out of place,
reminding me a bit of my old headmaster who had the same impatient
intensity as of a wound-up spring waiting to uncoil . . . I was for ever
in awe of him. Not scared, but never relaxed; always on the edge of trying
to be very articulate so as not to waste his time. As if it was necessary to
be constantly alert, as he was, never to miss the main chance, whatever
it may be. And I don't mean that in a derogatory sense at all, rather that
he grasped a situation, recognized the usability of a relationship, and saw
people's potential clearer than they saw it themselves.

Frances Partridge was a good deal less impressed. In June 1946
Carrington arranged for 'the Tycoons' – Lane and Geoffrey Smith,
the series' prospective printer – to visit her at Ham Spray, her house
in the Berkshire downs. Both writer and illustrator were in a nervous
state of mind – the costs of the project were steadily rising, so much

so that there was talk of having to charge four guineas a volume –
but, according to Chopping, 'Mr Lane was in rather a frivolous
mood, preferring to talk about the number of choc ices they
had eaten on the journey.' Frances Partridge was less charitable, and
her lethal observations are quintessential Bloomsbury in their old-
fashioned snobbery and high-minded disdain for trade. The two
men arrived in a 'smooth, long-nosed Bentley', which was bad
enough, but worse was to come. 'Allen Lane, a stocky figure squeezed
into a smart suit of palest grey, was purely and simply the millionaire in an American film,' she recalled years later. 'He appeared to
be acting a part, an important element of which was manifesting
the "common touch" by revealing a passion for choc ices. Yet I'm
sure he never ceased thinking of himself as the personification of
power through money, benevolent but not to be "had". This for
some reason made him rather pathetic.' As they were leaving, she
reminded him that they had met in the 1920s, when he was a Bodley
Head rep and she was helping out at the Bloomsbury bookshop run
by Francis Birrell and David Garnett, and 'his millionaire pomposity
crumpled just a fraction at this reminder of his boyish diffident self'.
Refreshing as it is to have a less reverential view of Lane, delivered
by a writer rather than a fellow publisher or colleague, one sees
exactly why Lane felt ill-at-ease in the company of upper-class,
Oxbridge-educated literati.

As the project inched its way forward, Chopping's forbearance
came close to breaking point. 'Really, Lane is the limit,' he
complained to Noël Carrington:

One doesn't mind being kept waiting several hours in a cold cattle market,
one forgives him for not answering an important letter about one's contract,
and then three months after completely ignoring all one's questions, one
even makes allowances for him when he doesn't answer one's second in-
vitation for the weekend, I must say one forgives all these as they crop
up, but now and again, when one reviews one's past achievements and
one's relationship with one's publisher, when perhaps one is not feeling
quite so indulgent, I find that I take a very poor view of it and I say
again that he is the limit. If I wasn't in the position of one employed by

him, and can't complain of his generosity or non-interference, I should tell him that he is appallingly rude, that many people think Penguin not only incompetent but crooked, and that I am getting tired of sticking up for him and championing his cause.

Nor was he well disposed to Frostie, who was left dealing with the practicalities: he thought her an 'enigma' and a 'menacingly grey eminence', whose role was 'uncomfortably equivocal, as if she had the ear of both sides, but the intimate cooperation of neither'.

By the end of the decade it had become obvious that *British Wild Flowers* was no longer a feasible proposition: the costs had soared — so much so that Tschichold warned that the firm might go bust if the project was not abandoned — and painted illustrations, however accurate, seemed dated when compared with the colour work on display in the New Naturalist books. By now Chopping had recovered his equanimity, and was better disposed to his publisher. 'Throughout Allen behaved impeccably, never angry, never sentimental, always just, always aloof, a little impatient perhaps of the slowness of others. One felt one had walked through the cold corridors of power in the publishing world, that one had felt the draught and come out into the open air again.' Lane, he declared, had 'foresight, energy and buried somewhere inside a warm, tough heart'. Frances Partridge was as implacable as ever. She and Chopping went to see Lane in his gaunt, ugly flat in Whitehall Court, with its huge leather armchairs, said to have belonged to Ribbentrop when he was the ambassador in London; he told them that Penguin could no longer continue with the project, and 'his innocent air of candour covering a businessman's astuteness faintly sickened me'. Her squeamishness seems unfair: according to Elizabeth Barber of the Society of Authors, who acted on behalf of the author and illustrator, 'no negotiation can ever have been conducted in a more sympathetic atmosphere', and Frances Partridge was paid £1,500 — a huge sum in those days — in compensation.

Lane came under attack from another quarter when he decided to close down Porpoise Books, a short-lived children's imprint. Grace Hogarth, a highly esteemed children's book editor, was employed to edit a series of hardback illustrated books, priced at 3s. 6d. in printings of 100,000 copies. The four titles published included Edward Ardizzone's *Paul the Hero of the Fire* and V. H. Drummond's *The Flying Postman*, but that was not enough. 'Allen Lane has decided, quite arbitrarily, to sack me, and has fired me as editor. The result is that some four or five artists have been left high and dry,' Grace Hogarth told the illustrator H. A. Rey. Some 150,000 copies of the published volumes were flogged off to a remainder merchant at 4d. each, eventually making their way to New Zealand; their editor's dismissal was an example of Lane's tendency to take someone on in a fit of enthusiasm, suddenly change his mind, and get rid of him or her with equal despatch ('It sounds as though Allen is prac- tising on his guillotine!' a colleague remarked when building works were in progress, and the office resounded with thuds).

The Penguin History of England was a longer-lasting and more successful series, but like Grace Hogarth its editor enjoyed an uneasy relationship with Lane, and like Richard Chopping he provided an entertaining if tendentious account of their relationship. Described by the Mass Observation observer as 'a dark, slim man, rather hunched, with the vitality of a Cockney', J. E. 'Jack' Morpurgo was a London boy; his family was Jewish, but he preferred to keep this under wraps. Educated at Christ's Hospital and at universities in America and Canada, he had had a good war, serving with the Eighth Army in India, North Africa and Greece. Servile and self- important, pompous and prone to persecution mania, he is the Uriah Heep of the Penguin story: in later years he claimed a far greater intimacy with Lane than was ever offered, saw himself, for no good reason, as the heir-apparent, and when neither intimacy nor inher- itance came his way, took his revenge by writing a biography of Lane in which protestations of love and admiration fail to disguise the bitterness and resentment of the spurned courtier. He had literary ambitions, and while serving as a soldier he published a story in *Penguin New Writing* and contributed to *Transatlantic*; in his biog- raphy of Lane, in which he appears in the third person, he claims that he was recommended to Lane by both John Lehmann and George Orwell, but it is obvious from the surviving correspondence that, despite the story in *PNW*, Lehmann had no idea who he was and thought little of his work, and no doubt Orwell would have looked equally baffled if questioned on the matter. Be that as it may, Tom Fairley, the editor of *Transatlantic*, got it into his head that he might be the man to succeed him, and arranged a meeting with Lane. 'We met in a tiny and untidy room,' Morpurgo recalled in his autobiography. 'Allen gave me a glass of white wine and glared suspiciously at my rank badges, my burnished Sam Browne and my campaign ribbons. I saw a brisk, handsome man in his early forties, looking like a yeoman farmer who had submitted himself to the scrupulous attentions of the best barber and most exclusive tailor in London.' Lane's tone was 'sharp and chilly', which Morpurgo put down to his discomfiture in the company of those who had fought in the war. Lane asked Morpurgo if he could hitch a lift to Whitehall Court in his taxi; they shook hands as they parted, and 'for the first time I saw what I was to see so many times in the coming years, a mischievous smile, the grin of a boy that knows that he has done wrong and does not regret it'.

Not long afterwards, Morpurgo was summoned to lunch at Silverbeck. Still working for the War Office's Public Relations Directorate, and still in uniform, he was driven down in a War Office car with an ATS driver at the wheel, and arrived 'just in time for the first of five gins' (a liking for drink was something they had in common). He was introduced to Lettice, 'a pretty, intelligent woman who appeared to have no interest in publishing and no knowledge of why it was that I had been invited'. Throughout the meal Lane fielded telephone calls and studiously ignored his guest, but when it was over he suggested a stroll in the garden. As was his way when interviewing prospective employees, Lane never mentioned publishing but talked instead about farming, a subject about which Morpurgo knew next to nothing, but as they were walking back to Morpurgo's car, Lane suddenly said, 'Come and work for me.' He was thinking of setting up a public relations department, something hitherto unknown in Penguin, and Morpurgo seemed the right man for the job.

All this was heady stuff for a twenty-seven-year-old major in need of a job, but then, in Lane-like fashion, a great silence descended, and Morpurgo heard nothing more about it. Lane proved evasive when he tried to get in touch; later Morpurgo discovered that he had, at the same time, offered the job to Fairley – 'but I soon learned that disloyalty of this kind, like the evasiveness with which he served me, was endemic to Allen's nature'. Morpurgo decided to look elsewhere, and was offered a job at the BBC. The threat of competition stung Lane into action, and he suggested that Morpurgo should attend an editorial meeting in Bill Williams's office at the Bureau of Current Affairs. It was attended by Dick, Bill Williams, Frostie, Glover, Edmund Segrave, the editor of the *Bookseller*, and Lane himself. Lane said little, but grunted, smiled or scowled as the mood took him, occasionally coming up with 'I met an old boy at a party last night. He has an idea for a book . . .' Dick, 'a larger, less mercurial version of Allen', puffed his pipe throughout and provided figures when needed; Lane later advised Morpurgo to 'pay no attention to Dick. He doesn't know anything about anything.' Glover delivered monosyllabic verdicts on books proposed for publication; Frostie was a 'fair-haired, bird-like woman' who seemed 'almost obsessively dedicated to Allen and to Penguin', so much so that 'when he nodded, she nodded, and when he glared she scowled'; Bill Williams provided a steady flow of gossip about authors in a voice that combined a Welsh accent with a slight stammer, and Morpurgo 'came to suspect that Allen kept him as a prompter and, as often was needed, a hatchet-man, and because the society was forever changing, an immutable'. The meeting over, Lane 'looked disparagingly at my military trappings' and finally offered him the job.

For a time Morpurgo moonlighted from the War Office before joining Penguin full-time in the autumn of 1945, working in a Nissen hut behind the main building in Harmondsworth. In addition to his public relations work, he edited and wrote much of *Penguins Progress*, which had been suspended during the war and was mailed free to Penguin readers, giving news and background information about forthcoming titles; and he succeeded Denys Kilham Roberts as editor of *Penguin Parade*, three issues of which were published after he took over. He also claimed to have made a modest contribution to musical education, though this has been disputed. Lane, in fidgety mood at an editorial meeting, suddenly burst out with 'I think we're getting into a rut' and demanded that someone come up with an idea. 'Come on, Jack, something to wake us up,' he said, rounding on the hapless Morpurgo. For no apparent reason, Morpurgo, who knew nothing about music, suggested Penguin Music Scores, small enough and portable enough to be carried by eager concert-goers. Gordon Jacob, who also claimed to have suggested the scores, was appointed series editor; landscape in format, with patterned paper covers, many of them created by Elizabeth Friedlander, the scores were objects of beauty in themselves.

Morpurgo was bright and energetic but, for whatever reason, his face didn't fit: when he rashly claimed credit for the way in which 'Penguin' had become synonymous with paperbacks, Lane rounded on him with 'and because of you, now every sleazy production published by shoddy publishers in Warrington is called a Penguin'. By the summer of 1947 Lane had decided that 'he's better out of the team'. After an editorial meeting in 117 Piccadilly, Lane, Dick, Frostie and Tanya Kent went out to lunch, Glover made his own way back to Harmondsworth, and Morpurgo and Bill Williams were left alone in Williams's office. Williams poured them both a large gin and said, 'AL thinks you would be even more use to us if you got some more experience elsewhere. Then you can come back.' 'I did not mince words with Morpurgo, nor did he show resentment of any kind,' the hatchet-man reported back to his master. 'I simply pointed out to him that he had no future in the firm, and that in his own interest he should look out for other work.'

But that was not the end of the story. Next morning, back in Harmondsworth, Lane popped his head round Morpurgo's door, assumed his 'naughty boy grin', and said, 'You are always nagging us about our shortage of history titles. Get us a History of England.' Advancing into the room, he perched on the edge of the desk and added, 'I don't want any of the grand old men. I want the historians who are going to be the grand old men in thirty years time.'

For the next three years Morpurgo busied himself commissioning titles for the Penguin History of England before moving on to the History of the World: few of the historians he commissioned are remembered today apart from J. H. Plumb, who eventually succeeded Morpurgo as advisory editor on the history list, but the History of England in particular was a critical and commercial success, and the books became required reading for sixth-formers, undergraduates and lay readers eager to learn about the Normans or the Stuarts without having to plough through a scholarly work as stout as a telephone directory. 'During all the period when I edited the History series I was also one of Allen Lane's very few confidants,' Morpurgo once claimed, though supporting evidence is not forthcoming. He left in 1950, but his involvement with Penguin, and with Lane, was far from over.

Despite the new series, Penguin continued to rely on hardback publishers to sub-license rights in a good many titles, and novels in particular. Harold Raymond at Chatto still had his reservations – 'I regard the cheap paper-covered book *à la* Penguin as one of the greatest dangers to the book trade,' he told Charles Prentice as late as 1944, adding that this was 'the result of close observation of the figures over a number of years' – but they did not prevent Chatto from joining in a scheme whereby a select group of publishers agreed to give Penguin the first offer of their books in exchange for an 'over-ride' royalty, paid directly to the publisher, and a guaranteed first printing of 100,000 copies of each title. Lane was beginning to worry about competition for paperback rights, and this was a way of keeping the enemy at bay. Chatto, Faber, Michael Joseph, Hamish Hamilton and Heinemann joined the group, and the first ten titles included J. B. Priestley's *Angel Pavement*, Lytton Strachey's *Eminent Victorians*, T. S. Eliot's *Selected Poems*, Maugham's *Cakes and Ale* and Raymond Chandler's *The Big Sleep*. According to Robert Lusty, then at Michael Joseph, the participating publishers were invited down to Silverbeck for a celebratory lunch. On arrival they were offered 'martinis of a strength and in quantities of unaccustomed prodigality', which were 'delivered to us on some conveyor belt system presided over by a Wodehousian butler acquired by Allen for the occasion'. Inflamed by drink, all those present made speeches; Lusty was driven back to Bloomsbury by A. S. Frere of Heinemann, singing sea shanties as they wove their way through the traffic. It was, all in all, a very Lane-like occasion.

15. An Estate of the Realm

Looking back on the books he read as a schoolboy in the Forties and early Fifties, the writer and editor John Gross has written that Penguins were 'indispensable', and how 'in those days the imprint seemed rather like the BBC: not so much a publisher as an estate of the realm'. Penguin, Arthur Calder-Marshall told listeners to the BBC's European Service in the summer of 1945, was a national institution, comparable with the BBC, Sadler's Wells or the Old Vic: its founder was 'a very simple man who has perceived a simple truth, out of which he has made a fortune – that people will choose the best, if they can afford it', and no other firm aroused 'such affection, such pride and almost a proprietory interest'. All this had been achieved in an astonishingly short period of time, but although success brought Lane both wealth and acclaim, the Fifties proved an uneasy and unexciting decade for his firm: a degree of smugness set in, the list was less exciting, and its standing as a benign monopoly came under siege from brasher, more populist competitors.

Lane's achievements received formal recognition in 1952, when he was knighted. His immediate reaction was to take to his bed for the day; in due course his mother accompanied him to Buckingham Palace, where his fellow-initiates included Hugh Casson and John Rothenstein, and then he set about answering the tidal wave of congratulatory letters. Letters were received from, among others, Feliks Topolski, David Astor, Lance Beales, the Duchess of Atholl, Ben Travers, Billy Collins, Sybil Thorndike, the Salvation Army, W. H. Smith's (Cairo branch), the Corner Stores in Stanwell Moor, Powers-Samas Accounting Machines and John Wilder Ltd, Agricultural Engineers. Victor Gollancz bit back any sense of pique he may have felt ('Very few honours given in my lifetime have been better deserved'); Sir Geoffrey Faber's letter gave particular pleasure, since he enquired after the Ayrshires on Priory Farm; Stanley

Morison hoped Lane would not now be too grand to join him in a glass or two in El Vino; Robert Maxwell combined congratulations with the suggestion of a meeting to discuss the possibility of his buying Penguin Books (Harry Paroissien had warned Lane that 'Captain Maxwell' had recently taken over the British Book Centre in New York, as a result of which they must 'keep a wary eye that bills are paid'); Ralph Tubbs's letter provoked a query about the boiler at Silverbeck; Harold Raymond, all doubts now seemingly cast aside, told him that only the night before he had thought to himself, 'Some day they'll knight Allen, and so they damn well ought . . . You hit on a good idea, and never wavered till you had put it across.' 'I bet you never imagined this would happen in the days of the old crypt in the Euston Road,' wrote Edward Young. 'How encouraging it is to know that the finest, best conceived and most adventurous publishing venture of the century has not passed unnoticed. Usually when someone one knows appears in the honours list, one says "Good God! What next?" . . .'

'Pride of place must go to the godmother who gave the name at the christening,' Lane modestly insisted, and if Joan Coles would pay a visit to Silverbeck, 'we would unroll the red carpet for the occasion'. 'Don't carry self-effacement to the point of denying your personal responsibility for this historic feat,' Bill Williams urged. 'In some ways you are a light-hearted character, and you have always been inclined to suggest that Penguins is a kind of immaculate conception, a mystical accomplishment in which you have played a subsidiary part.' All this was very satisfactory, and so too were Lane's finances: that same year he was reckoned to own assets worth nearly £215,000, consisting of 37,500 shares in Penguin, valued at £187,000, a half share in Priory Farm worth £12,500, a half share in two houses worth £3,000, and insurance policies valued at £12,000; on top of which he paid himself a salary of £5,000 a year.

Boardroom paintings are as emblematic of business success as knighthoods, and Lane was not immune to their allure: to his credit, he opted for a group painting, with himself to one side, and it was hung on the staircase at Harmondsworth where everyone could see it. Entitled *After the Conference*, and painted in the mid-Fifties,

Rodrigo Moynihan's canvas was, in effect, a work of fiction, in that those portrayed had never been assembled in one room together, let alone attended an imaginary editorial meeting. It featured such names from the recent past as John Lehmann, Jack Morpurgo, Michael Abercrombie and Gordon Jacob as well as Dick, Frostie, Bill Williams, Nikolaus Pevsner, E. V. Rieu, A. J. Ayer, A. S. B. Glover and Eleanor Graham, each of whom had a separate sitting with the artist. A. J. Ayer later remarked that 'it might have been called a conversation piece if any of us had seemed to be conversing', but since some of those included had never met, this was not a possibility; and the room in which they were portrayed was neither the boardroom at Harmondsworth nor Bill Williams's new office at the Arts Council, but the senior common room at the Royal College of Art. Dick was appalled by the size of the painting, and worked out that it had cost the firm a shilling per square inch. His worries were not entirely absurd: for all its success, Penguin still lived off its overdraft, and Harmondsworth, Silverbeck, Priory Farm and Lane's Bentley were owned, in the last resort, by Martins Bank.

Moynihan's painting was a mythological work in more ways than one, in that it looked back to a Penguin world which, during the course of the decade, became ever more embattled, and was populated by characters whose connection with the firm would cease or become increasingly tenuous over the next few years. A decade that began with Attlee as Prime Minister and ration books an everyday item ended with Harold Macmillan's boast that 'You've never had it so good' and the post-Suez wave of Angry Young Men: young people in particular had more money to spend, and not necessarily on books. The Queen's Coronation in 1953 had famously boosted the sale of television sets, and three years later the BBC's own benign monopoly was broken with the introduction of commercial television. Penguin's position was also under siege – and in what was, in terms of sales at least, the most valuable section of the market.

Moynihan's painting was also misleading in that it suggested that Penguin was exclusively highbrow and literary in its tastes and terms of reference, and in the years since Lane's death the firm's reputation has, to some extent, been hijacked by those who look back to a golden age as mythical as *After the Conference*. Reflecting its founder's taste, the list had always had a solid middlebrow basis, from Agatha Christie and Ethel Mannin in the pre-war years to, in the 1950s, such strong sellers as Monica Dickens, John Wyndham, Henry Cecil, C. S. Forester, Ngaio Marsh, Margery Allingham, P. G. Wodehouse and Pierre Daninos's two books about Major Thompson, devoured in huge quantities on this side of the English Channel for their admiring evocation of an England that was rapidly slipping out of sight. And the early Pelicans in particular were aimed at the lay reader; far from being works of original scholarship, they were designed to act as introductions to their subjects, written by experts in clear and accessible prose.

Penguin's pre-war imitators and rivals had soon vanished from the scene, but a far stronger contender soon appeared. Sporting a logo designed by Mervyn Peake, Pan had been set up in 1944 by Alan Bott and the Book Society, but three years later it was taken over by a consortium of Collins, Macmillan and Hodder; over the years its ownership changed, most notably when Billy Collins, anticipating a trend, decided to paperback his books 'in-house' under the Fontana imprint and withdrew from the Pan consortium, but its backers were invariably large, well-established firms with extensive middlebrow lists there to be exploited. The original Pans were in a larger format than Penguins, but before long they adopted the more familiar pocket size: under an agreement with the Board of Trade, the firm was allowed to print in France provided half the print-run was earmarked for export, and the manner in which, once a fortnight, finished copies were carried by barge from Paris and across the English Channel was celebrated by Lane's old associate Robert Gibbings in *Coming Down the Seine*.

Not only did Pan and its successors present a challenge in the middlebrow market, but, from the very beginning, they used full-colour picture illustrations on their covers. Lane had already shown his displeasure over Penguin Inc.'s picture covers, and over the next few years the brow level of Penguin publications and their physical appearance provoked endless and agonized debate as Lane and his colleagues tried to adjust to a rapidly changing market and to

competition from within and without the book trade. Pandering to
the mass market was, Williams warned Lane, 'a process which,
inevitably, leads to lower standards . . . Your entire success – and,
indeed, your reputation, your knighthood too – has been based on
a steadfast refusal to bid for the masses . . . One of my fears is the
erosion of values by the American fever for expansion.' Anti-
American attitudes were widespread in Britain until the mid-Fifties,
but seemed increasingly irrelevant as the country succumbed to rock
and roll, stumpy imitation skyscrapers, Wimpy Bars and badly-cut
English-made blue jeans; in Williams's case they went hand-in-hand
with a nostalgia for the high-minded austerity of the Attlee years,
prompting his admission that if 'Britain was about to become luxu-
riously supplied with nylon legs and television sets, I should take a
pessimistic view of the prospects of cultural activities. The fact is
that poverty promotes serious reflection upon the less material values
and therefore instigates an attention to serious books, music and the
arts, which is absent in more prosperous times.' Penguins, Beatrice
Warde declared, were tailor-made for the 'financially impoverished
élite', and Williams would have approved her claim that 'They have
never talked down, or printed down, to their public because that
public was never envisaged in terms of Caliban, or as an amorphous
something called the proletariat.'

Like other commentators before and since, Williams liked to
compare Penguin with the BBC, and with the Third Programme
in particular. He had a far more genial spirit than Lord Reith, but
with his Nonconformist background he might well have shared the
former Director-General's Calvinist belief that the higher and the
lower instincts battled for supremacy within the individual, and
within society at large, and that it was imperative to 'wipe out as
much as we can of the barbarian in case it may get control of us'.
Hostile to frivolity and the corrupting effects of American culture
and an advocate of centralized planning run by experts, Reith
believed in 'giving people what one believes they should like *and
will come to like*', and that the 'best way to give the public what
it wants is to reject the express policy of giving the public what it
wants' but provide it instead with something 'slightly better than

it now thinks it likes'. Williams was too sceptical to share Reith's conviction, integral to his insistence that a single radio station should serve the whole nation, that if high culture and elevated ideas were made available to all, the great majority would rise to the occasion; but both he and Lane shared his belief in the liberating potential of ideas and the need to banish ignorance, his disdain for popularity as an arbiter of culture, and his longing to make 'the wisdom of the wise and the amenities of culture available without discrimination'. Lane, on the other hand, would not have approved of Reith's disdain for commerce, and his publishing genius lay in his ability to combine a Reithian commitment to the highest possible standards with a hard-headed realization that he must do so within the disciplines of a business.

Williams was appointed Secretary-General to the Arts Council in 1951, by which time he had become a firm believer in the idea of 'cultural diffusion': the best should be made available to those who were willing and able to absorb it, and although these would, inevitably, represent an educated or ambitious minority, the benign effects would, with luck, trickle down to the world at large. Cyril Connolly may have devoted *Horizon* editorials to mocking those writers who became 'culture diffusionists', squandering their talents by working for publishing or the BBC, but such ideas were prevalent in post-war broadcasting. Departing from Reith's model of one radio station that would cater to all brow levels, whether they liked it or not, the Controller of Home Programmes drew up, in 1943, plans for a programme aimed at a 'highly intelligent minority audience' with a taste for 'critical discussions of art, drama, music and literature; poetry and prose readings of the less popular type; experiments in radio drama, programmes in foreign languages etc.' By the late 1930s Reith's elevated and educative National Programme had begun to fray at the edges as string quartets and donnish lectures learned to coexist with variety programmes and comedy turns, and his dream of a single, unifying service gave way in the face of popular demand.

William Haley, the man responsible for dividing the listening world between the Third Programme (highbrow), the Home Service (middlebrow) and the Light Programme (lowbrow), was a keen exponent of the notion that culture and learning would, if all went well, filter down from one brow level to another, with Light listeners tuning into the Home and then, greatly daring, sampling something on the Third. A year older than Lane, Haley had started life as a copytaker on *The Times*, worked as a reporter on the *Manchester Evening News* and served as Managing Editor of the *Manchester Guardian* before becoming Editor-in-Chief and, later, the Director-General of the BBC. According to a colleague, his 'reverence for knowledge was all the greater for his not having been to university'; he believed that nothing should be broadcast on the Third 'until we are satisfied that we have assembled the best body of people capable of doing it at the time', a very Lane-like sentiment. Broadcasting was destined to be 'the prime re-educative agency of the post-war world', and when the Third began broadcasting in 1946 the critic Edward Sackville-West declared that it 'may well become the greatest educative and civilizing force England has known since the secularization of the theatre in the sixteenth century', while Harman Grisewood, who succeeded George Barnes as Controller of the Third, suggested that 'what is at stake is something fundamental to our society. It is what I call the principle of refinement . . . the attempt at perfection in a Christian sense.'

As an occasional broadcaster and critic, Bill Williams endorsed Haley's vision of the BBC as a pyramid, with the Third at the top, the Light at the bottom, and aspirant listeners at all levels benefiting from whatever trickled down from the tier above, while at the same time inching their ways towards the apex: the Third, he told *Observer* readers, 'had left the Philistine speechless', and promised to 'redeem radio from Americanization and the threat of "commercials"'. Haley's belief in 'crutches' coincided with Williams's view of Penguin: and, as if to emphasize the similarities, John Hersey's *Hiroshima* was read on the Third, Neville Coghill's translation of *The Canterbury Tales*, one of the most successful and popular of all the Penguin Classics, was first commissioned by the Third, and after the demise of *Penguin New Writing* John Lehmann resurfaced on the Third with the broadcasting equivalent of a literary magazine entitled

New Soundings. And the composer Alexander Goehr's suggestion that 'the Third Programme was founded on Labour England. Its imagined listener was a hard-working, Labour-voting schoolmaster in (say) Derby, who was interested in international theatre, new music, philosophy, politics and painting' was strikingly similar, in its kind but condescending way, to Marghanita Laski's evocation of the herbivorous Penguin reader as someone who 'tends to read the *Observer*, use the public libraries, join the Film Society, go to concerts and art exhibitions, look critically at architecture and watch birds'.

Support for Bill Williams's view of Penguin was forthcoming, later in the Fifties, from a young North Country academic, a working-class graduate of a red-brick university who seemed to embody the ideal reader. 'I bought my first Penguin twenty-five years ago, during a week's hiking between youth hostels,' Richard Hoggart recalled: he was then sixteen, at grammar school, and a member of 'the generation which became intellectually active in the mid-Thirties, too young to have direct memories of the First World War but greatly concerned with the movement towards the next'. 'The volumes we knew best still come to mind being pushed into the pockets of Montague Burton sports coats or into cycle panniers or rucksacks or kitbags. I still have some Pelicans which I bought at the Leeds University bookshop before the war and which went through North Africa and Italy,' he continued. Another young man, also from Leeds, had similar recollections. Keith Waterhouse has recalled how 'back in the 1940s I was never seen in public without a dog-eared Pelican stuffed into the pocket of my leather-patched sports jacket, and I always made sure that the title – Freud's *Psychopathology of Everyday Life*, as it might be – was visible', adding that when it came to impressing the girls, 'a well-chosen Pelican in the pocket could be as effective an ice-breaker as a box of Black Magic. Threepence cheaper, too.'

Hoggart made his name with *The Uses of Literacy*, published by Chatto in 1957 and paperbacked by Penguin the following year; and although it contains few specific references to Penguins, it is not hard to see why Lane so admired it, not least for its insights into aspirant Penguin-readers (Williams, curiously enough, was less keen, doubting its conclusions and suggesting it should have been titled *The Uses of Illiteracy*). Hoggart identified himself with the 'uprooted and the anxious', with scholarship boys like himself who found themselves uneasily suspended between the working-class world in which they grew up, and the intellectual life opened up by their education. 'They have, in some degree, lost the hold on one kind of life, and failed to reach the one to which they aspire,' he suggested: hampered by a 'poor background and inadequate training in handling ideas', they tend to have 'a precarious tenancy in several near-intellectual worlds', be hostile to authority, read the *New Statesman*, inveigh against a debased popular press and the advertising business, and 'overestimate the satisfactions of intellectuals'. Such people, Hoggart went on,

tend to read bitterly ironic or agonized literature – Waugh, Huxley, Kafka and Greene. They own the Penguin selection from Eliot, as well as some other Penguins and Pelicans; they used to take *Penguin New Writing* and now subscribe to *Encounter*. They know a little, but often only from reviews and short articles, about Frazer and Marx; they probably own a copy of the Pelican edition of Freud's *Psychopathology of Everyday Life*. They some-times listen to talks on the Third Programme with titles like 'The Cult of Evil in Contemporary Literature' . . .

Their homes had 'usually lost the cluttered homeliness of their origins', and 'the result is often an eye-on-the-teacher style of furnishing like their favourite styles in literature; rooms whose pattern is decided by the needs of the tenants to be culturally *persona grata*'. Hoggart's insight is reminiscent of Lane's hope that the look and contents of Penguins would be such that their owners would happily leave them on display when the vicar called by, rather than stuffing them shamefacedly under the sofa cushions. Since 'so much is designed for effect, for culturally keeping up with the Koestlers', idealism was combined with ambition and pretension: they 'lean so intensely towards culture precisely because they over-value it, even see it sometimes as a substitute for the religious belief which they cannot quite face as a serious possibility . . . Culture is a sign of disinterested goodness, of brains and imagination used to give liberty and poise. Behind the often strange forms of striving is a wish for the assumed freedom, for the power and command over himself, of the "really cultured" man.' In the nineteenth and early twentieth centuries this 'earnest minority' from the working and lower-middle classes subscribed to Robert Blatchford's *Clarion*, read Shaw and Wells and Henry George's *Progress and Poverty*, joined cycling clubs, Mutual Improvement Societies and Mechanics' Institutes, attended WEA classes and University Extension courses, and, in the Thirties, subscribed to the Peace Pledge Union and the Left Book Club; but now, Hoggart believed, 'as society comes nearer to the danger of reducing the larger part of the population to a condition of obediently receptive passivity, their eyes glued to television sets, pin-ups and cinema screens, these few, because they're asking important questions, have a special value'. Like Bill Williams, Hoggart thought it unlikely that 'a majority in any one class will have strongly intellectual pursuits', and that, challenged by 'the myriad voices of the trivial and synthetic sirens', the market they embodied was unlikely to expand in the years ahead.

Many of Hoggart's exemplary readers almost certainly listened to the Third Programme, but by the mid-Fifties the Third was being attacked in the popular Press as 'precious', 'donnish' and 'esoteric', and Ian Jacob, the new Director-General, seemed to sympathize with its critics. Never as adamant as Bill Williams, Lane employed the BBC analogy when, acting the devil's advocate, he suggested that since Ian Jacob was prepared to embrace the Light as well as the Third, Penguin should consider publishing the literary equivalents of *Take It from Here* or *Music While You Work*. He was not, he claimed, opposed to such a move in principle. 'Some years ago,' he confessed in an internal memo, 'I suggested that there was a lot of money to be made if we lowered our sights and produced a series outside our existing Pelican/Penguin range, into which we could put such titles as we knew we could sell but which we didn't want to have associated with our existing imprints.' He compared Penguin in the old days to the Old Vic under Lilian Baylis, when overheads were kept to the minimum and the staff consisted of no more than a handful of people: but Penguin had become far larger, paying pensions and better wages, and the bills had somehow to be paid.

Williams's reaction was one of jocular unease. 'Parrot Books', he suggested, might be the perfect imprint for 'health books, phrenology books and nonsense of that kind', as well as novelists like Peter Cheyney, 'or creatures of even lower breeding': but, above all, they must prevent the Parrots from 'contaminating the other birds in the aviary' as Gresham's Law – whereby bad money drives out the good – moved remorselessly into action. A few years earlier a series of 'Penguin Outlines' had been suggested, designed for readers who might be daunted by a Pelican. 'The increase of the second-rate tends to diminish the market for the first-rate,' Williams declared, before moving on to a conclusion of which Reith and Haley would have approved. 'Our policy at present is to make a large number of readers *reach upward* until they get into the Pelican class. If an easier option were offered them, they might not reach so avidly.'

Despite his insistence that 'America, in Penguin matters, should remain a British colony', Williams confessed to a secret yearning to publish Westerns, several of which were added to the list, while Lane himself urged Frostie to see if she couldn't persuade Cape to sell Ian Fleming's next James Bond novel to Penguin rather than Pan, since 'we could do very well with him on our list'. Quite what distinguished a Penguin novel from one published by Pan or Corgi was often hard to define, but a pattern was emerging whereby publishers like Pan and Corgi tended to far outsell Penguin on a few bestselling titles, but could offer nothing comparable by way of a large and steady-selling backlist. Riding high on the boom in war books, Paul Brickhill's *The Dam Busters* was the first Pan to sell a million copies; in 1955, the year in which Lane contemplated snatching Fleming away, Pan sold 8 million books and had 150 titles in print, whereas Penguin sold 10 million books with a backlist of 1,000. Whether the crossword and puzzle books, or the miscellaneous words published in the short-lived, yellow-covered Ptarmigan series, or the practical Penguin Handbooks, were any better than their Pan equivalents is a matter for the experts; what set them apart was the elegance and distinction of their typography and production, and jackets which, while too restrained and old-fashioned for some, had an indubitable distinction.

But for all their distinction, Penguin jackets were beginning to seem, to booksellers at least, unhelpfully old-fashioned. Pan were popular with the wholesalers, and it made sense to display a new Pan or Corgi face out in the shops in the hope that casual browsers would be tempted by the four-colour illustrations on the covers, but Penguins, with their identical lettering jackets, were in danger of being shelved spine-out, and deprived of full-frontal exposure: creating shops within shops, devoted exclusively to the sale of Penguins, proved a huge success both at home and abroad, but could only be a temporary expedient. Replying to his letter of congratulation in 1952, Lane had told Edward Young that he had sometimes considered changing the standard design, 'but despite the fact that both Charles Prentice and Tschichold had a crack at it, we realized that your fundamentals were so good that it would be folly to interfere with them to any appreciable extent'. If changes now had to be made, much of the responsibility would fall on the shoulders of Jan Tschichold's chosen heir-apparent, Hans Schmoller.

Precise, formal and anxious, with corrugated hair and what Richard Hoggart described as a 'crinkly smile', Schmoller shared his predecessor's liking for bow ties as well as his elegant perfectionism, but was less impatient and more tolerant; and if he seemed, at times, humourless and irascible, no one doubted his dedication to Penguin. He had been born in Berlin in 1916 into a Jewish family; as a young man he had been prevented from attending a university and had instead been apprenticed to a Jewish firm of book printers, studying calligraphy and typography in the evenings. In 1937 he had left Germany and come to England before emigrating to Basutoland, where he worked for a firm of printers attached to a Catholic mission for nine years and was interned for a time in South Africa as an enemy alien, before moving back to England in 1949. He wrote to Oliver Simon at the Curwen Press, pointing out a wrong font in one of his productions; Simon offered him a job in return, and when Tschichold returned to Switzerland in 1949 he moved to Penguin, becoming head of production in 1956. Known as 'half-point Schmoller' (his own epithet), he was a stickler for detail, and involved himself in every aspect of how Penguin looked, from the books themselves to – as Lane put it – 'the "In" and "Out" signs at the gates', and the choice of cutlery and glass in the new directors' dining-room at Harmondsworth. Margaret Clark remembered the Bauhaus chairs in his office, and how, in a fit of pique, he hurled an unpaginated typescript out of the window, leaving the pages to blow about in the wind. 'Who has changed the typeface on these statements?' he wanted to know on one occasion; he became incandescent with rage when a local printer ran off some internal memos, and had them withdrawn. 'There were those at Penguin who swore that he could distinguish between a Garamond full point and a Bembo at two hundred paces,' an admirer recalled. He was exemplary in his insistence on the highest possible standards of editing, design and production, and in his devotion to a consistent and pervasive 'image' of Penguin: an editorial colleague, Oliver Caldecott, thought him 'Penguin's conscience on any matter where he detected that a colleague (even Allen Lane himself) was about to treat an author, a supplier or another member of staff unfairly or incorrectly'. He was also responsible for the beautiful patterned paper jackets which adorned the Penguin Scores and the marvellous series of Penguin Poets which, unencumbered by scholarly apparatus, introduced generations of readers to poets from Donne and Hopkins to Auden and Graves. He was admired rather than loved, and when the receptionist at Harmondsworth greeted the genial Caldecott by his Christian name, Schmoller ruefully confessed that 'I've been here twenty years, and they never call me Hans.' For all his teutonic formality, he wooed and married Tanya Kent; he was, perhaps, too austere to be part of Lane's inner circle, but Lane valued his dedication and his perfectionism, and found that Schmoller's experience gave his 'judgement a balance which is lacking in others, which is why I find talking over such questions as these with you so comforting'.

Schmoller instinctively preferred the typographical to the picture jacket, but the original horizontal bands, so recently perfected by Tschichold, were replaced with vertical bands with, in due course, tasteful woodcuts or devices placed between, while the standard Pelican cover came to consist of a pale blue border running round the edge of the jacket; the back panel of both displayed a postage-stamp-sized author photograph and a brief biography. Such quiet good taste was far removed from the dramatic, magazine-like illustrations used by Pan to illustrate Ian Fleming or bestselling war memoirs like *The Wooden Horse* or *The Colditz Story*. Lane was prepared to garland in green the penguin on the front cover of Edward Young's *One of Our Submarines*, published in 1954 as the thousandth Penguin: it went on to sell 350,000 copies, which seemed to justify the refusal to follow Pan's example, but when, a couple of years later, Penguin paperbacked *The Cruel Sea*, Nicholas Monsarrat's bestselling novel about life on the Atlantic convoys, Lane bent with the wind and gave it a feeble full-colour cover. For a reprint of Colette's *Gigi and the Cat*, Penguin filled the entire jacket with a still from the hugely successful film of *Gigi*, but even the steamiest novels were modestly attired: Alberto Moravia's *The Woman of Rome*, believed by schoolboys at the time to be the most torrid novel ever written, carried an unornamented 'horizontal' jacket, and whereas the Pan edition of Alan Sillitoe's *Saturday Night and Sunday Morning* had a suitably moody full-colour illustration on its cover, the Penguin edition of John Braine's *Room at the Top*, also a film tie-in, was embellished with a black-and-white cut-out of Laurence Harvey, the star of the film, sandwiched between vertical bands of orange.

Although Bill Williams, Frostie, Glover and Schmoller were unanimous in their opposition to picture jackets, feeling that they would dilute Penguin's image and lead to a lowering of editorial standards – Williams confessed that he could 'feel no great heartbreak' if Penguin lost out to Pan as a result – Lane was torn both ways. He famously detested and despised the American taste for 'breastsellers', muttered under his breath about 'bosoms and bottoms', and told Harry Paroissien, with some relish, that the jacket of *The Cruel Sea*, published in the year of Suez, had been loathed by the reps, all of whom agreed that 'like Anthony Eden, we have sacrificed a reputation which it has taken us many years to build up'; but Bill Williams suspected him of 'secretly pining' after picture covers. Dick had long favoured picture covers – 'Although I know it will put up our production costs, I think we should experiment with this style of production,' he had urged Lane back in 1947 – and as early as 1949 Lane had told Frostie, 'I think we could safely move away from our standard design especially if we have the Jan Tschichold stamp on everything.' After spending some weeks travelling round the States and Canada with Paroissien, Lane wrote a memo to the doubters back home in which he admitted to being 'acutely aware' of the preference in both countries for colour jackets and a larger text typeface. 'I think we have got to lay this picture cover ghost one way or the other,' declared Paroissien, who had recently elicited a description of Jeeves from P. G. Wodehouse (tall, dark, black jacket, striped trousers) and forwarded it to Schmoller: in vain, since Schmoller, remembering Wodehouse's Berlin broadcasts, refused to work on this batch of titles, which had to be designed by someone else. Paroissien favoured a trial run, but 'why should we panic in face of a competition we never intended to appease or imitate?' Bill Williams wanted to know, and his fellow-sceptics repeated Lane's own belief that, unlike their rivals, Penguins were instantly recognizable, and all the better for it, and that to reset in a larger type would merely increase the bulk and price of the books.

Later in 1957 it was decided to try picture jackets with a batch of books rather than the occasional title, and Hans Schmoller got in touch with Abram Games. Described by David Gentleman as 'one of the last great British poster designers', Games lectured at the Royal College of Art in Richard Guyatt's influential School of Graphic Design, together with Edward Ardizzone, Edward Bawden and Reynolds Stone. His famous wartime posters had included 'Grow Your Own Food', since when he had designed a stamp for the 1948 London Olympics and the symbols for the Festival of Britain and Keep Britain Tidy. Over thirty Penguin jackets appeared under his aegis – some, like Gabriel Chevalier's *Clochemerle* novels, designed by Games himself, some by the illustrators he commissioned, including Hans Unger. Far removed from the magazine-illustration covers favoured by Pan or Corgi, they were adorned with bright, elegant, rather stylized four-colour artwork, oddly reminiscent of the work produced for Penguin Inc. in the 1940s. But they ended up by pleasing no one, being too tasteful for the vulgarians and too radical for the old guard; and whereas Penguins had always been shelved apart from the paperback riff-raff, these were displayed along-side them. 'They haven't a single friend in the trade,' Bill Rapley told Bill Williams, who promptly passed the news on. 'We have now definitely decided against picture covers, and when the existing titles run out they will appear in the old orange and white,' a relieved Lane informed Harry Paroissien. 'Everybody seems quite relieved that the decision has been made.' The evil hour had merely been postponed, and the vexed matter of jackets, and what did or did not constitute a Penguin book, was to cause havoc and unhappiness in the years ahead.

16. Flirting and Foreign Parts

Lane's home life, like that of the office, was harmonious on the surface but permeated by a vague sense of unease and impending change; and although he seemed cool and in control, beyond the reach of other people, tribulations took their toll. He suffered a 'crack-up' after old Mr Williams Lane died in early 1950, Frostie reporting him as 'suffering very much from an anti-climax after his father's death and the accumulation of unworked-off tension'. He took himself off to recuperate in the South of France. 'I know myself better than most people think I do,' he told Tanya Kent: he had become nervy and irritable of late, 'strained of face and twitchy of finger', and he was determined to change his life once he got back to England.

The loss of his mother, some eight years later, would prove a far heavier blow. After her husband's death she had moved from Oxfordshire to South Cottage, a stone's throw from Silverbeck. She was generally regarded as a formidable old lady, and Penguin staff jumped to when she rang in to speak to 'my son' or 'my son Richard'. She liked a restorative drink in the evening, and Lane kept her fridge stocked with half bottles of champagne, many of which he helped to drain on his way home from the office. She died in the drawing-room at Silverbeck in March 1958, and her death prompted a massive clear-out and division of spoils between the two brothers: among the items shipped out to Dick, then living in Australia, were his RNVR uniform plus epaulettes, a sola topi, a set of silver spurs, a model cannon, a bush knife, two silver porringers, three powder horns, a soup tureen, a grandfather clock, miniatures of Dickens and Tennyson, a piano and a refectory table from Lancaster Gate; a pair of duelling pistols, specially requested by Dick, had mysteriously disappeared.

'Look at poor old Allen Lane in this week's *Sunday Times*, looking

a tired old man of seventy,' Agatha Christie remarked two years
after he had been knighted, and signs of wear and tear could probably be put down to overwork and domestic unease. Lane's health
seemed sound enough, apart from the occasional twinge of gout,
but every now and then Bill Williams urged him to visit 'our old
friend' Karl Bluth, a German émigré doctor and a friend of
Brecht and Heidegger who combined medicine with the writing
of poems and plays, played the piano in the garage of his home
in Hampstead, and numbered Arthur Koestler and Peter Watson of
Horizon among his patients. He made sure that Estrid Bannister
had her vitamin injections, and Lettice's friend Anna Kavan her
controlled doses of heroin: Williams urged Lane to allow Bluth to
examine his 'filters', and claimed to be a new man whenever he
allowed himself to be 'decarbonized' and have his 'tappets' adjusted.
Whenever Lane's trousers became too tight, he paid a visit to
Champney's, returning home leaner and more fractious. After one
visit he decided to lay off the booze, and asked Harry Paroissien
to send him a vegetable-shredder from the States: like other ex-
pats at the time, Paroissien and his wife Eileen were subjected to
a constant stream of requests for luxuries unavailable in post-war
England, from nylons and cortisone cream to an electric blender,
spare parts for Lane's Sunbeam electric razor and a machine for
clearing the leaves from the swimming-pool in which his children
spent so much of their time in summer. He was devoted to his
daughters, and as family holidays became a thing of the past, he
liked to take one or other of the two older girls with him when
he went on his travels: the *Young Elizabethan*, a magazine for teenage
girls, included an account of a bicycling holiday he and Clare had
taken on the Cherbourg peninsula, though the carefully posed
photographs – Lane looking disconcertingly Germanic in knee-
length shorts and long white socks – were taken near Silverbeck.
Anna, the third daughter, had a mild form of Down's Syndrome;
for a time it seemed as though this might bring her parents closer
together, but by the mid-Fifties their marriage was unravelling.

One day in 1955 the German publisher Ledig Rowohlt came to
stay at Silverbeck, bringing with him his mistress, Susanne Lepsius.

According to office gossip, at the end of the weekend Rowohlt left for Germany with Lettice Lane, who was not averse to the occasional affair, while Susanne stayed behind at Silverbeck. Whatever the truth of the matter, Susanne Lepsius became, and remained, a fixture in Lane's life; Lettice moved out of Silverbeck, and three years went by before she and Lane met again. Some eighteen years younger than Lane, Susanne Lepsius remains a curiously elusive figure. It was said that after leaving Rowohlt she was briefly married to an Englishman in order to get a British passport and be able to spend more time with Lane; she is variously described as tall, slim and slight, with a pale, rather fleshy face and a strong German accent; Richard Hoggart found her serious and solid, like 'a piece of mobile furniture', while George Weidenfeld thought she had a touch of Sonia Brownell about her; one of Lane's young editors, who got to know her well, thought her sexy rather than beautiful, and her attitude towards Lane one of chilly detachment. Cultivated and well-read, she dabbled in antiques, imported Meissen china, and encouraged Lane's urge to collect, with particular emphasis on snuffboxes; her detractors suggest that she palmed him off with inferior goods, and lined her pockets in the process. She lived for a time in Lane's flat in Whitehall Court, and visiting publishers were sometimes disconcerted to find black underwear draped about the bathroom; a Penguin employee remembers the lingering smell of her 'over-sweet perfume', and how the atmosphere of Whitehall Court was 'cold to the point of sinister'. In due course Lane bought her a flat in Notting Hill, where they held literary evenings to introduce her to the publishing world. Lane, Susanne, Bill Williams and Estrid Bannister spent holidays together in Estrid Bannister's cottage at Rosscarbery in County Cork; it proved a convivial retreat, but nothing was quite the same after Estrid Bannister, devoted though she was to her long-standing lover, fell in love with and married an Irish fisherman, much to Bill Williams's loudly voiced distress.

The Rowohlt connection having proved ephemeral, and Lane providing a modest allowance – so modest that, or so it was said, many of her clothes were second-hand – Lettice worked for a time in the handkerchief department of Harrods; eventually she took a flat in Holland Park, where the girls spent their holidays from school. Adrift in the vastness of Silverbeck, Lane was looked after for a time by the gardener and his wife: the house soon became dirty and cold – Lane saw no point in keeping the Aga on – and he told Dick that when he eventually asked his mother and his cousin Ducka Puxley if they would like to move in, 'they accepted with alacrity'.

Friends remarked how odd it was that so neat and well turned-out a man was prepared to live in the squalor that descended on Silverbeck after Lettice's departure. 'We must remember that it's important to be kind to each other,' Bill Williams wrote to Lane in Rosscarbery, after noticing how unhappy he seemed. 'Part of my own recent sadness has been the realization that a private problem was invading your life and, to some extent, usurping the devotion we had always had in common' – the shared devotion being, of course, to Penguin Books, that 'rare and precious enterprise'. Lane's melancholy must have been obvious to all. Writing from the SS *Oronsay en route* from Australia to England, where he planned to spend the next three months at Silverbeck, Dick said that he had heard some 'most disturbing reports' about his brother's state of mind, and offered some bracing words of advice. To enjoy a 'better existence', he warned, Lane would have to cooperate with those around him: 'If you are going to dig in your toes and stick out your jaw and say that not only are you capable of looking after your own affairs but also those of all your family and relations, not to mention a couple of hundred employees, we shall get nowhere.'

On holiday in Ireland in the summer of 1956, Lane got up early one morning while the children and his sister Nora were still asleep, sat down by a window overlooking an estuary, and poured out his woes to Frostie. 'Our marriage was not a happy one, and but for the children I doubt if we would have kept it up for as long as we did,' he told her. Over the last few years he had lost interest in everything, at home and in the office, on the grounds that 'it all seemed so pointless'. 'I didn't love Lettice. My brother was making a mess of everything I gave him to do. The bickering in the office forced me back into my shell, and I thought, "Well, let them get on with it."' But the 'German invasion' had forced things into the

open. 'Much as my mother likes to be with me, I can see that it
is not a good thing in the long run,' he conceded: he had decided
to leave Silverbeck and 'strike out on my own', and was eager to
make Whitehall Court less 'club-like'. As for Frostie, 'I feel closer
to you than I have ever done, and I'm grateful for your great understanding during this period when I have been particularly difficult
to deal with.' In a letter to Dick he referred to 'the rather sticky
period of the last eighteen months or so, which took their toll',
but assured him that he was now back on top form.

Although Lane was perfectly happy to be seen around with
Susanne and enjoyed her company, it may well be that he saw her
as little more than a 'trophy' mistress, an accessory fitting a man of
his standing in the world; nor does it seem likely that he was in
love with her, or even found her particularly attractive. 'Susanne is
in Germany, so I too am living a life of bachelordom, but unlike
you I find that I thrive on it,' he admitted to Paroissien, three years
into the affair; they spent less and less time together, and, he told
Frostie, 'I feel very badly about Susanne, but I am convinced that
marriage would spell disaster. She is a complement to me in many
ways, but in other ways we are vastly separated.' By now there was
no more talk of divorcing Lettice, or making a legal separation. 'She
wants to come back, but I'm sure that would be a mistake,' he told
Joan Collihole. 'Although I'm a bit lonely at times, it's a small price
for the freedom which I enjoy.' As for Susanne, 'I do of course miss
her very much, but the alternative, that of marrying her, would
have been impossible. As an amusing companion she has no equal,
but as a wife she would have driven me round the bend.'

It may well be that travel gave Lane a good deal more pleasure
than women, and both his wealth and his job enabled him to indulge
his wanderlust at a time when currency restrictions put foreign parts
out of reach for all but the most well-heeled. In 1951, for instance,
he took seven weeks off and travelled to Iraq to visit Agatha Christie
and Max Mallowan, then on a dig at the ancient city of Nimrud.
Reading Henry Miller 'with mixed feelings' as he went, he took a
boat from Piraeus to Limassol, heavily laden with wine, potatoes,
tractors and a consignment of Penguins, travelled on to Beirut in

an Egyptian cargo boat crammed with donkeys, was outraged by the ignorance of Beirut booksellers, took a taxi to Damascus, and finally made it to Baghdad, where the booksellers were a good deal better informed. Once on site he tried (and failed) to fool Mallowan by burying a bogus artefact; he was present when the Ashurbanipal Stela was unearthed, and in the evenings Agatha Christie read them the first draft of *The Mousetrap*, written in her tent. Back in England, Lane sent a Stilton to his hosts to thank them for their hospitality; he and Lettice revisited the site in later years, bearing with them another ceremonial Stilton.

Later that year he made a business trip to Nigeria and the Gold Coast. The BOAC plane served 'cocktails on the house' and boasted 'a kitchen complete with an oven and two stewards and a stewardess to dish out the grub'; they landed at Tripoli, where dinner was served in a nearby hotel, and 'lots of gin' was downed in Lagos. Africa, he confided to his diary, was the market of the future. On his return he was invited round to the Colonial Office and asked for his views. The Cold War was at its height, and the Government was keen to counteract Soviet and Communist propaganda in Africa: while recognizing that Lane was unlikely to accept 'Colonial Office tutelage' on what he should or should not publish, it was felt that Penguins could have a useful role to play in what was referred to as 'ideological defence in immature communities'. Penguin's leftish leanings were a drawback, but according to his interlocutor at the Colonial Office, Lane seemed anxious to start new series for the under-developed countries, and was 'determined that it would be a mistake to write down for West Africa': so 'provided Lane in his zeal to sell his wares does not resort to Zilliacus and [D. N.] Pritt, his scheme should at least fill the vacuum with something whole-some. If the African is reading an abridged version of *Adam Bede*, he isn't reading the products of Rosary Gardens' (i.e. Communist Party publications). No more was heard from the Colonial Office, and although Lane's vision of publishing textbooks for the African market was pre-empted by educational publishers like Longmans and Heinemann Educational Books, he did publish fourteen titles in the Penguin West African Library, as well as the Penguin African

Library, launched in 1962; the Communists, on the other hand, may have drawn comfort from Andrew Rothstein's notorious Pelican, *A History of the USSR*, which ridiculed the notion of slave labourers in the Gulag and was widely regarded as a piece of Soviet propaganda. Lane retained his interest in publishing for what would later become known as the Third World – writing from Ceylon two years later, he told Frostie that 'the old order is changing so rapidly that we could really afford to ignore the European population and concentrate on the Ceylonese' – but it would be left to others to put his intimations to practical effect.

Lane visited the West Indies in 1952, Ceylon and Australia in 1953, and met Hemingway, an old drinking companion, in Cuba the following year: his reading matter on that Caribbean cruise, he told Frostie, consisted of Rupert Hart-Davis's biography of Hugh Walpole, Laurens van der Post's *Voyage to the Interior*, and a manual on rabbit-keeping. Equipped with eight Van Heusen drip-dry shirts, two of which he brought home unopened in their cellophane bags, he toured the world in eighty days in 1957, visiting Russia and China and returning home via Sydney and San Francisco. His Russian and Chinese diaries make tedious reading, short on human interest and crammed with meetings with long-forgotten dignitaries and editors from state publishing houses. The plane from Prague to Moscow had no seatbelts and an unpressurized cabin, making it hard to breathe at times; in Moscow he found 'a complete absence of vitality, of sparkle, of enthusiasm'. China was preferable, not least because he had as a travelling companion Esmé Barton: the widow of the journalist George Steer, who had alerted the world to the German bombing of Guernica, she satisfied Lane's liking for loud, strong women who bossed him around. Never a 'finicky eater', he happily sampled the food on offer, but was defeated by 'a brew called goat's wine' in Canton, and had to fall back on his own supplies. Back in Europe, he developed a soft spot for the Dordogne and struck up a friendship with Estrid Bannister's friend Philip Oyler, the author of *The Generous Earth*, a proto-hippie with long white hair and beard who grew his own tobacco, brewed his own wine and lived with a girlfriend half his age.

One country he always enjoyed visiting was Australia: its inhabitants may have contracted an unfortunate taste for American paperbacks, but he valued its vast potential as a market, and the fact that Nora lived in Sydney made it all the easier to combine business with pleasure. During the war, Penguins had been sold and manufactured under licence by the Australian firm of Lothian, but after the war Lane decided to set up an office of his own. After being demobbed from the Navy, Bob Maynard had worked for a while for the United Nations in London, and Lane used to visit him from time to time in the Berkeley or Brown's Hotel 'to satisfy himself that the Government gin was fit for overseas visitors' consumption'. Maynard was keen to return to Penguin, but whereas he dreamed of opening a branch in South Africa, Lane decided that he should make for Australia. Dick was fiercely opposed to the idea, seeing it as yet another example of profligate impetuosity, but by the time he had made his opinions known Maynard and his wife were steaming towards the Antipodes. Consisting of a tin shack in the suburbs of Melbourne, lacking any form of insulation and blazingly hot in summer, Penguin Australia opened in 1946. Maynard and his wife ordered, packed and despatched the books; and when not on the road or in the warehouse – two years after their arrival, a pre-war Vauxhall was shipped out for their use – they sent home food parcels to their half-frozen and under-nourished colleagues in Harmondsworth.

In the same year in which the Vauxhall was landed, Dick turned up in Australia on a visit. On the boat out he had met Elizabeth Snow, and they were married in Sydney, with Bob Maynard as best man; her father, Sir Edgar Snow, owned the Sydney equivalent of Selfridge's, and although, in later years, Dick would often complain about how badly he had been treated by his older brother in terms of salary, pension and ownership of shares, his money problems were, from now on, a thing of the past. Bob Maynard, in the meantime, plodded dutifully on. In 1953 Lane paid his first visit to Australia: unaware, before his arrival, of the size or shape of the country, he asked Maynard if he would be at the quayside in Perth to meet him off the boat, with his Vauxhall at the ready. He soon realized that, for all his sterling qualities and long service, Maynard was not the man to convert an overheated shack into a modern, smooth-running publishing operation. Convinced that Maynard was not equipped to deal with academics and educational authorities, and that as a salesman he lacked the necessary fire, he began to whittle away at his confidence and authority. Dick was put in charge, and Maynard's days were numbered. 'I am tired of being kicked around and I am coming home for a showdown,' he told Frostie, but Lane refused to be cornered. 'No, no, no. Don't do that on my account. I won't be here. Don't do that,' he begged, when Maynard rang from Melbourne to suggest that he should come to England to discuss his future. They were the last words Maynard ever heard from Lane in his capacity as employer. Shortly afterwards, to the fury of many Australian booksellers, Maynard was dismissed – but that was not the end of the story. Some years later, Lane went to stay with the Maynards in Melbourne; he apologized for what he had done, and in his will he left a sum to be settled on their blind daughter, Laura.

Dick was appalled by what had happened, and – in Maynard's company at least – referred to his brother thereafter, with heavy irony, as the 'Noble Knight'. With Maynard removed from the scene, Dick was left in charge. Whether he accompanied Lane on a visit to the outback to see an author named Arthur Upfield remains unclear – according to the publisher Alan Hill, Lane and Upfield engaged in a 'fearful drinking bout' which left the outback author 'senseless on the bedroom floor' – but before long Dick's own position was in doubt. There was talk of his returning to Harmondsworth, and the problems that would inevitably entail. Writing to Harry Paroissien, Lane confessed he had no idea what to do with Dick: he had made 'such a mess' of the farm that he could not bear to confine him to the cows, and in an effort to remedy matters he had taken on, as a farm manager, Sydney Goldsack's son, who was now living in Dick's half of Priory Farm. Nor was Lane alone in his views. Bill Williams wrote to say that all the members of the 'coffee meeting' – an informal meeting of senior editors – were worried about what would happen if, after his return from Australia, Dick was left in charge when Lane was on holiday or on one of his long world trips. Morale would plummet, and there would be 'an unreasonable application of the brakes': it was essential that they should feel free to press ahead 'without the restraints which Dick invariably imposes'. Lane entirely agreed. 'If it were not for the ties of blood and sentiment, we should be making radical changes' in Australia, he told Paroissien. 'There must be some parting of the ways between my brother and myself, certainly as far as the English company is concerned,' he confessed. Dick felt bruised, rejected and hard done by, and was well aware that, with his brother's active connivance, he had become an embarrassment and a laughing-stock in Harmondsworth. Writing to Lane about a 'spot of bother' with his health – he had had a kidney operation, and went on to itemize details of enemas, diarrhoea and the like – he felt compelled to add, 'for heaven's sake don't treat this as a business letter and send it to all your colleagues for comment'; he felt hurt when Lane failed, as promised, to meet him off the boat at Tilbury, quibbled over the costs of fares and whether Penguin should pay those of his wife and daughter, and claimed that, in monetary terms, Lane had given him a 'very raw deal indeed', refusing him a pension scheme or a salary increase, and forcing him to live off capital. Matters would get worse, but in the meantime Lane offered an olive branch by suggesting that Dick – still, just, in charge of Penguin Australia – might like to take the Bentley back with him as 'passenger's luggage', and tried to explain their differences on the grounds that 'we are entirely different characters, and when we run in double harness, it is like hitching two entirely different types of horse to the same vehicle. You are by nature steady-going, conservative and full of the sterling virtues, whereas I am more mercurial, much less reliable, and inconsistent . . .'

Finding the right man to run the Australian business was not easy, but Lane liked the country and felt very much at home there. America was, as ever, a very different matter. Every now and then Lane would appear in the States, visiting publishers in New York and Boston, and keeping on eye on the new Penguin Inc. office and warehouse, housed in an old mill in Baltimore: not only were the overheads far lower than in New York, but Baltimore was one of the first container ports on the east coast of America, and Penguin took full advantage of this. Harry Paroissien had been running the shop since 1949. 'In a short space of time he has really done something astonishing,' Blanche Knopf reported back to Lane two years after Paroissien's arrival, but unlike Ballantine, or Enoch and Weybright, he had no desire to publish on his own account. Penguin Inc.'s publishing programme was restricted to an edition of Shakespeare and the printing, for copyright reasons, of titles by Bernard Shaw and Robert Graves: everything else was imported from Harmondsworth. It was a well-run business, and it consistently returned profits to the parent company. Alun Davies, who worked there as a young man, remembered it as a slice of England set down on the East Coast, seemingly divorced from American publishing as a whole: there was no question of dealing with the dreaded magazine distributors, or selling titles on sale or return. Lane seemed ill-at-ease in the American publishing world, confessing to Paroissien that 'There is something about the American character which I find very difficult to understand', and that 'It is really the magnitude of the operation in the paperbound business which has always scared me.' When not voicing his loyalty – 'My aim is, and has been, to serve you and the Penguin idea faithfully and well. I am ready to bow out whenever you want me to' – Paroissien devoted as much of his long letters home to the minutiae of the English book trade ('Dorking North station would repay regular visits') as he did to the American; while Lane, in return, interlaced gossip and publishing strategy with tips about dustproof floors and a request for some Roco Oil Bare Floor Sweep.

Over half Penguin Inc.'s sales were to colleges and universities, and Paroissien was the first publisher in the States to promote his books through college reps; but before long other American 'trade' publishers were casting covetous eyes on the college market. Weybright and Enoch were already producing their own equivalents of Pelicans and Penguin Classics at the New American Library, and in 1952 Jason Epstein, a young editor at Doubleday, invented the notion of the 'egghead', 'trade' or 'quality' paperback. Aimed at students and cerebral lay readers, and printed in modest quantities in the larger 'B' format, trade paperbacks were more expensive and better produced than mass-market paperbacks, and Epstein's Anchor Books were soon being emulated by Random House's Vintage and other up-market lists.

As a pioneer in the field, Penguin Inc. began to seem a desirable property to other American publishers, and although Paroissien invariably looked askance at their advances, and was to prove adept at guarding his patch, some kind of tie-up with a New York or Boston publisher made sense in terms of selling Penguins to the world at large. It was rumoured that Random House was keen to buy Penguin Inc., and that some kind of merger with the *Encyclopaedia Britannica* was imminent; Morris Ernst, Lane's old friend from his Bodley Head days, reported in 1958 that 'Penguin is the chief topic of gossip on the book Rialto'. 'A modest exhibitionist, a common-sense logician, a warm-hearted curmudgeon', in Victor Weybright's opinion, Ernst adored name-dropping and publishing gossip, liked nothing more than broking and fixing deals and – if his letters are anything to go by – exuded an oleaginous servility, at least where Lane was concerned. Lane had no illusions about Ernst – he told Paroissien that he fully expected him to put a phone call through to Sam Goldwyn or the President during the course of a meeting, and was 'quite aware that Morris is not altogether honest in his dealings with me' – but he liked and valued him enough to publish his autobiography, *The Best is Yet*; and before long Ernst was hard at work on his behalf, trying to broker a deal whereby Penguin Inc. and an American publisher could work together to their mutual advantage.

Lane's dealings with various American publishers make an unedifying tale, showing him at his most devious and inconsistent, and the ingredients were always the same. The publishers inevitably wanted to buy a half share in Penguin Inc., and Lane resented losing control; they were reluctant to limit themselves to importing and selling copies brought over from England, and wanted to be able to publish Penguins written by Americans and tailored for the American market; they insisted on being free to design, sell and market Penguins in the American manner, however distasteful this might seem on the other side of the Atlantic; and Harry Paroissien, who dreaded losing out, was always at Lane's right hand, casting doubts on the value and viability of the Americans, and the character of those involved. Lane wanted the sales and the status that would flow from a connection with a major American publisher, but was not prepared to loosen his grip, and his underhand methods did grave damage to his reputation within the gossipy, incestuous world of New York publishing.

Ernst's son-in-law, Mike Bessie, was an editor at Harper's, a long-established firm that combined commercial clout with a gentlemanly reputation; in a memo to his colleagues he described Paroissien as a 'mighty impressive fellow' who thought Penguins were under-exploited in the bookshops, and was keen to work with an established 'trade' publisher. Negotiations broke down when Harper's insisted on a share in the equity of Penguin Inc., but when Ernst learned that Bessie and two of his colleagues, Pat Knopf and Hiram Haydn, were leaving the firm and setting up on their own, his exuberance knew no bounds. 'You will look around the fabulous American publishers for years before you will find anything as exciting, honourable and interested in your type of editorial taste,' he told Paroissien apropos the new firm of Atheneum; dropping heavy hints as he went – 'If I were a director of Penguin England – a function I would greatly enjoy' – he hurried to convince Lane to throw in his lot with the new firm. 'If he goes on with all this backwards bending he will be permanently tilted aft,' Paroissien remarked in one of his letters home. D. C. Heath, a firm of educational publishers, had recently been appointed to sell Penguins in the college market, and it was agreed that Atheneum should, on a commission basis, sell Penguins to wholesalers and booksellers.

No sooner had the knot been tied than Lane began to chafe at its restraints. He was not best pleased when Fred Warburg told him over lunch that, according to Victor Gollancz, it was rumoured in New York that Atheneum had bought up Penguin Inc.; Paroissien fanned the flames, telling Lane that he was 'convinced that Pat and Mike are fundamentally interested in money and status, and that is why I would consign all Mike's and Morris's high-toned protestations to the trash can. We can either run the business as we have been doing for the past ten years, putting the Penguin idea first and accepting the financial limitations, or we can go all out for an American-type enterprise. I do not believe there is a compromise.'

It had been agreed that the arrangement with Atheneum would run for three years from 1958, but within a short time Lane was flirting with other publishers. Jason Epstein had earlier suggested that he might leave Doubleday in order to sell and distribute Penguins in the States, and one day in 1960 Lane came home to find Epstein and Barney Rosset of the Grove Press 'sitting on the doorstep': Epstein had left Doubleday, and they had flown over to discuss the possibility of working with Penguin. Nothing came of it: although Epstein thought Lane 'a fine publisher, as sly as he was affable', Lane dismissed his visitors as a 'couple of clever alecks'. That evening, Bennett Cerf of Random House rang Epstein from New York, told him that 'Lane's bankers would no more let him sell his American branch than the Queen would let Prince Philip sell Canada', and offered him a job at Random House instead.

The Atheneum connection came to an end in 1961. Morris Ernst posted off a lachrymose note of regret – there was a possibility of Pocket Books distributing Penguins, and 'I shudder at the idea that Penguins may be sandwiched between breasts etc. on the jackets' – but Lane's mind was elsewhere. He was deep in discussions with Cass Canfield of Harper's, and both men seemed ecstatic at the prospect of coming together. 'I have never been more interested in any publishing project,' Canfield told Lane. 'Like you, I am really enthusiastic about this project, in fact I cannot think of one that has interested me more since I set out on the Penguin path,' Lane replied. Quite unaware that Lane was carrying on an identical flirtation with Lovell Thompson of Houghton Mifflin, Canfield, the most upright and patrician of American publishers, made arrangements for a formal announcement to be made in New York, at which Lane would address the senior management and sales force of Harper & Row. Letters of agreement had been exchanged at the Century Club, but half an hour before Lane was due to step on to the podium, he rang

Cass Canfield. 'Sorry, I can't be with you, the deal's off,' Canfield was told – followed by a click, as the line went dead.

Back in London, Lane dictated an apologetic letter to Canfield ('I don't think I have ever been faced with such a difficult letter to write') and, as he often did when reluctant to face the consequences of his own behaviour, scuttled off to his newly-acquired 'beach hut' in Spain, leaving Schmoller and Paroissien to clear up the mess. He continued to dither, telling Schmoller that he was 'heartily fed up' with Houghton Mifflin, and that 'as of now, I would be quite content to revert to Harper's'. Houghton Mifflin eventually acquired 49 per cent of Penguin Inc., and Lane was made a director of the Boston-based firm, but although the marriage lasted until 1966 he could not rest until he had bought back their stake and severed the connection. 'How could I work with a man like that?' Cass Canfield asked a friend: his equanimity restored, he joined colleagues from Atheneum and Pocket Books in sending Lovell Thompson of Houghton Mifflin a black-bordered card of condolence. Morris Ernst, unctuous and long-winded to the end, wrote to say that he 'would be less than frank if I did not say that the tactics pursued by you, no doubt on the advice of Harry, have resulted in less than an honourable and tidy image for your good self and your great enterprise'. Harry Paroissien had won the day, and Penguin Inc. continued much as before.

Nor was Lane's flirtatiousness confined to the States. He tantalized himself and his colleagues with talk of working part-time or stopping work altogether when he reached sixty, pondered on possible heirs-apparent, many of whom had no experience of publishing in particular or business in general, and would present no threat to himself, and enjoyed, almost as an end in itself, discussing possible mergers or even the sale of Penguin to an endless succession of companies and tycoons, from Cecil King and Roy Thomson to Neville Blond, the founder of the Royal Court. Lane had two reasons for contemplating a possible sale of all or part of Penguin: although, in later years, he pretended indifference to what happened after his death, he wanted to minimize death duties; and he wanted to go on running the firm after any sale, and ensure that those who took over Penguin would remain true to its principles when he finally departed the scene – impossible dreams that have beguiled and deluded a good many otherwise shrewd and hard-headed publishers in the years since his death.

The City was beginning to show an interest in publishing, partly on the reasonable grounds that the educational market was a 'growth industry' and partly from the more dubious belief that there was some mysterious 'synergy' between the book trade and the world of entertainment, and before long large corporations would be taking over the most eminent publishing houses on both sides of the Atlantic. The omens were not all good – Rupert Hart-Davis had burned his fingers when he sold his firm to Heinemann, and would do so again before abandoning the trade altogether – but temptation was too strong to be ignored. In 1957 Thomas Tilling, a bus company which already owned a sizeable chunk of Heinemann, offered Lane £400,000 for the firm: Lane told Paroissien that he was seeing its boss, Lionel Fraser, but 'though I am not unsympathetic to the idea, I shall want to know a great deal more about what is expected of me, and what interference I might expect of them'. 'I don't like the idea of being put in a position in which I was not in control of my operation,' he told A. S. Frere of Heinemann: 'I value my freedom of action more than the idea of being a publishing tycoon.' Bill Williams learned that Longmans were prepared to offer £500,000, and both Collins and Odhams expressed interest. 'As to what happens to the firm *after* your demise, you've never really given a bugger, and I don't blame you,' he told his old friend after urging him not to reduce his own holding to less than 51 per cent. 'But if you lost control of it in your lifetime, you'd break what you use for a heart.'

Writing 'on a bright sunny morning in the Dordogne', Lane told Williams that 'we have enjoyed the best and happiest years of the firm; what we have to do in the few years left to us is to see that the principles on which it was founded are going to be maintained into the foreseeable future'. Much to Williams's relief, the negotiations with Tillings fizzled out. 'I am now definitely decided against letting go of control,' Lane informed an equally relieved Harry

Paroissien, 'as I think there might be a grave danger of changing the whole character of the firm if the financial voice was in a position to speak loudly.' Nowadays we tend to look askance at hard-boiled businessmen who affect to be swayed by anything other than profit, suspecting them of humbuggery, naivety or both, but in Lane's case – and that of some other tycoons with whom he had dealings – such cynicism would have been misplaced.

But not always, alas. A year or so later Lane began discussions with Geoffrey Crowther, the editor of *The Economist* and a Trustee of the *News Chronicle*, about the possibility of Penguin being sold to the group of which the magazine formed a part. 'You would not find that we were interested in profits exclusively or even primarily,' the former editor of *Transatlantic* told him. 'I have never hesitated with *The Economist* to take action that would reduce the immediate profits if it seemed the right or the interesting thing to do, and I have a great belief that in doing so one gets more profit in the end.' 'I attach less importance to legal covenants than I do to an understanding on principle,' Crowther continued. 'If we can agree, on the one hand, that you won't walk out on the firm until it is in safe hands, and on the other, that when it is, we won't try to hold you, that would be enough for me. But to satisfy my colleagues I think we ought to have some sort of agreement on paper . . .' Such noble sentiments were all very well, but shortly afterwards an outraged Lane broke off negotiations when he learned that Crowther and his fellow-trustee, Lord Layton, had sold the *News Chronicle* and the *Star* to the right-wing *Daily Mail*: the *News Chronicle*, like Penguin Books, had been a pillar of the liberal left, and if Crowther and his colleagues could so blithely sell it off to the enemy camp, how could he trust any assurances they might give about the future of Penguin Books? Disillusioned on that particular front, he held equally fruitless discussions with *The Times*, and with David Astor at the *Observer* and Laurence Scott at the *Manchester Guardian*, both of whose papers were owned by trusts of a kind that might better preserve the Penguin ethos.

In the meantime, Ben Travers had put him up for the Garrick, and he had been made a director of Bumpus, the famous but old-fashioned bookshop then being revitalized by an energetic book-seller named Tony Godwin. He was in touch once more with Lettice, and a new generation of young editors would soon be making their mark on the firm, but all was not well. 'I haven't a clue what I'm going to do next. I've got the firm, the farm, the Zoo, Bumpus, and a lot of acquaintances, a few friends, an enormous capacity for enjoyment but a rather empty personal life,' he confided to Joan Collihole. That may have been the case, but huge changes were around the corner, not all of them to his taste.

17. Changing the Guard

One of the melancholy truths of institutional life is that many of those involved come to think of themselves as indispensable and indestructible, yet after their departure – whether voluntary or enforced – the waters close over so quickly that it is as if they had never been; and Penguin was no exception. 'You and Bill must realize, as so many of our publishing colleagues do, what your contributions amount to and, as Bill has said so often, we must never part. We are a trinity without which the firm would be quite different,' Lane told Frostie from a Caribbean cruise ship: but the trinity's days were numbered, and a new generation was waiting to make its mark.

Frostie's reaction is not recorded, but Bill Williams was happy to go along with such sentiments, whatever the truth of the situation. 'During our many years of comradeship we have never been closer than we are now and, as we both realize, we have reached this harmony of outlook without even making a conscious effort to do so,' he told Lane, and later he confided that 'Nothing in my life has been as rewarding, as exhilarating, or as worthwhile as my place at your side – at your side and two paces to the rear. I hope I shall maintain that stance and posture till I pass on – to publish Penguins in Paradise!' As for taking on new members of staff, 'I don't think we need any additional chaps on the editorial side. We are an effective, if mixed, team. You are constantly burgeoning new and fruitful ideas; I play the elder statesman with some success, and do a fair amount of keeping authors sweet; Frostie when she is on form is a persuasive go-between, a good judge of a book and equally bright on the ideas side; Glover makes a most serviceable encyclopaedia . . .' And, as if that weren't enough, 'You have an incandescent quality which I relish very much indeed, even in its more exasperating aspects!'

But for all his talk of editing Penguins in Paradise, Williams's attention was elsewhere for much of the time, and, shrewd as he was, he was becoming out of touch and out of date. After Lane's death he confessed that he found his work on the Arts Council more interesting and more important than his Penguin connection, and he relished the perks of life as a cultural bureaucrat. Dennis Foreman remembered him as a 'curt, big, bluff organizer, like a football manager in the field of culture, socially oriented rather than arts oriented'; John Curtis, a young Penguin colleague, thought of him as 'a very powerful *éminence rouge*', with a finger in every pie (in due course these would include a Trusteeship of the National Gallery); in Richard Hoggart's opinion, he was the last 'dominant' Secretary-General of the Arts, famed for telling an over-active Chairman, 'You are the admiral; I am the captain. Now get off my bridge.' Kenneth Clark, when Chairman, was granted one short interview a week with the Secretary-General, and handed a glass of sherry; he was not allowed a secretary, but Williams 'said that his own secretary would bring me in such letters as it was appropriate for me to see, together with his answers'. Exercising such power in the ornate and gilt surroundings of the Astors' old house in St James's Square was heady stuff, and Penguin may have seemed, by comparison, dingy and sub-fusc.

Lane still valued Williams as a drinking partner, but had no illusions about his value to, or interest in, the firm; and, with their sixtieth birthdays looming, both Williams and Glover seemed ever more dispensable. 'There is no question that Glover has a malign influence in the firm,' Lane told Dick in December 1957. 'He hasn't a single member of his staff with any creative ability. WEW is weak and drifts with the stream.' Nine months later, he told Frostie that he wanted both men to be out of the firm within the next two to three years, by the end of which time she would be 'the only permanent officer on the watch': giving Williams a further lease of life would depend on whether or not he had encouraged a new generation of editors, 'and I don't think this will be easy for him'. Williams had been made a director in 1957, but he had, in Lane's opinion, 'become increasingly unreliable, and at times I doubt his loyalty'.

Though unsparing of her colleagues, Frostie alone seemed immune to criticism; but her health remained a constant source of worry, and although she worked herself as hard as ever, she was increasingly out of touch with younger writers and publishing editors. She had problems with her breathing, but Lane thought her ailments were essentially 'psychosomatic'; and throughout the Fifties he was forever dropping her fond but worried notes, suggesting an 'overhaul' in the London Clinic, urging her to work more from home, begging her not to fret when a nervous or physical break-down resulted in her being out of the office for weeks on end. 'The trouble is that she has no idea of how to organize her life, and if she goes on I can see nothing but a series of breakdowns,' he told Paroissien. Bill Williams was equally anxious. Writing to Lane after one particularly bad bout, he reported, with relief, that she was calmer and 'not getting into people's hair in the office': part of the problem, as he saw it, lay in her devotion to Lane, and 'she would work best if she were not having to see you several times a day, and could be left alone for several days on end'. Her laughter became ever more hysterical, and still more so when Lane was present; she burst into tears when Hilary Rubinstein, then a young editor at Gollancz, told her over lunch that they were not prepared to license some Dorothy Sayers novels to Penguin. As her appearances in the office became increasingly intermittent, a degree of paranoia set in: she felt that her contribution to the firm's original publishing was neglected and overlooked, and as Penguin politics became more Machiavellian, she worried that she too might fall victim to a conspiracy of courtiers. 'So little credit seems to come to me for the initiation of so many aspects of Puffins (probably unknown to you), the majority of handbooks, including their initi-ation, planning with the author, encouragement and criticism and detailed work,' she told Lane in a memo which was almost certainly never sent. She went on to cite her close involvement with Elizabeth David's *Mediterranean Food* – she and Lane had defied the disapproval of their colleagues by starting a cookery list, and she had commis-sioned John Minton to draw the cover – and reminded him of how she had brought to the firm two books by Kenneth Clark, *The*

Meaning of Art and *Landscape into Art*, as well as Herbert Read's
Modern Art. Lane had suggested that, given the state of her health,
she should no longer attend policy meetings, and should try to disassociate herself as much as possible from the politics of office life,
but 'I shouldn't be human if I didn't feel a certain difficulty in
cutting myself away . . . This is not the way I thought things would
go.' As for the editorial meetings held in Bill Williams's office, 'I,
more than anyone, have been responsible for making them happen
– even to the extent of carrying that little white suitcase in which
everything was put when we used to meet up in London.' 'I am a
fighter, but not for myself,' she told him in another note in which
she suggested that Glover and Schmoller were closer in spirit to
university presses than to the 'interpretative amateurism' she cherished at Penguin. She felt vulnerable and exposed, for 'if the attitudes which have been expressed about Bill (via Glover on his own
and on behalf of the junior staff) also represent the general attitude
to me, then it is unrealistic to expect it to work. There is no point
in having *two* people outside the house who are objects of hostility
and contempt.' It was hard for her to struggle on 'with the feeling,
like Bill, that I have no backing, and am only tolerated'.

Relief seemed on hand when, in the summer of 1957, Frostie
announced her engagement, so averting her 'personal nightmare' of
'ending up in some Earl's Court rooming-house'. Harry Kemp was
a minor poet, and the author of seven slim volumes; he had been
a protégé of Robert Graves and Laura Riding, and had lived with
them for a time with his first wife. According to his obituarist in
the *Independent*, he was 'a small, ruddy-faced man, old fashioned in
his dress, credulous in his judgements'; the author of 'cool, well-
shaped poems', he was a 'lively raconteur with a roving and satirical
eye'. His eye proved rather too roving, but for the time being Bill
Williams seemed impressed: Frostie, he told Lane, had brought her
'prospective mate' into the office, and he seemed 'very agreeable:
good-looking in an athletic sort of way, nicely mannered, and easy
and intelligent in conversation'. The happy couple planned to live
in Lewes, and 'thank God she has got someone to cry on instead
of us!' Harold Raymond wrote to the bride-to-be with his

congratulations, and professed himself amazed that no one had snapped her up before: 'I should have thought someone would have clubbed you if he couldn't have persuaded you. Young men can't be what they were in my time!' Frostie busied herself flat-hunting: according to Bill Williams, Kemp did nothing but watch cricket, 'and contents himself with exclaiming "bad show!" when she reports that flats have been snatched from under her nose'.

Once installed in Lewes, Frostie came into the office far less often, but books and files and papers were sent to her in a steady flow. She was made a director of the firm, and for a time, Lane told Paroissien, she seemed happy and 'the complete woman of affairs'; but before long the old problems had returned, and Lane was begging her not to overdo it, reminding her that 'at the age of 42, you shouldn't have to be humping great baskets of books half across London'. He sent her to a health farm, and wrote a stern note to her negligent spouse: her current condition was 'a very serious matter which brooks of no further delay', and he asked Kemp to come and see him about it. Referring to her 'current breakdown', Williams told Lane that she had lost her 'drive and sense of proportion', and had become 'more and more fussy, more and more unable to distinguish between the important and the trivial, and more and more inclined to rattle the juniors'. She found it impossible to delegate, and carried everything in her head or on 'sundry scraps of paper'. Her work, he declared, should be divided between a newly appointed team of young editors who were waiting in the wings.

Alan Glover, much to his distress, was seen as an irrelevance, and was increasingly ignored. When he learned that Lane, without consulting him, had arranged for John Curtis to 'have a go' at a proposed series of Picture Pelicans, he gave vent to his feelings with 'deep and bitter regret'. 'In the face of this humiliation which you have seen fit to impose on me before not only my equals, I cannot suppose that I am performing any useful purpose here at all, or without a complete loss of self-respect stay here.' If Lane so wished, he was ready to 'walk out without any further ado'. No answer was forthcoming, so he returned to the matter a few days later. 'It sometimes seems to me,' he wrote, 'and I don't think I'm unique in having the feeling, that you sometimes think that people in the firm are wrong just *because* they're in the firm, whereas anything that comes from an outsider is valuable and exciting just *because* it comes from outside.'

With Glover due to retire in 1960, Bill Williams and Eunice Frost fast fading from the scene, and the new generation of editors still in their twenties, Lane began to look elsewhere for an editorial right-hand man. 'We can spot the chaps who want to "go into publishing" in the belief that it is a round of cocktail parties and boy friends,' Paroissien once warned him, pandering to Lane's reservations about the Eton and Oxford school of publisher, and in due course a possible alternative presented itself. While on holiday in Spain in 1957 Lane read, on Frostie's recommendation, *The Uses of Literacy*. It was, he told her, a first-class piece of work, and although he knew nothing about the author, 'I have a hunch he's the man we may be looking for on the editorial side.' Richard Hoggart had no practical experience of publishing, and no desire to abandon the academic life, but over the years he was to become a kind of guru or sounding-board for Lane. 'I was almost an archetype of the audience he was after,' he later wrote. 'But I was an articulate archetype, so he could learn more because I could talk to him about it.' He remembered Lane 'sitting in his chauffeur-driven car, and he would talk in the most extraordinarily innocent way about ideas and society and so on'. In Hoggart's opinion, Lane 'needed to be in contact with people whose insights he respected, who seemed to know things he didn't know about intellectual, social or cultural life': looking back on Lane thirty years after his death, Hoggart saw him as a man driven on by a spirit of rebellion, who wanted to reach readers not by diluting or over-simplifying but through an Orwellian belief in the virtues of 'clear, firm speech' – and 'today, when the very existence of a "common reader" is denied, this splendid conviction needs to be assessed afresh'.

Despite Lane's bias towards non-publishers, it seemed more likely that an heir-apparent might be found among the younger generation of Penguin editors, then in their mid-twenties. John Curtis had already been with the firm five years when Dieter Pevsner and Tom Maschler joined in 1958, and all three went on to become well-known figures in the trade. The son of Nikolaus, Dieter Pevsner joined from university and went on to make his mark as a non-fiction editor, looking after a new generation of Penguin Specials and Pelicans on politics, psychology, archaeology, religion and history, while John Curtis, in true Penguin fashion, combined his editorial labours with publicity and design before moving on to Weidenfeld & Nicolson; but whereas Pevsner would remain with the firm for the rest of Lane's life, Maschler shot through like a comet, presaging a future that Lane would find hard to accept and making a greater impact on the firm than his brief tenure might suggest.

Lean, dark and endowed with vulpine good looks, a devotee of corduroy jackets, open-necked shirts and slip-on shoes at a time when publishing offices were staffed by men in fiery tweeds or, in Penguin's case, grey suits, white shirts and unalarming ties, Maschler was to become the most stylish and charismatic publisher of his generation, whose imprimatur was coveted by authors and venerated by literary agents, newspapermen, television producers, booksellers, literary editors and even the odd member of the reading public; a few years later, by which time he had converted an ailing Jonathan Cape into the most modish and sought-after imprint in literary London, a journalist wrote of how, when Maschler turned up at a publishing party, the room stiffened as if a wolf had been let loose in a flock of sheep. He was in his mid-twenties when he came to Penguin. His father, Kurt Maschler, was a publisher who had come to Britain from Berlin to escape the Nazis, and was well known as a publisher of art books and children's books. Tom Maschler had decided against going to university, and after a brief spell with André Deutsch had moved on to MacGibbon & Kee. There he had edited a collection of essays entitled *Declaration*, which brought him a certain *réclame* in the literary world: its contributors included John Osborne, Kenneth Tynan, Colin Wilson, John Wain, Lindsay Anderson, Doris Lessing and other writers of the Angry Young Man school, and it went on to sell some 20,000 copies in hardback. Lane must have heard about *Declaration*; if not, Maschler was drawn to his attention by the formidable Blanche Knopf, who described her protégé as 'the most brilliant young man I had seen in a very long time'.

Despite his youth and relative inexperience, Maschler displayed an enviable insouciance in his dealings with Lane: so much so that it seemed as though he was interviewing Lane for a job, rather than vice versa. 'I wonder whether you could telephone me at my office and let me know where and when I could reach you, since I would prefer to discuss the matter personally with you,' he told his future employer. Paul Scherer, then working on the sales side, remembered how after Maschler had joined the phone rang in the middle of a meeting. Lane picked it up. 'I thought I said I wasn't taking any calls,' he told the switchboard operator, but to no avail. In due course the receiver was passed to Lane's most junior editor. 'Oh, hello, darling,' Maschler began, before embarking on a long and amorous conversation: Scherer likes to think that he lay on the floor at the time, but this could be wishful thinking.

Bill Williams may have reported Maschler as working 'with more ardour than direction', but Lane recognized and valued his qualities, and he quickly began to make his mark. He was, nominally, Frostie's editorial assistant, buying in new fiction; but she was hardly ever in the office – Maschler claims that she never came into the office at all during his two years at Penguin, but was seldom off the phone – and before long he was dabbling in foreign rights, looking after the play list, building up a line of authors in translation, and trying to persuade Lane to engage in the kind of co-edition publishing pioneered by his father. He soon discovered that for all her assiduity and the books she humped across London, Frostie was hopelessly out of touch with younger writers of the age and type he had published in *Declaration*, and was taking too long to make up her mind about books submitted to the firm: 'You've only had it so far for two years and six weeks!' Hilary Rubinstein complained apropos Nadine Gordimer's *The Lying Days*, on offer from Gollancz. Penguin had turned down Amis's *Lucky Jim*; Lane himself had cast a cold eye on such 'doubtful starters' as *Catcher in the Rye* and Brian Moore's *The Lonely Passion of Judith Hearne*; and when Maschler reported back on a meeting with André Deutsch about books he might buy for the Penguin list, Frostie's reaction was entirely negative: V. S. Naipaul's *The Suffrage of Elvira* had already been rejected, with no chance of an appeal, George Mikes was out of the question ('No – rejected'), and Maschler's special pleading on behalf of Brian Moore's *The Feast of Lupercal* ('Do we *really* want to turn this down?') fell on deaf ears. But all was not in vain. He outraged Hamish Hamilton by turning down the latest Angela Thirkell, took on David Storey, William Golding's *Lord of the Flies* and John Braine's best-selling *Room at the Top*, and, making good use of his European connections, translations of Camus, Sartre, Brecht and Musil. He also revived the ailing play list: a keen habitué of the Royal Court, and a friend of Tynan, Tony Richardson and George Devine, he stretched his remit to include original work as well as reprints and published new plays by the new school of 'kitchen sink' dramatists such as Arnold Wesker and Bernard Kops under the imprint of New English Dramatists: the first volume sold over 200,000 copies, and the covers were decorated with interlinking triangles of colour, reminiscent of G-Plan furniture or the modern Danish kitchenware promoted in the 1950s by Estrid Bannister. For the time being at least, Lane was infatuated by his new appointment, whose irreverence and scorn for the accepted wisdom reflected his own: Maschler was a regular visitor to Silverbeck, he went with Lane to Switzerland to interview graphic artists for a possible series of illustrated books, and even Bill Williams ruefully noted 'how easily the impact of poor Frostie has dissolved', and that 'the cleaning-up operation was both desirable and overdue'.

Much to Lane's irritation, Maschler's stay at Penguin was all too brief. Early in 1960, Lane was diagnosed with jaundice and whipped off to the Edward VII Hospital in Windsor. While recuperating, he was visited by Tom Maschler, who told him that he would be giving in his notice since he had been offered a job in publishing which it would be madness to decline. He could not, he wrote to Lane afterwards, tell him which firm he was joining since this would 'embarrass the publisher *enormously* should it be discovered at this point'; but all would be revealed in due course, and in the meantime he would like to recommend in his place a friend named Tony Godwin. Infuriated as he was to lose a potential heir-apparent – 'Well. What am I going to do?' he demanded when Maschler broke the news – Lane agreed to see Godwin, despite some reservations about his being a bookseller without publishing experience. He already knew him, both in person and by reputation, as a bookseller, and Charles Pick of Michael Joseph had warmly recommended him as a possible Penguin editor. Maschler drove a nervous Godwin down to the hospital for his initial interview, and departed to contemplate his future as an editorial director of Jonathan Cape.

A small, wiry, energetic figure with bright blue eyes, Godwin was then about forty. In later years he was invariably togged out in an open-necked shirt and jeans, topped by a bush of frizzy grey hair, but in those days he was a more clerkly figure, clad in a sober grey suit and smoking cigarettes through a holder. In the late Thirties he had worked for Gordon Fraser in Paris, which gave him a life-long interest in modern painting. During the war he had served in an artillery regiment, rising to captain and seeing action in Italy and Normandy. Demobbed in 1946, and lacking a university degree and formal qualifications, he sold books off a barrow – as did his contemporary Paul Hamlyn, at exactly the same time – before deciding to open a bookshop. He borrowed £2,000 from friends, and opened Better Books in the Charing Cross Road.

Twenty years earlier, Allen Lane had complained about the dowdy exclusivity of English bookshops; Better Books was deliberately undowdy, but although Godwin made a point of employing literate assistants who knew what he had in stock, and promoted poetry readings, coffee-drinking and the like, Better Books might well have alarmed middlebrow book-lovers. John Sewell painted an imitation Matisse fascia board; Ronald Searle and others drew and designed the advertisements that appeared in the Tube, the Arts Theatre programmes and the *New Statesman*; the basement was decorated in unbooksellerish hues of silver and black. Fired by his success, Godwin opened another bookshop in the City, and in 1959 he was asked to work his magic on Bumpus. The quintessential 'carriage trade' bookseller, Bumpus had been run since the 1920s by the venerable and much-loved J. G. Wilson. It had recently been taken over by a consortium of publishers, including Allen Lane, Robert Lusty of Hutchinson, Alan White of Methuen and Jocelyn (Jock) Gibb, a benign and heavily tweeded gentleman publisher of the old school who shared Lane's passion for farming, and spent much of his time in the office telephoning the bailiffs on his farms in Scotland and discussing milk yields with his baffled employees. Godwin inherited fifty employees, many of them over seventy years old, customers' accounts which had not been settled since the early 1930s, and losses of £1,800 a month. Faced with such horrors, he moved the shop from Oxford Street round the corner into Baker Street – not a wise move, since under the terms of the lease he was not allowed to hang out a sign or a fascia board – sacked most of the staff, bought the Book Society, and edited and redesigned its magazine, *The Bookman*.

Godwin's bedside interview with Lane must have gone well, for – much to the surprise of their colleagues at Bumpus, none of whom had been consulted by Lane, their fellow-director, or their ebullient employee – it was announced that he would be joining Penguin in an editorial capacity forthwith, and that he would continue working for Bumpus and the Book Society until September 1960. Reporting that Penguin was in 'disarray' after Maschler's departure, Lane announced that Godwin would begin by 'picking up some of the threads' from his predecessor, but this was not good enough for the new arrival. Godwin was not pleased by a piece in the *Bookseller* which reported that he was replacing Maschler as 'an editor at Penguin Books'. 'I feel this was a bit much,' he complained to his new boss: he thought he had been taken on to replace Eunice Frost, whereas Maschler was 'on a par with Ditta [i.e. Dieter Pevsner: spelling was never Godwin's strong point] and the other young editors', and such an announcement would not help him in his dealings with hardback editors, literary agents and the like. Lane confided to Frostie that he had had 'a bit of a bleat' from Godwin, who felt it would be 'a retrograde step to move from MD of Bumpus into Tom's shoes'. Godwin, in the meantime, wrote Lane a memo in which he stressed the importance of maintaining Penguin's

standards and providing 'paperbacks for the literate': it was essential
not to allow the firm's 'unique role and identity to be diluted by
the demands of sales', but it was equally important, if Penguin was
not to lose out to its brasher rivals in terms of display and shelf
space, that the sales and marketing side of the business should be
developed and expanded. 'You know, the best day's business I ever
did was hiring Tony Godwin,' Lane informed Charles Pick later that
year at the Frankfurt Book Fair. A few years later, he would be
singing a different tune; but for the time being at least the future
looked rosy.

Lane was equally euphoric about another new appointment made
at this time. Whereas Godwin, like Lane himself, had worked his
way up from the bottom, C. M. Woodhouse was the quintessence
of what Henry Fairlie had recently termed the 'Establishment', and
the kind of man whom Lane had hitherto shunned as a possible
colleague. A baronet, educated at Winchester and New College,
Oxford, with a good war behind him – he had been parachuted
into Greece and blown up the all-important Gorgopotamos viaduct,
severely disrupting supplies to Rommel's forces in North Africa –
'Monty' Woodhouse was an old-fashioned, liberal-minded, scholarly
public servant who combined his duties as a Conservative MP with
writing, reviewing and a devotion to modern Greece. He had been
introduced to Lane by Alan Pryce-Jones, Stanley Morison's successor
as editor of the *Times Literary Supplement*, and had little experience
of business and none whatsoever of publishing.

For whatever reason, Lane saw Woodhouse as a potential right-
hand man, albeit one who came into the office on a part-time basis
and would combine publishing with his parliamentary duties. 'I am
more sure than ever that he is the right man,' Lane informed Frostie,
and George Weidenfeld was reported as telling New York publishers
that Woodhouse had taken over the running of Penguin: but the
honeymoon was brief. A bad start was made when Lane complained
that, with Maschler's departure, the other editors at a sales conference chaired by Woodhouse 'said their pieces like a group of boys
at school': Woodhouse bridled on their behalf, pointing out that
'the criticism would have been more justified if you had given me

any idea beforehand of what you did expect'. A month or two after taking up the reins, Woodhouse was complaining that the job was far bigger than expected, and the machine a good deal less smooth-running. He was heavily involved in a Finance Bill and a Standing Committee, and found it impossible to give more time to the firm; Lane complained that Woodhouse had failed to brief himself adequately for the spring sales conference, and that it was impossible for him to do a proper job running the editorial department on three days a week. 'In the circumstances, I think it would be better if you made other plans as from the autumn,' Lane memoed his new colleague. 'I have no comment on your decision,' Woodhouse replied. 'I would like to put on record that, according to my diary, there have only been four working days since Easter on which I did not spend at least half the day, generally more, either at Harmondsworth or at Holborn' (where Penguin had, briefly, a small London office above an ironmonger's shop).

Tony Godwin remembered Woodhouse as 'one of the nicest men I've ever met', albeit one who was 'addicted to gentle civil service procedures and a dyed-in-the-wool conservative', and noted how Lane failed to hide 'a terrible courteous impatience for the poor sweet man'; Tom Maschler's only recorded comment was a laconic 'P. G.?' scrawled against his superior's name, and only a year or two after Woodhouse's departure Lane referred to him as 'the governmental type whose name escapes me'.

Woodhouse's tenure at Penguin was, as he ruefully admitted in his memoirs, 'brief and uneasy'. While in Ghana on parliamentary business he had been told by an indignant reader that the words 'Not for Sale in the USA or Canada', printed on the back of the Penguin edition of Stanley Kaufmann's novel *The Philanderer*, somehow suggested that Penguin was unloading pornography on the African market; on his return to England he had suggested more 'emollient' wording might be in order, and this, he concluded, 'was the sum total of my success with Allen Lane'. His only other recorded contribution to Penguin history was to express some reservations, as voiced by some junior members of staff, about the desirability of publishing the unexpurgated version of D. H. Lawrence's

Lady Chatterley's Lover. Lane, he recalled, 'was furious, and told me to mind my own business': which was just as well, perhaps, since Lady Chatterley was about to make a fortune for Penguin and its founder, and attract more attention than any book ever published by the firm.

18. Lady Chatterley Goes on Trial

First published in full in Florence in 1928, Lawrence's most no-torious novel·was available for the law-abiding in expurgated form from Heinemann, the publishers of his collected works. Bolder spirits smuggled in unexpurgated editions, printed and published on the Continent, but these were regularly intercepted by Customs; between 1950 and 1960 nineteen different printings had been referred to the Director of Public Prosecutions, seventeen destruc-tion orders had been issued by magistrates, and a London book-seller had been prosecuted for selling an edition printed in Sweden.

Penguin had published thirteen Lawrence titles since the war, and it was decided to publish a further seven, including *Lady Chatterley's Lover*, in 1960, to coincide with the thirtieth anniversary of their author's death. F. R. Leavis, the most influential academic critic of the day, had acclaimed Lawrence as the only major novelist of recent times and the last exemplar of the Great Tradition, and although, as it turned out, Leavis thought *Lady Chatterley's Lover* his least impressive novel, to reprint a batch of the novels made good sense in literary as well as commercial terms. Alwyn Birch of Heinemann had told Lane that although the police had several times enquired about the possibility, they had no intention of publishing an un-expurgated edition of *Lady Chatterley*, so Penguin had the field to itself. At an editorial meeting John Curtis wondered aloud which edition Penguin would be publishing: no easy matter, since Lawrence had written three versions, the last of which was most heavily peppered with four-letter words. 'I remember AL looking up with those piercing eyes of his,' he recalled, 'but on this occasion his face also revealed a surprised glance: for it was apparent that up until this moment he had not taken this issue on board.' Lane may have stumbled inadvertently into what was to prove the most sensational episode of his career, but once the alternatives had been pointed out he was adamant that Penguin should publish the unexpurgated *Lady Chatterley*.

Interviewed on the subject some years later, Lane declared that 'there's a time in a publishing firm, especially when things are going well, when to chuck a jemmy in the works is a very good thing because it gives everyone a lift', and publishing *Lady Chatterley's Lover* appealed to his sense of mischief, even though his own tastes tended to the puritanical. 'My own view has always been to refuse to give way on anything I have published on grounds of politics, religion, morals or what have you,' he told Dick. 'I don't see myself in the role of crusader,' he claimed, 'but I thought that if ever a book had been designed to be a test book for the Act, this was it.' The 'Act' was Roy Jenkins's Obscene Publications Act, passed the previous year: the prosecution of *Lady Chatterley's Lover* under the terms of the Act was to become the most celebrated trial in publishing history, and its publication one of the milestones marking the way from the sober, strait-laced Fifties to the permissiveness of the Swinging Sixties.

Until the passing of the Act, obscenity was still a common-law offence, and was defined in terms laid down by Lord Chief Justice Cockburn in 1868, viz. 'Whether the tendency of the matters charged . . . is to deprave and corrupt those whose minds are open to such immoral influences.' Enforcing the law was a random and variegated business. In the 1940s the Metropolitan Police thought up the 'disclaimer' system, used to dispose of books which no one would dream of defending on literary grounds − no summons was issued, there was no hearing before a magistrate, and the offending articles were taken away and burned − and until the passing of the Act most supposedly obscene publications were dealt with by destruction orders or the occasional prosecution followed by a trial, either before a magistrate or before a judge and jury. Egged on by a zealous Home Secretary, Sir David Maxwell-Fyfe, a latterday Joynson-Hicks, and by worrying stories in the Press about the unmentionable things to be found in imported American horror comics and pulp fiction, prosecutions reached a new high in the mid-Fifties. In 1954 alone, 167,000 books and magazines were destroyed; local magistrates vented their fury on the postcards of Donald McGill; copies of *Madame Bovary*, *Moll Flanders* and the works of J. P. Sartre were consigned to the flames, the victims of local destruction orders; a magistrate in Swindon ordered the incineration of *The Decameron*; Customs officers confiscated Pepys's Diary and *Tristram Shandy* when not riffling through travellers' suitcases in search of Olympia Press editions of works by Henry Miller and Frank Harris. Bearing in mind the fate of Zola's first English publisher, Henry Vizetelly – prosecuted in 1889 for publishing *La Terre*, he died in prison – Penguin worried about including *Germinal* and Rabelais in Penguin Classics before deciding to run the risk.

Most of the publishers involved were fly-by-night outfits or unabashed pornographers, but mainstream practitioners became alarmed when, in 1954, some of their more respectable colleagues received summonses and were hauled into the dock. Mrs Webb of Hutchinson was charged with the publication of a novel entitled *September in Quinze*; she and her fellow-directors were fined £500 apiece, the Recorder of London declaring it essential to 'take a very solid stand against this sort of thing, and realize how important it is for the youth of this country to be protected, and that the fountain of our national blood should not be polluted at its source'. A. S. Frere of Heinemann was the next to be put on trial after Walter Baxter's *The Image and the Search* had been excoriated by John Gordon in the *Sunday Express*: some said that Lord Beaverbrook was taking his revenge on Frere for refusing to publish a book attacking the Windsors. The prosecution was led by a florid Old Etonian, Mervyn Griffith-Jones QC, later described by Roy Jenkins as 'that indefatigable scourge of the impure': he asked the jury, in language that would soon become familiar to Lane and his fellow-defendants, 'When Christmas comes, would you go out and buy copies of the book and hand them round as presents to the girls in the office – and if not, why not? The answer is that it is not the type of book they ought to read.'

Some comfort could be drawn, however, from the acquittal of Secker & Warburg, the original publisher of the novel that had made 'Monty' Woodhouse's Ghanaian interlocutor so indignant. A

keen young policeman on the Isle of Man had spotted a copy of
The Philanderer in a local bookshop, and the firm's managing director,
Fred Warburg, received a summons. Warburg elected for trial by
jury, which was more expensive and, potentially, more punitive than
appearing before a magistrate; but whereas Mrs Webb and A. S.
Frere had suffered the indignity of appearing in the dock, Mr Justice
Stable allowed the defendant to sit in the well of his court at the
Old Bailey, alongside his solicitor. Malcolm Muggeridge and Graham
Greene hovered in the corridors outside, primed to give evidence
on Warburg's behalf, but neither was called to the witness-box. Mr
Justice Stable's summing-up, printed in full in the Penguin edition
of the book, suggested that, at last, the tide was beginning to turn
in favour of a more liberal view of such matters. He had already
told the jury to take the book home and, rather than concentrate
on the purple passages, to read it as a whole. They must, he told
them, consider the meaning of obscenity in terms of the modern
day: and the fact that a book was not suitable for a fourteen-year-
old girl did not necessarily mean that to make it available to adults
should be a criminal offence.

As a direct result of the 1954 prosecutions, the Society of Authors
set up a Committee to look into the vexed issue of obscene
publications: A. P. Herbert was in the chair, C. H. Rolph, the
pseudonym of a policeman turned campaigning journalist, acted as
Secretary, and the members included V. S. Pritchett, Walter Allen,
Sir Gerald Barry, Roy Jenkins, H. E. Bates, A. D. Peters, Herbert
Read, W. A. R. (Billy) Collins and Norman St John Stevas. Stevas
was given the job of drafting a bill based on their deliberations, and
this was presented, unsuccessfully, as a private member's bill, by Roy
Jenkins and Lord Lambton in 1955. Four years later Jenkins tried
again, and the Obscene Publications Act passed into law.

The Act provided a new test of obscenity, and allowed a defence
of the public good. The work in question had to be considered in
its entirety; expert witnesses could be called to prove that the work
could be published 'for the public good on the ground that it is in
the interests of science, literature, art or learning'; there was a time
limit on prosecutions; booksellers, widely regarded as the most

vulnerable link in the chain, were given the defence of 'innocent dissemination'; the penalties for the guilty, hitherto unlimited, were restricted to a fine or three years in prison; and publishers were given the right to appeal against destruction orders.

All this was well and good, but the Act had yet to be tested out on a serious work of literature. As Lane readied himself to publish *Lady Chatterley*, the Act had been cited in over forty prosecutions – all of them confined to such works as *The Ladies Directory*, a guide to prostitutes and their services, or self-evident pornography like *Heaven, Hell and the Whore*. In 1958, however, George Weidenfeld had bought the British rights in Nabokov's *Lolita*, bravely pre-empting a long line of other publishers who were waiting for Roy Jenkins's Bill to become law. Gerald Gardiner, a future Labour Lord Chancellor and a passionate devotee of free speech, had master-minded Weidenfeld's campaign, and was determined to outwit Sir Theobald 'Toby' Mathew, the Director of Public Prosecutions. A letter was sent to *The Times* in support of publication, signed by a long list of eminent writers, academics and public figures, Allen Lane among them; Weidenfeld sent a copy from the very modest first printing to the DPP, and told him that unless he heard to the contrary he would publish by October 1960. Some nerve-racking days intervened, but eventually Weidenfeld was summoned to the phone, in the middle of a party, and told that the book would not be prosecuted. The celebrations became more frenzied than before, and the firm went on to sell over 200,000 copies in hardback.

Lane may have been ready to test the Act, but he was equally anxious not to spend time in prison. His decision to press ahead received a welcome boost when, in 1959, an unexpurgated edition of *Lady Chatterley* was, at last, published in New York: and, as with *Ulysses*, where America led, Lane might safely follow. With the approval of Frieda Lawrence and Laurence Pollinger, the literary agent to the estate, Knopf were the publishers of the expurgated edition, and formally controlled the volume rights, but three years after Frieda's death, Barney Rosset of Grove Press decided to go ahead with an unexpurgated edition, with a preface by the poet Archibald MacLeish and an introduction by Mark Schorer, a respected academic. Rosset sold a large number of copies to a book club, and since this involved sending copies through the post he became liable to prosecution under the so-called Comstock Law, which declared it a federal offence to send obscene material through the US Mails. The Post Office seized twenty-four cartons of books, and although Rosset was found guilty his appeal was upheld by Judge Bryan and he was free to publish in the States. The fact that he had no rights in the book left him at the mercy of paperback publishers eager to cash in. Within eight days of Judge Bryan's decision Pocket Books had brought out an unexpurgated edition of their own; they were followed by Dell, Pyramid and New English Library, and a vicious bookshop battle ensued.

In January 1960 the board of Penguin agreed to publication, and Laurence Pollinger accepted an advance of £1,000. It was decided to print 200,000 copies, with an August publication date; later on, to counter suggestions that Penguin was cashing in on pornography, Hans Schmoller pointed out to Michael Rubinstein, Penguin's assiduous solicitor, that such high expectations were far from unique: Lawrence's *Sons and Lovers*, first published in Penguin in 1948, had sold 321,000 copies, *The Woman of Rome* 715,000, the *Odyssey* 965,000, *Clochemerle* 430,000, *One of Our Submarines* 350,000 and *Room at the Top* 190,000. Hazell, Watson & Viney agreed to print the book, but although they produced a dummy copy, proceedings ground to a halt when a compositor complained to the Head Reader. After an acrimonious board meeting, the firm reluctantly withdrew: they had, a director later explained, been left paying the bills after *Night and Day* collapsed in 1937, and were reluctant to run the risk again. Help was to hand in the form of Sir Isaac Pitman, who told Lane and 'Rab' Butler that he would be more than happy to print the book 'as a matter of principle', though he would be using Western Printing Services, run by Anthony Rowe, rather than the firm that bore his name. Since WPS had printed *Ulysses* for The Bodley Head, Pitman's intervention lent continuity to the proceedings.

Lane's resolve to press ahead with publication was matched by an equal determination on the part of the authorities to prosecute.

Pitman told Lane that 'Rab' Butler had written to say that he, for one, would welcome publication, but he may well have been a lone voice in both the Government and the Conservative Party. A month after Penguin had decided to go ahead, the Attorney General, Sir Reginald Manningham-Buller (waggishly referred to as 'Bullying-Manner'), was asked in the House of Commons whether he could give Penguin an assurance that they would not be prosecuted should they decide to publish, and replied with an emphatic 'No'. The Government claimed later that the decision on whether or not to prosecute was entirely a matter for the Director of Public Prosecutions, and had nothing to do with the Attorney-General, but although this was formally the case, the evidence suggests otherwise.

The DPP's attention had been drawn to the book by advertisements in the trade press, and by a letter from the Chief Constable of Peterborough. Sir Toby Mathew's nephew told Anthony Rowe that his uncle was determined to prosecute; Mathew sought the advice of the Senior Treasury Counsel, who suggested that he should initiate proceedings under the Obscene Publications Act. Maurice Crump, Sir Toby's Deputy at the DPP, informed Mervyn Griffith-Jones that the Department was reluctant to act as a censor of new books, but 'in the case of an old-timer like *Lady Chatterley's Lover* the situation is different': he advised against announcing a decision about whether or not to prosecute 'for fear of creating a precedent and thereby acting as censors', but thought its likelihood could 'be percolated to the publishers through the Home Office'. After reading the first three chapters on the train to Southampton, the Attorney-General told Sir Toby that 'if the remainder of the work is of the same character, I have no doubt that you were right to start proceedings'; the Solicitor-General, who had also dipped into the book at Sir Reginald's suggestion, helpfully weighed in on the side of prosecution.

Readying his ammunition, Sir Toby passed a copy of *Lady Chatterley*, imported from the Continent, to Mr Crump in the DPP, and asked him for his views. Mr Crump thought it in essence a 'trashy novelette', and took exception to Lawrence's failure to tell the reader about Connie Chatterley's everyday life – 'whether she rode, hunted, played tennis or golf . . . She is little more than a female body into whose acts of love-making we are invited to pry.' And the same could be said of her lover, the gamekeeper Mellors: how, Mr Crump wanted to know, 'did he spend his time when not game-keeping? Did he visit the local? Read, smoke, garden, do good works?' Mr Crump was equally severe about Lawrence's prose. 'Not only is his characterization poor, but it is in places also inaccurate or ungrammatical.' He was particularly incensed by the fact that 'the necktie Chatterley was wearing on p. 14 is described as being "careful". "Drive a careful car" might be a slogan for Mr Marples, but it would hardly earn him a prize for literature' – 'Ernie' Marples being Harold Macmillan's cheeky-chappie Minister of Transport, who had recently opened Britain's first stretch of motorway, and was much concerned with improving the national standard of driving.

Mr Crump was not the only literary critic whose opinion was sought. Yellowing back numbers of literary magazines were scoured for hostile reactions to the book from T. S. Eliot and Lord David Cecil, but little use was made of their views; anxious to secure the services of hostile witnesses, the DPP approached Helen Gardner, an Oxford don and an authority on the metaphysical poets, and Noël Annan, the Provost of King's, Cambridge: to Sir Toby's disappointment, both wrote back to say they would welcome publication ('Snub No. 2,' Mr Crump scribbled in the margin of Annan's letter). An official also visited John Holroyd-Reece, now resident at Chilham Castle in Kent, and came away more confused than ever. Holroyd-Reece claimed that although Lawrence himself had asked him to publish *Lady Chatterley*, he had refused to do so since it was not 'up to the standards of the books he was accustomed to publishing', while the four-letter words were 'completely unnecessary and indeed distasteful, and were merely put in to annoy Frieda'; but for all that he supported its publication. 'While Mr Holroyd-Reece is an extremely interesting and knowledgeable person to talk to, he makes it almost impossible to get a word in edgeways,' the exhausted official reported back; Holroyd-Reece, who also happened to be Michael Rubinstein's godfather, sent a full account of the meeting to Lane, typed up on sheets of virulent yellow paper.

Michael Rubinstein was convinced that Penguin could produce 'a most formidable company of witnesses' to speak out on the novel's behalf: he thought it unlikely that a jury would find it obscene, but if they did Lane would face no more than a nominal fine. Jeremy Hutchinson and Richard du Cann produced a list of potential witnesses, and Rubinstein set about writing to some 300 eminent writers, academics, churchmen and public figures to drum up support. Bill Williams, in the meantime, was duplicating Rubinstein's efforts and receiving, for the most part, welcome letters of support. Aldous Huxley wrote from California, declaring *Lady Chatterley* 'an essentially wholesome book', and offering to come over at his own expense if needed as a witness; whatever the views expressed earlier in *After False Gods*, T. S. Eliot said he would 'regard its suppression as deplorable'; Bertrand Russell regarded any prosecution as 'wholly regrettable and misguided'; John Betjeman pronounced Lawrence to be 'one of the most outstanding novelists of this century', and *Lady Chatterley* one of his best; Harold Nicolson admitted that 'What really enrages me about this prosecution is that it should be brought against Penguin Books who, of all publishers, have conferred the greatest benefit on the present generation of readers and promoted the circulation of the best in English literature.' Stephen Spender, John Lehmann, Tom Driberg, Melvin Lasky, Kingsley Amis, A. J. Ayer, J. B. Priestley and Rupert Hart-Davis assured Williams of their support, but not all were convinced. Graham Greene thought it ridiculous to prosecute, but confessed that 'I find some parts of the book rather absurd, and for that reason I would prefer not to be called in case I was forced into any admission harmful to the Penguin cause'; Compton Mackenzie hoped that Penguin wouldn't be involved in a 'tiresome case', since 'I don't think *Lady Chatterley's Lover* is worth it'; Evelyn Waugh remembered the book as being 'dull, absurd in places and pretentious', while its author 'had very meagre gifts'; Victor Gollancz read it with 'unutterable boredom', but 'could not imagine a more deplorable piece of topsy-turveydom than that *Lady Chatterley* should be condemned and the really vile *Lolita* get through'; after expressing amazement at having been approached in the first place, Enid Blyton revealed that she had never read it, and that 'my husband said NO at once'.

With both sides flexing their muscles, Lane paid a visit to Scotland Yard before leaving in early August for his villa in Spain. Despite a predictable lack of support from W. H. Smith, subscription orders were nearing the 200,000 mark; all this was highly encouraging, but, with prosecution threatened, Penguin felt it would be wrong at this stage to involve booksellers, who could hardly plead 'innocent dissemination' if caught stocking so notorious a work. The ingenious Rubinstein suggested that twelve copies should be made available to the police at Penguin's High Holborn office: this would constitute 'limited publication', and the matter could be resolved before Penguin proceeded to 'full' publication. With Lane away, it was agreed that Bill Williams and Hans Schmoller, as directors of the company, would be responsible for the handing over. Detective Inspector Monahan duly turned up at the Penguin office, and Bill Williams handed over the twelve copies, one or more of which would be passed on to the DPP; no sooner had he done so than he had an attack of cold feet – what would his colleagues at the Arts Council think of it all? – and asked Inspector Monahan to replace his name with Schmoller's in the record. Schmoller, who combined devotion to the firm with a nervous disposition, wrote for the record a meticulous, minute-by-minute account of the proceedings in his immaculate italic hand, and carefully stored it away in the files.

Lane had barely stepped off the aeroplane in Málaga before Michael Rubinstein rang Harmondsworth to say that Richard du Cann, one of the barristers he had briefed on Penguin's behalf, insisted that any further distribution of books should be halted at once: the matter was now *sub judice*; no review copies should be sent out, and copies sent out to booksellers and wholesalers should be returned at Penguin's expense. A summons was served at Harmondsworth, and received on behalf of the company by Ron Blass, the warehouse manager; Hans Schmoller's nerves were further shredded when Leonard Russell revealed in the *Sunday Times* that the book was due to be published on 25 August, that Scotland Yard

Frostie in her cartwheel hat:
photograph by Lotte Meintner–Graf

AL the publishing statesman

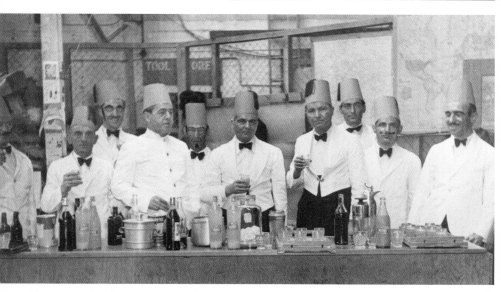

Christmas drinks at Harmondsworth, *c.* 1947. Left to right: Jimmy Holmes,
Bill Rapley, Peter Kite, Bill Williams (minus bow tie), Stan Olney, AL, Dick,
John Overton, Bob Hill, Jack Summers

From left, *c.* 1955: Bernhard Baer, E.V. Rieu, John Cramer (?), Grace Hogarth, Noel Carrington, unknown, unknown, Roger Maxwell (?), J. Overton, Gordon Jaco J. E. Morpurgo, R. B. Fishenden, Ralph Hill, A. S. B. Glover.
Front (seated on sofa): Bill Williams, Lettice Lane, Dick, AL, Estrid Bannister, Edward Crankshaw

'Editorial meeting': meetings involving all those depicted here never took place.
The photograph was, perhaps, a dummy run for Rodrigo Moynihan's painting, and
was taken in Bill Williams's office at 117 Piccadilly, c. 1950.
From left: R. B. Fishenden, Noel Carrington, AL, A. S. B. Glover, E. V. Rieu, Frostie,
A. W. Haslett (?), Michael Abercrombie (?), Bill Williams (sitting), Eleanor Graham,
C. A. Mace, J. E. Morpurgo, Nikolaus Pevsner

Dick Lane puzzling over a typescript, with chequebook to hand

Edward Young signs copies of *One of Our Submarines*, published in 1954 as the thousandth Penguin

A window display of the book. Jan Tschichold's refinement of Young's original Penguin cover was decorated with laurel leaves

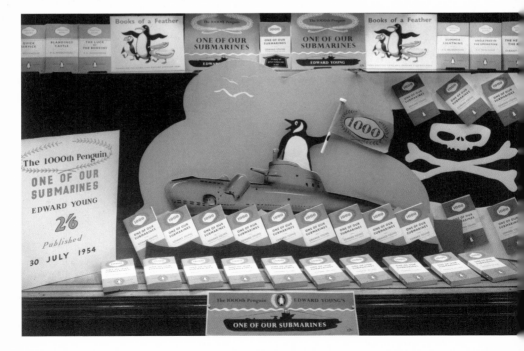

Garden party at Silverbeck to celebrate the twenty-first anniversary of Penguin in 1956. From left: unknown, Ashton Allen, AL, Bill Williams, Stan Olney

Penguin party at 117 Piccadilly, 1950. Among those photographed are: Lettice Lane, Estrid Bannister, Bill Williams, Eunice Frost, Hans and Tanya Schmoller. At the back, far left, is Denys Kilham Roberts, editor of *Penguin Parade*, and in front of him, without glasses, J. M. Richards, author of *An Introduction to Modern Architecture*

Clare Lane and AL on their bikes. The picture was taken near Silverbeck to illustrate an article about a bicycling holiday they had recently enjoyed in Normandy

Kaye Webb with the creator of
Paddington Bear, Michael Bond

Crowds gather to buy copies
of *Lady Chatterley's Lover*.
Below: a protester prepares to
ignite a copy, matches in one
hand and tongs in the other

Nikolaus Pevsner
hemmed in by *The
Buildings of England*

Tony Godwin puts his
feet up, 1963: photograph
by Fay Godwin

Prague airport: H. F. Paroissien, Hans Schmoller, Lettice and AL, and
Leslie Paisner (Penguin's legal adviser)

AL and Lettice greet guests at
the Stationers' Hall, 1969

The meeting of past and future:
AL and Tom Maschler

Birthday
celebrations

AL with his library of signed copies, Silverbeck

had asked for copies, and that Penguin would mount a sturdy defence if prosecuted. Anxious at being left in charge at such a critical moment, Schmoller and Bill Williams cabled their leader in Spain: 'LEGAL ACTION IMMINENT STOP ADVISE YOUR IMMEDIATE RETURN.' Lane came back to find his colleagues holding an emergency board meeting in the library at Silverbeck and ready to concede defeat, but he had no intention of giving up the fight. Rubinstein wrote to ask whether any of the Penguin directors had a criminal record (Lane had to confess to a driving offence), and whether anyone knew what Lawrence meant when he had Sir Clifford Chatterley say, 'If a man likes to have his wife, as Benvenuto Cellini says, "in the Italian way", well that is a matter of taste.'

Much time was spent, on both sides, worrying about how and whether copies of the book should be provided to the jury and other interested parties. It was agreed that eight copies could be set aside for those members of the Press who would be covering the trial, on the strict understanding that these would be returned at once should the prosecution succeed, and Rubinstein suggested that these should be bound in jackets from other Lawrence titles in Penguin: all, including *Lady Chatterley*, had a uniform look, with Schmoller's vertical orange bands and, in between, an engraving by Stephen Russ of Lawrence's emblem of a phoenix rising from the flames. Journalists were known to be hardened cynics and men of the world, but others were more vulnerable or easily corrupted. Mr Simpson of HMSO was reluctant to have copies made for the jury and members of the court since 'the copying process would have to be undertaken by a staff composed mainly of young girls', and he recommended instead that Mr Crump should acquire Continental editions via the Swiss or German police; Mr Crump's particular worry was that if the prosecution failed the book would then be 'offered openly and persuasively to every child or teenager who has 3s. 6d. in his or her pocket. This is a fearsome thought.' A *Lady Chatterley* that was on sale to discerning and well-heeled men of the world for a guinea or 30s. was a very different matter from a cheap edition which could be bought by the young and the hoi-polloi. Penguin could not have been more cooperative throughout. 'Normally one would not expect the publisher to volunteer any assistance to the prosecution,' Mr Simpson remarked to Mr Crump, 'but one gets the impression that the publishers have invited, or at least welcomed, these proceedings to be instituted.'

With publication suspended for the duration, the trial began on 20 October at the Old Bailey: it was the second case, after *The Ladies' Directory*, to come before a judge and jury under the provisions of the Act. Court No. 1 had poor acoustics, and according to Mollie Panter-Downes, who was covering the case for the *New Yorker*, 'the whole place sighed and croaked and groaned disconcertingly at every footfall'. The judge, Mr Justice Byrne, was, according to Miss Panter-Downes, a 'lean figure in a close grey wig that oddly simulated a bristling crew cut'. A devout Roman Catholic, he was felt to favour the prosecution case; for some reason his wife, equally ill-disposed, sat alongside him throughout, raising her eyebrows as yet another literary man (or woman) shambled into the witness-box to give evidence for the defence. The judge's copy of the offending work was carried into court in a specially made silk bag, with the more shocking passages heavily underscored in purple ink. The jury consisted of nine men and three women; Lane and Hans Schmoller were allowed, like Fredric Warburg before them, to sit in the well of the court, and from the Press box Mollie Panter-Downes observed Lane to be 'a compactly-built grey-haired man with a quietly pugnacious expression'.

The defence team consisted of Gerald Gardiner, assisted by Jeremy Hutchinson and Richard du Cann. A tall, austere-looking figure, Gardiner was renowned for the clarity of his intellect and his cold, dispassionate delivery. He had only joined the defence at the last minute, and was already acting on behalf of Randolph Churchill in a slander case against the mustachioed Tory MP Sir Gerald Nabarro, who had accused him of cowardice for attacking Sir Anthony Eden over his handling of the Suez crisis; and while the jury was settling down in the court-room to read *Lady Chatterley* – despite defence pleas about the hardness of the seats, the embarrassment of reading such a work in public, and the problem of slow readers, Mr Justice Byrne had refused to allow the jury to do their reading at home, and three days had to be set aside for the business – he nipped across to an adjoining court-room and concluded his business there. Jeremy Hutchinson remembered Lane as a 'perfect' client, never complaining and more than happy to murmur 'Over to you . . .'; and after it was all over, Lane, true to form, asked him whether he might be interested in a senior post at Penguin Books.

The prosecuting counsel, Mervyn Griffith-Jones, proved to be the most memorable character in the case: not surprisingly, since he had much in common with Sergeant Buzfuz and other barristers of the rubicund, sarcastic and orotund school. Tough, pompous and likeable, according to Jeremy Hutchinson, he was genuinely outraged at such a book being made available at a cheap price: asked by a colleague how he decided whether or not to prosecute, he declared that 'I put my feet up on the desk and start reading. If I get an erection, we prosecute,' so he must have found *Lady Chatterley's Lover* inflammatory, and all the more dangerous in paperback. 'The prosecuting counsel is a bit fearsome,' Lane told Harry Paroissien: Mollie Panter-Downes observed that he had 'the sort of well-boned good looks – full-chinned and brought into period by his wig – that you often see in English eighteenth-century family portraits of country squires and their spaniels regarding each other with mutual satisfaction', while Sybille Bedford, doing a comparable job for *Esquire*, noted 'high cheek-bones, a florid colour, a strong jaw and a thin mouth', and 'a voice quivering with thin-lipped scorn'.

However deep his disapproval, Griffith-Jones's opening speech was, in Montgomery Hyde's opinion, 'scrupulously fair'. He began by explaining the new Act, telling the jury that if they decided that *Lady Chatterley* was not obscene, and unlikely to 'deprave and corrupt', they must decide in its favour; if, on the other hand, they thought it was obscene, they must then decide whether publication could be considered to be in the public good, bearing in mind the views of the expert witnesses produced by the defence. That duty done, Griffith-Jones rose to rhetorical heights. 'Would you approve your young sons, young daughters – because girls can read as well

as boys – reading this book?' he asked the jury, in words that doubtless haunted him for the rest of his career, and achieved instant fame
well beyond the court-room. 'Is it a book you would have lying
around in your own house? Is it a book you would even wish your
wife or your servants to read?' The reference to servants had, in
C. H. Rolph's opinion, 'a visible – and risible – effect on the jury,
and may well have been the first nail in the prosecution's coffin',
and would be nimbly exploited by Gerald Gardiner in his closing
speech for the defence. As yet undaunted, Griffith-Jones then
summoned his one and only prosecution witness – Detective-
Inspector Monahan, who confirmed that he had taken receipt of
twelve copies of the book from Hans Schmoller and served a
summons on Ron Blass a week later, and briskly departed the scene.

After an opening speech for the defence, in which Gerald Gardiner
made much of how Allen Lane had left school at sixteen and of
his desire to make good books available to ordinary people, with
special reference to Pelicans, the Penguin Classics, the Penguin
Shakespeare and the Shaw Million, the thirty-six expert witnesses
for the defence were summoned for cross-examination. They were,
in Richard Hoggart's opinion, reassuringly un-bohemian, consisting
as they did of 'eminent and elderly men of letters, none of whom
would frighten a jury with farouche manners or beliefs', and 'equally
elderly lady dons, impregnable in tweed costumes and sensible shoes';
and the first to be called was indeed a lady don, the same Helen
Gardner whom the DPP had tried to enlist in their cause. The
Bishop of Woolwich famously declared that this was a book that
all Christians should read, a remark that provoked mirth and banner
headlines in the popular press. Eager to hold the book up to ridicule
while at the same time exercising his histrionic gifts, Griffith-Jones
read out what Malcolm Muggeridge later declared to be 'the most
hilariously fatuous dialogue ever to be written in the English
language' ('Sir Malcolm gave a little squirting laugh, and became
Scotch and lewd. "Honour! How was the going, eh? Good, my
boy, what?" "Good!" "I'll bet it was! Ha-ha! My daughter, chip off
the old block, what! I never went back on a good bit of fucking,
myself. Though her mother, oh, holy saints!" He rolled his eyes up

to heaven. "But you warmed her up, oh, you warmed her up, I can see that. Ha-ha! My blood in her! You set fire to her haystack all right!"'). 'Do you think any future generation reading that conversation would get anything approaching an accurate picture of the way in which Royal Academicians conducted their conversation?' Griffith-Jones asked Graham Hough of Cambridge University, but although Hough conceded that this was 'the one utterly, disastrously bad passage in the book', he would go no further than that.

Other defence witnesses included C. V. Wedgwood, Bill Williams, Roy Jenkins, Cecil Day Lewis, Stephen Potter, Noël Annan and Dilys Powell. Rebecca West gave forth 'in singing tones, like a prophetess intoning from the walls of Troy', while E. M. Forster, looking more mole-like than ever in a fawn gabardine mac, was barely visible above the rim of the witness-box; T. S. Eliot patrolled the corridors outside, waiting in vain to be called, and Sir Stanley Unwin was visibly put out when Griffith-Jones showed no interest in his views, dismissing him with a peremptory 'No questions'. An over-confident Griffith-Jones had assumed that to ridicule and humiliate the expert witnesses would be an easy matter, but he could not have been more mistaken: and worse was to come.

Although some listeners were puzzled by his claim that *Lady Chatterley* was an essentially 'puritan' piece of work, it was widely agreed that by far the most impressive expert witness was Richard Hoggart: Sybille Bedford found him the 'most quietly and fervently assured' of all the witnesses, and considered his evidence, given on the second day, to be the turning-point of the trial. Years later, trying to explain why he had been chosen, Hoggart imagined Lane saying to himself, 'I'm going to have someone for the defence who is not posh, not middle-class, not Oxbridge – a sort of sub-fusc university lecturer from the provinces, a sort of "ee-by-gum" character.' Griffith-Jones did his best to patronize Hoggart – 'The question is quite a simple one to answer without another lecture,' he sneered at one stage, adding, 'You are not at Leicester University at the moment' – but Sybille Bedford thought his attempts at 'gentlemanly superiority' were thwarted by Hoggart's 'earnest and friendly' answers. After it was all over, Lane commissioned an introduction to *Lady Chatterley* from her most persuasive advocate.

Although it has sometimes been claimed, presumably by those who neither followed the proceedings nor read the detailed accounts of the trial by C. H. Rolph and Montgomery Hyde, that he had been so unnerved by his cross-examination during the *Whispering Gallery* trial that he vowed never to appear in court again, and left Bill Williams to make the case on his behalf, Lane was called on the fourth day, following Raymond Williams, St John Stevas and the frustrated Sir Stanley Unwin: as Bill Williams remembered, 'he was manifestly ill-at-ease and, indeed, declined to face the fast bowling as an opening bat and went in much lower down'. He told Jeremy Hutchinson how his 'idea was to produce a book which would sell at the price of ten cigarettes, which would give no excuse for anyone not being able to buy it, and would be the type of book which they would get if they had gone on to further education'. Penguins were designed, in part, to provide 'another form of education' for 'people like myself who left school when they were sixteen'; he had always wanted to 'make Penguin a University Press in paperback' and to that end he had published some 3,500 titles and sold about 250 million books in all. He was not, he declared, in the business of publishing expurgated editions of books, and only two novels – Robert Tressell's *The Ragged Trousered Philanthropists* and a pre-war Penguin Special of *The Good Soldier Schweik* – had not been published in full. (In fact, the Penguin edition of Gide's *If It Die* had appeared with two small cuts, the Penguin Classic *Daphnis and Chloë* had been mildly trimmed, and a wartime edition of J. Meade Falkner's *The Nebuly Coat* had, to the distress of his admirers, been deprived of many of its architectural and topographical asides.) Griffith-Jones, whose interventions and cross-examinations had become increasingly sporadic as the trial wore on, tried to catch him out by referring to an article in the *Manchester Guardian* in which Lane had been quoted as saying that *Lady Chatterley* was 'no great novel', but his attempted ambush came to naught.

Despite a summing up by the judge which made plain his own views on the matter, the jurors brought back a verdict of not guilty.

No sooner had the cheering died down than Gerald Gardiner sprang to his feet to ask that Penguin should be awarded costs amounting to some £13,000 in what had always been regarded as a test case (back in the summer, Mr Crump had reminded a colleague in Customs and Excise that 'publication was by arrangement to provide the basis of a test case'). According to C. H. Rolph, Mr Justice Byrne 'smiled, a little enigmatically, pushed back his chair' and refused to make any order as to costs: but none of the expert witnesses asked for a fee, and with *Lady Chatterley's Lover* selling in its thousands as soon as the verdict was announced – vast queues formed outside bookshops, and Western Printing Services were joined by two other printers, including Hazell's, in rushing out batches of 300,000 copies of a book that went on to sell some 3 million copies – Penguin could afford to go without.

A celebratory party was held at the Arts Council, and the letters of congratulation flooded in. T. S. Eliot admitted to being 'both disappointed and relieved' that he had not been called; Julian Symons told Lane that his 'stand was magnificently courageous'; Michael Rubinstein's father, Harold, a well-known literary lawyer, suggested that 'Michael has avenged his firm's (and father's) defeat thirty-three years ago, when *The Well of Loneliness* was banned under the old law'; anticipating those who saw the verdict as a preamble to the liberalization of the Sixties – Hugh Carleton Greene's regime at the BBC, John Trevelyan's labours at the British Board of Film Censors, the end of the Lord Chamberlain's role as theatrical censor – John Braine wrote that 'because you had the courage to do what you felt to be right as a publisher, you have made the lot of the professional writer – and, in particular, the professional novelist – a great deal easier. I for one shall always feel very much in your debt.' The young seemed less impressed: Lane's daughter Clare thought *Lady Chatterley* 'all right, but a bit old-fashioned'; Max Hastings, still a schoolboy at Charterhouse, told his mother, Anne Scott-James, who had appeared as a defence witness, that all the boys had rushed out to buy a copy, 'but I am sorry to tell you, Mummy, that now we have read it we all *definitely* think it should be banned'.

The *Sunday Express, Daily Telegraph* and *Evening Standard* were outraged by the verdict; *The Times* wondered why the prosecution hadn't produced its own team of expert witnesses; fourteen Tory MPs put down an amendment to the Queen's Speech demanding the repeal of the Obscene Publications Act. Nor did all academics agree with their colleagues about the virtues of the book. F. R. Leavis told Michael Rubinstein that he could 'see no reason for Sir Allen's knight errantry unless he had the golden fleece in view', and refused to autograph Lane's copy of *The Common Pursuit*, recently reissued in the new, larger-format Peregrine imprint, on the grounds that 'I do not think Sir Allen Lane did a service to literature, civilization or Lawrence in the business of *Lady Chatterley's Lover*'; more in a spirit of mischief than disapproval, John Sparrow, the Warden of All Souls, and the economist Andrew Shonfield wrote articles in *Encounter* suggesting that a passage from the novel quoted by Griffith-Jones in his concluding address referred, in fact, to an act of buggery, and that the jury might not have been so lenient had they been alerted to this. Nor were some members of the public happy about the outcome. 'You are a disgrace to the name of Lane,' wrote a correspondent from Bath; another, from Edgbaston, suggested that Lane should give his 'tainted money' to charity, and that 'in this way you may lighten your sentence on the Day of Judgement'; a third cherished 'a lurking feeling that whenever you now have occasion to mix with the better class of people, you will experience an uncomfortable feeling of being unobtrusively shunned'.

Shunned or not, Lane's Christmas book that year, sent out to some 200 people, was a clothbound copy of C. H. Rolph's account of the trial, later reissued in paperback. Sir Theobald Mathew was among its recipients: as were A. S. B. Glover, who quickly pointed out an error in the prelims, and Sir Stanley Unwin, who, commenting on Paul Hogarth's drawings in the text, wished that 'the portrait of myself was more recognizable. That kind of a drawing calls for a paper with more finish . . .' Lane commissioned Stephen Russ to design a plate for his house in Spain, now renamed El Fénix in honour of Lawrence, and prepared to reap the rewards of *Lady Chatterley's Lover* – a book he had taken on and published without any involvement on the part of Tony Godwin, who had only recently joined the firm, and whose own eagerness to extend the frontiers of permissible reading would, paradoxically, sour and destroy his relations with Lane.

The trial was a turning-point, and after it was over previously forbidden works like *The Ginger Man* and *The Kama Sutra* were finally published in this country. As John Sutherland has pointed out, a certain caution still prevailed: John Calder, a bolder publisher than most, issued Henry Miller's 'Tropics' and William Burroughs's *The Naked Lunch* initially as expensive hardbacks; the Mayflower paperback of *Fanny Hill* was pulped following a prosecution headed by Mervyn Griffith-Jones, but Hubert Selby's *Last Exit to Brooklyn* was reprieved on appeal after a trial in which the seventy-seven-year-old Sir Basil Blackwell, called as a prosecution witness, confessed to having been depraved and corrupted by his reading of the work. Like it or not, Lane's persistence had radically altered the climate of opinion in Britain.

19. Penguin Goes Public

By the late Fifties Lane had taken to submitting handwriting samples from prospective employees to a professional graphologist: Ruth Simon had introduced him to graphology, and it was enjoying a vogue in the City and the business world. No doubt the energetic scrawls of both Godwin and Maschler were sent off for expert analysis; and, not to be outdone, Lane posted off an anonymous example of his own firm but spidery scrawl for diagnosis. 'He is by nature warm, sensual and imaginative, but has developed a cold, competitive and combative outlook, which of necessity brings him to the front,' the expert declared, adding that 'His whole life is a hunting expedition, and although he is a successful hunter he is not satisfied – indeed, he is not satisfiable.'

Interviewed on the radio not long after the Chatterley trial, Lane revealed that he hadn't lost his temper for ten years; he was, he admitted, solitary by nature, a man who didn't like to be intruded on and was reluctant to allow other people to get too close. Colleagues and fellow-publishers hurried to offer their own interpretations of Lane's elusive, paradoxical nature. 'Relishing conviviality, he was terrified of intimacy, and though he had experienced tragedy he dared not lighten its burden by sharing it with others. Being intellectually incapable of analysing his own success, he was forever worrying that it would be snatched from him by someone whose cunning outstripped his own,' J. E. Morpurgo suggested three years after Lane's death, adding that he got rid of those he no longer liked or needed 'with a ruthlessness that was all the more vicious if they had come close to discovering the frontier which he himself could not define: the frontier between his private and his professional nature'. Peter Calvocoressi, then at Chatto & Windus, saw something of Lane at this time, and found him 'not an easy man to know outside his own close circle of friends. Although he liked talking and was a careful listener, there was also a sense of reserve, an unforthcoming watchfulness which came close to suspiciousness. Even in a *tête à tête* he left you wondering what he was thinking.' Tony Godwin remembered him as 'a stocky man in a conservative blue business suit with the freshly starched tips of a handkerchief peeping up out of his breast pocket and shirt cuffs that were always immaculate and secured by posh cufflinks . . . A trim, vigorous, cordial figure, he could easily have filled the bill as one of Conrad's sea captains. But the final impression one carried away was of his jaw muscles, like steel hawsers and as unyielding.'

The writer and publisher Raleigh Trevelyan was exposed to Lane at his most capricious. Although Godwin offered him a job at Penguin, he already knew Lane. He and his friend John Guest, an editor at Longmans, had met Lane and Bill Williams when stranded in Paris by an impenetrable fog, and they had travelled back to London together by train. 'I want you to go to Aleppo,' Lane told Trevelyan soon after he joined the firm: while staying there recently with Freya Stark he had met the art historians Hugh Honour and John Fleming and had suggested that they should edit a new illustrated series to be entitled Style and Civilization, and since Trevelyan was a cultivated man with a knowledge of things Italian, he was perfectly equipped to carry matters forward. After some initial bafflement about why he should be expected to travel to Syria – it turned out that Lane had met Freya Stark in Asolo, where Lettice had taken a house, and not in Aleppo – Trevelyan happily obliged. Back in England, he saw a fair amount of Lane socially as well as professionally. He visited Lane and Susanne Lepsius in Whitehall Court, and the three of them spent long weekends together in Fowey, where Lane had sailed with his brother John before the war, and Trevelyan had recently bought a house. But then, quite suddenly, the friendship was withdrawn. Robert Lusty had told Trevelyan that if things didn't work out at Penguin, he could have his job back at Hutchinson; Lane was not pleased when he learned this, and still less so when the offer was taken up. When Trevelyan went to say goodbye, Lane barely looked up from the balance sheet spread out on the desk before him.

No doubt it made cheerful reading. The phenomenal sales of
Lady Chatterley's Lover had a dramatic effect on Penguin's figures for
1960: pre-tax profits were three times those of the previous year at
£364,000, and profit margins increased from 9.3 per cent of turnover
to 18.5 per cent. Lawrence's novel helped to make Lane a millionaire when, in the spring of 1961, he decided to turn Penguin into
a public company. 'I should hate people to think that we were going
public on the strength of *Lady Chatterley's Lover*, as if this were our
one and only chance,' he declared, but there was no doubt that
publishing such a huge bestseller had made the firm attractive to
investors at a time when the stock market was already riding high.
Lane's approach to the whole business was hard-headed and ruthlessly unsentimental. Michael Rubinstein had performed wonders
with *Lady Chatterley*, but he was a literary rather than a commercial lawyer, and was replaced by Leslie Paisner, a practitioner 'well
versed in the ways of jungle life east of St Paul's'; and Lane used
the planned sale of shares to acquire Dick's holding in the company,
and finally sever his connection with it.

Irrespective of any sale of shares, Lane was keen to reorganize
Penguin's Australian operations without his 'plodding' brother's
involvement; Dick continued to feel undervalued and hard done by,
pointing out more than once that although he had provided the
initial capital with which the firm had been funded, helped sort out
Penguin Inc. after the war, and taken over the running of Australia
after the sacking of Bob Maynard, neither his salary nor his pension
reflected his long service or the success of the company: on a visit
to England, he had stayed two nights at Whitehall Court, and 'received
a note from the accounts department suggesting I ought to pay for
the privilege'. His sense of grievance was to be inflamed still further
when Penguin went public. Lane had been advised to reorganize the
capital structure of the firm, and to buy Dick out and insist on his
resignation as a precondition of his doing so. Dick had told him that
so long as he could provide for his wife and daughter, he would be
happy to retire early, since his health was poor and he was reluctant
to take orders from recently appointed directors.

In the spring of 1961 Dick received a letter in which Lane asked him if he would accept £200,000 for his shares in the company: at present Lane himself owned 50.018 per cent of the shares, and his children's trust a further 24.9 per cent; he felt uneasy about not owning 51 per cent or more of the shares himself, and had made his offer to Dick on the misleading assumption that the shares would fetch between 8s. and 9s. each if put on the market. Dick was not unsympathetic, but as Lane piled on the pressure he dug in his heels and became increasingly resentful. A revised offer of £220,000, to include the shares, compensation for loss of office, a year's salary and the cost of a trip to England, was followed by a cable which read 'ESSENTIAL YOU RESIGN AS DIRECTOR OF AND CEASE CONNECTION WITH ENGLISH AND AUSTRALIAN COMPANIES', and another demanding 'URGENT YOU RESIGN AUSTRALIA UNCONDI-TIONALLY'. 'OK LETS THROW THE WHOLE THING AWAY,' Dick cabled back. 'I DON'T WANT TO SELL MY SHARES OR RESIGN AS A DIRECTOR UNDER YOUR CONDITIONS.' 'You may think I feel a little bitter about things. Well, I am,' he told Lane. Dick rang from Australia to say that despite his poor health, he was keen to go on working: could he not be re-elected to the board of Penguin Australia after his formal resig-nation, and was there no way his compensation could be increased from £10,000 to £15,000? But resistance proved in vain, and Dick's shares were duly acquired. In April Lane announced that Penguin was to become a public company; Lane intended to keep 51 per cent of the shares in his own hands and 19 per cent with the family trusts, and 750,000 ordinary shares – 30 per cent of the total – were offered to subscribers at 12s. each. In the event, the shares were over-subscribed by 150 times; from some 150,000 applications, 3,450 were chosen by ballot, getting 200 shares each. Demand was such that by the end of the first day of dealing the price had risen to 17s. 3d. per share.

Lane had become a millionaire overnight. 'For the first time since I started my career I found black ink being used by the bank,' Lane informed Dick, and he had paid off the overdraft on Priory Farm. He told Leslie Paisner that Dick felt hard done by, and complained that he hadn't been told the truth about the value of his own holding, but nevertheless a celebratory 'stag dinner' was held at the Marie Antoinette Room in the Savoy at which Lane, his lawyer, his financial advisers and male members of the Penguin old guard tucked into lobster thermidor, caviare and pâté de foie gras, washed down by magnums of Lanson 1953. Lane and Penguin Books had indeed come a long way since Dick had borrowed his parent's insurance money to fund the fledgling firm.

With money in his pocket, Lane embarked on a brief flirtation which, like his dealings with Cass Canfield at Harper & Row, revealed him at his most whimsical and irresponsible. His old friend Jonathan Cape had died in 1960, still in harness at the age of eighty; Wren Howard, the firm's co-founder, was in his late sixties, and although the firm had been the most stylish and innovative of literary publishers during the Twenties and Thirties, it had begun to lose vigour and direction. 'That old carp Cape' (Bill Williams's epithet) had owned seventh-twelfths of the firm, and Wren Howard five-twelfths: Howard and his son Michael had exercised their option to increase their holding to seven-twelfths on Jonathan's death, but that left 41.7 per cent of the shares, which would have to be sold to pay death duties. Nor was life much happier on the far side of Bedford Square. Michael Joseph had sold his firm to Illustrated Newspapers in 1954; seven years later they sold it on to Roy Thomson, the heavily bespectacled Canadian Press tycoon who had recently bought the *Sunday Times*. Charles Pick and Peter Hebdon, the firm's two managing directors, and Roland Gant, the editorial director, were extremely unhappy about the takeover, and reluctant to renew their contracts. One day in December 1961, Lane had lunch with Charles Pick and John Wyndham, a Michael Joseph author whose novel *The Day of the Triffids* had been a bestseller for Penguin. According to Pick, Lane had assumed that Wyndham was a member of the Egremont family, and lost interest once he learned that his real name was Harris: this sounds improbable, but either way the conversation had far more to do with publishing politics than with science fiction. When Pick revealed how unhappy he and his two colleagues were about the Thomson takeover, Lane – seemingly on an impulse –

suggested that he and the 'Trinity' should form a partnership, buy up the ownerless shares in Cape, and install Messrs Pick, Hebdon and Gant to run the firm: none of them had money of their own to invest, but he would be happy to put up £25,000 of his own money, and would in any case be seeing Cape's lawyer that very afternoon. Lane's only proviso was that, as he told Pick, 'I will not have anything to do with Maschler.' Maschler had been made a director of Cape in July, but since, under the proposed scheme, Roland Gant would be the editorial director, Pick was happy to go along with this.

The 'Trinity' travelled up to Hampstead Garden Suburb to see Wren Howard, who seemed happy enough with what was proposed, while Pick approached Norman Collins, the novelist and former colleague of Victor Gollancz: Collins was keen to get back into publishing, saw possible benefits for Associated Television, which he had founded with Lew Grade and A. D. Peters, was prepared to put up another £25,000, and – apropos the removal of Maschler – told Pick that 'He's either a publishing genius or he'll lose us a lot of money.' Heartened by such rapid and positive progress, the 'Trinity' prepared to hand in their resignations, while Lane headed off to his house by the sea in Spain, a modest whitewashed building with marble floors, Moorish features and a phoenix weathervane. It was agreed that Pick, Hebdon and Gant should be appointed working directors, that Lane and Norman Collins should join the board in due course, and that Wren Howard should remain as Chairman for another year. All this appeared in the *Bookseller*, where Lane was reported as saying that 'it would be a pity to let the Americans get too big a toehold here': that same year both W. H. Allen and Rupert Hart-Davis had been bought by American publishers – Heinemann had sold Hart-Davis to Harcourt Brace Jovanovich – and Billy Collins had been in touch with Lane about the possible takeover of Pan by New American Library, which had itself just been taken over by the *Times–Mirror* group of Los Angeles: a move which had been bitterly opposed by Victor Weybright, and led to his departure from the firm and the severing of an increasingly acrimonious relationship with Kurt Enoch. Cape, it seemed, was to be saved from an equally dreadful fate. Pick cabled El Fénix to say that Norman Collins had agreed to increase his stake to £40,000 if Lane would do the same, and five days after Christmas, he cabled again with the news that he and his two fellow-directors had been given until 1 January to sign their new service contracts, and that they would resign once Lane cabled his continuing support: this must have been forthcoming, since all three gave in their notices at Michael Joseph, and the resignations were announced in the *Bookseller*. The lawyers and accountants got to work, and the future of Cape and the 'Trinity' seemed assured.

While all this was going on, Tom Maschler was in New York, on his first buying trip for Jonathan Cape. Wren Howard's son Michael thought it might be polite to keep him informed, and wrote to tell him the news. Maschler, who had just bought the British rights in Joseph Heller's *Catch 22*, rang as soon as he received Howard's letter. 'Where does this leave me?' he wanted to know; Howard, doubtless intimidated by the molten mix of anger and righteous indignation heading in his direction, told him, 'We haven't discussed that yet.' Back in London, Maschler was determined to save his job, but thought his chances of doing so were slim. He insisted on a meeting with the 'Trinity': Peter Hebdon told him he would have to go, but after the meeting was over Wren Howard clapped his hands together and, much to Maschler's gratitude and relief, told his young colleague that the deal was off. An embarrassed Wren Howard then had to tell all those involved that he could take things no further. Cables winged their way to Spain: 'DEADLOCK OVER TOM STOP NEGOTIATIONS ENDED' (Charles Pick); 'GREAT REGRETS OUR PROJECTED ASSOCIATION PROVES UNWORKABLE STOP NEGOTIATIONS NOW DISCONTINUED' (Wren Howard). Pick and Gant discovered when Lane was due back from Spain, and met him at Heathrow to urge him into battle on their behalf – but to no avail. Soured by the experience, Pick believed that Lane felt no sense of responsibility for what had happened: 'he shrugged it off as a setback, but not a setback to his career, and he wanted to wash his hands of the situation'. Before long, however, Pick and Gant had moved on to Heinemann – Pick as managing director, Gant as editorial director – while Peter Hebdon returned to Michael Joseph as its managing director.

Quite why Tom Maschler had roused such hostility in his old boss remains a mystery. According to Charles Pick, Maschler had lost him so much money at Penguin that 'he would never put his money where Tom Maschler was', but none of that rings true. By the late Fifties paperback firms were beginning to pay hardback publishers higher and more competitive advances than they had in the past – as Lane himself confessed in 1958, 'we are, whether we like it or not, in a tough, highly competitive industry, and we have to fight every inch of the way, from the facing of colossal advances if we are to keep books away from Pan, Corgi, Ace, Panther etc. to the real struggle to retain space at the retail outlet' – but Penguin could still afford to stay aloof; and there is no evidence to suggest that Maschler paid, or was in a position to pay, 'colossal advances' or, like Godwin in the years to come, to insist on providing his books with expensive four-colour jackets. Writing under the pseudonym of Mark Caine, Maschler had published, with Hutchinson, a Machiavellian manual entitled *The S-Man*: it was rumoured by some that Maschler had then paid himself over the odds to buy the paperback rights for Penguin, and that Lane took a dim view of the matter, but in fact the rights were acquired by Maschler's good friend Tony Godwin: the book had been taken on in secret, and Lane only discovered who its author was when tipped off by Robert Lusty, its original publisher. Some said that Lane took against Maschler because he was Jewish, but there is no evidence that he was remotely anti-semitic, and he was more than happy to number Hans Schmoller and Nikolaus Pevsner among his colleagues. Maschler himself believes that Lane had seen him as his heir-apparent, and was so put out by his leaving Penguin that he determined on revenge, but although Lane could and did turn against his favourites if they failed to come up to scratch or seemed no longer right for the job, this had not been the case with Maschler; nor, Krishna Menon always excepted, was Lane a great grudge-bearer, preferring to put the past behind him and move on to other things. One other possibility occurs. Maschler was good-looking, attractive and charismatic, and it could be that he had become too friendly with Susanne Lepsius. Raleigh Trevelyan believes that Lane may have turned against him because he was jealous of his friendship with Susanne, chaste as it was, and Maschler too may have excited the ire of Jove. Whatever the truth of the matter, Maschler's departure was Penguin's loss: within a very short time he had revived Cape's reputation as the most exciting publisher in London, and as such he would soon be banging on Penguin's door, demanding that they compete for the rights in his books with the same energy and commitment as their more overtly commercial rivals. The problematic shares, in the meantime, were acquired by Sidney Bernstein of Granada.

'I realize that this is the close of a phase of my life, and I find that I like it that way,' Lane told Frostie on Good Friday 1961. 'The pace is getting too hot for me, and the young group with a little schooling will be able to stand up to it far better than I would be able to.' He was right about the changing pace of life, but he would not accept its implementation with such equanimity.

20. The Rise and Fall of Tony Godwin

Al Alvarez once wrote of Tony Godwin that he was, above all else, 'a writer's publisher, bored by administration, irritated by office politics, and most happy when dealing with the text and its creator'. 'Inexhaustible, sprightly and buzzing with energy', and possessed of an astonishing attention to detail, he would get up at the crack of dawn to work on an author's book and stagger into the office weighed down with notes as long as the book itself: he was, for Alvarez and many others, 'the platonic ideal of a reader', a publisher who 'made me feel that no one had ever before really *read* anything I had written', and, as Giles Gordon recalled, knew 'instinctively rather than analytically' what was wrong with a book. Charles Clark, who joined Penguin as an editor in 1960, thought Godwin 'the best uneducated mind' he had ever worked with, unencumbered by academic baggage and able to get straight to the essence of a book; and after his death, Mordecai Richler wrote that he had been 'revered, admired, loved and, now and again, feared' by his authors. And, like all the best publishers, he combined a readiness to put in long hours working on a typescript with trust in 'hunch' or the intuitive sense of whether or not a book is right for a list: Peter Buckman, one of his young editors, remembers Godwin telling him that he must learn to 'sniff' and sample a book before taking matters any further.

Godwin had spent his working life as a bookseller, and once installed at Penguin he put his experience and his almost intuitive sense of how and why books sold at the disposal of his authors. He emphasized the importance of marketing in order that Penguin could compete with brasher, more crudely commercial rivals, insisted on brighter, sexier advertisements and display material, arranged competitions for booksellers, 'the inconspicuous of the trade', and insisted that his young editors go out on the road with the reps; but he saw the author and the author's work as being of overriding value and importance, and the publisher's *raison d'être*. 'The author may be illiterate. I don't give a damn. They have got talent which, to me, is a damn sight more important than a great many other qualities,' he told Hans Schmoller. 'Writers are not like business people. We may be publishers, but basically we tend to think like business people, and we must remember, if we are going to keep authors, that they are talented people with large egos and difficult to deal with. Successful publishing is when the publisher remembers that the author comes first no matter what the cost to internal administration.'

Godwin's seemingly insouciant approach to costs would be held against him at a future date, and his attitude to authors was far closer to that of an originating than a reprint publisher. Whereas Bill Williams and Frostie were so convinced of Penguin's innate superiority, and so accustomed to enjoying a near monopoly, that they barely deigned to notice the competition, vulgar and ill-bred as it was, Godwin was intuitively aware that the publishing world was about to change in ways that would eventually make it impossible for Penguin, for all its strengths and virtues, to continue as before. 'At the moment paperback publishers are cashing in on the past sixty years of creative writing and publishing,' he once wrote in the *Times Literary Supplement*. 'Unless they take over some of the responsibilities for discovering and encouraging new talent, the present literary scene will be denuded within the next decade.' Godwin wanted to gratify his own editorial urges, to work – as Williams and Frost and Glover had done before him – with authors on their books, as well as buying the rights in novels already published by other firms; but he was also uneasily aware that as rival publishers set up their own paperback imprints, they would revert the rights in books formerly licensed to Penguin in order to publish them themselves, and that as these rival lists grew stronger and more assured, Penguin, vulnerable as never before, could no longer automatically assume that they would be offered the reprint rights.

Before long Godwin would be making his mark as an original publisher, reviving, in particular, the Penguin Specials list; but he had joined the firm in 1960 as an 'advisory fiction editor', and although he was promoted to Chief Editor later that year, he concentrated his energies at first on the fiction list. In a memo to Lane he announced that

the Penguin fiction policy is to publish good fiction where there is a reasonable chance of selling the minimum economic number; to publish and help build young British authors of promise even when a loss may occasionally be envisaged; to publish books of a reasonable literary level of which there is a jolly good chance of selling extremely well; to publish those works and authors whom we consider to be our social duty to make available in a Penguin edition even though it may involve us in a financial loss – and to equate one against the other to produce a list which has an overall balance . . .

– a variant on 'swings and roundabouts' with which Lane could hardly disagree. Over the next few years such famous names of the period as Iris Murdoch, Angus Wilson, Malcolm Bradbury, Edna O'Brien and C. P. Snow were added to the Penguin fiction list, along with Americans like Truman Capote, Saul Bellow, Peter de Vries and John Cheever; writing to Lane three years after he joined, Godwin listed Harper Lee's *To Kill a Mockingbird*, Malcolm Lowry's *Under the Volcano*, Lynne Reid Banks's *The L-Shaped Room* and Camus's *The Outsider* among the novels in which he had bought the paperback rights, pointed out that the number of reprints and new titles taken on had soared since his arrival, and wondered whether, in the circumstances, a rise from £3,500 to £5,000 a year might not be in order. He shared Lane's belief in publishing all – or a sizeable proportion – of an author's work, whether it be that of Virginia Woolf or F. Scott Fitzgerald; and despite Heinemann's part-ownership of Pan, Charles Pick was persuaded to license to Penguin a batch of novels by Graham Greene, for which Godwin offered £50,000, and two batches by Somerset Maugham, sold for £65,000 *in toto*. Nor did Godwin neglect the middlebrow market: Daphne du Maurier and H. E. Bates became Penguin authors, and a million copies were printed of Richard Gordon's four 'Doctor' novels, with Godwin himself supervising the sales and marketing campaign. But, like all good publishers, he was far from infallible: he turned down *Catch*

22, which went on to sell in vast quantities for Corgi, one of the imprints that was nibbling at Penguin's heels; and when Gollancz asked for an advance three times more than Penguin were used to paying for John le Carré's *The Spy Who Came in from the Cold*, he and Dieter Pevsner decided not to make an offer, and the book was sold to Clarence Paget at Pan for £1,750.

Giles Gordon, who joined Penguin as an editor in 1966, described Godwin as 'a manic jack-in-the-box' and 'an abrasive, shock-haired little man, a kind of pocket grey-haired Struwwelpeter'; the literary agent George Greenfield remembered him as 'often very prickly, with lightning changes from cold rudeness to a warm, blue-eyed smile', and how 'he was almost always as taut as a violin string'. Volatile, impatient and often irascible – his temper was not improved by ill health, and he was to die of asthma while still in his fifties – he was not the easiest of colleagues or employers, reducing secretaries to tears with what one of his victims described as his 'brusque and bullying manner'; but he provided a much-needed burst of colour, energy and enthusiasm in a firm which was in danger of becoming somnolent, smug and out of touch. Like Lane, he had a mischievous streak, and liked to wind people up, Lane among them; like Lane before him, he had a passion for starting new series. Peregrine Books, a larger-format equivalent of the American 'egghead' or 'college' paperback, pricier than the average Pelican and printed on better paper, was launched in 1961, and is best remembered for reprinting academic literary critics like Empson and F. R. Leavis, sub-leased from Chatto's then flourishing list of literary criticism; the Penguin English Library provided a home for English-language classics, debarred by definition from the Penguin Classics list; the new Penguin Modern Classics list was launched with novels by Ronald Firbank, Carson McCullers and Nathaniel West, as well as Cyril Connolly's *Enemies of Promise*, and later included works by Camus, Sartre, Brecht, Svevo, Gide and Thomas Mann; the Penguin Modern Poets offered a selection of three poets per volume, the tenth of which, devoted to the Liverpool Poets, sold over 50,000 copies; the thirteen volumes of Style and Civilization were joined, in due course, by the Penguin African Library, Political Leaders of the Twentieth Century, Modern European Poets and a brand-new Penguin Shakespeare.

Like Lane, Godwin was instinctively a man of the left, and, like Lane in the late 1930s, he and Dieter Pevsner were happy to use Penguin Specials as a branch of campaigning journalism. Godwin asked Bertrand Russell to write about the threat of nuclear weapons, and *Has Man a Future?* duly made its way on to his desk; the campaign against capital punishment found a voice in *Hanged by the Neck* by Arthur Koestler and C. H. Rolph and Leslie Hale's *Hanged in Error*; Nora Beloff's *The General Says No* discussed the familiar problem of Britain's relations with what was then called the Common Market, Colin Buchanan worried over *Traffic in Towns*, and Wayland Young delved into *The Profumo Affair*. Like *Private Eye* and the Angry Young Men, Godwin sided with those who ridiculed the 'Establishment', and deplored the 'thirteen wasted years' of Conservative government: responding to a widespread feeling that post-war Britain was hopelessly bogged down by antiquated class distinctions, a divisive educational system and an economy blighted by bone-headed management and primeval trade unions, and that the country had somehow lost any sense of purpose and direction, a series entitled Britain in the Sixties sought to discover what was wrong with a whole range of national institutions. Michael Shanks's Pelican on *The Stagnant Society*, commissioned by Bill Williams and originally published as a Penguin Special in 1961, brooded on the malaise of the British economy, soon to be revitalized (or so some thought) by the meritocratic Harold Wilson, and J. K. Galbraith's *The Affluent Society* and Vance Packard's *The Hidden Persuaders* were both taken on before Godwin's arrival: Dieter Pevsner, with Godwin's full support, was responsible for commissioning the great majority of the Penguin Specials, devoted to such topical issues as apartheid, Cyprus and Algeria, while the Pelican list included writings which set the intellectual tone of the 1960s, including R. D. Laing's *The Divided Self*.

Not all Godwin's colleagues shared his radical sympathies. Meaburn Staniland, a scholarly figure who masterminded blurbs and briefly employed the young Clive James to match author photographs to their potted biographies, wrote to suggest that Godwin's non-fiction commissions were often too ephemeral and left-wing, too concerned with Africa and South America, and that he worried about the elevation of 'sociology to the level of a religion'. Godwin wrote angrily back about the threat to the environment from pollution – he shared Lane's admiration for Rachel Carson's *Silent Spring* – and the spread of nuclear and biological weapons. 'I give you that cliché that "the proper study of mankind is man",' he wrote. 'And that includes sociology as well as psychology and history, comparative history and anthropology. The tradition of sociology in England is new and weak; the ability of English sociologists to write in reasonable English is limited. Nevertheless it is our job to try to get good books out of them.' It was nonsensical of Staniland to suggest that the Penguin African Library was being published from a misplaced sense of guilt: 'the fact of the matter is that the African continent exists, and the extent of ignorance on the subject is very considerable'.

Godwin's leftish leanings were accompanied by a genuine – and very Lane-like – desire to bring the best to as many people as possible. Writing in the *TLS*, he savaged Fredric Warburg for his disdainful use of the word 'commodity' when referring to paperbacks. All books, Godwin claimed, were 'commodities': the implication of what Warburg had written was that 'a book must have been vulgarized in some way to enjoy considerable appeal. And the corollary is that the only books of true merit are the ones with only a minority appeal. What rubbish! There isn't necessarily any correlation between the merit and popularity of a book.' Warburg, he claimed, snobbishly equated price with quality. 'There is something very gingerly about the manner in which Mr Warburg handles the word "commodity". You can almost picture his wry distaste . . . If the commodity is not produced with the intention of selling it, what is publishing supposed to be about?'

So far so good, in Lane's book at least: rather more problematic, though, was the vexed issue of covers. After the experiment with Abram Games's full-colour covers, Lane had reverted, with relief, to the familiar orange and white vertical bands: but however strong the urgings of Frostie and Bill Williams, he must have known that changes would have to be made. The early Sixties saw the rise of the graphic designer, of glossy magazines like Mark Boxer's *Queen* and the *Sunday Times*'s colour supplement which made effective use of bold, brightly coloured lettering and forceful visual images, designed to intrigue and entice; advertisers and magazine editors discarded illustrators and wood engravers in favour of photographs and montages in which line drawings, half-tones and lettering were cunningly interlaced. Such developments were hard to ignore at a time when Penguin was more vulnerable to competition than ever before – not just from rival paperback publishers, but from television, magazines and other aspirants after the leisure time and the spare cash of a generation generously endowed with both. John Curtis, briefly doubling up as the art editor, commissioned jackets that combined photographs and graphic effects as well as giving work to young designers like Derek Birdsall and, with Hans Schmoller's blessing, artists like Quentin Blake and David Gentleman, whose drawings were to feature on innumerable jackets; but it was Godwin's appointment of Germano Facetti as Art Director in 1961 that inaugurated sweeping changes. A good-looking, crew-cut survivor of Mauthausen concentration camp – he had been sent there at the age of seventeen for taking part in the Italian Resistance – Facetti had worked as a designer for the architect Ernesto Rogers in Milan and for Olivetti before moving on to magazines: his work for Penguin seems, in retrospect, both tasteful and austere, but Hans Schmoller, who dismissed him as a 'failed architect', resented his appointment and claimed that his jackets, many of them full-colour half-tones, destroyed the unity that had hitherto existed between the jacket and the text.

Facetti's opening gambit was to ask Romek Marber, a graphic artist who had recently designed some covers for *The Economist*, to design a new 'grid' or layout for the crime series, still clad in its pre-war uniform of green and white horizontal bands. Ranged left, in the fashion of the time, with the bottom two-thirds left free for an illustration, Marbek's elegant grid set a pattern that would be used for Penguins, Penguin Specials, Pelicans and Penguin Modern Classics, and was adapted by Facetti for the black-backed Penguin Classics and the new Penguin English Library. His decision to jettison the coloured borders and woodcut roundels of Penguin Classics in favour of four-colour reproductions from paintings may have appealed to students and book-buyers, but provoked howls of anguish from Hampstead. 'Rieu blew up on the phone about Tony's proposals for the classics,' Harry Paroissien told Lane. 'The old boy was bloodying and buggering all over the place.' 'Oh my poor series, of which I used to be so proud,' Rieu exclaimed after he had been sent a copy of Euripides with a Facetti cover. J. M. Cohen had stood down as the Classics editorial adviser in 1963, and no doubt it came as a relief to both sides when Rieu retired the following year, and was replaced by Betty Radice and Robert Baldick.

Rieu was not the only one to take a dim view of the new jackets, and worse was to come when Godwin decided to revolutionize fiction covers, retaining Tschichold's penguin and an overall impression of orange (or green, in the case of crime) while making full use of photographers, designers and the techniques of advertising. Collins had commissioned Raymond Hawkey to redesign all Agatha Christie's covers – to such good effect, in Godwin's opinion, that the Penguin crime list could no longer compete, despite Romek Marber's reforms. Facetti, Godwin decided, was too conservative, too tasteful, to master-mind the fiction list: he needed someone more abrasive, more eye-catching, more in touch with the younger generation.

In 1964 Godwin appointed Alan Aldridge to look after the fiction list, reporting to him in his new offices in John Street, off Theobald's Road, rather than to Facetti in Harmondsworth. Decked out in bell-bottomed trousers, floral waistcoat and bleached shoulder-length hair, Aldridge was, by training, a commercial artist, a devotee of pop culture and psychedelic art who went on to design *The Beatles Illustrated Lyrics* and *The Butterfly Ball*; and his work – much of which looks tawdry and far more dated than Tschichold's or Schmoller's austere abstractions – was calculated to render the old guard apoplectic with rage. 'Where, sir, are Penguins going?' a long-serving rep wrote to Lane. 'Make no mistake, sir, many of our covers are as dishonest as some of those used by our competitors in the past. Our marketing methods are, for the most part, garish, cheap and nasty; our overall policy, which used to stand for excellence above all else, has degen-erated to what seems to me a deliberate courting of the "pop" market and its dishonesty of presentation.' Evidently unimpressed by the books as well as their covers, he was 'deeply disturbed that my reputation is being held to ransom by an editorial policy (or should I say lack of one) in which I can see little resemblance to the Penguin I know and love. We have a wonderful reputation. I can't stand by and see it ruined.' Or, as Hans Schmoller put it four years after Lane's death, 'It was not until the 1960s that paperbacks were drawn into, and sometimes carried along rudderless by, the visual deluge that, these days, threatens to drown us with its constantly changing swirls of graphic fashion and the unscrupulous plundering of past styles, with its fondness for pastiche and all the other appurtenances and clichés of pop and camp art.'

Some authors were equally unamused. Lane offered to fly out to Antibes after Charles Pick had written from Heinemann to say that Graham Greene thought his covers 'beyond belief' and was threatening to withdraw the licences from Penguin; Candida Donadio, Saul Bellow's literary agent, told Godwin that her author had taken a 'violent dislike' to his jackets, describing them as 'junk', 'cheapjack' and 'faggy'; John Masters, like Greene, threatened to withdraw. Anthony Powell was understandably upset when Godwin wrote to say that Penguin would no longer be using Osbert Lancaster's entirely apposite drawings on the covers of his books: quite apart from their suitability, neither he nor Lancaster had been consulted about the change. 'Mr Powell's whole attitude was condescending,' Godwin told the *Evening Standard*. 'His letters were most unpleasant.' 'It seems to me that you are clearly out of sorts with Penguin. It makes me wonder whether you really want to continue with a publisher that you clearly seem to dislike,' he informed his affronted author, who decamped to the Fontana list, where a series of elegant and appropriate jackets by Mark Boxer soon awaited him.

Nor were the jackets the only bone of contention. A charismatic figure who infected others with his own energy and enthusiasm, Godwin attracted to him a praetorian guard of young, idealistic editors, many of them fresh from university and lacking any experience of business or publishing. They kept themselves apart from the old guard, favouring different pubs and greasy spoons, and the

gulf widened still further when Godwin moved his headquarters
from Harmondsworth to John Street. Penguin seemed, at times, to
be divided into two camps: the old guard – Paroissien, Ron Blass
and Lane himself, with Bill Williams and Frostie hovering in the
wings – disapproved of and resented Godwin and all he stood for,
while some of the newcomers looked down on the old-timers as
antediluvian survivors from a vanished age, hopelessly out of touch
with the changing literary, cultural and social scene. But it would
be misleading to over-emphasize the gulf: many of the 'old guard'
were young in years – Ron Blass was in his forties, and Chris Dolley,
who had joined Penguin in 1962, a good deal younger – and editors
like Dieter Pevsner, Charles Clark, Nikos Stangos and Oliver
Caldecott were at home in both camps; as was Jim Cochrane, a
young editor who did not share the left-wing views of most of his
John Street colleagues.

For Lane himself, Godwin felt a wary admiration. He found him
'an extraordinary mixture of overweening vanity and genuine
simplicity', someone who felt himself to be 'a man apart' yet often
suffered agonies of doubt, and was both unassuming and self-
regarding. Godwin had always hero-worshipped him, and 'from
talking to him there was never any doubt in my mind of his editorial flair, with one exception a far stronger flair than any other
publisher I have known'. He respected his 'granite shrewdness' and
his 'infectious enthusiasm', thought him 'marvellous company and a
boon companion' who relished 'mischievous jokes' and appeared to
prefer gossip to serious conversation, and remembered how, if anyone
suggested a new book or series, 'Out would come a scrap of paper;
there'd be a small pause as he unscrewed his large fountain pen, and
then he'd start scribbling away, making financial calculations.' But he
felt that, by the time he joined the firm, Lane's brilliance as a publisher
was no longer apparent. Lane liked to quote Israel Sieff, the dynamic
head of Marks & Spencer, to the effect that 'Quality counts', and
like Sieff he saw himself as being above the fray, dispensing advice
to the senior staff. 'Allen's mind seemed to have closed some time
during my period at Penguin,' Godwin believed: he took little real
interest in the editorial side of the business, suggested new titles with

a 'perfunctory diffidence', and only became really excited when pondering the possibility of selling cheap and simple paperbacks in the African market, and when Godwin bought his second batch of Somerset Maughams.

Although Lane became steadily more disenchanted with Godwin, they were agreed on the desirability of founding a hardback imprint within Penguin: but their reasons for doing so could not have been more different. Penguin had always published a certain number of titles and series in hardback – apart from the Pelican History of Art and the Buildings of England, sheets of Penguin Classics and the Penguin History of England had been bound in boards for the library market – and Lane, as he grew older, may have yearned for the respectability and status still associated with the hardback book. In 1961 he had discussed, over lunch with Stanley Morison and Robin Darwin of the Royal College of Art, the possibility of Penguin producing elegant, finely produced hardbacks along the lines of Francis Meynell's Nonesuch Press or Rupert Hart-Davis's Reynard Library, and although nothing came of it the dream still lingered. Godwin's approach reflected his worries about changes in the publishing world, and how Penguin could best react to them: in this respect at least he seemed far more prescient than Lane, anticipating much of what has happened since his lonely death in New York in 1976. The post-war 'group' arrangement, whereby particular publishers gave Penguin the first option on their books, was still in force – by the early Sixties the group consisted of Cape, Chatto, Hamish Hamilton, Michael Joseph and Secker – but Faber's decision to set up its own paperback list, and revert titles hitherto published by Penguin, suggested that it was unlikely to continue for ever. There was also the vexed matter of royalties. A younger and more aggressive breed of literary agents began to argue that authors should receive a full royalty on the paperback editions of their books (as was the case if the paperback was published by the originating hardback publisher) rather than allowing the hardback publisher 50 per cent of any paperback royalties (as was the case if the paperback rights were licensed to a third party, such as Penguin), and this removed any incentive for the hardback publisher to license rights to Penguin

– or, indeed, any other paperback imprint operating at one remove.

With Penguin vulnerable to losing the rights in the books it published under licence, whether they be last week's bestsellers or steady backlist items that seemed to have 'belonged' to the firm since time immemorial, it became all the more important to commission and publish titles in which Penguin, and not some other publisher, held the 'volume' rights. That was all very well, but – then as now – authors liked to be published in hardback as well as paperback, and without an 'in-house' hardback imprint, Penguin ran the risk of taking on an author, perhaps for his first book, and then losing him to a publisher who was in a position to publish in both hard and paper. Anticipating the movement of the Seventies and Eighties into what became known as 'vertical' publishing, whereby hardback publishers bought or set up paperback imprints, and vice versa, Godwin saw a hardback list as a means of guaranteeing a steady supply of saleable titles which could then be reissued in paperback, and meeting agents' objections by offering a full royalty on both. Billy Collins was pioneering this approach with his Fontana list, but neither Lane's brief ownership of shares in Methuen, nor his contemplating a takeover from Thomas Tilling of Secker & Warburg and Rupert Hart-Davis's admirable but unprofitable list, seems to have been motivated by a desire to do the same thing in reverse at Penguin.

Godwin's strategic reasons for wanting to start a hardback list coincided with Lane's nostalgia for the kind of publishing he had been involved with at The Bodley Head. Although Godwin later revealed plans for Penguin to publish original fiction, it was agreed that the new list should consist of non-fiction titles only. Harry Paroissien suggested that the new imprint should be called Allen Lane The Penguin Press, a self-conscious echo of John Lane The Bodley Head, and premises were acquired one afternoon in the summer of 1965 when Lane noticed that Bertram Rota, the antiquarian booksellers, were moving out of the old Vigo Street offices that had once housed The Bodley Head – they had become rather scruffy in the intervening years – and decided, with a flash of his old impulsiveness, to acquire the lease there and then. 'I felt it was very fitting to go in a full circle and end up where I began nearly fifty years ago,' he wrote to Dick in Australia.

In Godwin's opinion, Lane showed no interest in the new firm until he spotted the For Let sign in Vigo Street, and displayed a 'complete incomprehension' of the notion of ALPP as a 'handmaiden of Penguins', regarding it instead as 'a sport, a hobby, an amusing self-indulgence', and 'a celebration and rounding-out of his own career in publishing'; and whereas Godwin believed that two years were needed in which to launch the list, Lane thought one was enough. The books published by Allen Lane The Penguin Press became known for their creamy paper and elegant design, if not for their saleability, and the first title on the list – 750 sets of *Bibliopola*, a two-volume, trilingual, linen-bound work by Siegfried Taubert, a German antiquarian bookseller and a future Director of the Frankfurt Book Fair – suggested that Lane had prevailed over Godwin by producing a book that would almost certainly have appealed to Stanley Morison and Robin Darwin, but had no potential whatsoever as a paperback: as the *Guardian* put it, 'Sir Allen Lane has returned to "conventional" publishing with a thud if not a bang.' At the 1966 sales conference Godwin had emphasized ALPP's editorial independence, and its readiness, at times, to take on books that might seem too specialized or rarefied for the Penguin list, but although ALPP produced only one really strong seller, both in hardback and in paperback – Ronald Blythe's *Akenfield*, commissioned by Godwin with his customary enthusiasm, but published after his departure from Penguin – *Bibliopola* proved a momentary aberration, and the list soon acquired a more modern, even modish look: Godwin's own opening batch included Hunter S. Thompson's *Hell's Angels*, Al Alvarez's *Beyond All This Fiddle*, Jules Feiffer's *The Great Comic Book Heroes*, Octavio Paz's *The Labyrinth of Solitude* and Studs Terkel's *Division Street: America*, and later offerings included works by academic heavyweights like Gunnar Myrdal and investigative journalists like Anthony Sampson.

Although Godwin once claimed that having one's own hardback imprint would reduce the number of huge advances paid out to other publishers, he was not averse to paying the larger advances that were now expected by authors and their agents. The old-fashioned Pelican author had been, more often than not, an other-worldly academic or passionate enthusiast who was either retired or attached to a university and was happy to be published by Penguin for the glory and a modest return; but many of those with whom Godwin had dealings were full-time professional writers who could not afford to be paid a few hundred pounds for several years' work. In his post-Penguin incarnations, Godwin acquired a reputation for extravagance and paying over the odds for books of a kind that, all too often, combined laudatory reviews with modest sales, and by doing so he led the way into a world in which advances bore little or no relation to the actual sales of a book. No doubt he realized, almost intuitively, that there is, more often than not, a great gulf set between what an author needs in order to write a book and what a publisher should sensibly pay: but whereas most publishers, happily following the advice of Sir Stanley Unwin, based their advances on the royalties that would accrue on sales of 40 per cent of the print-run, and refused to take into account any possible earnings from subsidiary rights, Godwin was prepared to pay large advances because, according to Al Alvarez, he believed that authors should be as free as possible of money worries: never an expensive luncher, unlike so many of his colleagues in the trade, 'he paid you the compliment of assuming that you would prefer a larger advance to the dubious privilege of sharing with him an over-priced, drunken meal'.

Competing with rival paperback publishers was not simply a matter of paying what became known as 'competitive' advances and kitting the books out with more 'commercial' jackets: it also involved, Godwin claimed, a readiness to spend money on marketing and promotion. A sales and marketing director was employed for the first time, in the form of Richard Holme, a graduate of Oxford and the Harvard Business School who had previously worked for Carr's biscuits and Unilever, and was regarded by the old guard as Godwin's henchman; although in later life he returned to business and was ennobled for contributions to the Liberal Democrat Party, he remembered Penguin as being far and away the most political place in which he ever worked, an impression confirmed by a junior editor, who recalled clusters of middle-aged, grey-suited men gathering in the corridors, muttering among themselves in low conspiratorial tones. With the impatience of youth, Holme thought Lane was increasingly out of touch with changes in the trade: his insistence on keeping prices as low as possible was, in Holme's opinion, unnecessary, counter-productive and out-of-date, in that modern paperback buyers were more likely to be seduced by an alluring picture cover than a bargain price; much as Lane resented having to accept returns from booksellers, he failed to realize that the higher the sales, the higher the potential for returns. Holme's time at Penguin was short – he reckoned he fell from grace when, on a trip to Bristol, Lane asked him who should be his heir-apparent, and he immediately suggested Tony Godwin – but he was best remembered for the part he played in promoting Len Deighton's thriller, *Funeral in Berlin*.

Deighton had been greatly disappointed by Penguin's handling of his last novel, *Horse Under Water*, which had sold over 90,000 copies before going out of print. It had, he told Godwin, represented 'a major opportunity for Penguin to demonstrate to the trade and to the public that it was alive to the new and vigorous ideas and methods' being used by other paperback firms, and Tom Maschler, Deighton's hardback publisher at Jonathan Cape, insisted that Penguin should try harder with the new book. In addition to a £5,000 advance, Maschler demanded a £5,000 promotion budget, and a first printing of 250,000 copies. Deighton was, he told Godwin, 'close to being the most desirable paperback property in England', and Penguin should be able to sell a million copies of *Funeral in Berlin*. 'I see no reason why Penguin should not publish him the way I believe others would,' Maschler insisted. As for the proposed publicity budget, 'I am not kidding. Len is not asking for favours or for the unreasonable. Penguin will profit, just as he will. Think about it.' Deighton then returned to the attack. If Penguin thought the proposed publicity budget was 'such a gigantic waste of money, then it would be fairer if they did not bid for my type of book, because this today is the sort of treatment I can expect. If Penguin Books can't see that printing 250,000 copies of *Funeral* will bring them a considerable return, they are living in the past.'

Godwin's correspondence with Maschler and Deighton has a curious fascination, showing Penguin poised between the world that Lane and Williams and Frostie had brought into being, and that of the aggressively marketed middlebrow bestseller (in that year alone Pan sold 6 million James Bonds). Godwin himself had mixed feelings: he told John Hitchin in the sales department that Deighton was a 'difficult and harassing author', but although 'I neither regard his books as literature, nor do I have any particularly passionate personal regard for them', he could not afford to lose such an author if Penguin was to publish bestselling novelists in paperback. 'If we are not prepared to promote top authors to the same extent as our competitors, then I really do think it is a waste of my time,' he concluded, taking care to send copies of his memo to Lane and Harry Paroissien. To promote *Funeral in Berlin*, Godwin and Richard Holme flew a planeload of journalists to Berlin. The chartered plane had been painted white, and carried a motif from the book jacket; the hacks drank black velvet on the flight over, and were met at the airport by Michael Caine, the star of the film version of the book, who took them on a tour of the Berlin Wall. The novel subscribed 283,000 copies, but Godwin's critics claimed that the cost of the exercise wiped out any possible profit; and Lane was said to be livid.

Whether Lane objected to the contents of Deighton's book is not recorded, but he found some of those now appearing on the list too gamey for his tastes. 'I am, as you know, something of a puritan by nature, and I find the passages in the book which you sent me disgusting,' he told Hans Schmoller apropos Jean Genet's *The Thief's Journal*, the rights in which Godwin had recently bought from Anthony Blond (along with Spike Milligan's *Puckoon*, which sold in huge quantities in Penguin). 'My own taste editorially is towards Maugham, Wells, Hemingway, Graham Greene and Evelyn Waugh, in the theatre to Shaw and Wilde and Noël Coward, typographically to Oliver Simon and Tschichold, in art to Turner and Ivon Hitchens, and I find myself out of sympathy with much of contemporary literature, theatre, typography and art.'

But it was neither a steamy novel nor a volume of louche memoirs that tipped Lane over the edge, bringing to a head all his resentment and unease about the changes that were being made to his firm. Godwin had decided to revive a Penguin tradition of publishing collections of cartoons by contemporary practitioners, among them Brockbank, Ronald Searle and André François, and in 1963 Jill Norman, a young editor who later looked after the Penguin cookery list, took on a collection by an iconoclastic French cartoonist called Siné. Siné's cartoons combined mockery of the Roman Catholic Church with sexual and lavatorial motifs: any editorial unease was partially allayed by enthusiastic endorsements from Ronald Searle, John Mortimer and A. J. P. Taylor, who wrote that 'his drawings are splendidly funny. He provides a valuable social comment on our times, and I cannot see why anyone should object to this volume. It is quite harmless.' Malcolm Muggeridge agreed to make a selection and write an introduction. 'As a hater of pornography and aspiring Christian I find his furious indignation over the present moral confusion in State and Church very much to my taste,' he told Jill Norman, adding that 'there is something very funny in the thought that a publishing house which made an enormous profit out of the perverse sexual ravings of D. H. Lawrence should fear to sully its reputation with Siné'. Godwin thought Muggeridge's initial selection disappointing, with 'very little of the savagery and the unique quality of his humour', but matters were remedied, and the book, now entitled *Massacre*, eventually went into production. Lane, who had his doubts, sent a copy to Arthur Crook, the editor of the *Times Literary Supplement*, who passed it round the office and reported back that no one seemed remotely shocked; the fact that Lane had sent it to him, and apparently accepted his endorsement, was, Godwin later suggested, indicative of his 'instinctive deference to the Establishment'.

Despite Arthur Crook's endorsement, Lane's hostility to the book had hardened. 'I agree with you. The drawings are nauseating,' he told Tanya Schmoller. 'I suggest that Hans and Harry might have a look at it, and if necessary a board meeting could be called to discuss it.' The meeting was held in September 1966, and was spread over two days. After reminding his fellow directors that they had a collective responsibility for the firm's publications, Lane conceded that

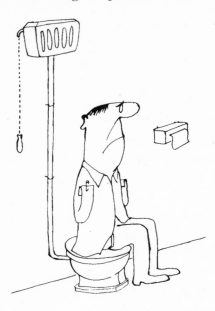

*One of the Siné cartoons that caused offence in
bookshops up and down the country.*

Arthur Crook had thought the cartoons 'rather good', and asked
Godwin to make his case. Godwin began by discussing the generation gap, and the difference in taste and attitudes between the under-
thirties and the over-forties. It was, he argued, unwise and impossible
to avert the gaze from the tendency towards greater explicitness in
matters of sex and religion, and cited Genet and Edna O'Brien as
examples of writers whose work might shock but should not therefore be ignored or condemned; it would be a disaster to withdraw
the book at this late stage. Harry Paroissien was firmly against publication, Godwin noting how Lane used him to voice his own views,
particularly when younger editors were present; Charles Clark, who
had a legal background, said that Ben Hooberman, a solicitor specializing in libel, obscenity and copyright matters, thought it highly
unlikely that the DPP would show any interest, or that Penguin
would be prosecuted for blasphemy (Lane's solicitor, Leslie Paisner,
on the other hand, thought the book should be withdrawn); Hans
Schmoller and Ron Blass voted against, but Dieter Pevsner, Charles

Clark, Richard Holme and the accountant Tony Walker were all in favour of pressing ahead. Lane and the old guard were outvoted, and publication of *Massacre* went ahead as planned.

No sooner had the book appeared than the office was deluged with correspondence from outraged clergymen and, more worryingly, indignant booksellers. 'I am confident you will disassociate yourself from this disgraceful production in clear and certain terms,' wrote the Revd A. R. Vine of the Church Federal Council, adding that he particularly objected to a crucified Christ 'leering at an undressing nun'; the Revd Ernest Payne of the Baptist Union thought it 'one of the most offensive books I have ever seen', and that it was both

blasphemous and pornographic. Such letters were forwarded to Lane, now brooding in his Spanish villa. But worse was to come. 'It seems extraordinary that a man with your business sense should wish to publish such a grotesquely blasphemous item,' declared Allen Figgis of Hodges Figgis, the Dublin booksellers; John Heffer of the well-known Cambridge firm declared himself 'horrified'; a Cheltenham bookseller was convinced that 'the person who can think up such muck as this must be mad'. Most damaging of all was a letter from Una Dillon, a doyenne of London bookselling. 'For the first time in my life I have decided against stocking a Penguin,' she told Lane: she had liked Siné's previous work, but this was blasphemous and 'in exceedingly bad taste'. Many of these booksellers were the friends of Lane's youth, with whom he had enjoyed good business relations for years past; and their outrage and disdain were hard to stomach. 'This letter is a somewhat difficult one for me to write,' he told

Allen Figgis. He sympathized with Figgis's views, but 'I have a young and energetic editorial staff, and I have tried my best to give it as free a hand as possible'.

Godwin, in the meantime, stoutly defended publication, declaring in a press release that 'Penguin has frequently published books without a consensus of agreement on the Board, for it has always been a major part of Penguin's policy to publish books across the widest range of taste.' But before long the ructions within Penguin had become public knowledge. 'When any old family concern, like the BBC, tries to get "with it", you can be sure that the results will be farcical,' reported *Private Eye*. Just as the BBC had lowered its standards to compete with ITV, so Penguin, 'alarmed by the paperback whizz kids flooding the market with titillating rubbish, have flung themselves into the fray. Now, as part of their Christmas fare, comes a grotesque book of cartoons by Siné. Penguin, like the BBC, is so incompetently run that those in authority did not realize the nature of the work until it was too late. Now a full-scale boardroom row has broken out, and resignations may follow.'

A month before publication, Lane told Godwin over dinner how much he disliked Siné's book, and wondered whether his colleague

would mind too much if 'he got someone on the QT to pick up the copies in the warehouse and dispose of them somewhere and report the book o/p'. No doubt Godwin assumed that Lane was joking, and thought no more about it, but some time in December George Nicholls, who worked in the warehouse at Harmondsworth, was woken by a phone call at midnight and told to report for duty at once. Standing in the dark outside the warehouse were Lane, Mr Bosley (his chauffeur), Mr Singleton (his farm manager), and 'another person who shall be nameless' (but could have been Susanne Lepsius, though many in the office assumed it must have been Ron Blass). 'George, that bloody board outvoted me, but I'll have my own back on them,' Lane told Nicholls before asking him to open up the warehouse: he was after 'those bloody Sinés', and was determined to pinch the lot. 'Crikey!' Nicholls exclaimed – his account of his midnight adventure reads like a cross between *Beano* and an Ealing Comedy – but he dutifully opened up, and the brown paper parcels of Siné were taken off the shelves, loaded into a van and driven away to Lane's farm: whether they were then burned or buried is a matter of debate. 'Now, we'll keep this a secret, we won't tell anybody, will we?' Lane told Nicholls as he prepared to drive off with his booty. 'You're the governor,' Nicholls replied. Next morning some 220 copies were found on the picking bench, overlooked the night before: Harry Paroissien took them away, declared the book out of print, and told the warehouse manager to put any returns 'under lock and key'.

Lane had drawn blood, and publicly humiliated his enemy. Godwin joined Lane, Charles Clark, Nikolaus Pevsner, Edward Boyle and Kingsley Amis on a Penguin promotional trip to Prague, during the course of which he told Clark that, after the Siné business, it would be impossible to patch up relations with Lane. Lane informed Charles Pick that since Godwin had 'asked to be relieved of the editorship of the fiction list and also the responsibility for covers', he was now dealing with fiction covers himself, and was 'engaged in a massive operation of correcting some trends'; he told Tanya Schmoller that the art department would be returning to Harmondsworth, and that 'Tony feels that he has been taking on too much. He has no agreement and wants one as editor. He has no desire ever to become managing director.'

Godwin, who had been preoccupied with launching Allen Lane The Penguin Press, was taken ill: working at Penguin put him under such physical and emotional strain that he often had to retire to bed for days on end, and he was rushed to hospital suffering from what proved to be a near-lethal asthma attack. When he came out of hospital – where he neither heard from nor was visited by any of his senior colleagues at Penguin – he took a fortnight's holiday in Spain. On his return he was met at Heathrow by a distraught Dieter Pevsner, who revealed that Lane planned to get rid of him: Pevsner had put up a fight on his colleague's behalf, but Lane seemed adamant. Back in the office, an uneasy calm prevailed until, after an editorial meeting, Lane suggested that they should meet for dinner. They met two days later at the Escargot. Halfway through the meal Lane suddenly said that Godwin must go: he wasn't prepared to argue or discuss the matter, but Leslie Paisner, his solicitor, would be in touch about compensation. Godwin knew Paisner to be 'an exceptionally tough lawyer': could they not, he wondered, talk things over as friends? Lane, 'now hostile and contemptuous', flatly refused: his attitude, Godwin later recalled, 'was that of a gentleman who has dismissed his butler, and was not disposed to be bothered personally over such incidentals as the length of service, compensation etc.' It was, Godwin felt, as though 'my very existence rankled, and his actions became dictated by venom'. He refused Lane's offer of a brandy: the two men went outside, Lane climbed into a chauffeur-driven car, which had evidently been circling round, and Godwin headed off for a restorative drink in a nearby pub. He was devastated by what had happened to him: he had never expected to be sacked, and – according to his wife Fay – it broke both his heart and his health.

A joint statement was prepared for release to the Press. Publishing, it declared, 'is still a matter of individual taste, skill and judgement, and it has become clear that the tastes of Mr Godwin and Sir Allen Lane are at certain points incompatible. In view of these difficulties Mr Godwin is, at Sir Allen's request, shortly resigning as a director and chief editor.' It had been agreed that neither side would talk to journalists, but within hours *The Times* was on the trail. According to Godwin, William Rees-Mogg overheard Lane boasting in the Garrick of how he had got rid of 'that shit Godwin', and a reporter had been sent down to Harmondsworth, where he talked to members of staff and, despite a denial from Lane, got the distinct impression that Godwin had been sacked; Ronald Segal, the editor of the Penguin African Library, claims that Godwin rang to tell him what had happened, and that Segal then spoke to a friend on *The Times*. A Pelican author who had suggested the Political Leaders of the Twentieth Century series and Specials like Paul Foot's *Immigration and Race in British Politics*, Segal was a close associate of Godwin, and thought his sacking 'a shoddy business as well as a disreputable return for his achievement in making Penguin a successful pioneer of new, often pioneering books'.

'The Godwin sacking farce continues its dreary course,' Godwin told John Berger, one of the authors he had brought to Allen Lane The Penguin Press. 'Allen Lane has made an unspeakable buffoon of himself. We sent out a joint statement and then agreed neither of us would talk. He then talked rapidly to everyone in sight. The main burden seems to be that I was sacked because I thought that Penguins should be popped into petrol stations and pubs, and published Penguins with naughty, racy covers. This has caused a certain degree of hilarity among the more intelligent British public.' According to *Private Eye*, the sacking came as no surprise: 'Sir Allen has long been known to become physically ill at the mention of Godwin. The mere mention of his name is liable to bring on a seizure.'

When not suffering a seizure, Lane seemed to relish the attention. 'I am an ancient old piece,' the 'vigorous and deeply tanned, white-haired and handsome' publisher informed Anne Batt of the *Daily Express*. 'Two years ago I thought I would just fade away and let the young people take over. I thought I was getting a bit fuddy-duddy and that it would be fun to be a farmer. Well, it wasn't.' 'Books and baked beans don't mix,' he continued. 'Books written by distinguished authors need a little dignity . . . It was the negation of everything I had set out to do. I was perfectly straight with them. I said, "Honestly, chums, this is just not on" . . . There's nothing more dispiriting than sitting back when you know something is going wrong and not taking any action. Once you plunge in, you throw away your sleeping pills and really start living again.' 'How refreshing,' Batt mused, 'to meet a businessman with ideals worth so much more to him than cash.' Conveniently forgetting how, a quarter of a century earlier, he had relied on Woolworth's to launch his new list, Lane told the *Daily Telegraph* that books should be sold in bookshops, 'and not in pubs, supermarkets and similar places'. 'I've got rid of the buggers,' Lane confided to a colleague as they took to the dance floor at an office outing, but his public pronouncements were more emollient. He assured *The Times* that he and Godwin were still friends, 'so much so that we concluded our meeting on Friday night over a bottle of wine': elsewhere the paper noted that Penguin's turnover had doubled between 1960 and 1967 and that the number of copies sold had risen from 17 million to 28 million, and quoted Tom Maschler as claiming that the 'virtually irreplaceable' Godwin had made a 'monumental and colossal' contribution to the firm, and (bearing in mind, perhaps, his own inadvertent contribution to Godwin's fall from grace) that Richard Holme's decision to fly the team of hacks to Berlin had probably doubled the sales of *Funeral in Berlin*. Although many of Maschler's most publicized bestsellers, *Catch 22* and Desmond Morris's *The Naked Ape* among them, were paperbacked by Corgi, some of the old guard felt that he continued to exercise an undue influence on the firm through the books he sold Penguin and the ways in which they were presented and promoted.

It only remained to sort out the terms of Godwin's departure. After reminding other members of the board that Godwin had no service contract, Lane went on to say that 'in view of the contribution which he has made over the past six years, I felt we should be generous': but what constituted generosity was a matter of debate. Matters came to a head in the ALPP offices in Vigo Street: a 'fretful' Lane sat in an upstairs room, Godwin, who was suffering a bad asthma attack and dosing himself with cortisone, remained on the ground floor, and Charles Clark shuttled between the two. Lane at first suggested £5,000, but Charles Clark and Dieter Pevsner felt he was owed three years' salary. Lane agreed to abide by Edward Boyle's decision; Boyle, who was eventually tracked down taking tea in Yorkshire, agreed with Pevsner and Clark, and a sum of £18,000 was decided upon. Leslie Paisner told Lane later that he should never have paid so much, and that no court would have awarded Godwin that amount had he brought a case for unfair dismissal. Lane offered to waive £6,500 in dividends rather than have the firm suffer from his folly: Godwin later claimed that he tried to wriggle out of his commitment, while at the same time recalling Lane's typical acts of impulsive generosity – how he had offered to lend him £1,000 to buy a house, given him the run of El Fénix, which Godwin loved, and lugged back a guitar from Spain for one of Godwin's daughters by his first marriage.

Looking back on Godwin's sacking ten years after the event, Dieter Pevsner and Oliver Caldecott, Godwin's eventual successor as fiction editor, wrote that Godwin's abrasive manner and his tendency to ride roughshod over his colleagues meant that 'when the chemical bond between himself and Allen Lane broke, the hostages he had given by accumulated slights and cheerful prodigality with others' money, and his first, nearly fatal illness, left him isolated and defence-less'. The old guard could barely disguise their delight, but a group of Penguin editors, including Oliver Caldecott, Charles Clark, Dieter Pevsner, Jim Cochrane, Giles Gordon, Tony Richardson, Kaye Webb, Jill Norman, Peter Wright and Robert Hutchison, published letters in *The Times* and the *Bookseller* in praise of Godwin's 'extraordinary achievements' and his 'intense concern for quality and purpose', adding that 'we know these feelings are shared by Sir Allen Lane and his fellow directors'. Godwin may have told a young colleague that he had been a victim of 'the arbitrary use of capitalist power', but by the end of the year he was installed as joint managing director of Weidenfeld & Nicolson, where he was soon competing with Tom Maschler as a stylish, exciting and much talked-about hardback editor. He remained, as Al Alvarez put it, 'a troublesome, unorthodox pres-ence' in the publishing world, and 'the fact that he was so much brighter and more dedicated than the average publisher may have influenced people, but did not win him many friends in the trade'.

Almost certainly, Lane had wanted to be shot of Godwin for some time: he disliked the way in which, as he saw it, the image and repu-tation of his life's work were being destroyed, and resented a sense that Godwin would like him to play a more passive or emeritus role in the firm. While the crisis was simmering he asked Arthur Crook if he might be interested in a job at Penguin. Crook, who saw his role as that of interceding between the old guard in Harmondsworth and Godwin's cohorts in central London, was 'wined and dined' so well that he found it impossible to resist a salary more than twice that he enjoyed as editor of *The Times Literary Supplement*, plus a car and the use of a flat. Lane invited him for a celebratory dinner at the Garrick, and after the meal they found themselves standing next to one another in the gents' urinals. Lane said how glad he was that Crook would be joining the team; and then, as they were washing their hands in adjoining basins, he asked him how long it would take for him to get rid of Tony Godwin. Since Godwin and Crook were close friends, it was not the most tactful of questions, and Crook hurriedly withdrew as a result: but it suggested the way Lane's mind was working.

Godwin's own ambitions and aspirations were less clear-cut. Morpurgo suggests that Godwin was intent on mounting a coup against Lane, and portrays him as a scheming revolutionary lurking in the wings with dagger drawn; Chris Dolley, a Cambridge graduate who had joined Penguin after working for Unilever in West Africa and succeeded Harry Paroissien in Baltimore before returning to England in 1967, was equally convinced that the 'Gang of Three' – Godwin, Holme and Tony Walker, 'a large, fat man who seemed to survive on enormous glasses of gin and Dubonnet' and who had helped Godwin on his barrow immediately after the war – were keen to sideline Lane, and made 'an ill-conceived and incompetent move to isolate him' in 1965. Godwin's allies and admirers, on the other hand, doubt very much whether Godwin ever planned to get rid of Lane, much as he might have wanted him to play an increasingly honorific role and to withdraw from a publishing world which he no longer understood or found congenial. Godwin, in their opinion, was above all an editor, uninterested in finance and well aware that he was in no way equipped to run a vast and complex concern like Penguin. 'At home,' Godwin's wife Fay recalled, 'Tony talked freely and exhaustively and exhaustingly about the problems at Penguin, but at no time did I ever hear even the remotest suggestion of getting rid of Allen Lane,' but Ron Blass remembered meeting Godwin on a beach in Hawaii, *en route* to Australia, and being asked for his support in 'neutralizing' Lane on the grounds that 'You're either with us or against us.' Dieter Pevsner cites, as an example of

Godwin's lack of interest in the financial aspects of the publishing business, how he disliked working on budgets and only once took part in the annual writing down and writing off of stock, an essential if hard-hearted publishing exercise which, given his passionate attachment to his authors and their books, he found too painful to endure. Fay Godwin, on the other hand, remembers him poring over computer printouts of sales in the evenings at home, and how he often said that although he would like to spend all his time working with authors on their books, he felt he had to involve himself in the practicalities of publishing in order to best advance their interests; and Jim Cochrane recalls how Godwin urged his young editors in John Street to think of themselves as publishers, and not just as editors.

'I have always felt more grateful to Allen than to anyone else I have ever known,' Godwin wrote after his departure from Penguin. Some years later, after Godwin had left Weidenfeld for a job with Harcourt Brace in New York, he spotted Harry Paroissien, the embodiment of the old guard, in a Manhattan restaurant. 'Allen Lane: I truly loved that man,' he told his old colleague. It made a fitting conclusion to a tale of two men who had so much in common, not least in their dedication to Penguin, but were torn apart by changes in the world around them, and by the impossibility of two such strong and dominant figures coexisting within the confines of a single firm.

21. Closing Time

By the early Sixties it no longer made sense for Lane to stay on at Silverbeck. Lettice was living in London on the modest allowance he gave her; the two older girls, Clare and Christine, were grown up and making their own way in the world; Susanne Lepsius had been provided with a flat in Notting Hill Gate and was less in evidence than before; a new runway was being built at Heathrow, and all around the house trees were being felled and the ground razed in readiness. He moved instead to the Old Mill House in West Drayton, an elegant three-storeyed red-brick Georgian building perched over a stream; only a few minutes' drive from Harmondsworth, it was converted into three self-contained flats, one of which was let to the Schmollers. Weekdays were spent in the Mill House or in Whitehall Court, weekends at Priory Farm, from where he would return to the office bearing eggs for sale to the staff.

His passion for farming was stronger than ever, and he spoke to his farm manager every morning from the office. 'Don't let's exclude farming talk: it is all too long since we had a natter on such things,' he wrote to Noël Carrington. He told Frostie that after consulting his 'soothsayer' he had come to realize that the only women he thought about were Lettice and Susanne – hardly cheering news for his most devoted colleague and correspondent – and that given his enjoyment of the farm, 'I've often wondered if Susanne would really be at ease with me.' He thought Lettice would like him back, but doubted if it would work. 'We were both unhappy when we were together and are much better with each other when we have our separate lives,' he went on, adding that 'one thing I have learned about myself is that I am one who dislikes any form of ties, although I like affection and a feeling of warmth'.

Material ties were another matter, and in 1965 he bought another farm in Chapmansford in Hampshire, not far from where Carrington farmed. Larger than Priory Farm, it was, he told Carrington, 'a gem', even if the buildings were in a poor state: its 522 acres included a trout stream, a tributary of the Test, and water meadows, and he planned to concentrate on beef and barley. 'The more I see of farming, the more I like it,' he told his old colleague. The Old Mill House was owned by the firm, but the farm at Hurstbourne Priors was not the only new purchase to be funded from the sale of Penguin shares. He bought some woods near Iddesleigh in Devon, which he had come to regard as his ancestral county, and the architect Edward Samuel designed him a sunny, well-lit house on the beach at Rosscarbery, the village in County Cork where he and Susanne had spent so many summers with Bill Williams and Estrid Bannister. From there, in the summer of 1964, he wrote to Nora, who had just returned to Australia after spending three months in England. The time they had spent together had been 'the most memorable and enjoyable moments' of his life. 'I can't tell you what your coming over here has meant to me,' he told her. 'Before you arrived I was in rather a depressed state, and I don't think that I could have realized at the time that it was possible for such a perfect relationship as ours to exist.' Relations with Dick may have soured over the years, but his devotion to Nora was a reminder of how, in the old days, the intensity of feeling between Lane and his siblings had seemed like an impenetrable barrier, excluding all outsiders, Lettice included.

That same year, Lettice came back. Their lives were to remain, at best, semi-detached. They spent holidays together in Spain, taking Anna with them more often than not, and getting to know full-time ex-pats like Gerald Brenan and Bill and Annie Davies, the immensely rich American socialites and friends of Hemingway, Kenneth Tynan and Cyril Connolly; Robert Lusty went to stay at El Fénix after the death of his wife, and his gloom was alleviated by Lane's 'mercurial effervescence' and regular samplings of 'the tinto and the blanco'. Lettice steered clear of Whitehall Court and the Old Mill House and spent most of her time at Priory Farm, where she had her own self-contained quarters. Years later she told an interviewer that Lane had been 'an impossible man to get away from, and an impossible man to live with', and that she 'wouldn't have married any other man – never': but although to outsiders – including Penguin employees – she seemed funny, clever, attractive and engaging, she was often short-tempered and sarcastic towards her errant spouse. 'What do you mean by "one of my authors"?' she snapped when Lane told her that he had invited the young historian Hugh Thomas to lunch: the implication being that, as a mere paperback publisher, he was not qualified to talk in such terms.

Lane's relations with Clare and Christine were far more harmonious, though he was never a demonstrative father, shied away from displays of emotion, and was happy to leave their schooling to Lettice (much of which had been paid for by old Mrs Williams Lane, at least until Penguin went public). One or other of them often accompanied him on his journeys to the States or Australia, combining travel to exotic places with minimal office duties; racked with guilt about his treatment of Lettice and his affair with Susanne, he took Clare out to drunken dinners at the Savoy, during the course of which he told her that it was quite normal for middle-aged men to chase other women, and tried to gain her absolution; jealous of having his family broken into, he resented her falling in love with Morpurgo's stepson, Michael, and was, for a time, tricky with his new son-in-law.

He remained, in his sixties, dapper and well-dressed enough to qualify as one of the nation's Top Ten Best Dressed Men: 'How shall I dazzle my audience today?' he would ask before setting out for the office. He never wore a hat, and, when invited to John Curtis's wedding in a synagogue, he borrowed one from his gardener and asked the lady in the Penguin canteen to steam it clean; he loved his collection of cars and was an enthusiastic motorist. He combined, as ever, parsimony with sudden bouts of unexpected generosity. He retained his passion for cheap hotels and travelled economy class, and expected his employees to follow his example, but when the young John Rolfe, who joined the firm in 1960 in a junior capacity, screwed up the courage to ask whether Penguin could possibly lend him the money to put down the deposit on a house, Lane, who was just about to leave for Spain, told him he could let him have £3,000 interest-free, and that he should discuss the details with the chief accountant. The accountant knew nothing about it, and persuaded Lane to reduce the loan to £1,000: but he had the last word, and made amends by leaving Rolfe £1,000 in his will. Others in the firm benefited from Lane's generosity in this way; and the staff at large benefited when, in 1964, he started the Penguin Pension Fund, putting in £100,000 of his own money to set the scheme in motion.

Giles Gordon remembered how Lane 'was forever to be seen bustling about the fragilely partitioned eggbox compartments of the glasshouse at Harmondsworth'. His eye for detail and his perfectionist instincts were as evident as ever – he worried about the brickwork and the landscaping of the new warehouse, and instructed Malcolm Kelley, then working in the warehouse and run off his feet, to take time off to count some recently planted poplars and replace the dead ones – and in many ways he was as sharp and innovative as ever: he was one of the first publishers to introduce an automated warehouse, and for all his tirades about selling books in pubs and suchlike places, he seemed perfectly happy to see Penguins on sale in supermarkets. He still got up early every morning, and bustled off to work: he commissioned Ralph Tubbs, who had recently completed Baden-Powell House in the Cromwell Road, to design the new front offices at Harmondsworth, and the twenty-fifth anniversary of Penguin was celebrated with a long-remembered party in the aquarium at the Frankfurt Zoo – an appropriate setting, since Penguin had been one of the few British publishers to take a stand at the first Frankfurt Book Fair in 1947.

And yet he seemed, at times, detached from and adrift in a rapidly changing world. By 1967 Penguin had 488 employees *in toto*, a far cry from the Crypt or even the post-war years. Tony Mott – whose first memory of Lane was of him bursting into Harry Paroissien's office with a cry of 'I've found a little man in Slough who can turn shirt cuffs for sixpence!' – remembers bumping into him outside the newly installed computer-room, and Lane saying, 'I have no idea what those sods are doing . . .' At publishing parties in Vigo

Street he often stood alone, with his back to the wall: Patrick Wright, who had recently joined Allen Lane The Penguin Press as its solitary rep, assumed that this neatly suited figure must be Mr Lane's chauffeur, and hurried to offer him a drink. At another Vigo Street party for literary agents, Tony Mott found Lane in the lavatory, perched on a bale of lavatory paper. 'Mott,' he asked, 'who are all those people out there?' 'But, Sir Allen, you invited them . . .' 'Why the hell did I do that? I don't know any of the fuckers.' He sent Mott out for a bottle of white wine which they drained together, Lane still perched on the lavatory paper; after which they returned to the party, where Lane dazzled the assembled agents with his urbanity and charm.

Lady Chatterley's Lover, Siné's cartoons and the sacking of Tony Godwin may have hit the headlines, but, according to Godwin, much of Lane's time and energy during the 1960s was devoted to setting up an educational list, and trying to sort out the Australian end of the business. Penguin had always been an educational publisher in that Pelicans, Penguin Classics and Penguins themselves were read and studied by schoolchildren and students as well as by those in search of pleasure and information: but in the early Sixties it was decided to publish specifically for the educational market, and for schools in particular. It was, and still is, a highly competitive and specialized area of publishing, dominated by huge firms like Longmans and Oxford University Press, and employing sales techniques and methods very different from those of 'trade' publishers like Penguin: books were sold by specialist sales forces through educational suppliers rather than bookshops, and liberal use was made of inspection copies. Quite who first came up with the suggestion that Penguin should enter these dangerous waters is a matter of debate: Chris Dolley said that he put the idea in Lane's head before leaving to run the Baltimore office; Morpurgo, a rival claimant, was sceptical at first on the grounds that educational publishing was outside Penguin's area of expertise, but was seduced by dreams of becoming Lane's deputy or even heir-apparent; some have suggested that Lane was so impressed by the vast profits being made by Longmans in particular that he was determined to tap this lucrative market for himself, making full use of the Penguin name in the process. His instinctive readiness to try something new, and a sense that educational publishing represented an extension of (rather than a distraction from) Penguin's role as a public educator, coincided with changes in the world of education at all levels. Great hopes and high ideals were vested in comprehensive education, and the Penguin Education list was to exploit the new fashion for 'child-centred' textbooks; the Robbins Report of 1963 had paved the way for a huge expansion of higher education, the new 'plate-glass' universities were opening their doors, and – as an example of how a backlist title could benefit from a rapidly expanding market – the Penguin Classics edition of Vasari's *Lives of the Artists* sold 10,000 copies a year after it had been adopted by Harold Wilson's new Open University.

As early as 1961, Jack Morpurgo, then the Director General of the National Book League in Albemarle Street, had written to Lane to suggest, for no apparent reason, that he should be appointed 'a sort of Minister plenipotentiary at Cabinet level', representing Penguin's interests overseas. After leaving Penguin, Morpurgo had worked for the Falcon Press, but bills were never paid and the company was wound up after its founder, Peter Baker, was arrested for forging Sir Bernard Docker's signature. Wearing, for much of the time, 'a smouldering expression, midway between a look of pleasure and a frown', he had spent four years with the Nuffield Foundation before moving on to the NBL in 1955, where he busied himself promoting books in schools and factories and travelling over-seas. Every now and then, he tells us, Lane would call in, some-times with Susanne Lepsius, for a drink and a gossip: he told Morpurgo that he regarded him as his 'human thermometer', but vague promises – 'Jack, you've been here long enough. You're coming back to Penguins' and 'I must have a second-in-command I can trust, just in case' – were never followed up. Morpurgo's minis-terial suggestion was similarly ignored, but a year later he returned to the attack. He was, he claimed, perfectly equipped to promote educational aspects of the Penguin list in the Commonwealth and what was becoming known as the Third World; and he could effect an introduction to the Nuffield Foundation, which was keen to be involved in scientific educational textbooks in the post-sputnik world, and would far prefer to deal with a firm like Penguin than with more conventional educational publishers. The notion of Morpurgo as a peripatetic ambassador was, once again, politely ignored, but the Nuffield Foundation was of interest. Meetings were held in Albemarle Street, and although he complained that he had 'as yet nothing in writing to prove my position as the merest lackey in the courts of Harmondsworth' and worried, pointedly, that Penguin might be sold to some predator like the property developer Charles Clore, 'who would not give a twopenny damn for the security of one who was not a director', Morpurgo was allowed to describe himself as 'education adviser' on the Penguin notepaper.

Although the Science Teaching Project, sponsored by the Nuffield Foundation, was launched in 1966, Morpurgo's involvement with the Penguin Education list was mortifyingly brief. Chris Dolley attended a meeting at the NBL along with Lane, Paroissien and Bill Williams, and walked out on the grounds that Morpurgo talked 'so much twaddle' that he could bear it no longer. 'With the best grace that I know I have removed myself from the scene,' Morpurgo wrote to Lane. He had, he admitted, failed to come up with any figures to support his proposals, but had used instead 'the knowledge that comes from experience . . . surely it is to use the instinctive shortcuts which come from experience that any organization takes on seniors instead of novices!' 'I would not wish it that bitterness should seem to be the sum of my reactions,' he continued, rising to Pecksniffian heights of unctuous eloquence. 'Disappointed and, I do not deny it, resentful of the circumstances of the conclusion I may be, but there are still those within the organization (and you first among them) whom I claim among my closest friends, and still I am devoted to the *ethos* of Penguin.' Before long the friendship between the two men, such as it was, would be shattered for ever; and after Dolley's departure for the States Penguin Education was run by a 'novice' in the form of Charles Clark, whose initial interview with Lane had been devoted, exclusively, to apples and apple-growing. The Penguin Education list went on to enjoy some phenomenal sales – the Success with English series, launched in 1968 as a venture into the highly competitive English as a Foreign Language or 'ELT' market, sold some 2 million copies overseas, much to the irritation of such long-established rivals as Longmans and Macmillan – but it was a mixed blessing: launching the series was hugely expensive, contributing to the cashflow crisis of the late Sixties; and, in the early years, the educational list was not sold in the UK by a specialist sales team but by the Penguin reps, who knew little about the educational market and were distracted from their main job of selling to the shops.

One advantage of Penguin Education was that Tony Godwin was neither interested nor involved: and the same applied to Puffin Books, which had the additional bonus of appealing more to Lane's imagination, and being run by one of the people in Penguin of whom he was most fond. Eleanor Graham retired in 1961: Margaret Clark had been assured by Lane and Monty Woodhouse that she would assume the vacant seat, but Tony Godwin, only recently arrived and flexing his muscles, told her, fairly brutally, that 'You haven't a hope in hell of getting the Puffin job.' She left for The Bodley Head, but not before she had persuaded her colleagues to buy the rights in Tolkien's *The Hobbit* – Eleanor Graham had long held out against it, greeting any mention with a 'grimace of distaste' – and the post she'd been promised was offered instead to a journalist and magazine editor, Kaye Webb. Buxom, ebullient and attractive, she had been married to Ronald Searle, who had recently left her to live in France, and had worked as assistant editor of *Lilliput* and edited the *Young Elizabethan*. Lane had met her first in El Vino or Champney's, and they had taken to each other at once. 'He was so beguiling – I longed to know more about him,' she recalled, while Lane, for his part, took to ringing her with job offers and arranging lunch dates. Kaye Webb and Ronald Searle were old friends of the Godwins, and Godwin often claimed that he had suggested her for the job: devious as ever, Lane used Godwin to get rid of Margaret Clark, so clearing the way for his own favoured candidate. Kaye Webb had energy, enthusiasm and the obsessive single-mindedness of the true publisher, and she had timed her arrival to perfection: the Sixties saw a boom in children's paperbacks as they gained acceptance in schools and libraries as well as in book-shops, and the Puffin backlist grew from 150 to around 800 titles. The number of titles published by Puffin doubled in her first year, and despite growing competition from rival paperback firms, Kaye Webb persuaded other publishers, including Billy Collins and the OUP, to license books to her. She published *Mary Poppins*, Dodie Smith's *A Hundred and One Dalmatians* and the works of Roald Dahl and Philippa Pearce; she broke with Penguin tradition by publishing original fiction, including William Mayne's *A Parcel of Time* and Clive King's bestselling *Stig of the Dump*, which had been turned down by every other publisher in London. In 1967 she founded the Puffin Club, which organized competitions, outings and parties, published a quarterly *Puffin Post*, and boasted 44,000 members within two years. Lane thoroughly approved, and invited Puffin readers to barbecues on his farms; he had always liked to think of Penguin readers as members of a club, waiting for the monthly list of new publications and attending Penguin exhibitions, and Kaye Webb's initiative appealed to this side of his character. She, for her part, reciprocated his affection, pointing out to his critics that he 'was not devious or dishonest. He just avoided unpleasantness', and loyally taking his side during the travails of the Godwin era.

'Why don't you chuck up Middlesex and retire to Hobart or Perth, where life goes at the right speed?' John Betjeman once asked him. Lane shared to the full Betjeman's love of the country, but Penguin Australia was not immune to the editorial problems that had bedevilled relations with Penguin Inc.: though this time they were not of Lane's making. On a visit to Australia in 1961, he decided that the Melbourne office should be encouraged to publish locally, and not be restricted simply to importing books from England. It was a fine idea in principle, but proved harder to put into practice. While in Sydney, he invited Geoffrey Dutton, Max Harris and Brian Stonier to lunch at Nora's house to discuss how best to set about it. Cultured and well-heeled, Dutton was an estab-lished writer and a senior lecturer in English at Adelaide University who knew everyone who needed to be known in the Australian

literary world; Max Harris was a bonhomous bookseller who had
earlier edited a literary magazine entitled, appropriately enough,
Angry Penguins, wrote a regular column on bookish matters in the
Australian, and anticipated its imminent popularity by commissioning
an *Australian Wine Guide*; Stonier provided the practical publishing
experience. All three were enthused by Lane's vision, even if, as
Dutton put it, 'in the best Lane tradition, we were to do all the
work ourselves and be paid very little'. 'There was always some
excitement about Lane,' Dutton recalled, 'some promise of
impending action. With his neatness and trimness and precise movements, he reminded me of a tennis player, but the balls he hit were
words, and although they came swiftly they came softly.' An editorial meeting was held in the Melbourne offices, after which Lane
returned to England and left them to get on with it. The first batch
of Australian Penguins were published in March 1963. The penguin
on the front cover was garlanded with boomerangs on either side,
which infuriated those authors who prided themselves on being
published by an international rather than a purely Australian firm:
so much so that Patrick White rang Dutton and ordered him to
'Get rid of those fucking boomerangs!'

Despite the high hopes, the Australian publishing programme was
blighted from the beginning by resentment and suspicion between
Harmondsworth and Melbourne. Lane seemed happy to take a back
seat, reminding Stonier that 'I promised to send you duplicates of
the signs we have on our toilets here. The one for the ladies' department is obvious. The other pair, which represents variations on a
Paris street urinal theme, are meant to be fixed to both sides of the
door . . .' Godwin, on the other hand, was determined not to 'lose
our controlling ability to direct and shape the Australian list'. He
worried that Australian production and design would not come up
to Hans Schmoller's high standards, and insisted that major authors
like Patrick White, already on the Penguin list, should continue to
be published from Harmondsworth, with Penguin Australia
indenting for as many copies as they thought they could sell;
Melbourne were upset by Godwin's apparent indifference to much-
admired Australian authors like Randolph Stow, by his refusal to

commit Harmondsworth to taking sizeable orders of Australian-originated books and by his insistence that they should cost such books on the basis of likely Australian sales, and regard any orders from England as so much jam on the bread, desirable in itself but not to be relied upon. Melbourne were so infuriated by Godwin's lack of interest in Donald Horne's *The Lucky Country* that they decided to go it alone, and went on to sell 250,000 copies in Australia; when Lane came out to open Penguin Australia's new Ringwood building, Dutton persuaded him to think again, and Godwin reluctantly agreed to take 15,000 for Britain, where it was published as *Australia in the Sixties*.

Worse was to follow when Godwin wrote to say that he was starting a new series of anthologies devoted to new writing in countries around the world – 'Foreigners still begin at Calais', ran the blurb to early numbers in the series, which included Raleigh Trevelyan's excellent *Italian Writing Today* – and he asked Dutton if he would edit the Australian volume. Dutton duly sent off his selection, which included stories by Patrick White and Randolph Stow, and poems by Judith Wright, Les Murray and A. D. Hope: after an interminable delay the typescript was returned by sea mail along with a damning report by the critic Francis Hope, who pronounced the book unpublishable. 'London Insults Our Best' ran a headline in the *Australian* on learning that Godwin had rejected Dutton's anthology as being of 'far too low a standard for us to publish' and had compared it with a school magazine: it was promptly sold to Billy Collins, who published it as a Fontana paperback original. In 1965 Tony Godwin, eager to make amends, paid a visit to Australia, where he was best remembered for taking a five-mile hike at midday in a heatwave, clad in heavy boots and knee-length shorts: but by then it was too late, and Dutton, Harris and Stonier handed in their notices and went off to found Sun books, a rival paperback concern. Lane wrote them a genial letter in which he said that, under the circumstances, he would have done exactly the same himself.

It was on his visit to Australia in 1961 that Lane came up with his most famous one-liner, indicative of both his ruthlessness and his awkward embarrassment when dealing face-to-face with disagreeable situations. The decision to publish for the Australian market coincided with Dick's long-awaited departure from Penguin Australia and his resignation as a director of the parent company; Ralph Vernon-Hunt of Pan had told Lane that he expected to sell 3 million books a year in Australia, as opposed to a million Penguins, and Lane was determined to make major changes. On arrival at Sydney airport he was frisked by Customs officials looking for copies of *Lady Chatterley's Lover*, which was still banned in Australia; writing from Melbourne, he told Harry Paroissien that he was having a 'gruelling time', that the existing management was in a 'state of chaos' and that sackings at all levels were imminent or in hand; it was rumoured that two senior executives were to lose their jobs, but no one knew who had drawn the short straws. Three of the top men from Penguin Australia saw him to the airport for his flight back to Britain, and still nothing had been said: but then, in the departure lounge – or, better still, at the foot of the steps leading up to the aeroplane itself – Lane turned to his escorts, said, 'You're out, you're in, you're out, and I'm off,' and hurried away to take his seat. According to some reports, Ron Blass had accompanied Lane to Australia, and was ordered to stay behind and sort out the mess: whatever the truth of the matter, it was on a trip back from Australia with Ron Blass that Lane enjoyed or endured the one real adventure of his life.

Dark-haired, tough and genial, not unlike one of the Kray twins in appearance at least, Ron Blass had no literary or social pretensions, and had started his working life with Penguin before the war as a van-driver. Lane had been impressed by the orderly and logical way in which he packed and unpacked the bales of books, and after the war, which he spent in the Navy, he returned to Penguin to work in the warehouse. He rose from being warehouse manager to sales director: he may not have read any of the books he housed and despatched, but he knew every aspect of the business, was nimble at doctoring booksellers' orders in an upward direction, was a brilliant negotiator with the firm's biggest accounts, so much so that Penguin continued to dominate the trade throughout the Sixties, and seemed happy to be used as a hatchet-man, summoning those about to be sacked to lunch at the nearby Berkeley Arms. In his sombre dark suits and crisp white shirts, he was very much one of Lane's cronies, sitting over long lunches in the directors' dining-room at Harmondsworth, trading gossip and innuendo in the febrile world of office politics and, according to Richard Holme, indulging in long, maudlin conversations on death and suicide; but he was also, unlike Harry Paroissien, on good terms with the jeans-wearing, open-necked Godwinites in John Street and Vigo Street. An enthu-siastic drinker, he liked nothing better than the occasional jaunt overseas; and, from Lane's point of view, he made a perfect travel-ling companion.

In the autumn of 1962 the two men went together on a business trip to Australia. Their business done in Melbourne, they spent a few days on the Great Barrier Reef before moving on to South Africa, via Mauritius; Lane, who had complained of boredom in Australia, suggested that they should break their journey home in Kenya, and spend a few days on safari. They hired a car in Nairobi, bought a cheap map of the country, and headed off to the Tsavo National Park, where other tourists were perched on Land Rovers, drinking gin and tonics and waiting for the animals to appear. This did little to alleviate Lane's boredom, so they drove on, spotting two foxes and a rabbit as they went. 'Well,' Lane told his travelling companion, 'I don't go much on this safari lark.' After passing a waterfall and two elephants, they came to a bridge bearing a notice which read 'No Crossing'. Using their fingers to calculate distance on the sixpenny map, they worked out that if they ignored the notice and headed on for another seventy miles, they would reach Malindi, on the Indian Ocean. Lane took the wheel, picking his way past a rhino and a giraffe, and before long they had lost all sense of time or direction. They drove into a dried-up gulch, and were trying to reverse their way out when they were deluged by a torrential trop-ical storm, and the car was up to its axles in sticky black mud. They decided to walk to the nearest village: Lane took his diary and a pencil, and Blass a packet of cigars, but they left everything else in the car, including their coats and their money. 'Don't worry,' Lane told his companion, 'round the next corner there'll be a melon stall,' but his optimism was misplaced. Gazelles and giraffes were their only companions as they squelched through the mud, and a wild pig ran in circles round them for mile after mile. Parched with thirst, they smashed open some coconuts and drank the milk. Blass, who was leading the way, tried to distract Lane's attention from some large feline footprints, but there was 'No need for you to do that, Ron – I saw them a long way back!' By now it was getting dark: Blass lit a fire, Lane wrote his diary, and, in the distance, the drums began to beat. 'I'm glad I'm here with you,' Lane told Blass. 'I'd rather be here with you than with anyone.'

They woke before dawn next day and resumed their walk. Their tongues had begun to swell from thirst, and they were beginning to lose heart when 'out from the trees came three of the blackest-looking people you've ever seen, pushing bicycles'. Lane was mounted on one bike and Blass on another, and somehow they were separated: Blass, very much a man of his time, fully expected to be put in a pot and eaten, but much to his relief he caught up with Lane in a nearby village of straw huts, where he found his leader drinking Fanta with the local chieftain. They were given eggs to eat, their socks were washed, and they were told that at midday a lorry was due on its weekly trip to Malindi. The two publishers scrambled into the front with the driver, pots, chickens and locals were crammed in the back, and they made their way, very slowly, to Malindi, where they booked into a hotel on the beach, had a shave and a meal, cabled the office to report their whereabouts, and flew on to Mombasa the following day in an elderly Dakota. Back in Nairobi, Lane held a party to celebrate, with champagne for the hotel staff.

The two safari-lovers went their own ways at Rome airport: Lane claimed to be in need of a holiday and headed off to the villa in Spain, while Blass went back to the office. In due course a Mr Gosling of the East African Automobile Association wrote to say that the abandoned Peugeot had been discovered, and that all their possessions were on their way back to England, along with some samples of the black mud in which the car had bogged down; Lane sent Chief Ishmael Kenga of Malindi a parcel of books in return for his help and hospitality, and ordered a copy of J. H. Patterson's classic *The Man-Eaters of Tsavo* for his travelling companion. 'They tell me you have been doing your safari on the handles of a push-bike,' Noël Carrington remarked. 'I call that trying to keep up with Collins, who went to bed with Elsa the Lioness, presumably to give her better publicity.' Billy Collins had indeed made a fortune from *Born Free*, and years later it was revealed that he had shared a bed with Joy Adamson, its formidable author.

Although he was never seen by Lane as an heir-apparent, their African adventures strengthened Blass's position in the court of Harmondsworth: he became Lane's closest confidant, a substitute son who drove him home after work and stopped off *en route* for a drink and a gossip as well as acting, when necessary, as both spy and hatchet-man. Lane continued to tantalize himself and others with talk of stepping down or taking a back seat, while his loyal retainers, never too sure where the future lay, jostled for position. Writing to congratulate Lord Beaverbrook on his eighty-fifth birthday, he recalled how, over dinner with Stanley Morison a year or two earlier, the press baron had told them how he kept out of the office as much as possible, but retained control through his senior executives. 'I cannot pretend that I have taken things so far myself, but since I saw you I have kept away from the office as much as possible, and I have found that far from losing touch I have a greater sense of personal control,' he told Beaverbrook ('I am very flattered to think that advice of mine may have played a small part in building up that immense organization you have imprinted on London,' the Beaver courteously replied). Bill Williams believed that after the battles with Godwin, 'Allen's buoyancy and resilience were not as effective and confident as they had once been, and for the first time in my long friendship with him I was becoming aware that he had had enough': but although a large part of Lane quite genuinely believed that, as he endlessly assured friends and colleagues, he longed to 'say goodbye to the rat race', he had, in the last resort, no wish to give up. When Chris Dolley accused him of having no inten-tion of retiring, or appointing an heir-apparent, Lane replied, 'Why should I? Let them sort it out when I am dead,' and he once told

Charles Clark that 'very few firms survive the death of their founder': Morpurgo, anxious to present Lane in his last years as a lonely, embittered figure, suggested that 'bitterness calcified his habitual indecisiveness, so that it was no longer a matter of his failing to make up his mind about what should happen to Penguin after his death. He just did not care.'

Despite the Woodhouse fiasco, he retained his fascination with Conservative politicians. 'I wondered whether circumstances would ever permit you to think of joining us in the expansion of the educational side,' he asked Edward Boyle, a portly, pink-faced and heavily chalk-striped former Minister of Education who combined patrician origins with liberal views and had stoutly defended the cause of comprehensive schools. In the spring of 1965 Boyle wrote, 'with considerable diffidence', to ask if he could possibly take up Lane's offer, since life on the Opposition benches was not proving too onerous. 'Do forgive me for writing, and if this letter finds its way into the w.p. basket, it will be only what I deserve,' he wrote. Unable to resist such self-deprecation, Lane appointed Boyle a member of the Penguin Board, and made him a trustee of his charitable trust, the Allen Lane Charitable Foundation, set up in the 1960s to help the underprivileged, including the deaf and the mentally handicapped, and to fund archaeological expeditions and the publication of books by young writers. Although he only came in twice a week, Boyle was scrupulous about attending meetings, briefly held the fort at ALPP after Godwin's departure, made his views known on editorial and publishing matters, and was popular and well-regarded by old guard and iconoclasts alike: even Harry Paroissien, never easily won round, found him 'most impressive in a quiet way'.

Boyle was a valuable addition, but he was a part-time Penguin, and was neither an heir-apparent nor a managing director in the making. More often than not, Lane confided his worries to Frostie, who was no longer working for the firm and took a dim view of Godwin and his cohorts. Who, he wondered from Spain in December 1966, just as the Godwin crisis was coming to a head, should be the new managing director? Neither Godwin nor Hans Schmoller was

keen; Paroissien 'badly wants it, but is quite unfitted for it'; he had
been talking to Arthur Crook, but 'I wonder if the ability to control
a staff of under a dozen can have fitted him to cope with our varied
assortment of bods?' Eight days later he was once again in touch:
Arthur Crook would like to join 'if he felt he would eventually step
into my shoes – but could he?' He couldn't see Boyle as a 'day-to-
day boss' – but what about Mike Randall of the *Daily Mail*? 'What
I find so difficult is having to explain how and why I am so redundant, and at pre-retirement age, too,' the fifty-one-year-old Frostie
replied, adding that she felt helpless as she watched 'you spinning
round from person to person', and worried about 'vulgarization' and
the 'abdication of standards' in the firm. In the meantime, a comic
example of talking at cross-purposes was provided by the granitic
figure of Lord Reith. Reith had been casting about for a role in life
ever since leaving the BBC, and in 1963 Robert Lusty, then a
Governor of the BBC, suggested to him that he should talk to Lane
about the future of Penguin. It was agreed that Lusty should pick
up Reith from his offices in the Great West Road – he was then
the Chairman of British Oxygen – and that they should travel on
together to Harmondsworth. Lusty was late, and Reith was in a foul
mood as they made their way to Lane's office. But any ill temper
was soon blown away by Lane, who was at his most charming and
gave the old curmudgeon a tour of the offices and the warehouse,
followed by lunch in the directors' dining-room. Reith was very
taken with his host, but somewhat surprised not to hear from him
again. 'Having so much enjoyed my visit to you, I had hoped that
I would have seen you before the long time that has passed,' he eventually wrote to Lane; and to Lusty he memoed, 'I have heard nothing
from that fellow Lane. I thought he wanted me to take it over.' But,
according to Lusty, there was a further twist to this tale of mutual
misunderstanding: assuming that Reith still exercised influence at the
BBC, Lane thought he had called to offer him a governorship, and
was puzzled to hear no more about it.

Not long before his downfall, Tony Godwin spent an evening
with Lane at the Old Mill House. They downed glass after glass of
white wine, and by half-past eleven Lane was well away. Godwin

had matched him glass for glass, but managed to stay comparatively sober; and later he wrote a chilling account of how, as the evening progressed, Lane made no effort to disguise his 'terrible contempt' for his colleagues, and for his most loyal lieutenant in particular. Bill Williams had earlier referred to 'poor miserable old Harry' as being 'spiritless, ineffective and supine' and 'overpaid and over-indulged for years': although Godwin himself thought Paroissien 'totally subservient', he was shocked by Lane's 'ruthless denigration of Harry on both personal and professional levels' – and equally shocked to learn how pitifully little the most loyal retainer of all, Eunice Frost, had earned over the years. Godwin was 'horrified' by this unwelcome glimpse of a character once summarized by Morpurgo as 'pathologically disloyal': what, he wondered, 'had given him this terrifying rancorous contempt for people'? Lane always retained a 'tremendously disciplined public persona', and he never let the mask slip again, at least in Godwin's presence: but it had provided a foretaste of what lay ahead for Godwin himself.

Whatever Lane's opinions in private, two of the old guard remained in harness: although he told Dick that Paroissien had been 'a great disappointment to me, and quite incapable of making up his mind on important issues', his long-serving lieutenant was made joint managing director with Chris Dolley after Godwin's dismissal in 1967; and Schmoller would remain with the firm for the rest of his working life, grumbling about the covers while applying to the texts the same high standards as ever. Frostie was no more than a sympathetic ear, but Bill Williams lingered on in the wings, worrying about his health and his pension and what the future held when the time came for him to retire from the Arts Council. Though no longer actively involved in Penguin affairs, he was, he had told Lane in the spring of 1963, thrilled that his old friend still wanted him to 'stick around', still more so since his salary would drop by some £4,000 a year when he left the Arts Council at the end of the year. Two years later, after suffering a stroke and a mild heart attack, he wrote to Paroissien to say that he was 'angry and appalled' by rumours that he had had to retire due to ill health; eager to prove that he was still in the swim, he wrote from New York to say that he had lunched with Victor Weybright, who was 'fatter than ever, and evidently propelled by some insatiable demon', and when he learned that Lane and Lord Goodman were considering a bid for an ITV franchise, he begged to be put on the board, since 'I know quite a lot about TV.' Throat cancer struck next, and although he was to outlive Lane by seven years, his eloquent, well-written letters struck a nostalgic, valedictory note. 'I accept the inevitable twilight, and feel nothing but thankfulness,' he told Lane at the end of a long letter in which he looked back to 'the enlightened boozing in the old Barcelona; the tantrums, the tears, the resignations', and declared, once again, how the two of them had 'a kinship together, almost (even) a twinship. We have separate identities, but we belong to the same totem, and I believe both of us have been conscious of that bond. I can only say that for you, as for no other man, I have always recognized and cherished a profound and abiding affection . . .' Such effusions had been frequent enough in the past, but this particular letter had been written in response to one from Lane himself, in which he too had waxed lyrical about their long association. Writing from Spain, he told a gratified Williams that he had been thinking of the old days, and their lunches at the Barcelona:

You know and I know exactly how much you have influenced both the enterprise and me over this period. I don't think either of us could have visualized what it was going to become, but both of us having a good streak of idealism and a certain toughness of purpose have made it very much in our own image. What happens after our time is beyond our control. As good gardeners or farmers we can only do our best to see that the soil is kept in good heart, free of weeds, and that the crops are not forced but allowed a natural growth in the knowledge that if these principles are followed our successors will continue to have the satisfaction from it that we have had ourselves.

No doubt he had particular individuals and types of book in mind when he referred to weeds and the forcing of crops, and these unwelcome developments had provoked an outburst of nostalgia: in the meantime, 'what I have valued most has been the close friendship we have enjoyed over these many years, and I look forward to many more years of companionship when we can sit and drink and talk of life and love'.

For all the talk of totems and twinship, Williams still liked to think of Lane as a philistine businessman, ill-at-ease with things of the mind and the finer effusions of the human spirit. Anthony Blond remembers how Lane's 'eyes glazed' when congratulated on a recent Pelican, and how Williams said, 'Now you've upset him. Don't you know he can't read?', which may have been meant as an affectionate joke but seems almost too insulting to be true; Richard Hoggart, a more reliable witness, described a meeting in Williams's office in St James's Square to discuss a donation from Lane to Hoggart's Centre for Contemporary Studies at Birmingham University, and how, after producing a bottle of hock from 'a well-stocked cupboard incorporated into his desk', Williams turned to Lane and said, 'Oh, give him what he wants, Allen. You've made a fortune by riding cultural change without understanding it.' Whatever his understanding, Lane was shrewd enough to know a good thing when he saw it: after Tony Godwin suggested that a Lowry painting which hung in the directors' dining-room might be presented to Bill Williams as a leaving present, since he was known to admire it, the picture suddenly vanished, reappearing soon after on the walls of the Old Mill House. Not unnaturally, Lane resented being patronized: Bruce Hepburn, a successful and popular sales manager, fell from grace when, during the course of an editorial meeting, he turned to Lane and said, apropos some literary matter, 'You wouldn't understand that, Sir Allen.'

Whereas Bill Williams combined condescension with clear-headedness, in that he never wanted or expected to be more than a right-hand man, Morpurgo patronized Lane while cherishing delusions of grandeur that combined self-importance and pathos in equal measure. Several times, in the years after Lane's death, he claimed to have been the heir-apparent – or, as he put it, 'the Prince of Wales'. 'I believe that I was the only person who was brought to the walls of Caernarvon Castle twice, the second time in the Sixties when, in the role of potential successor, I attended several sales and editorial meetings, at least once as Chairman,' he told Steve Hare, striking an appropriate note of bathos as he did so. In his perceptive but self-serving biography of Lane he claims the 'dubious distinction of being the only man who twice mounted the steps and twice was tripped before he reached the throne'. 'On the first occasion,' he informed *New Statesman* readers, 'I was pulled back before I was proclaimed; on the second I was presented to the populace – then pushed into the moat. Allen Lane never forgave me for knowing how to swim – which seems to confirm Williams's opinion that he was a sadist.' No member of the 'populace' can recall Morpurgo being presented to them from the walls of Caernarvon Castle, or anywhere else for that matter: no doubt it was as spurious as Morpurgo's repeated claim to have been 'one of Allen Lane's very few confidants'.

Morpurgo's expectations, unrealistic as they always were, may have become inflamed when Clare Lane fell in love with his stepson Michael, then at Sandhurst and later to achieve fame as a writer of children's books. As it turned out, the young couple's decision to get married had quite the opposite effect. Far from cementing Morpurgo's tenuous foothold in the firm, it drove the two men irrevocably apart, so much so that, according to Morpurgo, they never spoke again: much to Lane's relief, no doubt, since he had come to loathe Morpurgo, and was glad to see the back of him at last. In Morpurgo's version of events, set down in his biography and elaborated in his memoirs, Harry Paroissien took him out to lunch, at Lane's request, and during the meal Morpurgo was informed that, on the basis of his salary at the National Book League, he could afford to give the newly-weds an annual allowance of £2,000 a year, which Lane would then match. Morpurgo was so infuriated by the suggestion that he, 'a salaried book-trade administrator and modestly successful author', should be expected to stump up the same amount as a publishing millionaire that he let out a cry of, 'To hell with you both, and to the lowest circles of Hell with Allen Lane!', stormed out of the restaurant and, on the grounds that he had sullied their friendship, never spoke to Lane again. The whole episode, he declared, was typical of Lane's 'zest for labyrinthine machination and the cowardice which made him prefer the use of hired assassins to face-to-face confrontation'. And with that Morpurgo disappeared from the Penguin story, resurfacing only when he wrote Lane's life some years after his subject's death. He left the National Book League in 1969 to become the Professor of American History at Leeds University: Robert Lusty, who commissioned the biography at Hutchinson, was considered by Lane to be 'about my oldest friend on this side of the Atlantic, apart from Bill', but it may be that he had no idea of Lane's real opinion of his former colleague.

Towards the end of Godwin's time, Lane had, in a deliberate attempt to reassert his control over editorial matters, paid Robert Lusty at Hutchinson £25,000 for the paperback rights in Svetlana Stalin's *Twenty Letters to a Friend*, buying the book over the phone without consulting anybody else; and after Godwin's departure, he infuriated his young left-wing editors by agreeing with Charles Pick of Heinemann that Penguin would publish the simultaneous paperback edition of Randolph and Winston Churchill's account of the Six Day War. For a time there was a stalemate, with the editors refusing to work on the book, but in the end Lane got his way: like a pre-war Penguin Special, the book was co-published within ten days of delivery of the typescript, and the first printing of the paperback amounted to 100,000 copies. Godwin's inheritance was, in part, being dismantled. David Pelham from *Harper's Bazaar* was appointed to look after fiction jackets ('If you're going to make changes, change 'em now. Chop!' Lane told him). Lane and Harry Paroissien had wanted to close down Allen Lane The Penguin Press, but Charles Clark persuaded them to think again, and he was deputed to run both ALPP and Penguin Education; and although Lane worried that Harry Paroissien was showing his age and seemed unable to deal with the younger generation, life seemed to have recovered much of its old flavour. To the historian Paul Addison, who met him at this time, he seemed to exude a sense of power, not unlike Sir Magnus Donners in Anthony Powell's 'Dance to the Music of Time', but he was never a pompous tycoon: he went on holiday to Morocco with Nora and his cousin Joan Collihole, smoked some hash, and was too dazed the following day to read a page of his book; meeting the recently knighted Rupert Hart-Davis for the first time since the death of Sir Rupert's third wife, the former Ruth Simon, 'he flung his arms round me and kissed me – in the Garrick Club, much to the amazement of the other members'. When visiting Joan Collihole and her sister Evelyn in Devon he seemed happy to hang about the kitchen or go shopping, lugging the groceries back by hand; *Dixon of Dock Green* was his favourite television programme, perhaps because its hero, played by Jack Warner, looked rather like him; he had a fish-tank in his office, and when his daughter Christine asked him what he did all day, he told her that he'd sit there 'with my feet on the desk and watch the fish'.

But no sooner had Penguin life improved than his health let him down. 'Why are you so scared by death and dissolution?' Frostie asked him after he had been laid low by an attack of jaundice in the early Sixties. 'I suppose because you are coming to it all rather late in life, and as one who has hardly known what it is to be ill.' In due course he had more reason to be scared. In July 1968 he wrote to Frostie to say that, far from being in Spain as expected, he was incarcerated in the Middlesex Hospital. 'In general terms,' he told her, 'it's innards towards the bottom end.' The diagnosis of bowel cancer seemed horribly appropriate: it was always said in the office that Lane's favourite book was F. A. Hornibrook's *The Culture of the Abdomen: The Cure of Obesity and Constipation etc.*, published by Heinemann in 1924, and when the poet and translator James Michie, then the editorial director of Heinemann, was taken to lunch at the Zoo to discuss the possibility of a job at Penguin, they talked about the weather for most of the meal until, at the coffee stage, Lane leaned forward and urged upon him the importance of regular bowel movements and the passing of a daily 'stool'. Kaye Webb wrote to say that she felt sick when Edward Boyle broke the news at an editorial meeting: she admired Lane for being so 'reticent and unfussy', but reminded him that 'people who love you will want to be fussing'. 'You must try to be the best, fastest-healing, miracle patient they've ever had,' she told him; nor need he worry about the office, 'because we'll work even harder . . .'

Lane's courage in dealing with what proved to be a fatal illness, and his reluctance to have attention drawn to his plight, provoked widespread admiration. 'Your stamina and your resolution will soon restore you to your usual volcanic form,' wrote Bill Williams: a month later, on his way to Lake Como, he wished that Lane could come with him 'so that we two wise old soldiers could sit in the sun and ruminate upon our campaigns and adventures'; Lane, for his part, told his old friend how much he had 'appreciated your visits to this rather dismal cell. Having enjoyed rude health up to the present time, it comes a bit hard to face some of the problems of mortality.' Lettice rang the hospital, and was surprised to learn that he was sitting up in bed and asking for newspapers: he was, she told Frostie, doing well but he had become very thin and 'looks about half of himself'. 'I sometimes think you must think I am very callous about Allen,' she went on, suspecting perhaps that her tone might seem insufficiently sympathetic, 'but he is so much part of me that the cruel part of me exactly fits him – I can exorcize myself through him.'

Among the members of staff who appeared at the Middlesex bearing flowers and chocolates was a new fiction editor named Judith Burnley. She had met Lane in Spain, when she was working on a woman's magazine: she had told him of her interest in short stories, and after her arrival at Penguin he had encouraged her to start a new series, Penguin Short Stories, which appeared four times a year over the next three years, and included work by established authors and novices, Shiva Naipaul among them: Tom Maschler had published new plays in the New English Dramatists, and Tony Godwin had planned to publish a hardback fiction list, but this constituted Penguin's first foray into original adult fiction since *Penguin New Writing*. Another, much older beneficiary of Lane's editorial hunches was also in touch: writing from Majorca, Robert Graves told Lane that he had 'always been deep in debt to Penguins, and to you personally: especially for commissioning *The Greek Myths*'. Figures from his past were always welcome, but Lane retained his interest in the present: Robert Hutchison, one of Godwin's young editors in John Street – Godwin had appointed him religious books editor after Hutchison told him he was prepared to give God 'the benefit of the doubt' – visited him in the Middlesex shortly after Mick Jagger had performed in an open-air concert in Hyde Park, and Lane was keen to hear all about it.

Lettice Lane once said of her husband's last three years that 'he had his hell here and now – it was horrible', and although he put on a brave face and still talked about the future, his involvement with the day-to-day running of Penguin could not continue as before. Reporting to Frostie from the Middlesex on an outbreak of civil war between old guard and Young Turks, he said that 'As far as I'm concerned, I've had enough, and have no intention of going back to the office. One could go on battling, but to what purpose? It's been a great adventure, best at the start when it was all a bit of a lark, but good too as the pattern began to form and we blossomed out in so many directions.' Of course he went back once he'd been let out, but not with the same energy or enthusiasm; and although Paroissien had proved a broken reed, he seemed happy enough to leave matters in the ambitious hands of Chris Dolley. A bouncing, ebullient figure with a permanent tan and a melon-shaped grin on his face, Dolley was keen on modern management techniques, knew about cashflow and budgets, and despised Penguin non-fiction editors in particular as unworldly, donnish 'red moles', middle-class sympathizers with the 1968 student revolts who had no understanding of business and no sense of financial responsibility, and wasted valuable resources publishing Maoist tracts and revolutionary handbooks, of which Carlos Marighela's *For the Liberation of Brazil*, with its bomb-making tips, was the most cited example; he believed that Penguin was being 'used as a soap-box', and nowhere more so than in the Latin American Library, edited by Richard Gott, with its books about South American radical priests and the followers of Che Guevara. Most of the Penguin editors returned his disdain in full, regarding him as a wide boy and a philistine, only interested in profit-and-loss accounts and moved by the dispiriting disciplines of the publishing accountant. They would have liked him even less had they known that while still in Baltimore he had urged an increasingly desperate Lane to sack the 'Gang of Three', and that Lane had begged him to come back and run Penguin.

Dolley's detractors, of whom there were many, were convinced that only death prevented Lane from becoming disillusioned with his new protégé; but for the time being he was happy to allow him his head. Dolley's subsequent claims that Penguin was in dire financial straits when he took command in the autumn of 1968 were certainly exaggerated – the firm remained in the black throughout the late 1960s, and the number of copies sold rose by 1.5 million a year between 1964 and 1970, with the biggest increase shown in 1969 – but he was right in his belief that the systems used were no longer adequate for running a firm of its size and complexity. According to Bill Williams, Lane 'never quite grasped the niceties of budgeting or the tidal mysteries of cashflow', but he was not unique in this respect among publishers of his generation, most of whom placed more faith in shrewdness and native wit than in the abstractions of accountants and management consultants. According to Dolley, there were no financial controls or management accounts; there was a negative cashflow, the warehouse was clogged with unsaleable books, suppliers could not be paid, and there was an overdraft of £600,000 at the bank (which was hardly unusual or surprising, since publishers inevitably have money paid out in the form of advances and production bills, and it takes time for the tide to flow back from booksellers and wholesalers). Margins had been steadily eroded since Godwin's arrival: books were under-priced and over-printed, with unbusinesslike editors committing the cardinal publishing sin of printing too many copies in order to get the low prices they were after. The huge investment involved in setting up Penguin Education had been a steady drain on funds, and – in Dolley's opinion – ALPP had been an expensive failure, producing books that sold modestly in hardback and had, for the most part, little paperback potential. After comparing costs with Ralph Vernon-Hunt, he realized that Penguin was paying more than its competitors for paper, typesetting, printing and binding, so reducing the margins still further; large advances had made matters even worse. He negotiated an immediate loan of a million pounds from the bank; margins on new books were increased and print-runs reduced, and Hans Schmoller was asked to renegotiate terms with the firm's suppliers.

Lane agreed that there had been far too much over-printing, but was too ill to be fully involved. He had always been keen to keep Penguin prices as low as possible, and his old-fashioned idealism had manifested itself in 1964 when Jim Callaghan, as Chancellor of the Exchequer, appealed to industry to exercise price restraint. 'You've heard what the Chancellor has said,' Lane told a pricing meeting. 'We're going to exercise price restraint. It's in the country's interest, and I think we should do it.' Lane's public-spiritedness may have cost Penguin dearly, since price increases were, for some years, pegged to 1964 levels. His words are touchingly evocative of a vanished world, ignorant of cashflow, management accounts and the stock control systems now being imposed by Dolley, Ray Maskery, the chief accountant, and John Rolfe: one has the sense of two different perceptions of life, one representing the past and the other the future, passing in a haze of mutual incomprehension.

Frostie, of course, was unimpressed by all she had heard of Dolley. 'I feel a deep sense of exhaustion at the thought of yet another palace upset in the cause of this succession fever,' she wrote. 'On what grounds is *he* likely to be the answer?' she wanted to know. 'What about Harry's expectations and situation? What qualities has CD got that are a *real* improvement on the two Tonys [Godwin and Walker]?' Lane was, she suggested, merely pretending to 'face a situation you don't want to face at all. You *insisted* on having your way in picking the Tonys even though all they stood for was so plainly wrong, and tagging after them was difficult enough for almost all their colleagues.'

Whatever Frostie's reservations, Dolley was in charge, and still more so when Harry Paroissien finally bowed out: but Lane's 'succession fever' was far from over, and became all the more heated when Robert Maxwell told his fellow MP Edward Boyle that he 'was only biding his time before having a go'. Richard Hoggart came up with a scheme whereby a consortium of universities would buy the shares in Penguin for two-thirds of their market value to ensure 'continuity of control and a guarantee that no quick profit would be made by anyone'; Lord Goodman bustled to and fro, and a meeting was held with Hoggart, Alan Bullock, Isaiah Berlin, Asa Briggs and other eminent academics, but although such a plan tickled Lane's vanity and his sense that Penguin was not a publishing firm like any other, it ground to a halt when it became apparent that individual universities could not guarantee to stay in the scheme. There was a suggestion that OUP and CUP should jointly acquire Penguin: more seriously, there were renewed discussions with Heinemann and the Thomas Tilling group, and – or so it was claimed after Lane's death – with Mark Longman, whose family firm had merged in 1968 with Pearson's, the owners of the *Financial Times*, to form Pearson Longman Ltd; Paul Hamlyn's pink Rolls-Royce was seen parked outside the Old Mill House, but he came to discuss a possible role in the firm rather than a takeover. Despite Lane's unhappy dealings with American publishers and his worries about British publishers being bought up by their American rivals, he seemed unconcerned when McGraw-Hill bought shares in the firm. 'You're welcome! Most welcome!' he told its President, Shelton Fisher, and before long McGraw-Hill had increased its holding in Penguin from 10 to 17 per cent. But even as the corporate publishers hovered in the wings, part of him wished that some way could be found for Christine and David Teale to be involved in the future running of the firm, young as they both were.

Lane's fiftieth anniversary as a publisher was marked with a flurry of dinners, speeches and presentations. Old Penguin, embodied in Noël Carrington, Bill Williams, Frostie, Eleanor Graham, Nikolaus Pevsner, Max Mallowan and E. V. Rieu, presented him with a painting of Priory Farm by S. R. Badmin, one of the artists featured in the post-war Puffin Picture Books (it was agreed that a John Piper would be too expensive); a publishers' dinner was held at the Garrick, graced by Robert Lusty, Bill Williams, Harold Raymond, Ian Parsons of Chatto, Hamish Hamilton, Arthur Crook, Billy Collins, Edmund Segrave, Desmond Flower, Jock Murray, Fred Warburg and Edward Young. Despite a recent admission that 'I'm not a very intelligent man, and I've really got away with murder', he was made a

Companion of Honour: he was too ill to receive it in person, but congratulations flowed in from Lord Thomson of Fleet, Harold Raymond, Agatha Christie and Baroness Budberg, who assured 'darling Allen' that 'H. G. [Wells] always said it was the best one'. Edward Boyle arranged a vast and formal dinner in the House of Commons, attended by, among others, Harold Evans, Lord Goodman, Kenneth Clark, Max Reinhardt, Norah Smallwood, Noël Carrington, Elliott Viney, Edward Young, John Lehmann and J. H. Plumb, who had been appointed Penguin's history advisory editor in 1961: the assembled throng was treated to a speech of mind-boggling pomposity by the don and civil servant Lord Redcliffe-Maude, a fellow-Bristolian, who spoke at length about his time at Eton and his experiences as the High Commissioner in Basutoland before admitting that he loathed paperbacks and only read them as a last resort.

Rather more to Lane's taste was a party at Vigo Street, suggested by Ethel Mannin and restricted to such old friends as Joan Coles (she who had first suggested the name Penguin), Ben Travers, Norman Clackson of sailing fame, Bill Williams, Frostie, Edmund Segrave, Bob Lusty, Christina Foyle and Peggy Rafferty, the proprietor of the Duke of York in Iddesleigh, where Lane was the patron and founder of the darts league. Having suggested the idea, Ethel Mannin was unable to attend. Writing to apologize, she revealed how far she had travelled from the advanced ideas of her youth. 'That's an incredibly dirty book The Bodley Head published, *My Father and Myself*,' she remarked of J. R. Ackerley's classic memoir. 'I wondered if you'd read it? I know anything goes nowadays, but the physical details are the very, very end, even in this post-Lady Chatterley era of depravity . . .'

Among other absentees were Kingsley Martin, who had just died, and J. B. Priestley, who a year or two earlier had expressed his regret that his relations with Penguin had not been as happy as they might have been. 'I always had the feeling that somebody there – certainly not you, and not Billy Williams, who is a friend of mine – was against me and my work: perhaps one of Dr Leavis's pupils,' he had written, bearing in mind, perhaps, the large number of Leavisites who had contributed to Boris Ford's multi-volume Pelican Guide to English Literature: back in the Fifties, both Lane and Williams had been keen to publish a Priestley Companion – 'Allen Lane is as ardent as I am about the pro-Priestley campaign,' Williams had told him – but matters had ground to a halt when Priestley's agent A. D. Peters ('a pretty tough nut', in Lane's opinion) insisted on an advance of £1,000 rather than the £500 offered to other authors in the series. Peters would certainly have been among the guests at a huge party held at Stationers' Hall. 'I'm all for lumping the lot, publishers, booksellers, critics, literary agents, printers and authors into one gigantic binge with lashings of good grub and booze and calling it a day,' Lane told Bill Williams, adding that what he dreaded above all else were 'pompous speeches'; and, ill and frail as he was, he stood by the door of the Stationers' Hall, shaking hands with an interminable stream of well-wishers. Lane's sentimentality, and his sense of the symbolic occasion, seldom let him down, and on 23 April 1969, exactly fifty years after he had joined The Bodley Head, Penguin finally published *Ulysses* in paperback. The advance – £75,000 – was the highest yet paid by a paperback publisher in this country: but the book had sold 420,000 copies by the end of the following year, and the wheel had come full circle.

Gratifying as it might be to meet John Gross and Stephen Spender to discuss the possibility of his backing a successor to *Encounter*, lunch with fellow-tycoons like Israel Sieff and Max Rayne, and put up the money needed to endow the Morison Room in the Cambridge University Library, given over to Stanley Morison's papers and work-in-progress, Lane was well aware that, though still only in his sixties, time was running out. His time in hospital had made him realize that his 'hold on life is on a leasehold basis and not a freehold, and that the tenancy is due to run out in the foreseeable future'; after one of his monthly lunches with Bill Williams, then recovering from his throat cancer, he told Dick that 'Our old pals are popping off like flies, and I realize that I now know more people on the other side than I do here.' He looked back with nostalgia to the old days and colleagues who no longer worked for the firm. He asked Bill Williams to write a history of Penguin, urging him,

three weeks before his death, to make it a top priority; he had lunch
with Edward Young to discuss a collection of reminiscences, and
asked Dick if he would make a contribution; although Kaye Webb
was not keen to reprint Eleanor Graham's slow-selling *Story of Jesus*,
he asked her to slip it through. 'I often think that our old and well-
weathered friendship deserves a bit of life together: talking, talking,
talking about what we have learned from so much living,' Bill
Williams told him; and they would sit for long hours together in
the garden at Priory Farm, drinking white wine and poring over
the past. He had had enough of city life, he told Williams, and was
happy to spend his days at Priory Farm: but he was constantly in
and out of hospital, and for the last year of his life a nurse lived in
at the farm, while Ron Blass bought him a second-hand Rolls-
Royce, large enough for him to lie down in the back. After a visit
to the Middlesex, Lettice told Frostie that he wouldn't allow her to
change his dressings: 'I really can't be of any use, except as a snappy
companion – and, after all, he has got Nora . . .' Frostie, devoted
as ever, sent him postcard views of Edwardian Bristol during his
last illness, as if she was steering him home.

'I am still making progress, but it will be some months before I
am completely mobile,' Lane wrote to Dick in February 1970, adding
that he had been thinking of taking a set of rooms in Albany, where
the three brothers had lived all those years before; a few days later
he wrote again to say that he would arrange for Cliff Bosley, his
chauffeur, to meet Dick when he arrived at Southampton on the
Canberra in May, and that although he was back in bed he was planning a trip to Spain. Such hopes were never realized: he died, quite
suddenly, on 7 July, and his ashes were taken to St Nectan's church
at Hartland to be buried alongside those of his parents and Uncle
John. Letters of condolence flooded in, the obituaries were long
and laudatory, and Richard Hoggart, Harry Paroissien and Robert
Lusty addressed a mighty throng at a memorial service in St Martin's
in the Fields. He left £1,216,474 in his will, the greater part of
which was left to the Allen Lane Foundation: Lettice was left nothing,
Lane fearing that she could all too easily fritter away a fortune, and
neither were his three daughters, all of whom, he felt, had been

adequately catered for by the trusts he had set up for them in the 1950s; £10,000 was left to the Society of Authors, the Royal Literary Fund, that lifeline for indigent authors, and the Book Trade Benevolent Fund, whose bungalows in Hertfordshire provided retirement homes for booksellers, most of whom had been wretchedly paid during their working lives, and £500 to the staff of the Garrick Club, where, before he was eventually made a member, the blackballs against his name had been unkindly compared with caviare in a teaspoon; there were some thirty bequests to friends and colleagues, gifts of books and paintings, and £10,000 to Bob Maynard's blind daughter in Australia. It had been a brief but busy life, and one that had brought pleasure and improvement to millions around the world.

Epilogue

The day after Lane's death, the merger of Penguin and Pearson Longman was announced: an American takeover by McGraw-Hill had been averted, and although Penguin was subsumed into Pearson Longman, and not the other way round, it remained a British institution. But, to some extent, that was neither here nor there: publishing was changing fast, and over the next thirty years Penguin would lose its unique identity and become, for better and for worse, no different from any other corporate publisher. As the flashes of orange faded from covers and spines and Pelican Books vanished into oblivion, Tschichold's penguin and the Penguin Classics lingered on as reminders of what seemed like a vanished age.

Many of the most famous names on the Penguin list disappeared as publishers set up their own paperback lists and reverted the rights, but Penguin acquired its own source of supply when Peter Mayer first set up Viking as a hardback imprint in the UK in 1984, then bought the long-established firms of Hamish Hamilton and Michael Joseph from the Thomson Organization in 1985, so enabling the firm to publish in both hardback and paperback, and pay their authors full royalties on both. Books were no longer re-set for paperback publication, so ensuring adherence to the standards set by Tschichold and Schmoller, but used the hardback setting instead; the traditional A-format was abandoned in favour of the larger B-format, which was good for the profit margins but maddened those readers who liked to slip a Penguin into a jacket pocket; books were published, in both hardback and paperback, that Lane would have disdained as 'breastsellers' and their covers were no better and no worse than those of the upstart rivals so despised by Frostie and Bill Williams. And Penguin became, at last, a presence in America as well as on this side of the Atlantic: Viking, founded in the 1920s by Lane's friend Harold Guinzburg, was acquired in 1975; as was the New American

Library, the creation of Victor Weybright and Kurt Enoch. The wheel had come full circle: it was an irony which Lane, that most mischievous of publishers, would surely have relished.

Reference Notes

Where it is obvious from the text who is writing to whom, I have given the date only (where known) of letters and office memos. Where identification is needed, I have used initials wherever possible: these should be self-explanatory, but the most recurrent are 'AL' (Allen Lane), 'EEF' (Eunice Frost), 'HPS' (Hans Schmoller), 'HFP' (Harry Paroissien), 'JEM' (J. E. 'Jack' Morpurgo), 'NC' (Noël Carrington), 'NP' (Nikolaus Pevsner), 'RL' (Richard or 'Dick' Lane), 'TG' (Tony Godwin), 'TK' (Tanya Kent, later Schmoller) and 'WEW' (William Emrys Williams). 'Bristol' refers to the Penguin files in Bristol University Library, of which Allen Lane's papers form a part; 'Bristol: EEF' to Eunice Frost's papers in the same library; 'HRHRC' to the Harry Ransom Humanities Research Center at the University of Texas at Austin; 'PRO' to the Public Record Office; 'Reading' to the Reading University Library. Full details of publications mentioned in the notes can be found in the Bibliography on page 442.

Chapter 1: Bristol Days

p.5 'a pleasant ruddy little man . . .': Williams, *Allen Lane: A Personal Portrait*, p.36.

p.6 'of the making of money . . .': 22 March 1950, Bristol.

p.7 'a number of my forebears . . .': to HFP, 24 February 1956, Bristol.

p.7 'ruthless . . .': Williams, *Allen Lane: A Personal Portrait*, p.36.

p.8 'awful compulsion . . .': to TK, March 1950, private collection.

p.8 'That our upbringing . . .': ibid.

p.9 'fairly religious family . . .': Lane, 'Reminiscences', Bristol.

p.10 'as dense as could be': Ducka and Pat Puxley interview with TK, 14 August 1970, Bristol.

p.10 'probably rather dull': interview with John Singleton, 1960.

p.10 'which allows me . . .': to RL, 5 November 1969, Bristol.

p.11 'Allen and I were likened . . .': Lane, 'Reminiscences', Bristol.

p.11 'old Martin who had . . .': November 1958, Bristol.

p.12 'Father appeared dressed as the Kaiser . . .': ibid.

p.13 'yanked back to the Grammar School . . .': interview with Heather Mansell-Jones, 1968.

p.14 'We have a library . . .': quoted in Hill, *The History of Bristol Grammar School*, p.190.

p.14 'a shorter, more substantial . . .': quoted ibid., p.191.

p.14 'real affection . . .': *Bristol Grammar School Chronicle*, December 1952.

p.15 'the street lighting . . .': quoted in Hill, *The History of Bristol Grammar School*, p.193.

p.15 'I wasn't very bright . . .': interview with Heather Mansell-Jones, 1968.

p.15 'an incipient smile . . .': 5 July 1970, Bristol.

p.16 'offers no crumb . . .': Danchev, *Oliver Franks*, p.9.

Chapter 2: Life with Uncle John

p.17 'mild affliction . . .': Travers, *A-Sitting on a Gate*, p.39.

p.18 'In this parish . . .': quoted in Lambert, *The Bodley Head*, p.6.

p.18 'I have always been in doubt . . .': Introduction to *The Life of Sir Thomas Bodley*, BH Christmas book, 1894.

p.19 'I bought it at the station . . .': quoted in Lambert, *The Bodley Head*, p.65.

p.21 'How doth the little busy Lane . . .': quoted ibid., p.67.

p.22 'You have covered yourself . . .': quoted in May, *John Lane and the Nineties*, p.166.

p.22 'Alert, well-groomed . . .': ibid., p.26.

p.22 'dim, bottle-glassed . . .': quoted in Lambert, *The Bodley Head*, p.188.

p.22 'knowledge of literature . . .': May, *John Lane and the Nineties*, p.226.

p.22 'his soft voice . . .': Travers, *A-Sitting on a Gate*, p.39.

p.23 'You are such a *fraud* . . .': quoted in Lambert, *The Bodley Head*, p.59.

p.23 'that villain Lane . . .': ibid.

p.23 'a tubby little pot-bellied bantam . . .': ibid., p.123.

p.23 'I think that authors . . .': Travers, *A-Sitting on a Gate*, p.40.

p.23 'one of the sacrifices . . .': quoted in Lambert, *The Bodley Head*, p.125.

p.25 'Will you procure me . . .': quoted ibid., p.162.

p.26 'his bright, intelligent eyes . . .': interview with TK, 3 December 1970, Bristol.

p.26 'humorous, well-dressed figure . . .': Hiscock, *Last Boat to Folly Bridge*, p.87.

p.26 'It is a far cry . . .': to Lawrence Cape, n.d., Bristol.

p.26 'flair amounts to anything . . .': interview with Heather Mansell-Jones, 1968.

p.28 'be affable and keep smiling . . .': 12 February 1922, Bristol.

p.28 'I like the writer . . .': n.d., Bristol.

p.28 'rather difficult to get on with . . .': interview with Heather Mansell-Jones, 1968.

p.28 'as easy a job . . .': to John Lane, 30 October 1964, Reading.

p.29 'within a week . . .': interview with TK, 11 October 1970, Bristol.

p.29 'Never lose an opportunity . . .': for the source for the quote, see Locke's *The Joyous Adventures of Aristide Pujol*.

p.29 'when he found them . . .': *Publishers' Circular and Booksellers' Record*, 5 January 1929.

p.30 'Young man, why waste . . .': ibid., 11 May 1929.

p.30 'fell on his hands . . .': ibid.

p.33 'a small man . . .': quoted in Lambert, *The Bodley Head*, p.213.

p.33 'an old-fashioned sea captain . . .': *Spectator*, 18 July 1970.

p.33 'worth publishing . . .': n.d., Reading.

p.33 '*might* have possibilities . . .': quoted in *Spectator*, 18 July 1970.

p.33 'Allen, my dear . . .': n.d., Reading.

p.33 'represented a man . . .': *Spectator*, 18 July 1970.

p.34 'never speaks': n.d., Reading.

p.34 'a man of boundless energy . . .': Mallowan, *Mallowan's Memoirs*, p.288.

p.34 'The burden of his seventy years . . .': May, *John Lane and the Nineties*, p.227.

p.34 'ancient: small and bearded . . .': quoted in Lambert, *The Bodley Head*, p.212.

Chapter 3: The Whispering Gallery

p.36 'The name on the manuscript . . .': 27 August 1926, Bristol.

p.37 'Who the dickens is Rodd? . . .': John William Dunbar, statement, n.d., private collection.

p.37 'give the boy every encouragement . . .': quoted in Lambert, *The Bodley Head*, p.220.

p.38 'as an act of good faith . . .': deposition of 11 January 1927, private collection.

p.38 'If I can tell . . .': AL statement in court, 18 December 1926.

p.38 'rather puts me in the cart . . .': 19 September 1926, Bristol.

p.38 'assure the Diarist . . .': 29 September 1926, Bristol.

p.39 'one of the most talked about . . .': 9 November 1926, private collection.

p.39 'I was starting to read . . .': Hesketh Pearson, deposition, Bristol.

p.40 'I do not mind . . .': ibid.

p.40 'it is no fabrication . . .: ibid.

p.40 'a pal's flat . . .': ibid.

p.41 'for the moment satisfied . . .': Basil Willett, deposition, Bristol.

p.41 'otherwise we shall have to sue . . .': ibid.

p.42 'if you will not do . . .': Lambert, *The Bodley Head*, p.225.

p.42 'Would you throw us over?': ibid., p.226.

p.43 'Daily Mail Exposure . . .': *Daily Mail*, 22 November 1926.

p.44 'The fate of *The Whispering Gallery* . . .': quoted in Ingrams, *God's Apology*, p.62.

p.44 'Perhaps the unkindest cut . . .': ibid.

p.44 'under the influence of champagne . . .': Pearson, *Hesketh Pearson by Himself*, p.212.

p.44 'appeared to be a reputable . . .': quoted in Ingrams, *God's Apology*, p.62.

p.44 'the youngest partner . . .': 26 November 1926, Bristol.

p.44 'deep regret that your name . . .': 24 November 1926, Bristol.

p.45 'I am afraid . . .': quoted in Hunter, *Nothing to Repent*, p.117.

p.45 'for no more consideration . . .': Pearson, *Hesketh Pearson*, p.216.

p.45 'Pat [Hastings] gravely warned . . .': quoted in Hunter, *Nothing to Repent*, p.117.

p.46 'Memoirs are a well-known . . .': quoted ibid., p.116.

p.46 'the foulest thing . . .': quoted in Ingrams, *God's Apology*, p.65.

p.46 'had to look at . . .': ibid.

p.46 'dirty little rats . . .': ibid.

p.47 'I did not say . . .': court proceedings, 18 December 1966, Bristol.

p.47 'because I could not think . . .': Pearson, *Hesketh Pearson*, p.221.

p.48 'you got yourself off . . .': ibid.

p.48 'consent to pay a farthing . . .': quoted in Lambert, *The Bodley Head*, p.228.

p.48 'the spunk of a boiled rabbit . . .': quoted in Hunter, *Nothing to Repent*, p.120.

p.48 'John Lane The Badly Had': Higham, *Literary Gent*, p.189.

p.48 'clever and alert': quoted in Lambert, *The Bodley Head*, p.220.

p.48 'No artist . . .': quoted in Ingrams, *God's Apology*, p.56.

p.49 'an act of insanity . . .': Pearson, *Hesketh Pearson*, p.211.

p.49 'Lord Beaverbrook, you remember . . .': 27 October 1926, Bristol.

p.49 'there is no question . . .': AL to T. S. Blakeney, 19 April 1968, Bristol.

Chapter 4: Goodbye to The Bodley Head

p.51 'an incredibly good-looking . . .': Mannin, *Young in the Twenties*, p.81.

p.52 'we drank a good deal of gin . . .': ibid.

p.52 'I am so liable . . .': quoted in Lambert, *The Bodley Head*, p.242.

p.52 'he told me . . .': Mannin, *Confessions and Impressions*, p.209.

p.52 'This is a very terrible book . . .': 18 January 1931, Bristol.

p.54 'it is sometimes unnecessary . . .': *Publishers' Circular and Booksellers' Record*, 11 May 1929.

p.56 'quite a social bird . . .': interview with Heather Mansell-Jones, 1968.

p.58 'the dirtiest, darkest . . .': Lane, 'Reminiscences', Bristol.

p.58 'There is little to indicate . . .': 16 May 1929, Bristol.

p.58 'You appear to be . . .': n.d., Bristol.

p.59 'I cherish always . . .': interview with TK, 11 October, 1970, Bristol.

p.59 'one of the greatest pleasures . . .': *Publishers' Circular and Booksellers' Record*, 5 January 1929.

p.59 'we put this remarkable piece . . .': Leonard Woolf, *Beginning Again*, p.178.

p.59 'Her table manners . . .': ibid., p.179.

p.60 'a great deal of unmitigated filth . . .': quoted in Travers, *Bound and Gagged*, p.24.

p.63 'Thus one half . . .': quoted in Richard Ellmann, *James Joyce* (New York: Oxford University Press, 1959), p.679.

p.64 'a book costing . . .': quoted in Travers, *Bound and Gagged*, p.43.

p.65 'Allen and I had fairly similar tastes . . .': interview with TK, 20 February 1971, Bristol.

p.66 'The trip had aged him . . .': Lane, 'Reminiscences', Bristol.

p.66 'Allen's last affair . . .': 6 July 1933, private collection.

p.66 'regarded his two brothers . . .': quoted in Rolfe, *Sixty Penguin Years Plus Two*.

p.67 'Candidly the situation . . .': Smedley, Rule & Co., 5 October 1932, Bristol.

p.68 'was of a very friendly nature . . .': 11 November 1933, Reading.

p.68 'conscious that there might have been . . .': Hiscock, *Last Boat to Folly Bridge*, p.86.

p.68 'We shall have to watch . . .': Bulcraig & Davis, 6 December 1929, Bristol.

p.68 'It is expecting too much . . .': Bulcraig & Davis, 6 May 1936.

p.69 'It is astonishing . . .': quoted in Lambert, *The Bodley Head*, p.268.

p.69 'thought it an amusing idea . . .': Unwin, *The Truth about a Publisher*, p.244.

p.69 '*Ultimately* it may be possible . . .': n.d., Bristol.

p.69 'If I had been a little wiser . . .': AL to EEF, 10 August 1956, Bristol: EEF.

p.69 'that it might be possible . . .': 7 April 1952, Bristol.

p.69 'a most unpleasant proceeding . . .': 8 October 1948, Bristol.

p.70 'the long and sentimental association . . .': n.d., Bristol.

Chapter 5: Hatching a Penguin

p.72 'as a means of awakening interest . . .': Carey, *The Intellectuals and the Masses*, p.109.

p.73 'My aim was to publish . . .': J. M. Dent, *The Memoirs of J. M. Dent*, p.124.

p.74 'murderous blow': Attenborough, *A Living Memory*, p.124.

p.75 'both socially desirable . . .': quoted in Hodges, *Gollancz*, p.50.

p.75 'How dare you!. . .': quoted in Edwards, *Victor Gollancz*, p.175.

p.77 'that urbane and picturesque international': Curtis Brown, *Contacts* (London: Cassell, 1935), p.178.

p.77 'personality bordering on that of an adventurer . . .': Enoch, *Memoirs Written for His Family*, p.80.

p.77 'somehow gave off a sinister vapour . . .': Higham, *Literary Gent*, p.191.

p.77 'creature of grandiose schemes . . .': *Stanley Morison*, p.215.

p.79 'as a result of detailed discussions . . .': Holroyd-Reece to Ved Mehta, n.d., Bristol.

p.80 'This is an age of cheapness . . .': quoted in Wilson, *First with the News*, p.326.

p.82 'This particular transaction . . .': quoted in Kingsford, *The Publishers' Association*, p.147.

p.82 'I can do nothing . . .': quoted in Mehta, *John Is Easy to Please*, p.88.

p.83 'arterial and by-pass roads . . .': Priestley, *English Journey*, p.401.

p.83 'The place to look for . . .': Orwell, *The Lion and the Unicorn*, p.67.

p.84 'Notice how . . .': Priestley, *English Journey*, p.402.

p.85 'a marked and regrettable characteristic . . .': Raymond, *Publishing and Bookselling*, p.48.

p.85 'Before the war . . .': quoted in Mountain, *Foyles*, p.93.

p.87 'From the moment . . .': *Penrose Annual*, 1938.

p.87 'a man who may be poor . . .': quoted in Wyatt, *Distinguished for Talent*, p.85.

p.88 'designed primarily . . .': *Bookseller*, 22 May 1935.

p.88 'quiet, "gentlemanly" publisher . . .': *Penrose Annual*, 1938.

p.88 'to discuss the new reading public . . .': letter to E. J. B. Rose, 7 November 1979, Bristol.

p.88 'he combined with a handsome appearance . . .': Dickson, *House of Words*, p.151.

p.89 'if we can't make money . . .': quoted ibid., p.153.

p.89 'a large, rugger-playing sort of figure . . .': interview with TK, 13 February 1971, Bristol.

p.89 '47 of [the delegates] . . .': Blackwell to E. J. B. Rose, 7 November 1979, Bristol.

p.89 'flaming mad': quoted in *The Penguin Collector*, December 1997.

p.89 'I have never been able . . .': n.d., Bristol.

p.90 'I have always thought it . . .': quoted in Hodges, *Gollancz*, p.30.

p.90 'a consistent and easily recognizable . . .': *Book Collector*, 1952.

p.90 'the first serious attempt . . .': *Penrose Annual*, 1938.

p.91 'dark little office . . .': *Book Collector*, 1952.

p.91 'elderly and benign . . .': Peggy Rafferty, *Penguin Collector*, 1976.

p.91 'As to the name . . .': 'The Paperback Revolution', in Briggs (ed.), *Essays in the History of Publishing*, p.294.

p.91 'a certain dignified flippancy': interview with John Singleton, 1960.

p.91 'in the old days . . .': letter to AL, 7 March 1969, Bristol.

p.91 'They had a cardboard model . . .': Mannin, *Young in the Twenties*, p.171.

p.92 'quick, alert, emphatic . . .': Lusty, *Bound to be Read*, p.67.

p.92 'How well I remember . . .': letter to AL, 6 January 1952, Bristol.

p.92 'by some percentage . . .': Elliott Viney to Steve Hare, 16 October 1994.

p.92 'In choosing these first ten titles . . .': *Bookseller*, 22 May 1935.

p.92 'Your suggestion of the sixpenny series . . .': 1 November 1934, Bristol.

p.93 'the book trade can afford . . .': Raymond, *Publishing and Bookselling*, p.24.

p.93 'It is best for everybody's sake . . .': quoted in St John, *William Heinemann*, p.282.

p.94 'Nobody can live . . .': ibid., p.283.

p.94 '*National Velvet* is now dead . . .': ibid., p.284.

p.94 'splendid value for sixpence . . .': *New English Review*, 5 March 1936.

p.95 'I shall be happy . . .': quoted in Morpurgo, *King Penguin*, p.90.

p.96 'It is said to be the most successful . . .': quoted in Edwards, *Victor Gollancz*, p.680.

p.96 'I refuse to be manacled . . .': quoted ibid., p.169.

p.96 'Victor exuded a greater dynamism . . .': ibid.

p.96 'one of the tightest-fisted old bastards . . .': quoted in Ziegler, *Rupert Hart-Davis*, p.88.

p.96 'A publisher of outstanding genius . . .': ibid.

p.96 'I went to see Jonathan . . .': interview with Alex Hamilton, *The Times*, 22 April 1969.

p.98 'Who's ever heard . . .': ibid.

p.99 'It's a flop . . .': Maddock interview with TK, 3 December 1970, Bristol.

p.99 'I don't know about these . . .': interview with Alex Hamilton, *The Times*, 22 April 1969.

Chapter 6: Pelicans Take Flight

p.101 'These Penguin books . . .': 22 July 1935, Bristol.

p.101 'Let me congratulate you . . .': 22 July 1935, Bristol.

p.101 'A PUBLISHING TRIUMPH': 28 July 1935.

p.101 'makes literature as fluid . . .': *Listener*, 1 April 1936.

p.102 'perfect reading for sixpence . . .': *Observer*, 18 March 1935.

p.102 'carried in a man's pocket . . .': *Saturday Review*, 10 August 1935.

p.102 'one of the great . . .': *Bookseller*, 8 August 1935.

p.102 '7/6 is too much . . .': *Daily Express*, 16 January 1936.

p.103 'though our general feeling is . . .': 4 October 1935, Reading.

p.104 'Chattos have been rather coy . . .': 11 October 1935, Reading.

p.104 'one of the interesting features . . .': 14 August 1935, Reading.

p.104 'it sounds rather a paying proposition . . .': 17 August 1935, Reading.

p.104 'I cannot see why . . .': 11 October 1930, Reading.

p.105 'I think it wrong . . .': 12 October 1939, Reading.

p.105 'as it seems to me . . .': 16 October 1939, Reading.

p.105 'As a member of the public . . .': *Times Literary Supplement*, 26 November 1938.

p.106 'from something that was only suitable . . .': for Margaret Cole's arguments, see *Listener*, 22 and 29 December 1937, 5 and 12 January 1938.

p.106 'if books are to be purchased . . .': *Times Literary Supplement*, 26 November 1938.

p.107 'the action of a very few . . .': ibid.

p.107 'to bring serious . . .': *Economist*, 3 December 1938.

p.108 'all among the skeletons . . .': *Penguin Collector*, December 1997.

p.108 'they had to have a curtain . . .': interview with TK, 10 February 1971, Bristol.

p.109 'represented an ideal . . .': Muspratt, *Fire of Youth*, p.171.

p.109 'square-jawed, tallish . . .': *Advertising World*, August 1938.

p.109 'was in love with all the Lanes . . .': Jean McFarlane to EEF, 16 February 1984, Bristol: EEF.

p.110 'Of one thing I'm sure . . .': interview with Heather Mansell-Jones, 1968.

p.110 'there is no fortune . . .': *Penrose Annual*, 1938.

p.111 '£10,000 a year . . .': *Star*, 7 October 1937.

p.111 'I wouldn't dream . . .': *Rover World*, August 1937.

p.111 'even the King Penguin . . .': *Bookseller*, 6 August 1936.

p.112 'Right, how much do you want . . .': quoted in Hare, *Allen Lane and the Penguin Editors*, p.57.

p.112 'Prepare for a shock . . .': quoted in Holroyd, *The Lure of Fantasy*, p.373.

p.113 'You can't protect . . .': interview with Alex Hamilton, *The Times*, 22 April 1969.

p.113 'some misgivings . . .': quoted in Rolfe, *Sixty Penguin Years Plus Two*.

p.113 'one of the greatest educationalists . . .': H. G. Wells to Beatrice Webb, 5 January 1940, in Smith (ed.), *The Correspondence of H. G. Wells*, p.263.

p.113 'which are to be similar . . .': 25 August 1936, Reading.

p.113 'Bookish Krishna Menon's . . .': quoted in Hare, *Allen Lane and the Penguin Editors*, p.51.

p.114 'When I first met Allen . . .': Williams, *Allen Lane: A Personal Portrait*, p.49.

p.114 'when you and I first discussed . . .': 27 April 1943, Bristol.

p.115 'an impressive and rather frightening figure . . .': Grant Duff, *The Parting of Ways*, p.102.

p.116 'wild-eyed, emaciated . . .': Lusty, *Bound to be Read*, p.66.

p.116 'I am dying . . .': ibid., p.68.

p.116 'defected to education . . .': quoted in Rolfe, *Sixty Penguin Years Plus Two*.

p.117 'the emergence of Penguin . . .': ibid.

p.117 'But Estrid, darling . . .': quoted in article on EB by Andro Linklater, *Sunday Telegraph* Colour Magazine, 23 January 1993.

p.118 'heavy cherub's face': Hoggart, *An Imagined Life*, p.89.

p.118 'not the man to wear hair shirts . . .': Edwards and Hare (eds.), *Pelican Books*, p.21.

p.118 'in a strictly extra-mural capacity . . .': Williams, *Allen Lane: A Personal Portrait*, p.12.

p.119 'an infuriating, mercurial colleague . . .': ibid., p.31.

p.119 'We are a funny pair . . .': 20 August 1954, Bristol.

p.119 'favourite posture . . .': *Penguins Progress*, 1940.

p.119 'Wistfully cynical . . .': Weidenfeld, *Remembering My Good Friends*, p.119.

p.119 'the largest and most powerful . . .': Lane, 'Reminiscences', Bristol.

p.119 'with a rod of iron': Zuckerman, *From Apes to Warlords*, p.37.

p.121 'bottleneck': George, *Krishna Menon*, p.151.

p.121 'a world which paralyses . . .': 30 September 1938, Bristol.

p.121 'I shall be most grateful . . .': 12 November 1938, Bristol.

p.121 'Last time when we met . . .': 22 December 1938, Bristol.

p.121 'voice seethed with venom . . .': *Observer*, 22 April 1973.

p.121 'The reason for our split . . .': quoted in Rolfe, *Sixty Penguin Years Plus Two*.

p.122 'a fact of enormous importance . . .': *Spectator*, 22 July 1938.

Chapter 7: Red Alert

p.123 'plain horrible': Elizabeth Creak to author.

p.124 'They strike me . . .': Lovat Dickson, 3 June 1937, Bristol: EEF.

p.125 'at the quixotic instigation . . .': n.d., Bristol: EEF.

p.125 'Deep as her devotion to you is . . .': 23 March 1953, Bristol.

p.126 'You don't need me . . .': 1 August 1958, Bristol.

p.126 'the ultimate . . .': Jean McFarlane to EEF, 16 February 1984, Bristol: EEF.

p.126 'while Allen was always charming . . .': quoted in Rolfe, *Sixty Penguin Years Plus Two*.

p.126 'We were breaking . . .': quoted in Wyatt, *Distinguished for Talent*, p.83.

p.127 'plain men, in cars . . .': *Penguins: A Retrospect, 1935–51*, p.6.

p.127 'genial gastronome called Carbonnel . . .': Williams, *Allen Lane: A Personal Portrait*, p.65.

p.128 'excellent chef': *Night and Day*, 28 October 1937.

p.128 'far more sherries . . .': interview with H. L. Beales, 1984, Bristol.

p.128 'a time of very high idealism . . .': 'How I Became a Literary Midwife', 19 May 1993, Bristol.

p.132 'help in the terribly urgent struggle . . .': *New Statesman*, 14 January 1939.

p.132 'almost incredible circulation . . .': ibid., p.231.

p.132 'I should explain . . .': ibid., p.211.

p.133 'slick books of reportage . . .': Orwell, 'Arthur Koestler', *Focus*, 1946.

p.133 'was diverting high-minded schoolteachers . . .': Taylor, *English History*, p.397.

p.133 'worked off their rebelliousness . . .': ibid.

p.133 'provide the indispensable basis . . .': quoted in Hynes, *The Auden Generation*, p.209.

p.134 'It was pretty obvious . . .': quoted in Rolfe, *Sixty Penguin Years Plus Two*.

p.135 'a tremendous fire-eater . . .': interview with TK, 10 February 1971, Bristol.

p.135 'with bitter irony . . .': Grant Duff, *The Parting of the Ways*, p.193.

p.135 'Are these Penguin Specials . . .': 6 March 1940, Bristol.

p.136 ' Someone Has Got To Clean Up . . .': *Daily Mirror*, 12 October 1938.

p.136 'kindly man with a receding chin . . .': quoted in Kershaw, *Making Friends with Hitler*, p.141.

p.136 'dreads war': ibid., p.193.

p.137 'tear it up if you like!': interview with TK, 15 February 1971, Bristol.

p.137 'Have you noticed the titles . . .': quoted in Joicey, 'Paperback Guide to Progress', p.34.

p.137 'To believe all evil . . .': ibid.

p.138 'Anti-fascists in high life . . .': *New English Weekly*, 21 July 1938.

p.138 'The people who read the *New Statesman* . . .: ibid.

p.138 'perhaps the most interesting . . .': interview with Alex Hamilton, *The Times*, 22 April 1969.

p.138 'there is some feeling . . .': 14 August 1938, Bristol.

p.138 'Your name is associated . . .': 16 August 1938, Bristol.

p.139 'I'll be damned . . .': quoted in Morpurgo, *King Penguin*, p.133.

p.139 'I shall firmly contradict . . .': 18 August 1938, Bristol.

p.139 'In the books on Science and Art . . .': *Left Review*, May 1938.

p.139 'I never discovered . . .': Haskell, *Balletomane at Large*, p.97.

p.140 'flair and judgement . . .': Richards, *Memoirs of an Unjust Fella*, p.133.

p.140 'violently hiccupping . . .': 15 December 1938, Bristol.

p.140 'iron determination . . .': McLean, *True to Type*, p.27.

p.141 'Cocky little sparrow . . .': NC interview with TK, 23 June 1970, Bristol.

p.141 'With the greatest skill . . .': 14 September 1960, Bristol.

p.142 'exactly the sort . . .': Pick, 'Memoirs', private collection.

p.143 'I was back where I started . . .': Julian Maclaren-Ross, *Memoirs of the Forties* (London: Alan Ross, 1965), p.37.

p.143 'I must say, though I says it myself . . .': 2 May 1938, Bristol.

p.144 'old man van Leer . . .': interview with TK, 10 February 1971, Bristol.

p.145 'to preach the Gospel . . .': 8 March 1939, Bristol: EEF.

p.146 'Let's see the boy . . .': quoted in Edwards and Hare (eds.), *Twenty-One Years*.

p.146 'I note that you are at school . . .': 25 October 1939, Bristol.

p.146 'It is obvious . . .': 23 June 1939, Bristol.

p.146 'I guarantee you . . .': Lane, 'Reminiscences', Bristol.

p.147 'the reason was not far to see . . .': n.d., private collection.

p.147 'in connection with a proposal . . .': 28 December 1938, Bristol.

p.147 'one of the greatest needs . . .': 11 August 1939, Bristol.

p.147 'this rather serious young man . . .': *Times of Ceylon*, 18 April 1939.

Chapter 8: Penguins Go to War

p.149 'They were like dynamite . . .': interview with Jack Kendle, 1984, Bristol.

p.151 'There is really an astonishing lack . . .': 1 February 1940, Bristol.

p.151 'Only much later . . .': Morpurgo, *King Penguin*, p.156.

p.152 'one of our greatest . . .': Admiral Sir George Creasey, Foreword to Edward Young, *One of Our Submarines* (London: Hart–Davis, 1952), p.6.

p.154 'Since my return from America . . .': 24 November 1941, Bristol.

p.154 'If the question of paper . . .': 24 November 1942, Bristol.

p.155 'the most expensive item . . .': Unwin, *The Truth about a Publisher*, p.272.

p.155 'I went to look . . .': quoted in *Penguin Collector*, July 2000.

p.155 'The Germans have done . . .': ibid.

p.156 'a general falling-off . . .': quoted in Hewison, *Under Siege*, p.22.

p.156 'The average intellectual level . . .': Orwell, 'Money and Guns', BBC Indian Service, 20 January 1942.

p.156 'the literary indifference . . .': quoted in Hewison, *Under Siege*, p.8.

p.156 'progressive decline . . .': ibid.

p.156 'Young people were buying books . . .': Unwin, *Publishing in Peace and War*, p.21.

p.157 'an uneasy mixture . . .': Clark, *The Other Half*, p.10.

p.158 'the Ministry of Information "suggests" . . .': *Tribune*, 7 July 1944.

p.158 'I have a distinct phobia . . .': AL to Hermon Ould, 15 December 1937, HRHRC.

p.158 'small nucleus . . .': *Daily Mail*, 26 January 1940.

p.159 'I can appreciate more than ever . . .': n.d., Bristol.

p.159 'only a mean-minded sergeant . . .': quoted in Edwards and Hare (eds.), *Pelican Books*, p.41.

p.159 'If you were to advertise . . .': 25 October 1939, Bristol.

p.160 'Here surely is an idea . . .': 10 August 1940, Bristol.

p.160 'My feeling is . . .': 25 September 1939, Bristol.

p.160 'The public seemed . . .': quoted in Peaker, *The Penguin Modern Painters*, p.18.

p.161 'At no time in the pre-war years . . .': quoted in Hewison, *Under Siege*, p.161.

p.161 'more and more Londoners . . .': ibid., p.60.

p.162 'There had not been . . .': quoted in Addison, *The Road to 1945*, p.148.

p.162 'a very vital personality . . .': ibid.

p.163 'paces his office . . .': *News Review*, 9 January 1941.

p.163 'Sooner or later . . .': quoted in Hare, *Allen Lane and the Penguin Editors*, p.110.

p.164 'Allen Lane in this matter . . .': quoted in Joicey, 'A Paperback Guide to Progress', p.41.

p.164 'Could you please arrange . . .': ibid.

p.164 'It seemed to me . . .': quoted in Pearson, *Penguins March On*, p.33.

p.166 'short, powerful-looking man . . .': quoted in Morpurgo, *King Penguin*, p.175.

p.167 'was the reason . . .': 10 August 1956, Bristol: EEF.

p.167 'somehow I got the idea . . .': ibid.

p.168 'Every time a stack of books . . .': interview with Jack Kendle, 1984, Bristol.

p.168 'I want you to meet . . .': Bob Maynard tape, 1984.

p.169 'After gazing idly . . .': 8 July 1943, private collection.

p.170 'loved John better . . .': *Spectator*, 18 July 1970.

p.170 'encased himself in a spiritual armour . . .': Morpurgo, *King Penguin*, p.186.

p.170 'I have got a little barrier . . .': interview with John Singleton, 1960.

Chapter 9: Branching Out

p.171 'I should love to appear . . .': 17 October 1938, Bristol.

p.172 'but what I really want . . .': 31 July 1941, Bristol.

p.172 'I think the Roman Catholic organization . . .': 23 February 1943, Smith (ed.), *The Correspondence of H. G. Wells*, p.372.

p.172 'It is delightful to find . . .': 16 June 1943, ibid., p.394.

p.173 'has interested me . . .': 27 November 1942, Bristol.

p.173 'These printing johnnies . . .': 21 March 1942, Bristol.

p.173 'I am afraid *Interglossa* . . .': 12 August 1944, Bristol.

p.174 'a spirit, a near-revolutionary mood . . .': Lehmann, *Thrown to the Woolfs*, p.49.

p.175 'George Orwell's story . . .': 28 October 1936, Bristol.

p.175 'thus giving the lie . . .': 14 November 1936, Bristol.

p.176 'an extremely harmonious . . .': Lehmann, *The Penguin New Writing*, p.9.

p.176 'an authority on the international control . . .': 9 August 1940, HRHRC.

p.176 'the advantage of backing . . .': n.d., HRHRC.

p.177 'I have no hesitation . . .': 11 October 1940, HRHRC.

p.177 'if the sales exceed . . .': 7 November 1940, HRHRC.

p.178 'It is only fair to tell you . . .': 29 March 1941, HRHRC.

p.178 'I was rather surprised . . .': 2 April 1941, HRHRC.

p.178 'it would be absurd . . .': 8 April 1941, HRHRC.

p.179 'among dockside workers . . .': 25 June 1941, HRHRC.

p.179 'I hope you won't think . . .': 5 June 1941, HRHRC.

p.179 'seemed entirely in contradiction . . .': 9 December 1941, HRHRC.

p.179 'impressed by your keenness . . .': 18 July 1945, HRHRC.

p.180 'I think we should . . .': 2 August 1945, HRHRC.

p.180 'I liked a great deal . . .': 31 December 1946, HRHRC.

p.180 'a venture that looked . . .': 3 January 1947, HRHRC.

p.180 'I do hope you will be able . . .': 6 March 1947, HRHRC.

p.180 'I am devoted to the little magazine . . .': 29 December 1949, HRHRC.

p.181 'It is the worst loss so far . . .': quoted in Lehmann, *The Ample Proposition*, p.75.

p.182 'everybody has had enough . . .': quoted in Hare, *Allen Lane and the Penguin Editors*, p.180.

p.182 'somewhat idealistic basis . . .': 15 January 1946, Bristol.

p.182 'the Baroness stormed in . . .': 1 February 1946, Bristol.

p.182 'with the present feeling . . .': 23 December 1947, Bristol.

p.183 'almost as beautiful . . .': quoted in David Garnett (ed.), *Carrington:*

Letters and Extracts from Her Diaries (London: Cape, 1970), p.23.

p.183   'a fine figure of a man . . .': Hale, *A Slender Reputation*, p.210.

p.185   'like a schoolboy . . .': NC interview with TK, 23 June 1970,
          Bristol.

p.185   'rather confused . . .': quoted in Hare, *Allen Lane and the Penguin
          Editors*, p.135.

p.185   'But this is absolutely tops! . . .': NC in *Penguin Collectors' Society
          Newsletter*, 1979.

p.187   'thin little books . . .': *Times Literary Supplement*, 14 April 1946.

p.187   'For some time . . .': June 1942, quoted in Peaker, *The Penguin
          Modern Painters*, p.10.

p.188   'I was very much excited . . .': 12 June 1942, Bristol.

p.188   'instead of carrying . . .': 31 January 1941, Bristol: EEF.

p.188   'The greater part of the work . . .': 30 May 1944, Bristol.

p.189   'the firm is now so well known . . .': AL to Bernhard Baer,
          22 August 1947, Bristol.

p.189   'If there are people . . .': 20 July 1942, Bristol.

p.189   'The old scheme seemed . . .': 22 January 1954, Bristol.

p.190   'They are an extraordinary example . . .': 22 April 1944, Bristol:
          EEF.

p.190   'a great service . . .': 18 March 1946, Bristol.

Chapter 10: *The New Jerusalem*

p.191   'London certainly seems . . .': 24 September 1940, private collection.

p.191   'discussing the possibility . . .': 1 February 1940, Bristol.

p.192   'a powerful solvent . . .': Taylor, *English History*, p.503.

p.192   'Progress and reaction . . .': Orwell, *The Lion and the Unicorn*, p.95.

p.193   'the opportunity should be taken . . .': quoted in Barnett, *The Audit
          of War*, p.19.

p.193   'we should proclaim . . .': ibid., p.20.

p.193   'consider means of perpetuating . . .': ibid.

p.193   'was always the New World . . .': quoted in Addison, *The Road to
          1945*, p.162.

p.193   'the way to victory . . .': quoted ibid., p.164.

p.194 'A new consciousness . . .': *Penguin New Writing*, No. 4.

p.194 'allowed itself to be deprived . . .': quoted in Calder, *The People's War*, p.509.

p.194 'print articles which . . .': *Partisan Review*, July–August 1941.

p.195 'the threepenny edition . . .': quoted in Calder, *The People's War*, p.137.

p.196 'a vision of a garden-city society . . .': Barnett, *The Audit of War*, p.11.

p.197 'emergence of a new kind of man . . .': quoted in Joicey, 'A Paperback Guide to Progress', p.37.

p.198 'We were anti-They . . .'; quoted in Addison, *The Road to 1945*, p.153.

p.199 'influence the tastes . . .': *Daily Herald*, 22 November 1950.

p.199 'revolution in the spirit of man . . .': quoted in Barnett, *The Audit of War*, p.17.

p.200 'Our cost of production . . .': quoted in Rolfe, *Sixty Penguin Years Plus Two*.

p.200 'I am more and more suspicious . . .': quoted in Addison, *The Road to 1945*, p.147.

p.201 'Will not such discussions . . .': quoted ibid.

p.201 'did not talk down . . .': Hoggart, *A Sort of Clowning*, p.61.

p.201 'voted Labour for the first time . . .': quoted in McKibbin, *Classes and Cultures*, p.453.

p.201 'Your bloody *Picture Post* . . .': Hopkinson, *Picture Post*, p.15.

p.202 'After the WEA . . .': Morpurgo, *King Penguin*, p.196.

p.202 'able piece of work . . .': 26 September 1946, Bristol.

p.202 'INTENSELY ANXIOUS . . .': 9 September 1946, Bristol.

p.202 'I am frantically excited . . .': 12 September 1946, Bristol.

p.203 'Now that Gollancz's . . .': 1 October 1948, Bristol.

p.203 'they will undoubtedly . . .': n.d., Bristol.

p.203 'much as some of us . . .': 9 October 1948, Bristol.

p.204 'I am fighting shy . . .': quoted in Rolfe, *Sixty Penguin Years Plus Two*.

p.204 'the demand is now . . .': quoted in Joicey, 'A Paperback Guide to Progress', p.44.

p.204 'a twentieth-century Attila . . .': 14 July 1949, Bristol.

p.204 'lose sales on any book . . .': 7 January 1946, Bristol.

p.204 'Well, have it your own way . . .': 10 January 1946, Bristol.

p.204 'genuine independent attraction . . .': 18 December 1939, Bristol.

p.204 'Topolski's cover for *Pygmalion* . . .': 30 January 1941, Bristol.

p.205 'so individual and masterly . . .': 5 March 1947, Bristol.

p.205 'The pleasant relations . . .': AL to Topolski, 28 November 1947, Bristol.

p.205 'provided Willie can do it . . .': Elliott Viney to Steve Hare, 16 October 1994.

p.205 'No venture which I have undertaken . . .': quoted in Holroyd, *The Lure of Fantasy*, p.374.

p.205 'We had sherry on a smooth lawn . . .': quoted in Barker, *Stanley Morison*, p.423.

p.206 'The tone of the Festival . . .': Sissons (ed.), *The Age of Austerity*, p.323.

Chapter 11: *Transatlantic Blues*

p.210 'I think I have come back . . .': to Louis Hacker, 5 August 1939, private collection.

p.212 'The paper got to be the same colour . . .': quoted in Davis, *Two-Bit Culture*, p.55.

p.213 'a quick and decisive "yes" . . .': Enoch, *Memoirs Written for His Family*, p.148.

p.213 'polite, serious young gentleman . . .': ibid., p.149.

p.214 'Kurt, in six months . . .': ibid., p.161.

p.215 'dovelike and forebearing . . .': quoted in Peaker, *The Penguin Modern Painters*, p.39.

p.215 'Penguins will be out of business . . .': EEF to AL, 15 July 1945, Bristol.

p.215 'the most lugubrious . . .': 4 July 1945, Bristol.

p.215 'devoid of the taste . . .': quoted in Rolfe, *Sixty Penguin Years Plus Two*.

p.216 'a stooge for Lane . . .': Weybright, *The Making of a Publisher*, p.172.

p.216 'the tall, apple-cheeked countryman . . .': ibid., p.180.

p.216 'moved among the workers . . .': ibid, p.184.

p.216 'put me on my guard . . .': Enoch, *Memoirs Written for His Family*, p.172.

p.216 'We will continue . . .': 24 January 1947, quoted in Bonn, *Heavy Traffic and High Culture*, p.9.

p.217 'I am convinced more than ever . . .': 10 October 1946, quoted in Davis, *Two-Bit Culture*, p.114.

p.218 'a "little Englishman" . . .': Weybright, *The Making of a Publisher*, p.174.

p.218 'Allen was as grim . . .': ibid., p.198.

p.218 'discharged his responsibilities . . .': Williams, *Allen Lane: A Personal Portrait*, p.70.

p.219 'The cover of *The Tyranny of Sex* . . .': 23 December 1947, Bristol.

p.219 'Whatever comes, we keep absolutely clear . . .': 23 February 1949, Bristol.

p.219 'that unpleasant couple . . .': 18 February 1949, Bristol.

p.219 'not quite such a squirt . . .': 13 February 1949, Bristol.

p.219 'not a bad egg': 17 February 1949, Bristol.

p.219 'after having ladled . . .': 15 January 1949, Bristol.

Chapter 12: Scenes from Office Life

p.221 'I'm afraid the pre-war spirit . . .': 16 April 1947, Bristol.

p.221 'there hasn't been a definite enough breakaway . . .': RL to AL, 5 August 1947, Bristol.

p.222 'Then there's no need . . .': R. J. Minney in *The Recorder*, 3 September 1947.

p.222 'although I dislike . . .': 5 August 1947, Bristol.

p.223 'You write a couple of letters . . .': 27 November 1945, Bristol.

p.223 'Sometimes I am rather under the impression . . .': 25 February 1953, Bristol.

p.224 'worked impulsively and restlessly . . .': Margaret Clark in Edwards and Hare (eds.), *Twenty-One Years*, p.37.

p.224 'dropped the twinkle . . .': Margaret Clark to author, 12 October 2004.

p.224 'he was bad at hatchet work . . .': Calvocoressi, *Threading My Way*, p.183.

p.224 'gay, volatile, insecure . . .': Williams, *Allen Lane: A Personal Portrait*, p.13.

p.225 'was good company . . .': ibid., p.20.

p.225 'eyebrows raised enquiringly . . .': ibid., p.16.

p.225 'Some word, some name . . .': address at AL's memorial service, 18 August 1970.

p.225 'nothing to cultivate . . .': Williams, *Allen Lane: A Personal Portrait*, p.18.

p.225 'an inveterate and diligent quizzer . . .': ibid., p.15.

p.226 'whether dictated or written . . .': ibid., p.37.

p.226 'did not appear . . .': McLean, *True to Type*, p.55.

p.226 'He had an easy, likeable way . . .': quoted in Hare, *Lost Causes*, p.47.

p.227 'I found that Harry . . .': 25 May 1950, Bristol.

p.227 'I am slow to give . . .': 25 February 1956, Bristol.

p.228 'nothing fancy . . .': AL to HFP, 23 April 1956, Bristol.

p.228 'On the other side of the Channel . . .': Margaret Clark interview with author.

p.228 'The plane trip . . .': 11 July 1950, Bristol.

p.229 'I want you to go on the road . . .': Herbert, 'Penguin in the Early Fifties', *Signal*, January 1993.

p.232 'say a dozen gins . . .': 7 November 1946, Bristol.

p.232 'we can have our own bottle . . .': 7 April 1947, Bristol.

p.232 'Oh, half and half . . .': McLean, *True to Type*, p.55.

p.232 'couldn't take the drink . . .': interview with TK, n.d., Bristol.

p.232 'this never kept me long . . .': 15 March 1948, Bristol.

p.232 'some (serious this time) . . .': 7 December 1948, Bristol.

p.234 'as likely as not . . .': *Penguin Collector*, December 2002.

p.234 'perfectly wicked to start . . .': 22 February 1944, Bristol.

p.235 'genuinely sorry . . .': 1 May 1949, Bristol.

Chapter 13: *The Search for Perfection*

p.236 'Each book which goes to press . . .': 13 July 1947, Bristol.

p.236 'the innate sense of quality': 17 June 1965, Bristol.

p.236 'blemishes . . .': 7 September 1949, Bristol.

p.237 'dark shirt, heavy tweed jacket . . .': *Tablet*, 22 July 1995.

p.238 'Though only twenty-eight . . .': *The Green Tree and the Dry*, p.152.

p.239 'the only man I have ever known . . .': Morpurgo, *Master of None*, p.180.

p.239 'You say on page 78 . . .': 3 February 1953, Bristol.

p.239 'It was, of course, "Silesian" . . .': 4 February 1953, Bristol.

p.239 'You say of your hero . . .': 12 November 1952, Bristol.

p.239 'strike those who are familiar . . .': 5 January 1945, Bristol.

p.239 'by far the most pleasant . . .': letter to Steve Hare, 11 February 1994.

p.240 'quizzical, mysterious air . . .': *Tablet*, 22 July 1995.

p.240 'be recompensed for their work . . .': 5 December 1954, Bristol.

p.240 'I do feel more and more . . .': 19 July 1949, Bristol.

p.240 'that old Buddhist': Margaret Clark interview with author.

p.241 'the typographical care . . .': Simon, *Printer and Playground*, p.106.

p.243 'I wanted to design books . . .': letter to Steve Hare, 11 February 1994.

p.244 'more difficult to design a book . . .': quoted in McLean, *True to Type*, p.34.

p.244 'Fine typefaces, bad composition . . .': quoted in McLean, *Jan Tschichold: Typographer*, p.146.

p.244 'produced a bland smile . . .': ibid., p.12.

p.245 'I think he could produce perfection . . .': 13 July 1947, Bristol.

p.245 'In your letter . . .': quoted in McLean, *True to Type*, p.12.

p.246 'squandered . . . brochures and leaflets . . .': Schmoller, *Two Titans*, p.63.

p.246 'had probably done more . . .': ibid., p.104.

p.246 'No British typographer . . .': Bartram, *Making Books*, p.64.

p.246 'My overall hunch . . .': 15 July 1949, Bristol.

p.247 'I feel far more constructive zeal . . .': 8 July 1947, Bristol.

p.247 'Bill, I think, feels rather lost . . .': July 1947, private collection.

p.248 'inner cabinet . . .': 14 July 1947, Bristol.

p.248 'in the unparalleled position . . .': 6 September 1948, Bristol.

p.249 'my permanent love . . .'; 10 September 1948, Bristol.

p.249 'We must jointly see . . .': 1 May 1949, Bristol.

p.249 'sources of infection': n.d., Bristol.

Chapter 14: Buildings and Classics

p.251 'bucked as a dog with two tails . . .': AL to Victor Weybright, 5 March 1946, Bristol.

p.252 'enslaved by the idiom . . .': quoted in Radice, *The Translator's Art*, p.21.

p.252 'I personally am not at all apprehensive . . .': 10 September 1947, Bristol.

p.252 'without hesitation . . .': 24 October 1947, Bristol.

p.252 'My dear Allen . . .': quoted in Hare, *Allen Lane and the Penguin Editors*, p.198.

p.253 'If I were asked . . .': 22 January 1964, Bristol.

p.253 'by husbanding our reserves . . .': 6 April 1948, HRHRC.

p.253 'You have done the King Penguins now . . .': NP interview with TK, n.d., Bristol.

p.254 'extraordinarily well . . .': 12 March 1942, Bristol.

p.255 'The journeys are just not human . . .': quoted in Cherry, *The Buildings of England*, p.9.

p.255 'Is there such a thing?': 5 October 1947, Bristol.

p.255 'succeeded in making several dents . . .': 9 November 1948, Bristol.

p.256 'I don't think he opened up . . .': interview with TK, n.d., Bristol.

p.256 'No, that's all right . . .': ibid.

p.256 'We are departing from our chosen function . . .': 3 December 1952, Bristol.

p.257 'publish a book of English wild flowers . . .': quoted in Hare, *Lost Causes*, p.36.

p.258 'very sweet character . . .': Partridge, *Everything to Lose*, p.85.

p.258 'A pocket Napoleon . . .': Hare, *Lost Causes*, p.18.

p.259 'Mr Lane was in rather a frivolous mood . . .': quoted ibid., p.41.

p.259 'smooth, long-nosed Bentley . . .': Partridge, *Everything to Lose*, p.18.

p.259 'Really, Lane is the limit . . .': 12 March 1946, Bristol.

p.260 'enigma . . .': Hare, *Lost Causes*, p.38.

p.260 'Throughout Allen behaved impeccably . . .': ibid., p.40.

p.260 'his innocent air . . .': Partridge, *Everything to Lose*, p.93.

p.260 'no negotiation . . .': Elizabeth Barber to AL, 26 October 1950, Bristol.

p.261 'Allen Lane has decided . . .': 20 January 1949, Bristol.

p.261 'It sounds as though Allen is practising . . .': Williams, *Allen Lane: A Personal Portrait*, p.14.

p.262 'We met in a tiny and untidy room . . .': Morpurgo, *Master of None*, p.176.

p.262 'just in time for the first of five gins . . .': ibid., p.177.

p.263 'but I soon learned . . .': ibid., p.179.

p.263 'a larger, less mercurial version . . .': ibid., p.196.

p.264 'I think we're getting into a rut . . .': ibid., p.224.

p.264 'and because of you . . .': Morpurgo, *King Penguin*, p.222.

p.264 'he's better out of the team . . .': AL to RL, 13 July 1947, Bristol.

p.264 'AL thinks you would be even more use . . .': Morpurgo, *Master of None*, p.198.

p.264 'I did not mince words . . .': 8 July 1947, Bristol.

p.264 'You are always nagging us . . .': Edwards and Hare (eds.), *Pelican Books*, p.48.

p.265 'During all the period . . .': Morpurgo to Steve Hare, 16 February 1995.

p.265 'I regard the cheap paper-covered book . . .': 18 December 1944, Reading.

p.265 'martinis of a strength . . .': Lusty, *Bound to be Read*, p.125.

Chapter 15: An Estate of the Realm

p.267 'indispensable . . .': John Gross, *A Double Thread* (London: Chatto & Windus, 2001), p.176.

p.267 'a very simple man . . .': BBC European Service, 29 July 1954.

p.267 'Very few honours . . .': 1 January 1952, Bristol.

p.268 'keep a wary eye . . .': 28 February 1952, Bristol.

p.268 'Some day they'll knight Allen . . .': 1 January 1952, Bristol.

p.268 'I bet you never imagined . . .': 29 January 1952, Bristol.

p.268 'Pride of place . . .': 20 February 1952, Bristol.

p.268 'Don't carry self-effacement . . .': 31 December 1951, Bristol.

p.269 'it might have been called . . .': Ayer, *More of My Life*, p.62.

p.271 'a process which, *inevitably* . . .': 4 November 1954, Bristol.

p.271 'Britain was about to become . . .': WEW to Victor Weybright, 6 March 1946, private collection.

p.271 'financially impoverished élite . . .': *Printing Review*, autumn 1956.

p.271 'wipe out as much as we can . . .': quoted in le Mahieu, *A Culture for Democracy*, p.144.

p.271 'giving people what one believes . . .': ibid.

p.272 'highly intelligent minority audience . . .': quoted in Carpenter, *The Envy of the World*, p.6.

p.273 'reverence for knowledge . . .': ibid., p.7.

p.273 'until we are satisfied . . .': ibid., p.9.

p.273 'may well become . . .': ibid., p.59.

p.273 'what is at stake . . .': ibid., p.97.

p.273 'had left the Philistine speechless . . .': quoted in Rolfe, *Sixty Penguin Years Plus Two*.

p.274 'the Third Programme was founded . . .': quoted in Carpenter, *The Envy of the World*, p.14.

p.274 'tends to read the *Observer* . . .': *Observer*, 29 July 1956.

p.274 'I bought my first Penguin . . .': *Penguins Progress, 1935–60*.

p.274 'back in the 1940s . . .': *Daily Mail*, 18 December 1989.

p.275 'They have, in some degree . . .': Hoggart, *The Uses of Literacy*, p.258.

p.275 'tend to read bitterly ironic . . .': ibid., p.257.

p.275 'lean so intensely . . .': ibid., p.259.

p.276 'as society comes nearer . . .': ibid., p.263.

p.276 'a majority in any one class . . .': ibid., p.281.

p.276 'Some years ago . . .': 21 February 1955, Bristol.

p.277 'Parrot Books . . .': 2 March 1955, Bristol.

p.277 'The increase of the second-rate . . .': 11 November 1954, Bristol.

p.277 'America, in Penguin matters . . .': WEW to AL, 4 November 1954, Bristol.

p.278 'but despite the fact . . .': 31 January 1952, Bristol.

p.279 'Who has changed the typeface . . .': Cinamon, 'Hans Schmoller', p.51.

p.279 'There were those at Penguin . . .': Bartram, *Making Books*, p.53.

p.279 'Penguin's conscience . . .': Cinamon, 'Hans Schmoller', p.40.

p.279 'I've been here twenty years . . .': ibid.

p.279 'judgement a balance . . .': 28 May 1957, private collection.

p.280 'feel no great heartbreak . . .': 23 March 1953.

p.280 'like Anthony Eden . . .': 23 November 1956, Bristol.

p.281 'Although I know . . .': 5 August 1947, Bristol.

p.281 'I think we could safely move away . . .': 1 May 1949, Bristol: EEF.

p.281 'acutely aware . . .': n.d., Bristol.

p.281 'I think we have . . .': HFP to AL, 14 September 1956, Bristol.

p.281 'why should we panic . . .': n.d., Bristol: EEF.

p.281 'one of the last great British poster designers . . .': *Penguin Collector*, December 1996.

p.282 'They haven't a single friend . . .': WEW to AL, 25 August 1957, Bristol.

p.282 'We have now definitely decided . . .': 13 March 1958, Bristol.

Chapter 16: Flirting and Foreign Parts

p.283 'suffering very much . . .': EEF to HFP, 27 February 1950, Bristol.

p.283 'I know myself better . . .': 12 March 1950, private collection.

p.283 'Look at poor old Allen Lane . . .': quoted in Morgan, *Agatha Christie*, p.400.

p.285 'a piece of mobile furniture . . .': author interview with Richard Hoggart.

p.285 'over-sweet perfume . . .': Margaret Clark to author, 12 October 2004.

p.286 'they accepted with alacrity . . .': 17 October 1955, Bristol.

p.286 'We must remember . . .': 9 August 1956, Bristol.

p.286 'most disturbing reports . . .': 5 May 1957, Bristol.

p.286 'Our marriage was not a happy one . . .': 10 August 1956, Bristol.

p.287 'the rather sticky period . . .': 14 May 1957, Bristol.

p.287 'Susanne is in Germany . . .': 11 February 1958, Bristol.

p.287 'I feel very badly about Susanne . . .': 1 August 1958, Bristol.

p.287 'She wants to come back . . .': n.d., private collection.

p.288 'cocktails on the house': diary, private collection.

p.288 'determined that it would be a mistake . . .': C. Y. Carstairs, Colonial Office memo, 7 September 1951, PRO.

p.288 'provided Lane in his zeal . . .': Mr MacLaren, Colonial Office memo, 20 September 1951, PRO.

p.289 'the old order is changing . . .': 7 January 1953, Bristol: EEF.

p.289 'a complete absence of vitality . . .': diary, private collection.

p.290 'to satisfy himself . . .': quoted in Dutton, *A Rare Bird*, p.2.

p.291 'I am tired of being kicked around . . .': 28 February 1955, Bristol: EEF.

p.291 'No, no, no . . .': Dutton, *A Rare Bird*, p.21.

p.291 'fearful drinking bout . . .': Hill, *The Pursuit of Publishing*, p.108.

p.291 'such a mess': 15 February 1956, Bristol.

p.292 'an unreasonable application . . .': 21 November 1956, Bristol.

p.292 'If it were not for the ties . . .': n.d., Bristol.

p.292 'a spot of bother . . .': n.d., Bristol.

p.292 'very raw deal indeed . . .': 5 May 1957, Bristol.

p.292 'we are entirely different . . .': 14 May 1957, Bristol.

p.293 'In a short space of time . . .': 29 October 1951, HRHRC.

p.293 'There is something about the American character . . .': 13 November 1956, Bristol.

p.293 'It is really the magnitude . . .': 19 May 1954, Bristol.

p.293 'My aim is, and has been . . .': 2 April 1960, private collection.

p.293 'Dorking North station . . .': 17 May 1956, Bristol.

p.294 'Penguin is the chief topic . . .': 8 September 1958, Bristol.

p.294 'A modest exhibitionist . . .': *The Making of a Publisher*, p.196.

p.294 'quite aware that Morris . . .': 7 November 1960, private collection.

p.295 'mighty impressive fellow': n.d., Bristol.

p.295 'You will look around . . .': 20 March 1959, private collection.

p.295 'If I were a director of Penguin England . . .': 24 August 1959, private collection.

p.295 'If he goes on with all this backwards bending . . .': 24 March 1959, Bristol.

p.295 'convinced that Pat and Mike . . .': 2 April 1960, private collection.

p.296 'sitting on the doorstep . . .': AL to Ernst, 12 September 1958, Bristol.

p.296 'a fine publisher . . .': Epstein, *Book Business*, p.83.

p.296 'Lane's bankers would no more let him sell . . .': ibid., p.84.

p.296 'I shudder at the idea . . .': 26 September 1961, private collection.

p.296 'I have never been more interested . . .': 30 November 1961, Bristol.

p.296 'Like you, I am really enthusiastic . . .': 4 December 1961, Bristol.

p.297 'Sorry, I can't be with you . . .': Canfield, *Up and Down and Around*, p.139.

p.297 'I don't think I have ever been faced . . .': 20 December 1961, Bristol.

p.297 'as of now, I would be quite content . . .': 31 December 1961, Bristol.

p.297 'How could I work . . .': quoted in Haydn, *Words and Faces*, p.130.

p.297 'would be less than frank . . .': 15 December 1961, Bristol.

p.298 'though I am not unsympathetic . . .': 20 June 1957, Bristol.

p.298 'I don't like the idea . . .': 27 June 1957, Bristol.

p.298 'As to what happens to the firm . . .': 28 May 1957, Bristol.

p.298 'on a bright sunny morning . . .': n.d., Bristol.

p.298 'I am now definitely decided . . .': 19 August 1958, Bristol.

p.299 'You would not find . . .': 12 August 1960, Bristol.

p.300 'I haven't a clue . . .': n.d., private collection.

Chapter 17: Changing the Guard

p.301 'You and Bill must realize . . .': n.d., Bristol.

p.301 'During our many years . . .': 20 April 1953, Bristol.

p.301 'Nothing in my life . . .': 20 August 1954, Bristol.

p.301 'I don't think we need any additional chaps . . .': 23 March 1953, Bristol.

p.302 'curt, big, bluff organizer . . .': quoted in Sinclair, *Arts and Cultures*, p.86.

p.302 'a very powerful *éminence rouge* . . .': ibid.

p.302 'You are the admiral . . .': Hoggart, *An Imagined Life*, p.229.

p.302 'said that his own secretary . . .': Clark, *The Other Half*, p.137.

p.302 'There is no question . . .': 31 December 1957, Bristol.

p.302 'the only permanent officer . . .': 1 August 1958, Bristol.

p.302 'become increasingly unreliable . . .': 7 March 1960, Bristol.

p.303 'The trouble is that she has no idea . . .': 11 February 1956, Bristol.

p.303 'not getting into people's hair . . .': 23 March 1958, Bristol.

p.303 'So little credit seems to come . . .': n.d., Bristol: EEF.

p.304 'I am a fighter . . .': n.d., Bristol: EEF.

p.304 'personal nightmare . . .': n.d., Bristol: EEF.

p.304 'prospective mate': 25 August 1957, Bristol.

p.305 'I should have thought . . .': 16 September 1957, Bristol: EEF.

p.305 'and contents himself . . .': n.d., Bristol.

p.305 'a very serious matter . . .': 16 November 1959, Bristol: EEF.

p.305 'current breakdown . . .': 18 December 1959, Bristol.

p.305 'deep and bitter regret . . .': 26 March 1958, Bristol.

p.306 'We can spot the chaps . . .': 30 April 1954, Bristol.

p.306 'I have a hunch . . .': 7 May 1937, Bristol.

p.306 'I was almost an archetype . . .': *Penguin Collector*, December 1993.

p.306 'needed to be in contact . . .': Hoggart, *An Imagined Life*, p.48.

p.308 'the most brilliant . . .': AL to HFP, 23 July 1958, Bristol.

p.308 'I wonder whether you could telephone . . .': n.d., Bristol.

p.308 'with more ardour than direction . . .': 8 August 1958, Bristol.

p.308 'You've only had it . . .': 7 December 1960, Bristol.

p.309 'how easily the impact . . .': 11 March 1960, Bristol.

p.309 'embarrass the publisher *enormously* . . .': 30 March 1960, Bristol.

p.310 'Well. What am I going to do? . . .': author interview with Tom Maschler.

p.311 'I feel this was a bit much . . .': 7 August 1960, Bristol.

p.311 'a bit of a bleat . . .': 12 August 1960, Bristol: EEF.

p.312 'paperbacks for the literate . . .': 25 July 1960, Bristol.

p.312 'You know, the best day's business . . .': interview with TK, 26 February 1971, Bristol.

p.312 'I am more sure than ever . . .': 24 December 1959, Bristol.

p.312 'said their pieces like a group of boys . . .': 27 June 1960, Bristol.

p.312 'the criticism would have been . . .': 4 July 1960, Bristol.

p.313 'In the circumstances . . .': n.d., Bristol.

p.313 'I have no comment . . .': 15 July 1960, Bristol.

p.313 'one of the nicest men . . .': n.d., Bristol.

p.313 'the governmental type . . .': AL to TK, 1963.

p.313 'brief and uneasy . . .': Woodhouse, *Something Ventured*, p.148.

p.313 'was the sum total . . .': ibid.

p.314 'was furious, and told me . . .': ibid.

Chapter 18: Lady Chatterley Goes on Trial

p.315 'I remember AL looking up . . .': quoted in Penguin Collectors Society, *Twenty-One Years*, p.48.

p.316 'there's a time in a publishing firm . . .': interview with Heather Mansell-Jones, 1968.

p.316 'My own view has always been . . .': 7 March 1960, Bristol.

p.316 'I don't see myself in the role of crusader . . .': quoted in Rolfe, *Sixty Penguin Years Plus Two*.

p.317 'that indefatigable scourge . . .': quoted in Sutherland, *Offensive Literature*, p.33.

p.320 'as a matter of principle . . .': Austin Strutt to Sir Theobald Mathew, 17 June 1960, PRO.

p.321 'in the case of an old-timer . . .': 13 July 1960, PRO.

p.321 'if the remainder of the work . . .': 20 August 1960, PRO.

p.321 'trashy novelette . . .': n.d., PRO.

p.322 'up to the standards . . .': notes on interview with Holroyd-Reece, 29 September 1960, PRO.

p.323 'a most formidable . . .': Rubinstein to Glover, 10 March 1960, Bristol.

p.323 'an essentially wholesome book': 9 October 1960, Bristol.

p.323 'regard its suppression as deplorable . . .': 19 August 1960, Bristol.

p.323 'wholly regrettable and misguided . . .': 19 August 1960, Bristol.

p.323 'one of the most outstanding novelists . . .': 17 August 1960, Bristol.

p.323 'What really enrages me . . .': 26 October 1960, Bristol.

p.323 'I find some parts of the book . . .': 22 August 1960, Bristol.

p.323 'tiresome case . . .': 15 August 1960, Bristol.

p.323 'dull, absurd in places . . .': to Michael Rubinstein, 21 August 1960, Bristol.

p.323 'unutterable boredom . . .': quoted in Edwards, *Victor Gollancz*, p.677.

p.324 'my husband said NO . . .': 20 August 1960, Bristol.

p.325 'If a man likes to have his wife . . .': 3 October 1960, Bristol.

p.325 'the copying process . . .': 21 September 1960, PRO.

p.325 'offered openly and persuasively . . .': Crump to Simpson, 22 September 1960, PRO.

p.326 'Normally one would not expect . . .': 21 September 1960, PRO.

p.326 'the whole place sighed . . .': *New Yorker*, 19 November 1960.

p.326 'lean figure in a close grey wig . . .': ibid.

p.327 'I put my feet up on the desk . . .': Hoggart, *An Imagined Life*, p.53.

p.327 'The prosecuting counsel . . .': 31 October 1960, Bristol.

p.327 'high cheek-bones . . .': *Esquire*, April 1961.

p.327 'scrupulously fair': Hyde, *The Lady Chatterley's Lover Trial*, p.16.

p.328 'a visible – and risible – effect . . .': Rolph, *The Trial of Lady Chatterley's Lover*, p.17.

p.328 'eminent and elderly . . .': Hoggart, *An Imagined Life*, p.54.

p.328 'the most hilariously fatuous dialogue . . .': *New Statesman*, 27 August 1960.

p.329 'in singing tones . . .': Mollie Panter-Downes, *New Yorker*, 19 November 1960.

p.329 'I'm going to have someone . . .': *Penguin Collector*, December 1993.

p.330 'he was manifestly ill-at-ease . . .': Williams, *Allen Lane: A Personal Portrait*, p.24.

p.331 'publication was by arrangement . . .': 21 June 1960, PRO.

p.331 'smiled, a little enigmatically . . .': Rolph, *The Trial of Lady Chatterley's Lover*, p.250.

p.331 'both disappointed and relieved . . .': 18 November 1960, Bristol.

p.331 'stand was magnificently courageous . . .': 15 November 1960, Bristol.

p.331 'Michael has avenged . . .': 19 November 1960, Bristol.

p.331 'because you had the courage . . .': 21 November 1960, Bristol.

p.331 'all right, but a bit old-fashioned . . .': n.d., Bristol.

p.331 'I am sorry to tell you . . .': Anne Scott-James to AL, 23 November 1960, Bristol.

p.332 'see no reason for Sir Allen . . .': quoted in Sutherland, *Offensive Literature*, p.25.

p.332 'the portrait of myself . . .': 27 March 1961, Bristol.

Chapter 19: Penguin Goes Public

p.334 'He is by nature warm . . .': 18 August 1956, Bristol.

p.334 'Relishing conviviality, he was terrified . . .': *New Statesman*, 4 May 1973.

p.334 'not an easy man . . .': Calvocoressi, *Threading My Way*, p.182.

p.335 'a stocky man in a conservative blue business suit . . .': *Observer*, 22 April 1973.

p.335 'I want you to go to Aleppo . . .': author interview with Raleigh Trevelyan.

p.336 'I should hate people to think . . .': quoted in de Bellaigue, *British Book Publishing as a Business*, p.30.

p.336 'well versed in the ways of jungle life . . .': AL to RL, 19 June 1961, Bristol.

p.336 'received a note from the accounts department . . .': 28 July 1960, Bristol.

p.337 'You may think I feel . . .': 28 July 1960, Bristol.

p.337 'For the first time . . .': 19 June 1961, Bristol.

p.338 'That old carp Cape': WEW to AL, 20 September 1949, Bristol.

p.339 'I will not have anything . . .': quoted in Pick, memoirs.

p.339 'He's either a publishing genius . . .': Pick, National Sound Archives tape.

p.339 'it would be a pity to let the Americans . . .': *Bookseller*, 13 January 1962.

p.340 'Where does this leave me?': author interview with Tom Maschler.

p.340 'DEADLOCK OVER TOM . . .': 7 June 1962, Bristol.

p.340 'GREAT REGRETS . . .': 8 February 1962, Bristol.

p.342 'I realize that . . .': Good Friday 1961, Bristol.

Chapter 20: The Rise and Fall of Tony Godwin

p.343 'a writer's publisher . . .': *London Review of Books*, 24 January 1980.

p.343 'instinctively rather than analytically . . .': Gordon, *Aren't We Due a Royalty Statement?*, p.89.

p.343 'the best uneducated mind . . .': interview with Charles Clark.

p.343 'revered, admired, loved . . .': *New York Times*, 3 May 1976.

p.343 'the inconspicuous of the trade . . .': TG to John Berger, 2 March 1967.

p.344 'The author may be illiterate . . .': 18 May 1962, Bristol.

p.344 'At the moment . . .': *Times Literary Supplement*, 17 June 1965.

p.345 'the Penguin fiction policy . . .': 30 August 1960.

p.346 'a manic jack-in-the-box . . .': Gordon, *Aren't We Due a Royalty Statement?*, p.87.

p.346 'often very prickly . . .': Greenfield, *Scribblers for Bread*, p.86.

p.346 'brusque and bullying manner': *Bookseller*, 9 February 1996.

p.348 'sociology to the level of a religion . . .': quoted in Rolfe, *Sixty Penguin Years Plus Two*.

p.348 'I give you that cliché . . .': ibid.

p.348 'a book must have been vulgarized . . .': *Times Literary Supplement*, 17 June 1965.

p.350 'Rieu blew up on the phone . . .': 1 April 1963, Bristol.

p.350 'Oh my poor series . . .': quoted in Radice, *The Translator's Art*, p.17.

p.350 'Where, sir, are Penguins going? . . .': 11 November 1966, Bristol.

p.351 'It was not until the 1960s . . .': 'The Paperback Revolution', in Briggs (ed.), *Essays in the History of Publishing*, p.303.

p.351 'beyond belief . . .': 11 April 1967, Bristol.

p.351 'junk . . .': Candida Donadio to TG, 12 September 1966, Bristol.

p.351 'Mr Powell's whole attitude . . .': *Evening Standard*, 8 September 1966.

p.352 'an extraordinary mixture . . .': memo, n.d., Bristol.

p.352 'Out would come a scrap of paper . . .': *Observer*, 22 April 1973.

p.352 'Allen's mind seemed to have closed . . .': memo, n.d., Bristol.

p.354 'I felt it was very fitting . . .': 28 September 1965, Bristol.

p.355 'complete incomprehension': memo, n.d., Bristol.

p.355 'Sir Allen Lane has returned . . .': *Guardian*, 1 September 1966.

p.356 'he paid you the compliment . . .': *London Review of Books*, 24 January 1980.

p.357 'a major opportunity for Penguin . . .': 30 December 1965, Bristol.

p.357 'close to being the most . . .': 30 December 1965, Bristol.

p.357 'such a gigantic waste . . .': 30 December 1965, Bristol.

p.358 'difficult and harassing author . . .': n.d., Bristol.

p.358 'I am, as you know . . .': 15 August 1966, private collection.

p.359 'his drawings are splendidly funny . . .': n.d., Bristol.

p.359 'As a hater of pornography . . .': 28 September 1966, Bristol.

p.359 'very little of the savagery . . .': 15 April 1964, Bristol.

p.359 'instinctive deference to the Establishment . . .': n.d., Bristol.

p.359 'I agree with you . . .': AL to TK, private collection.

p.360 'rather good': minutes of board meeting, 5 October 1966, Bristol.

p.361 'I am confident you will . . .': 5 December 1966, Bristol.

p.361 'one of the most offensive . . .': 30 November 1966, Bristol.

p.361 'It seems extraordinary . . .': 10 November 1966.

p.361 'horrified': 2 December 1966, Bristol.

p.361 'the person who can think up such muck . . .': Cantrell's bookshop to AL, 24 November 1966, Bristol.

p.361 'For the first time in my life . . .': 7 November 1966, Bristol.

p.361 'This letter is a somewhat difficult one . . .': 17 November 1966, Bristol.

p.362 'Penguin has frequently published . . .': n.d., Bristol.

p.362 'When any old family concern . . .': *Private Eye*, 9 December 1966.

p.362 'he got someone on the QT . . .': TG memo, n.d., Bristol.

p.363 'George, that bloody board outvoted me . . .': George Nicholls statement to TK, 9 October 1970, Bristol.

p.363 'asked to be relieved . . .': 13 April 1967, Bristol.

p.363 'Tony feels that he has been taking . . .': 18 December 1966, private collection.

p.364 'an exceptionally tough lawyer . . .': TG statement, n.d., Bristol.

p.364 'that shit Godwin': ibid.

p.365 'a shoddy business . . .': Segal to Steve Hare, 29 September 1994.

p.365 'The Godwin sacking farce . . .': 10 May 1967, Bristol.

p.365 'Sir Allen has long been known . . .': *Private Eye*, 12 May 1967.

p.365 'I am an ancient old piece . . .': *Daily Express*, 8 May 1967.

p.365 'and not in pubs . . .': *Daily Telegraph*, 8 May 1967.

p.366 'I've got rid of the buggers . . .': author interview with Betty Hartel.

p.366 'so much so that we concluded . . .': *The Times*, 8 May 1967.

p.366 'in view of the contribution . . .': 24 August 1967, Bristol.

p.367 'when the chemical bond . . .': *Bookseller*, 27 March 1976.

p.367 'the arbitrary use of capitalist power': author interview with Robert Hutchison.

p.367 'a troublesome, unorthodox presence . . .': *London Review of Books*, 24 January 1980.

p.367 'wined and dined': Arthur Crook, *Listener*, 15 November 1979.

p.368 'a large, fat man . . .': Dolley statement to Steve Hare, n.d.

p.368 'At home, Tony talked freely . . .': *Guardian*, 8 November 1979.

p.369 'I have always felt more grateful . . .': memo, n.d., Bristol.

p.369 'Allen Lane: I truly . . .': Morpurgo, *King Penguin*, p.353.

Chapter 21: Closing Time

p.370 'Don't let's exclude farming talk . . .': 17 June 1963, Bristol.

p.370 'I've often wondered if Susanne . . .': 17 May 1961, Bristol: EEF.

p.371 'a gem . . .': 5 October 1965.

p.371 'the most memorable and enjoyable moments . . .': 16 August 1964, Bristol.

p.371 'mercurial effervescence . . .': Lusty to AL, 17 August 1962, Bristol.

p.372 'an impossible man . . .': Lettice Lane interview with Steve Hare, 8 April 1994.

p.372 'What do you mean by "one of my authors"? . . .': author interview with Christine and David Teale.

p.372 'How shall I dazzle my audience today? . . .': ibid.

p.373 'was forever to be seen . . .': Gordon, *Aren't We Due a Royalty Statement?*, p.49.

p.373 'I've found a little man in Slough . . .': author interview with Tony Mott.

p.375 'a sort of Minister plenipotentiary . . .': 28 January 1961, Bristol.

p.375 'a smouldering expression . . .': *Books*, the NBL's magazine, quoted in Norrie, *Sixty Precarious Years*.

p.375 'human thermometer . . .': Morpurgo, *Master of None*, p.230.

p.375 'Jack, you've been here long enough . . .': ibid., p.233.

p.376 'as yet nothing in writing . . .': 28 March 1963, Bristol.

p.376 'so much twaddle': Dolley statement to Steve Hare, n.d.

p.376 'With the best grace . . .': 13 September 1963, Bristol.

p.377 'You haven't a hope in hell . . .': Margaret Clark to author, 9 October 2004.

p.377 'grimace of distaste': Margaret Clark to Steve Hare, 1 June 1994.

p.377 'He was so beguiling . . .': *Penguin Collector*, December 1999.

p.378 'was not devious or dishonest . . .': ibid.

p.378 'Why don't you chuck up Middlesex . . .': 6 December 1962, Bristol.

p.379 'in the best Lane tradition . . .': Dutton, *Snow on the Saltbush*, p.257.

p.379 'Get rid of those fucking boomerangs! . . .': quoted in Dutton, *A Rare Bird*, p.52.

p.379 'I promised to send you duplicates . . .': 12 December 1962, private collection.

p.379 'lose our controlling ability . . .': memo, n.d., Bristol.

p.380 'London Insults Our Best . . .': *Australian*, 10 October 1964.

p.380 'far too low a standard . . .': TG memo, n.d. (1964), Bristol.

p.381 'gruelling time . . .': 3 July 1961, private collection.

p.382 'Well, I don't go much on this safari lark . . .': *et seq.*, Ron Blass interviewed by Kaye Webb, n.d., Bristol.

p.384 'They tell me you have been doing your safari . . .': 30 November 1962, Bristol.

p.384 'I cannot pretend . . .': 25 May 1964, private collection.

p.384 'I am very flattered . . .': 5 June 1964, private collection.

p.384 'Allen's buoyancy and resilience . . .': Williams, *Allen Lane: A Personal Portrait*, p.89.

p.384 'Why should I . . .': Dolley to Steve Hare, 22 August 1994.

p.385 'very few firms survive . . .': author interview with Charles Clark.

p.385 'bitterness calcified . . .': *New Statesman*, 4 May 1973.

p.385 'I wondered whether . . .': n.d., Bristol.

p.385 'with considerable diffidence . . .': 10 March 1965, Bristol.

p.385 'most impressive in a quiet way . . .': 15 April 1965, Bristol.

p.386 'badly wants it, but is quite unfitted . . .': 14 December 1966, Bristol: EEF.

p.386 'if he felt he would eventually . . .': 12 December 1966, Bristol: EEF.

p.386 'What *I* find so difficult . . .': n.d., Bristol: EEF.

p.386 'Having so much enjoyed . . .': 23 September 1963, Bristol.

p.386 'I have heard nothing . . .': Lusty, *Bound to be Read*, p.225.

p.387 'terrible contempt . . .': statement by TG, n.d., Bristol.

p.387 'spiritless, ineffective and supine . . .': n.d., Bristol.

p.387 'a great disappointment to me . . .': 16 December 1966, Bristol.

p.387 'stick around': 11 February 1963, Bristol.

p.387 'angry and appalled': 14 April 1965, Bristol.

p.388 'fatter than ever . . .': WEW to AL, 20 September 1966, Bristol.

p.388 'I know quite a lot about TV . . .': WEW to AL, 13 February 1967, Bristol.

p.388 'I accept the inevitable twilight . . .': 20 April 1965, Bristol.

p.388 'You know and I know . . .': 14 April 1965, Bristol.

p.389 'eyes glazed . . .': Blond, *The Book Book*, p.81.

p.389 'a well-stocked cupboard . . .': Hoggart, *An Imagined Life*, p.90.

p.389 'You wouldn't understand . . .': author interview with Doug Rust.

p.389 'I believe that I was the only person . . .': Morpurgo to Steve Hare, 16 February 1995.

p.390 'dubious distinction . . .': Morpurgo, *King Penguin*, p.284.

p.390 'On the first occasion . . .': *New Statesman*, 4 May 1973.

p.390 'a salaried book-trade administrator . . .': Morpurgo, *King Penguin*, p.307.

p.390 'To hell with you both . . .': Morpurgo, *Master of None*, p.256.

p.391 'about my oldest friend . . .': AL to HFP, 10 January 1956, Bristol.

p.391 'If you're going to make changes . . .': David Pelham interview, 1984, Bristol.

p.392 'he flung his arms round me . . .': Hart-Davis to EEF, 6 September 1971, Bristol: EEF.

p.392 'with my feet on the desk . . .': author interview with Christine and David Teale.

p.392 'Why are you so scared . . .': 4 January 1966, Bristol.

p.392 'In general terms . . .': 12 July 1968, Bristol: EEF.

p.392 'reticent and unfussy . . .': n.d., Bristol.

p.393 'Your stamina and your resolution . . .': 24 July 1968, Bristol.

p.393 'appreciated your visits . . .': 28 August 1968.

p.393 'looks about half of himself . . .': 6 August 1968, Bristol: EEF.

p.393 'always been deep in debt . . .': Easter 1968, Bristol.

p.394 'the benefit of the doubt': author interview with Robert Hutchison.

p.394 'he had his hell here and now . . .': Lettice Lane interview with Steve Hare, 8 April 1994.

p.394 'As far as I'm concerned . . .': 7 August 1968, Bristol: EEF.

p.395 'never quite grasped . . .': Williams, *Allen Lane: A Personal Portrait*, p.59.

p.396 'You've heard what the Chancellor . . .': quoted in Rolfe, *Sixty Penguin Years Plus Two*.

p.396 'I feel a deep sense of exhaustion . . .': n.d., Bristol: EEF.

p.396 'was only biding his time . . .': AL to EEF, 6 January 1969, Bristol: EEF.

p.397 'You're welcome! . . .': author interview with Gordon Graham.

p.398 'darling Allen . . .': 16 June 1969, Bristol.

p.398 'That's an incredibly dirty book . . .': 19 April 1969, Bristol.

p.398 'I always had the feeling . . .': 4 August 1966, Bristol.

p.399 'Allen Lane is as ardent as I am . . .': 14 July 1950, Bristol.

p.399 'a pretty tough nut': AL to WEW, 26 May 1964, Bristol.

p.399 'I'm all for lumping the lot . . .': 17 December 1968, Bristol.

p.399 'hold on life is on a leasehold basis . . .': AL to EEF, 4 January 1969, Bristol: EEF.

p.399 'Our old pals are popping off . . .': 9 December 1969, Bristol.

p.400 'I often think that our old and well-weathered friendship . . .': 22 June 1969, Bristol.

p.400 'I really can't be of any use . . .': 16 May 1969, Bristol: EEF.

p.400 'I am still making progress . . .': 2 February 1970, Bristol: EEF.

Bibliography

Addison, Paul, *British Politics and the Second World War*, London: Jonathan Cape, 1975.

Attenborough, John, *Hodder & Stoughton, Publishers: 1868–1975*, London: Hodder, 1975.

Ayer, A. J., *More of My Life*, London: Collins, 1984.

Barber, Michael, *Anthony Powell: A Life*, London: Duckworth, 2004.

Barker, Nicolas, *Stanley Morison*, London: Macmillan, 1972.

Barnett, Correlli, *The Audit of War: The Illusion and Reality of Britain as a Great Nation*, London: Macmillan, 1986.

Bartram, Alan, *Making Books: Design in British Publishing since 1945*, London: British Library, 1999.

Bishop, Morchard, *The Green Tree and the Dry*, London: Jonathan Cape, 1939.

Blond, Anthony, *The Book Book*, London: Jonathan Cape, 1985.

Blond, Anthony, *Jew Made in England*, London: Timewell Press, 2004.

Bonn, Thomas L., *Heavy Traffic and High Culture: New American Library as Literary Gatekeeper in the Paperback Revolution*, Carbondale: Southern Illinois UP, 1989.

Box, Muriel, *Rebel Advocate: A Biography of Gerald Gardiner*, London: Gollancz, 1983.

Briggs, Asa (ed.), *Essays in the History of Publishing*, Harlow: Longman, 1984.

Brophy, John, *Britain Needs Books*, London: National Book Council, 1942.

Brown, Iain D., *Tony Godwin: Publishing Genius, 1960–67*, MA thesis, School of Advanced Study, University of London, 1996.

Calder, Angus, *The People's War: Britain 1939–45*, London: Jonathan Cape, 1969.

Calvocoressi, Peter, *Threading My Way*, London: Duckworth, 1994.

Canfield, Cass, *Up and Down and Around: A Publisher Recalls the Time of his Life*, London: Collins, 1972.

Carey, John, *The Intellectuals and the Masses: Pride and Prejudice among the*

Literary Intelligentsia 1880–1939, London: Faber, 1992.

Carpenter, Humphrey, *The Envy of the World: Fifty Years of the Third Programme*, London: Weidenfeld & Nicolson, 1996.

Carter, John, 'The Typography of the Cheap Reprint Series', in *Typography* No. 7, 1938.

Cerf, Bennett, *At Random*, New York: Random House, 1977.

Cherry, Bridget, *The Buildings of England, Ireland, Scotland and Wales: A Short History and Bibliography*, Penguin Collectors' Society, 1998.

Cinamon, Gerald (ed.), 'Hans Schmoller: His Life and Work', in *Monotype Recorder*, New Series, No. 6, April 1987.

Clark, Kenneth, *The Other Half: A Self-Portrait*, London: John Murray, 1977.

Clark, Margaret (ed.), *Signal 70: Approaches to Children's Books*, Stroud: The Thimble Press, 1993.

Crutchley, Brooke, *To Be a Printer*, London: The Bodley Head, 1980.

Danchev, Alex, *Oliver Franks: Founding Father*, Oxford: OUP, 1993.

Davis, Kenneth C., *Two-Bit Culture: The Paperbacking of America*, Boston: Houghton Mifflin, 1984.

de Bellaigue, Eric, *British Book Publishing as a Business since the 1960s*, London: British Library, 2004.

Dent, J. M., *The Memoirs of J. M. Dent*, London: Dent, 1928.

Dickson, Lovat, *The House of Words*, London: Macmillan, 1963.

Duff, Shiela Grant, *The Parting of Ways: A Personal Account of the Thirties*, London: Peter Owen, 1982.

Dutton, Geoffrey, *Snow on the Saltbush: The Australian Literary Experience*, Ringwood: Viking Australia, 1984.

Dutton, Geoffrey, *A Rare Bird: Penguin Books in Australia 1946–96*, Ringwood: Penguin Australia, 1996.

Edwards, Russell, *The Penguin Classics*, Miscellany 9, Penguin Collectors' Society, June 1994.

Edwards, Russell, and Hall, David J., *'So Much Admired': Die Insel-Bucherei and the King Penguin Series*, Edinburgh: Salvia Books, 1988.

Edwards, Russell, and Hare, Steve (eds.), *Twenty-One Years*, Miscellany 10, Penguin Collectors' Society, July 1995.

Edwards, Russell, and Hare, Steve (eds.), *Pelican Books: A Sixtieth Anniversary Celebration*, Miscellany 12, Penguin Collectors' Society, 1997.

Edwards, Ruth Dudley, *Victor Gollancz: A Biography*, London: Gollancz, 1987.

Ellmann, Richard, *James Joyce's Ulysses: A Short History*, Harmondsworth: Penguin, 1969 (written to accompany the first Penguin publication of *Ulysses*).

Enoch, Kurt, *Memoirs Written for His Family*, New York: privately published, 1984.

Epstein, Jason, *Book Business: Publishing Past, Present and Future*, New York: Norton, 2001.

Ernst, Morris, *The Best is Yet*, New York: Harper, 1945.

Feather, John, *A History of British Publishing*, London: Croom Helm, 1988.

Flower, Desmond, *The Paperback: Its Past, Present and Future*, Arborfield, 1959.

Flower, Desmond, *Fellows in Foolscap: Memoirs of a Publisher*, London: Hale, 1991.

Frederiksen, Erik Ellegaard, *The Typography of Penguin Books* (translated by K. B. Almlund), Penguin Collectors' Society, 2004.

Fussell, Paul, *Wartime: Understanding and Behavior in the Second World War*, New York: OUP, 1989.

Games, Stephen (ed.), *Pevsner on Art and Architecture: The Radio Talks*, London: Methuen, 2002.

George, T. J. S., *Krishna Menon: A Biography*, London: Jonathan Cape, 1963.

Good, Estrid Bannister, *Smorrebrod and Cherry Blossom: An Autobiography*, privately published, 1992.

Gordon, Giles, *Aren't We Due a Royalty Statement? A Stern Account of Literary, Publishing and Theatrical Folk*, London: Chatto & Windus, 1993.

Graham, Tim, *Penguins in Print: A Bibliography*, Penguin Collectors' Society, 2003.

Green, Evelyne, *The Pictorial Cover: 1960–1980*, Manchester Polytechnic Central Library, 1981.

Greenfield, George, *Scribblers for Bread*, London: Hodder, 1989.

Hale, Kathleen, *A Slender Reputation: An Autobiography*, London: Warne, 1994.

Hare, Steve (ed.), *Allen Lane and the Penguin Editors 1935–1970*, Harmondsworth: Penguin, 1995.

Hare, Steve (ed.), *Father and Son*, Penguin Collectors' Society, 1999.

Hare, Steve (ed.), *Lost Causes*, Penguin Collectors' Society, 1998.

Haskell, Arnold, *Balletomane at Large: An Autobiography*, London: Heinemann, 1972.

Haydn, Hiram, *Words and Faces*, New York: Harcourt Brace, 1974.

Hermann, Frank, *Low Profile: A Life in the World of Books*, Nottingham: Plough Press, 2002.

Hewison, Robert, *Under Siege: Literary Life in London, 1939–45*, London: Weidenfeld & Nicolson, 1977.

Higham, David, *Literary Gent*, London: Jonathan Cape, 1978.

Hill, Alan, *The Pursuit of Publishing*, London: John Murray, 1988.

Hill, C. P., *The History of Bristol Grammar School*, London: Pitman, 1951.

Hiscock, Eric, *Last Boat to Folly Bridge*, London: Cassell, 1951.

Hodges, Sheila, *Gollancz: The Story of a Publishing House 1928–1978*, London: Gollancz, 1978.

Hoggart, Richard, *The Uses of Literacy*, London: Chatto & Windus, 1957.

Hoggart, Richard, *A Sort of Clowning. Life and Times: 1940–59*, London: Chatto & Windus, 1990.

Hoggart, Richard, *An Imagined Life. Life and Times: 1959–91*, London: Chatto & Windus, 1992.

Holroyd, Michael, *The Lure of Fantasy: Bernard Shaw, Volume III, 1918–1950*, London: Chatto & Windus, 1991.

Holroyd, Michael, 'The Whispering Gallery', in *Works on Paper*, London: Little, Brown, 2002.

Hopkinson, Tom, *Picture Post 1938–50*, Harmondsworth: Penguin, 1970.

Hopkinson, Tom, *Of This Our Time: A Journalist's Story*, London: Hutchinson, 1982.

Howard, Michael, *Jonathan Cape, Publisher*, London: Jonathan Cape, 1971.

Hunter, Ian, *Nothing to Report: The Life of Hesketh Pearson*, London: Hamish Hamilton, 1987.

Hyde, H. Montgomery, *The Lady Chatterley's Lover Trial*, London: The Bodley Head, 1990.

Hynes, Samuel, *The Auden Generation: Literature and Politics in England in the 1930s*, London: The Bodley Head, 1976.

Ingrams, Richard, *God's Apology: A Chronicle of Three Friends*, London: André Deutsch, 1977.

Joicey, Nicholas, 'A Paperback Guide to Progress: Penguin Books 1935– c. 1951', in *Twentieth Century British History*, Vol. 4, No. 1, 1993.

Joy, Thomas, *Mostly Joy: A Bookman's Story*, London: Michael Joseph, 1971.

Keir, David, *The House of Collins*, London: Collins, 1952.

Kershaw, Ian, *Making Friends with Hitler: Lord Londonderry and Britain's Road to War*, London: Allen Lane, 2004.

Kingsford, R. J. L., *The Publishers' Association 1896–1946*, Cambridge: CUP, 1970.

Laity, Paul (ed.), *Left Book Club Anthology*, London: Gollancz, 2001.

Lambert, J. W., and Ratcliffe, Michael, *The Bodley Head 1887–1987*, London: The Bodley Head, 1987.

Landau, Rom, *Love for a Country: Contemplations and Conversations*, London: Nicholson & Watson, 1939.

Lane, Richard, unpublished 'Reminiscences', Bristol University Library.

le Mahieu, D. L., *A Culture for Democracy: Mass Communication and the Cultivated Mind*, Oxford: OUP, 1988.

Lehmann, John, *The Whispering Gallery*, London: Longman, 1955.

Lehmann, John, *I Am My Brother*, London: Longman, 1960.

Lehmann, John, *The Ample Proposition*, London: Eyre & Spottiswoode, 1966.

Lehmann, John, *Thrown to the Woolfs*, London: Weidenfeld & Nicolson, 1978.

Lehmann, John, and Fuller, Roy (eds.), *The Penguin New Writing: An Anthology*, Harmondsworth: Penguin, 1985.

Loxley, Simon, *Type: The Secret History of Letters*, London: I. B. Tauris, 2004.

Lusty, Robert, *Bound to be Read*, London: Jonathan Cape, 1975.

McCleery, Alistair, 'The Return of the Book Publisher', in *Book History*, Vol. 5, Pennsylvania State University Press, 2002.

McKibbin, Ross, *Classes and Cultures: England 1918–1951*, Oxford: OUP, 1998.

McLaine, Ian, *Ministry of Morale: Home Front Morale and the Ministry of Information in World War II*, London: Allen & Unwin, 1979.

McLean, Ruari, *Modern Book Design: From William Morris to the Present Day*, London: Faber, 1958.

McLean, Ruari, *Jan Tschichold: Typographer*, London: Lund Humphries, 1975.

McLean, Ruari, *Jan Tschichold: A Life in Typography*, London: Lund Humphries, 1997.

McLean, Ruari, *True to Type*, London: Werner Shaw, 2000.

Mallowan, Max, *Mallowan's Memoirs*, London: Collins, 1977.

Mannin, Ethel, *Confessions and Impressions*, London: Jarrolds, 1930.

Mannin, Ethel, *Young in the Twenties*, London: Hutchinson, 1971.

Manvell, Roger, Introduction to *The Penguin Film Review*, London: Scolar Press, 1977.

Mardersteig, Giovanni, *The Officina Bodoni*, Verona: Edizioni Valdonega, 1980.

Marwick, Arthur, *British Society Since 1945*, London: Allen Lane, 1982.

Maschler, Tom, *Publisher*, London: Picador, 2005.

May, J. Lewis, *John Lane and the Nineties*, The Bodley Head, 1936.

Mehta, Ved, *John is Easy to Please: Encounters with the Written and the Spoken Word*, London: Secker & Warburg, 1971.

Moran, James, *The Double Crown Club: A History of Fifty Years*, London: Westerham Press, 1974.

Morgan, Janet, *Agatha Christie: A Biography*, London: Collins, 1984.

Morgan, Kenneth O., *The People's Peace*, Oxford: OUP, 1990.

Morpurgo, J. E., *Allen Lane: King Penguin*, London: Hutchinson, 1979.

Morpurgo, J. E., *Master of None: An Autobiography*, Manchester: Carcanet, 1990.

Mountain, Penny, and Foyle, Christopher, *Foyles: A Celebration*, London: Foyles, 2003.

Mowl, Timothy, *Stylistic Cold Wars: Betjeman versus Pevsner*, London: John Murray, 2000.

Muspratt, Eric, *Fire of Youth: The Story of Forty-five Years' Wandering*, London: Duckworth, 1948.

Norrie, Ian, *Mumby's Publishing and Bookselling in the Twentieth Century*, London: Bell & Hyman, 1982.

Norrie, Ian, *Sixty Precarious Years: A Short History of the National Book League 1925–1985*, London: National Book League, 1985.

Nowell-Smith, Simon, *The House of Cassell 1848–1958*, London: Cassell, 1958.

Orwell, George, *The Lion and the Unicorn: Socialism and the English Character*, London: Secker, 1941.

Partridge, Frances, *Everything to Lose: Diaries 1945–1960*, London: Gollancz, 1985.

Peaker, Carol, *The Penguin Modern Painters: A History*, Penguin Collectors' Society, 2001.

Pearson, Hesketh, *Hesketh Pearson by Himself*, London: Heinemann, 1965.

Pearson, Joe, *Penguins March On: Books for the Forces during World War II*, Penguin Collectors' Society, 1996.

Penguin Books, *Penguins: A Retrospect 1935–51*, Harmondsworth: Penguin, 1951.

Penguin Books, *Penguins Progress 1935–60*, Harmondsworth: Penguin, 1960.

Penguin Books, *Fifty Penguin Years*, Harmondsworth: Penguin, 1985.

Pepper, Terence, *Howard Coster's Celebrity Portraits*, London: National Portrait Gallery, 1985.

Petersen, Clarence, *The Bantam Story: Thirty Years of Paperback Publishing*, New York: Bantam, 1970.

Pevsner, Nikolaus, 'Some Words on the Completion of The Buildings of England', in *Staffordshire*, Harmondsworth: Penguin, 1974.

Pick, Charles, unpublished memoirs (private collection).

Powers, Alan, *Front Cover: Great Book Jacket and Cover Design*, London: Mitchell Beazley, 2001.

Priestley, J. B., *English Journey*, London: Heinemann, 1934.

Radice, William, and Reynolds, Barbara, *The Translator's Art: Essays in Honour of Betty Radice*, Harmondsworth: Penguin, 1987.

Rafferty, Peggy, *Food for the Duke*, Badger Press, 1983.

Raymond, Harold, *Publishing and Bookselling*, London: Dent, 1938.

Richards, J. M., *Memoirs of an Unjust Fella*, London: Weidenfeld & Nicolson, 1980.

Rolfe, John, with Cox, Wendy, *Sixty Penguin Years Plus Two: an Eccentric Chronicle Written for His Friends*, privately published, n.d.

Rolph, C. H., *The Trial of Lady Chatterley's Lover*, Harmondsworth: Penguin, 1961.

Rolph, C. H., *Books in the Dock*, London: André Deutsch, 1969.

Rose, Jonathan, *The Intellectual Life of the Working Classes*, New Haven and London: Yale University Press, 2001.

St John, John, *William Heinemann: A Century of Publishing*, London: Heinemann, 1990.

Schick, Frank L., *The Paperbound Book in America: The History of Paperbacks and their European Background*, New York: Bowker, 1958.

Schiffrin, André, *The Business of Books*, London: Verso, 2000.

Schmoller, Hans, *Two Titans: Mardersteig and Tschichold*, New York: The Typophiles, 1990.

Schreuders, Piet, *The Book of Paperbacks: A Visual History of the Paperback*, London: Virgin, 1980.

Simon, Oliver, *Printer and Playground: An Autobiography*, London: Faber, 1956.

Sinclair, Andrew, *Arts and Cultures: The History of the Fifty Years of the Arts Council in Great Britain*, London: Sinclair-Stevenson, 1995.

Sissons, Michael, and French, Philip (eds.), *The Age of Austerity*, London: Hodder, 1963.

Smith, David C. (ed.), *The Correspondence of H. G. Wells. Vol. 4: 1935–46*, London: Pickering & Chatto, 1998.

Smith, Harold S. (ed.), *War and Social Change: British Society in the Second World War*, Manchester: Manchester University Press, 1986.

Spencer, Herbert, 'Penguin on the March', in *Typographica* 5, June 1962.

Sutcliffe, Peter, *The Oxford University Press: an Informal History*, Oxford: OUP, 1978.

Sutherland, John, *Offensive Literature: Censorship in Britain, 1960–1982*, London: Junction Books, 1982.

Sutherland, John, *Fiction and the Fiction Industry*, London: Athlone Press, 1978.

Sutherland, John, *Reading the Decades: Fifty Years of the Nation's Bestselling Books*, London: BBC Books, 2002.

Taylor, A. J. P., *English History 1914–1945*, Oxford: OUP, 1965.

Tebbel, John, *Between Covers: The Rise and Transformation of Book Publishing in America*, New York: OUP, 1987.

Tolley, A. J., *John Lehmann: A Tribute*, Ottawa: Carleton University Press, 1987.

Topolski, Feliks, *Fourteen Letters*, London: Faber, 1988.

Travers, Ben, *A-Sitting on a Gate: Autobiography*, London: W. H. Allen, 1978.

Travis, Alan, *Bound and Gagged: A Secret History of Obscenity in Britain*, London: Profile Books, 2000.

Unwin, Philip, *The Publishing Unwins*, London: Heinemann, 1972.

Unwin, Stanley, *Publishing in Peace and War*, London: Allen & Unwin, 1944.

Unwin, Stanley, *The Truth About a Publisher*, London: Allen & Unwin, 1960.

Wallis, Philip, *At the Sign of the Ship: Notes on the House of Longman 1724–1974*, Harlow: Longman, 1974.

Warburg, Fredric, *An Occupation for Gentlemen*, London: Hutchinson, 1959.

Warburg, Fredric, *All Authors are Equal*, London: Hutchinson, 1973.

Watson, Graham, *Book Society*, London: André Deutsch, 1980.

Weidenfeld, George, *Remembering My Good Friends: An Autobiography*, London: Collins, 1994.

Weight, R., 'State, Intelligentsia and the Promotion of National Culture in Britain', in *Historical Research: the Bulletin of the Institute of Historical Research*, 1996.

West, W. J. (ed.), *Orwell: The War Broadcasts*, London: Duckworth and BBC Books, 1985.

Weybright, Victor, *The Making of a Publisher*, London: Weidenfeld & Nicolson, 1968.

Whitehead, Ella and John (eds.), *John Lehmann's 'New Writing': An Author Index*, Edwin Mellen Press, 1990.

Whitehead, Kate, *The Third Programme: A Literary History*, Oxford: OUP, 1989.

Williams, Gertrude, *W. E. Williams: Educator Extraordinary*, Penguin Collectors' Society, 2000.

Williams, Raymond, *The Long Revolution*, London: Chatto & Windus, 1961.

Williams, W. E., *Allen Lane: A Personal Portrait*, London: The Bodley Head, 1973.

Wilson, Charles, *First with the News: The History of W. H. Smith 1792–1972*, London: Jonathan Cape, 1985.

Woodhouse, C. M., *Something Ventured*, London: Granada, 1982.

Woolf, Leonard, *Beginning Again*, London: The Hogarth Press, 1964.

Wyatt, Woodrow, *Distinguished for Talent*, London: Hutchinson, 1958.

Ziegler, Philip, *Rupert Hart-Davis: Man of Letters*, London: Chatto & Windus, 2004.

Zuckerman, Solly, *From Apes to Warlords: An Autobiography*, London: Hutchinson, 1978.

Index

Abercrombie, Michael, 269
Abyssinia, 129
Ackerley, Joe Randolph: *My Father and Myself*, 398
Ackermann, Rudolph, 145
Acland, Sir Richard, 197, 199; *Unser Kampf*, 199
Adam, Sir Ronald, 162
Adams, Evangeline, 58
Adamson, Joy, 384
Addison, Paul, 198, 391
Adelphi (magazine), 48
Aden, 146
Adprint, 144–5
Africa: AL's interest in, 288
Agate, James, 102, 107
Albany, Piccadilly, 57–8
Albatross Verlag (publishers): Continental Editions, 76–9; Enoch and, 140–2
Aldridge, Alan, 350
Allen & Unwin (publishers): founded, 27; wartime losses through bombing, 155; publishes Hogben, 172–3
Allen, Ashton, 225
Allen Lane Charitable Foundation, 385, 400
Allen Lane The Penguin Press (ALPP): launched, 20, 21, 354–6, 363; Boyle and, 385; proposed closure, 391; expensiveness, 395
Allen, W. H. (publishers), 339
Alvarez, Al, 343, 356, 367
American Civil Liberties Union, 62
Amis, (Sir) Kingsley, 363; *Lucky Jim*, 308

Anchor Books (USA), 294
Angell, Norman: *The Great Illusion*, 135
Annan, Noel (*later* Baron), 322, 329
Annenberg family, 209
Apuleius: *The Golden Ass*, 46
Architectural Review, 253–4
Ardizzone, Edward, 281; *Paul the Hero of the Fire*, 261
Army Bureau of Current Affairs (ABCA; *later* Bureau of Current Affairs), 160–2, 200–201, 234
Army Education Corps, 161
Arno, Peter, 60
Arnold, H. A. W.: with Bodley Head, 86; proposes sixpenny paperbacks to AL, 86; on AL's return from Ripon Hall conference, 89; visits Holy Trinity crypt, 108
Arnold, Matthew, 73
'Art for the People' scheme, 161, 188
Asquith, Anthony, 182
Asquith, Herbert Henry, 1st Earl of Oxford and Asquith, 40
Associated Television, 339
Astor, David, 4, 195, 243, 299
Athenaeum Printing Works, Redhill, 92
Atheneum (US publishers), 295–7
Atholl, Katharine Marjory Stewart-Murray, Duchess of, 137–8
Atkins, Robert, 53
Attlee, Clement (*later* 1st Earl), 192, 201–2
Auden, W. H.: in Spanish Civil War, 130; decamps to USA, 194
Australia: Dick in, 34–5, 229, 290–91,

Australia (*cont.*)
336; AL visits, 289–90, 372,
380–81; AL opens branch in,
290–91; Nora in, 371; AL's interest
in, 374, 378–80
Avon Books (USA), 209
Ayer, (Sir) A. J., 246, 248, 269

Baer, Bernhard, 189, 226
Bagnold, Enid: *National Velvet*, 93–4
Baker, John, 81
Baker, Peter, 375
Balcon, Michael, 182, 201
Baldick, Robert, 350
Balfour, Arthur James, 1st Earl, 40
Ballantine, Betty, 210, 214
Ballantine, Ian, 210–15, 219, 293
Balogh, Thomas (*later* Baron), 197
Baltimore, Maryland, 292–3
Bannister, Estrid, 117, 233, 284–5,
309, 371
Bantam Books (USA), 217
Barber, Elizabeth, 260
Barbirolli, Sir John, 182
Barcelona (restaurant), Soho, 127–8
Barker, Nicolas, 77
Barnes, George, 273
Barnett, Correlli, 196
Barrow, R. H.: *The Romans*, 236
Barry, (Sir) Gerald, 130, 134, 206
Bartholomew, Harry Guy, 130
Bartlett, Vernon, 131
Barton, Esmé, 289
Barton, J. E., 14
Bartram, Alan, 246
Bates, Ralph: *Lean Men*, 138–9
Batt, Anne, 365
Bawden, Edward, 144, 145, 185, 189,
281
Baxter, Walter: *The Image and the
Search*, 317
Beach, Sylvia, 61–2, 64, 77

Beales, H. Lance, 118–19, 128, 145,
166, 172, 210
Beardsley, Aubrey, 19–20
Beaverbrook, William Maxwell
Aitken, 1st Baron: and publication
of *The Whispering Gallery*, 49;
success, 72; requisitions
Harmondsworth in war, 168; and
prosecution of Baxter's *The Image
and the Search*, 317; eighty-fifth
birthday, 384
Beddington, Jack, 90, 254
Bedford, Sybille, 327, 329
Beerbohm, (Sir) Max, 145
Bell, Clive, 189
Bellow, Saul, 215, 351
Beloff, Nora: *The General Says No*, 347
Benckendorff, Count, 182
Benedict, Ruth, 215
Benn, Ernest (publisher): Sixpenny
Library, 75; Holroyd-Reece works
for, 77; AL acquires title from, 96
Bennett, Arnold, 22; Ethel Mannin
admires, 51; supports publication
of *Ulysses*, 62; *A Man from the
North*, 24
Bentwich, Norman, 57
Beowulf: transl. by David Wright, 252
Berger, John, 365
Berlin, Sir Isaiah, 219, 397
Bernal, J. D., 171
Bernstein, Sidney (*later* Baron), 158,
342
Bertram, Anthony, 183; *Design*, 140
Bessie, Mike, 295–6
Betjeman, (Sir) John, 139, 189, 227,
236, 253–4, 323, 378
Better Books (bookshop), 310
Bevan, Aneurin, 7, 257
Beveridge, William, Baron, 4, 192,
196; Report (1942), 195
Bevin, Ernest, 133, 204, 249

Bibliopola, 355

Bihalji-Merin, O. ('Peter Thoene'): *Modern German Art*, 139

Binder, Pearl, 36, 184, 234

Birch, Alwyn, 315

Bird, Frank, 167

Bird, Nora (*née* Lane; AL's sister): born, 8; inheritance from Annie, 49; accompanies AL to Aden and India, 146–7; marriage, 167; made temporary director of Penguin, 170; in New York, 211; in Australia, 371; holiday in Morocco with AL, 391; and AL's decline, 400; left nothing in AL's will, 400

Birdsall, Derek, 349

Birkenhead, F. E. Smith, 1st Earl of, 39

Birrell, Francis, 259

Bishop, Morchard: *The Green Tree and the Dry*, 238

Black, Mischa, 206

Blackwell, Sir Basil, 56, 82, 88–9, 333

Blackwood's (publishers): wartime losses, 155

Blake, Quentin, 349

Blass, Ron, 324, 328, 352, 360, 363, 368, 381–4, 400

Blast (magazine), 19

Blatchford, Robert, 276

Blond, Anthony, 358, 389

Blond, Neville, 297

Bluth, Dr Karl, 284

Blythe, Ronald: *Akenfield*, 355

Blyton, Enid, 324

Bodkin, Sir Archibald, 61

Bodley Head, The (publishers): AL joins, 5, 13, 16, 25; founded, 6, 18–21; in First World War, 12; publications, 24–5; staff, 27; incorporated as limited company, 32, 103; publishes Agatha Christie, 33–4; financial difficulties, 35, 36, 54, 59, 67–9, 103; and publication and court case of *The Whispering Gallery*, 36–48; Greenwood runs, 52; buys in rights from other publishers, 55–6; Modern Library, 56; publishes topical books, 56–7; Twentieth Century Library, 57, 116, 138; Penguin Books launched from, 60, 68; publishes *Ulysses*, 64–5; voluntary liquidation and rescue by Unwin and others, 69, 88; provides titles for first Penguins, 98; ends connection with Penguin, 103

Bodley, Sir Thomas, 18

Bone, L. Russell, 254

Boni & Liveright (US publishers), 36, 38, 62

book clubs, 81–2, 132–3

Book Export Scheme, 227

Book of the Month Club, 81

Book Production War Economy Agreement, 154

Book Society, 81, 84, 89, 270, 311

book tokens: proposed, 80

Book Trade Benevolent Fund, 401

Bookman, The (magazine), 311

Bookseller (magazine), 82, 88, 92, 102, 111, 145, 311, 339–40, 367

Booksellers' Association: opposes direct selling to readers, 107

Boots lending library, 79

Bosley, Cliff, 363

Bosschère, Jean de, 46

Boston, Mass., 292

Boswell, Ronald (*born* Bussweiller): joins Bodley Head, 32; publishes topical books, 56; and Bodley Head economies, 67; leaves Bodley Head, 68; Krishna Menon edits

Boswell, Ronald (*born* Bussweiller) (*cont.*)
  books for, 116; publishes Mowrer, 134
Bott, Alan, 81, 140, 270
Bottome, Phyllis: *The Mortal Storm*, 137; *Our New Order or Hitler's*, 200
Boulenger, E. G.: *The Wonders of Sea Life*, 185
Bouquet, A. C., 147
Boxer, Mark, 349, 351
Boyle, Sir Edward (*later* Baron), 363, 385–6, 392, 396, 398
Braine, John, 331; *Room at the Top*, 280, 309
Brandstetter, Oscar, 78
Braque, Georges, 189
Bray: Hind's Head, 145, 165
Brenan, Gerald, 371
Brickhill, Paul: *The Dam Busters*, 277
Briggs, Asa, Baron, 397
Bristol, 8–9, 11–12; St Mary Radcliffe church, 8, 12
Bristol Grammar School, 13–14
Britain: post-war political ideals, 191–2; overseas book trade, 233–4
'Britain Can Make It' exhibition, 200
British Book Centre, New York, 268
British Broadcasting Corporation (BBC): founded, 79; ethos, 271–3; Third Programme, 271–4, 276
Brockbank (cartoonist), 359
Brogan, D. W., 183
Broster, D. K.: *Sir Isumbras at the Ford*, 154
Brown, Curtis (literary agent), 77
Bryan, Judge (USA), 320
Buchanan, Colin: *Traffic in Towns*, 347
Buck, Pearl S.: *The Good Earth*, 208
Buckman, Peter, 343
Budberg, Moura, Baroness, 181, 185, 398

Buildings of England, The (Penguin series), 253, 353
Bulloch, J. M., 101
Bullock, Alan, Baron, 397
Bumpus (bookseller), 99, 299, 310
Bureau of Current Affairs *see* Army Bureau of Current Affairs
Burnley, Judith, 393
Burra, Edward, 189
Burroughs, William: *The Naked Lunch*, 333
Butler, Richard Austen (*later* Baron), 192, 320–21; Education Act (1944), 196
Butt, Dame Clara, 10
Byrne, Sir Laurence Austin (Mr Justice), 326–7, 330–31

Caine, Mark *see* Maschler, Tom
Caine, Michael, 358
Caldecott, Oliver, 279, 352, 367
Calder, John, 333
Calder, Ritchie (*later* Baron Ritchie-Calder), 131
Calder-Marshall, Arthur, 131, 267
Caldwell, Erskine: *God's Little Acre*, 217
Callaghan, James (*later* Baron), 396
Calvocoressi, Peter, 334
Cammaerts, Emile, 25
Campbell, Roy, 129
Campbell-Bannerman, Sir Henry, 32
Canfield, Cass, 209, 296–7, 338
Cape, Jonathan: on flair, 26; and Maurois' *Byron*, 56; publishes James Joyce works, 63; Travellers' Library, 74; publishes Radclyffe Hall, 77; character and behaviour, 96–7; agreement with Penguin, 96–8, 104, 353; Florin Library, 104; complains of non-payment of royalties, 145; refuses to cooperate with Penguin on children's books,

187; Maschler joins and reforms, 307, 310, 342; death, 338; AL offers to part-purchase company, 339–40

Carbonnel, Señor (of Barcelona restaurant), 127–8

Cardus, Neville, 182

Carey, John, 72

Carnegie, Dale: *How to Win Friends and Influence People*, 209

Carr, Edward Hallett, 130, 195

Carr-Gomme, Hubert, 32, 38–9, 57

Carrington, Noël, 141, 183–6, 232, 257–9, 370–71, 384

Carson, Rachel: *Silent Spring*, 236, 348

Carter, John, 141

Carthage (ship), 65

'Cassandra' *see* Connor, Bill

Cassell (publishers), 80, 93

Casson, Sir Hugh, 206; *Homes by the Million*, 200

Castle, Barbara (*later* Baroness), 115

Castor, Père, 184

Catholic Herald, 137

Cecil, Lord David, 322

Cecil, Edgar Robert Gascoyne-Cecil, Viscount, 40

Central Council for Army Education, 161

Centre for Contemporary Studies, Birmingham University, 389

Cerf, Bennett, 62, 64, 214, 296

Ceylon (Sri Lanka), 289

Chadwick, Paxton: *Pond Life*, 186; *Wild Animals in Britain*, 186; *Wild Flowers*, 185–6

Chalmers-Mitchell, Sir Peter, 119–20, 137

Chamberlain, Houston Stewart: *The Foundation of the Nineteenth Century*, 24

Chamberlain, Neville, 130, 146, 149, 192

Champneys health farm, Tring, 109, 284

Chapell, Mr (of W. H. Smith), 80–81

Chapman, Frederick, 20

Chapmansford, Hampshire, 371

Chatto & Windus (publishers): author works for, 3; Phoenix Library, 74, 91, 104; in group agreement with Penguin Books, 92–3, 103–4, 265, 353; and first Penguin titles, 98; publish *Night and Day*, 128; Zodiac Books, 144

Chaucer, Geoffrey: *The Canterbury Tales*, 273

Cherry-Garrard, Apsley: *The Worst Journey in the World*, 112

Chesterton, G. K., 22, 49; *Orthodoxy*, 24

Chevalier, Gabriel: *Clochemerle*, 281

Cheyney, Peter, 102, 249, 277

Childe, V. Gordon: *What Happened in History*, 171–2

China: AL visits, 289

Chopping, Richard, 257–61

Christie, Agatha: changes publishers, 33–4, 55; friendship with AL, 33, 71; marriage to Mallowan, 34; on AL as head of family, 66; on AL's reaction to death of brother John, 170; as Christine's godmother, 215; on AL's ageing appearance, 284; AL visits Iraq with, 287; covers redesigned, 350; *The Mousetrap*, 288; *Murder on the Links*, 98; *The Mysterious Affair at Styles*, 33–4, 98

Churchill, Randolph, 326; account of Six Day War (with son Winston), 391

Churchill, (Sir) Winston S.: and *The Whispering Gallery*, 36, 40; subscribes to *Ulysses*, 61; disapproves of Londonderry's views,

Churchill, (Sir) Winston S. (*cont.*)
136; Topolski drawing of, 150;
wartime premiership, 192–3;
accepts Beveridge Report, 196;
suspicion of ABCA influence, 200
cinema: as rival to books and reading,
79
Clackson, Norman, 111–12
Clarion (magazine), 276
Clark, Charles: on Penguin staff, 343,
352; praises Godwin, 343, 367;
favours publication of Siné
cartoons, 360–61, 363; in Prague,
363; and Godwin's dismissal and
compensation, 366–7; runs
Penguin Education, 376, 391; and
AL's impending retirement, 385;
runs Allen Lane the Penguin Press,
391
Clark, Kenneth (*later* Baron): in
wartime Ministry of Information,
157, 187, 196; co-founds Pilgrim
Trust, 160; preserves National
Gallery paintings in war, 160; and
wartime arts, 162, 187–8; in Tots
and Quots club, 171; and Eunice
Frost, 188–9, 303; oversees
Penguin Modern Painters, 188–90;
and post-war reconstruction, 196;
supports Pevsner, 254; disapproves
of Pelican History of Art, 256; as
Chairman of Arts Council, 302;
Landscape into Art, 304; *Meaning of
Art*, 304
Clark, Margaret, 223–4, 279, 377
Clark, R. & R. (printers), 205
Cleland, John: *Fanny Hill*, 333
Clore, Charles, 376
Cochrane, Jim, 352, 367, 369
Cockburn, Sir Alexander (Lord Chief
Justice), 316
Cockburn, Claud ('Frank Pitcairn'),

129–30, 131, 135
Coghill, Neville, 273
Cohen, J. M., 252, 350
Cole, G. D. H., 106, 133; *The
Meaning of Marxism*, 203
Cole, Margaret, 106
Coles, Joan, 91, 109, 268
Colette: *Gigi and the Cat*, 280
Collihole, Evelyn, 148, 392
Collihole, Joan, 148, 166–7, 287, 300,
391–2
Collins, Norman, 96, 339–40
Collins (publishers): as family firm, 2;
publish Agatha Christie, 33–4;
Pocket Classics series, 73; attempt
'Sevenpenny' series of hardback
books, 80; sell books through
Woolworth's, 99; White Circle list
(thrillers), 102, 106; New
Naturalist series, 140, 257; Britain
in Pictures series, 144; publish
wartime memoirs, 151–2; consider
purchasing Penguin, 298
Collins, W. A. R. ('Billy'): as gentleman publisher, 27; and Agatha
Christie, 34; and wartime publication regulations, 154; and natural
history books, 257; and Pan paperbacks, 270; and takeover of Pan,
339; inaugurates Fontana books,
354; licenses books to Puffin, 378;
publishes Australian anthology, 380;
and Joy Adamson, 384
Colonial Office: discusses Africa
situation with AL, 288
Common Wealth Party, 197–8
Communism: appeal in 1930s, 129–30,
132–3; and *Penguin New Writing*,
138–9; publications on, 203
Comstock Law (USA), 320
Connolly, Cyril: on biographies, 1;
on popular taste, 81, 84; patronizes

Champneys health farm, 109;
wartime debating, 158; edits
Horizon, 159, 175, 194, 272; and
demise of *Horizon*, 181; wartime
attitude, 194
Connor, Bill ('Cassandra'), 130, 135,
136; *The English at War*, 195
Conservative Party, 192, 201–2
Cooke, Alistair, 158, 183
Cooper, Barbara, 180
Cooper, Duff (*later* 1st Viscount
Norwich), 193, 199
Corgi (paperback books), 277–8, 366
Cornford, John, 129
Corvo, Baron *see* Rolfe, Frederick
Coster, Howard, 145
Costin (butler), 51
Cotham Vale, Bristol, 8–9, 12
Council for the Encouragement of
Music and the Arts (CEMA; *later*
Arts Council), 160–62
Country Life (magazine), 184
Cowell, W. S. (printer), 184
Crankshaw, Edward, 182
Crawford, Mr (headmaster), 10
Crawford, William, 158
Creak, Elizabeth, 168
Cripps, Sir Stafford, 132, 206
Criterion (magazine), 72, 175
Crockett, T. H., 28, 32, 42–3, 57
Croft, Freeman Wills, 239
Croft, Henry Page, 1st Baron, 162
Cronin, A. J., 84
Crook, Arthur, 359–60, 367–8, 386
Crowther, Geoffrey, 182, 299
Crowther, J. G., 139
Crump, Maurice, 321–2, 325–6, 331
Cudlipp, Hugh, 130
Current Affairs (magazine), 201
Curtis Bennett, Sir Henry, 47
Curtis Circulating Company (USA),
214

Curtis, John, 302, 305–7, 315, 349, 372
Curwen, Harold: *Printing*, 185

Daily Herald, 82, 199
Daily Mail: attacks *The Whispering
Gallery*, 39, 41, 43–4, 46–7;
founded, 72; offers works of
Shakespeare, 82; political stand-
point, 130; organizes wartime
Savoy lunch, 158
Daily Mirror, 130, 156, 195
Dalton, Hugh (*later* Baron), 133
Daphnis and Chloë, 330
Darwin, Robin, 353, 355
David, Elizabeth: *Mediterranean Food*,
303
Davidson, John, 19
Davies, Alun, 293
Davies, Bill and Annie, 371
Davies, Bob, 108, 110, 228
Davis, Sir Edmund, 76, 78
Dawson, Geoffrey, 130, 195
Day Lewis, Cecil, 158, 329
Decachord, The (magazine), 124
Deeping, Warwick: *Sorrell and Son*,
80
de Graff, Robert, 208
Deighton, Len: *Funeral in Berlin*,
357–8, 366
Dell, Ethel M., 106
Dell (US publishers), 209, 320
Dent, J. M.: founds Everyman's
Library, 73, 117; interest in
typography, 241
Deutsch, André: character, 2
Dicks, John: Illustrated Novels, 72
Dickson, Rache Lovat, 88
Dillon, Una, 361
Disney, Walt: 'Silly Symphonies'
series, 59
Divorce of Lady X, The (film), 146
Docker, Sir Bernard, 375

Dodd, Mead (New York publishers), 55

Dolley, Chris, 352, 368, 374, 376, 384, 387, 394–6

Donadio, Candida, 351

dos Passos, John, 183

Double Crown Club, 141, 183, 244

Douglas, James, 63

Drinkwater, John and Daisy, 29

Drummond, H. V.: *The Flying Postman*, 261

Drummond, Lindsay: made director of Bodley Head, 32; and Bodley Head economies, 67; leaves Bodley Head, 68; and *New Writing*, 174–5

du Cann, Richard, 323–4, 326

du Gard, Roger Martin, 55

Dunbar, John Willis, 36–7

Dutton, Geoffrey, 378–80

Economist (magazine), 107, 299

Eden, Anthony (*later* 1st Earl of Avon), 280, 326

Editions Penguin (French), 150

Editions Pingouin, 150

Edizioni di Pinguino, 150

Education Act (1944), 196

Edward, Prince of Wales (*later* King Edward VIII and Duke of Windsor), 31–2

Egerton, George (i.e. Mrs Egerton Clairmonte): *Keynotes*, 21

Egoist Press, 61

Eichberg, Julius, 21

Eliot, T. S.: recommends Joyce's *Ulysses* to Woolfs, 60; agrees to publish *Finnegans Wake*, 63; political views, 129, 191; edits *Criterion*, 175; view of *Lady Chatterley's Lover*, 322–3; at *Lady Chatterley* trial, 329, 331

Ellis, Henry Havelock, 62

Emmett, Roland, 206

Enoch, Kurt: and Albatross Verlag, 76–9; association with AL, 77, 140–42, 212; leaves Germany for Paris, 78, 140–41; interned, 212; in USA, 212–16, 218–19; relations with Weybright, 215–16, 218–19, 339; Eunice Frost on, 219; and New American Library, 219, 293, 403

Epstein, Jason, 293–4, 296

Ernst, Morris, 62, 64, 219, 294, 296–7; *The Best is Yet*, 294

Evans, Charles, 93–4

Evans, Sir Ifor, 159–60, 162, 233

Evening Standard, 51, 102, 145, 192

Everyman's Library: founded, 73–4, 117; out-of-print books in wartime, 155; design, 241; classical titles, 252

Excess Profits Tax, 155

Eyre & Spottiswoode (publishers): wartime losses, 155

Faber & Faber (publishers), 265

Faber Gallery, 190

Faber, Sir Geoffrey, 156–7, 267

Facetti, Germano, 349–50

Fact (magazine), 131

Fairley, Tom, 262–3

Falcon Press, 375

Falfield, 53

Falkner, J. Meade: *The Nebuly Coat*, 330

Festival of Britain (1951), 206

Field, Marshall III, 214

Figgis, Allen, 361–2

First Editions Club, 29, 53

Fishenden, R. B., 145, 189

Fisher, James, 140, 257

Fisher, Shelton, 397

Flanner, Janet, 183

Fleming, Ian: James Bond books, 277, 280, 358

Fleming, John, 335

Fleuron (magazine), 242

Flower, Desmond, 93

Flower, Sir Newman, 93

Foges, Wolfgang, 144

Fontana books, 354

Foot, Michael, 195, 202; *Guilty Men* (with others), 195

Forces Book Club, 163–4

Ford, Boris, 399

Ford, Ford Madox: *The Good Soldier*, 25

Foreman, Dennis, 302

Forester, C. S., 55

Forster, E. M., 329

Forward March (movement), 197, 199

Fox, Ralph, 57

Foyle, Christina, 51–2, 85, 156

Foyle's bookshop, London: lending library, 79

France: AL visits, 66, 232, 236, 283; staff outings to, 111, 228

France, Anatole, 24, 30–31

François, André, 359

Frankfurt Zoo, 373

Franklin, Cecil, 113

Frankly Speaking (radio programme), 15

Franks, Oliver, Baron, 16

Fraser, Gordon, 310; *Furniture*, 200

Fraser, Lionel, 298

Frayn, Michael, 198, 206

Freedman, Barnett, 141

Frere, A. S., 266, 298, 317–18

Freud, Sigmund: *Totem and Taboo*, 121

Friedlander, Elizabeth, 264

Frost, Eunice: character and background, 123–4, 125–6; leaves Penguin, 123, 385; works for Penguin, 123–6; lunches at Barcelona restaurant, 128; at Hind's Head celebration, 146; and Penguin's wartime publications, 149, 159; and AL's marriage, 167, 235; moves to Silverbeck in war, 168; and Lehmann's CV, 176; and *Penguin New Writing*, 180; works on Penguin Modern Painters, 188–9; and Hersey's *Hiroshima*, 202; in USA, 214; and AL's breach with Weybright, 218; attends staff meetings, 230; Tatyana Kent stays with, 234; Glover on, 240; relations with AL, 248–9; responsibilities at Penguin, 248; health, 249, 303–5; view of colleagues, 249–50; Richard Chopping on, 260; at editorial meeting with Morpurgo, 263; in *After the Conference* painting, 269; and AL's hopes to publish Ian Fleming's James Bond book, 277; and Penguin cover designs, 280–81, 348, 402; on AL's reaction to father's death, 283; AL confides in, 286–7, 370, 385, 387; letter from AL in Ceylon, 289; AL assures of importance to Penguin, 301–2; engagement and marriage to Kemp, 304–5; made director of Penguin, 305; diminishing role, 306; failures of judgement, 308–9; Maschler works with, 308–9; and Godwin's appointment, 311, 385; and Woodhouse's appointment, 312; and AL's changing pace of life, 342; confidence in Penguin superiority, 344; disapproves of Godwin, 352; and succession to AL, 386; low earnings, 387; and AL's health worries, 392; and AL's final illness, 393–4, 400; and AL's reluctance to return to management, 394; on Dolley's administration, 396

Fry, Maxwell, 140, 196–7
Fussell, Paul, 159
Fyvel, Tosco, 195

Galbraith, J. K.: *The Affluent Society*, 347
Gale, Mr (Penguin office manager), 223
Gallagher, William: *The Case for Communism*, 203
Gallico, Paul, 183
Games, Abram, 281, 348
Gant, Roland, 338–40
Gardiner, Gerald (*later* Baron), 319, 326, 328, 331
Gardner, Helen, 322, 328
Gardner, James, 185
Garnett, David, 185, 259
Garnett, Eve: *The Family from One End Street*, 187
Garratt, G. T.: *Mussolini's Roman Empire*, 134, 137
Garrick Club, London, 299, 364, 368, 392, 397, 401
Garvin, J. L., 39, 195
General elections: (1945), 20; (1951), 206
Genet, Jean: *The Thief's Journal*, 358, 360
Gentleman, David, 281, 349
George, G. T.: *They Betrayed Czechoslovakia*, 136
George, Henry: *Progress and Poverty*, 276
Germany, 136–7
Gibb, Jocelyn (Jock), 311
Gibbings, Robert, 143; *Coming Down the Seine*, 270
Gide, André: *If It Die*, 330
Gill, Eric, 57, 65
Girodias, Maurice, 141
Glazebrook, Ben, 30

Glover, A. S. B. (Alan McDougall): on Mme Tabouis, 135; encyclopedic learning and perfectionism, 237–9, 246, 301; joins Penguin, 237–9, 241; supports Penguin staff, 240; and Williams, 248, 263; attends editorial meetings, 263; in Moynihan group painting, 269; opposes pictorial jackets, 280; AL disparages, 302, 305; Eunice Frost on, 304; retirement and subsequent activities, 306; receives copy of Rolph's book on *Lady Chatterley* trial, 332; works with authors, 344
Godwin, Fay, 364, 368–9
Godwin, Tony: public interest in, 2; on Penguin's loss of literary near-monopoly, 3; proposes Bodley Head join Penguin group, 69; on AL's hostility to Krishna Menon, 121; at Bumpus, 300; bookselling, 310–11; Maschler recommends to AL, 310; joins Penguin, 311–12, 343–4; praises Woodhouse, 313; and publication of *Lady Chatterley's Lover*, 332; handwriting, 334; on AL's appearance, 335; acquires rights to Maschler's *The S-Man*, 341; insists on four-colour jackets, 341, 349–51; belief in and support for authors, 343–4; qualities and character, 343, 346, 367; editorial policy, 344–8, 353–4, 358–9; political stance, 347–8; coterie of young editors, 351, 369; moves to John Street, 351; AL's view of, 352–3; view of AL, 352–3, 369; launches hardback imprint and list (Allen Lane The Penguin Press), 354–6, 363; and 'vertical' publishing, 354; policy on authors' advances, 356; and Deighton's *Funeral in Berlin*, 358;

supports Siné cartoons, 359–60, 362; ill health, 363, 366; dismissed by AL, 364–6; compensation payment, 366–7; subsequent publishing posts, 367, 369; supposed plotting against AL, 368; on AL's educational and Australian interests, 374; uninterested in Penguin Education, 377; and Australian list, 379–80; and appointment of new managing director, 385; and AL's disdain for colleagues, 386–7; suggests giving Lowry painting to Williams, 389; plans fiction list, 393

Goehr, Alexander, 274

Gold Coast (Ghana): AL visits, 288

Goldfinger, Ernö, 140, 207; (ed., with E. J. Carter): *The County of London Plan*, 200

Golding, Louis, 85; *The Jewish Problem*, 136

Golding, (Sir) William: *Lord of the Flies*, 309

Goldsack, Sydney, 99, 249, 291

Gollancz, Sir Israel, 29

Gollancz, (Sir) Victor; character, 4, 96; advertisements, 54–5; publishes paperbacks, 75; and Holroyd-Reece, 77; book jackets and design, 90, 134; on launch of Penguins, 95–6; reputation, 101; political stance, 132–4, 198, 202; publishes Orwell, 131; wartime paper allocation, 153; publishes Victory Books ('Yellow Perils'), 195; and publication of Hersey's *Hiroshima*, 202–3; on AL's knighthood, 267; on rumoured sale of Penguin Inc., 295; on *Lady Chatterley's Lover*, 323; *see also* Left Book Club

Gombrich, E. H.: *Caricature*, 145

Goodchild, G. H., 154; *Keeping Poultry and Rabbits on Scraps*, 149

Goodman, Arnold, Baron, 388, 397

Gordimer, Nadine: *The Lying Days*, 308

Gordon, Giles, 346, 367, 373

Gordon, John, 317

Gosling (of East African AA), 383

Gott, Richard, 394

Grade, Lew, 339

Graham, Eleanor, 186–7, 269, 377; *Story of Jesus*, 400

Grant, Cary, 10

Grant, Duncan, 189

Grant Duff, Shiela, 115, 135, 136; *Europe and the Czechs*, 135

Graves, Robert, 252; version of *The Golden Ass*, 46, 252–3; translates Suetonius's *Twelve Caesars*, 252; and Harry Kemp, 304; *The Greek Myths*, 393

Great Crash (1929), 56, 80

Greene, Colonel (of *Infantry Journal*), 213

Greene, Graham, 157, 318, 323, 351

Greene, Hugh Carleton, 331

Greenfield, George, 346

Greenwood, C. J., 52

Grierson, John, 131

Griffith, Hubert: *Seeing Soviet Russia*, 56

Griffith-Jones, Mervyn, 317, 321, 327–9, 332, 333

Grigson, Geoffrey, 175, 189

Grisewood, Harman, 273

Gross, John, 267, 399

Grosset & Dunlop (US reprint publishers), 214

Grove Press, 319

Guest, John, 335

Guild Books, 163–4

Guinzburg, Harold, 402

Guyatt, Richard, 281

Haining Report, 161
Haldane, J. B. S., 120
Hale, Kathleen, 183, 257; *Orlando's Evening Out*, 186
Haley, Sir William, 4, 272–3, 277
Hall, Radclyffe: *The Well of Loneliness*, 62, 77, 331
Hall, W. F. (Chicago printers), 217–18
Hamilton, Hamish: as gentleman publisher, 27; agreement with Penguin, 265, 353; publishing company bought by Mayer, 402
Hamlett, Colonel 'Dane', 45
Hamlyn, Paul, 310, 397
Hanley, James: *Boy*, 52
Harcourt Brace (Jovanovich) (New York publishers), 339, 369
Hardy, Thomas, 14, 29, 103
Hare, Steve, 390
Harmondsworth, Middlesex: Penguin Books move to, 126–7
Harper & Row (US publishers), 295–6, 338
Harrap, Walter, 163
Harris, Frank, 45–6
Harris, Max, 378–80
Harrison, G. B., 36, 159
Harrisson, Tom, 131, 196, 229; *Britain by Mass Observation* (with Charles Madge), 136, 229
Hart, (Sir) Basil Liddell, 137
Hart-Davis (Sir) Rupert: as gentleman publisher, 27; on Jonathan Cape, 96; AL buys rights of Young's *One of Our Submarines* from, 152; biography of Hugh Walpole, 289; sells publishing house, 298, 339, 354; Reynard Library, 353; AL meets in later years, 392
Hart-Davis, Ruth, Lady (*née* Simon), 392
Hartland, north Devon, 18

Harvey, Laurence, 280
Harvey, Wilfred, 69
Hašek, Jaroslav: *The Good Soldier Schweik*, 137, 330
Haskell, Arnold, 139
Hastings, (Sir) Max, 331
Hastings, Mrs (governess), 10
Hastings, Sir Patrick, 45–6
Hawkey, Raymond, 350
Haydn, Hiram, 295
Hazell, Raymond, 66, 92, 93, 246
Hazell, Watson & Viney (printers), 172, 244, 320, 331
Heal, Ambrose, 29
Heath, D. C. (educational publishers), 295
Heaton, Peter, 232; *Sailing*, 112
Hebdon, Peter, 338–41
Hedges, David, 229
Heffer, John, 361
Heinemann, William (publisher): as new publisher, 21; Windmill Library, 74; hostility to Penguin Books, 93–4; interest in typography, 241; agreement with Penguin, 265; buys Hart-Davis, 298; publishes *Lady Chatterley's Lover*, 315; sells Hart-Davis, 339; Pick and Gant join, 340–41; proposed purchase of Penguin, 397
Heller, Joseph: *Catch 22*, 340, 345–6
Hemingway, Ernest, 289
Hendy, Sir Philip, 189
Hepburn, Bruce, 389
Herbert, (Sir) Alan P., 157, 318
Herbert, David, 229
Hersey, John: *Hiroshima*, 202–3, 273
Hess, Dame Myra, 160
Higham, David (literary agent), 48, 77
Hill, Alan, 291
Hines, Muriel, 53

Hiscock, Eric, 26, 68

Hitler, Adolf, 56, 129–30, 135–6, 150

Hodder & Stoughton (publishers): Yellow Jackets (series), 74; wartime losses, 155

Hogarth, Grace, 260–61

Hogarth, Paul, 332

Hogarth Press, 60, 104, 175

Hogben, Lancelot, 120; *Interglossa*, 173; *Mathematics for the Million*, 172; *Science for the Citizen*, 172

Hogg, Quintin (*later* Baron Hailsham): *The Case for Conservatism*, 203

Hoggart, Richard: on Williams, 118; background, 119; on importance of Penguins in war, 159, 274; on Schmoller, 278; on Susanne Lepsius, 285; on Williams at Arts Council, 302; as adviser to AL, 306; and trial of *Lady Chatterley's Lover*, 328, 329; on Williams's deprecation of AL, 389; proposes universities purchase Penguin, 396–7; address at AL's memorial service, 400; *The Uses of Literacy*, 274–6, 306

Holme, Richard, Baron, 356–8, 361, 366, 368, 382

Holmes, Jimmy, 228, 242

Holroyd, Michael, 48

Holroyd-Reece, John (*né* Hermann Riess), 76–9, 141, 183, 219, 322

Holtby, Winifred, 57

Holy Trinity (church), Marylebone, 107–8

Homer: *Iliad* (transl. Rieu), 252; *Odyssey* (transl. Rieu), 251

Honour, Hugh, 335

Hooberman, Ben, 360

Hope, A. D., 380

Hope, Francis, 380

Hope-Wallace, Philip, 161

Hopkinson, Tom, 131, 179, 196–7, 202

Horizon (magazine), 160, 175–7, 181, 272

Horne, Donald: *The Lucky Country* (in England as *Australia in the Sixties*), 380

Hornibrook, F. A.: *The Culture of the Abdomen*, 392

Horovitz, Bela, 190

Hough, Graham, 329

Houghton Mifflin (US publishers), 296–7

How the Jap Army Fights (USA), 213

Howard, Michael (Wren's son), 338, 340

Howard, Wren, 69, 89, 96, 154, 157, 338–40

Howell, D. I. John, 45

Huebsch, Ben, 55

Hulton, Sir Edward, 196–7

Human Body, The (Puffin Picture Book), 186

Humphreys, Christmas, 237

Hunter, Norman: *The Incredible Adventures of Professor Branestawm*, 54

Hurstbourne Priors: AL buys farm, 371

Hutchinson, George, 75

Hutchinson, Jeremy (*later* Baron), 323, 326–7, 330

Hutchinson, Walter, 75, 116

Hutchinson (publishers): starts sixpenny list (Toucan Books), 102; wartime losses, 155; fined for publishing *September in Quinze*, 317

Hutchison, Robert, 367, 393–4

Huxley, Aldous, 323

Huxley, Sir Julian, 120, 140, 196–7, 257; *Essays in Popular Science*, 120

Hyde, Harford Montgomery, 327, 330

Iddesleigh, Devon, 371
Illustrated Classics, 143
Illustrated Newspapers, 338
India: AL travels in, 147
Indian and Colonial Library, 24
Infantry Journal, 213, 214
Information, Ministry of, 157–8, 193
Insel Verlag, 143–4
Iraq: AL visits with Mallowans, 287–8
Isherwood, Christopher, 194

Jackson, Holbrook, 141, 146; *The
    Eighteen Nineties*, 146
Jackson, Lt-Col. (of Services Central
    Book Depot), 162–3
Jacob, Gordon, 264, 269
Jacob, Ian, 276
Jagger, Mick, 394
James, Clive, 347
Jameson, Storm, 131
Japan: annexes Manchuria, 129
Jenkins, Herbert, 24
Jenkins, Roy (*later* Baron), 316–19
Jennings, Sir Ivor: at school with AL,
    16; *The British Constitution*, 16
Jerrold, Douglas, 75, 133, 153
Joad, C. E. M., 75; *Why War?*, 136
John Lane The Bodley Head
    (imprint), 354
Johnson, Lionel, 19
Johnston, Edward, 90
Jonas, Robert, 217
Jones, Elwyn, 234
Jones, Thomas, 160
Joseph, Michael: and Ethel Mannin,
    52; and Charles Pick, 141–2;
    agreement with Penguin, 265, 353;
    company sold, 338, 402
Joy, Thomas, 80
Joyce, James: *Ulysses*, 60–65, 70, 77,
    319–20, 399
Joynson-Hicks, Sir William (*later* 1st

Viscount Brentford), 63
Kahane, Jack, 141
Kauffer, McKnight, 208, 243
Kaufmann, Stanley: *The Philanderer*,
    313, 318
Kavan, Anna, 284
Kelley, Malcolm, 373
Kelmscott Press, 241
Kemp, Eunice *see* Frost, Eunice
Kemp, Harry, 304–5
Kenga, Chief Ishmael, 383
Kent, Tatyana (*later* Schmoller; Tanya;
    TK), 233–4, 279, 283, 359, 363
Kenya, 382–3
Keynes, Geoffrey, 141
Keynes, John Maynard, Baron, 106,
    160–61, 192, 196; *The Economic
    Consequences of the Peace*, 130
Kilham Roberts, Denys, 142, 174,
    263
King, Cecil, 130, 297
King, Clive: *Stig of the Dump*, 378
King Penguins, 143–5, 253–4, 256
Kingsmill, Hugh, 45–6, 48
Kipling, Rudyard: *Just So Stories*, 76
Kitchen, C. H. B.: *Death of My Aunt*,
    105
Kite, Peter, 108
Kitto, H. D. F.: *The Greeks*, 236
Klee, Paul, 189
Knickerbocker, H. R.: *Germany:
    Fascist or Soviet?*, 56
Knight, Mr (butler), 67, 148
Knopf, Alfred, 55, 155, 233
Knopf, Blanche, 55, 253, 293
Knopf, Pat, 295
Knopf (US publishing house), 202, 319
Koestler, Arthur, 120, 129, 195, 284;
    Hanged by the Neck, 347
Korda, Sir Alexander, 145, 158
Krishna Menon, V. K., 56, 113–16,
    120–21, 138, 341

Labour Party: in 1930s, 129–33;
expels Pritt, 137; post-war government, 191, 201–2; in wartime
coalition, 192–3, 198
Laing, R. D.: *The Divided Self*, 347
Lamb, Lynton, 145
Lambton, Antony, Viscount, 318
Lancaster, (Sir) Osbert, 351
Lanchester, Elsa, 52, 151, 191
Lane, Sir Allen: reputation and influence, 2, 198–9, 202, 221; and
nature of publishing, 3–4; character and behaviour, 4, 97, 109, 146,
221, 224–9, 334–5; changes name
from Williams, 5; family background, 5–6, 27; joins Bodley
Head, 5, 13, 16, 25–6; farming
interests and practices, 6, 13,
165–6, 186, 370–71; attachment to
family, 8; birth and christening, 8;
upbringing and family life, 8–12;
appearance and dress, 9–10, 17, 26,
52, 115, 147, 258, 335, 372; relations with brother Dick, 9, 11,
110, 170, 222–3, 291–2, 336–7,
371; schooling, 10–11, 13–16;
sense of mischief, 15; early earnings, 27–8; social life and manner,
28–9, 51–2, 55–6, 67, 226, 233,
374; collects signed copies of all
Penguins, 30; knowledge of
French, 30–31; evening studies, 31;
joins Territorial Army, 31; claims
inheritance on John Lane's death,
35; and *The Whispering Gallery*
case, 46–7, 49; inherits majority
shareholding in Bodley Head,
49–50; annuity from 'American
Trust', 52; theatre-going, 53; attitude to publicity, 54; reading, 54,
225–6, 236, 392; in USA, 55, 208,
212, 214, 218; involvement in

Bodley Head work, 57, 59;
consults fortune-tellers, 58; moves
to Paddington, 58; personal risk-
taking, 59–60; publishes *Ulysses*,
64–5; home life with siblings,
66–7; love affair, 66; travels and
holidays in Europe, 66, 232, 283,
289; loses Bodley Head, 69; and
birth of Penguin Books, 71, 78–9,
84, 90–93; and earlier paperback
publishers, 78–9; and middle-class
readership, 83–5; Arnold suggests
sixpenny paperbacks to, 86–8;
non-smoking, 87; suggests
Woolworth's as sales outlet, 89;
and Penguin design, 90–91; and
booksellers' resistance to selling
Penguins, 98–9; and early success
of Penguins, 106–7; advocates
direct selling to readers, 107; rents
crypt of Holy Trinity, Marylebone
as book warehouse, 107; helps
pack and unpack books, 109;
office conditions, 109; visits
Champneys health farm, 109; acts
of generosity, 110–11, 228, 291,
367, 372–3; discomfits Jean
Osborne, 110; finances and earnings, 110–11, 268, 336–8; cruises
with parents, 111; sailing, 111–12,
335; takes staff to France, 111,
228; as director of London Zoo,
120; dismisses Krishna Menon,
121; on popular demand for intelligent books, 122; employs Eunice
Frost as secretary, 125–6; moves to
Harmondsworth, 126–7; political
views, 128, 137, 198, 288–9, 385;
and topical political matters, 134;
business trips to Paris, 142; predicts
war, 146; travels to Aden and
India, 146–7, 184; moves to

Lane, Sir Allen (*cont.*)
    Silverbeck, 147–8; and outbreak
    of war, 149; skiing, 150; cycling
    in wartime, 151; wartime services
    and activities, 151–2; book supply
    and publishing in war, 157,
    163–5; disdain for Publishers'
    Association and trade bodies, 157,
    164; wartime debating and talks,
    158–9; marriage to Lettice, 166–8;
    sex life, 167; children, 168, 234–5;
    domestic life, 168; and brother
    John's death, 169–70; reserve, 170,
    227; supports *Penguin New
    Writing*, 173, 176–81; welcomes
    Puffin Picture Books, 184–6;
    paintings collection, 188, 389; and
    post-war ideals, 191, 198, 207;
    influence, 198–9, 202; and
    Penguin in USA, 209–20; and
    management of Penguin, 221–6,
    247; instinct for books, 226; rela-
    tions with Williams, 227, 388–9,
    393; staff relations, 230–31; drink-
    ing, 231–2; attends Nuremberg
    war crimes trials, 234; deteriorat-
    ing marriage relations, 235, 284;
    perfectionism, 236–7, 373; Glover
    sends advice to, 240; improves
    design and appearance of
    Penguins, 242–3, 245–6; and
    Pevsner's Buildings of England
    series, 254–6; and *British Wild
    Flowers*, 257–9; Richard
    Chopping's view of, 258–60;
    knighthood, 267–8; in Moynihan's
    boardroom painting, 268–9; ideals,
    271–2; considers publishing lighter
    works, 276; ambivalence over
    picture jackets, 280–82; reaction
    to parents' deaths, 283; devotion
    to daughters, 284, 372; health

    concerns, 284; antique collecting,
    285; domestic life after Lettice's
    departure, 285–6; relations with
    Susanne Lepsius, 285, 287; visits
    Iraq with Mallowans, 287–8; world
    travels, 288–90, 372; dealings with
    US publishers, 294, 296–7; consid-
    ers selling Penguin, 297–9; house
    in Spain, 297, 332, 371, 383, 385;
    resumes relations with Lettice, 300,
    371–2; sense of emptiness, 300;
    view of Williams and Frost, 301–3;
    jaundice, 309, 392; in takeover of
    Bumpus, 311; on Woodhouse,
    312–13; and publication of *Lady
    Chatterley's Lover*, 316, 319–20,
    324–5, 332–3; attends trial of *Lady
    Chatterley's Lover*, 326–7, 330; and
    graphology, 334; turns Penguin
    into public company, 336–7; offers
    to part-purchase Cape, 339–40;
    hostility to Maschler, 341–2; view
    of Godwin, 352–3; favours
    Penguin hardbacks, 353; and Allen
    Lane The Penguin Press, 354–6;
    pricing policy, 357, 396; conserva-
    tive tastes, 358; opposes publication
    of Siné cartoons, 359–63; removes
    and destroys copies of Siné book,
    362–3; dismisses Godwin, 364–8;
    moves to Old Mill House, West
    Drayton, 370; property purchases,
    370–71; motoring, 372; innova-
    tions, 373; educational interests,
    374–8; isolation, 374; sackings in
    Australia, 381; lost in Kenya,
    382–3; resists retirement, 384–5;
    holiday in Morocco, 391; bowel
    cancer, 392–4; inadequate under-
    standing of financial control,
    395–6; succession question, 396;
    fiftieth anniversary as publisher

celebrated, 397–9; made
Companion of Honour, 398; death
and burial, 400; will, 400–401
Lane, Anna (AL's daughter): birth,
168; mild Down's syndrome, 284;
in Spain with AL, 371
Lane, Annie (*née* Eichberg; John
Lane's wife): in Bath during First
World War, 12; marriage, 12,
24–5; writing, 22; on Pat Puxley,
28; at AL's meeting with Shaw, 30;
wealth, 32; and husband's death
and funeral, 34–5; as majority
shareholder in Bodley Head, 36;
death and will, 49–50, 52
Lane, Christine (AL's daughter) *see*
Teale, Christine
Lane, Clare (AL's daughter) *see*
Morpurgo, Clare
Lane, Elizabeth (*née* Snow; Dick's
wife), 290
Lane, John (AL's brother): schooling,
15; inheritance from Annie, 49,
52; works for insurance company
in London, 53; stays with AL in
Paddington, 58, 66–7; represents
Bodley Head on world tour, 65–6;
hard work at Penguin, 108; character and personality, 110; sailing,
111; naval war service, 152–3, 169;
resents AL's marriage, 167; death in
war, 169–70
Lane, John (publisher): founds Bodley
Head, 6, 17–21; birth and death
dates, 8; in Bath in First World
War, 12–13, 25; courtship and
marriage, 12, 21–2; invites AL to
join Bodley Head, 13, 16, 17;
background and character, 17–18;
collecting, 18; instinctive literary
sense, 22–3; working conditions,
22; appearance, 23, 33; builds up

Bodley Head, 24–5; AL lives with,
28; encourages AL in career, 29;
publishes Agatha Christie, 33;
death, 34, 68; paintings sold, 51;
reputation, 54; works in publishing, 54, 59; interest in typography,
241
Lane, Lettice, Lady (*née* Orr): background, 166; marriage to AL,
166–8; visits USA with AL, 218;
lives at Silverbeck, 221; attends
party for Prescott, 232; invites
Tatyana Kent to Silverbeck, 234;
deteriorating marriage relations,
235, 284–5; Morpurgo meets, 262;
affairs, 285; life after split from AL,
285–6; AL resumes relations with,
300, 371–2; makes home in
London, 370; manner, 372; on
AL's illness, 393–4, 400; left nothing in AL's will, 400
Lane, Lewis (John Lane's father),
17–18, 126
Lane, Nora (AL's sister) *see* Bird, Nora
Lane, Richard (Dick; AL's brother):
birth, 8; relations with AL, 9, 11,
110, 170, 222, 291–2, 336–7, 371;
upbringing and education, 10–12,
15; attends John Lane's Devon
funeral, 34–5; in Australia, 34–5,
229, 290–2, 336; inheritance from
Annie, 49; acting, 53; career difficulties, 53–4; works for Bodley
Head, 54, 65; moves to Paddington
with AL, 58, 66–7; sees brother
John off on world tour, 65–6; and
marketing of first Penguins, 98;
and Penguin's finances, 103; hard
work at Penguin, 109; character,
110; fishing, 111; selects
Harmondsworth as home for
Penguin, 127; lunches at Barcelona

Lane, Richard (Dick; AL's brother) (*cont.*)

restaurant, 128; lives at Silverbeck, 147–8, 221; at wine-tasting, 150; cycling in wartime, 151; naval war service, 151–2, 169; resents AL's marriage, 167; ship torpedoed, 169; visits New York, 169, 211–12, 216; and brother John's death, 170; interest in farming, 185, 221; and Hersey's *Hiroshima*, 202; and Shaw's affection for AL, 204; cans raspberries, 206; dogwood tree memorial, 218; as director of Penguin, 221; and management of Penguin, 221–3, 248; practicality, 221; car used by Penguin rep, 229; on working conditions, 230; drinking, 231–2; staff view of, 231; attends AL's birthday dinner (1946), 233; and Pevsner's use of car, 255; at editorial meeting with Morpurgo, 263; in *After the Conference* painting, 269; favours picture covers, 281; receives personal items after mother's death, 283; advice to AL after split from Lettice, 286–7; marriage to Elizabeth, 290; opposes opening branch in Australia, 290; and publication of *Lady Chatterley's Lover*, 316; AL acquires holdings in Penguin, 336–8; ill-health, 336–7; AL writes to in decline, 400; 'Reminiscences', 9

Laski, Harold, 115, 132, 139, 193; *Where Do We Go from Here?*, 199

Laski, Marghanita, 274

Latin American Library, 394

Laughton, Charles, 52

Lawrence & Wishart (publishers), 137

Lawrence, D. H.: *Lady Chatterley's Lover*: trial and acquittal, 1, 326–32; published by Penguin, 314, 315–16; published in USA, 319–20; literary qualities, 321–2; prosecution planned, 321–3, 325; supported by literary figures, 323; pre-publication subscription orders, 324; sales, 331, 336; effect of publication, 333; banned in Australia, 381

Lawrence, Frieda, 319, 322

Layton, Walter Thomas, 1st Baron, 299

Leacock, Stephen, 24

Leavis, F. R., 61, 315, 332, 346, 398–9

Leavis, Queenie: *Fiction and the Reading Public*, 81

le Carré, John: *The Spy Who Came in from the Cold*, 346

Lee, Jennie, Baroness, 7

Left Book Club (Gollancz), 106, 132–4, 195, 203

Left Review, 122, 139

Le Gallienne, Richard, 18, 23

Lehmann, John: and *Penguin New Writing*, 124, 138, 142, 150, 173, 176–81; AL's relations with, 174; background, 174; edits *New Writing*, 174–5; founds *London Magazine*, 181; manner, 183; on emerging wartime ideals, 194; and Morpurgo, 261–2; in *After the Conference* painting, 269; Third Programme *New Soundings*, 273–4; 'New Writing in England', 176

Lehmann, Rosamond, 176

Leighton, Frederic, Baron, 20

Lenin, Vladimir I., in *The Whispering Gallery*, 36, 39

Léon, Paul, 77

Leonardo da Vinci, 79

Lepsius, Susanne, 284–5, 287, 335, 342, 363, 370, 375

Leslie, Doris, 57

Leverhulme Trust: supports Pevsner's *Buildings of England* series, 256

Lewis, D. B. Wyndham ('Timothy Shy'), 150

Lewis, Wyndham, 19, 129

libraries (lending), 79–80

Lilliput (magazine), 131

Lindsay, Alexander Dunlop (*later* 1st Baron), 162, 197

Linklater, Eric, 96; *Poet's Pub*, 98

Lippmann, Walter, 215

Literary Guild, 81

Little Review (USA), 61

Lloyd George, David (*later* 1st Earl), 40

Locke, W. J., 21, 29

London: bombed in war, 191

London Magazine, 181

London Mercury (magazine), 175

London Zoo, 119–20

Longfellow, Henry Wadsworth, 22

Longman, Mark, 397

Longmans (publishers): burnt in war, 155; offers to buy Penguin, 298; educational publishing, 374, 377

Lorant, Stefan, 131; *I Was Hitler's Prisoner*, 135

Lord Chamberlain: theatrical censorship role ends, 331

Lorimer, E. O.: *What Hitler Wants*, 136

Lothian (Australian publishers), 290

Low, (Sir) David, 131, 133; *Europe Since Versailles*, 212

Lowry, L. S., 389

Lubetkin, Berthold, 119

Lund Humphries, 243

Lusty, Sir Robert: on early sixpenny paperbacks, 75; and launch of Penguin, 92; on Krishna Menon, 116; on AL's manner, 225; on publishers' group supplying titles to Penguin, 265; in takeover of Bumpus, 311; offers to re-employ Raleigh Trevelyan, 335; stays at El Fénix (Spain), 371; and Lord Reith, 386; and AL's relations with Morpurgo, 391; sells rights of Svetlana Stalin book to AL, 391; address at AL's memorial service, 400

MacDonald, Ramsay, 129

McGraw-Hill (US publishers), 397, 401

Machell, Roger, 30

Mackenzie, (Sir) Compton, 323

Maclaren-Ross, Julian, 142–3

McLean, Ruari: on Eunice Frost, 126; shares flat with Young, 127; on AL's determination, 140; on AL's instinct for books, 226; on AL's drinking, 232; praises Glover, 239; war service, 239; on Overton, 242; on Tschichold, 244, 246

MacLeish, Archibald, 319

Macmillan, Harold (*later* 1st Earl of Stockton), 103, 157, 192

Macmillan, Hugh Pattison, Baron, 159, 161

Macmillan (publishers), 21, 377

Maddock, Llywelyn, 26, 99

Madge, Charles, 131; *see also* Harrisson, Tom

Mallowan, Sir Max, 34, 71, 87, 287–8

Manchester Guardian, 130

Mannin, Ethel: friendship with AL, 51–2; and Penguin design, 91–2; on AL's proposed magazine on current affairs, 138; celebrates AL's fiftieth anniversary as publisher, 398

Manningham-Buller, Sir Reginald (*later* Viscount Dilhorne), 321

Mansfield, Kathleen, 30

Manutius, Aldus, 75

Manvell, Roger, 182

Marber, Romek, 349–50

Mardersteig, Hans (or Giovanni), 76–9

Margesson, David, 201

Marighela, Carlos: *For the Liberation of Brazil*, 394

Marples, Ernest (*later* Baron), 322

Martin, Kingsley, 4, 131, 398

Marx, Enid, 185

Maschler, Kurt, 190, 307

Maschler, Tom: public interest in, 2; qualities, 307–8; works at Penguin, 308–9; resigns from Penguin, 309–11, 342; on Woodhouse, 313; handwriting, 334; and proposed sale of Cape, 339–40; AL's hostility to, 341–2; and Len Deighton, 357–8; sells book rights to Penguin, 366; supports Godwin, 366; publishes plays, 393; (ed.) *Declaration*, 307; *The S-Man* (by 'Mark Caine'), 341

Maskery, Ray, 396

Mason, Kenneth A.: *An Anthology of Animal Poetry*, 146

Mass Observation, 131, 229–30, 261

Masters, John, 351

Mathew, Sir Theobald ('Toby'), 319, 321–2, 332

Mathews, Elkin, 18, 20–21

Matisse, Henri, 65

Maugham, Somerset, 353

Maupassant, Guy de: 'Boule de Suif', 236

Maurois, André: AL meets, 31; and Penguin Paris, 142; *Ariel*, 92; *Byron*, 56; *The Silence of Colonel Bramble*, 31

Maxwell, Robert, 26, 268, 396

Maxwell, William, 112, 205

Maxwell-Fyfe, Sir David (*later* Earl of Kilmuir), 316

May, Lewis: on Annie Eichberg Lane, 22; meets Anatole France, 30; on John Lane in later years, 34; plays in *Hamlet*, 53

Mayer, Peter, 402

Maynard, Bob: service with Penguin, 108; AL aids wife during illness and pregnancy, 110; and Dunkirk evacuation, 152; as production manager, 152, 154; wartime economies, 154; runs foul of German censors, 165; meets Lettice, 168; designs jackets, 179; temporary work for UN, 290; dismissed in Australia, 291, 336

Maynard, Laura (Bob's blind daughter), 291, 401

Mayor, F. M.: *The Rector's Daughter*, 179

Mehta, Ved, 6, 79

Melville, Herman: *Typee*, 143

Mencken, H. L., 55

Mentor (US publishing house), 219

Methuen (publishers), 251–2, 354

Meynell, Francis, 64, 242, 353

Michie, James, 177, 392

Mikes, George, 309

Miller, Henry, 287, 333

Milligan, Spike: *Puckoon*, 358

Minton, John, 180, 303

Mitchison, Naomi, 57

Mitford, Nancy, 49

Moberley Pool (wartime paper allocation), 153

Modern European Poets, 347

Monahan, Detective Inspector, 324, 328

Mondadori, Arnoldo, 76

Monotype Corporation, 241–2, 245

Monsarrat, Nicholas: *The Cruel Sea*, 280

Moore, Brian: *The Feast of Lupercal*, 309; *The Lonely Passion of Judith Hearne*, 308

Moore, Henry, 189

Moravia, Alberto: *The Woman of Rome*, 280

Morison, Stanley: and Holroyd-Reece, 77; designs jackets for Gollancz, 89, 134, 245; type design, 90; left-wing and Catholic views, 130, 195; on War Economy Committee, 154; influence at *Times*, 195; and Shaw's ninetieth birthday celebrations, 205–6; imprisoned as conscientious objector in First War, 238; as typographical adviser, 241–2; on AL's knighthood, 267–8; and Penguin hardbacks, 353; and publication of *Bibliopola*, 355; and Beaverbrook in old age, 384; papers kept at Cambridge, 399

Morley, Frank, 89

Morocco, 391

Morpurgo, Clare (*née* Lane; AL's daughter): birth, 168; appearance, 170; holidays in France with AL, 284; on *Lady Chatterley's Lover*, 331; independence, 370; marriage to Michael Morpurgo, 372, 390; relations with AL, 372; left nothing in AL's will, 400

Morpurgo, J. E.: marriage, 25; writes biography of AL, 25, 261, 390–91; on AL's friendship with Hesketh Pearson, 37; and AL's bid to buy Bodley Head, 69; on AL's relations with Richard, 110; on Penguin's move to Harmondsworth, 127; on AL's travels, 147; on AL's wartime activities, 151; on AL's wartime debating, 158; and death of AL's

brother John, 170; on Glover, 239; dismissed, 247, 264; character and qualities, 261–2; edits Penguin History of England, 261, 264–5; relations with AL, 261, 265; joins Penguin, 263; suggests Penguin Music Scores, 264; in *After the Conference* painting, 269; on AL's character, 334; on Godwin, 368; advocates educational publishing, 374–6; on AL in later years, 385; on AL's disdain for colleagues, 387; patronizes AL, 389; self-aggrandisement, 389–90; AL dislikes, 390

Morpurgo, Michael, 372, 390

Morrell, Janet, 238

Morris, William, 74, 241

Morrison, Herbert (*later* Baron), 133

Mortimer, John, 359

Mortimer, Raymond, 189

Mott, Tony, 373–4

Mowrer, Edgar: *Germany Puts the Clock Back*, 56, 134; *Mowrer in China*, 136

Moynihan, Rodrigo: *After the Conference* (painting), 268–70

Muggeridge, Malcolm, 129, 318, 328, 359

Mundanus paperbacks, 75

Munich Agreement (1938), 130, 135, 147

Murray, John ('Jock'), 27, 141

Murray, John (publishers), 2, 21, 184

Murray, Kate, 58

Murray, Les, 380

Murry, John Middleton, 48

Muspratt, Eric, 108–9, 111

Mussolini, Benito, 129

Myrdal, Gunnar, 355

Nabokov, Vladimir: *Lolita*, 198, 319, 323

Naipaul, Shiva, 393
Naipaul, (Sir) Vidya S.: *The Suffrage of Elvira*, 309
Nash, Paul, 189
National Book League, 375–6, 390–91
National Gallery, London, 160
National government (1931), 129
National Health Service, 196
Nazi-Soviet Pact (1939), 136, 195
Nazis: degenerate art exhibition, 139; typographic preferences, 243
Nehru, Jawaharal (Pandit), 114, 147; *Autobiography*, 69
Nelson (publishing house), 73–4, 155
Neurath, Eva, 144
Neurath, Walter, 144, 190
New American Library, 219, 293, 339, 402–3
New English Dramatists, 309
New English Library, 320
New Pocket Library, 24
New Soldier Handbook, The (USA), 213
New Statesman (journal), 131, 138
New Verse (magazine), 176
New Writing, 175–7; *see also Penguin New Writing*
New York: AL in, 208, 212, 292
Newnes, Sir George, 72
Newnes (publishers), 184
News Chronicle, 130, 299
newspapers: popularity, 79; offer cheap books, 81–2; political stance, 130–31
Newton, Eric, 117, 189
Nicholls, George, 362–3
Nichols, Beverley, 51
Nicholson, Ben, 189
Nicolson, (Sir) Harold, 193, 323; *Why Britain is at War*, 150, 211
Nigeria: AL visits, 288
Night and Day (magazine), 128 & n, 320

1941 Committee, 196–7
Nonesuch Press, 242, 353
Norman, Jill, 359, 367
Northcliffe, Alfred Harmsworth, Viscount, 39, 72
Norwood, Cyril, 14
novels: publication and prices, 72–3
Now (magazine), 175–6
Nuffield Foundation, 376
Nuremberg Trials, 234

Obelisk Press, 141
Oberon, Merle, 145
O'Brien, Edna, 360
Obscene Publications Act (1959), 141, 316, 318–19, 321, 326, 332
Observer (newspaper): praises first Penguins, 102
Odhams Press, 298
Odyssey Press (Hamburg), 77
Old Mill House, West Drayton, 370–71
Olney, Stanley: with Bodley Head, 85; visits Holy Trinity crypt, 108; in wartime, 149, 152, 154; and management of Penguin, 222; leaves Penguin, 224–5; AL disparages, 249
Olympia Press, 141
Orr, Sir Charles, 166
Orwell, George: on effect of Penguins, 94–5; patronizes Barcelona (restaurant), 128; reservations on USSR, 129; in Spanish Civil War, 129; on working classes, 131; criticizes Duchess of Atholl's views on Spanish Civil War, 138; published by Penguin, 139; on reading in wartime, 156–7; criticizes wartime Ministry of Information, 158; contributes to *Penguin New Writing*, 177; on wartime press opinions,

194; edits Searchlight Books, 195; journalism, 195; and Morpurgo, 261; *Homage to Catalonia*, 133, 139; *The Lion and the Unicorn*, 83–4, 192, 195; *1984*, 158; *The Road to Wigan Pier*, 131, 133

Osborne, Jean, 109–10, 126, 166–8

Overton, John (*né* Hans Oberndorfer), 242–3

Ovid: *Amores*, 46

Oxford University Press, 3, 374, 378; acquires World's Classics, 73

Oyler, Philip, 289

Packard, Vance: *The Hidden Persuaders*, 347

Paget, Clarence, 346

Paisner, Leslie, 336–7, 360, 364, 366

Pan books, 270, 277–8, 280, 339, 358, 381

Panter-Downes, Mollie, 161, 326–7

Pantheon Books (USA), 213

paperback books: despised, 74–5; authors' payments on, 104 & n; in USA, 208–11, 215, 219, 293–4

Parker, John: *Labour Marches On*, 203

Parkes, James: *God and Human Progress*, 199; *God in a World at War*, 199

Paroissien, Eileen, 227, 284

Paroissien, Harry: in USA, 219, 229, 268, 281, 293; character and background, 226–7; position at Penguin, 247–9, 293; warns AL of Maxwell in USA, 268; opposes decorative jackets, 280–82, 350; sends goods to AL from USA, 284; and Susanne's absence from AL, 287; and Dick's position in Australia, 291–2; and deals with US publishers, 294–5, 297; and AL's view of Frost, 303, 305; and

AL's recruiting staff, 306; told of *Lady Chatterley* trial, 327; disapproves of Godwin, 352; suggests Allen Lane The Penguin Press as new imprint, 354; and book promotion, 358; opposes publication of Siné, 360, 363; and Godwin's devotion to AL, 369; and Penguin Education, 376; AL writes to from Australia, 381; on Boyle, 385; ambitions to be new managing director, 386; AL denigrates, 387, 394; appointed joint managing director, 387; and Morpurgo's resentment of AL, 390; proposes closing down Allen Lane The Penguin Press, 391; retires, 396; address at AL's memorial service, 400

Parsons, Ian, 27, 141, 144

Partridge, Frances: *British Wild Flowers*, 257–60

Pasmore, Victor, 189

Paternoster Row, London: bombed in war, 155

Patterson, J. H.: *The Man-Eaters of Tsavo*, 384

Payne, Revd Ernest, 361

Peake, Mervyn, 270

Pearson, Gladys, 37

Pearson, Hesketh: and publication of *The Whispering Gallery*, 36–49; *Modern Men and Manners*, 48; *Parallel Lives*, 48

Pearson Longman Ltd, 397, 402

Pegasus Press (Paris), 77

Peggy Bedford (roadhouse), 149

Pelham, David, 391

Pelican Books: precursors, 75; inaugurated, 112–13; advisory panel, 114–20; publish original works, 114; first list, 120; praised, 122;

Pelican Books (*cont.*)
    readership, 270; cover designs, 280;
    cease publication, 402
Pelican History of Art, 256, 353
Pelican Specials, 139–40
Penguin (boat), 6, 111–12, 152
Penguin African Library, 288–9, 346,
    348
Penguin Australia, 290, 292, 378, 381
Penguin Books: rivals, 3–4; publicity,
    54; launched from Bodley Head,
    60, 68; takes over distribution of
    Bodley Head titles, 69; origins and
    precursors, 71, 74–5, 78–9, 89;
    success and reputation, 71; reader-
    ship and social class, 72, 84–5,
    229–30, 270–71, 274; colour
    coding, 78; owes money to Bodley
    Head, 88; design and appearance,
    89–91, 140, 237, 241–6, 255–6,
    275, 277–80, 402; name, 91; first
    ten titles, 92, 96–8, 100; and
    'group' arrangement with other
    publishers, 92, 96–8, 103–4, 265,
    353; booksellers' initial reluctance
    to stock, 98; first reactions to and
    success of, 101–6; profits, 102–3,
    336; second batch, 102; payments
    to authors, 104–5; warehousing,
    107–8; profit-sharing scheme for
    staff, 111; staff outings to France,
    111, 228; move to Harmonds-
    worth, 126–7; print-runs and sales,
    145; wartime publications and
    sales, 149–50, 153–4, 157, 159,
    161–2, 171, 189–90, 195–6,
    199–200; thousandth title, 152;
    price raised to 9d in war, 154;
    second-hand copies donated to
    Forces, 163; post-war magazines,
    182–3; children's books, 184–6,
    377–8; wartime dominance, 198;
    influence and educational value,
    202, 267, 274–5; 'Millions' (or
    'Tens'), 205; in USA, 209–19;
    management, 221–6, 247; office
    and working conditions, 230; staff
    relations, 230–31, 240; editorial
    scrupulousness, 237, 241;
    Composition Rules, 246; overseas
    trade, 247; natural history books
    fail, 257; agreement with group of
    publishers, 265–6, 353–4; board-
    room painting (*After the
    Conference*), 268–70; bank overdraft,
    269; list, 270; post-war competi-
    tors, 270–71; pictorial coloured
    cover design, 280–82, 348–51; AL
    considers selling, 297–9; senior staff
    changes, 301–12; agree to publish
    Lady Chatterley's Lover, 320; sales
    figures, 320; cooperate in *Lady
    Chatterley* case, 326; incorporated
    as public company, 336–7; fiction
    list, 345; divided by Godwin, 352;
    hardback original books, 353–6;
    authors' advances, 356; marketing
    methods, 357–8; Pension Fund,
    373; staff numbers, 373; twenty-
    fifth anniversary, 373; educational
    list, 374–7; political emphasis, 394;
    financial control reformed by
    Dolley, 395–6; proposed university
    purchase of, 396–7; merger with
    Pearson Longman, 402
Penguin Books Inc. (USA): set up,
    210–11, 213–19; picture covers,
    270; operations, 292–4; deals with
    US publishers, 294–7
Penguin Classics, 251–3, 353, 402
Penguin Dictionary of Quotations (ed.
    Cohen), 252
Penguin Education, 375–7, 395
Penguin English Library, 346

Penguin Film Review, 182

Penguin Handbooks, 150, 277

Penguin Hansard, 149

Penguin History of England, 261, 264–5, 353

Penguin Modern Classics, 346

Penguin Modern Painters, 150, 161, 189–90

Penguin Music Magazine, 182

Penguin Music Scores, 264, 279

Penguin New Writing: Eunice Frost works on, 124; success, 142, 177–8, 181; publication, 150, 177–80; wartime censorship of, 158; AL supports, 173, 176–9; design, 179; ceases publication, 181; Morpurgo publishes story in, 261–2

Penguin Parade (magazine), 142, 263

Penguin Paris, 142

Penguin Poets, 150, 279

Penguin Prints, 189, 226

Penguin Science News (magazine), 182

Penguin Shakespeare, 347

Penguin Short Stories, 393

Penguin Specials: policy, 134; qualities, 135–6; numbers of titles, 137; AL admires, 138; French and German translations, 142; and magazine publishing, 181; in war, 199–200; discontinued (1945), 203; readership, 229; Godwin revives, 344, 347

Penguin West African Library, 288

Penguins Progress (magazine), 112, 181, 263

Penrose Annual, 87, 134, 244

Peregrine Books, 346

Peters, A. D., 157, 339, 399

Petherick, Maurice, 200

Pevsner, Dieter, 306–7, 311, 346–7, 352, 360, 364, 366–8

Pevsner, Lola, 253, 255

Pevsner, (Sir) Nikolaus: Richards recommends to AL, 140; edits King Penguins, 145, 254; and Penguin's cars, 229; on AL's drinking, 232; edits the Buildings of England Series, 253–6; attends party at Priory Farm, 256–7; and Pelican History of Art, 256; in *After the Conference* painting, 269; on promotional trip to Prague, 363; *An Outline of European Architecture*, 254

Phaidon Press, 190, 256

Pick, Charles: replaces Holroyd-Reece in Paris, 141–2; negotiates release of Pevsner in war, 254; recommends Godwin to AL, 310–12; and takeover of Michael Joseph, 338–41; and AL's hostility to Maschler, 339, 341; and Grahame Greene's objection to pictorial covers, 351; and Godwin's giving up fiction list, 363; and Churchills' account of Six Day War, 391

Pick, Frank, 90

Picture Pelicans, 305

Picture Post (magazine), 131, 192, 196, 199, 201

Pilgrim Trust, 160

Pipe, June, 168

Piper, John, 189, 254, 397

Pirandello, Luigi, 55

Pitcairn, Frank *see* Cockburn, Claud

Pitkin, Walter: *What's That Plane?*, 213

Pitman, Sir Isaac, 320–21

Planning, Design and Art Series (Penguin), 200

Plumb, (Sir) John H., 265

Pocket Books (USA), 208–9, 212–14, 217, 296–7, 320

Pocket Classics, 73
Poetry (London) (magazine), 175
Political and Economic Planning (PEP), 196
Political Leaders of the Twentieth Century series, 346–7
Pollinger, Laurence, 319–20
Popular Library (USA), 209
Porpoise Books, 260
Postgate, Raymond, 155
Potter, Stephen, 329
Pound, Ezra, 19, 61
Powell, Anthony, 191, 351
Powell, Dilys, 329
Powell, Michael, 182
Powers, Eileen: *Medieval People*, 251
Powys, John Cowper, 55
Powys, T. F.: *Mr Weston's Good Wine*, 103–4
Prague, 363
Prentice, Charles, 242, 265, 278
Prescott, Clifford, 99–100, 232
Priestley, J. B.: on John Lane, 34–5; selects for Book Society, 81; praises first Penguins, 101; opposes purchase tax on publishers, 157; politics, 192; on post-war plans, 193, 197; wartime broadcasts, 195; absent from AL's 50th anniversary as publisher, 398; relations with Penguin, 398–9; *English Journey*, 83–4, 126
Priory Farm, near Reading, 165–6, 268, 269, 291, 337, 370
Prisoner of War Book Service, 165
Prisoner of War, The (magazine), 165
Pritchett, (Sir) Victor S., 177
Pritt, D. N., 288; *Choose Your Future*, 137; *Light on Moscow*, 136–7; *Must the War Spread?*, 137
Private Eye (magazine), 362, 365
Pryce-Jones, Alan, 312

Ptarmigan series, 277
Publishers' Association: Stanley Unwin's involvement, 58; Gollancz's hostility to, 95–6; AL's disdain for, 157
Puffin Books, 150, 187, 377–8
Puffin Picture Books, 185–7
Puffin Post, 378
Puffin Story Books, 187
Punch (magazine), 20
Purchase Tax, 157
Puxley, Ducka (AL's cousin), 10, 27, 286
Puxley, Pat, 27
Pyramid (US publishers), 320

Queen (magazine), 349
Quennell, (Sir) Peter, 157
Quigly, Isabel, 228–9, 237, 240

Rabelais, François, 317
Radice, Betty, 350
radio: as rival to books and reading, 79
Rainsford, W. H.: *That Girl March*, 27
Randall, Mike, 386
Random House (US publishers), 62–3, 214, 294, 296
Ransome, Arthur, 187
Rapley, Bill, 108, 169, 225, 282
Raverat, Gwen, 143
Ravilious, Eric, 74
Raymond, Harold: proposes book tokens, 80; on non-readers, 85; reservations on paperbacks, 92–4, 141, 265; agrees to cooperate with Penguin, 103; praises AL's Penguin achievement, 268; congratulates Eunice Frost on marriage, 304; congratulates AL on CH, 398
Rayne, Max, Baron, 399
Raynes Park, 27

Read, (Sir) Herbert, 101, 139, 189;
  Modern Art, 304
Readers' Union, 81, 106
Redcliffe-Maud, John, Baron, 398
Redesdale, David Freeman-Mitford,
  2nd Baron, 24
Redouté, Pierre-Joseph: *A Book of
  Roses* (King Penguin), 144
Reed, (Sir) Arthur, 157
Rees-Mogg, William (*later* Baron),
  364
Reinhardt, Max, 70
Reith, John, Baron, 79, 271–2, 277,
  386
Reprint Society, 140
Rey, H. A., 261
Reynard Library, 353
Richards, Grant, 73, 241
Richards, J. M., 189, 253–4; *The
  Modern Movement in Architecture*,
  140
Richardson, Tony, 367
Richler, Mordecai, 343
Ricketts, Charles, 19
Riding, Laura, 304
Rieu, E. V.: translations of classics,
  251–3; in *After the Conference* paint-
  ing, 269; opposes changed Penguin
  covers, 350
Rieu, Nellie, 251
Right Book Club, 133
Ripon Hall, near Oxford, 88–9
Robbins Report (1963), 375
Robinson, John, Bishop of
  Woolwich, 328
Robinson, W. Heath, 54
Rodd, Peter, 49
Rodd, Sir James Rennell (*later* 1st
  Baron): and publication of *The
  Whispering Gallery*, 36–7, 41–4, 47,
  49
Rogers, Ernesto, 349

Rohmer, Sax, 249
Rolfe, Frederick (Baron Corvo), 23
Rolfe, John, 372–3, 396
Rolph, C. H. (C. R. Hewitt), 61,
  318, 328, 330–32; *Hanged in Error*
  (with Leslie Hale), 347
Ross, Alan, 181
Rosscarbery, Co. Cork, 286, 371
Rosset, Barney, 296, 319–20
Rota, Bertram (antiquarian book-
  seller), 354
Rothenstein, Sir John, 117, 160, 189
Rothermere, Harold Sidney
  Harmsworth, 1st Viscount, 39, 130
Rothstein, Andrew: *A History of the
  USSR*, 289
Rowe, Anthony, 320–21
Rowohlt, Ledig, 284–5
Roy, David, 89, 157
Royal Literary Fund, 401
Rubinstein, Harold, 113, 331
Rubinstein, Hilary, 303, 308
Rubinstein, Michael, 320, 322–5, 331,
  336
Rubinstein, Nash (solicitors), 113, 121
Ruskin, John, 101, 106
Russ, Stephen, 325, 332
Russell, Bertrand, 75, 323; *Has Man a
  Future?*, 347
Russell, Gordon, 196, 253; *The Story
  of Furniture*, 185
Russell, Leonard, 324
Russia: AL visits, 289
Russian Review, 181

Sackville-West, Edward, 161, 189, 273
Sackville-West, Vita: *All Passion Spent*,
  105; *The Edwardians*, 105
Saki (H. H. Munro), 24
Salinger, J. D., 30; *The Catcher in the
  Rye*, 308
Sampson, Anthony, 355

Samuel, Edward, 371

Sargent, (Sir) Malcolm, 161

Saroyan, William, 183

Sartre, Jean Paul, 30

Sassoon, Philip, 29

Savile Club, London, 120

Saville-Sneath, R. A.: *Aircraft Recognition*, 150, 213

Savoy (magazine), 20

Sayers, Dorothy L., 245, 252, 303; *The Unpleasantness at the Bellona Club*, 95, 98

Scherer, Paul, 308

Schmoller, Hans: printing and design standards, 245–6, 279, 402; designs Buildings of England volumes, 255; and Pevsner's view of AL, 256; character and appearance, 278–9; book jacket designs, 279–80; refuses to work on Wodehouse titles, 281; and AL's broken deal with Canfield, 297; Eunice Frost on, 304; and publication of *Lady Chatterley's Lover*, 320; and prosecution of *Lady Chatterley's Lover*, 324–6, 328; Godwin and, 344; and pictorial covers, 349, 351; and Genet's *The Thief's Journal*, 358; opposes publication of Siné cartoons, 360; rents flat in Old Mill House, 370; remains with Penguin until retirement, 387; negotiates terms with Penguin's suppliers, 396

Schmoller, Tanya *see* Kent, Tatyana

Schorer, Mark, 319

Science Teaching Project, 376

Scott, Laurence, 299

Scott-James, Anne (*later* Lady Lancaster), 331

Scrutiny (magazine), 72

Searle, Ronald, 145, 310, 359, 377

Secker & Warburg (publishers): Adelphi Library, 74; publish Orwell, 133; wartime losses, 155; acquitted over publication of *The Philanderer*, 317–18; agreement with Penguin, 353; takeover by Tillings, 354

Segal, Ronald, 364–5

Segrave, Edmund, 110, 263

Selby, Hubert: *Last Exit to Brooklyn*, 333

Selfridge, Gordon, 29

Selfridges (London store): sells early Penguins, 98, 100

Selwyn & Blunt (publishers), 116

Senior, Elizabeth, 144

Services Central Book Depot, 162–4

Services Committee for the Welfare of the Forces, 163

Sette of Odd Volumes (club), 22

Sewell, John, 310

Shakespeare & Co. (Paris bookshop), 61

Shakespeare, William: published by Penguin, 347

Shanks, Michael: *The Stagnant Society*, 347

Shannon, C. H., 19

Shaw, George Bernard: AL meets, 30; and Hesketh Pearson, 45; imaginary conversations with Chesterton, 49; readership, 73; works sold by *Daily Herald*, 82; supports Penguin Books, 82; published by Penguin, 112, 205–6; suggests Cherry-Garrard book to AL, 112; praises USSR, 129; and AL's trip to India, 147; wartime losses, 155; advocates spelling reform, 172; friendship with AL, 204–5, 232; objects to Topolski's illustrations, 204–5; political views,

204; awarded 'Million', 205–6; ninetieth birthday, 205; death, 206; asked for autograph by AL's daughter, 234–5; *Androcles and the Lion*, 172; *The Intelligent Woman's Guide to Socialism*, 113, 135; *Major Barbara*, 239; *Plays Pleasant and Unpleasant*, 204; *Pygmalion*, 204

Shell Guides, 254

Shelvankar, K. S.: *The Problem of India*, 199

Shonfield, (Sir) Andrew, 332

Shorter, Clement, 39

Shy, Timothy *see* Lewis, D. B. Wyndham

Sieff, Israel, 352, 399

Signet (US publishing house), 219

Sillitoe, Alan: *Saturday Night and Sunday Morning*, 280

Silverbeck (house), Harmondsworth, 7, 147–8, 168, 228, 232, 234, 265, 269

Simon & Schuster (US publishers), 209, 214

Simon, André, 53

Simon, Oliver, 77, 241–3, 278, 358

Simon, Ruth, 334

Simpkin Marshall (book wholesalers), 26, 99, 156

Simpson (of HMSO), 325–6

Siné (cartoonist): *Massacre*: publishing controversy, 359–62; stock destroyed, 363

Singleton (farm manager), 363

Smallwood, Norah, 123

Smith, Geoffrey, 184, 258

Smith, Matthew, 189

Smith, Phyllis Barclay: *British Birds on Lake, River and Stream* (King Penguin), 144

Smith, W. H. (booksellers), 72, 79, 89, 99, 131, 169, 324

Smithers, Leonard, 20

Snow, Sir Edgar, 290

Soane, Sir John, 107

Society of Authors, 318, 401

South America: Penguins marketed in, 233–4

Southwick Street, London, 58

Soviet Union (USSR): admired by Left, 129, 132; Cold War attitudes to, 182

Spain: AL's house in (El Fénix), 297, 367, 371, 383, 385

Spanish Civil War (1936–9), 129–30, 137–8

Sparrow, John, 332

Spectator (journal), 122, 131

Spencer, Stanley, 189

Spender, (Sir) Stephen, 129, 131, 175–7, 181, 399

Spring, Howard, 101

Stable, Sir Wintringham Norton (Mr Justice), 318

Stalin, Josef, 132, 181, 204

Stalin, Svetlana (*née* Alliluyeva): *Twenty Letters to a Friend*, 391

Stangos, Nikos, 352

Staniland, Meaburn, 347

Stapledon, Olaf: *Last and First Men*, 251

Stark, Freya, 335

Stead, W. T., 73, 186

Steed, Henry Wickham, 134

Steer, George, 289

Stein, Gertrude, 55

Sterne, Laurence: *A Sentimental Journey*, 143

Stevas, Norman St John (*later* Baron St John of Fawsley), 318, 330

Stone, Irving: *Lust for Life*, 55

Stone, Reynolds, 78, 141, 245, 281

Stonier, Brian, 378–80

Stonier, G. W., 177

Stopes, Marie, 62
Storey, David, 309
Stow, Randolph, 379–80
Strachey, John, 132
Strand Magazine, 72
Straus, Ralph, 52
Style and Civilization series (Penguin), 346
Success with English series, 377
Sudermann, Hermann: *The Song of Songs*, 24
Summers, Jack, 108
Sun books (Australia), 380
Sunday Chronicle, 38
Sunday Times: colour supplement, 349
Sutherland, Graham, 189
Sutherland, John, 333
Swaffer, Hannen, 202
Symonds, John Addington, 19
Symons, A. J. A., 29, 53, 127
Symons, Julian, 175, 331

Tablet (journal), 137
Tabouis, Geneviève: *Blackmail or War*, 134, 138
Talbot Square, Paddington, 58, 66, 147
Tambimuttu, James Meary, 175
Taubert, Siegfried, 355
Tauchnitz, Christian Bernhard (publisher): cheap editions, 76; merges with Albatross, 78
Tawney, Richard Henry, 133, 157
Taylor, A. J. P., 133, 192, 359
Taylor, W. G., 69
Teale, Christine (*née* Lane; AL's daughter): marriage, 2; birth, 168; godparents, 215; independence, 370; relations with AL, 372; and AL's activities in later years, 392; and management of Penguin, 397; left nothing in AL's will, 400
Teale, David, 2, 397

Tellisford House (school), 10, 13
Temple, William, Archbishop of Canterbury: *Christianity and the Social Order*, 199
Thames & Hudson (publishers), 144, 190, 256
Thatcher, Margaret, Baroness, 4
Things We can See, The (Penguin series), 200
Thirkell, Angela, 308
Thoene, Peter *see* Bihalji-Merin, O.
Thomas, Hugh (*later* Baron), 372
Thompson, Lovell, 296–7
Thomson, Roy, 1st Baron, 297, 338, 398
Tilling, Thomas (company), 298, 354, 397
Times, The, 112, 130, 195, 364–7
Times of Ceylon, 147
Times Literary Supplement: ignores first Penguins, 101; reservations over cheap paperbacks, 105, 107, 112; and Siné's cartoons, 359
Tit-Bits (magazine), 72
Todd, Barbara Euphan: *Worzel Gummidge*, 187
Tolkien, J. R. R.: *The Hobbit*, 377
Topolski, Feliks, 150, 204
Tots and Quots club, 171
Town and Country Planning, Ministry of, 196
Transatlantic (magazine), 182, 261–2
Travers, Ben, 17, 22–4, 28–9, 60, 68, 299
Tressell, Robert: *The Ragged Trousered Philanthropists*, 330
Trevelyan, John, 331
Trevelyan, Raleigh, 335, 342; *Italian Writing Today*, 380
Trollope, Anthony, 155
Tschichold, Jan: typographical designs for Penguin, 90, 237, 241, 243–5,

278–9, 281, 350, 358, 402; background, 243; perfectionism, 244–5; remoteness from Penguin inner circle, 247; and costs of *British Wild Flowers*, 260; and Schmoller, 279

Tubbs, Ralph, 140, 206, 256, 268, 373; *The Englishman Builds*, 207; *Living in Cities*, 200

Tunnicliffe, C. F., 185

Twentieth-Century Verse (magazine), 175

Unger, Hans, 281

United States of America: AL visits, 55, 208, 212, 214, 218, 289, 292, 372; *Ulysses* published in, 62–3; paperback publishing in, 208–11, 215, 219, 293–4; Penguins sold in, 209, 211–13, 215–19; books imported from England, 211; overseas book sales, 233–4; college market for books, 293, 295; publishers' takeover deals for Penguin Inc., 294–6; obscenity law in, 319–20

Unwin, Philip, 69, 106, 157

Unwin, Sir Stanley: character, 27; on Bodley Head's insolvency, 35; appoints Greenwood to run Bodley Head, 52; helps rescue Bodley Head, 69; on Albatross's Aryan clause, 78; organizes Ripon Hall conference (1934), 88–9; unhelpfulness on launch of Penguins, 95, 105; and wartime publication difficulties, 153–4, 157; on decline in literary taste, 156; attitude to Penguin, 157; and Hogben's *Interglossa*, 173; not questioned at *Lady Chatterley's Lover* trial, 329–30; criticizes Rolph's

book on *Lady Chatterley* trial, 332; policy on authors' advances, 356

Unwin, T. Fisher, 27

Upfield, Arthur, 291

van der Post, (Sir) Laurens: *Voyage to the Interior*, 289

Vanderbilt, Gloria, 55

Vasari, Giorgio: *Lives of the Artists*, 375

Venables, Bernard, 226; *Fish and Fishing*, 185

Vernon-Hunt, Ralph, 381, 395

Vigo Street, London, 21, 25, 32–3, 57, 85, 91, 354–5, 373–4

Viking Press (New York), 6, 55, 62; as British hardback imprint, 402

Vine, Revd A. R., 361

Viney, Elliott, 165

Vintage books (USA), 294

Vizetelly, Henry, 317

Völkischer Beobachter: blacklists Bodley Head, 56

Waddington, C. H., 182; *The Scientific Attitude*, 200

Walker, Tony, 361, 368

Walpole, Hugh, 81, 85, 109, 289

War Artists Advisory Committee, 187

Warburg, Fredric: as gentleman publisher, 27; and transfer of Bodley Head to Unwin, 69; publishes Orwell, 133; publishes Searchlight Books, 195; on rumour of sale of Penguin Inc., 295; acquitted over publication of *The Philanderer*, 318, 326; Godwin criticizes, 348

Ward, Barbara, 203

Ward, Robert Barrington, 195

Warde, Beatrice, 77, 205, 271

Warner, Jack, 392

Warner, Rex, 252

Waterhouse, Keith, 274

Watson, Peter, 175, 284

Watson, William, 20, 23

Watt, A. P., 3

Waugh, Evelyn: mocks Connolly, 109; political views, 129, 191; read in wartime, 156; on *Lady Chatterley's Lover*, 323; *Edmund Campion*, 239

Weaver, Harriet, 60–61, 63

Webb, Beatrice and Sidney (*later* Baron and Lady Passfield), 129

Webb, Kaye, 187, 367, 377–8, 392, 400

Webb, Mrs (of Hutchinsons), 317–18

Wedgwood, Dame C. V., 329

Week, The (journal), 131

Wegner, Max Christian, 76

Weidenfeld & Nicolson (publishers), 2, 367

Weidenfeld, George, Baron: character, 2; on Beales, 119; publishes *Lolita*, 198, 319; on Gerald Barry, 206; on Susanne Lepsius, 285; on Woodhouse at Penguin, 312

Wells, H. G., 22, 73, 172; *Crux Ansata*, 172; *Kipps*, 74; *The New Machiavelli*, 24; *The Rights of Man*, 172; *A Short History of the World*, 113

West Indies: AL visits, 289

West, (Dame) Rebecca: supports publication of *Ulysses*, 62; as defence witness in *Lady Chatterley's Lover* trial, 329

Western Printing Services, 320, 331

Weybright, Victor, 202, 215–19, 251, 293–4, 339, 388, 403

Wheeler-Bennett, Sir John, 212

Whispering Gallery, The (Hesketh Pearson): publication and court case, 36–49, 60

White, Alan, 311

White, Gwen: *Book of Toys*, 145

White, Patrick, 379–80

White, Timothy (chemists), 79

Wilde, Oscar, 19–20, 43

Willett, Basil, 24, 32–3, 40–42, 44, 46, 50, 57, 69, 85

Williams, Camilla (*née* Lane; AL's mother): relations with AL, 5–6; background, 7–8; on AL's upbringing and education, 10; relations with John Lane, 12–13; death, 283; moves into Silverbeck, 286–7; pays for granddaughters' education, 372

Williams, Gertrude (*née* Rosenblum), 116, 162, 167, 201

Williams, Raymond, 330

Williams Lane, Samuel Allen Gardiner (AL's father), 5–6, 8, 12; death, 283

Williams, William Emrys: on AL's parents, 5, 7; memoir of AL, 12; and AL's bid to buy Bodley Head, 69; on launch of Pelican, 114, 122; AL meets, 116, 118; character and career, 116–18; relations with Estrid Bannister, 117; independence of Penguin, 118; relations with AL, 118–19, 227, 371, 388–9, 393; works for Penguin, 122, 123; on Eunice Frost, 125, 303, 309; on Harmondsworth, 127; lunches at Barcelona restaurant, 128; attends Double Crown Club, 141; at Hind's Head celebration, 146; wartime activities, 160–64, 200; and publication of *Penguin New Writing*, 178; and *Russian Review*, 181–2; and 'Art for the People' scheme, 188; and Eunice Frost's overwork, 188; and publication of Gallagher's *Case for Communism*,

203; and AL's breach with Weybright, 218; on AL's character, 224–6; drinking, 230; attends AL's birthday dinner (1946), 233; and Tatyana Kent, 234; Glover criticizes, 240; advises AL, 246–7; in Penguin management, 247–8; works for Unesco, 248; AL's view of, 249, 302, 304; supports Graves's translation of *The Golden Ass*, 252–3; and Clark's opposition to Pelican History of Art, 256; at editorial meeting with Morpurgo, 263; dismisses Morpurgo, 264; on AL's knighthood, 268; ideals, 271–2, 274, 276–7; as Secretary-General to Arts Council, 272, 302; view of BBC, 272–3; on Hoggart's *Uses of Literacy*, 274–5; opposes publishing lighter books, 277; and Penguin cover design, 280–82, 348, 402; and AL's health, 284, 393; and Estrid Bannister's marriage, 285; and Longmans' offer for Penguin, 298; importance to company, 301, 306; qualities, 302; and Eunice Frost's engagement to Harry Kemp, 304–5; on Maschler, 308; and publication of *Lady Chatterley's Lover*, 323–5; as defence witness in *Lady Chatterley* case, 329, 330; confidence in Penguin superiority, 344; disapproves of Godwin, 352; and Penguin Education, 376; on AL's declining resilience, 384; retirement, 387–8; throat cancer, 388, 399; on AL's lack of financial understanding, 395; Priestley on, 398–9; AL requests to write history of Penguin, 399–400; with AL in last months, 400

Williams Lane family, 5–6

Wilmot, Ernest, 15

Wilson, Edmund, 62

Wilson, Harold (*later* Baron), 347

Wilson, J. G., 99, 311

Wine and Food Society, 53

Wintringham, Tom: *People's War*, 199; *New Ways of War*, 212

Wodehouse, (Sir) P. G., 281

Wolff, Kurt, 213

Wolpe, Berthold, 255–6

Wood, Kingsley, 157

Woodcock, George, 175–6

Woodhouse, (Sir) C. M. ('Monty'), 312–13, 377, 385

Woodruff, Douglas, 203

Woolf, Leonard: and James Joyce's *Ulysses*, 60–61; and success of Penguin Books, 104–5; at Hogarth Press, 175; *Barbarians at the Gates*, 132

Woolf, Virginia: and James Joyce's *Ulysses*, 60–61; and popular taste, 84; at Hogarth Press, 175

Woolsey, Justice John M., 63

Woolworth's: sells Bodley Head books, 59; as cheap sales outlet, 80, 82–3, 89; sells early Penguins, 99, 210, 365

Workers' Educational Association, 73, 116–17

World War II: AL predicts, 146; outbreak, 149; publication difficulties and restrictions, 152–8; reading resurgence, 156, 159; propaganda, 158; arts and music in, 160–1; books supply in, 163–4; future planning and changing political and social values, 192–201

World's Classics (series), 73, 252

Worsley, T. C., 130

Wright, Basil, 182

Wright, David, 252

Wright, Judith, 380
Wright, Patrick, 374
Wright, Peter, 367
Wyatt, Woodrow (*later* Baron), 87
Wyndham, John, 338

Year's Poetry, The (ed. Kilham Roberts and Lehmann), 174
Yellow Book, The (magazine), 19–20, 23
Young, Edward: on Ronald Boswell, 32; and publication of *Ulysses*, 64; Olney supervises, 86; and AL's non-smoking rule, 87; designs for Penguin, 91, 92, 140, 242, 278; on Holy Trinity crypt, 108; in charge of production, 109; Jean Osborne on, 110; visits Penguin Pool, London Zoo, 119; travels to Harmondsworth, 127; and Shiela Grant Duff, 135; leaves Penguin for Reprint Society, 140; press advertising, 140; designs Illustrated Classics, 143; visits van Leer in Holland, 144; at Hind's Head celebration, 145–6; war service as submarine commander, 152; congratulates AL on knighthood, 268; AL meets in late years, 400; *One of Our Submarines*, 152, 280
Young Elizabethan (magazine), 284
Young, Wayland: *The Profumo Affair*, 347

Zilliacus, Konni, 203–4, 288
Zola, Emile: *Germinal*, 317
Zuckerman, Solly, Baron, 119–20, 171; *Science in War*, 171